ASCENT®

CENTER FOR TECHNICAL KNOWLEDGE



# Autodesk® Vault Professional 2025 Administrator Essentials

*Learning Guide*

*Edition 1.0*

## Trademarks



## Disclaimer



Published by
ASCENT Center for Technical Knowledge
630 Peter Jefferson Parkway, Suite 175
Charlottesville, VA 22911

866-527-2368

www.ascented.com

AS-VLT2501-PES1NU-SG // IS-VLT2501-PES1NU-SG

# Contents

## Chapter 4: Lifecycle States 4-1



## Chapter 5: Revision Management 5-1



## Chapter 6: Managing Properties 6-1

# Preface

The *Autodesk® Vault Professional 2025: Administrator Essentials* guide introduces Autodesk Vault Professional 2025 to CAD administrators. The focus of this learning guide is to teach administrators how to set up and manage categories, lifecycles, revisions, file naming schemes, items, bills of materials (BOMs), and the engineering change order (ECO) process.

This guide is intended for administrators with some knowledge of Autodesk Vault Professional's data management capabilities. The hands-on practices included in this guide reinforce usage of items, BOM and ECO features, and automated workflows.

### Important:

Refer to the *Course and Classroom Setup* section for installing the practice files, setting up the database, and understanding the dependencies between course practices.

### Topics Covered

- Introduction to Autodesk Vault Professional
- Managing Categories
- Lifecycle Management
- Revision Management
- File Naming Schemes
- Working with Items
- Managing Change
- Working with Bills of Materials
- Administering Autodesk Vault Professional
- Reporting
- Thin Client

### Prerequisites

- Access to the 2025 version of the software, to ensure compatibility with this guide. Future software updates that are released by Autodesk may include changes that are not reflected in this guide. The practices and files included with this guide might not be compatible with prior versions (e.g., 2024).
- A good working knowledge of Autodesk CAD programs and working knowledge of Autodesk Vault Basic and Autodesk Vault document management features.

# Installation and Setup

## Classroom Environment

The courseware is intended for use in an instructor-led environment. If you plan to use the courseware on your own in a non-classroom environment, you must set up Autodesk Vault correctly. Before you set up your system, you should be aware of the following:

- Do not use a production vault for the practices. It is recommended that you set up a separate vault on a separate vault server.
- If you plan to repeat a practice, you must remove any files that were added to the vault when you previously completed the practice. It is recommended that you delete the entire vault and start again with a new vault.
- Do not attempt these practices on a production vault server until you are familiar with the procedures that are covered.

You must install and run this courseware from individual computers. You cannot run the courseware from a shared server. **DO NOT install the courseware on a computer that stores working vault data.**

## Overview of Installing the Courseware

The following steps describe how to install the courseware.

1. Install Autodesk Vault Professional Client and Autodesk Vault Professional Server on each computer.
2. Install the course datasets on each computer.
3. If Autodesk Vault has been previously used on the computer, restore default settings for the user interface.

## Installing Autodesk Vault

Install both Autodesk Vault Professional Client and Autodesk Vault Professional Server on each computer. See the Autodesk Vault installation help for installation instructions.

If you are using any of the following Autodesk software applications in conjunction with Autodesk Vault, they must be installed before installing Autodesk Vault.

- Autodesk Inventor
- AutoCAD
- AutoCAD Mechanical
- AutoCAD Electrical
- Autodesk Civil 3D
- Autodesk Revit

## Installing the Practice Files

To install the data files for the practices:

1. Download the practice files .zip file using the link provided on the Practice Files page in this guide.
2. Unzip the .zip file to the C: drive. A *Vault Professional Admin* folder is created and contains all the files that you will need. The path for all the files should be *C:\Vault Professional Admin*.
3. The remaining files are required to restore the database. The instructions for this are detailed below.

   ***WARNING:** The following procedure will overwrite the current datasets and file stores in your current vault. Be sure to back up any necessary vaults that might be required at a later time.*

## Restore the Backup

1. Click **Start>Autodesk Data Management>Autodesk Data Management Server Console 2025**.
2. In the *Log In* dialog box:
   - For *User Name*, enter **administrator**.
   - Leave the *Password* field blank.
   - Click **OK**.
   - The Autodesk Data Management Server Console displays.
3. Select **Tools>Backup and Restore**.
4. Select **Restore**, then click **Next**.

5. In the *Backup and Restore Wizard* dialog box, click the ellipses (three dots) button next to the *Select backup directory for restore:* field, navigate to the location on your local C: drive where the practice files were extracted (*C:\Vault Professional Admin*) and click **OK**, then set the following:
   - *Database data location:* **Default Restore Location**
   - *File Store location:* **Original Restore Location**

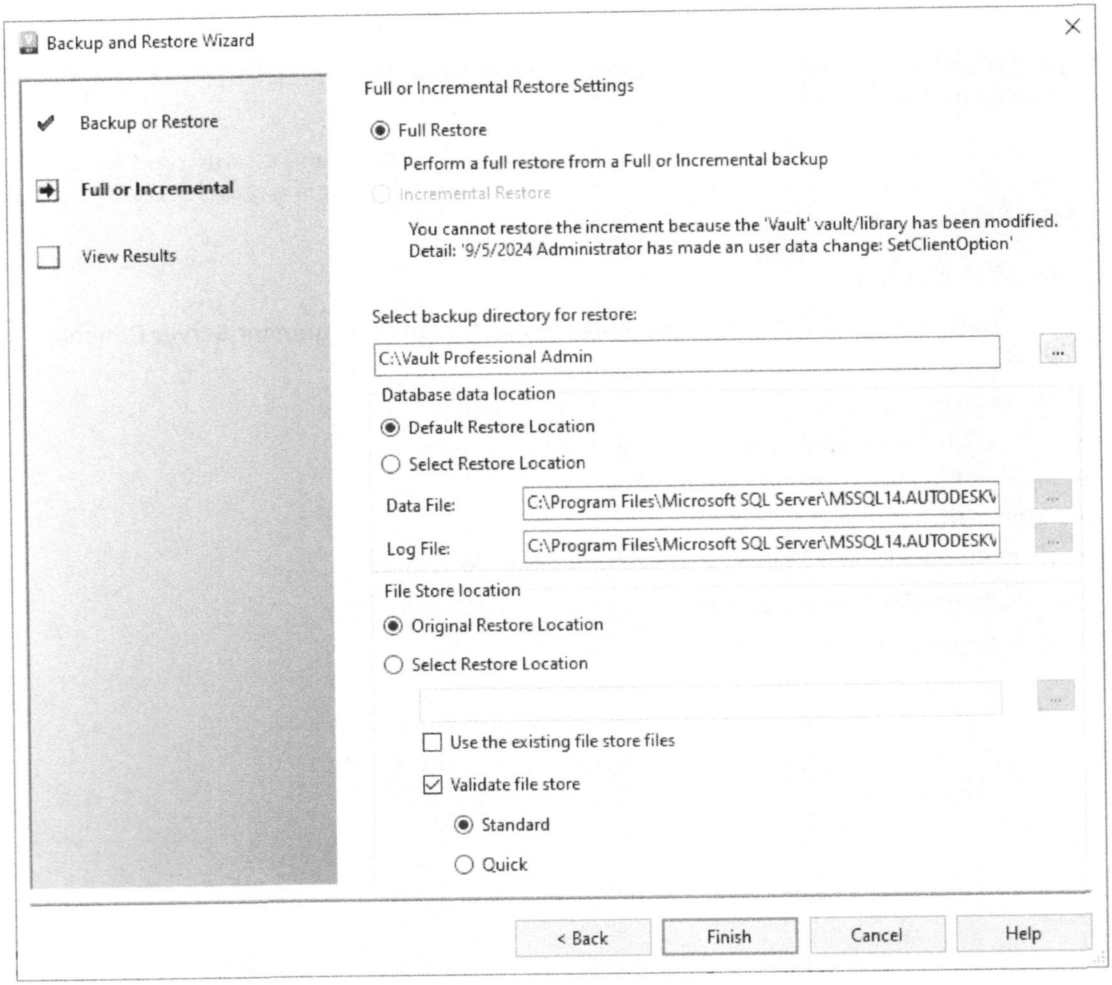


6. Click **Finish**.
7. In the prompt that displays, click **Yes** (as shown below) **only if you are sure that you want to delete the current datasets**.

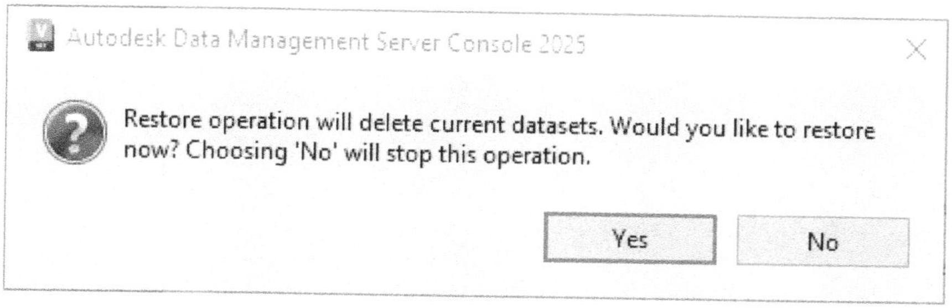


8. The *Restore Progress* dialog box displays the progress for restoring the database.
9. In the *Backup and Restore Wizard* dialog box, click **Close**.
10. In the *Autodesk Data Management Server Console* dialog box, click **File>Exit**.
11. Launch Vault Client and select **Tools>Administration>Global Settings**. In the *Integrations* tab, select the **Enable Job Server** checkbox, as shown in the image below. Click **Close**.

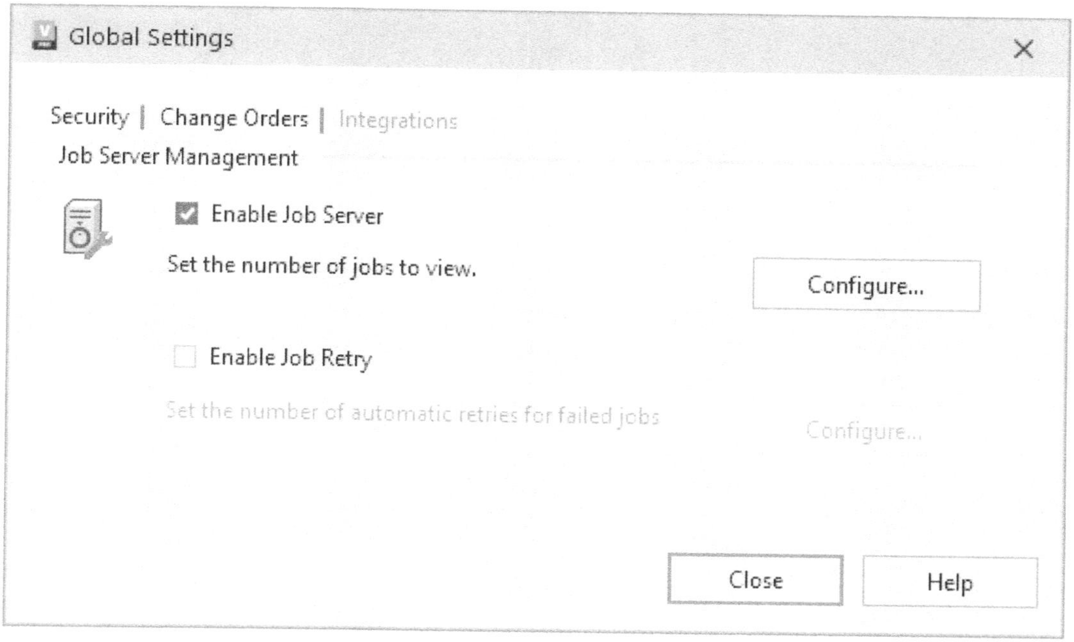

# In This Guide

The following highlights the key features of this guide.

| Feature | Description |
|---|---|
| **Practice Files** | The Practice Files page includes a link to the practice files and instructions on how to download and install them. The practice files are required to complete the practices in this guide. |
| **Chapters** | A chapter consists of the following: Learning Objectives, Instructional Content, and Practices.<br>• **Learning Objectives** define the skills you can acquire by learning the content provided in the chapter.<br>• **Instructional Content**, which begins right after Learning Objectives, refers to the descriptive and procedural information related to various topics. Each main topic introduces a product feature, discusses various aspects of that feature, and provides step-by-step procedures on how to use that feature. Where relevant, examples, figures, helpful hints, and notes are provided.<br>• **Practice** for a topic follows the instructional content. Practices enable you to use the software to perform a hands-on review of a topic. It is required that you download the practice files (using the link found on the Practice Files page) prior to starting the first practice. |
| **Appendices** | Appendices provide additional information to the main course content. It could be in the form of instructional content, practices, tables, projects, or skills assessment. |

# Practice Files

To download the practice files for this guide, use the following steps:

1. Type the URL *exactly as shown below* into the address bar of your Internet browser to access the Course File Download page.

   ***Note: If you are using the ebook, you do not have to type the URL. Instead, you can access the page simply by clicking the URL below.***

   **https://www.ascented.com/getfile/id/octarrhenaPF**

2. On the Course File Download page, click the **DOWNLOAD NOW** button, as shown below, to download the .ZIP file that contains the practice files.

3. Once the download is complete, unzip the file and extract its contents.

   **The recommended practice files folder location is:**
   *C:\Vault Professional Admin*

   ***Note: It is recommended that you do not change the location of the practice files folder. Doing so may cause errors when completing the practices.***

4. To set up the database, refer to the *Course and Classroom Setup* section.

**Stay Informed!**

To receive information about upcoming events, promotional offers, and complimentary webcasts, visit:

**www.ASCENTed.com/updates**

Chapter 1

# Introduction to Autodesk Vault Professional

This chapter provides an overview of the Autodesk® Vault Professional software, its features, functions, and benefits, and the Autodesk Vault Professional user interface.

## Learning Objectives

- Describe the benefits and functionality of Autodesk Vault Professional.
- Identify the user interface elements and navigate the user interface.

# 1.1 Autodesk Vault Professional Overview

In this chapter, you learn about the basic features and functionalities of Vault Professional, and its advantages as a design data management system.

With Vault Professional, you can implement an automated release and change management process with complete tracking of bills of materials (BOMs) and related design information. Figure 1–1 shows the Vault Professional interface.

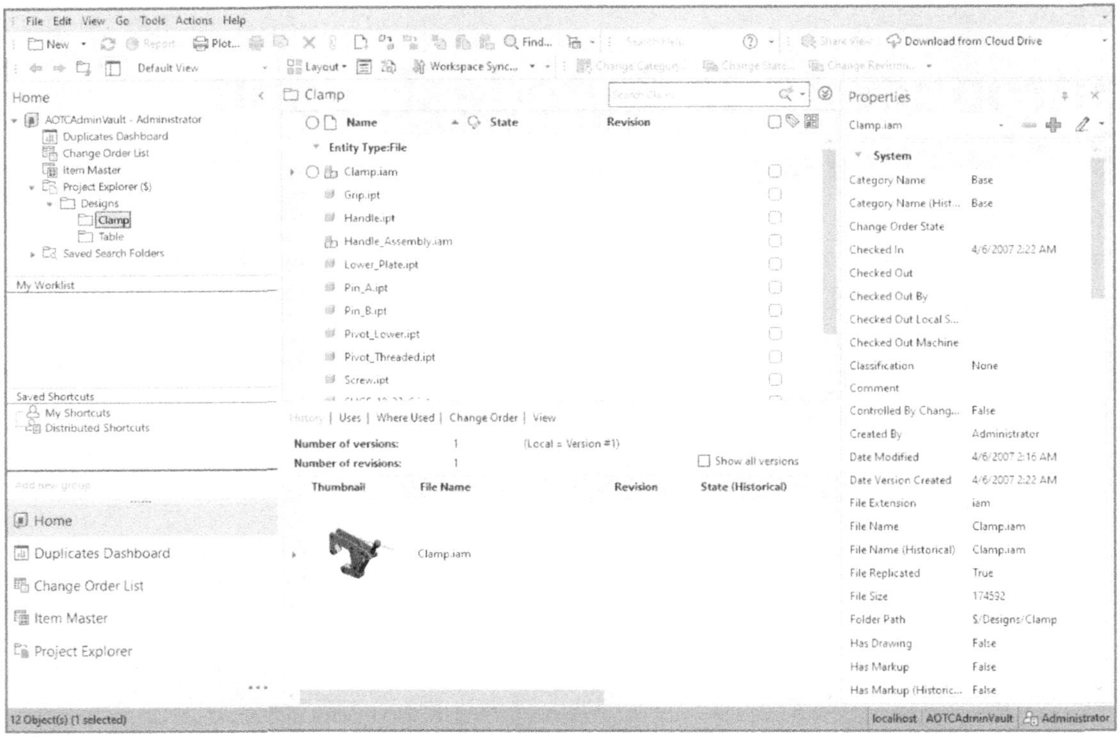


**Figure 1–1**

# About Autodesk Vault Professional

Autodesk Vault Professional can use vault files as item data, making vault files available to an extended design team that can include personnel from departments outside of engineering.

Autodesk Vault Professional helps you manage your vault data by creating and tracking change orders, managing bills of materials, and working with item revisions and lifecycles to oversee files throughout the design and manufacturing process.

## Benefits of Autodesk Vault Professional

When designers and engineers place their data files in a vault, Autodesk Vault Professional connects these files to item numbers that can integrate with ERP systems. Thus Autodesk Vault Professional is a gateway connecting two different parts of a company: the design/engineering team and the extended product team.

## Example of How to Use Autodesk Vault Professional

With Autodesk Vault Professional, more users can connect directly to the files in the vault, assign items to these files, enable other users in a larger team to work with the items, view items using visualization files, and manage these items as they move through their lifecycle from design to manufacturing to completion.

# Autodesk Vault Professional Functions

Autodesk Vault Professional automates the release management process by managing engineering changes and bills of materials. You use Autodesk Vault Professional to manage items throughout their lifecycle.

## Manage Items

| Function | Description |
|---|---|
| Create Items | With Autodesk Vault Professional, you can create items by assigning items to data files or by creating new items. |
| Delete Items | When an item has reached the end of its lifecycle and is no longer used, you can delete it from the *Item Master*. |
| Organize Items | Using the *Item Master* list, you can quickly search, sort, and filter items, and customize how the item list is viewed. |
| Add User-Defined Properties to Items | In addition to the default properties for each item, you can add user-defined properties (fields) to item records. |
| Where Used | You can analyze where items are used and check item dependencies before editing an item or requesting an engineering change order. |
| Track Item Revisions | A flexible revision numbering scheme keeps track of the history of items. You can use a predefined number of letter schemes, or use the ASME Y14.35M scheme. You can use secondary and tertiary schemes to track data with even more detail. |

## Bill of Materials (BOM)

| Function | Description |
|---|---|
| Link Items | A BOM is built automatically when an assembly file in the vault is assigned an item.<br>You can also link items together to create your own BOM that includes newly created items. |
| Edit BOMs | You can edit materials and quantities for any design. You can override quantities in a BOM. |
| Units of Measure | Autodesk Vault Professional and Autodesk® Inventor® support the same units of measure, so any units of measure used in Inventor are automatically transferred to Autodesk Vault Professional BOMs. You can also specify the base measure of items, including mass, volume, quantity, and length. |
| Property Mapping | You can map CAD properties in design files in Autodesk Vault to item properties. These CAD properties are carried over to corresponding items in Autodesk Vault Professional that can be used in the *Item Master* list and in the BOM. |

## Engineering Change Orders (ECOs)

| Function | Description |
|---|---|
| Manage ECOs | You can create ECOs and send them to members of the team. You can also attach notes and red-lined drawings to ECOs.<br>ECOs are reviewed and tracked by members of the team then can be rejected, approved, or withdrawn. The status of these ECOs is shown graphically and can be tracked to ensure that change orders are not forgotten or misplaced. |
| Set Up Routes | You can set up routing lists with email support. You can use these lists to ensure that the right team members are notified of changes. |

## Item Lifecycle

Every item is tracked with indicators that show the state of the item (**Work in Progress**, **Released**, **In Review**, and **Obsolete**). Revisions increment automatically in some cases when an item changes state. This process ensures that correct revision control is used. Generally, items are in a **Work in Progress** state when edited and in a **Released** state when released to manufacturing.

## Manage Security

Users receive system access based on their departments, positions, and roles. Security features prevent inadvertent changes and enable only authorized users to access or edit data. Certain functions, such as creating new numbering schemes, mapping CAD properties to item properties, and editing users, are restricted to administrators.

## Example of Linking Design Data

The design work on an ICU valve is nearing completion and released by the design team. As part of managing the valve data, you need to set up the packaged product. You add an item representing the final packaged assembly, an item representing the packaging itself, and another item representing the product specification sheet. You link these items to the assembly design data to form a BOM for all the components then release the items to manufacturing.

Based on an ECO, a new revision of the ICU valve packaged assembly has spare O-rings (as shown in Figure 1–2), and the ICU valve buttons are no longer painted.

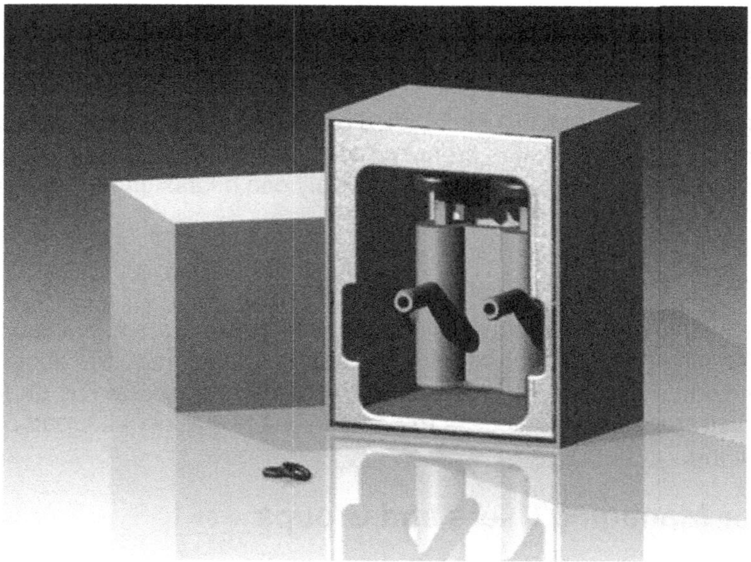

**Figure 1–2**

# Security and Users

You can control who has access to certain features in Autodesk Vault by assigning users different roles and permissions.

## Add Users

> ***Note:*** *When you add a new user, you should include their email address so that they can receive automatic notification of ECOs.*

As a Vault administrator, you can add, modify, and disable users from the system. You can group users with similar roles and manage permissions and roles for both groups and individual users.

You can also add users from a domain.

 

## Specify Roles

In addition to the numerous Administrator, Content Center, and Document predefined roles, Autodesk Vault Professional has the following predefined roles: Change Order Editor (Levels 1 and 2), ERP Manager, Item Editor (Levels 1 and 2), Item Reviewer, Custom Object Consumer, Custom Object Editor (Levels 1 and 2), and Custom Object Manager (Levels 1 and 2). You can also create your own custom roles. You can do this by creating a new role, editing a role, or copying an existing role to then edit. For example, you can copy the Document Editor Level 2 role and then remove the Folder Create permission so that users cannot create their own folders within the vault. Users can be assigned roles based on their required level of access in the company.

## Role-Based Permissions

Users are assigned Vault task permissions based on the role they are assigned by an administrator. Administrators can also create Access Control lists for any folder in a vault. Folder permissions such as Full Access and Read-Only can be assigned to groups or individual users.

## Example

New employees join the company and require access to design data in the vault. The administrator adds new users and sets their roles based on their required access to vault and Vault Professional data. However, because the new employees are training during the first two weeks, the administrator sets their access to certain sensitive folders as read-only until they have finished training.

## Guidelines for Managing Users and Groups

User permissions can be controlled for individual users or for groups of users. Follow these guidelines to manage groups efficiently:

- **Assign most permissions at group level:** If you use groups, consider assigning most permissions at the group level and not for each individual user. For example, to assign most users the Document Editor (Level 1) role, create a group, add the users, and assign the group the Document Editor (Level 1) role. If one or two users also need to be Content Center Editors, either create another group for those users or assign the permissions at the user level. You will be able to manage users more easily if you are consistent with the way that you assign permissions.
- **Disable permissions at the group level:** If a group is no longer required or you want to stop access for all of the users that belong to just that group, you can disable the group, removing permissions assigned to the group.

## How To: Adding a New User

The following steps describe how to add a new user and assign the user to a group.

1. In Autodesk Vault, select the **Tools>Administration>Global Settings** or in ADMS Console, click **Tools>Administration**. For access through ADMS, click the *Security* tab if not already displayed (there is only one tab when accessing through Vault), as shown in Figure 1–3.

   ***Note:*** *You can access the user management tools through either ADMS Console or Autodesk Vault. By administering users through Autodesk Vault, you can manage users from any computer on which Autodesk Vault is installed rather than through ADMS Console, which runs only on the Vault server.*

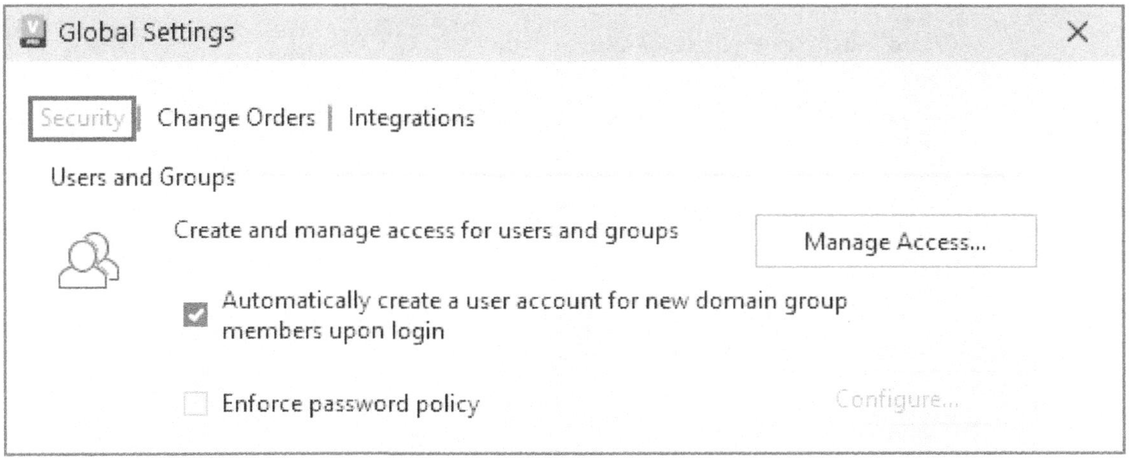


**Figure 1–3**

2. Select the **Enforce password policy** option (as shown in Figure 1–4) to enforce a password policy that can prevent unauthorized access and provide protection against potential security breaches. Click **Configure** and in the *Configure Password Policy* dialog box, select the required password settings and click **OK**. Administrators can enforce users to create passwords that meet specific criteria such as a minimum length, a combination of uppercase and lowercase letters, numbers, and special characters.

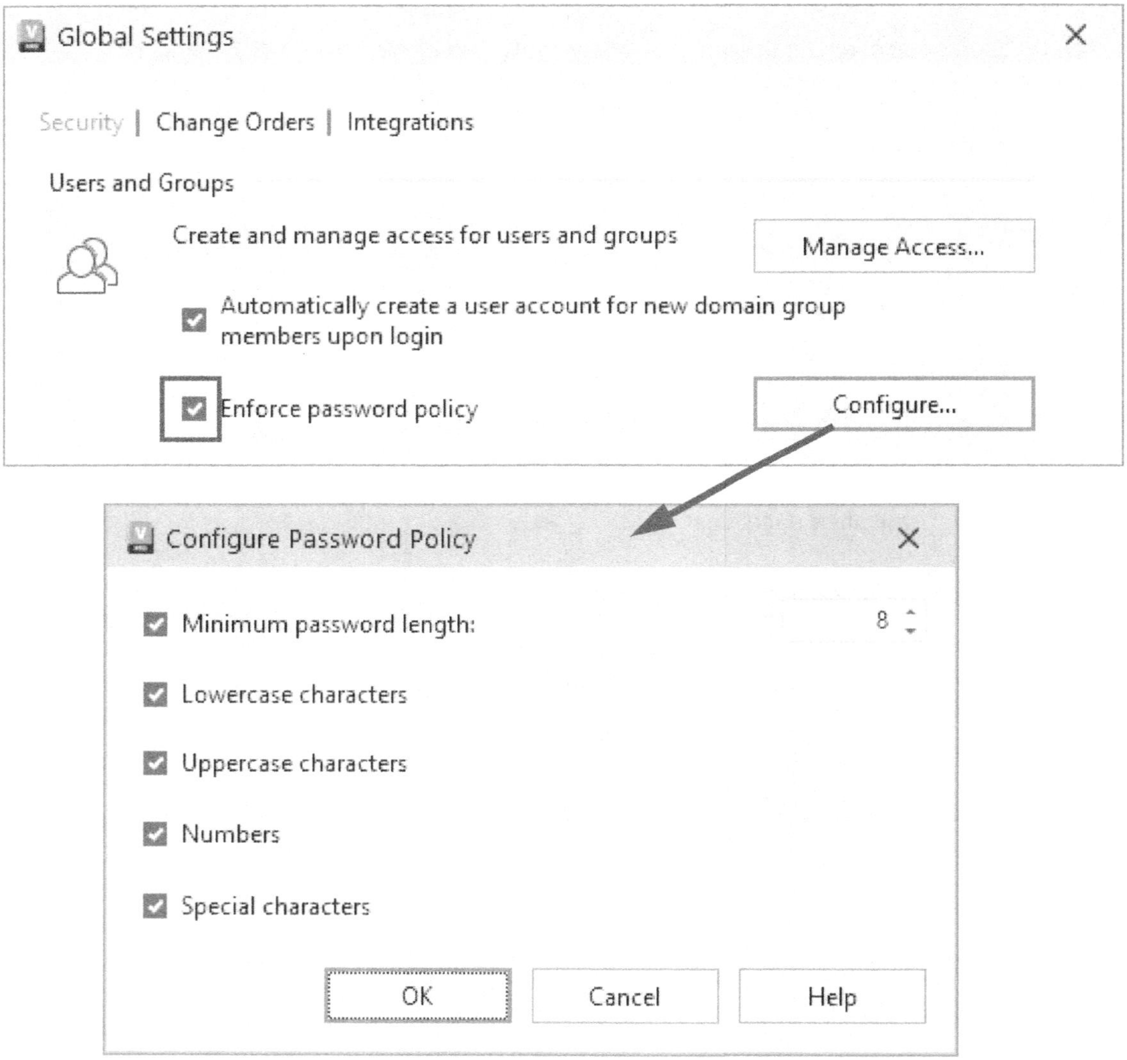


**Figure 1–4**

3. Click **Manage Access...** to display the *User and Group Management* dialog box shown in Figure 1–5.

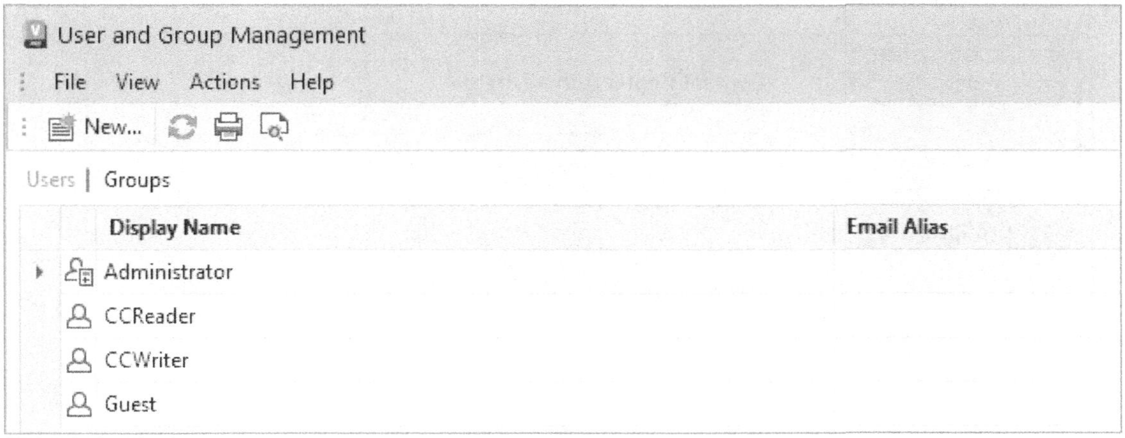


**Figure 1–5**

4. On the *Users* tab, click **New**. In the *New User Profile* dialog box (shown in Figure 1–6), fill in the user data such as the *Display Name*, *Email Alias*, *First Name*, and *Last Name*.

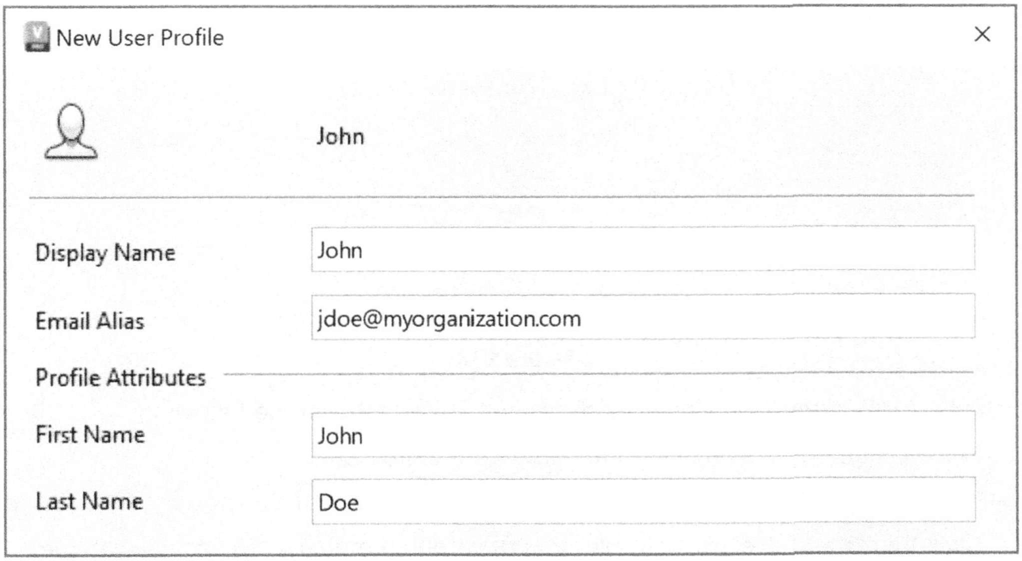


**Figure 1–6**

5. Select **Accounts** to set the authentication method, such as Vault Account or Autodesk ID. You can set the password as well.

6. If you are controlling permissions using groups, do not enter roles or vaults. If a few users require special permissions, click **Roles** and **Vaults** (shown in Figure 1–7) and specify the roles and vaults at the user level.

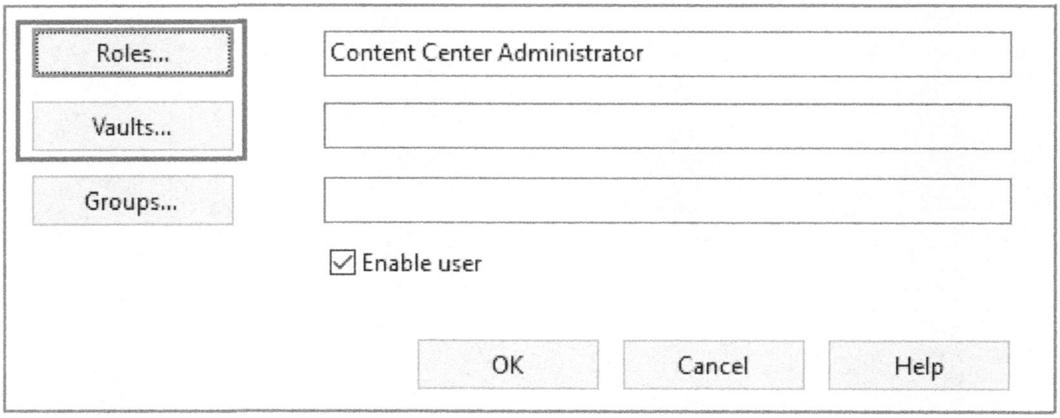


**Figure 1–7**

7. To create a new group, on the *Security* tab, select **Manage Access...**.
8. In the *User and Group Management* dialog box, select the *Groups* tab, then click **New**, as shown in Figure 1–8.

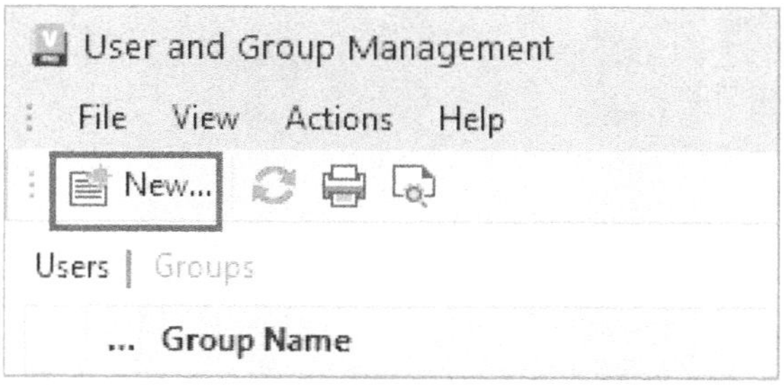


**Figure 1–8**

9. In the *New Group Profile* dialog box (shown in Figure 1–9), set the following:
   a. In the *Group Name* field, enter the name for the group.
   b. Click **Roles** and select the roles to apply to all members of the group.
   c. Click **Vaults** and specify the vaults that the group members can access with the selected roles.
   d. To add existing users to the group, click **Add**.

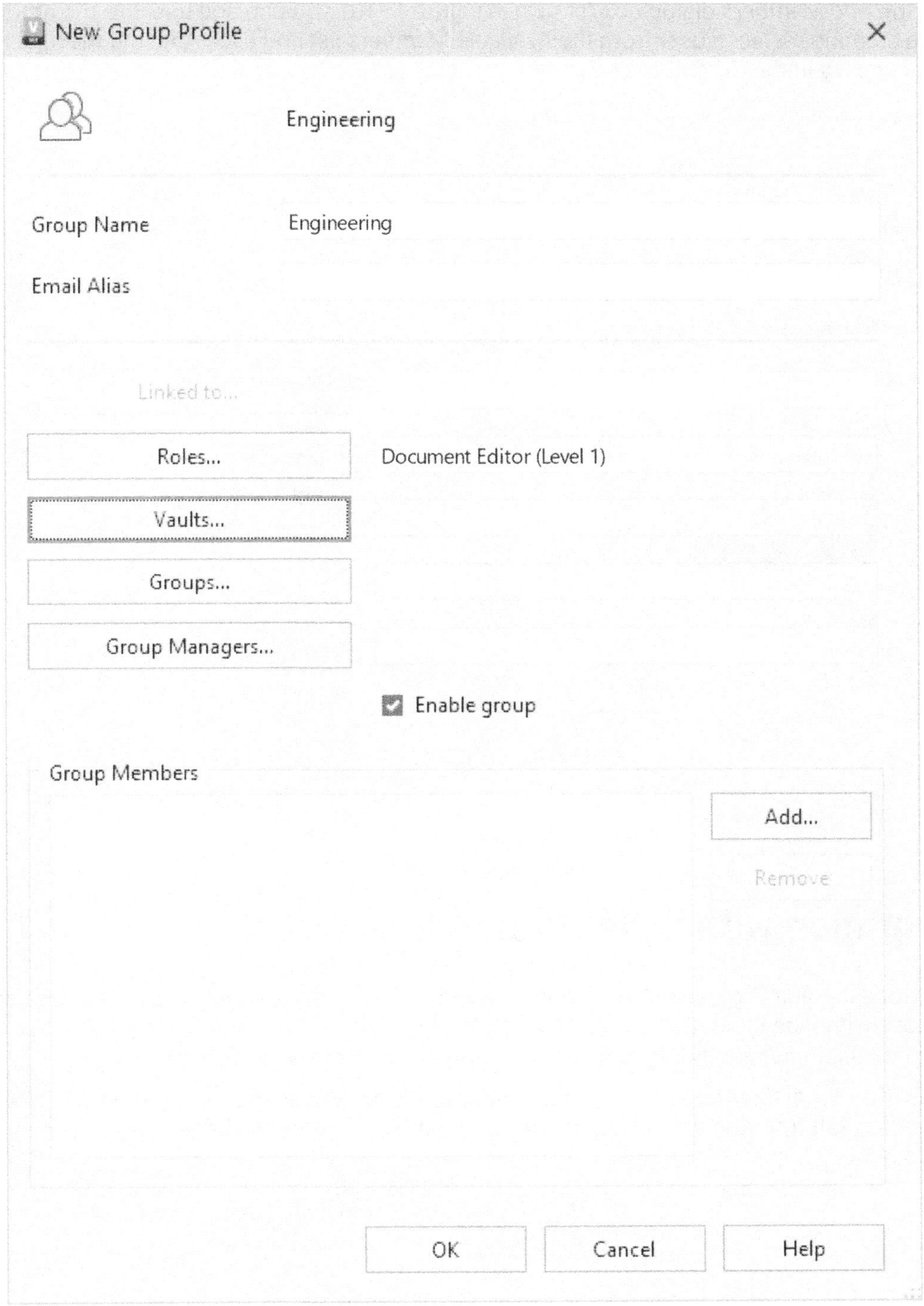
New Group Profile
Engineering
Group Name
Engineering
Email Alias
Linked to...
Roles...
Document Editor (Level 1)
Vaults...
Groups...
Group Managers...
Enable group
Group Members
Add...
Remove
OK
Cancel
Help

**Figure 1–9**

10. In the *Add Members* dialog box (shown in Figure 1–10), you can add users to the group you are creating. Select a user from the *Available Members* list and click **Add** and the user name will display in the *Current Members* list.

    ***Note:*** *A group requires at least one member to be added.*

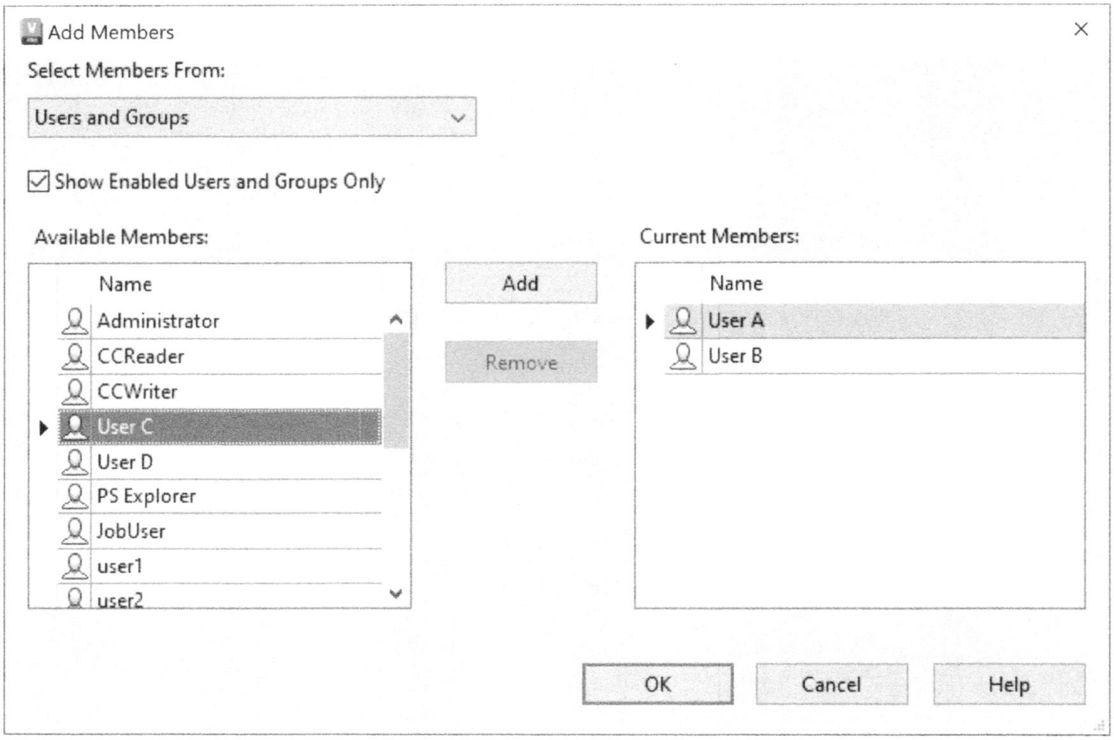


**Figure 1–10**

# Integration with Other Products

The Autodesk Vault Professional software is a web services-based application. The application interfaces with files located in a vault file store and database. The file store and database were created during installation or migrated from another Autodesk Vault release.

Vault Professional integrates with the applications that produced the files in the vault. You can access the vault from the design application or open files created by these applications in Vault Professional.

## Autodesk Inventor

Vault Professional integrates with Autodesk Inventor. Vault Professional reads Autodesk® Inventor® files and the relationships amongst these files. The items' type and BOM information is built on this data.

- Inventor can control BOM data. By assigning BOM structure properties to components, such as phantom or inseparable, Inventor influences how the Vault Professional application reads and builds its BOMs for those items.
- You can transfer custom properties between Inventor and Vault Professional.
- Vault Professional fully supports all units of measure used by Inventor.

## AutoCAD-Based Products

Autodesk Vault Professional integrates with other design applications and reads data in AutoCAD® drawing (DWG™) files. The following list outlines how AutoCAD-based applications work with Autodesk Vault Professional.

- External references (xrefs) are added as attachments to items in Vault Professional when the parent drawings are assigned items.
- Vault Professional can read drawing files and map their properties to item properties.
- Vault Professional can read projects, drawings, and properties from Autodesk® Civil 3D® drawing files, and it can map their properties to item properties. Vault Professional also provides Autodesk Civil 3D software users with additional project management functionality by displaying a Project tree in the Prospector tab. This enables the Autodesk Civil 3D software users to safely share their drawing files and individual AEC objects with other team members.
- Vault Professional reads BOM data in AutoCAD® Mechanical drawing files. It uses this data to create BOM data and determine object types.
- If the vault is set to enforce file locking, you cannot check out a drawing from the vault unless its lifecycle state is set to **Work in Progress**.

## Autodesk Revit

The Autodesk Vault Professional software with Revit Vault Add-in offers Autodesk Revit users with file security, version control, and multi-user support. Autodesk Vault integrates with Autodesk® Revit® Architecture, Autodesk® Revit® MEP, and Autodesk® Revit® Structure.

# 1.2 User Interface

In Autodesk Vault Professional, you typically begin in the *Navigation* pane. This pane contains one or more objects that essentially behave as folders, because they contain other objects.

When you select one of these folders, the data in the selected folder displays in the main pane. You then work in the main pane. When a record in the main pane is selected, it is previewed in the *Preview* pane.

The main features of the Vault Professional user interface are shown in Figure 1–11 and described in the following table.

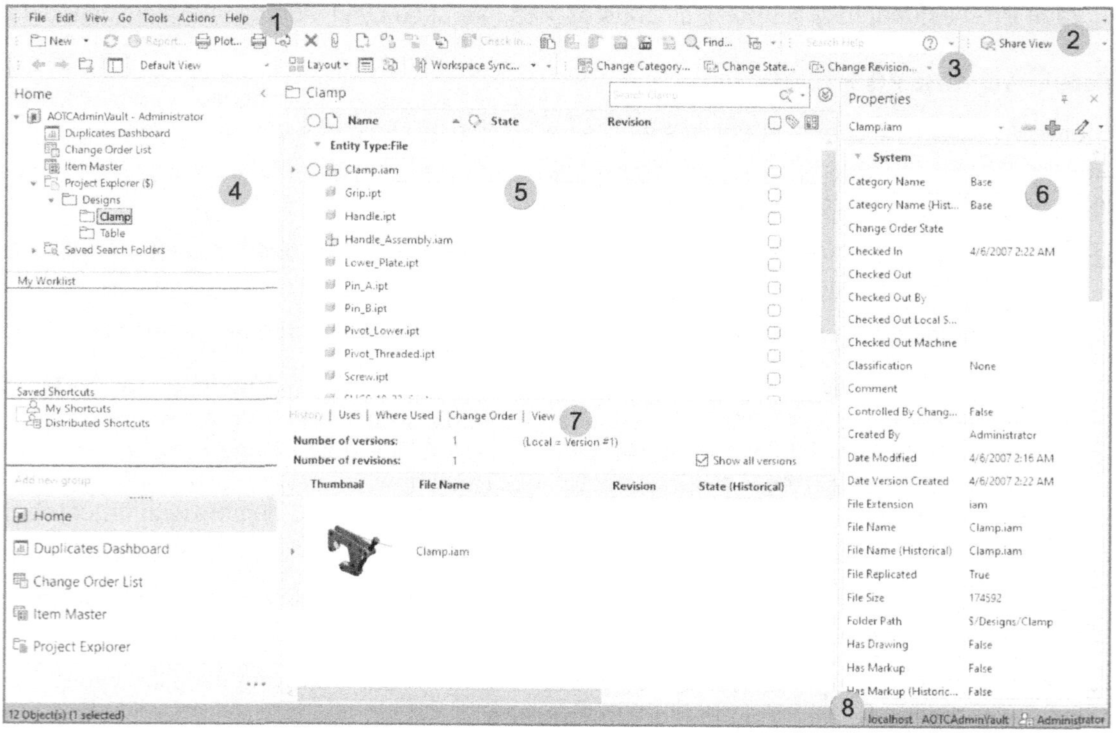


**Figure 1–11**

| | |
|---|---|
| 1 | **Main menu:** Contains the commands used in Vault Professional. |
| 2 | **Standard toolbar:** The Standard toolbar provides quick access to common commands depending on the environment. |
| 3 | **Secondary toolbars:** An Advanced and Behavior toolbar provides quick access to other common commands depending on the environment. |
| 4 | **Navigation pane:** Contains folders and subfolders for different environments, shortcuts for searches, and filters. The work environment (All Folders, *Item Master*, *Change Order List*, or Vault Explorer) is determined by the selection in the *Navigation* pane. |
| 5 | **Main pane:** Contains the primary list of data, which changes based on the current work environment. It can be a list of items, a list of files in the vault, or a list of ECOs. Depending on the type of environment, the records for these lists can be selected, previewed in more detail, and edited. |
| 6 | **Properties grid:** Contains all properties of a selected file. |
| 7 | **Preview pane:** Shows a preview of the selected record in the main pane. The different tabs are logically organized views of details of the record and change, depending on the environment. |
| 8 | **Status bar:** Shows information such as the number of records in the main pane, the number of records selected, the user name, and the name of the vault in which the user is logged. |

# About the Navigation Pane

The *Navigation* pane is the starting point in the Autodesk Vault Professional user interface. Use the *Navigation* pane to go directly to required data.

Using the main workflows, you can work efficiently with Autodesk Vault Professional and quickly locate the data you require.

## Navigation Pane Areas

| Screen Element | Description |
|---|---|
| **Home** | The upper part of the *Navigation* pane shows the folders you can click. These folders can be filtered so that only the *Item Master* or only Project Explorer is visible.<br>In Figure 1–12, the *Home* view is shown, where all possible folders for navigation are visible.<br>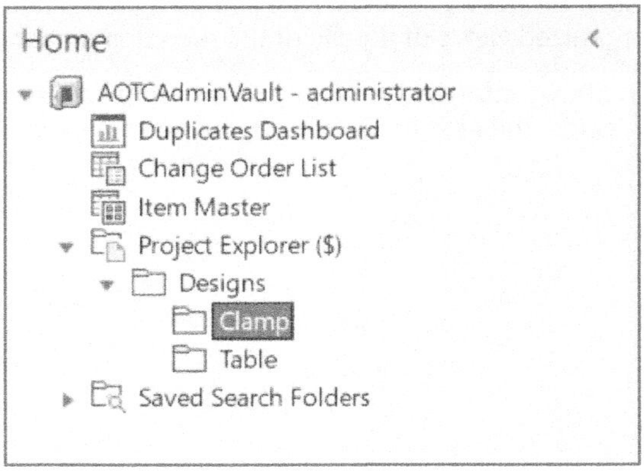<br><br>**Figure 1–12**<br>Three major work environments exist in Vault Professional:<br>• Items<br>• Change orders<br>• Project Explorer<br>By clicking the folders, you change the work environment displayed, which affects the main pane and the *Preview* pane. |
| **Saved Search Folders** | In the previous image, saved searches are also visible.<br>These saved searches are environment specific. For example, if you create a search in the *Item Master* for the word *Valve* then save this search, it displays under *Saved Search Folders*. Clicking this *Valve* folder brings up the *Item Master* work environment and displays the filtered items containing the word *Valve*. |

| Screen Element | Description |
|---|---|
| **My Worklist** | ECOs requiring your attention or action are listed under *My Worklist* together with the due date (as shown in Figure 1–13). Clicking the listed item brings up the *Change Order List* work environment with the ECO highlighted.   **Figure 1–13** |
| **Saved Shortcuts** | You can create group folders in the *Saved Shortcuts* area (shown in Figure 1–14). You can fill these folders with shortcuts to items, documents, files in the vault, and ECO. Clicking the links takes you to the selected objects. 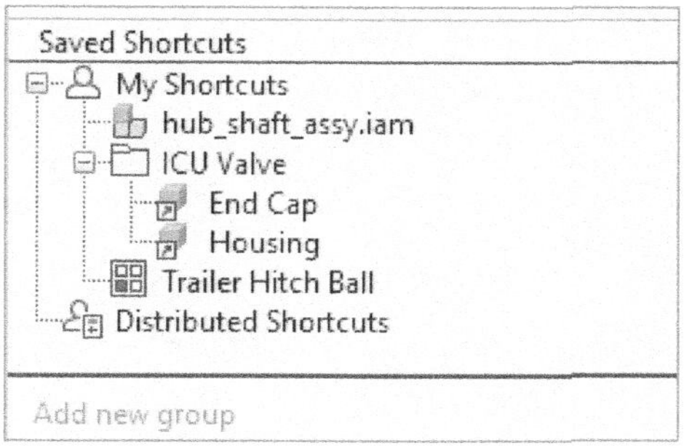  **Figure 1–14** |
| **Navigation Pane Buttons** | Buttons in the *Navigation* pane (shown in Figure 1–15 and located in the lower-left corner of the main interface screen) filter the folders at the top of the *Navigation* pane. For example, clicking **Project Explorer** removes all folders except those displayed in Project Explorer. 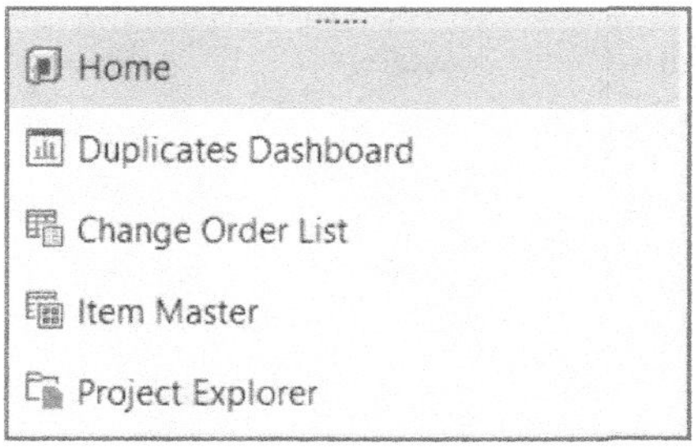  **Figure 1–15** <br><br> **Tip:** Use these buttons to filter the folders saved under *My Search Folders*. In the main pane, you see the results of searches for all work environments. However, when you click a button such as **Project Explorer**, only search results for the Project Explorer environment display. |

# About the Main Pane

The main pane changes based on the work environment and how the view is customized. Use the main pane to sort, filter, and view records in the list.

The main pane lists records of objects. These objects can be items, files in the vault, or ECOs, based on the work environment.

You can customize the main pane to show different fields and to filter the list based on different criteria. You can also use Find to quickly search a list.

## Example of the Item Master

When working with items, the *Item Master* (shown in Figure 1–16) is displayed in the main pane.

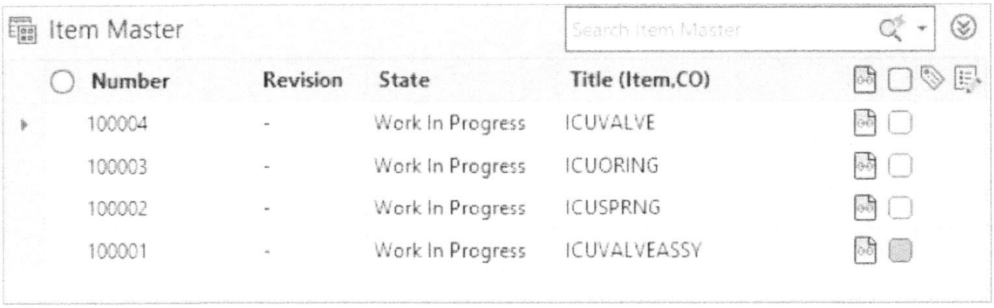


**Figure 1–16**

## Example of the Change Order List

ECOs are listed in the *Change Order List* (shown in Figure 1–17).

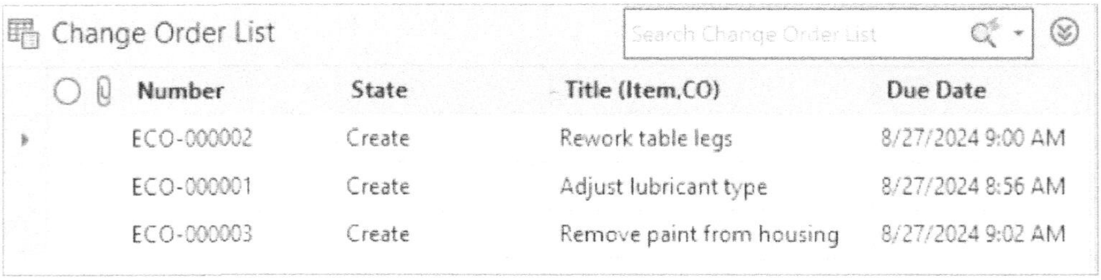


**Figure 1–17**

## Example of Files in a Vault Folder

Files and their properties are listed when a vault folder is selected in the *Navigation* pane, as shown in Figure 1–18.

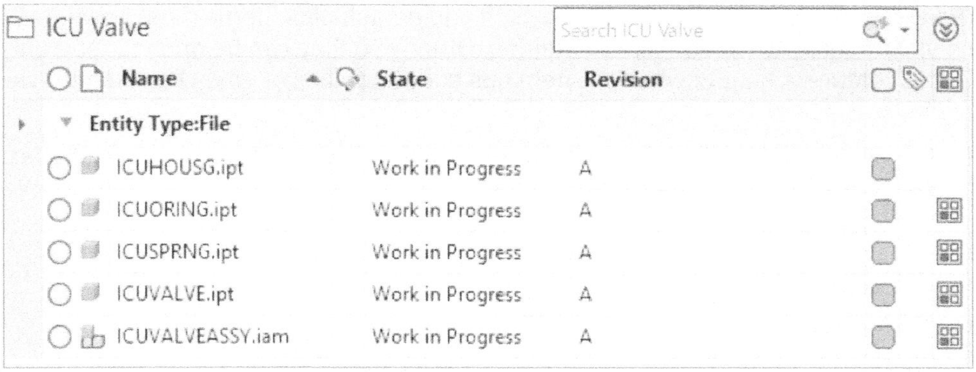


**Figure 1–18**

# About the Item Record Dialog Box

Along with the major interface panes, one of the most commonly used interface elements in Vault Professional is the *Item Record* dialog box. Use the *Item Record* dialog box to view (**Open**) or edit (**Edit**) items and their BOMs, and to attach and detach files. Items must be in the **Work In Progress** state in order to open them for editing. Otherwise they can be opened read-only for viewing. This feature is helpful when the item has a lot of details or when you want to view the associated files.

Using the *Item Record* interface (shown in Figure 1–19) you can edit an item's properties, including the item's BOM, attach and detach files, and view change orders associated with that item.

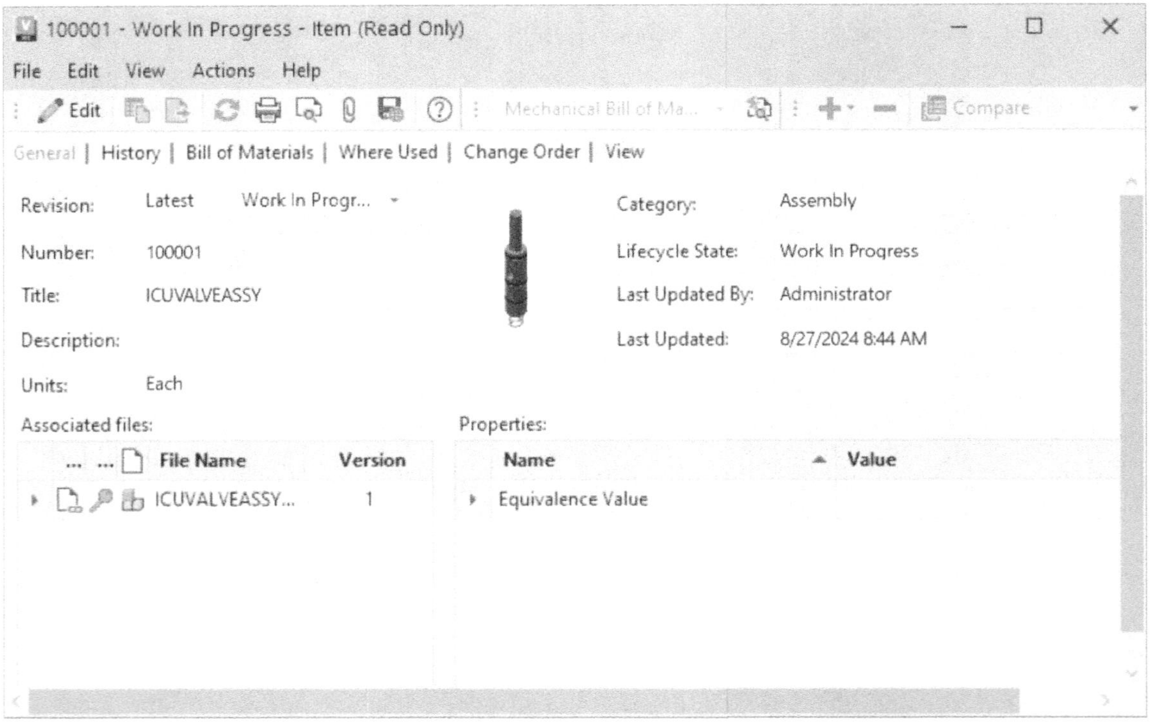


Figure 1–19

 

## Example of the Item Record Interface

You create a new item such as lubricant in the *Item Master*. In the *Item Master*, you double-click an item representing an assembly to open it and click **Edit** for editing. You add the lubricant item in the assembly item's BOM. When you have completed the task, you click **Save and Close** to save the changes and exit the *Edit Item Record* dialog box (shown in Figure 1–20).

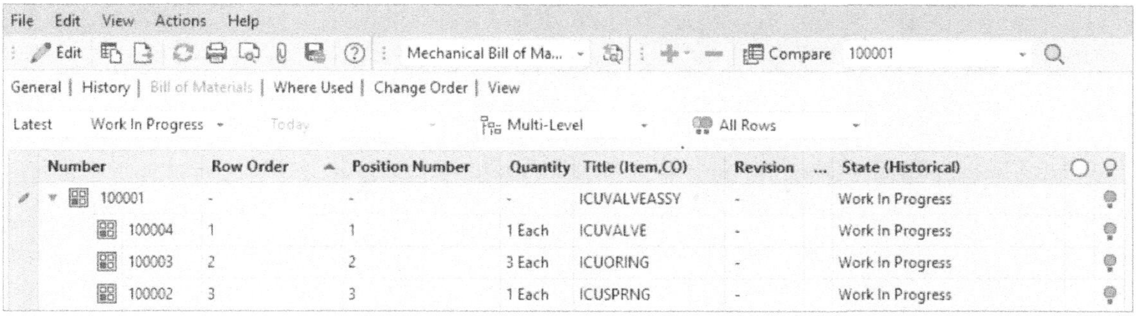


**Figure 1–20**

Chapter

2

# Organizing and Populating a Vault

In this chapter, you learn how Autodesk® Inventor® files, and other files are organized for best results with Autodesk® Vault. You then learn how to prepare existing projects and upload them to a Vault using Autodesk Autoloader.

## Learning Objectives

- Describe how Inventor project, model, library, and Content Center files are organized for the best results with Vault.
- Add existing models to a vault using Autodesk Autoloader.

# 2.1 How Autodesk Inventor Files Are Organized

A typical Autodesk Inventor design includes a large number of files. You can use Autodesk Autoloader to help organize your existing models before uploading them to the vault, or you can organize the files manually before you upload them. Regardless of which method you use, you should know how Autodesk Inventor uses the project file to find files and how regular model files and library files are organized.

Figure 2–1 displays a number of designs added to a vault. The files are organized in the vault to match the local working folder structure when the files were uploaded to the vault.

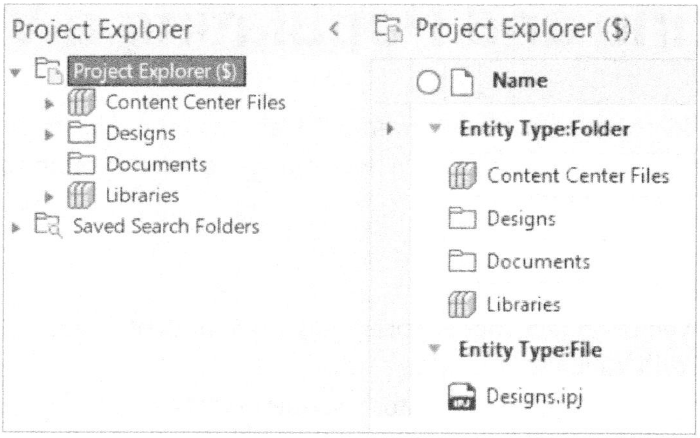


**Figure 2–1**

## About Project Files

Autodesk Inventor uses project files to organize and locate related files. Before you upload files to a vault or try to fix resolution issues, you must learn how Autodesk Inventor uses the project file to locate the files in a design.

### Project Files Defined

Autodesk Inventor uses project files to organize storage locations for related files in a design. For example, when you open an assembly in Autodesk Inventor, it looks for the component files relative to the locations specified in the project file. When you place a part from the Content Center, the generated part is stored in a folder relative to the top-level folder specified in the project file. A project file is set up to correspond with the way the files are organized in the vault.

You must create a Vault project file when you want to work with designs that will be managed using Autodesk Vault. This project file format is only available if you have Autodesk Vault installed. The Workspace, Libraries, and Content Center Files entries specify where Inventor searches for files. All paths are defined relative to a project file location using "**.**" as shown in Figure 2–2.

**Figure 2–2**

| | |
|---|---|
| 1 | A Vault project file is required for managing designs stored in the vault. |
| 2 | The local working folder is mapped to the root folder in the vault. All files in the design are typically located under this folder. |
| 3 | The *Workspace* folder is the top-level folder for the models and drawings you create for all designs stored in the vault. You create subfolders under here to organize your designs. |
| 4 | Library files in the vault are copied to folders under this local folder. Files in these folders cannot be edited. |
| 5 | Files generated from the Content Center are stored under this folder when copied from the vault. |

Autodesk Inventor uses the copy of the project file in the local working folder when you work with files you have checked out from the vault. Therefore, the paths in the project file must correspond to the way that files are organized in the local working folder. When you get files from the vault, the vault structure is reproduced in the local working folder.

## Project File Location

The project file should be located one folder above all other model and library file folders. A folder beneath the project file folder holds all designs with folders for each design.

Figure 2–3 displays the layout of a typical vault working folder. The project file, **Designs.ipj**, is located in the root folder (*VaultWorkingFolder*). The *Designs* folder is the workspace folder in the project file and is located under the project file. It contains folders for different designs. The *Content Center Files* and *Libraries* folders are also located under the project file but outside of the workspace folder.

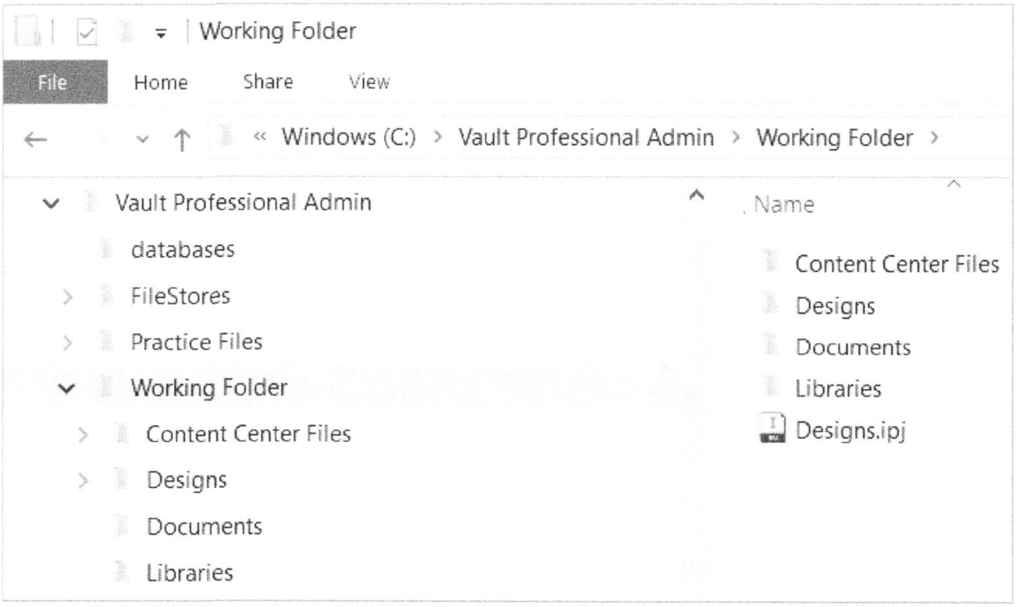


**Figure 2–3**

## Use a Single Project File

There are many ways to organize Autodesk Inventor project and model files. Some users have one project file for all designs; other users have one project file for each design. With Vault, a single project file should be used so you need to manage just one project file and do not have to switch project files when moving from one design to another.

 

## Frequently Used Subfolders

Frequently used subfolders are shortcuts defined in the project file to give you quick access to designs and library parts in your local working folders. A project file is displayed in the project file editor. The **Frequently Used Subfolders** entry of the project file contains paths to frequently used design and library folders, as shown in Figure 2–4.

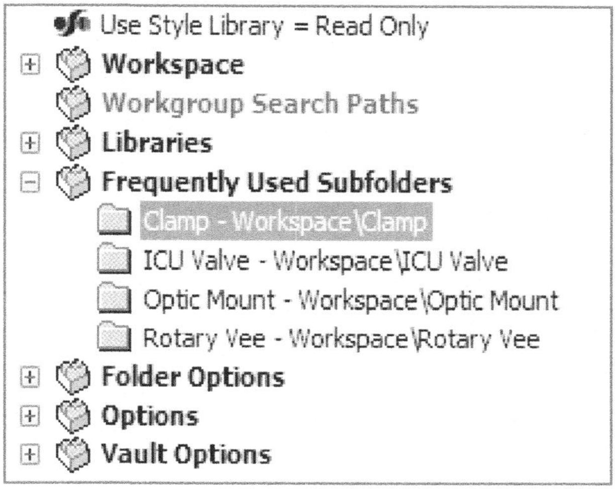


**Figure 2–4**

Frequently used subfolders are displayed when you browse for a file in Autodesk Inventor, making it easier to navigate to specific designs or libraries.

## Mapping Project Folders

When you check in files or add new files to the vault, the files are copied from the local working folder to folders in the vault. Inventor determines where to copy the files by looking in the project file. The vault folders are specified by mapping each local search path to a vault folder.

A typical folder mapping is shown in Figure 2–5. The *Project Root* folder is where the project file is stored. In the example shown, the local *Project Root* folder is mapped to the root folder of the vault. Therefore, the project file is copied to the root of the vault, and model files will be copied to their respective folders relative to the root folder in the vault. Each library path in the project file is also mapped to a vault folder. In Figure 2–5, files in the local path named *Library* are copied to the *Libraries* folder in the vault, and files in the local *Content Center Files* path are copied to the *Content Center Files* folder in the vault.

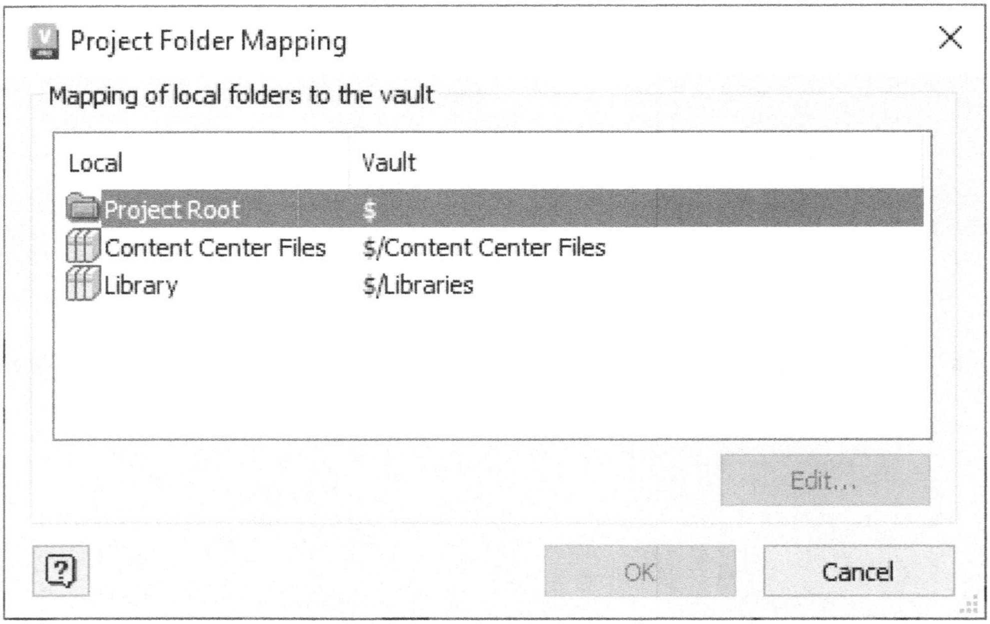


**Figure 2–5**

The mapping information is stored as XML data in the project file. For example, the mapping for the *Library* folder corresponding to the previous figure is displayed in Figure 2–6. The local path and the vault path are both specified.

```
<ProjectPath pathtype="Library">
  <PathName>Library</PathName> (1)
  <Path>.\Libraries</Path> (2)
  <VaultPath>$/Libraries</VaultPath> (3)
</ProjectPath>
```

**Figure 2–6**

| | |
|---|---|
| 1 | Path name in project file. |
| 2 | Local folder path. This folder is relative to the folder containing the project file. |
| 3 | Corresponding vault folder path. The folder structure under this folder matches the folder structure under the local folder path. |

# About Model Files

There are many ways to organize model files. The method you select must be compatible with the project file and with Vault. In this section, you learn how model files are organized for the best results with Autodesk Vault.

## How Inventor Model Files Are Organized

For best results, model files are organized in folders under a single project file, as shown in Figure 2–7.

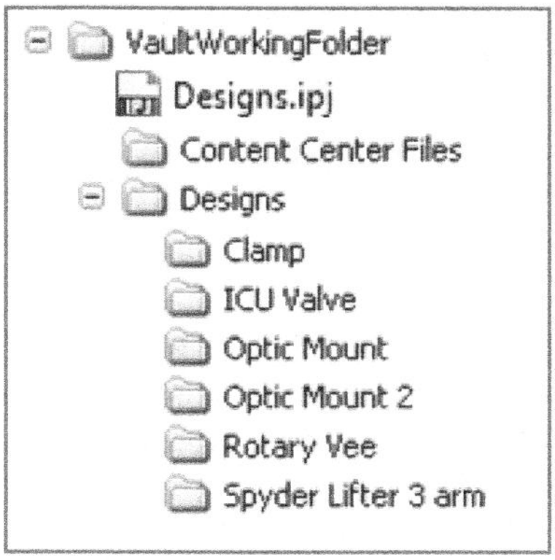


**Figure 2–7**

The same folder structure is used in the vault. When you retrieve files to your local working folder, they are copied to the same relative location and they open successfully in Inventor. For example, the corresponding vault is organized as shown. A single project file is located in the root of the vault.

Folders for the designs, libraries, and Content Center parts are one level below. You can further organize your files using subfolders under these top-level folders. When you get files from the vault, they are copied to the local working folder with the same structure and can be opened successfully, as shown in Figure 2–8.

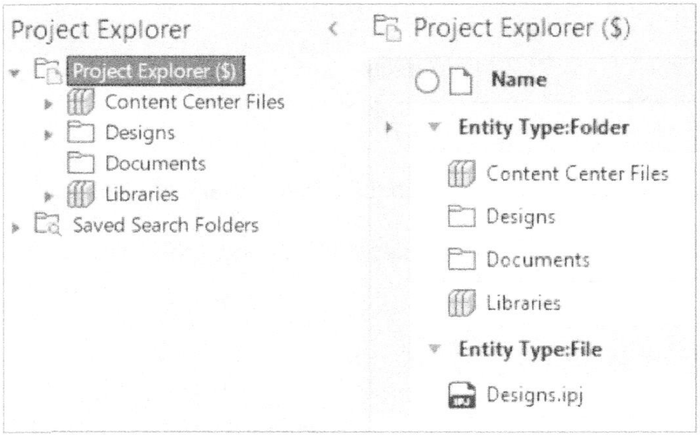


**Figure 2–8**

## Project File Settings for Model Files

The **Workspace** path specifies the location of a top-level folder for all non-library model files. Files for different designs are stored in folders under the *Workspace* folder. If model files are saved outside of the *Workspace* folder, Autodesk Inventor will not find them.

In the project file, the workspace is set as a relative path to the folder that contains the project file, as shown in Figure 2–9.

**Figure 2–9**

## How Common Parts Are Organized

If a part or subassembly is used in more than one design, the file should be stored in a separate folder from the designs in which the part is used, and then it should be referenced in each design. If the part or assembly rarely or never changes, the file can be stored in a library folder so that it cannot be modified by users.

The vault is used as a centralized storage area for all of your files including common parts and library parts and assemblies. Upload all of your library and common components to the vault so that Inventor users can place them in their designs using the **Place from Vault** command. Figure 2–10 displays a folder named *Common Parts*, which contains parts that are included in a number of designs.

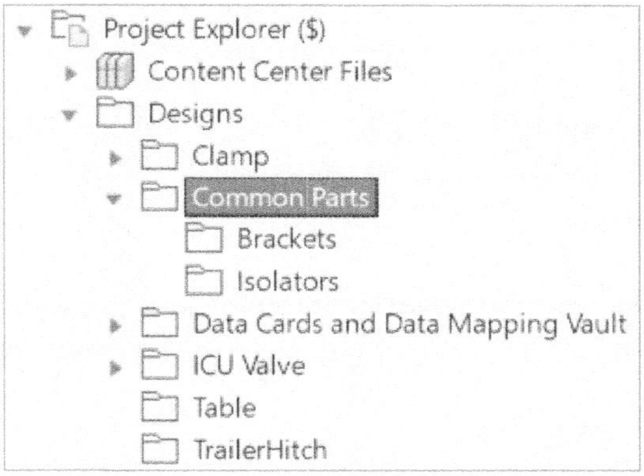


**Figure 2–10**

# About Library Files

Library files are parts or subassemblies that do not normally change. In Autodesk Inventor, library files are treated as read-only files that are not normally versioned.

Typically, library files are used in more than one design. Common purchased components, Content Center files, and iParts are typical library components. Autodesk Inventor includes a wide selection of library parts in the Content Center libraries. You can also get library parts and assemblies from component manufacturers or create them yourself. Any file can be designated as a library file, including regular Inventor parts and assemblies and AutoCAD® drawing files. You must set up and organize library components correctly so that they work with the vault.

## About Library Folders

Files that are stored in library folders in the vault are designated as library files. Library folders are similar to regular folders except that files in library folders are treated as library files and cannot be modified while stored in a library folder. Library folders must be created directly under the root of the vault, because you cannot create them under a regular folder.

Library folders use a different icon than regular folders. Note that subfolders are used to group library parts into meaningful categories. You can create any level of nested library folders to help organize the files, as shown in Figure 2–11.

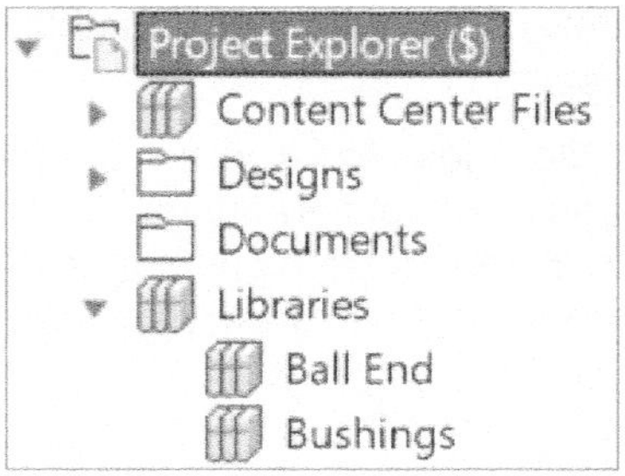


**Figure 2–11**

When a user retrieves a design from the vault and the design contains library files, the library files are copied into the working folder to the same relative location and folder as in the vault.

## iParts in the Vault

Figure 2–12 displays an iPart factory, **Heim Bushing.ipt**, in a library folder. Note that a unique icon is used to distinguish a factory from other file formats. iPart children also have unique icons.

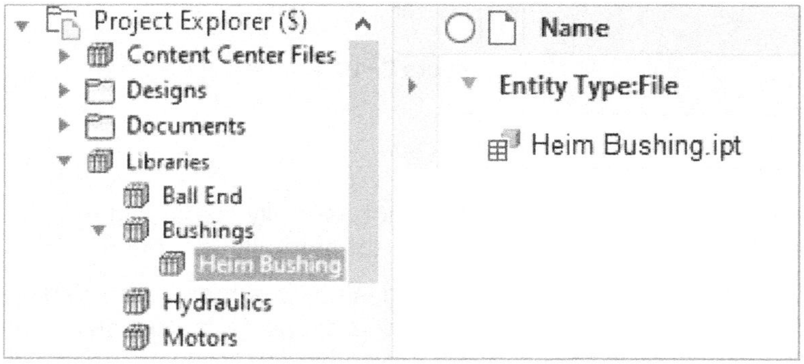


**Figure 2–12**

## Project Files Settings for Library Parts

When you open a model, Autodesk Inventor looks for library files in the locations specified in the project file. Figure 2–13 displays a project file with a single **Libraries** path that points to the top-level *Library* folder. The library path is relative because the *Library* folder is beneath the folder containing the project file.

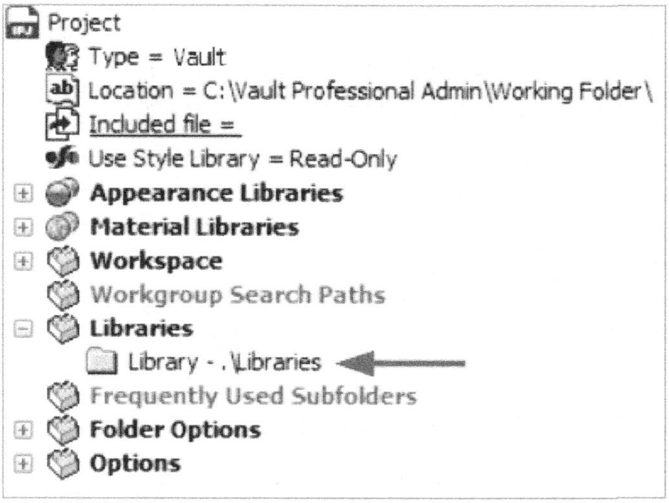


**Figure 2–13**

## Importance of Relative Paths

Because all design files, including library files, are stored in the vault, all paths in a vault project file should be defined relative to the folder containing the project file. When you use relative paths, the entire local working folder structure is portable; it can be located in any location on a user's computer. If you use absolute paths to local folders such as *G:\Libraries*, or UNC names such as *\\PartServer\Libraries*, each user must have the same setup on their computer if they want to share the same project file from the vault.

# About Content Center Files

Content Center files are parts that you often use in more than one design. They are similar to other library files and you need to set them up correctly to work with Autodesk Vault.

## About Content Center Files and Vault

Content Center files are parts that are placed from the Content Center libraries. The Content Center libraries are databases that store definitions of parts. A part file is not created until you first place the selected part in your design. Because many designs use identical instances of a part (for example, a common fastener), you normally store the resulting part file in a common folder that is outside of your designs so that many designs can reference one copy of the library part. When you place the part from the Content Center in another model, the folder in which you store Content Center parts is checked before a new part file is created. If the part already exists, the design references the existing part instead of creating another.

When you use Autodesk Vault to manage documents for a design team, you should install the Content Center libraries with the Autodesk Data Management Server (ADMS) rather than as Inventor Desktop Content.

## How Content Center Files Are Organized

As with user-defined library components, you share Content Center files between designs but you do not modify them. In the same way that you use the top-level *Libraries* folder, you specify a storage location for Content Center parts in the project file that is outside the *Designs* folder. Because you cannot modify parts generated from the Content Center, you store them in library folders in the vault. When you store a design in the vault or get versions of a design, parts placed from the Content Center act in a similar manner to other library parts.

You can organize Content Center files in many ways. However, for best results when using the vault, you should organize these files in the same way that you organize library files. Figure 2–14 displays the recommended folder structure for storing Content Center files. The *Content Center Files* folder is located directly under the project file but outside of the folder where regular design files are stored.

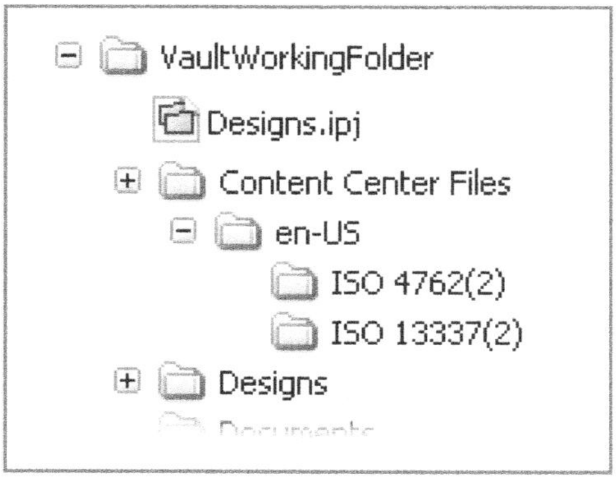


**Figure 2–14**

## Content Center Files in the Vault

Parts generated from the Content Center libraries are stored in the vault using the same folder structure below your working folder. When you create a part from the Content Center, the part is placed in a folder below the *Content Center Files* folder. The folder name reflects the family name of the part in the Content Center, as shown in Figure 2–15. In the vault, the local *Content Center Files* folder is mapped to a library folder one level below the root folder in the vault.

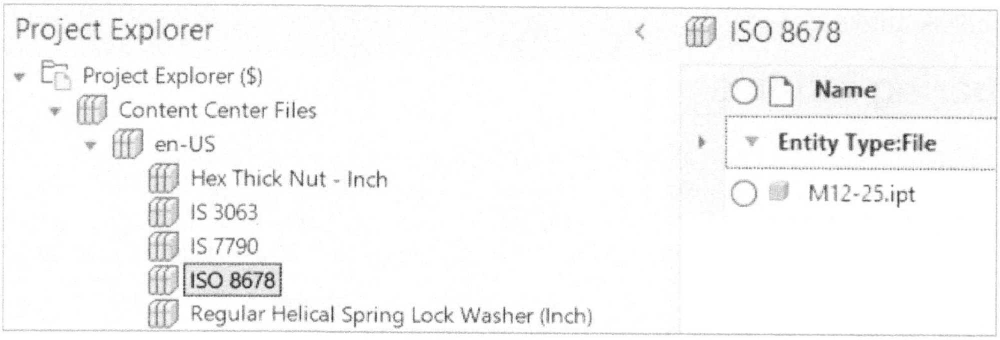


**Figure 2–15**

## Project File Settings for Content Center Parts

In the Autodesk Inventor project file editor, the *Content Center Files* path is set to the folder that you created for the Content Center files. Because the *Content Center Files* folder is beneath the project file, the path is relative to the project file as shown in Figure 2–16. The *Content Center Files* folder should be located outside the folder specified for user-defined library components.

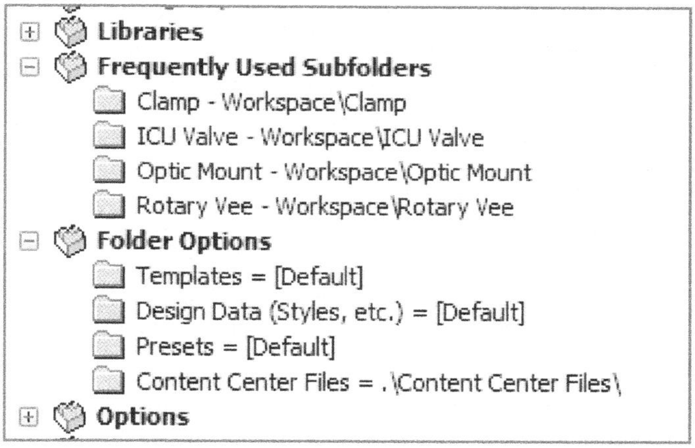


**Figure 2–16**

# 2.2 Adding Existing Models to a Vault

In this chapter, you learn how to prepare existing designs and add them to a vault using Autodesk Autoloader, a software that prepares, analyzes, and uploads Autodesk Inventor files to a vault. Many companies have existing Inventor designs that they need to add to the vault. You can use several methods to add your existing designs to the vault, depending on whether you want to manually prepare and upload the designs or use a more automated method such as Autodesk Autoloader.

## Preparing Models

The method you use to prepare data depends on the method you use to upload data to the vault. When you use Autodesk Autoloader to upload data, there is little preparation required because Autoloader reorganizes the files for you. If Autodesk Autoloader finds problems with some file relationships, you are required to fix the problems before using Autoloader to upload the files to the vault.

### Planning the Vault Structure

Before you upload existing model data, you must plan how you want to store your model files, library files, Content Center files, non-model files, and other data in the vault. If you use Autodesk Autoloader to upload your data, the software creates a single project file and the top-level vault folders for you. All that you need to create are subfolders to organize the files for each design. The structure and project file that Autoloader creates ensures that you can successfully work on your designs in Autodesk Inventor.

It is not a requirement that you have a single project file for all your designs before uploading files to a vault with Autodesk Autoloader. You can run Autoloader for each project file to upload the designs managed by the project file. It is highly recommended that you place all designs uploaded to the vault under the single vault project file created when you first upload files to a new vault using Autoloader.

### Preparing Project Files

When you run Autodesk Autoloader, you select an existing folder to upload. You then select a project file associated with the designs in the selected folder and its subfolders. The selected project file is used to validate file references in the designs in the selected folder before they are uploaded to the vault. Autodesk Autoloader reads any type of project file including Single-User, Shared, Semi-Isolated, and Vault.

Autoloader uses all defined paths in the project file to determine which files to upload. Each design in the selected folder and its subfolders is examined for dependent files. Autoloader checks that all dependent files can be found in the scope of the search paths so that models correctly resolve after uploading to the vault. All dependent files are added to the list of files to upload. Because Autoloader supports all project file formats, it locates all referenced files in the *Workspace*, *Workgroup*, *Libraries*, and *Content Center Files* search paths.

 

Existing projects can be organized in many different ways. Because Autoloader works with one project file at a time, run Autoloader once for each project file. If you already use a single project file for all of your designs, all designs can be uploaded at once using Autoloader. If you use multiple project files, you must run Autoloader for each project file.

You do not need to convert your existing project files to a Vault-type project file before you work with Autoloader. Autoloader creates a new Vault project file for you and adds it to the vault. The new project file is ready to use, including the correct search paths and folder mappings.

## Common Project File Problem

Although your existing projects can resolve correctly when you open the file in Autodesk Inventor, you might have to add additional search paths if Autodesk Autoloader cannot find files. For example, in Figure 2–17, the project file is located in the same folder as the main assembly, **Winch.iam**. The project file has *Workgroup* search paths to the *Motors* and *Hydraulics* folders, which are not located below the project file location. The project file does not contain a *Workspace* path. The main assembly opens successfully in Autodesk Inventor. However, when Autodesk Autoloader searches for files, the main assembly is not found because none of the search paths in the project file include the location of the main assembly file.

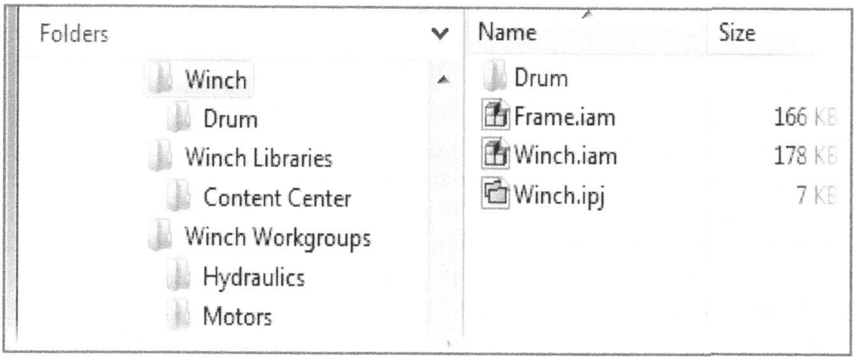


**Figure 2–17**

To fix the project file, add a *Workspace* path to the existing project file, and then run Autodesk Autoloader again.

## Solving File Resolution Problems

You cannot upload designs that fail to fully resolve. If Autoloader cannot find child files, you must either locate them and resolve the problem or remove the child part's reference from the parent file.

You can check your designs by opening each master assembly, drawing, and presentation file in Autodesk Inventor to ensure that all files are found. This can be a lengthy process, especially for large designs with many parent files. Alternatively, use Autodesk Autoloader to find resolution problems because it identifies just the issues that you need to resolve. Resolve the problem files and then run Autoloader again to recheck the data.

## Duplicate File Names

Although you can store files with the same name in the vault, it is recommended that you use unique filenames. If files are different, they should have different names. If the same file is used in more than one model, place the file in a common folder from which you can use the file in many designs. If the file is used by many designs and is rarely or never modified, move the file to a library folder so that it is protected from unintended changes, as shown in Figure 2–18.

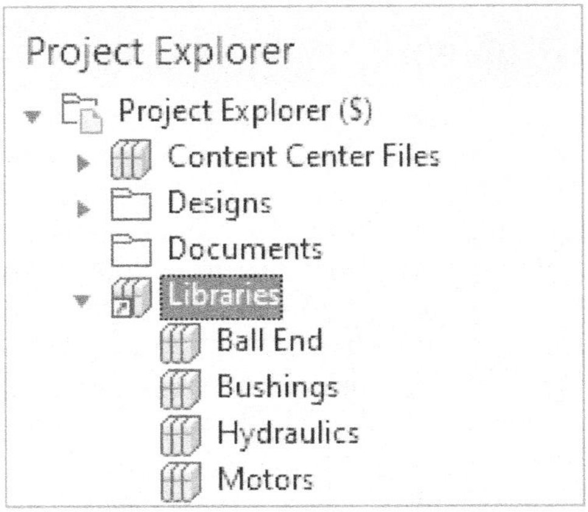


**Figure 2–18**

If you need to rename files, upload the files to the vault and then use the Vault renaming utility to rename the files rather than renaming the files in File Explorer and manually repairing the references. To add files with duplicate names to the vault, toggle off the **Enforce Unique File Names** setting in the vault and then add the files. In Vault, search for duplicate filenames. If the files are different, rename them. After renaming, toggle on **Enforce Unique File Names**. The option to enforce unique filenames in a vault is located in the *Vault Settings* dialog box (**Tools>Administration>Vault Settings**). In the *Vault Settings* dialog box, navigate to the Files tab>File Options area and click **Define**, as shown in Figure 2–19.

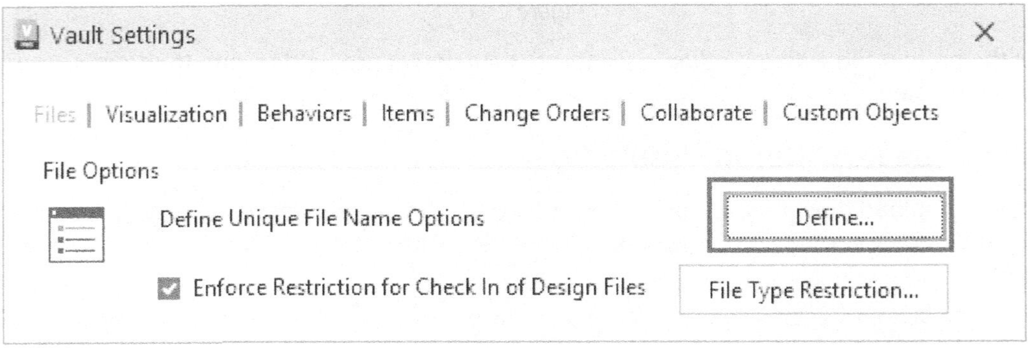


**Figure 2–19**

In the *File Name Options* dialog box, select **Enforce unique file name**, as shown in Figure 2–20. If using Autoloader, the **Enforce Unique File Names** option must be disabled.

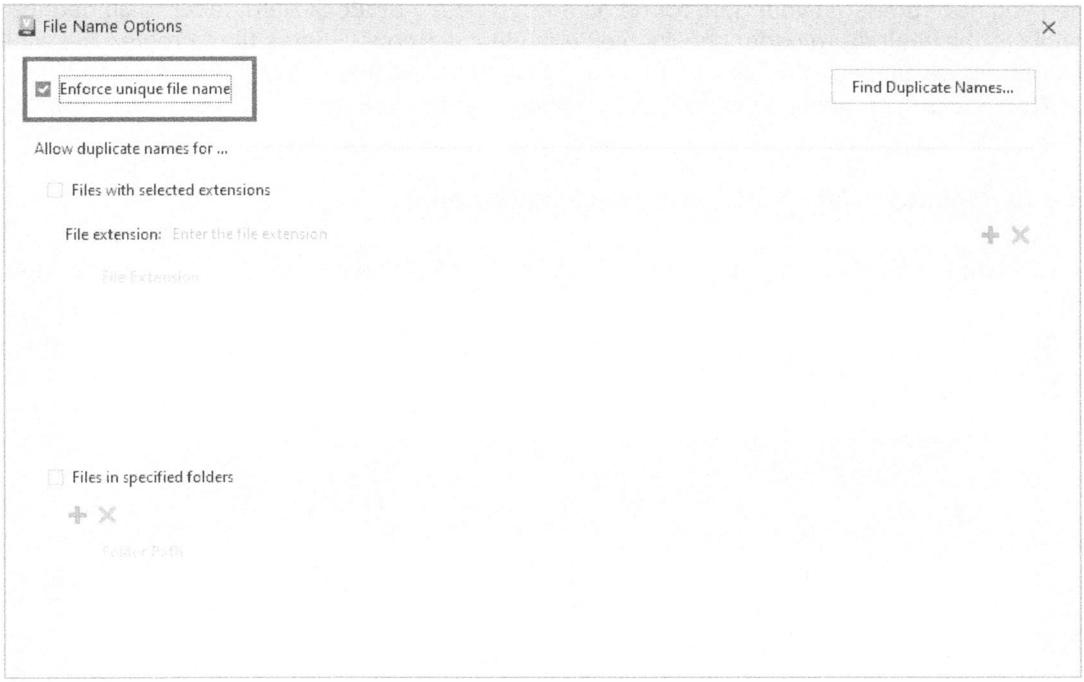


**Figure 2–20**

To consolidate duplicate files into one shared file, add your designs to the vault and then reorganize the files. Vault understands file relationships; therefore, you can move files without breaking links. To find where a file is used, view the *Where Used* information in Vault Explorer and record where each file is used. Delete all but one copy of the file, move the one copy from its current folder to a common folder, and then check out each dependent file and resolve the links. Use the **File Replace** operation where appropriate.

## Migrating Files

If you want to migrate your design files to the latest release of Autodesk Inventor, you can migrate the files before or after you add them to the vault. To migrate files, schedule a migration task using the Task Scheduler in Inventor. The scheduled task opens all files from a local or vault folder, migrates the files, and saves them back to the same local or vault location.

You are not required to migrate Autodesk Inventor files before uploading them to the vault; however, Autoloader will not upload Inventor files older than R10 (must be migrated first) and AutoCAD files older than R14.

# Uploading Models

When you have prepared your data for uploading, you use Autodesk Autoloader to upload the models to the vault. Autoloader checks file dependencies, consolidates files, creates the vault folder structure, uploads the files, and creates a vault project file. The resulting vault folder structure and project file ensure that you can successfully work with Autodesk Inventor and Vault.

## How To: Upload to Vault with Autodesk Autoloader

The following steps describe how to upload an existing Autodesk Inventor design to the vault using Autodesk Autoloader.

1. Organize the folder structure of your existing designs as you want them to display in the vault. (as shown in Figure 2–21)

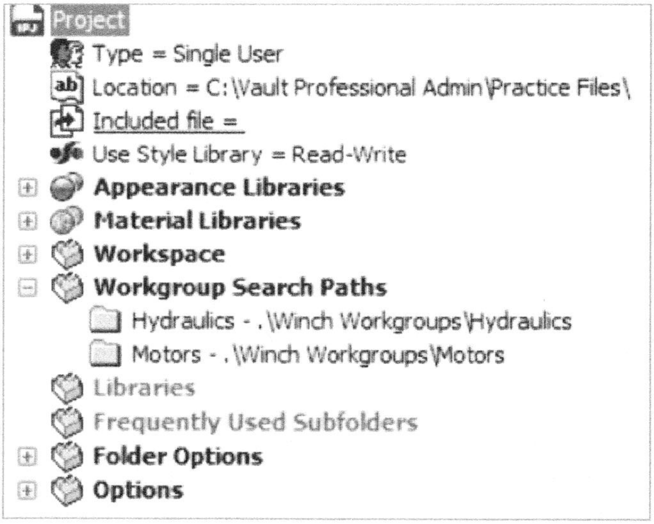


**Figure 2–21**

2. Start Autodesk Autoloader.
3. Select the top-level folder containing the designs you want to upload to the vault.
4. In the *Select Project* dialog box, select the project file that manages the files to be uploaded, as shown in Figure 2–22.

 

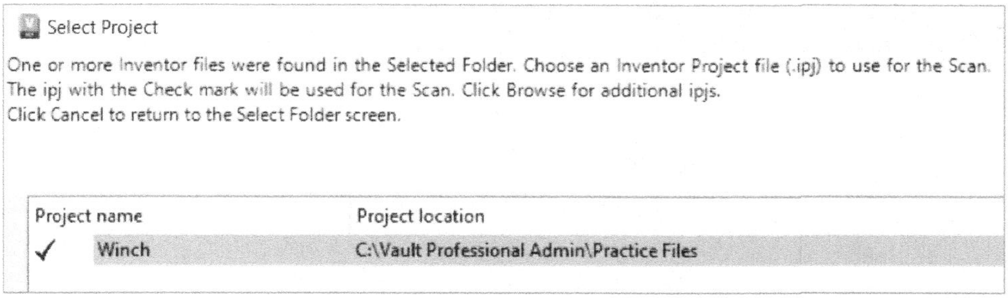


**Figure 2–22**

5. Click **Scan** (as shown in Figure 2–23) to scan all files in the project folders and confirm file relationships.

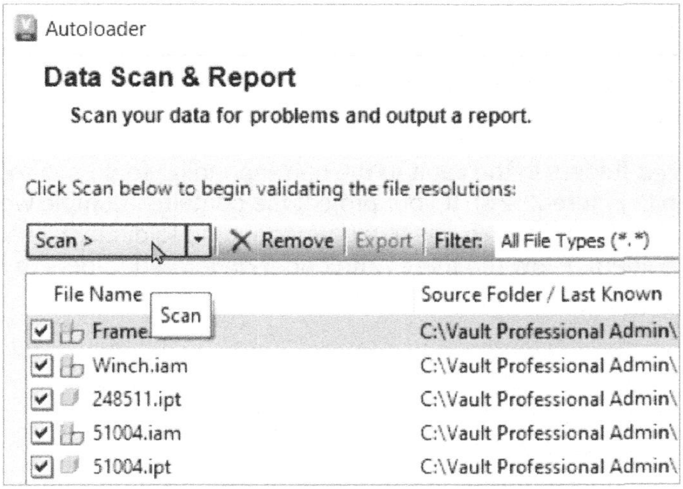


**Figure 2–23**

6. If required, fix any reported problems. Missing files and file resolution issues are reported (as shown in Figure 2–24). You are not required to abandon the Autoloader session. Open the files in their associated CAD application and repair the reported issues.

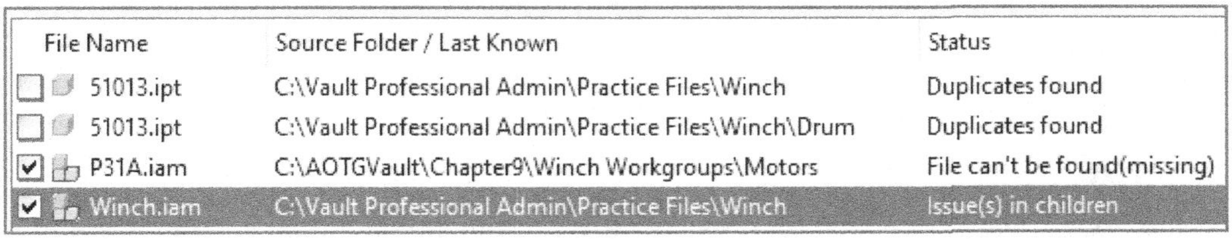


**Figure 2–24**

7. Return to Autoloader and rescan the files. You can only proceed when all reported issues have been resolved. The problem files can also be excluded from the selection set and loaded by hand later.

8. In the drop-down list, select **Find duplicates** (as shown in Figure 2–25). This will help identify any identical files that might cause confusion later in the process.

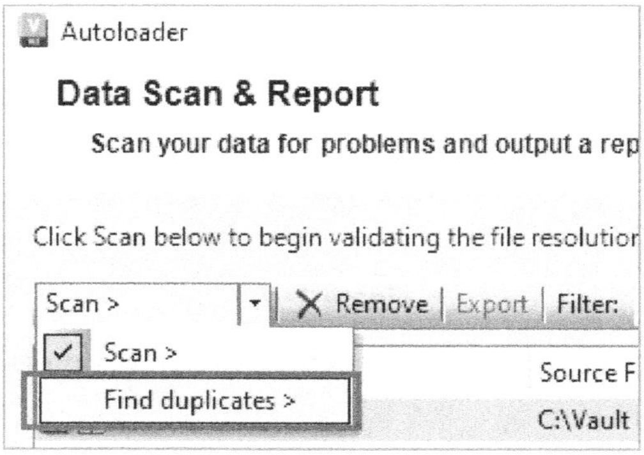


**Figure 2–25**

9. Once all issues have been resolved, click **Next**.
10. Log in to the vault.
11. Map the generated folders in the vault to the corresponding folders in the existing project folder (as shown in Figure 2–26). If your project file contains multiple workgroup or library search paths, you must map each one to a corresponding folder in the vault. You can create additional vault folders below the three Autoloader-generated folders to help organize the data in the vault.

    ***Note:*** *During the mapping step, selecting to map 'Winch' to 'Products' in the vault will put 'Winch' under 'Products'. If mapping the 'Winch' folder to a 'Winch' folder in the vault, select the **Direct Mapping** option at the bottom of the Browse Vault For Folder dialog box.*

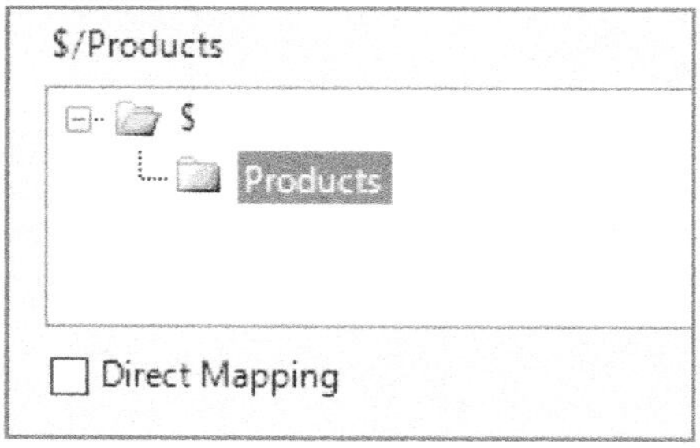


**Figure 2–26**

12. Click **Next**.
13. On the *Copy & File Redirection Progress* page, wait until the operation is complete and click **Next**.
14. Upload the files to the vault. You can optionally generate a visualization file of each CAD file before it is uploaded to the vault. Once uploaded, the Autoloader Progress and Report page notes the report location and filename to review the details of the upload.

## Autoloader Results

When you use Autoloader to upload files to a new vault, Autoloader organizes the files based on the recommended vault structure. Figure 2–27 displays the results of using Autoloader to upload several designs. Autoloader creates a new Vault project file, and creates two top-level library folders, *Content Center Files* and *Libraries*, along with a single top-level *Designs* folder. The project file contains the correct search paths and folder mappings. You should not have to edit the project file unless you want to add frequently used subfolders. You can get a copy of the project file to your working folder and immediately start working with the model files.

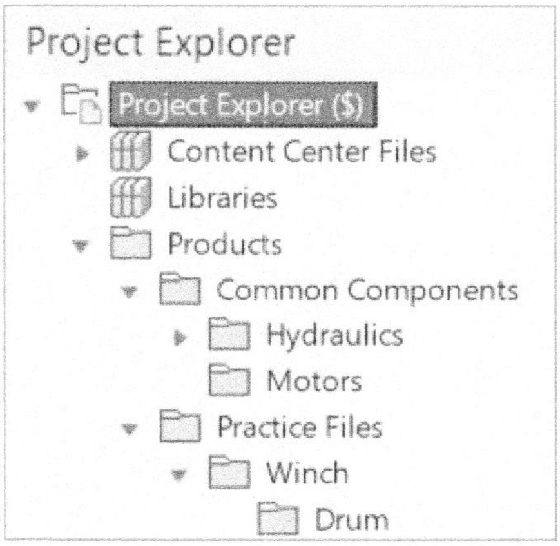


**Figure 2–27**

## Uploading Non-Inventor Data

By default, all files in and below the selected folder are uploaded to the vault (as shown in Figure 2–28). File relationships between Autodesk Inventor documents are maintained, as are external reference relationships between DWG files. Other files, such as images, documents, and spreadsheets are also uploaded, but are not automatically attached to other documents in the vault. If required, you must manually attach them to the appropriate file after you upload the files to the vault.

In Autoloader, you can upload all files found in or below the selected folder or limit the upload to Autodesk Inventor files or DWG-based files. You can also control the upload status for each file.

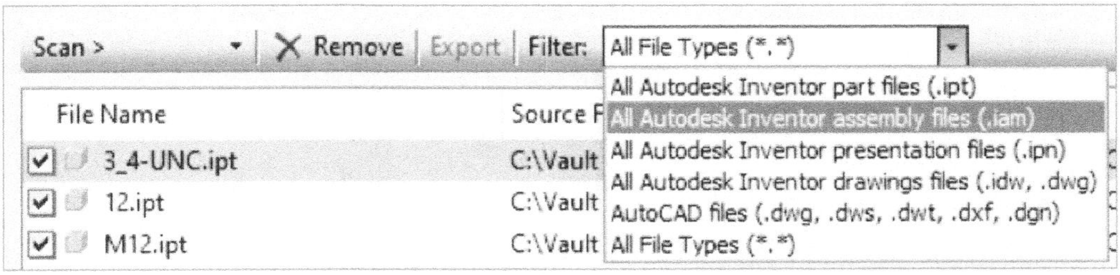


**Figure 2–28**

## Adding Visualization Files

You can also generate DWF or DWFx files for all CAD files uploaded to the vault. This can take a considerable amount of time for large datasets. You can run Autoloader multiple times with subsets filtered by file format to reduce the time for any one upload.

Another approach is to use the Task Scheduler to check out and then immediately check in all files after you have uploaded all files without DWF attachments. DWF files are created when the files are checked back in to the vault.

# Practice 2a
# Add Existing Projects to a Vault

In this practice, you prepare a project for uploading and then upload the design to an empty vault using Autodesk Autoloader, as shown in Figure 2–29.

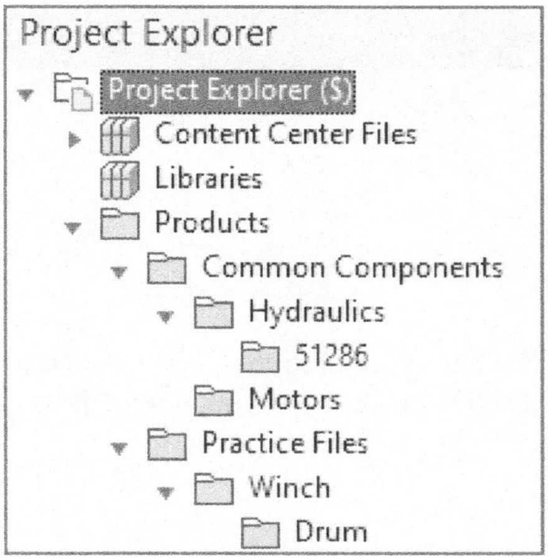


***The completed practice***

**Figure 2–29**

## Task 1: Create a new vault.

1. Exit Autodesk Inventor if it is running.
2. Start Autodesk Data Management Server Console using one of the following options:
   - **Start>Autodesk Data Management >Autodesk Data Management Server Console**
   - Double-click on the Autodesk Data Management Server Console icon on your desktop
3. Log in as **administrator**. Leave the *Password* field blank.

4. In the left pane, expand your computer name's node, right-click on the *Vaults* folder and select **Create**, as shown in Figure 2–30.

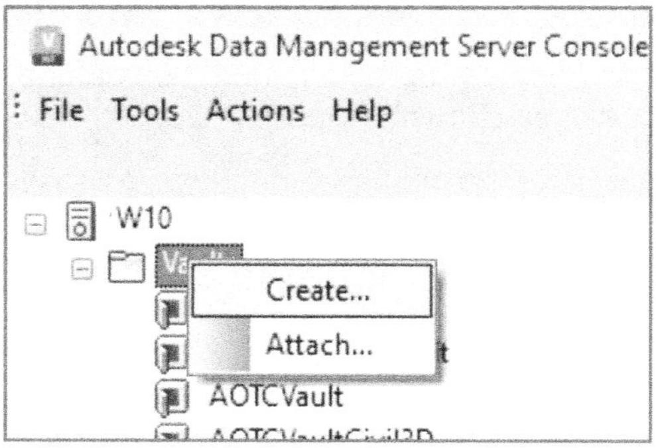


**Figure 2–30**

5. In the *Create Vault* dialog box (shown in Figure 2–31), for *New Vault Name*, type **UploadVault**. Click **OK**. When the vault is created, click **OK** to close the message box.

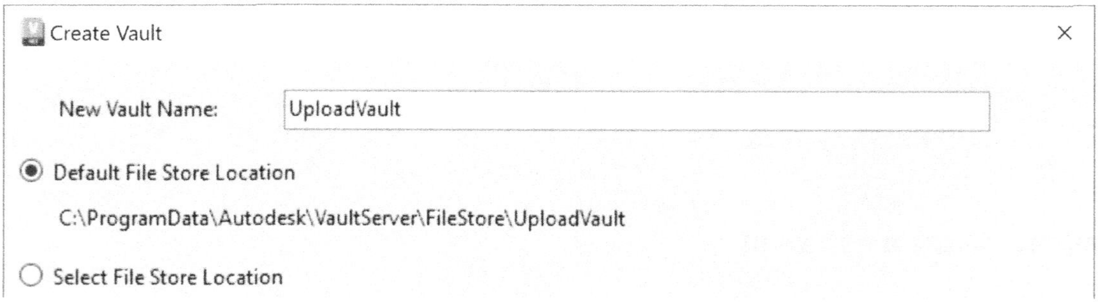


**Figure 2–31**

6. Exit Autodesk Data Management Server Console.

## Task 2: Edit Inventor project file.

1. In File Explorer, navigate to the folder *C:\Vault Professional Admin\Practice Files*. Right-click on **Winch.ipj** and select **Edit**. In the *Edit Project* window, view the project file's entries for **Workgroup Search Paths** (as shown in Figure 2–32). The *Hydraulics* and *Motors* folders are located below the *Winch Workgroups* folder.

   ***Note:*** *Note that if using Windows 11 you may not be able to right-click and select* ***Edit****. If this occurs, launch Inventor and access the Project File dialog box. Then click* ***Browse*** *and navigate to the C:\Vault Professional Admin>Practice Files folder and select the* ***Winch.ipj*** *file. This will activate the* ***Winch.ipj*** *project file and provide access to make edits.*

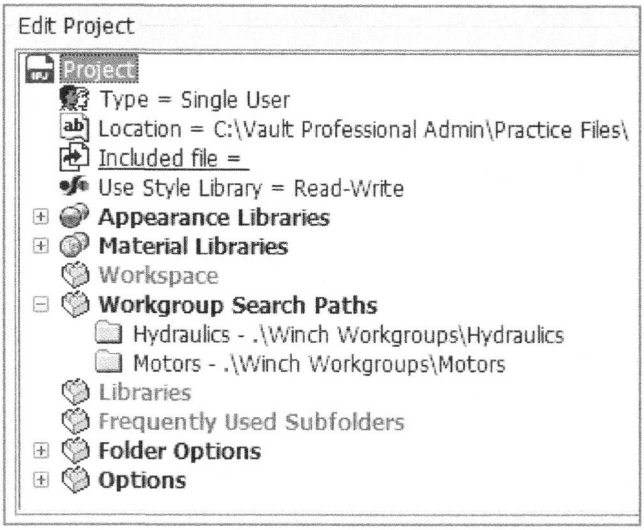


**Figure 2–32**

2. In the *Edit Project* window, right-click on **Workspace** and select **Add Path** (as shown in Figure 2–33). In the location, enter **.\Winch** (a period, followed by \Winch). Press <Enter>.

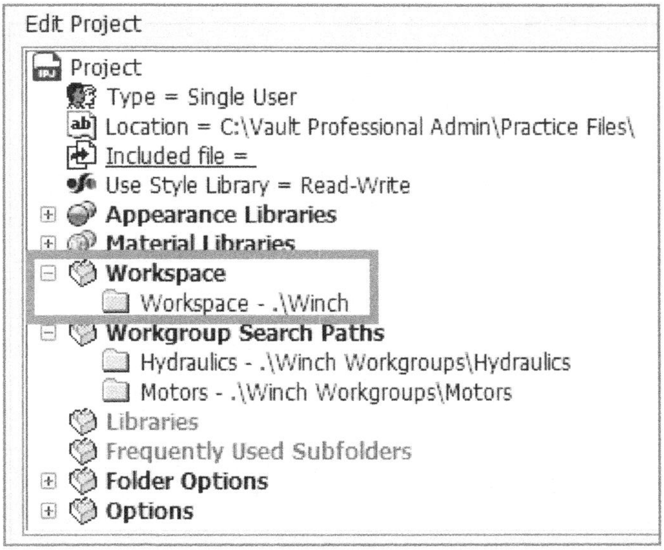


**Figure 2–33**

3. Click the plus sign (+) to expand **Folder Options** (as shown in Figure 2–34) and view the *Content Center Files* path.

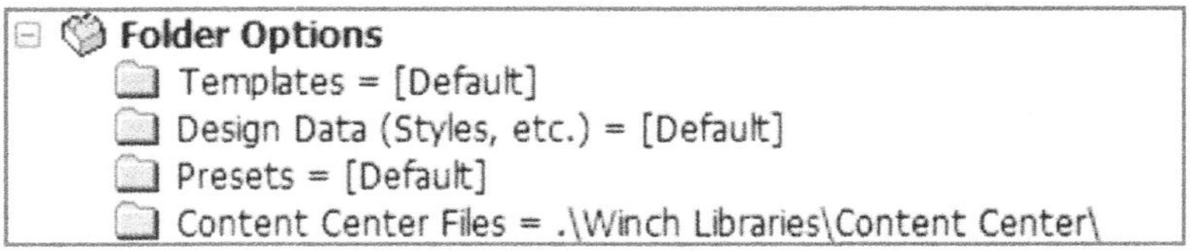


**Figure 2–34**

***Note:*** *If the supplied data folders were not installed to their default location, you might have to select a new path for the Content Center files.*

4. Click **Save**. Click **Close** to close the *Edit Project* window.

## Task 3: Start Autoloader and check file dependencies.

1. Start Autodesk Autoloader from the Windows *Start* menu>*Autodesk Data Management* folder. On the Welcome page, click **Next**.
2. On the *Select Data Source* page, click **Select Folder**, as shown in Figure 2–35.

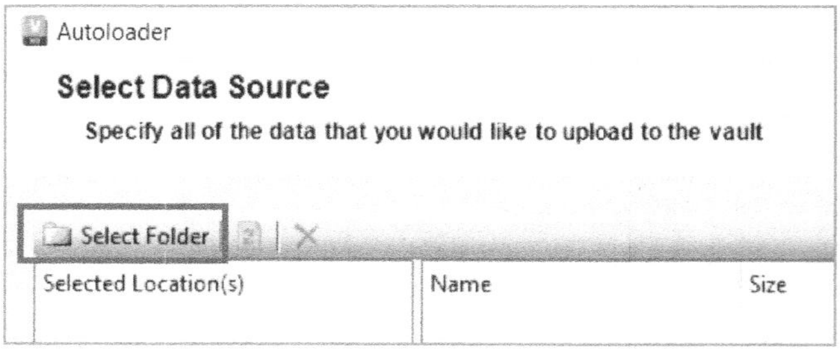


**Figure 2–35**

3. In the *Browse For Folder* dialog box, navigate to the *C:\Vault Professional Admin\Practice Files* folder.
4. Click **OK**.
5. In the *Select Project* dialog box, ensure that the **Winch** project file is shown as the active project file, as shown in Figure 2–36. If not, activate it.

**Figure 2–36**

6. Click **OK**.
7. In the *Autoloader* dialog box, click **Next**.

8. On the *Data Scan & Report* page, click **Scan**, as shown in Figure 2–37.

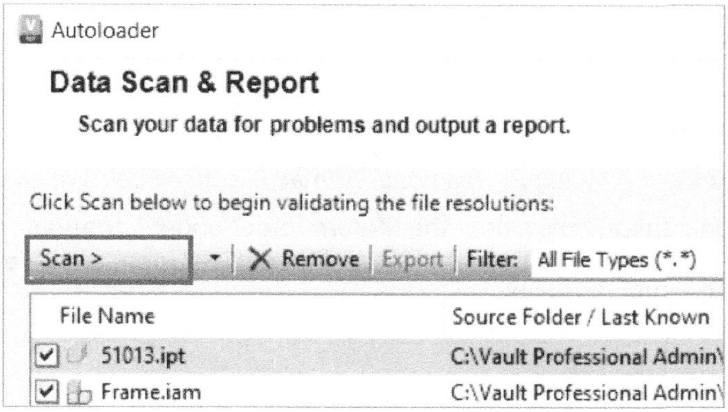


**Figure 2–37**

9. When the scan is complete, click **OK** to close the message box.
10. Note that **Next** is unavailable, indicating that there was a problem in one or more files. Click the *Status* column header to sort by status, and then scroll through the files and view the *Status* column, shown in Figure 2–38.

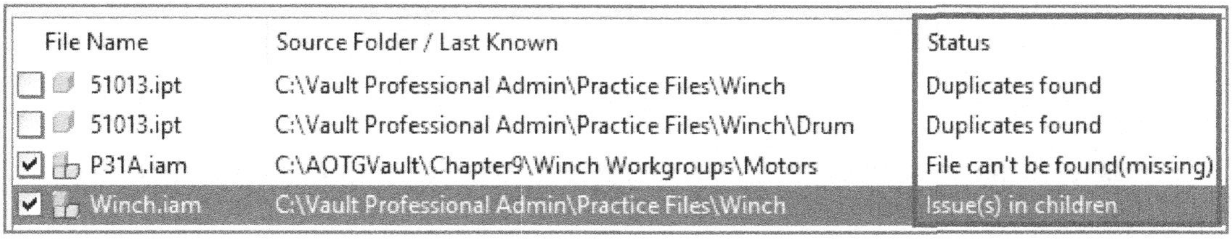


**Figure 2–38**

11. In the *File Name* column, click **Winch.iam**. Click **>>** to expand the *Autoloader* dialog box, if not already expanded.
12. On the *File Dependencies* tab, expand **Winch.iam** and select **P31A.iam**. The file resolution issue for **Winch.iam** is that **P31A.iam** cannot be found, as shown in Figure 2–39.

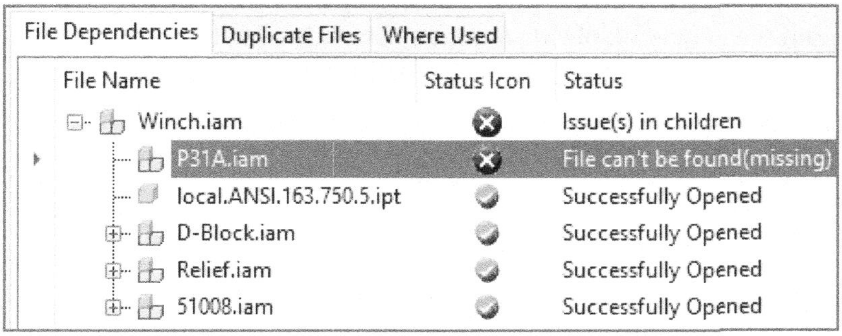


**Figure 2–39**

## Task 4: Solve the file resolution problem.

1. Start Autodesk Inventor.
2. Select **File>Manage>Projects** and ensure that **Winch.ipj** (under *C:\Vault Professional Admin\Practice Files*) is the active project file.
3. Open **Winch.iam** from *C:\Vault Professional Admin\Practice Files\Winch*.
4. In the *Resolve Link* dialog box, select the *Motors* folder under Locations, as shown in Figure 2–40. Select **P31B.iam** from the list and then click **Open**. Click **Yes** if you are prompted to update the assembly.

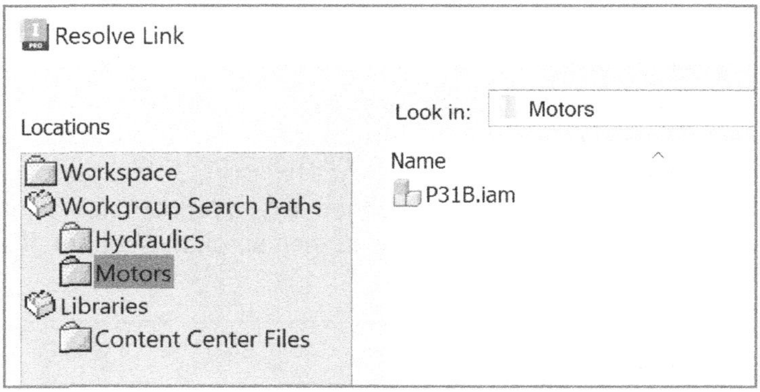


**Figure 2–40**

5. Click **Save**. In the *Save* dialog box, click **OK**. Update the data format if prompted.
6. Close the file.

## Task 5: Solve the duplicate files problem.

1. Switch to the Autodesk Autoloader. Click **Scan**.

   *Note: If you cannot restart the scan, click **Back** and **Next** again to return to the Data Scan & Report page. Click **Scan** to rescan the files.*

   The **Winch.iam** file is now resolved without errors; however, the scan reports duplicates in the examined files (two different **51013.ipt** files are referenced), as shown in Figure 2–41.

   *Note: Click on the Status column header to sort to view the duplicate files adjacent to each other.*

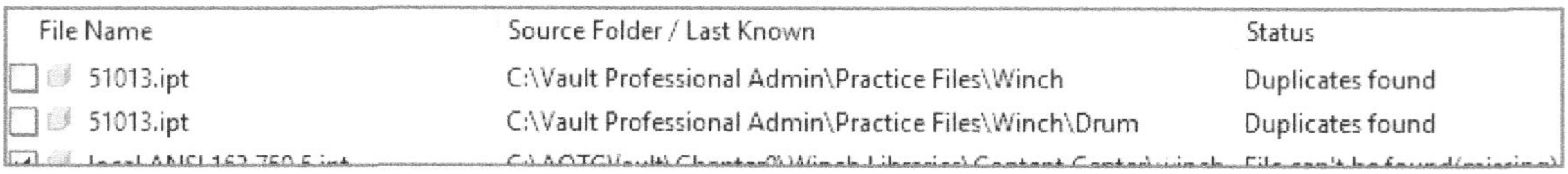


**Figure 2–41**

2. In the *File Name* column, click the first **51013.ipt** row. In the details pane at the bottom of the dialog box, click the *Duplicate Files* tab. The location of each **51013.ipt** file is displayed, as shown in Figure 2–42. This is where you analyze which file you want to keep, and which one needs to be replaced in the model and then deleted in the folder. In this case you will keep the file in the Drum folder.

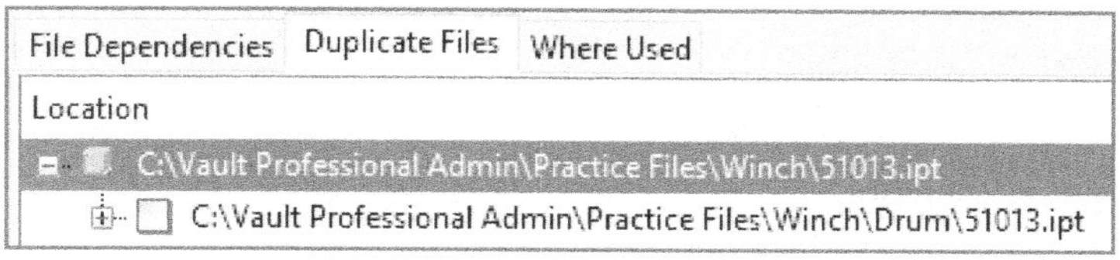


**Figure 2–42**

3. Switch to Autodesk Inventor. Open ***Frame.iam***. The project file should map you directly to the folder where **Frame.iam** is located. If it does not, navigate to *C:\Vault Profesisonal Admin\Practice Files\Winch*.

4. In the model browser, select **51013:3**. On the ribbon, select the *Assemble* tab and select **Component>Replace>Replace All** as shown in Figure 2–43.

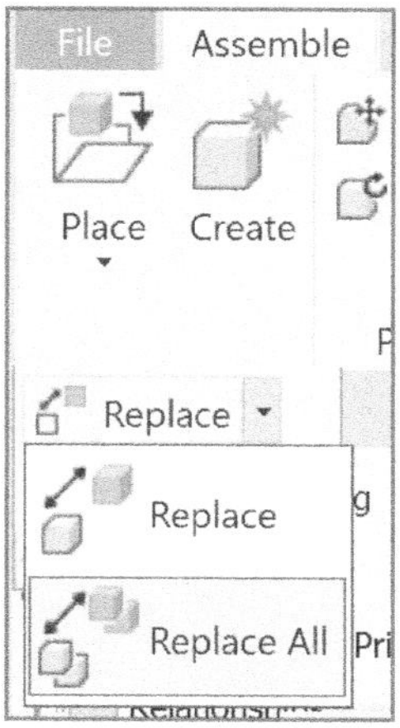


**Figure 2–43**

5. In the *Place Component* dialog box, browse to the *Drum* folder and select **51013.ipt**. Click **Open**.

6. Save the file. Close **Frame.iam**. Update the data format if prompted.

   - The original **...\Winch\51013.ipt** file is no longer referenced in the assembly.

7. In File Explorer, browse to the *C:\Vault Professional Admin\Practice Files\Winch* folder. Delete **51013.ipt**.

8. Switch to Autodesk Autoloader. Scan the files again. All files are opened and resolved successfully. No duplicate files are found.

   ***Note:*** *If Scan is grayed out, click the* ***Back*** *button, then* ***Next*** *and* ***Scan*** *will be available.*

## Task 6: Map folders and complete the upload.

The local drive folders (in which the files are located) must be mapped to the proper folder structure in the Vault database to ensure that the files are stored in the proper structure when they are uploaded to Vault. This task steps you through the mapping and uploading process.

1. Click **Next**. Log in to the vault.
   - For *User Name*, enter **administrator**.
   - Leave the *Password* blank.
   - For *Vault*, select **UploadVault**.
   - Click **OK**.
2. On the *Map Vault Folders* page, note that the project file's search paths are listed on the left and the new vault folders are on the right. Note that three new folders are created below the root folder in the vault, *Content Center Files*, *Designs*, and *Libraries*.
3. Under *Resultant Vault View,* select the *Designs* folder. Click **Rename**. In the *Rename Folder* dialog box, enter **Products**, as shown in Figure 2–44. Click **OK** to rename the vault folder.

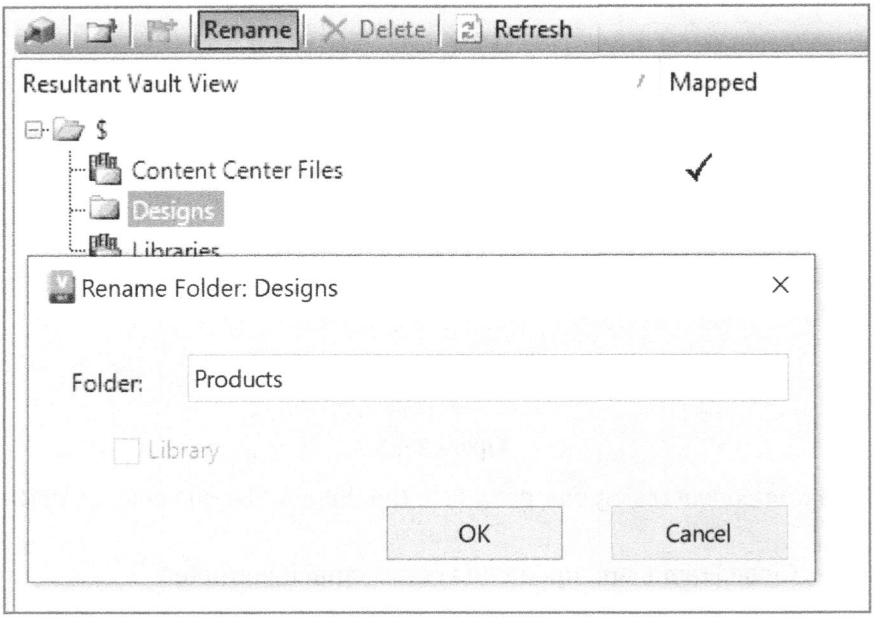


**Figure 2–44**

 

4. Under *Folder to Check In*, double-click **Practice Files**, as shown in Figure 2–45.

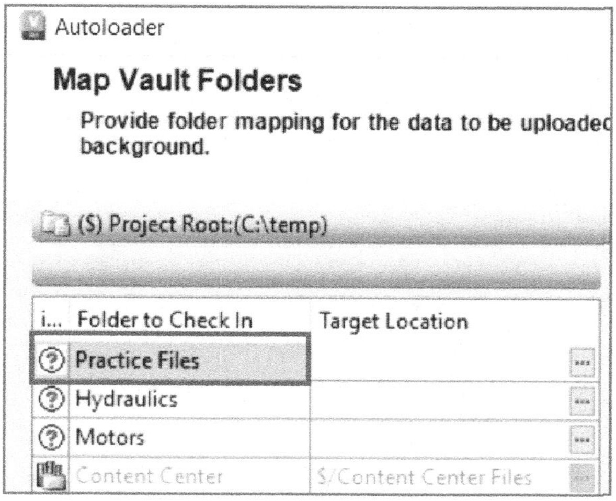


Figure 2–45

5. In the *Browse Vault for Folder* dialog box, select the **Products** folder and ensure that the **Direct Mapping** checkbox is not selected, as shown in Figure 2–46.

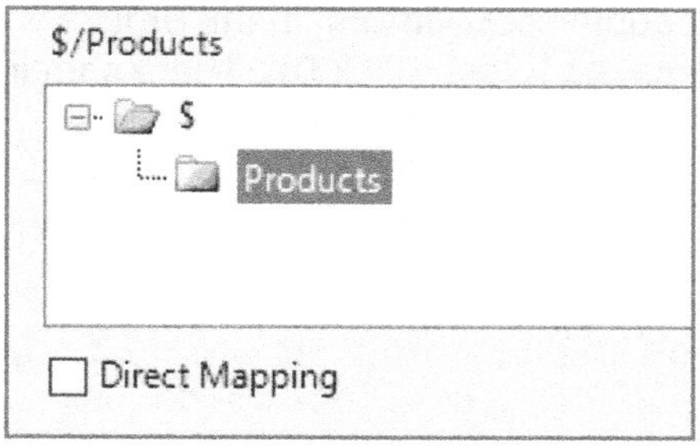


Figure 2–46

6. Click **OK**. The workspace folder from the project file is mapped to the new folder in the vault, as shown in Figure 2–47.

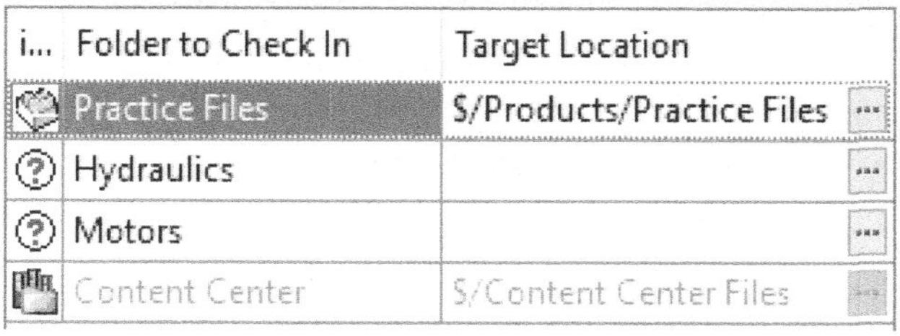


Figure 2–47

7. Under *Folder to Check In*, double-click **Hydraulics**. In the *Browse Vault for Folder* dialog box, select the *Products* folder. Click **New Folder**.
8. In the *Create Folder* dialog box, enter **Common Components**. Click **OK**. There should now be a *Common Components* folder under the *Products* folder.
9. In the *Browse Vault for Folder* dialog box, click **Common Components**. Click **OK**. A *Hydraulics* subfolder is created automatically, as shown in Figure 2–48.

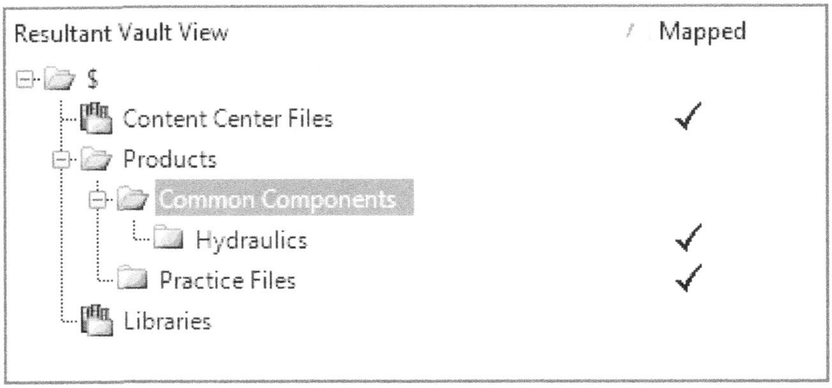


**Figure 2–48**

10. Under *Folder to Check In,* double-click **Motors**. In the *Browse Vault for Folder* dialog box, select the *Common Components* folder. Click **OK**. There should be a *Motors* folder under *Common Components*, as shown in Figure 2–49.

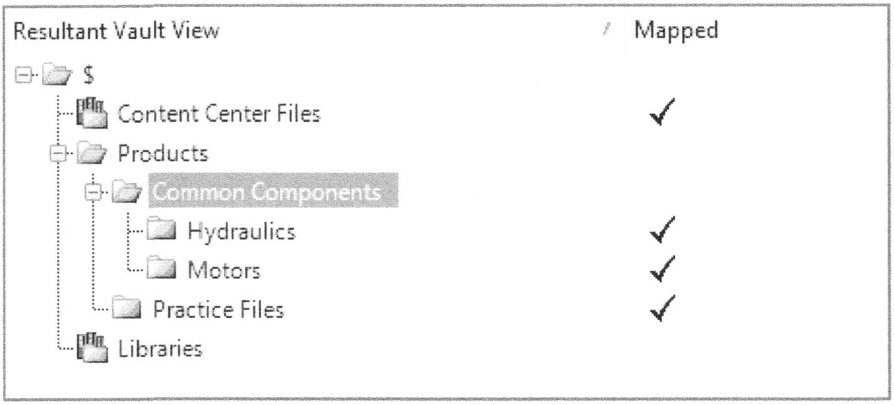


**Figure 2–49**

11. Click **Next**.

12. On the *Copy & File Redirection Progress* page, wait until the operation is complete. The *Status* area will state *Completed Successfully* when complete. Click **Next**.
13. On the *Specify Data Subsets* page (shown in Figure 2–50), examine the resulting structure of files in the vault.

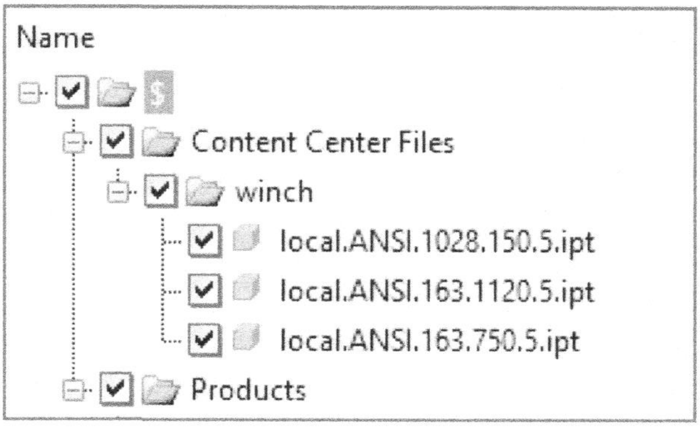


**Figure 2–50**

14. Click **Upload**.
15. On the *Autoloader Progress & Report* page, make note of the report location and filename once the upload is complete. It is located in the *Status* area at the bottom of the dialog box. This report can be used to validate what files were uploaded or to analyze errors.
16. Click **Done**.

## Task 7: Review the results.

1. Start Autodesk Vault.
   - For *User Name*, enter **administrator**.
   - Leave the *Password* blank.
   - For *Vault*, select **UploadVault**.
   - Click **OK**.
2. In the root folder of the vault, *Project Explorer ($)*, note that there is a project file named **Designs.ipj**.

3. View the contents of the other folders shown in Figure 2–51.

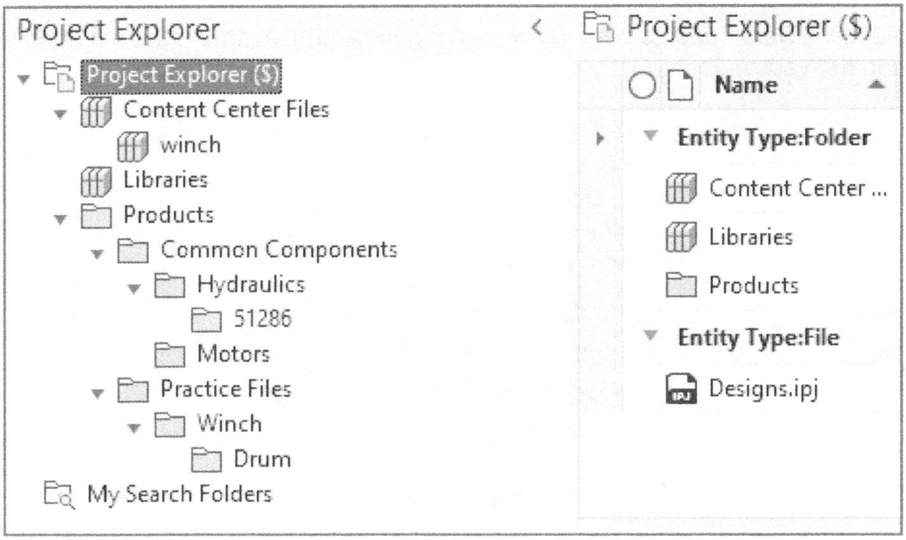


**Figure 2–51**

4. Exit Autodesk Vault Client.

**End of practice**

Chapter 3

# Managing Categories

Categories enable the grouping of documents by predetermined labels. Grouping by category also provides a means for assigning a defined set of behaviors and rules to objects, such as automatically assigning user-defined properties or life cycle definitions. Category assignment can be set up to happen automatically during check in based on rules, or a user can manually change a category.

## Learning Objectives

- Change a file or folder category.
- Create and edit categories.
- Assign rules to categories.

# 3.1 Categories and Rules

Categories in Autodesk® Vault Professional software are a powerful method of not only classifying different types of files or folders but automatically assigning other behaviors. Combined with rules, as users add new files to the vault or migrate from Autodesk Vault, lifecycle definitions and states, revision schemes and revision levels, and specific properties can be automatically assigned to the files. This ensures a very high level of both consistency and completeness to the data.

If you have Autodesk Vault Professional software, you can also configure categories to items and custom objects.

## Categories

On one level, categories are a very simple way of grouping different files or folders based on how your company creates, uses, and manages those files or folders. A very common example is that of files created by CAD applications and those created by word processing and graphics applications. Historically and functionally, the process for creating and releasing a set of models and drawings that represent a product or component has been very different than supporting documentation such as specifications and graphics used by marketing and sales. The CAD-generated files often go through a more formal, multi-step review and change process where as the supporting documentation can be managed in a simpler 'Work In Progress' or 'Released' fashion.

Categories give you the flexibility to categorize the files or folders in a way that best suits your organization. With categories you can:

- Visually identify different types of file groupings or purposes.
- Assign one or more lifecycle states based on the category and specify the default lifecycle definition and state for a new or migrated file.
- Assign one or more revisions based on the category and specify the default revision scheme and initial revision for a new or migrated file.
- Assign a set of existing properties or metadata to the file based on the category.

### Predefined File Categories

There are four pre-configured file categories shipped with Autodesk Vault. The details are listed in the following table.

| Name | Glyph | Description |
|---|---|---|
| **Base** | | Default category for migrated data and new files if no other rules are setup. |
| **Engineering** | | Data created for design purposes. Use this for the management of CAD-based files, such as Inventor, if you are going to use multiple file categories and have more formal lifecycle management needs. |

| Name | Glyph | Description |
|---|---|---|
| **Office** | | General data created by word processors, spreadsheet and image files. Use this for the management of office-type files if you are going to use multiple categories. |
| **Standard** | | Standard design data created by any application. Use this for the management of any file formats if you are going to only use a single category and have simpler lifecycle management needs. |

The predefined categories use the following lifecycle definitions, revision schemes, and property sets.

| Name | Lifecycle Definitions | Revision Schemes | Property Set |
|---|---|---|---|
| **Base** | • None (opt-out scheme) | • None (opt out scheme) | Biased towards Inventor file property mapped user-defined properties. |
| **Engineering** | • Flexible Release Process<br>• Long Lead Time Release Process<br>• None (opt out scheme) | • Standard Alphabetic Format<br>• None (opt out scheme) | Biased towards Inventor file property mapped user-defined properties. |
| **Office** | • Simple Release Process<br>• None (opt out scheme) | • Standard Numeric Format<br>• None (opt out scheme) | Biased toward standard file property mapped user-defined properties. |
| **Standard** | • Basic Release Process<br>• Simple Release Process<br>• None (opt out scheme) | • Standard Alphabetic Format<br>• None (opt out scheme) | Biased towards Inventor file property mapped user-defined properties. |

## Assigning Categories

When a file is added to the vault or a user migrates from Autodesk Vault Basic to Autodesk Vault Professional, files are automatically assigned the default category. For the default configuration this is the **Base** category. This can be changed by the Administrator.

## Predefined Folder Categories

There is one pre-configured folder category shipped with Autodesk Vault. The details are listed in the following table.

| Name | Glyph | Description |
|---|---|---|
| **Folder** | | Default category for migrated data and new folders if no other rules are set up. |

# Change Category Command

The **Change Category** command enables the authorized user to change the current category to a new one. The file must not be a state that locks the file and the user must have the permission to change the category. For example, a file which is in a **Released** state cannot change category.

Changing the category of a file will apply the default lifecycle state definition and state and the default revision scheme and revision if they have not been previously assigned. If they are, changing the category will not change the current state or revision. If the file was assigned a lifecycle definition and revision scheme in the current category, changing the category will not change the lifecycle definition or revision scheme. They must be manually changed after the category change.

## How To: Change Category

To change the category of a file, use the following steps.

1. Before you attempt to revise a file, you should determine whether you have permission to do so. You must be at least a Document Manager (Level 1) to revise a file. If you attempt to change the category and do not have permission to do so, you will not be informed until after you dismiss the *Change Category* dialog box (i.e., there is no precheck). You can have this permission as a user or by being a member of a group that has this permission. It is always best to manage permission at the group level if possible.
2. The file must not be locked. Changing the category will create a new file version and new file versions cannot be created if the file is locked. Ensure that the file is not in a **Released** state if it has a lifecycle definition and state associated with it.

3. Select the file or group of files from the main pane that are to be changed, as shown in Figure 3–1. If you need to change a set of related files, you can use the options in the dialog box to select these for you. If the files are not related, use the <Shift> + select or <Ctrl> + select option to select the files from the list.

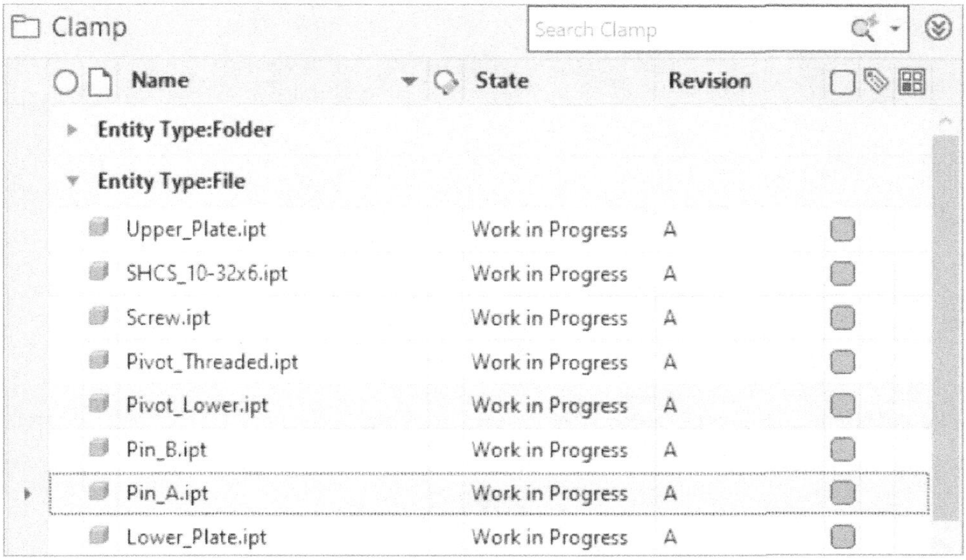


**Figure 3–1**

4. Select **Change Category** from the *Actions* menu as shown in Figure 3–2.

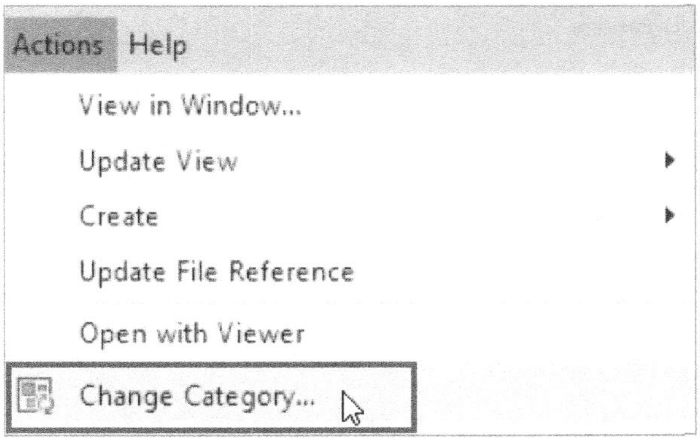


**Figure 3–2**

***Note:** You can also change categories in Autodesk Inventor by selecting **Change Category** from either the Vault tab>Control panel or from the shortcut menu in the Autodesk Vault Browser, as shown in Figure 3–3.*

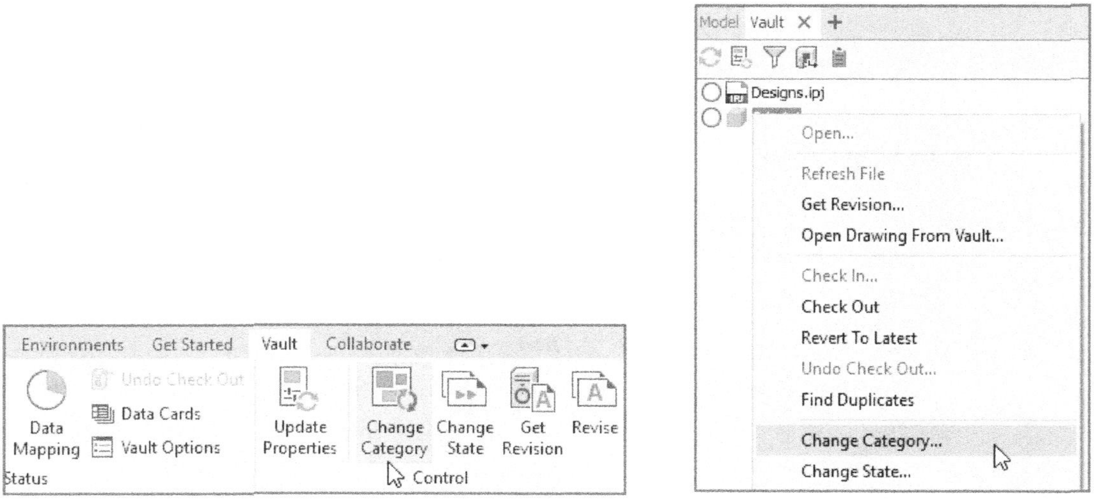


**Figure 3–3**

5. The *Change Category* dialog box shown in Figure 3–4 displays.

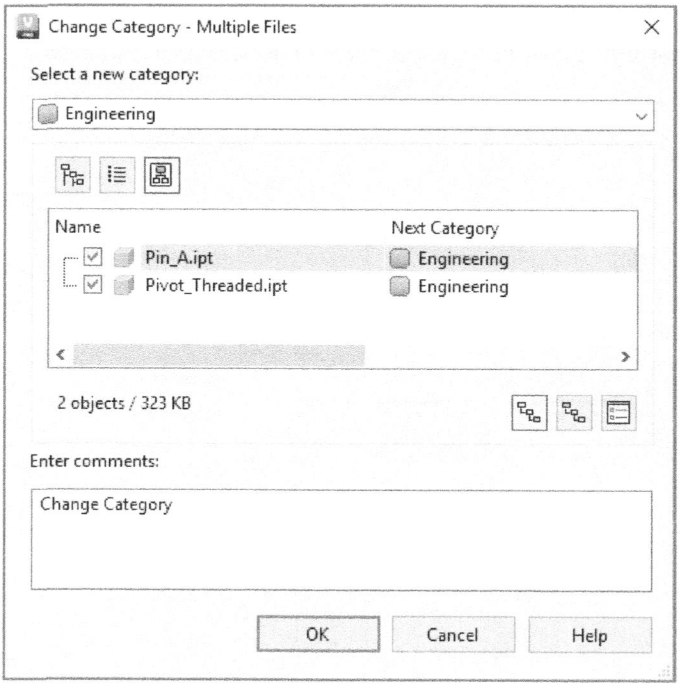


**Figure 3–4**

6. In the *Select a new category* section, select a new category from the drop-down list, as shown in Figure 3–5. Alternatively, you can change the category in the *New Category* column for each individual file.

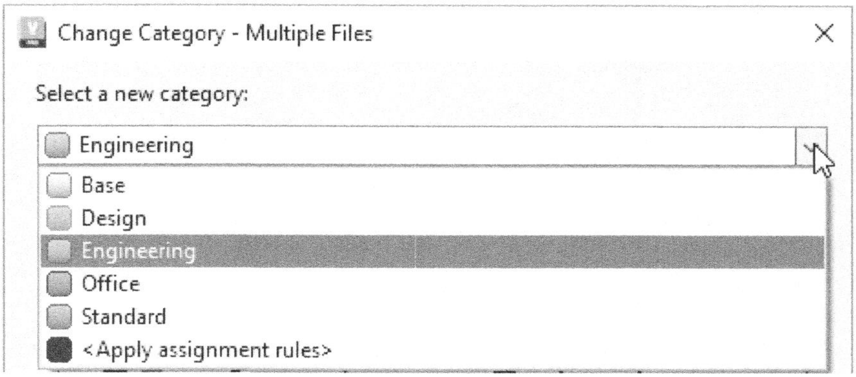


**Figure 3–5**

7. Use the View buttons (shown in Figure 3–6) to change the view to help understand file relationships.

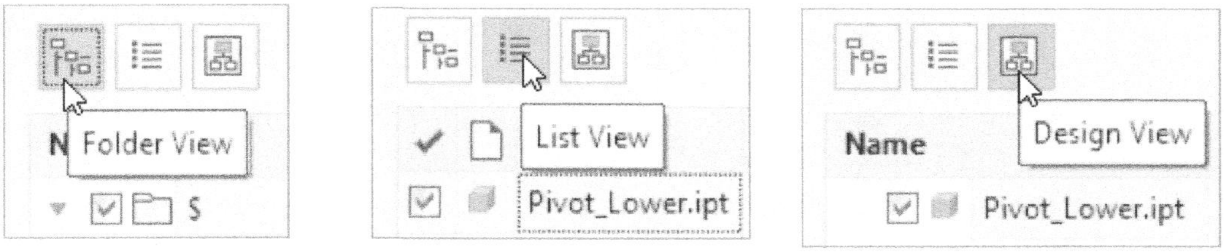


**Figure 3–6**

8. Use the Parent/Child selection buttons (shown in Figure 3–7) to modify the selection.

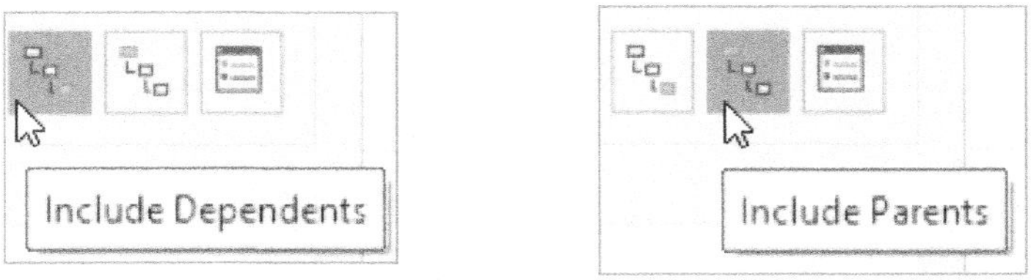


**Figure 3–7**

9. Select **Settings** to display the *Settings* dialog box shown in Figure 3–8. Here you can refine the selection of related files.

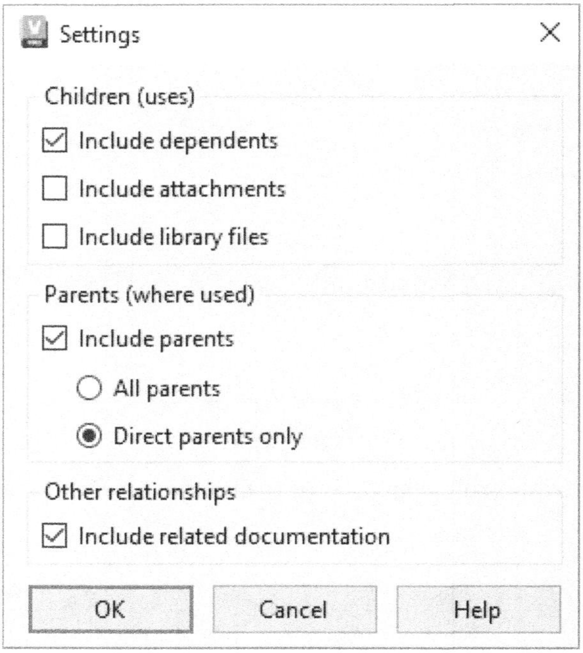


**Figure 3–8**

10. In the *Enter comments* area (shown in Figure 3–9), accept the default comment, select a comment from the drop-down list (if configured), or enter a custom comment.

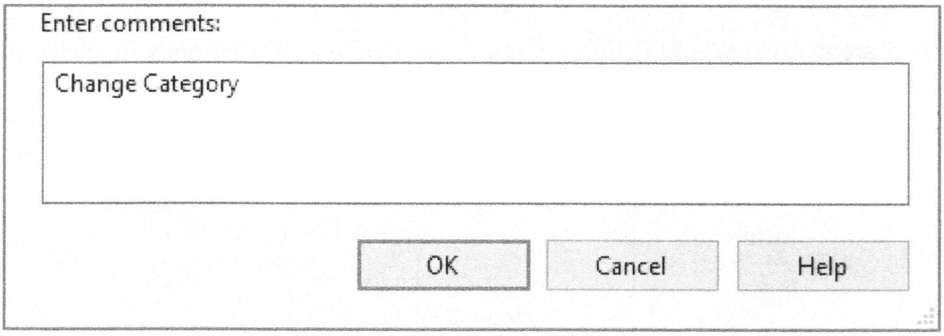


**Figure 3–9**

11. Click **OK** to complete the procedure.

# Rules

Rules enable you to automatically categorize a file based on one or more file property values. This gives you the ability to assign a category to a file when it is added to the vault using Autodesk Vault explorer or the CAD add-ins.

Rules work like the Advanced Find workflow in that you can specify a list of conditions to be met based on the system, user-defined property values, or filename values of the file being added. For example:

- Assign the file to the Engineering category if the filename ends with either 'IPT', 'IAM', or 'DWG'.
- Assign the file to the Office category if the user-defined property Category contains 'document'.
- Assign the file to the Standard category if the user-defined property Title contains 'Specification'.

# 3.2 Managing Categories and Rules

The Administrator can create and configure categories to specify the category glyph, lifecycle definitions, revision schemes, and property sets that will be assigned when a file is assigned a category. The Administrator can also create and manage a set of rules to automatically assign a file to a category when it is added to the system.

## Managing Categories

The Administrator can manage the set of categories using the *Configure Categories* dialog box shown in Figure 3–10.

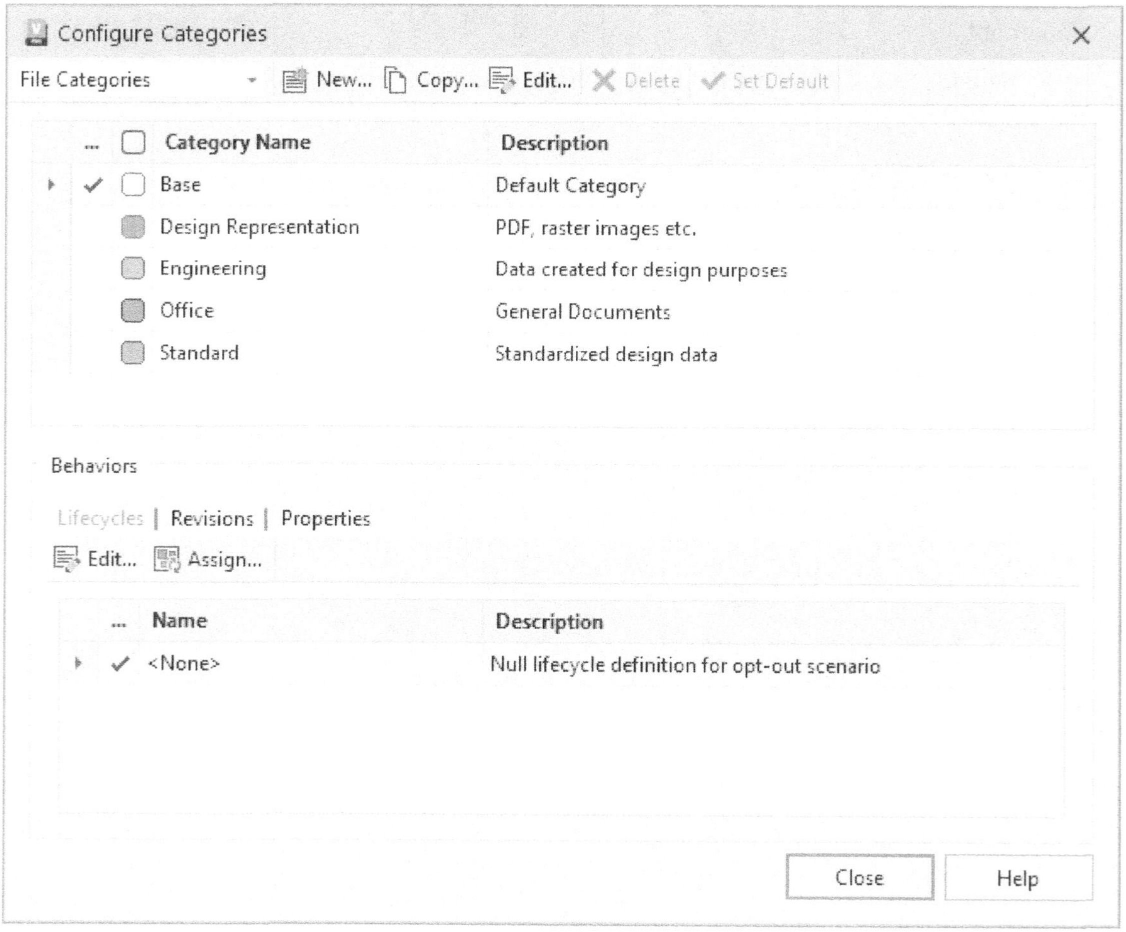


**Figure 3–10**

New categories can be created and existing categories can be edited. Categories that are not required and have not been used can be deleted. The category assigned to new files during migration or in the absence of any rule can be changed.

## How To: Create a New Category

If the categories provided do not meet your requirements, you can create a new one by completing the following steps.

1. In the *Tools* menu, select **Administration>Vault Settings**, as shown in Figure 3–11.

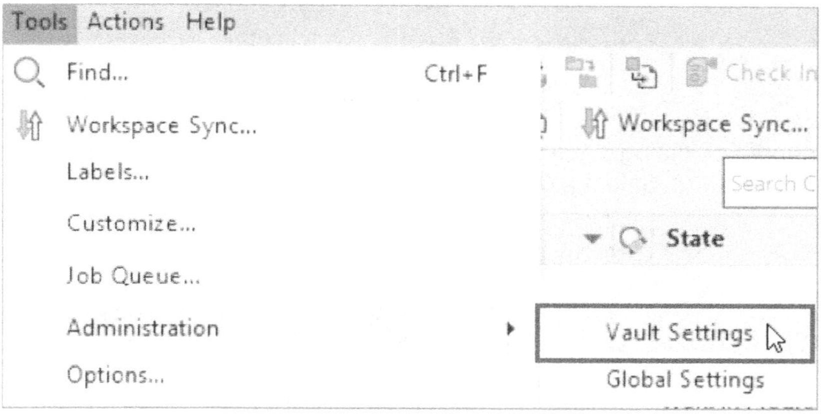


**Figure 3–11**

2. Select the *Behaviors* tab and select **Categories**, as shown in Figure 3–12.

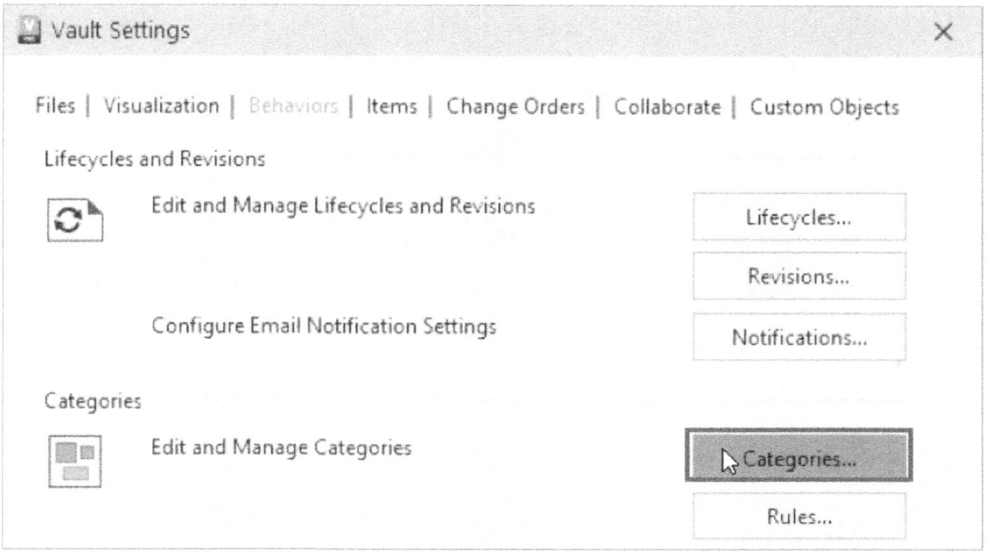


**Figure 3–12**

3. In the *Configure Categories* dialog box, select either **File Categories** or **Folder Categories** from the drop-down list and then select **New**, as shown in Figure 3–13.

   ***Note:*** *If you are using Autodesk Vault Professional software, you can also create Item Categories and Custom Object Categories.*

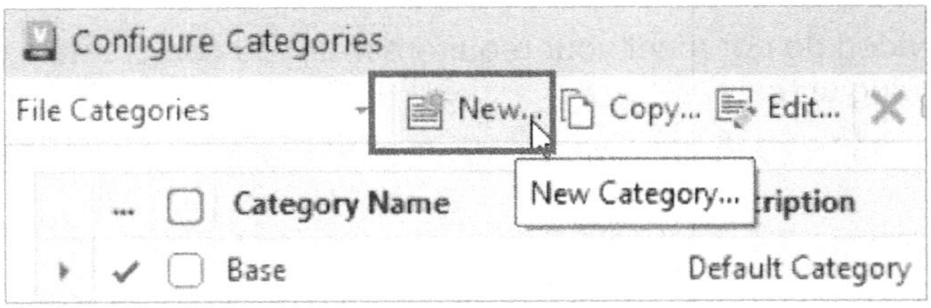


**Figure 3–13**

4. In the *Category Edit* dialog box, enter a *Name* and *Description* for your new category, as shown in Figure 3–14. Select a *Color* for the new category and click **OK**.

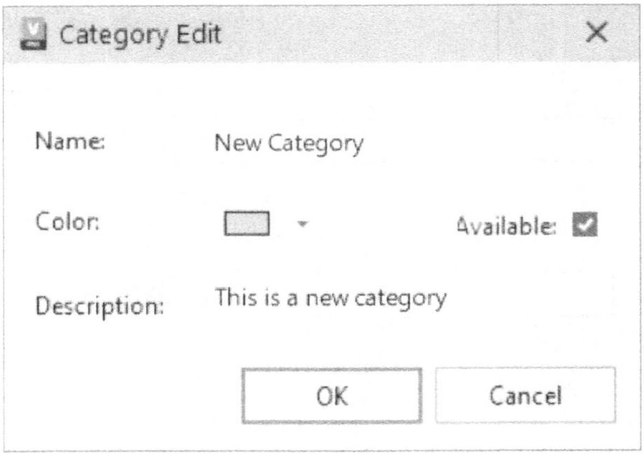


**Figure 3–14**

## How To: Edit Categories

Once you have a base category defined, or for any of the existing categories, do the following to edit the category:

1. In the *Tools* menu, select **Administration>Vault Settings**, as shown in Figure 3–15.

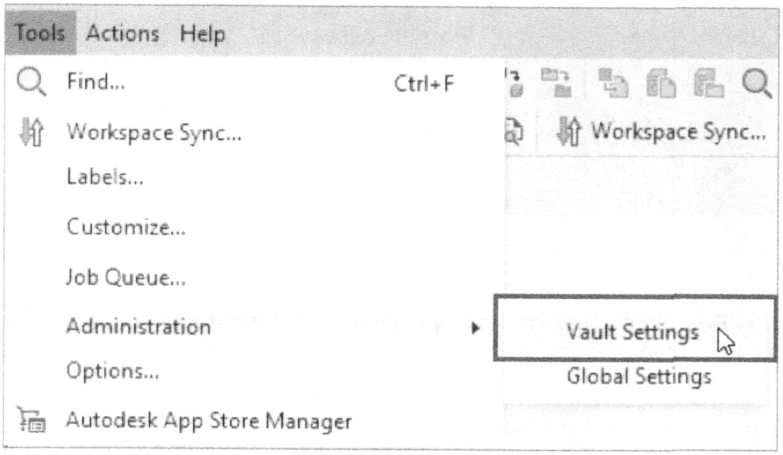


**Figure 3–15**

2. Select the *Behaviors* tab and select **Categories**, as shown in Figure 3–16.

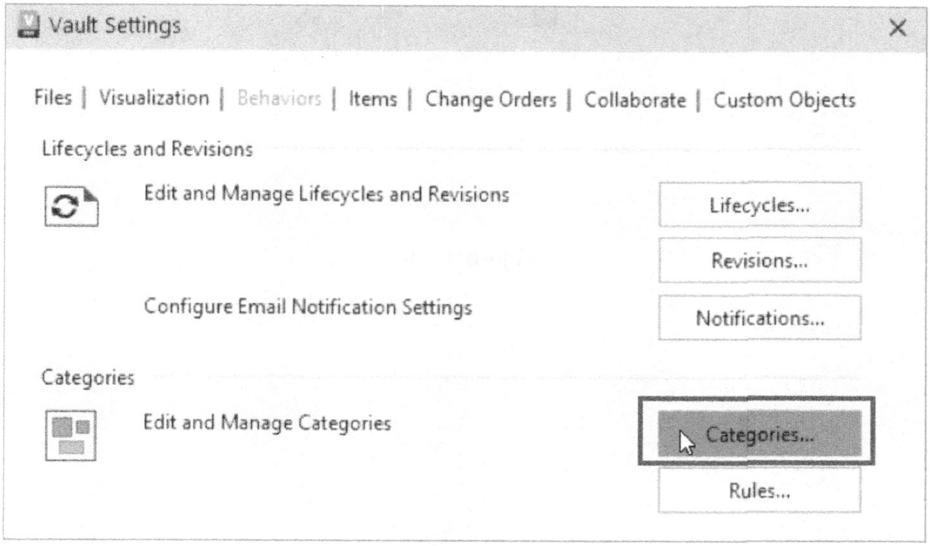


**Figure 3–16**

3. In the *Configure Categories* dialog box, select either **File Categories** or **Folder Categories** from the drop-down list, then select the category you want to edit and select **Edit**, as shown in Figure 3–17.

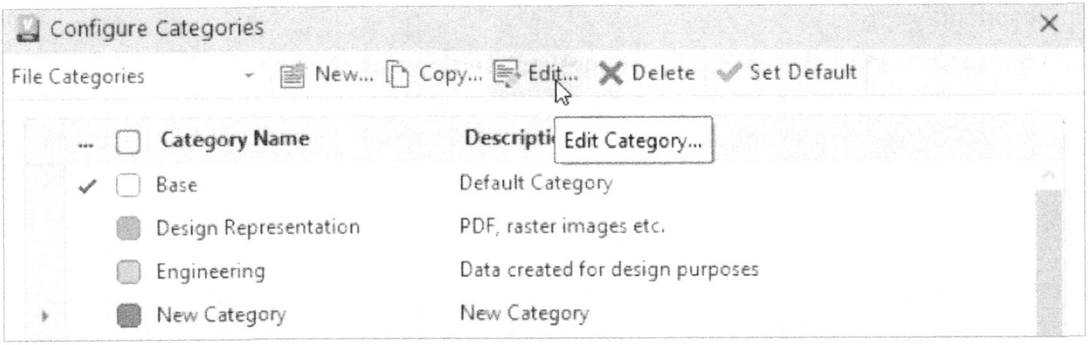


**Figure 3–17**

4. In the *Category Edit* dialog box, make any changes to the category and click **OK**, as shown in Figure 3–18.

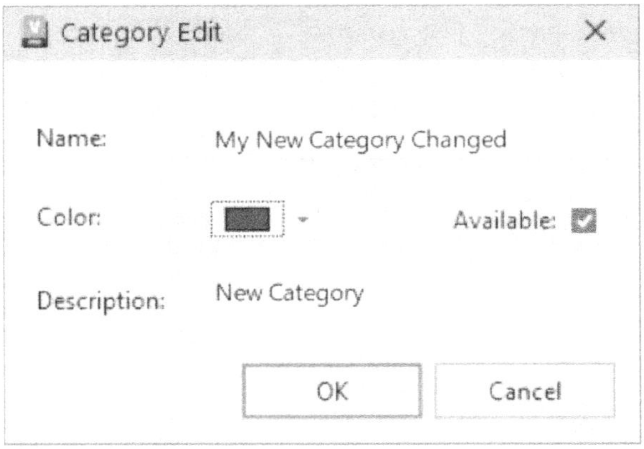


**Figure 3–18**

 

## How To: Apply Rules for Categories

Once you have a new category defined, or for any of the existing categories, do the following to apply a rule to the category.

1. In the *Tools* menu, select **Administration>Vault Settings**, as shown in Figure 3–19.

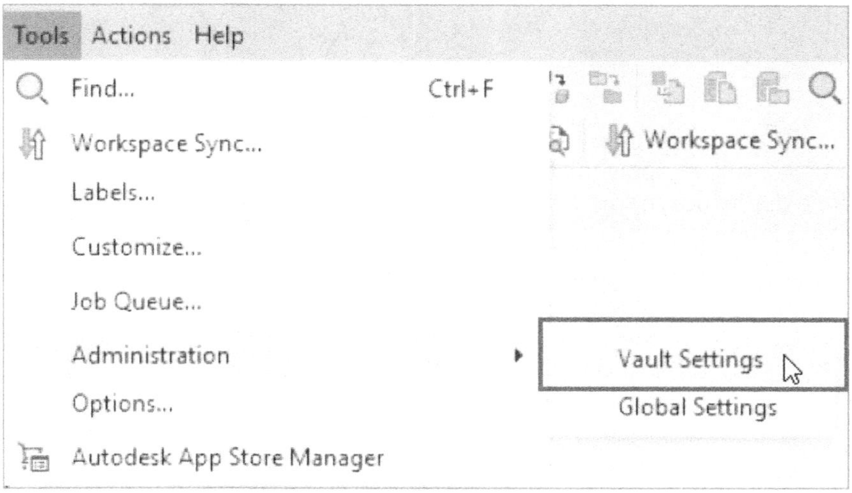


**Figure 3–19**

2. Select the *Behaviors* tab and select **Rules**, as shown in Figure 3–20.

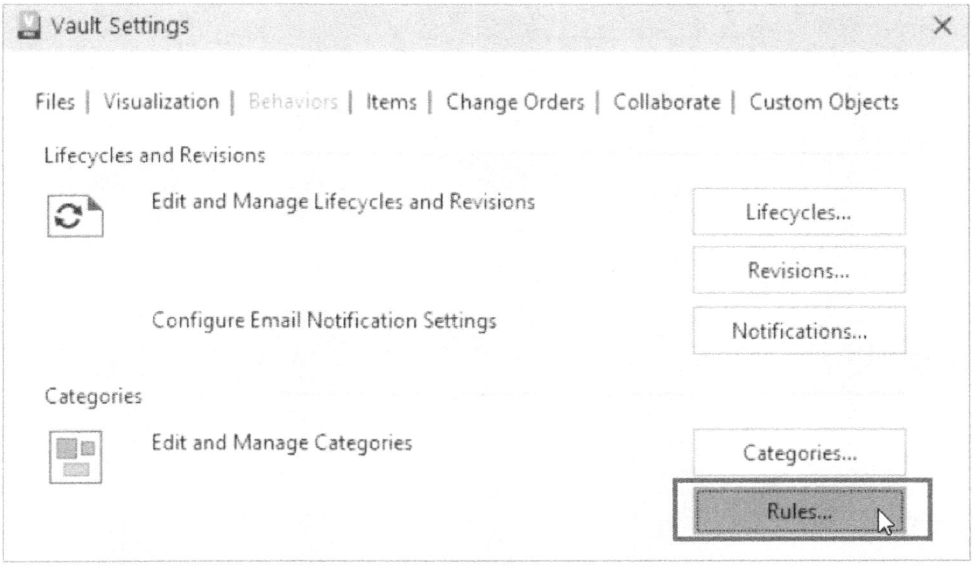


**Figure 3–20**

3. In the *Assignment Rules* dialog box, select **New**, as shown in Figure 3–21.

**Figure 3–21**

4. You will make a rule to apply the Engineering category to all Autodesk Inventor part files. In the *Edit Rule* dialog box, name the rule **Inventor Parts** and select the **Engineering** category, as shown in Figure 3–22.

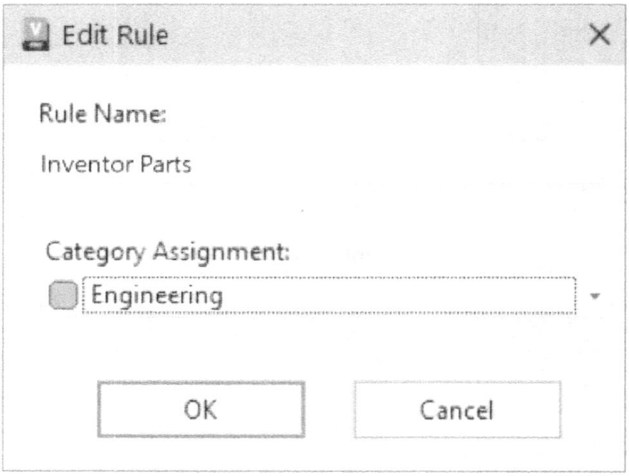


**Figure 3–22**

5. Once you click **OK**, the new *Inventor Parts* rule is added to the list. Select it to add the criteria as follows and as shown in Figure 3–23:
   - *Property:* **File Name**
   - *Condition:* **ends with**
   - *Value:* **.ipt**

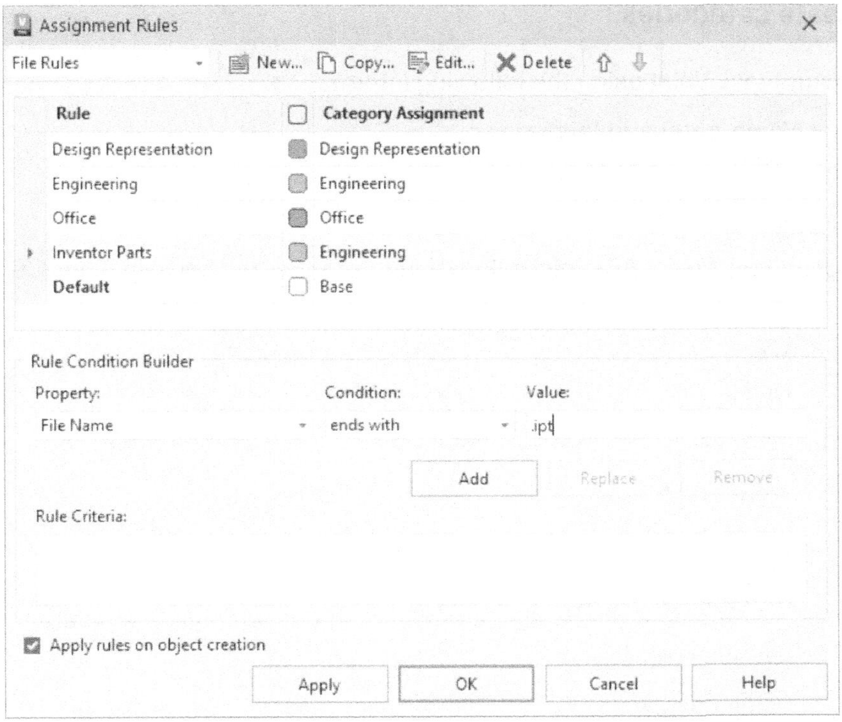


**Figure 3–23**

6. Click **Add** and the criteria is added automatically in the *Rule Criteria* section, as shown in Figure 3–24. Check the **Apply rules on object creation** option. Checking this box will place all new Autodesk Inventor parts in the *Engineering* category when they are checked in. Once this is complete, click **OK**.

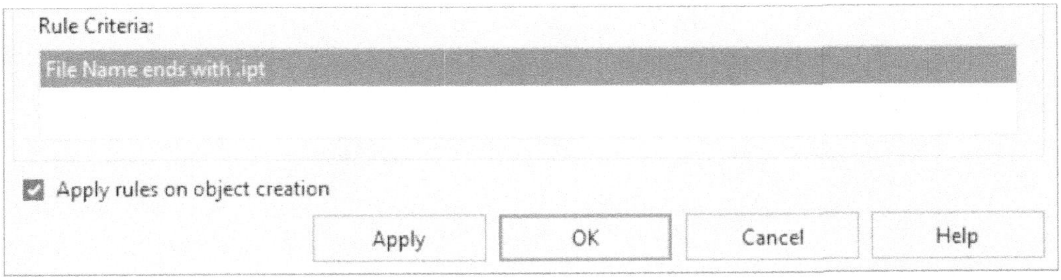


**Figure 3–24**

# Practice 3a
# Manage Categories

In this practice, you learn to create your own category and at least one rule to apply this new category to files you can check in.

## Task 1: Create categories.

1. Log in to Autodesk Vault using the following information:
   - For *User Name*, enter **administrator**.
   - Leave the *Password* field blank.
   - For *Vault*, select **AOTCVault**.
2. In the *Tools* menu, select **Administration>Vault Settings**, as shown in Figure 3–25.

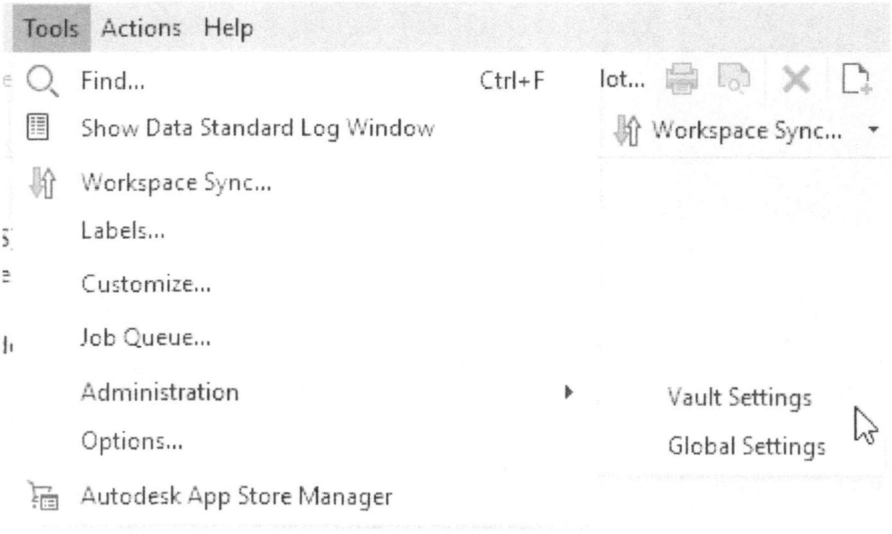


**Figure 3–25**

3. In the *Behaviors* tab, select **Categories**.

4. In the top left of the *Configure Categories* dialog box, select **File Categories**, as shown in Figure 3–26.

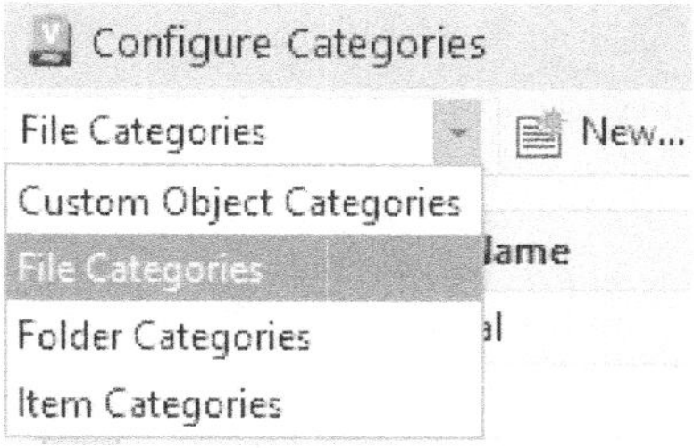


**Figure 3–26**

5. Click **New**. In the *Category Edit* dialog box, set the following, as shown in Figure 3–27:
   - For *Name*, enter **Survey**.
   - For *Color*, select **Green**.
   - For *Description*, enter **Survey Drawings**.
   - Click **OK**.

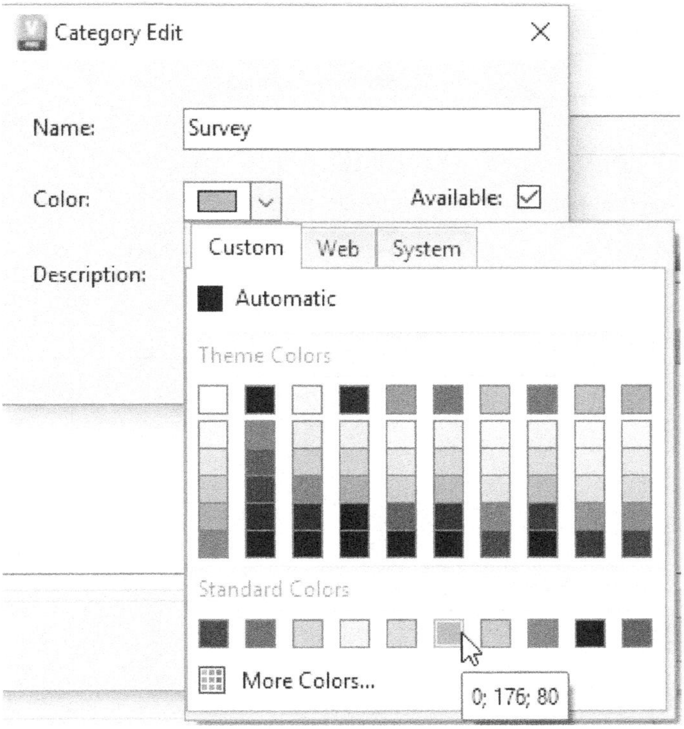


**Figure 3–27**

6. Click **New** again. In the *Category Edit* dialog box, set the following:
   - For *Name*, enter **Civil**.
   - For *Color*, select **Blue**.
   - For *Description*, enter **Civil Drawings**.
   - Click **OK**.
7. Click **New** again. In the *Category Edit* dialog box set the following:
   - For *Name*, enter **Architectural**.
   - For *Color*, select **Purple**.
   - For *Description*, enter **Architectural Drawings**.
   - Click **OK**.
8. In the *Configure Categories* dialog box (shown in Figure 3–28), view the new categories you added.

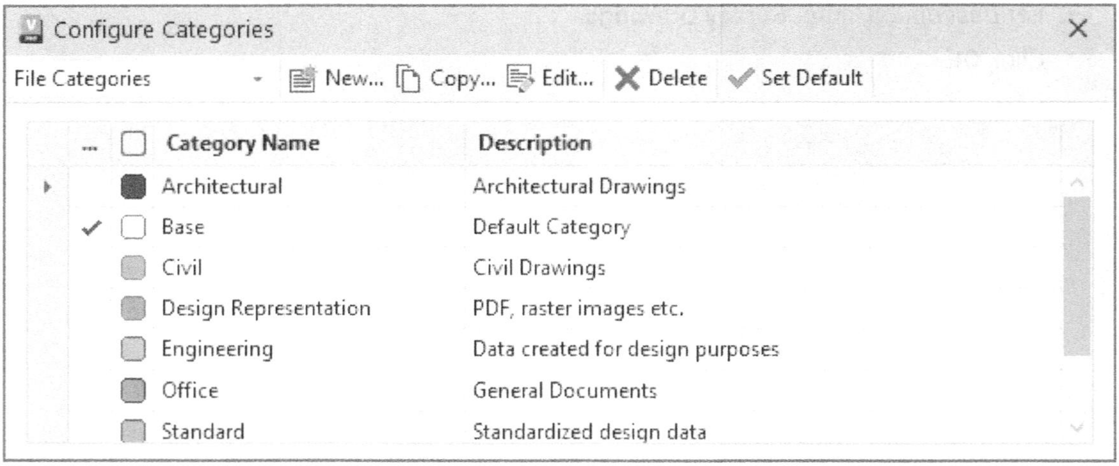


**Figure 3–28**

9. Close the *Configure Categories* dialog box.

## Task 2: Apply rules.

1. In the *Behaviors* tab of the Vault Settings, click **Rules**.
2. In the top left of the *Assignment Rules* dialog box, select **File Rules**, as shown in Figure 3–29.

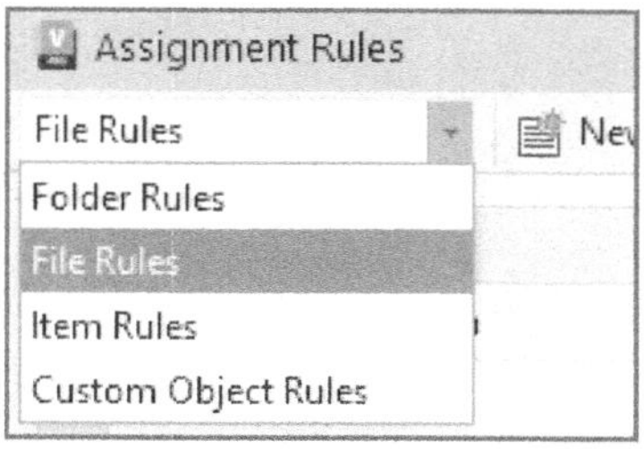


**Figure 3–29**

3. Click **New**.
4. In the *Edit Rule* dialog box:
   - For *Rule Name*, enter **Survey**.
   - For *Category Assignment*, select **Survey**.
   - Click **OK**.
5. In the *Assignment Rules* dialog box, in the *Rule Condition Builder* area, do the following, as shown in Figure 3–30:
   - For *Property*, select **File Name**.
   - For *Condition*, select **starts with**.
   - For *Value*, enter **V-**.
   - Click **Add**.

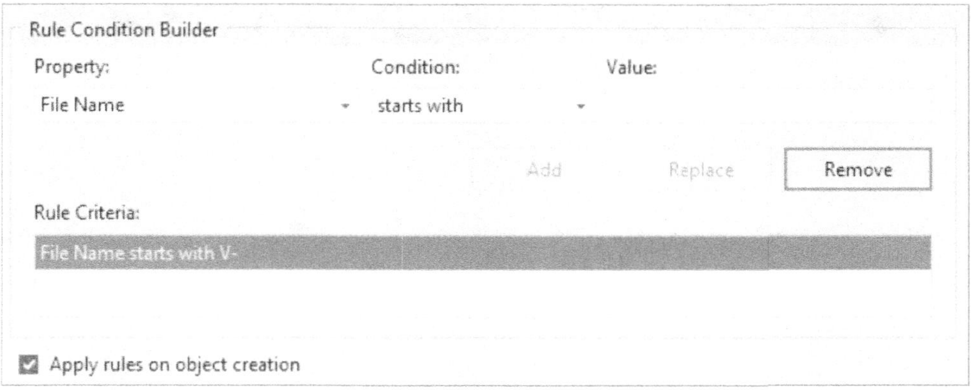


**Figure 3–30**

6. Repeat Steps 3 to 5 to create a *Rule Name* of **Architectural** (as shown in Figure 3–31) with a *Value* of **A-**, and again to create a *Rule Name* of **Civil** with a *Value* of **C-**.

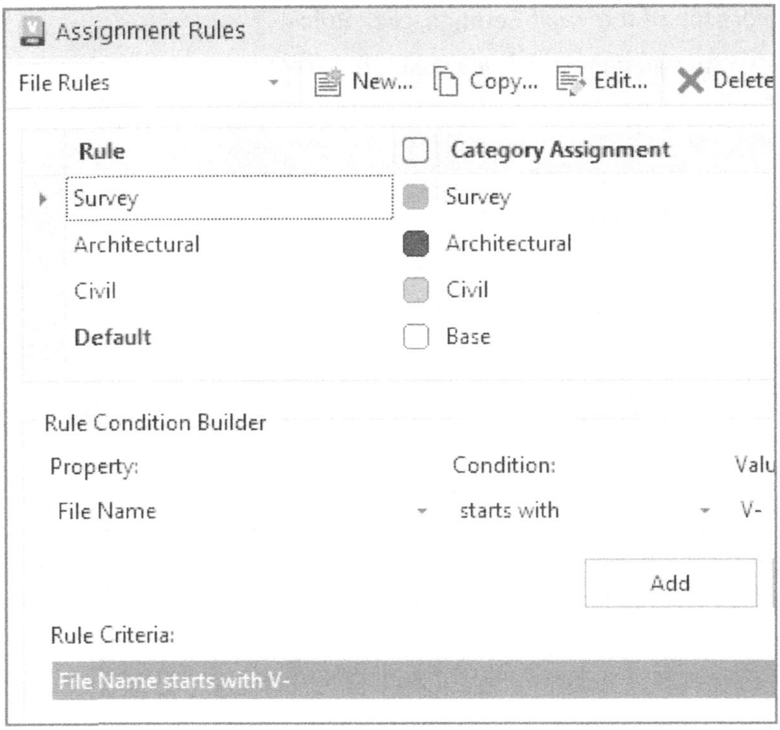


**Figure 3–31**

7. Ensure the **Apply rules on object creation** option is selected.
8. Click **Apply**, then click **OK** to exit the dialog box.
9. Close all dialog boxes and exit Autodesk Vault.

**End of practice**

Chapter

4

# Lifecycle States

Lifecycle management refers to the process a company uses to track its products from inception through retirement. As a product is conceived, defined, designed, tested, revised, and produced, it will transit various stages that are often quite specific to a particular company. Autodesk® Vault Professional enables lifecycle management by applying a uniform set of behaviors to project data in the lifecycle management process. Along with uniformity, Autodesk Vault Professional is a tool that enables configuration of states, transitions, and other aspects of lifecycle management so that companies can tailor the tool to best fit their processes. In this chapter, you will learn about lifecycle management, what default lifecycle definitions and states are available out-of-the-box and how to configure them or create a new lifecycle definition and set of states to meet your organization's needs. You will learn how to change the lifecycle state of a Vault object using the lifecycle definitions and states.

## Learning Objectives

- Describe the default out-of-the-box lifecycle definitions and how they could be applied for different situations.
- Describe the default out-of-the-box lifecycle states and how they could be used to control data access.
- Create a new lifecycle definition and set of associated lifecycle states.
- Plan for the configuration of lifecycle definitions and associated states.
- Configure the states of a lifecycle definition.
- Apply the lifecycle definition to project data.
- Change the lifecycle state of a file.
- Understand how the lifecycle state settings affect the ability to read and modify files.

# 4.1 Lifecycle Definitions and States

A lifecycle definition is an engine that can be configured to automatically assign security, behaviors, and properties to Vault objects based on where the object is in the life of the design process. This functionality enables you to streamline your work environment by removing the overhead involved in managing groups of files, custom objects, or an entire project. Several lifecycle definitions are included with the "out-of-the-box" installation. These range from a simple release process where project data is either editable or locked for editing to a more complex process involving long-lead time manufacturing, the review of project data before it is released, and the ability to short cut the formal release process for simple project data changes. They are designed to fit those processes seen in many companies from small shops to large corporations.

Each of these lifecycle definitions comprise two or more lifecycle states. A lifecycle state represents a certain point in the lifecycle of vault data. Common lifecycle states include **Work in Progress**, **Review**, and **Released**. Lifecycle states control the ability to view and modify project data. Transitions from one state to the next control how new versions are created and other activities. There are controls for specifying required conditions before a transition can be made.

These sets of lifecycle definitions and states cover many possible processes. If one does not fit your organization, a new definition with its unique set of states can be created.

## Lifecycle Definitions

A lifecycle definition uses states to identify the state of an object in the project lifecycle. Examples of states are **Work in Progress**, **For Review**, and **Released**. An object moves from one state to another based on the lifecycle definition transition rules. These transition rules determine when the state change occurs, and whether the change can occur manually or automatically (or both), based on criteria determined by the administrator. The lifecycle definition also determines if any other automatic behaviors occur based on a state change.

For example, a lifecycle definition can be configured to automatically revise a file when it moves from a **Work in Progress** state to a **Review** state. Alternatively, if a user changes a folder's status to **Obsolete**, the lifecycle definition can automatically apply security settings to the folder so that only an administrator can modify the folder and its contents or reinstate the folder for use.

Lifecycles can be used with files, project folders, items, and custom objects.

## Predefined Lifecycle Definitions

Several lifecycle definitions are included with the "out-of-the-box" installation that will assist administrators in assigning definitions to Vault content without having to create them. The lifecycle definitions are located in the *Vault Settings* dialog box, in the *Behaviors* tab. The following table lists the various lifecycle definitions.

| Lifecycle Definition | Description |
|---|---|
| **Basic Release Process** | Basic manufacturing lifecycle process for release control. This definition can be used with most manufacturing project content. |
| **Item Release Process** | For use with the Vault Professional software. Basic item lifecycle process for release control. This definition can be used with all items and includes the following states:<br>• **Work in Progress**<br>• **In Review**<br>• **Released**<br>• **Quick-Change**<br>• **Obsolete** |
| **Flexible Release Process** | Flexible manufacturing lifecycle process for release control. This definition includes all of the *Basic Release Process* states and a **Quick Change** state for editing released data. |
| **Simple Release Process** | A generic lifecycle process for many different types of project data. This definition consists of a **Work in Progress** state and a **Released** state. |
| **Long Lead Time Release Process** | Best suited for long lead time manufacturing projects. This definition includes a **Pre-Release** state indicating that the project data has been sent to manufacturing but is still in a state of change. |
| **Long Lead Time Release Process with Change Order** | Best suited for long lead time manufacturing projects directed by change orders. This definition includes the **Work in Progress**, **Review**, and **Pre-Release** states. The **Pre-Release** state indicates that a file has been sent to manufacturing but is still in a state of change. When there are no more change orders for the file, it moves to a **Released** state. From there, the file can return to the **Pre-Release** state through a **Quick Change**. |
| **Design Representation Process** | All PDF files created for document control are automatically assigned to the *Design Representation* category. A dedicated category enables administrators to manage their rules, lifecycles, and properties independent of the associated design files. |
| **<None>** | This definition enables any category to assign a null definition to opt out of using a lifecycle definition but to still retain category behavior. |

## Predefined Lifecycle States

The following table lists the various predefined lifecycle states.

| State Name | Description |
|---|---|
| **Work In Progress** | Sometimes known by the abbreviation "WIP", this is the state most commonly associated with the editing of the files. The editing, and often viewing, of files in this state is usually restricted to a small group of individuals, usually in the Engineering function. |
| **For Review** | This is the state that usually precedes the release of a design to manufacturing. In this state, more users can interact with the data, but generally no editing is permitted. This state enables users to evaluate new designs and changes to existing designs, before they are re-released to manufacturing. |
| **Released** | In this state, a broad range of groups in the organization now can read the data but usually editing is not permitted or at a minimum restricted to a very small group under controlled conditions. |
| **Obsolete** | This state is associated with designs that are no longer active. The products they are associated with are no longer being manufactured or are in a maintenance state. Access to these designs is more restricted and usually no edits can be made to them. |
| **Quick-Change** | This state is common in processes where there needs to be a quick yet controlled method of updating files without going through a formal review to release process. For example, files with typographical errors but no fundamental form, fit, or function changes. Modifications are generally permitted by a very small group of people. |
| **Pre-Release** | In processes where there are a large number of files, for example large assemblies or a product, this state enables the organization to approve the design or changes to the design but not designate them as released to manufacturing. Access can be permitted to a large group, but modification is usually prohibited and the ability to move them to the Released state is also restricted. |

In addition to edit ability, there is a set of rules regarding what happens to object revisions when an object is transitioned from one state to the next, who can make these transitions, and other considerations.

## Considerations Using the Predefined Definitions

Each of the predefined lifecycle definitions use one or more of the default states. There are a minimum set of rules governing transitions between states and object editing or viewing in a given state. These form the basic rules of the definition and can be adequate for your organization.

It is likely that you will need to configure the lifecycle definitions and states. This could range from minor tuning to major changes in the default states. Alternatively, you might need to create your own lifecycle definitions with their associated states, transitions, rules, and actions.

# Viewing Lifecycle Definitions

Viewing lifecycle definitions is an administrative task done through the *Vault Settings* dialog box. In the *Tools* menu, select **Administration>Vault Settings** and then select the *Behaviors* tab of this dialog box. You can access the *Lifecycle Definitions* dialog box (shown in Figure 4–1) by selecting **Lifecycles** in the *Lifecycles and Revisions* section. From here, you can choose to create new definitions, copy an existing definition, and edit or delete a definition from the *Lifecycle Definitions* toolbar.

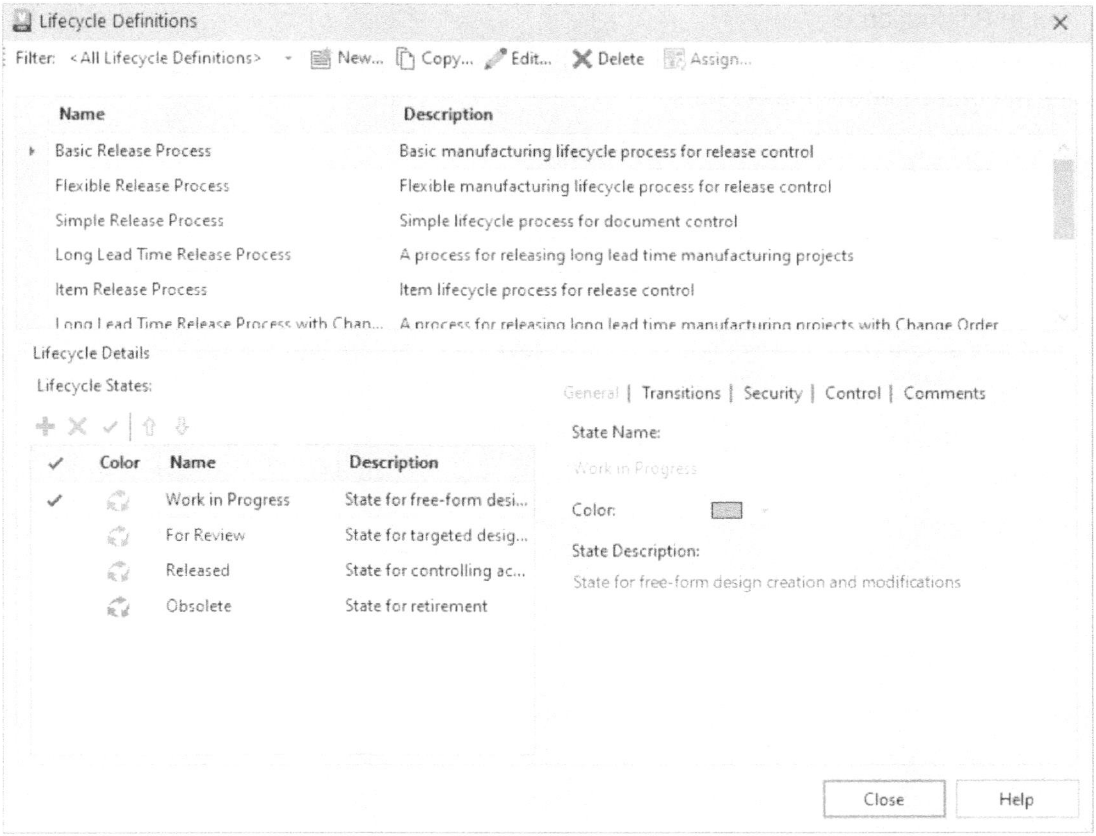


**Figure 4–1**

# Creating a New Lifecycle Definition

In some cases, it might be desirable to create a new lifecycle definition and set of states. For example, in a small organization there have been three states traditionally used to describe the files used to manufacture the product:

- Development
- Manufacturing
- Out of Production

This is a simple but effective process for the organization, and they want to use these lifecycle states rather than one of the defaults.

## How To: Create a New Lifecycle Definition

Follow these steps to create a new lifecycle definition called **Company Default**:

1. In the *Vault Settings* dialog box, select the *Behaviors* tab, then select **Lifecycles** in the *Lifecycles and Revisions* section to display the *Lifecycle Definitions* dialog box.
2. In the *Lifecycle Definitions* dialog box, click **New** (as shown in Figure 4–2) to display the *Lifecycle Definition* dialog box.

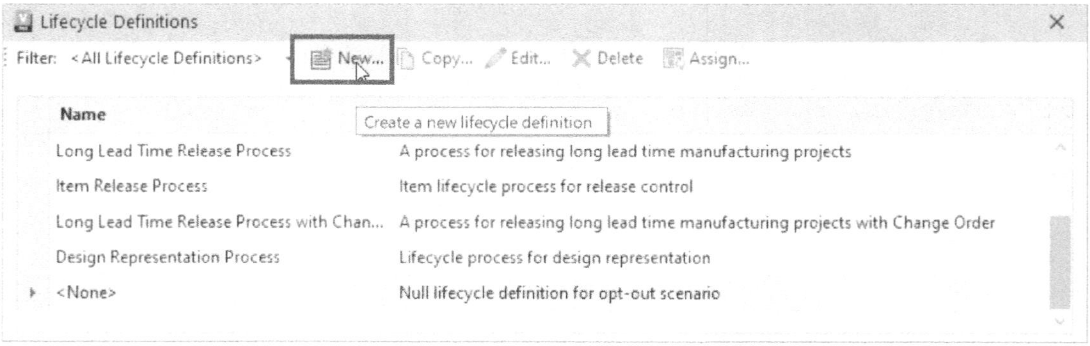


**Figure 4–2**

3. Enter a name and description for the new lifecycle definition.
4. In the *Category* drop-down list, select the categories you want to assign to the new lifecycle definition.

5. In the *Lifecycle Details* section, select plus (+) as shown in Figure 4–3 to display the *New Lifecycle State* dialog box.

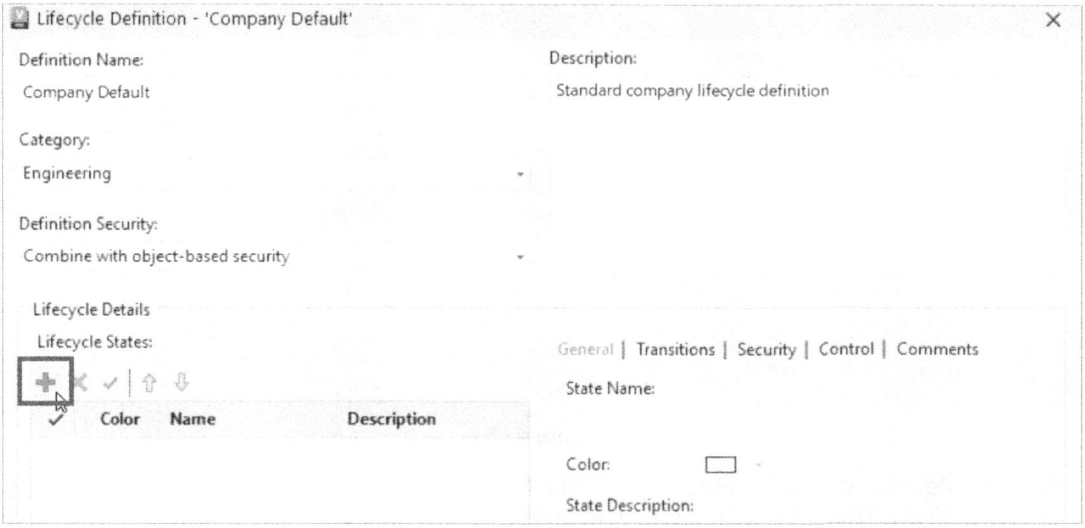


**Figure 4–3**

6. In the *New Lifecycle State* dialog box, enter a name and description for this state and select a color, as shown in Figure 4–4. Click **OK** to close this dialog box and return to the *Lifecycle Definition* dialog box.

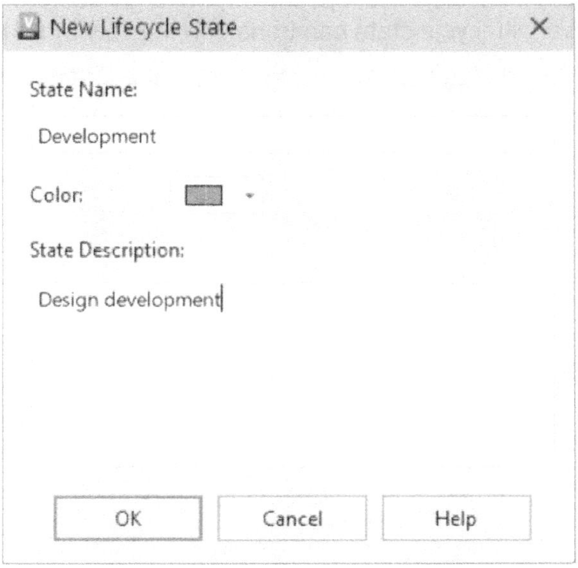


**Figure 4–4**

- Note that the first state defined is assigned the default state.

7. Repeat the process for the remaining states. If a different default state is required, select the desired state and select the checkmark to set it as the default state for the lifecycle definition, as shown in Figure 4–5.

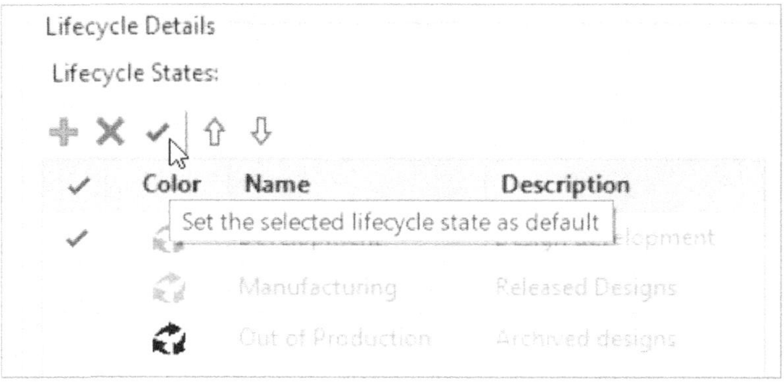


**Figure 4–5**

8. Reorder lifecycle states by selecting a state in the *Lifecycle Details* view and clicking the up or down arrow. The order of the lifecycle states determines the order in which they display in the *Change State* dialog box.
9. Click **Apply** to apply the new states for the new definition.
10. Click **OK** to close this dialog box and return the *Lifecycle Definitions* dialog box.
11. Before closing this dialog box, look through each tab in the right to see the default information for a given lifecycle state. Specifically, for a given state there is no lifecycle state security and every lifecycle state can transition to every other lifecycle state.
12. Click **Close** to close this dialog box and return to the *Vault Settings* dialog box.

## Scope of Configuration

Each lifecycle definition has a set of lifecycle states. In Figure 4–6, you can see the states associated with the **Basic Release Process** lifecycle definition. You can see that this lifecycle definition has a lifecycle state called **Work in Progress** associated with it.

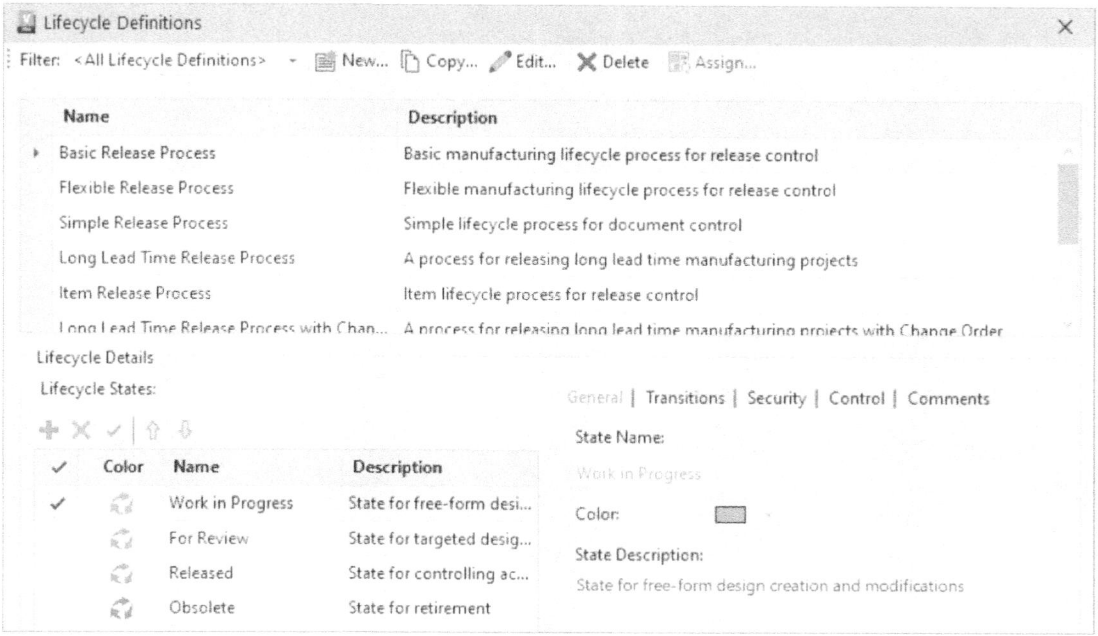


**Figure 4–6**

Figure 4–7 below shows the states associated with the **Flexible Release Process** lifecycle definition. This lifecycle definition also has a lifecycle state called **Work in Progress** associated with it. While they can have the same name, these are two independent lifecycle states and the rules and actions associated with the customization of one of them does not affect the other.

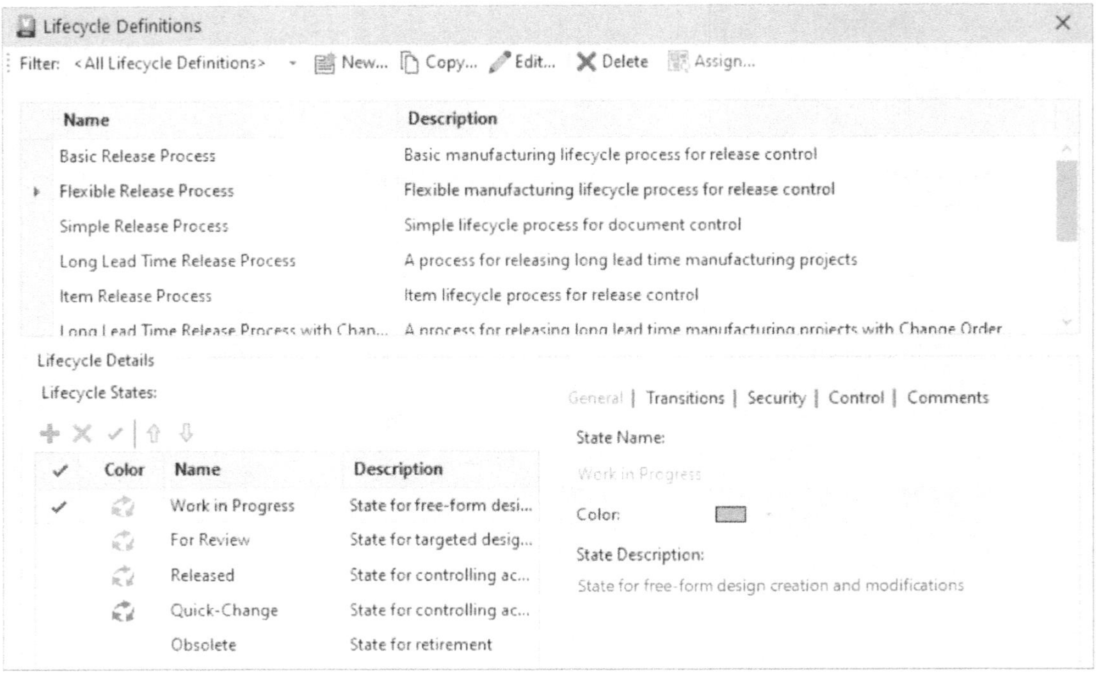


**Figure 4–7**

# Practice 4a
# Create New Lifecycle Definition

In this practice, you will create a new lifecycle definition named **Standard Process** with three states: **Development**, **Manufacturing**, and **Out of Production**, as shown in Figure 4–8.

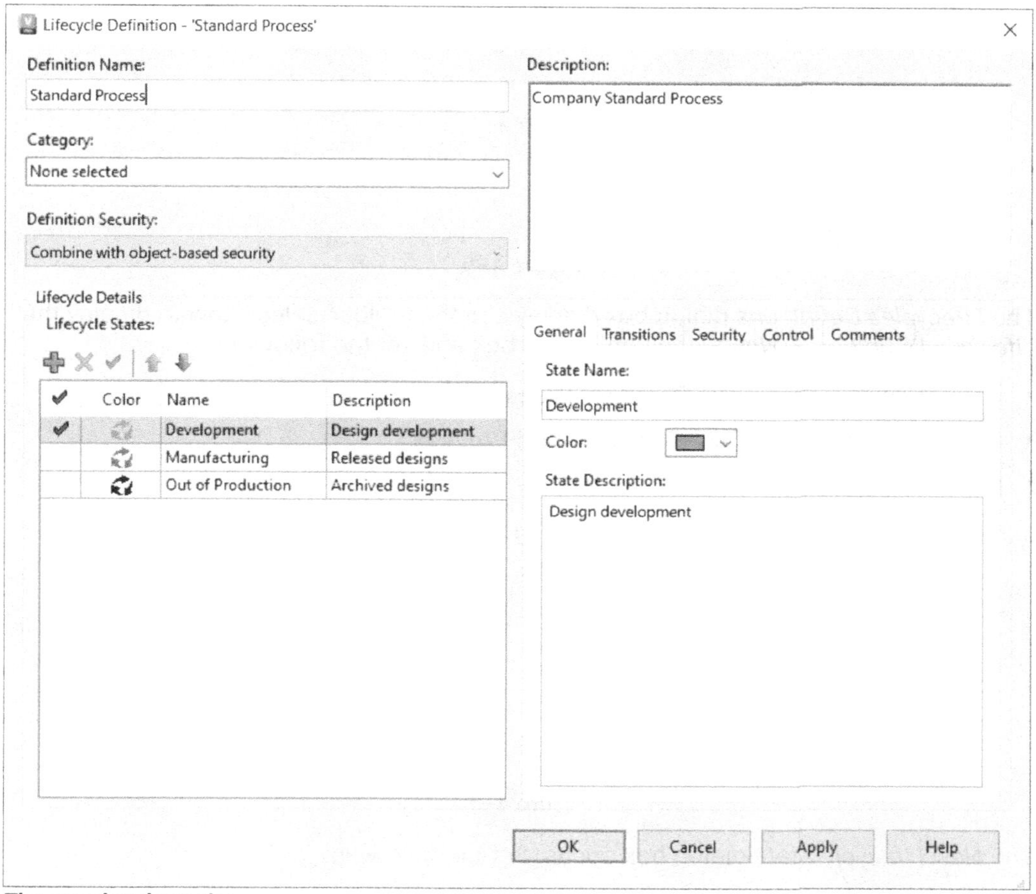


***The completed practice***

**Figure 4–8**

## Task 1: Create a new Lifecycle Definition.

1. If not already logged in, log in to Autodesk Vault using the following information:
    - For *User Name*, enter **administrator**.
    - Leave the *Password* field blank.
    - For *Vault*, select **AOTCVault**.

2. In the *Tools* menu, select **Administration>Vault Settings** to display the *Vault Settings* dialog box.
3. Select the *Behaviors* tab and then select **Lifecycles** in the *Lifecycles and Revisions* section, as shown in Figure 4–9.

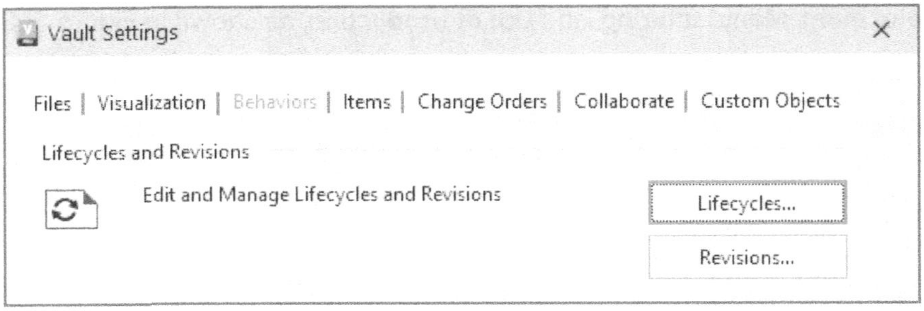


**Figure 4–9**

4. The *Lifecycles Definitions* dialog box displays. In the toolbar, select **New** to display the *Lifecycle Definition – 'New Definition'* dialog box and set the following:
   - For *Definition Name*, enter **Standard Process**.
   - For *Description*, enter **Company Standard Process**.
   - For *Category*, leave as **None selected**.
5. In the *Lifecycle Details* section, click plus (+) shown in Figure 4–10.

**Figure 4–10**

6. The *New Lifecycle State* dialog box opens. Set the following:
   - For *State Name*, enter **Development**.
   - For *Color*, select **Green**.
   - For *State Description*, enter **Design development**.
   - Click **OK** to return to the previous dialog box.
7. Repeat the process using the following information:
   - For *State Name*, enter **Manufacturing**.
   - For *Color*, select **Blue**.
   - For *State Description*, enter **Released designs**.

8. Repeat the process again using the following information:
   - For *State Name*, enter **Out of Production**.
   - For *Color*, select **Black**.
   - For *State Description*, enter **Archived designs**.
9. Examine the three states. Note that they display in blue text (as shown in Figure 4–11), which means they have not yet been applied.

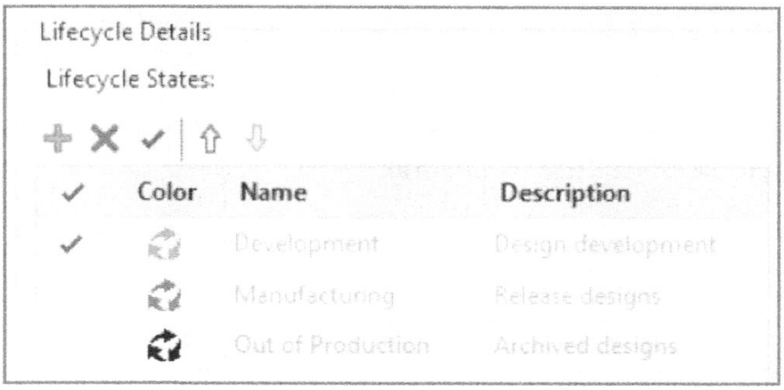


**Figure 4–11**

***Note:*** *The next step would be to configure the three lifecycle states. This will be done in the next practice.*

10. Click **Apply** to apply the three new lifecycle states, then click **OK** to dismiss the *Lifecycle Definition* dialog box. Note that the new lifecycle definition named **Standard Process** has been added as shown in Figure 4–12.

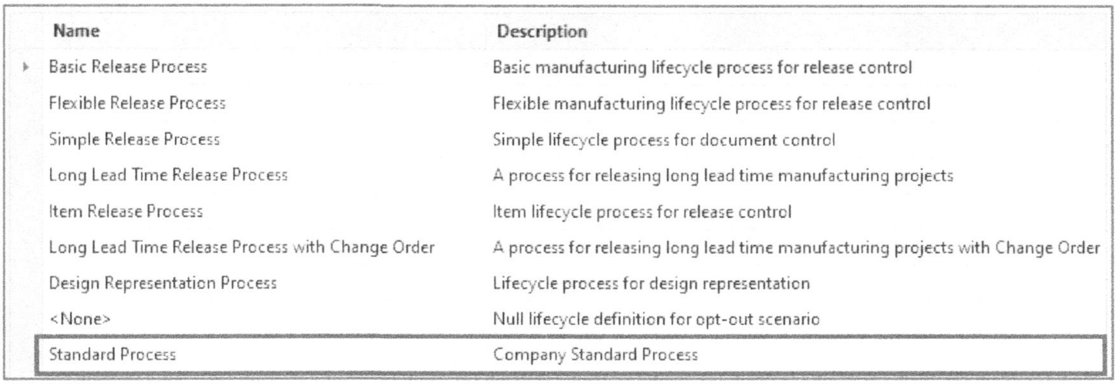

| Name | Description |
|---|---|
| Basic Release Process | Basic manufacturing lifecycle process for release control |
| Flexible Release Process | Flexible manufacturing lifecycle process for release control |
| Simple Release Process | Simple lifecycle process for document control |
| Long Lead Time Release Process | A process for releasing long lead time manufacturing projects |
| Item Release Process | Item lifecycle process for release control |
| Long Lead Time Release Process with Change Order | A process for releasing long lead time manufacturing projects with Change Order |
| Design Representation Process | Lifecycle process for design representation |
| <None> | Null lifecycle definition for opt-out scenario |
| Standard Process | Company Standard Process |

**Figure 4–12**

11. Click **Close** to close the dialog box and return to the *Vault Settings* dialog box. Click **Close** again to close this dialog box.

**End of practice**

# 4.2 Configuring Lifecycle States

The ability to define lifecycle definitions and behaviors enables you to customize your workflow environment to classify data based on their lifecycle status in the work process. This section will cover the following:

- Configure the lifecycle state to specify which users and groups can read, modify, and delete files which are in that state.
- Specify which actions should be taken when a file transitions from one lifecycle state to another.
- Specify which users and groups can transition a file from one lifecycle state to another or if the transition should be permitted by anyone.
- Specify which files versions for a given revision should be removed in a Purge operation.
- Configure the default comments added when a lifecycle state transition occurs.

## Setting Up

In order to effectively configure a lifecycle definition's lifecycle states, it is critical to do some upfront planning. For example, different users can have different abilities to read or modify files in a given lifecycle state. One lifecycle state can transition to any other lifecycle state but some of these transitions might not make sense in your process and should not be permitted.

Figure 4–13 shows an example of a lifecycle definition and the important considerations that must be planned before configuring one of the default lifecycle definitions or creating a new one.

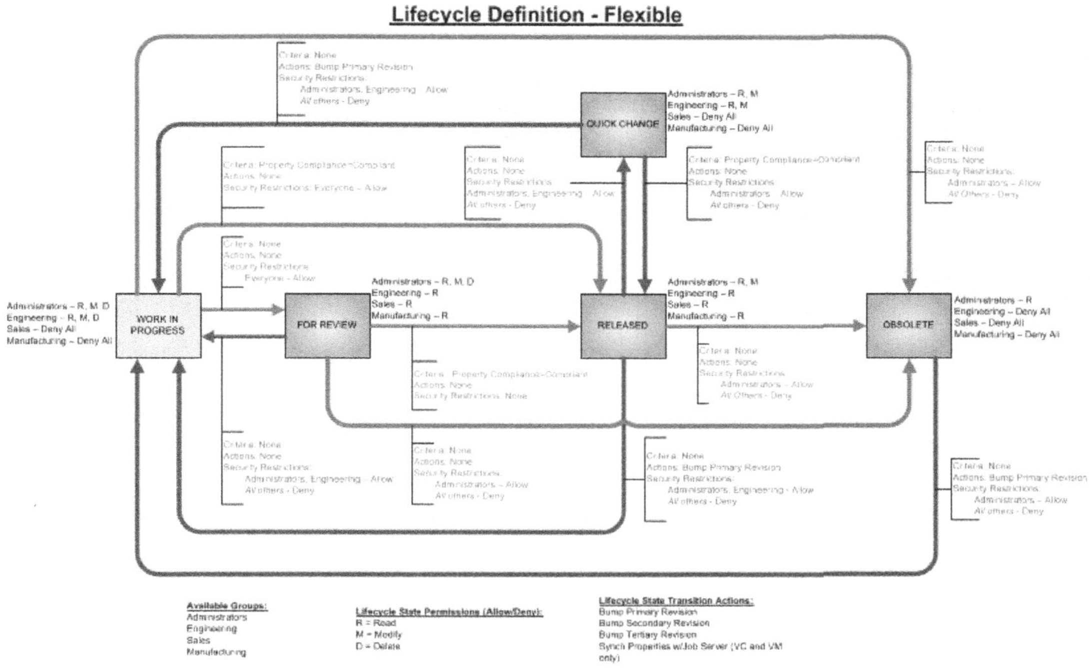


**Figure 4–13**

## Groups

It is important to think of the different groups in your organization and what access you will want them to have for files in different lifecycle states. For example, in the **Work In Progress** state, you probably only want the Engineering group and a few special users to be able to read or edit files. This special group of users can be administrators or department managers. In the **Released** state, it is common to grant access to all users but permit none, or only a small group, the ability to modify them.

Similarly, different groups of users will have different ability to transition between the lifecycle states. For example, you will likely have only a small group of users that can release a set of new or revised files to manufacturing. It is unlikely you will permit the users in the marketing or sales team to have this ability.

## Access Control Lists (ACLs)

The access control list enables you to add and remove members to control who has access to certain files, folders, items, and custom objects. You can also control whether the member can only view the content, modify the content, or delete the content.

A file, folder, or custom object that does not have an access control list defined uses object-based security.

Object-based security can be overridden. An override of security means that the ACL still exists on the object but it is being overridden by a newly defined ACL. This is called an override access control list or an override ACL.

As long as an override ACL exists, the object-based security is ignored. If the user removes the override ACL, then the object-based security becomes the new security. If an override ACL is active, only members and users in the ACL list have permissions to modify the object as shown in Figure 4–14.

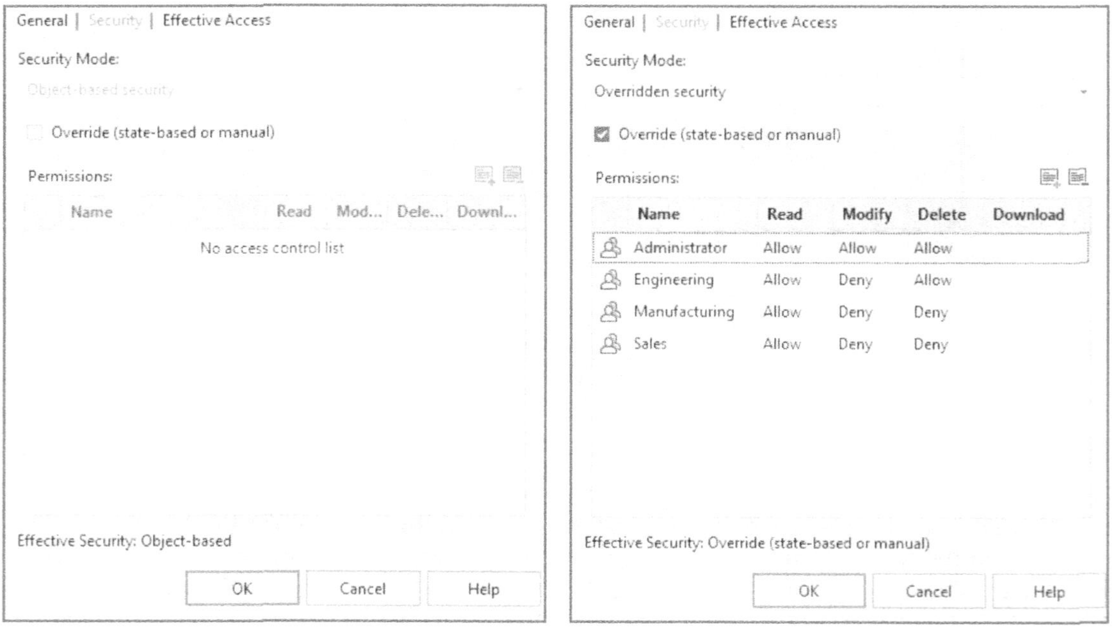


**Figure 4–14**

## How To: View Object Security

Examine file, folder, item, and custom object security through the context menu. You must be an administrator to view object security.

1. Right-click on a file, folder, item, or custom object in Vault and select **Details**.

 

2. In the *Details* dialog box, select the *Security* tab as shown in Figure 4–15.

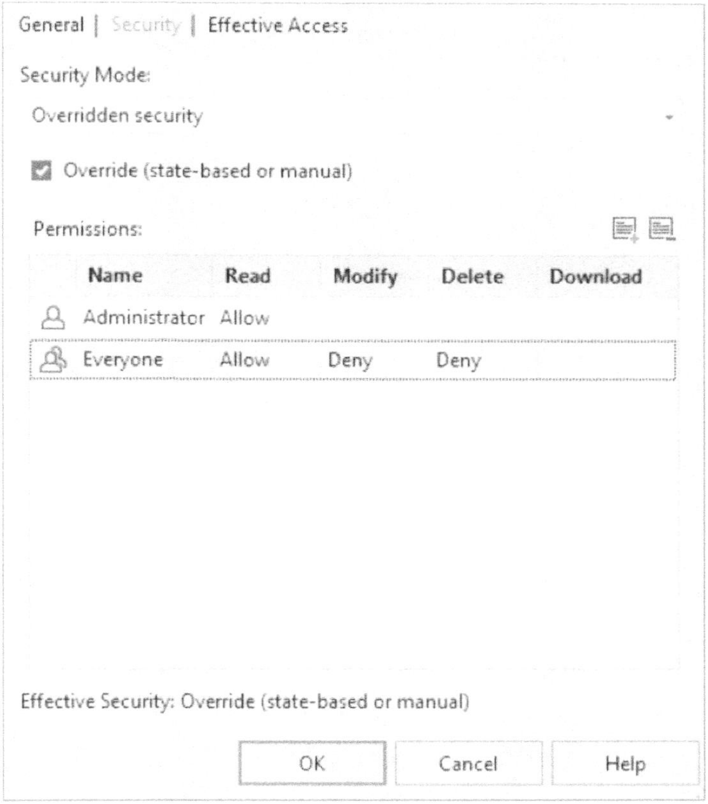


**Figure 4–15**

- **Security Mode:** Shows the security precedence for the selected object.
    - **Object-based security:** Security derived from the object. This is the default option and is the only option available if no other security is defined.

  ***Note:*** *Items do not have object-based security.*

    - **State-based security:** Security available when a state-based access control list (ACL) exists and is combined with object-based security.
    - **Overridden security:** Security available when a state-based ACL is overriding object-based security, or when the administrator sets a manual override on the object.
- **Permissions:** The ACL shows which groups and users are granted access to the selected object and their respective permissions.
- **Effective Security:** Security currently in use by the object (found at the bottom of the dialog box). In the example above, **Override (state-based or manual)** security is in effect.

3. Select the *Effective Access* tab (as shown in Figure 4–16) to view user permissions for the object.

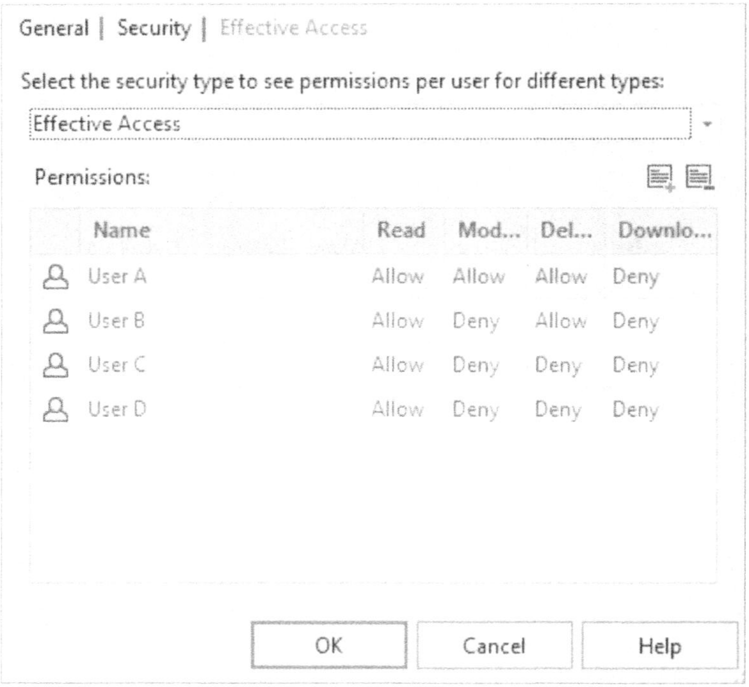


**Figure 4–16**

## Security Type

Select a security type to see a user's effective permissions for that security mode. This is primarily useful when both object-based security and state-based security are applied, and the administrator wants to finder a user's effective permissions.

> **Note:** *Only individual user permissions can be viewed. Groups cannot be added in the Effective Access tab.*

## Permissions

The permissions list in the *Effective Access* tab is empty by default. Add and remove members from the list to view the type of access they have to the object under the selected security type. Change the security type to see how permissions are impacted.

> **Note:** *The Effective Access tab is for viewing security permissions only. Adding and removing members does not change security permissions for the object. Permission changes must be performed in the Security tab.*

# Configuring Lifecycle State Security

Configuring security is an important step in the configuration. By default, no security beyond that which is determined by permissions assigned to each individual object is enforced for files in a given lifecycle state, as shown in Figure 4–17.

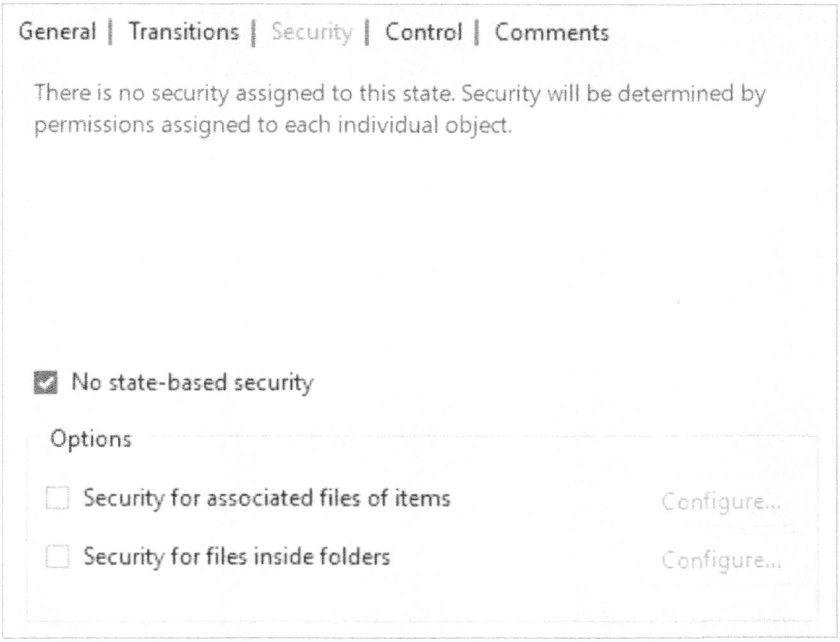


**Figure 4–17**

For lifecycle definitions created in the 2017 software release and greater, Autodesk Vault uses a dual-gate security model that combines object security with state security. Users must have role permission and combined object and state-based permissions to access a Vault object. Administrators can control individual access to a Vault object based on organizational area or business line. For example, an administrator can ensure that a group has read, write, and delete permissions and at the same time, deny permissions to certain members of the group while in various lifecycle states.

For *Definition Security*, select one of the following options as shown in Figure 4–18:

- **Combine with object-based security:** Any state-based security defined for individual states within this lifecycle definition combine with the object-based security set on the object. In other words, the combined security becomes the effective security for the entity.
- **Override object-based security:** Any state-based security defined for individual states within this lifecycle definition override the object-based security set on the object. In other words, state-based security becomes the effective security for the entity.

> ***Note:** Vaults migrated from Vault 2016 or earlier use **Override object-based security** as the default setting so that legacy (single-gate) security is maintained. However, all new vaults use **Combine with object-based security** as the default security setting, which is a dual-gate security setting. Change this setting at any time to mimic legacy (single-gate) security.*

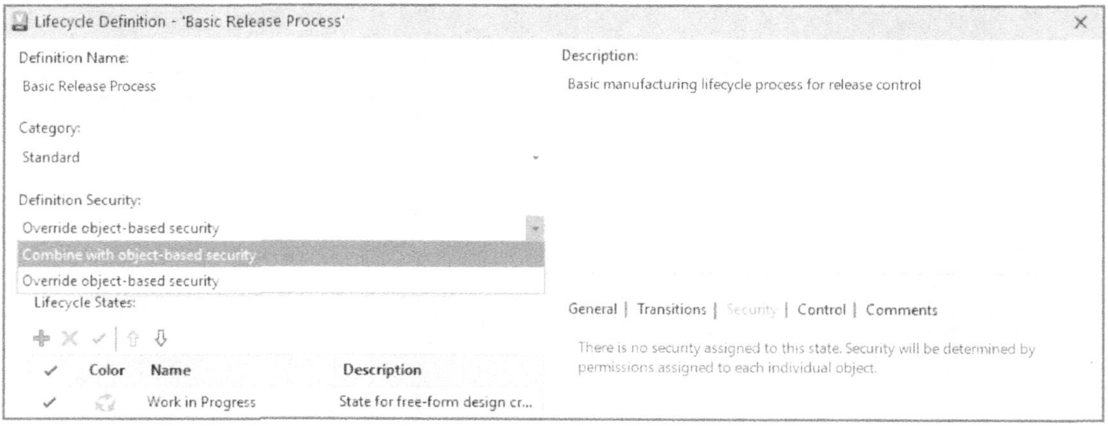


**Figure 4–18**

# Defining State-Based Security

## How To: Access Security for a Lifecycle State

1. Select **Tools>Administration>Vault Settings**.
2. In the *Vault Settings* dialog box, select the *Behaviors* tab and select **Lifecycles**.
3. In the *Lifecycle Definitions* dialog box, select the name of the lifecycle definition and click **Edit**. The selected definition name displays in the title bar.
4. Select the state for which you want to define security.
5. Select the *Security* tab to display the current security settings for that state.

## How To: Disable State-Based Security

1. Click **No state-based security** if you don't want to assign security for the state. Security is determined by the permissions assigned to the object.

## How To: Add a Member or Group Permission to a Lifecycle State

1. In the *Security* tab, clear the **No state-based security** checkbox if it is selected.
2. Click **Add**.
3. In the *Add Members* dialog box, select the member or group from the *Available Members* list and click **Add**. The selected name is moved to the *Current Members* list.

   ***Note:*** *Filter the Available Members list by selecting a qualifier from the Select Members From list.*

   From the *Current Members* list, select one or more members and then click **Remove** to modify the current members list.
4. Click **OK**.

## How To: Edit Member or Group Permissions

1. In the *Lifecycle Definition* dialog box, select the state from the Lifecycle States list.
2. In the *Security* tab, select the member or group to edit.
3. In the *Permissions* dialog box, enable or disable the **Allow** and **Deny** checkboxes for each permission.

| Permission | Access |
|---|---|
| **Read** | • **Allow:** States can be viewed.<br>• **Deny:** States cannot be viewed. If a member is denied read access, then they are not permitted Modify or Delete access either.<br>• **None:** State cannot be viewed. |
| **Modify** | • **Allow:** States can be modified.<br>• **Deny:** State cannot be modified.<br>• **None:** State cannot be modified. |
| **Delete** | • **Allow:** State can be deleted<br>• **Deny:** State cannot be deleted.<br>• **None:** State cannot be deleted. |

4. Click **OK**.

# Configuring Lifecycle State Transitions

Each lifecycle state has the ability to transition to every other lifecycle state. There are several considerations dealing with the ability for a lifecycle state to be changed or transitioned to another state. These are:

- **Criteria:** Are there property considerations governing the state transition? Criteria could also include a condition, such as not permitting a transition to In Review if the file is not associated to a change order.
- **Actions:** What actions, if any, should be performed when making the state transition. The actions include checking that the dependent child files, dependent child folders, contained files, linked files, linked folders, or linked custom objects are released. Actions can also include incrementing revision values, synchronizing properties, and creating visualization representation files.
- **Custom Job Types:** What custom jobs should be assigned to the transition?
- **Security:** Which user or groups are permitted the ability to transition from one state to the next?

Each of these considerations are displayed in their own tab in the *Transition* dialog box, as shown in Figure 4–19.

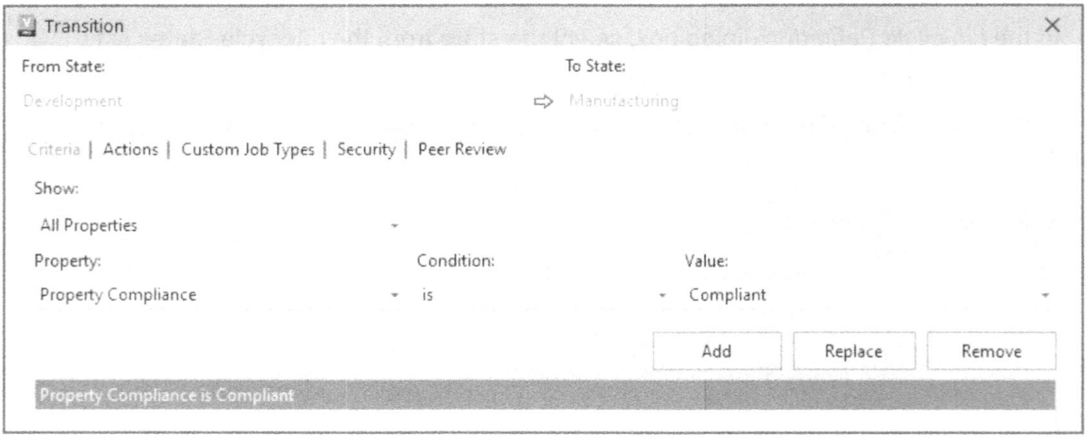


**Figure 4–19**

## Transition Criteria

Specifying criteria is much like the Advanced Find capability. You can specify if one or more of the system or user-defined properties associated with the file meet specific criteria. If all of the criteria are met, the transition can take place. If one or more of the criteria are not met, then the user is warned and cannot make the transition until the criteria are met or the lifecycle definition is changed.

The only default criteria that are set for some of the lifecycle state transitions in the default lifecycle definitions are property compliance. A property is said to be compliant if its value meets one or more criteria itself.

For example, the property Description must have a value between 10 and 20 characters long and the property Cost must have a numeric value greater than zero. If the individual conditions are true, then the two properties are compliant. All properties that have compliance criteria must be compliant in order for the Property Compliance property to be compliant. This is a useful way of making sure that the important properties associated with a file are filled out correctly before the lifecycle state can be transitioned.

## How To: Configure Transition Criteria

To configure the criteria that must be met before a file can transition into a new lifecycle state, do the following:

1. In the *Vault Settings* dialog box, select the *Behaviors* tab.
2. Select **Lifecycles** in the *Lifecycles and Revisions* section to display the *Lifecycle Definitions* dialog box shown in Figure 4–20.
3. Select the lifecycle definition to be customized.
4. Select **Edit** to display the *Lifecycle Definition* dialog box for the selected definition.
5. Select the lifecycle state from the list of *Lifecycle States* to be configured.
6. Select the *Transitions* tab to display a list of all of the lifecycle transitions for the selected lifecycle definition.

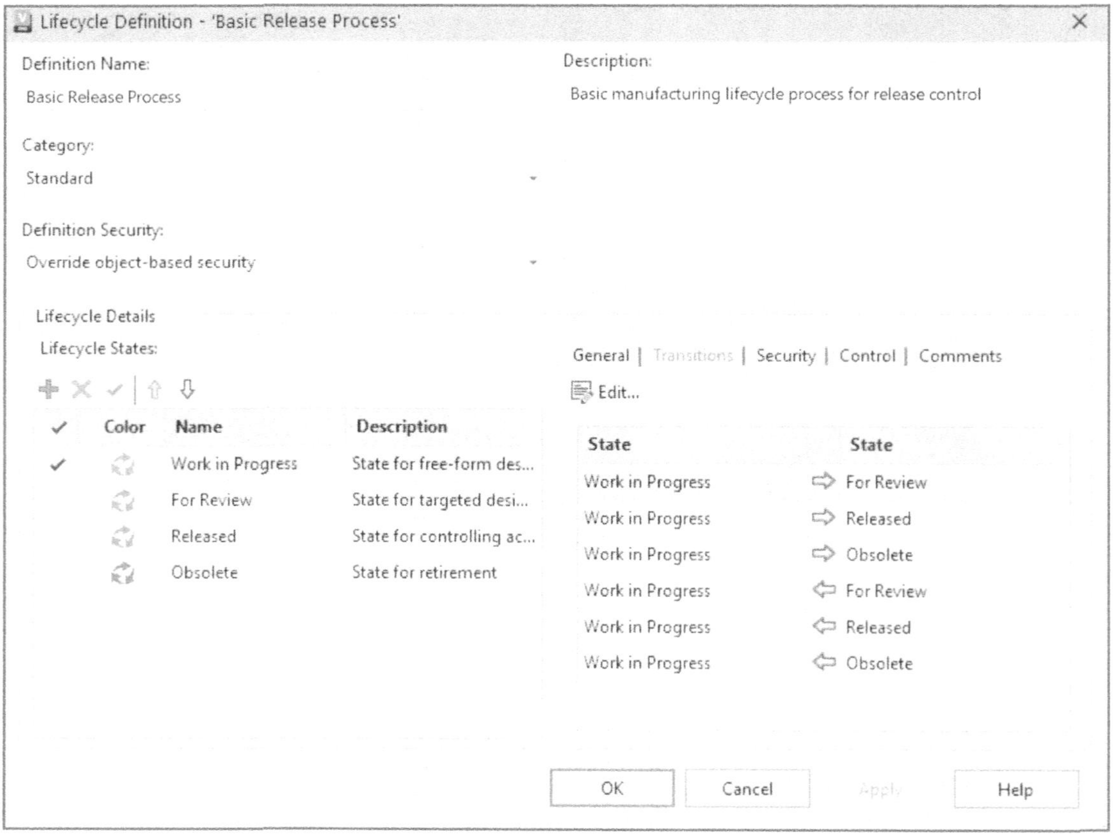


**Figure 4–20**

7. Select the transition to edit.
8. Select **Edit** to display the *Transition* dialog box.

9. Select the *Criteria* tab, as shown in Figure 4–21.

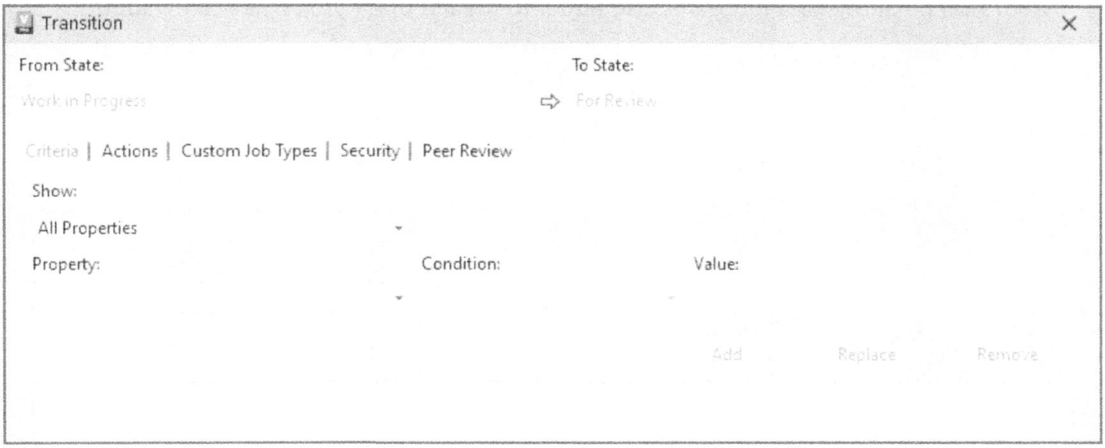


**Figure 4–21**

10. If required, filter which properties display based on a certain entity class using the *Show* drop-down list. For example, you can configure it so that only **File Properties** are shown in the *Property* drop-down list.

11. In the *Property* drop-down list (shown in Figure 4–22), select the property to evaluate.

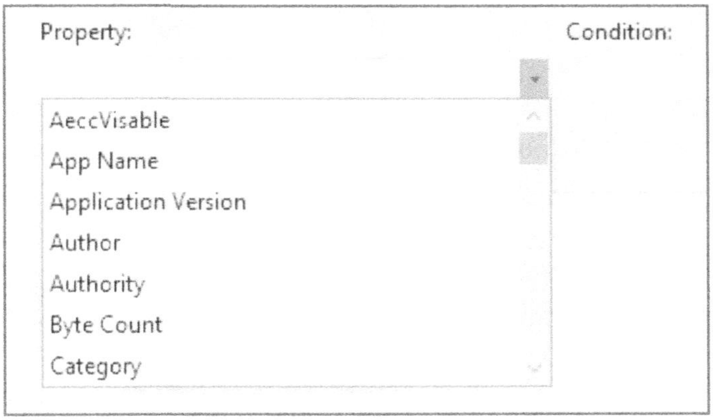


**Figure 4–22**

12. Specify the condition and value for that property.
13. Select **Add** as shown in Figure 4–23 to add it to the list of all properties to evaluate.

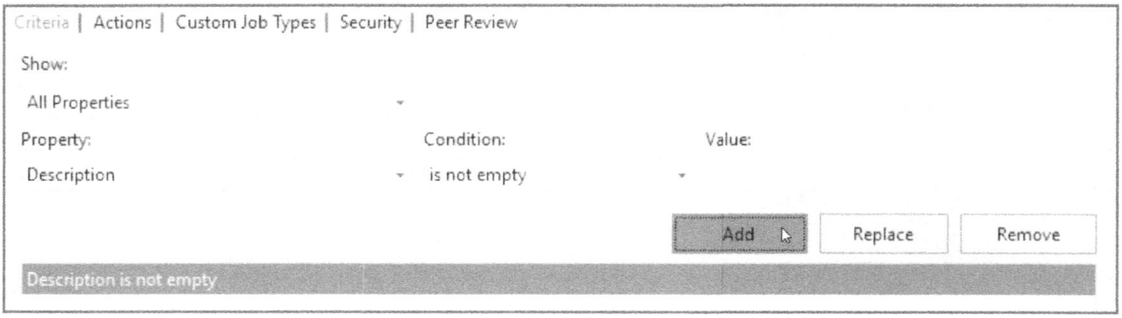


**Figure 4–23**

14. Repeat the previous three steps to add additional criteria.
15. Click **OK** to dismiss this dialog box and return to the *Lifecycle Definition* dialog box for the selected lifecycle definition.
16. Configure the remaining transitions for the selected lifecycle state.

    ***Note:*** *Every transition is shown for a given lifecycle state. For example, if you select State 1, you will find a transition from State 1 to State 2 and a transition from State 2 to State 1. Similarly, if you select State 2, you will find a transition from State 2 to State 1 and from State 1 to State 2. You only need to configure a particular state transition once. You do not need to configure it for every possible state transition. They are shown on every state transition for convenience.*

17. Click **OK** to dismiss this dialog box and return to the *Lifecycle Definitions* dialog box.
18. Click **Close** to dismiss this dialog box and return to the *Vault Settings* dialog box.

## Transition Actions

Actions are method of both automating process and enforcing rules associated with changing a file revision when moving from one lifecycle state to the other. When planning, some of the questions include:

- When transitioning from one state to another, is a new revision of the file created and of what kind?
- When making the transition, are there system level tasks that should be initiated?
- When transitioning to a released state, are checks on the state of the dependent children, content, or linked data required?
- If mapped property values should be synchronized by the Job Server.
- If both property values should be synchronized and visualization files updated by the Job Server.

The example in Figure 4–24 shows the actions that are performed in a lifecycle definition where the state transition is from the **Released** state to the **Work in Progress** state. In this case, the primary revision is bumped. So if the file were released at revision **A**, its revision would change to **B** when the state transition occurs. No properties would be synchronized by the Job Server and no release state checks would be performed.

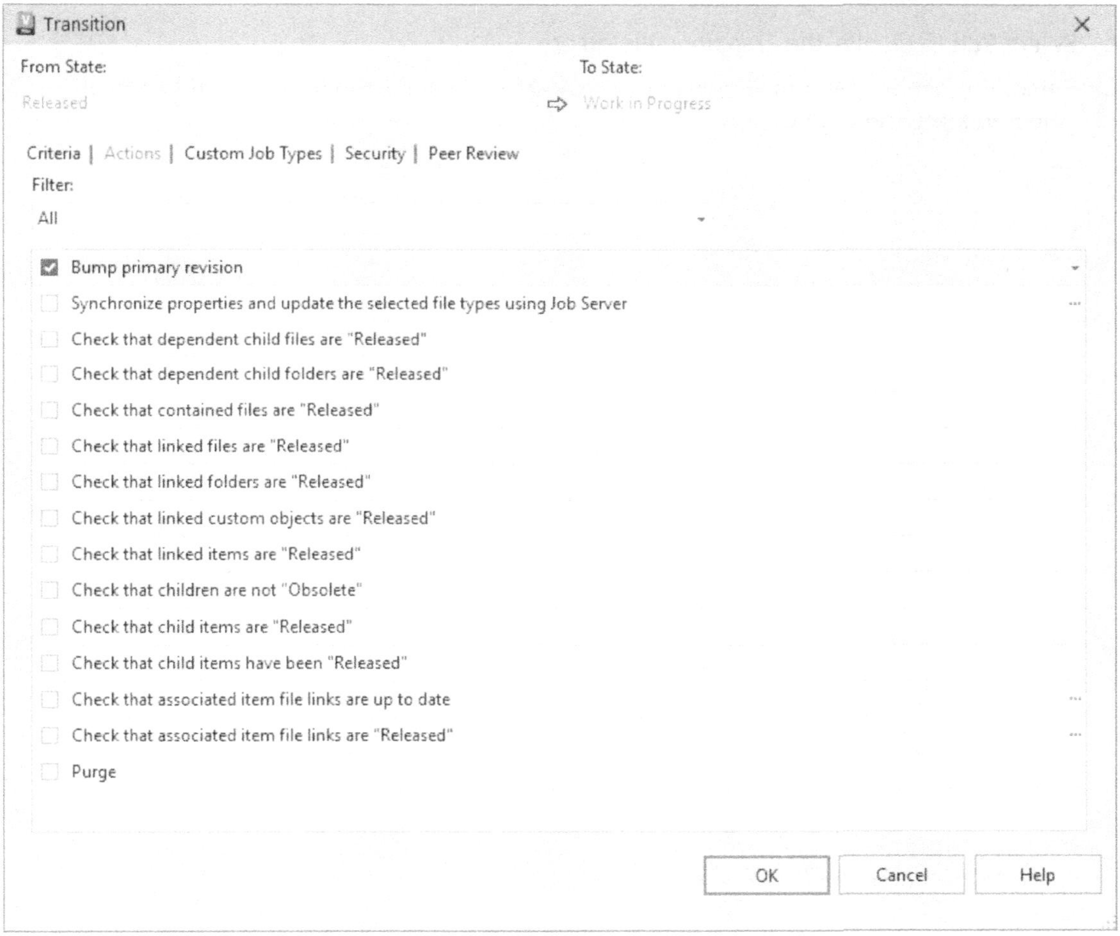


**Figure 4–24**

## How To: Configure Transition Actions

The following steps enable you to configure the actions that take place when a lifecycle state transition occurs:

1. In the *Vault Settings* dialog box, select the *Behaviors* tab.
2. Select **Lifecycles** in the *Lifecycles and Revisions* section to display the *Lifecycle Definitions* dialog box.
3. Select the lifecycle definition to be customized.

4. Select **Edit** to display the *Lifecycle Definition* dialog box for the selected definition.
5. Select the lifecycle state from the list of *Lifecycle States* to be configured.
6. Select the *Transitions* tab to display a list of all of the lifecycle transitions for the selected lifecycle definition.
7. Select the required state transition.
8. Select **Edit** to display the *Transition* dialog box.
9. Select the *Actions* tab (as shown in Figure 4–25) to display the actions initiated by the selected state transition.

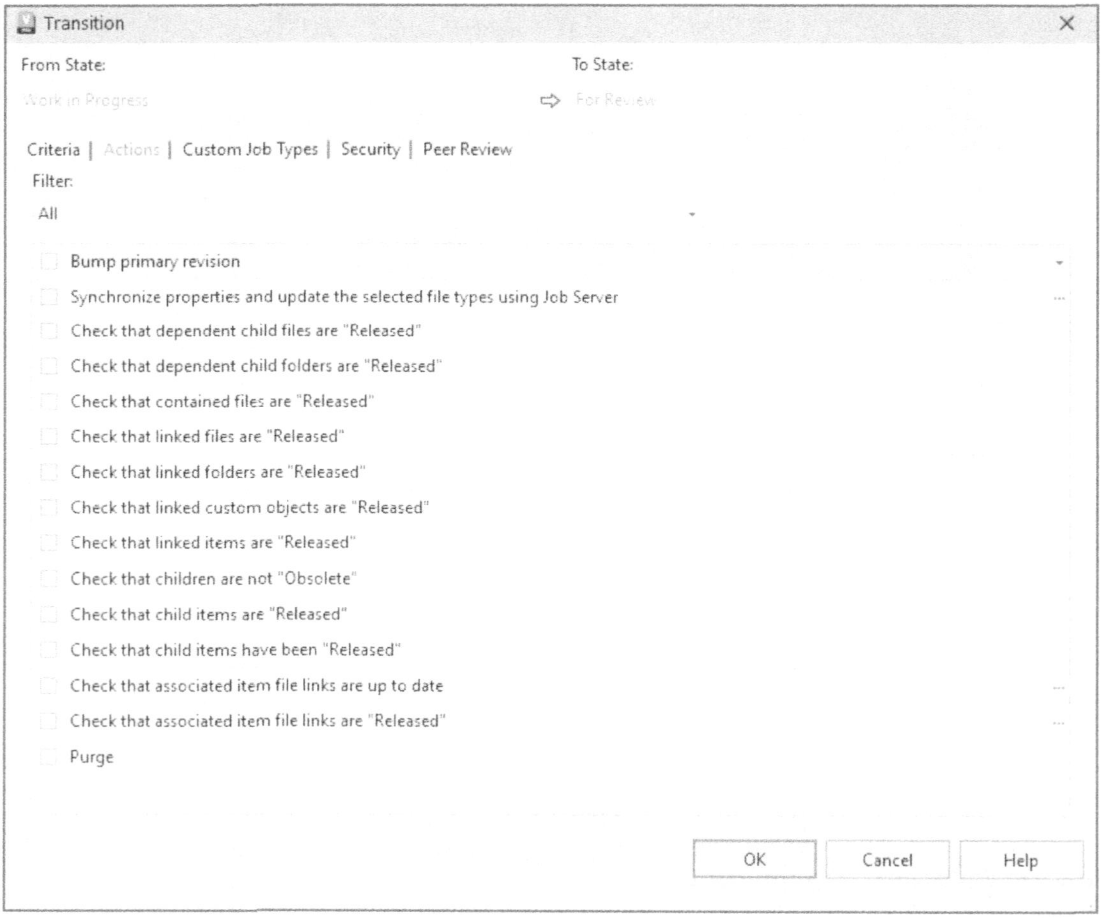


**Figure 4–25**

10. The default actions are shown. None are selected.
11. If required, select an entity class in the *Filter* drop-down list to show only the actions available for that entity class (e.g., select **Folders** to only see actions available for folder state transitions).

12. To specify a revision bump action, select the drop-down list to see the possible actions. Select the required action as shown in Figure 4–26.

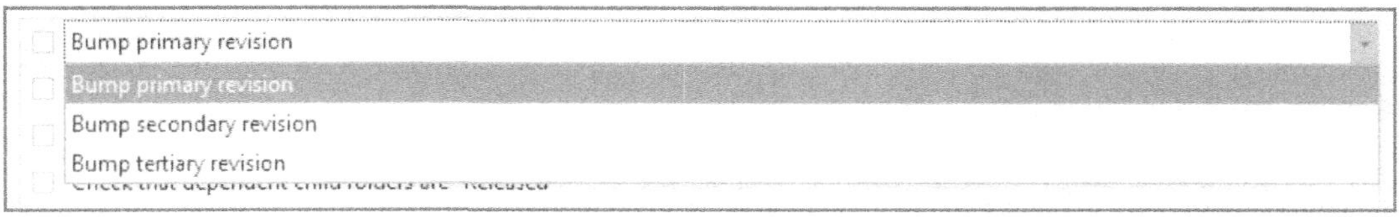


**Figure 4–26**

13. To specify a *Job Server* action, select the drop-down list to see the possible actions. Select the required action as shown in Figure 4–27.

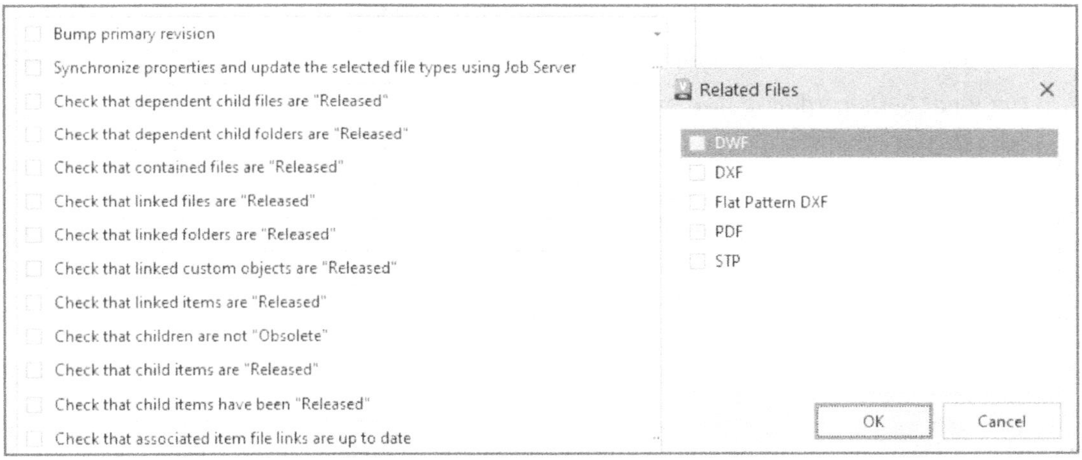


**Figure 4–27**

14. Review the final choices as shown in Figure 4–28.

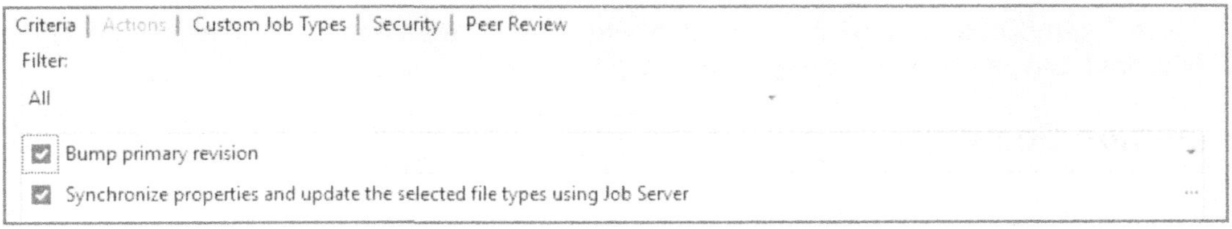


**Figure 4–28**

15. To specify release restrictions, select one or more of the options that check that the state of the dependent children, content, or linked data is set to released.

16. Click **OK** to dismiss this dialog box and return to the *Lifecycle Definition* dialog box for the selected lifecycle definition.

17. Configure the remaining transitions for the selected lifecycle state.
18. Click **OK** to dismiss this dialog box and return to the *Lifecycle Definitions* dialog box.
19. Click **Close** to dismiss this dialog box and return to the *Vault Settings* dialog box.

## Transition Custom Job Types

Custom jobs can be created to automate processes during a transition. Two steps are necessary to create a custom job. First, a programmer must create the custom job and install it within the vault extensions. Then, an administrator adds it to the transition.

### How To: Configure Transition Custom Job Types

The following steps enable you to associate a custom job with a state transition:

1. Click **Tools>Administration>Vault Settings**.
2. In the *Vault Settings* dialog box, select the *Behaviors* tab and select **Lifecycles**.
3. In the *Lifecycle Definitions* dialog box, select a lifecycle definition (e.g., Basic Release Process) and click **Edit**. The selected definition name displays in the title bar.
4. From the *Lifecycle States* list, select the lifecycle state to edit and then select the *Transitions* tab.
5. Select the desired transition, then click **Edit** to open the *Transitions* dialog box. Select the *Custom Job Types* tab.
6. Click **Add** and enter a name in the *Add to Input New Custom Job Type Name* field. Click **OK**.

   ***Note:*** *A typical naming convention is to add as a prefix your company name to any job types.*

7. Click **OK** to exit the *Transitions* dialog box.
8. This custom job type will initiate whenever an object transitions through this lifecycle.

   To enable this custom job on other transitions, repeat steps 3 to 5 and specify an existing custom job type instead of creating a new custom job.

## Transition Security

The last consideration for lifecycle transitions is which set of users and groups can initiate a state transition, if any is permitted to perform the state change. These are important questions for this topic:

- Does the state transition make sense for your process?
- If so, which set of users and groups can perform the transition? For example, in the default state **In Review** is it permitted to change the state to **Obsolete**? If so, who can do it? If not, then no one user or group can perform the transition.

Figure 4–29 shows that when releasing a new design or major design change, only the **Administrator** group has the ability to initiate the transition.

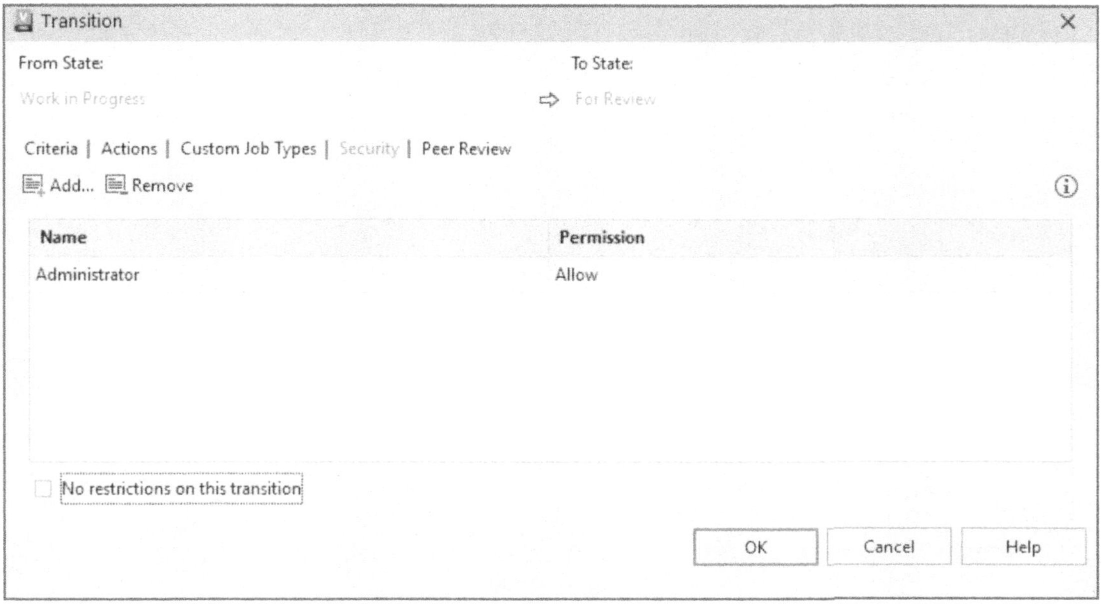


**Figure 4–29**

## How To: Configure Transition Security

The following steps enable you to specify which users and groups can initiate a state transition:

1. In the *Vault Settings* dialog box, select the *Behaviors* tab.
2. Select **Lifecycles** in the *Lifecycles and Revisions* section to display the *Lifecycle Definitions* dialog box.
3. Select the lifecycle definition to be customized.
4. Select **Edit** to display the *Lifecycles Definition* dialog box for the selected definition.
5. Select the lifecycle state from the list of *Lifecycle States* to be configured.
6. Select the *Transitions* tab to display a list of all of the lifecycle transitions for the selected lifecycle definition.
7. Select the required state transition.
8. Select **Edit** to display the *Transition* dialog box.

9. Select the *Security* tab to display the default security, as shown in Figure 4–30.

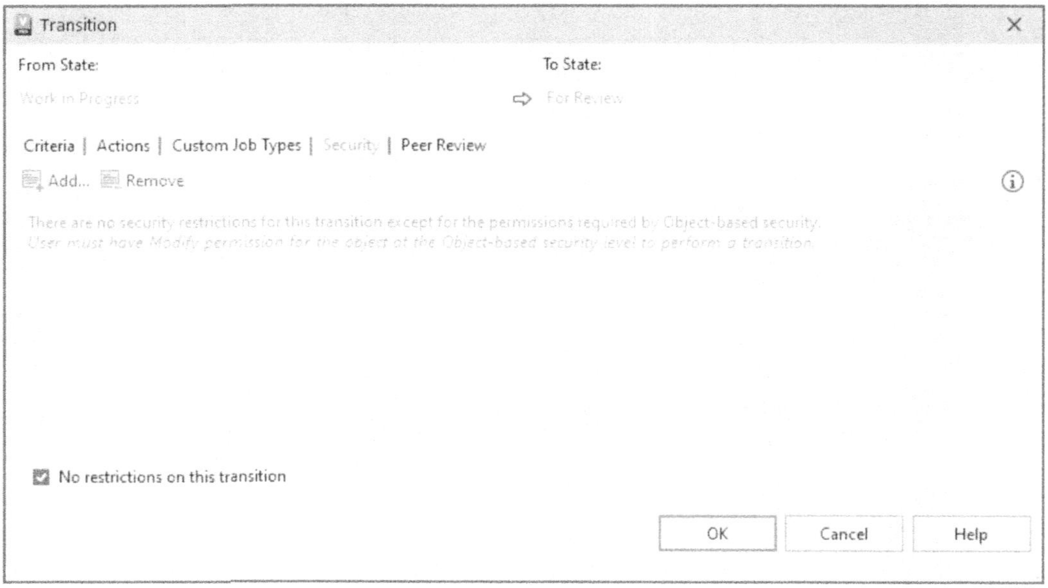


Figure 4–30

10. To configure security, first clear the checkbox for the **No restrictions on this transition** option, as shown in Figure 4–31.

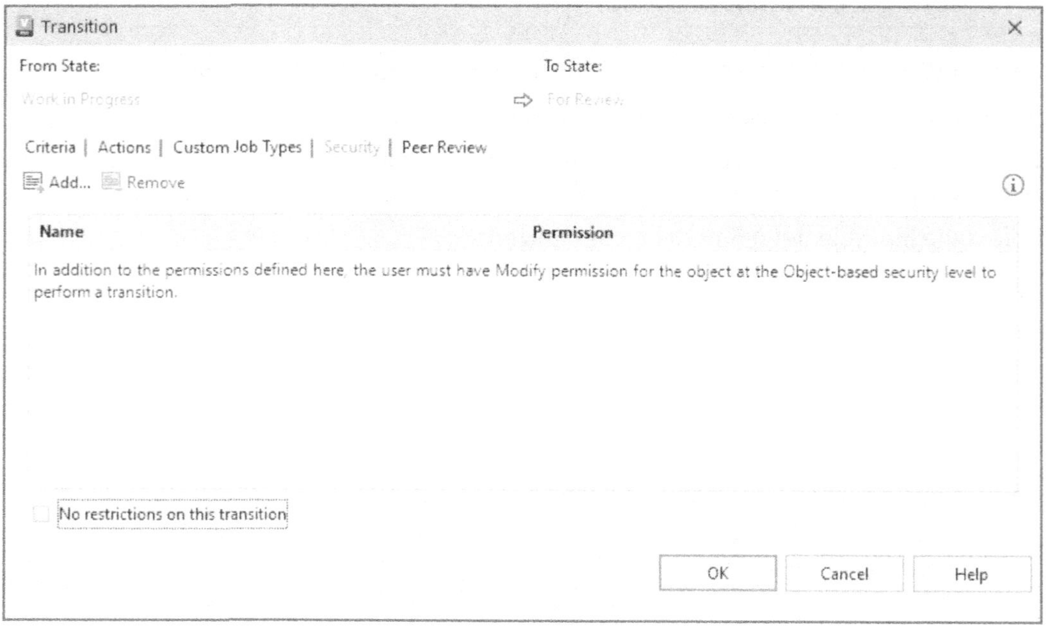


Figure 4–31

- The tab changes to enable you to specify which users and groups can perform the transition.

11. Select **Add** to display the *Add Members* dialog box.
12. Select the users and groups from the *Available Members* list that are granted or denied permission to perform the lifecycle change. Select **Add**, to add them to the *Current Members* list as shown in Figure 4–32.

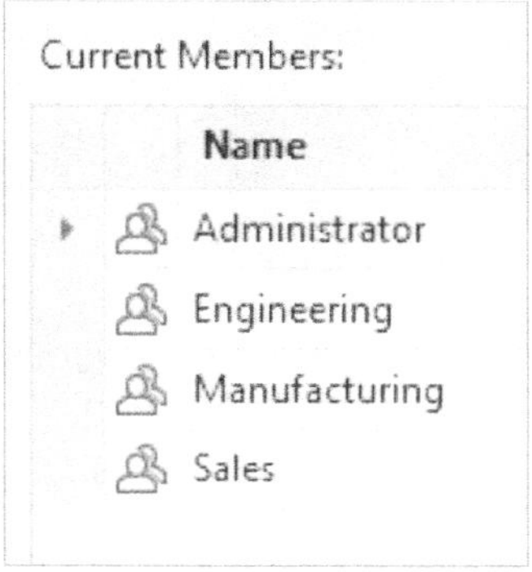


**Figure 4–32**

13. Click **OK** to return to the *Transition* dialog box with the selected members, as shown in Figure 4–33.

***Note:*** *By default, all members are permitted rights to change the file's lifecycle state. However, anyone who is not a member of a group or explicitly added as a member will be denied the ability to perform the state transition.*

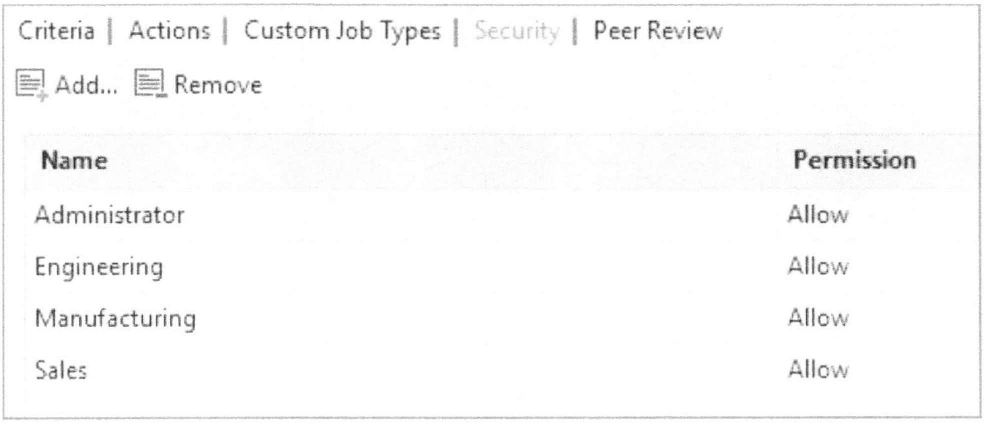


**Figure 4–33**

14. For each user or group, specify if they are permitted or denied the ability to change the file's state as shown in Figure 4–34.

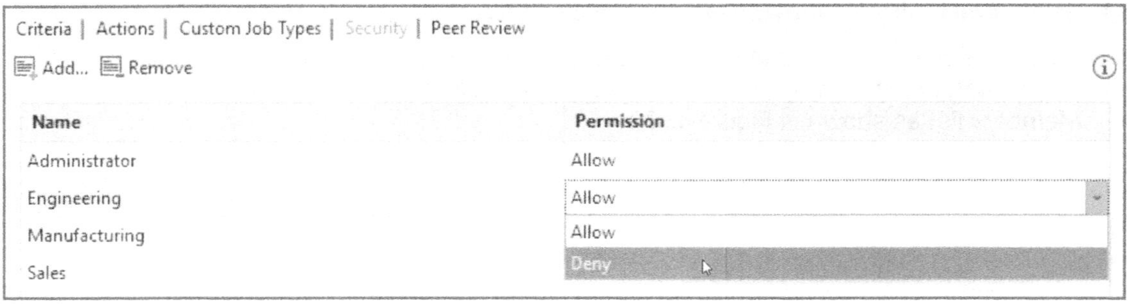


Figure 4–34

15. When done, review the final selections. Click **OK** to dismiss this dialog box and return to the *Lifecycle Definition* dialog box for this state transition.
16. Configure the remaining transitions for the selected lifecycle state.
17. Click **OK** to dismiss this dialog box and return to the *Lifecycle Definitions* dialog box.
18. Click **Close** to dismiss this dialog box and return to the *Vault Settings* dialog box.

## Creating the Transition Guidelines

Figure 4–35 shows how a tool like Microsoft Visio can be used to plan and manage the lifecycle definition's transitions.

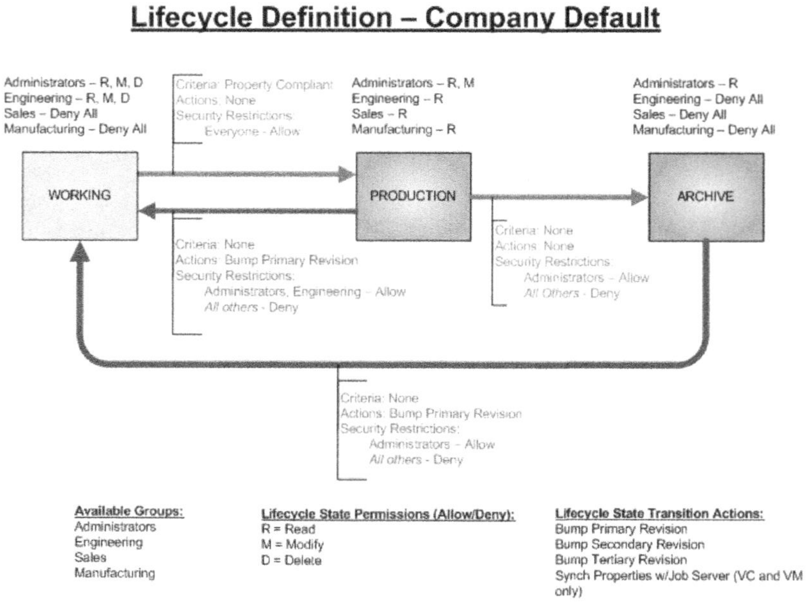


Figure 4–35

# Control and Comments Settings

There are two more settings that can be configured for a given lifecycle state.

## Control

The *Control* tab (shown in Figure 4–36) contains the settings that determine what happens during a **Purge** operation.

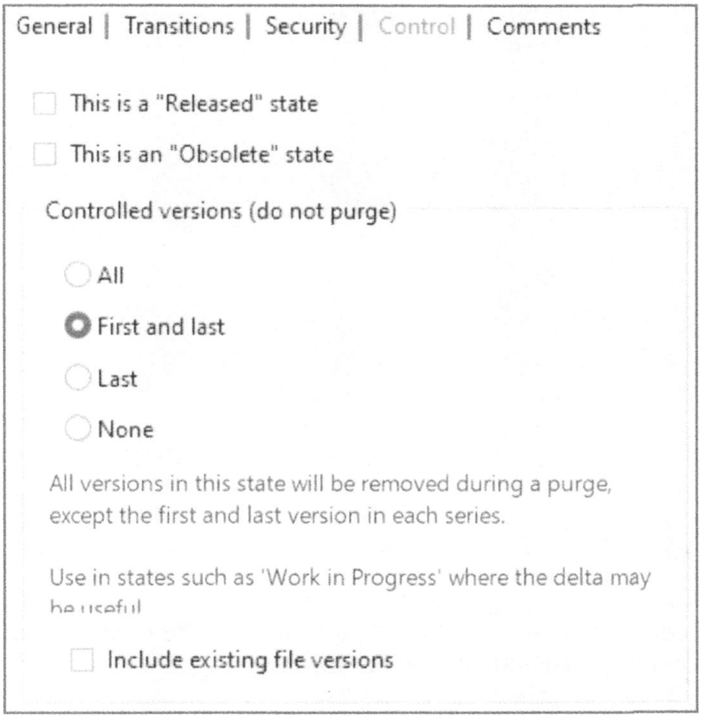


**Figure 4–36**

As you learned earlier, file versions are created every time you check a file in after being edited. File versions mark major milestones, for example release of a set of files representing a new product, or the subsequent major modification of one of those files for form, fit, and function purposes. For each revision, there can be many versions as files are checked out, modified, and checked in on a daily basis, a new user makes a modification to a files, etc. For the selected state, the radio buttons (**All**, **First and last**, **Last**, **None**) control which versions of a file will be kept if a purge occurs.

 

## Comments

When an object is transitioned from one lifecycle state to another, a comment is added. The *Comments* tab controls what comment is added. Figure 4–37 shows the dialog box that is presented to the user when transitioning to the **For Review** state.

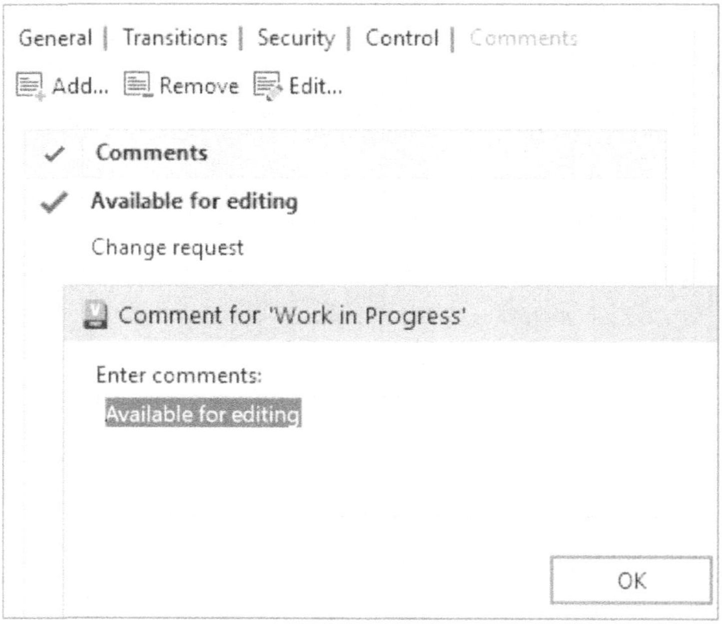


**Figure 4–37**

The *Comments* tab has a list of suggested text strings to use as a default. The user is free to add or replace this comment with one of their own. Figure 4–38 shows the suggested and default comment for a state transitioning to **For Review**.

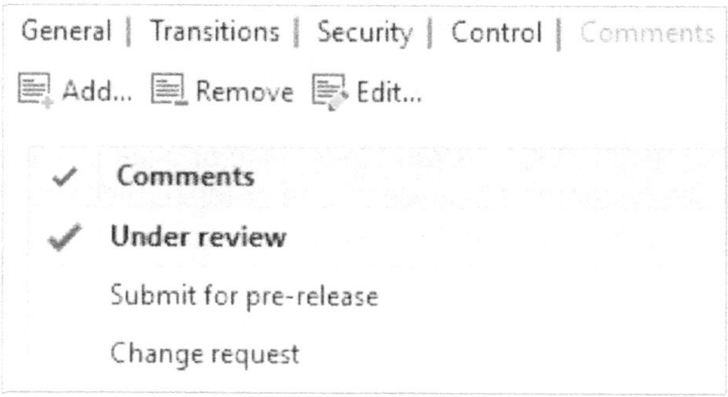


**Figure 4–38**

## How To: Configure Control and Comments

The following steps enable you to specify which objects are removed during a purge operation and the default comment text for the state being transitioned to:

1. In the *Vault Settings* dialog box, select the *Behaviors* tab.
2. Select **Lifecycles** in the *Lifecycles and Revisions* section to display the *Lifecycle Definitions* dialog box.
3. Select the lifecycle definition to be customized.
4. Select **Edit** to display the *Lifecycles Definition* dialog box for the selected definition.
5. Select the lifecycle state from the list of *Lifecycle States* to be configured.
6. Select the *Control* tab to display the settings for controlled versions as shown in Figure 4–39.

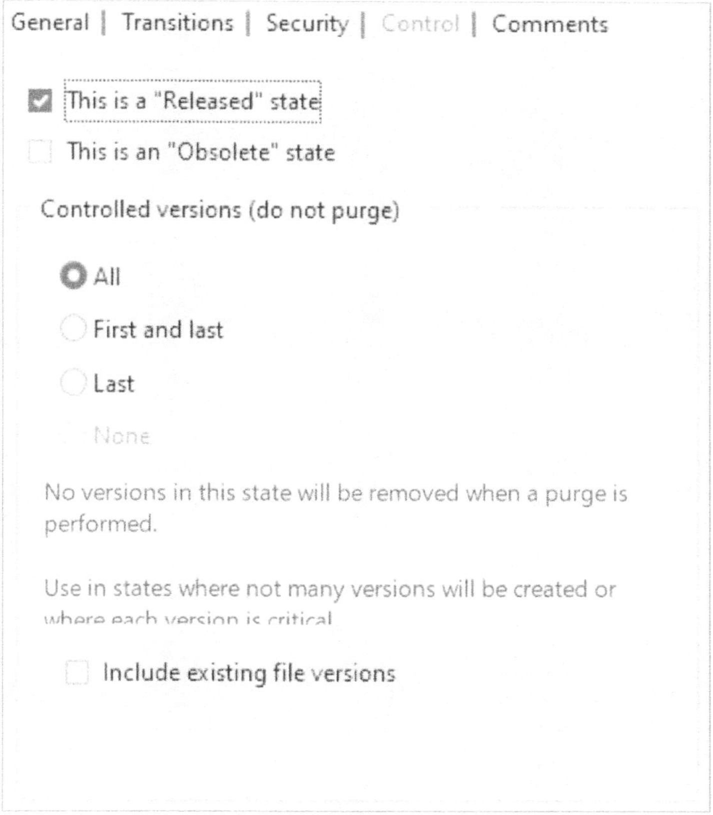


**Figure 4–39**

7. First, determine whether this state represents a released or obsolete condition. If it is a **Released** or **Obsolete** state, select the appropriate checkbox.

8. Determine which versions should not be purged. Select the different radio buttons (shown in Figure 4–40) to get details about each selection.
   - **All:** No versions in this state are removed when a purge is performed. This option is recommended for states where not many versions are created or where each version is critical.
   - **First and last:** All versions in this state are removed during a purge, except the first and last version in each series. Use this option for states where the changes between the first and last versions are not important.
   - **Last:** All versions in this state are removed during a purge, except the last version in each series. This option is recommended for states where a record that the file was in the state is important.
   - **None:** No version in this state will be retained after the purge has been performed.

   ***Note:*** *No record of the file being in this state will exist after the purge.*

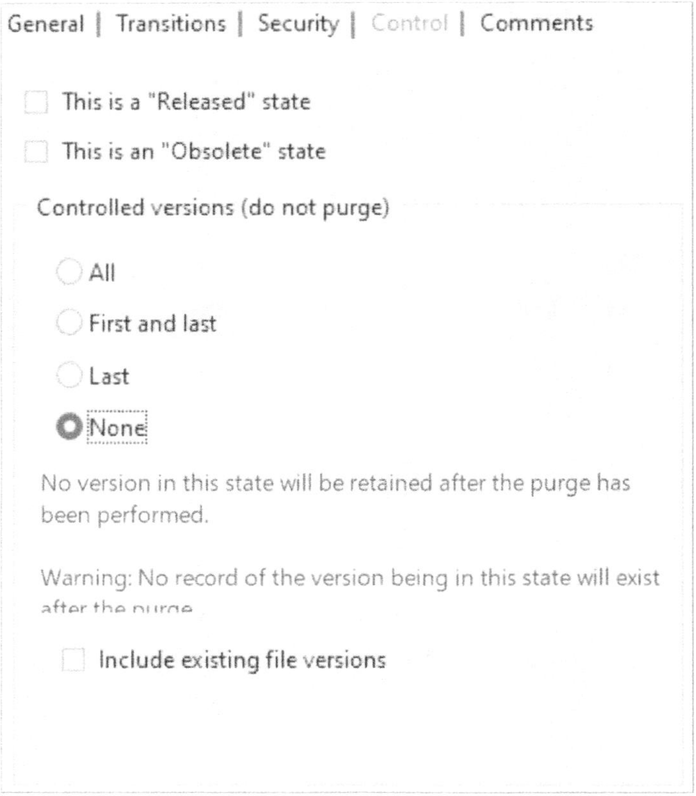


**Figure 4–40**

9. Select the *Comments* tab to display the list of default comments (if any) pre-populated for this state.

10. Select the comment to set as default or select **Add** to add a new comment, as shown in Figure 4–41.

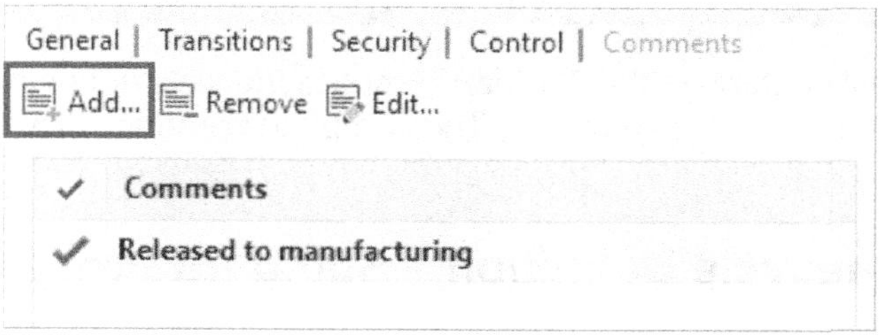


**Figure 4–41**

11. To create a new default comment, enter the text in the *Enter comments* field. Click **OK** as shown in Figure 4–42 to close this dialog box.

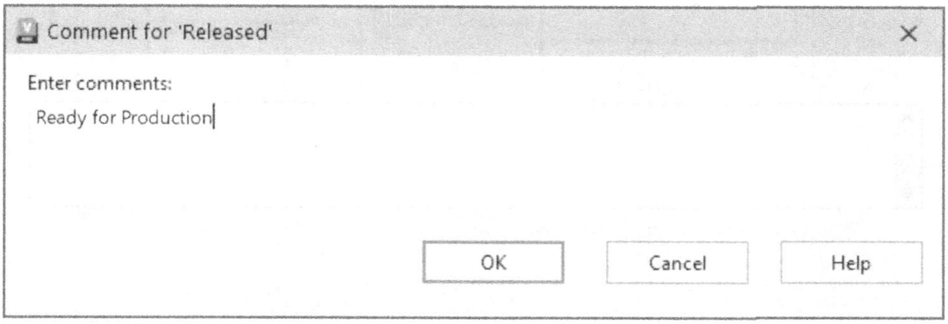


**Figure 4–42**

12. Double-click on the new comment if one was added (as shown in Figure 4–43), to make it the new default.
    - Note that you could also edit an existing comment rather than add a new one or remove a current one so it no longer displays in the drop-down list.

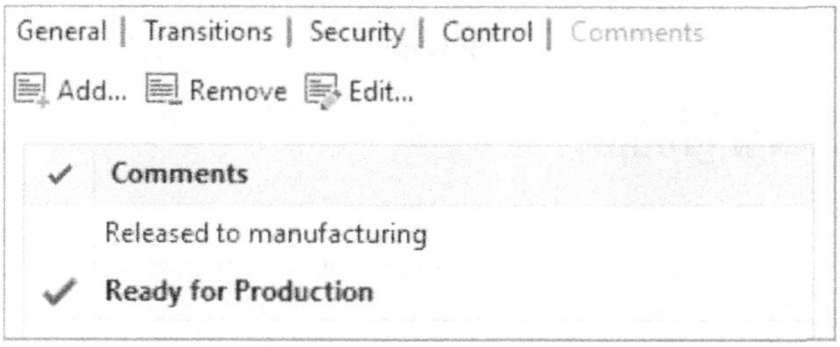


**Figure 4–43**

13. Configure the remaining transitions for the selected lifecycle state.
14. Click **OK** to close this dialog box and return to the *Lifecycle Definitions* dialog box.
15. Click **Close** to dismiss this dialog box and return to the *Vault Settings* dialog box.

# Practice 4b
# Lifecycle Definition

In this practice, you will customize the **Standard Process** lifecycle definition that you created in ***Practice 4a Create New Lifecycle Definition***. The completed practice displays as shown below in Figure 4–44.

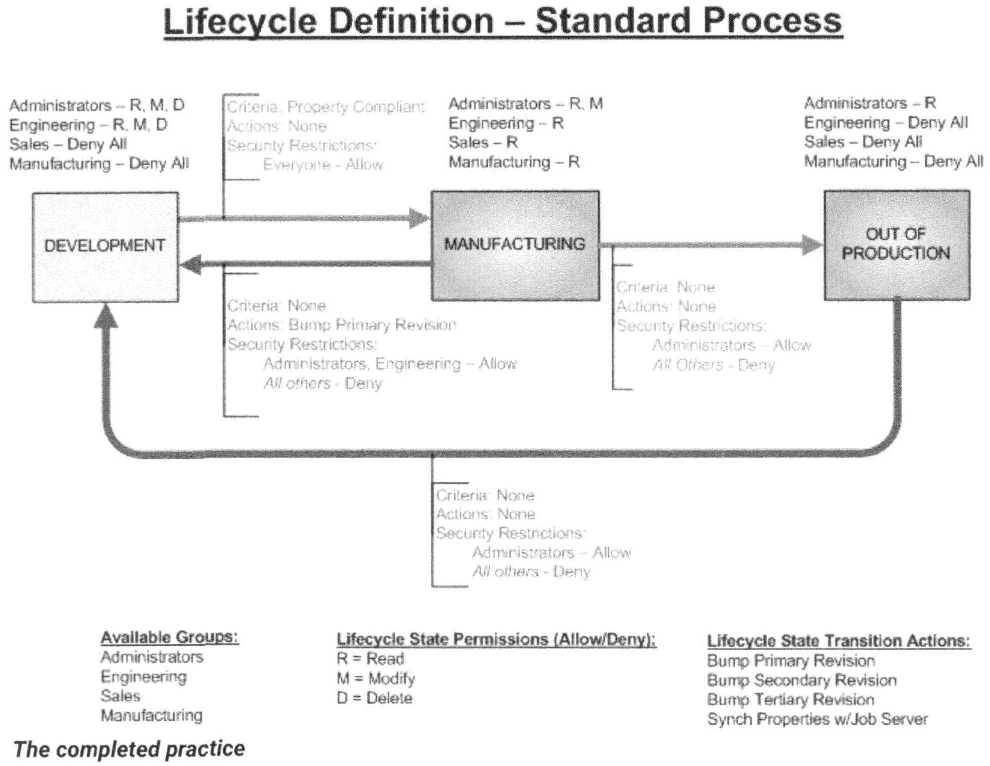


**Figure 4–44**

## Task 1: Create four new groups.

1. In the *Tools* menu, select **Administration>Global Settings** to open the *Global Settings* dialog box.
2. Select **Manage Access** in the *Users and Groups* section of the *Security* tab to display the *User and Group Management* dialog box.

 

3. Create a group called **Administrator**, and in the group definition, specify a role of *Administrator* with *User A* as a member using the following steps:
   a. Select the *Groups* tab and click **New**. The *New Group Profile* dialog box displays.
   b. In the New *Group Profile* dialog box, for the *Group Name*, type **Administrator**.
   c. Click **Roles**. The *Add Roles* dialog box displays.
   d. Select the **Administrator** checkbox, then click **OK**.
   e. In the *New Group Profile* dialog box, click **Add** to display the *Add Members* dialog box.
   f. Select **User A** from the *Available Members* list then click **Add** (as shown in Figure 4–45) to add this user to the *Current Members* list.

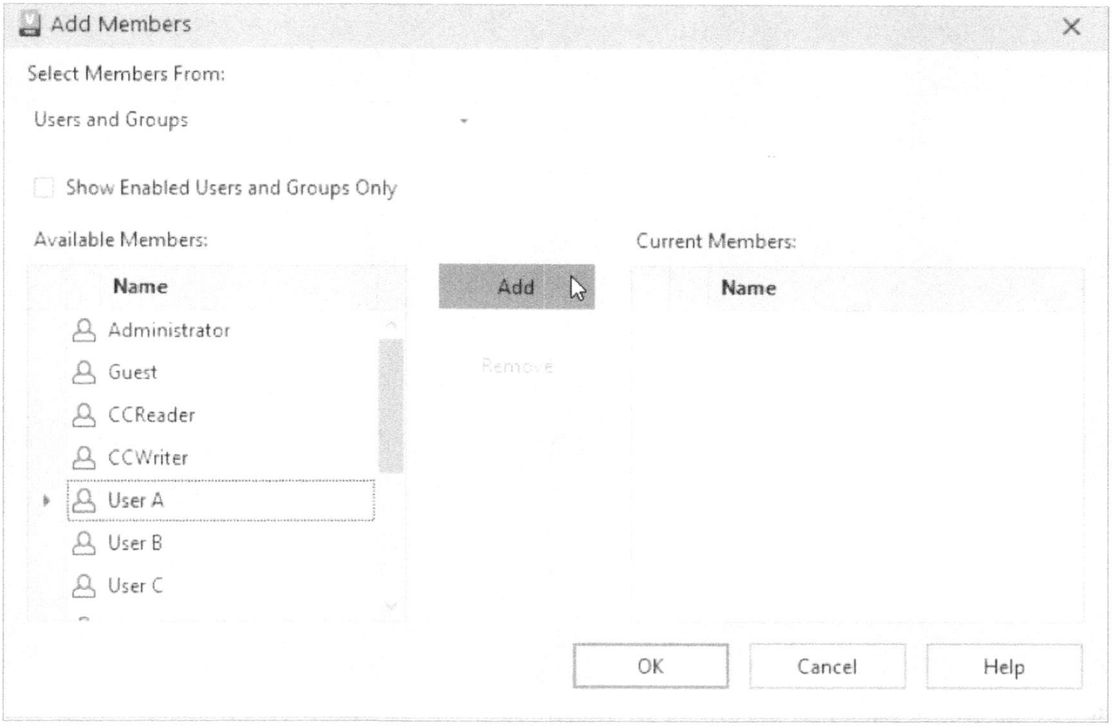


**Figure 4–45**

**g.** Click **OK** to dismiss the *Add Members* dialog box.

***Note:*** *Your New Group Profile dialog box should display as shown in Figure 4–46.*

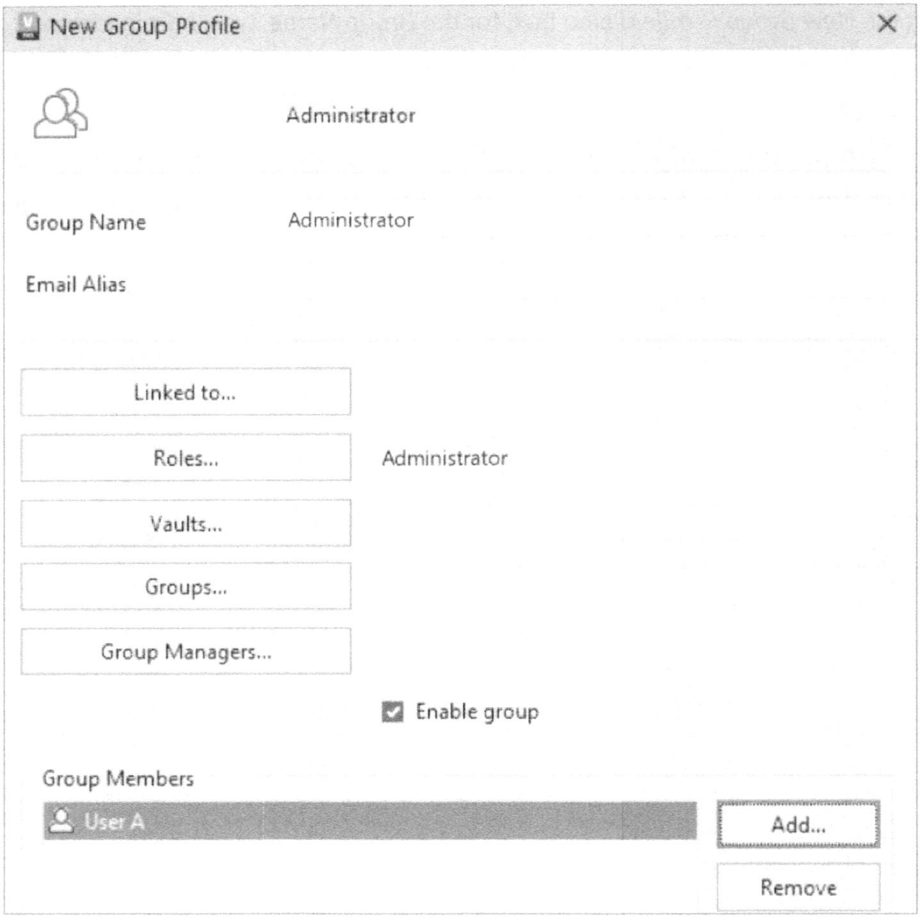


**Figure 4–46**

**h.** Click **OK** to dismiss the *New Group Profile* dialog box to return to the *User and Group Management* dialog box.

4. In this step, you create a group called **Engineering** defined with a role of Document Editor Level 2 and Document Manager Level 2 with User B as a member.
    a. Ensure you are on the *Groups* tab then click **New**. The *New Group Profile* dialog box displays.
    b. In the *New Group Profile* dialog box, for the Group Name, type Engineering.
    c. Click **Roles**. The *Add Roles* dialog box displays.
    d. Select the checkboxes for **Document Editor Level 2** and **Document Manager Level 2** then click **OK**.
    e. In the *New Group Profile* dialog box, click **Add** to display the *Add Members* dialog box.
    f. Select **User B** from the Available Members list then click **Add** to add this to the *Current Members* list, as shown in Figure 4–47.

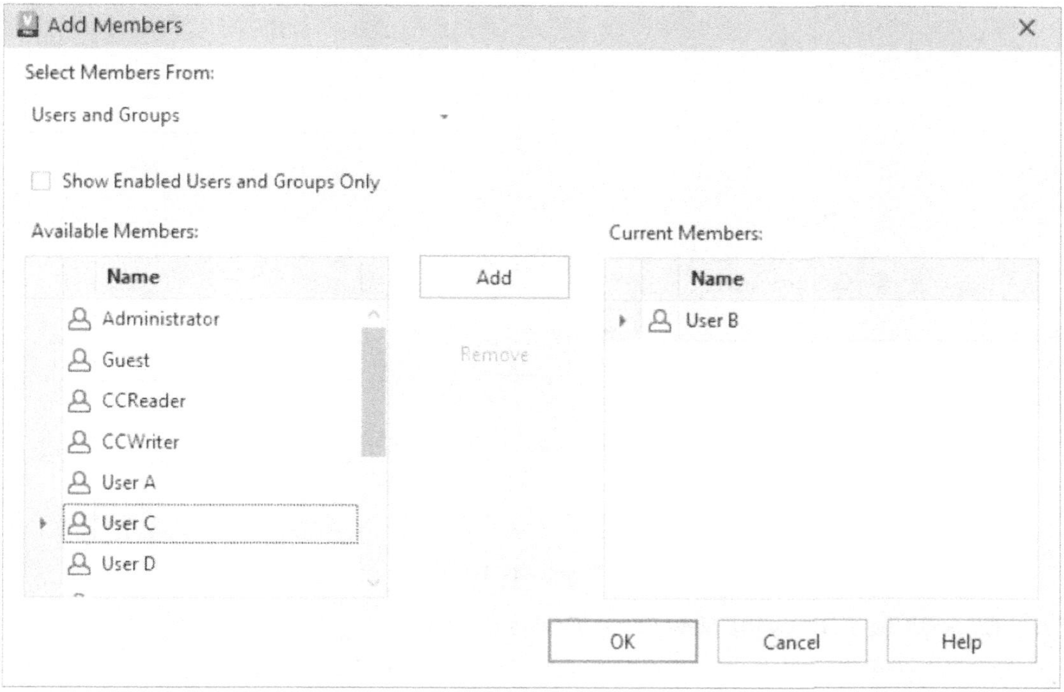


**Figure 4–47**

g. Click **OK** to dismiss the *Add Members* dialog box.

***Note:*** *Your New Group Profile dialog box should look as shown in Figure 4–48.*

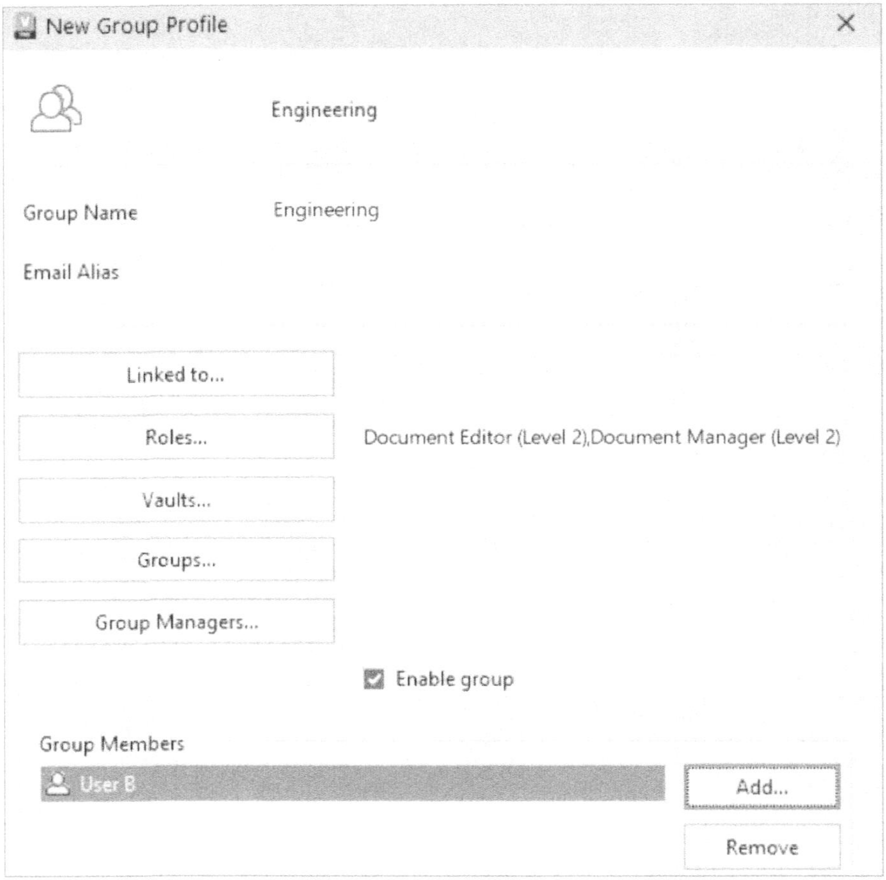


**Figure 4–48**

h. Click **OK** to dismiss the *New Group Profile* dialog box.

5. In this step, you create a group called **Manufacturing** defined with a role of Document Editor Level 2 and Document Manager Level 2 with User C as a member.
   a. Ensure you are on the *Groups* tab and click **New**. The *New Group Profile* dialog box displays.
   b. In the *New Group Profile* dialog box, for the Group Name, type **Manufacturing**.
   c. Click **Roles**. The *Add Roles* dialog box displays.
   d. Select the checkboxes for **Document Editor Level 2** and **Document Manager Level 2** then click **OK**.
   e. In the *New Group Profile* dialog box, click **Add** to display the *Add Members* dialog box.
   f. Select **User C** from the Available Members list then click **Add** (as shown in Figure 4–49) to add this user to the *Current Members* list.

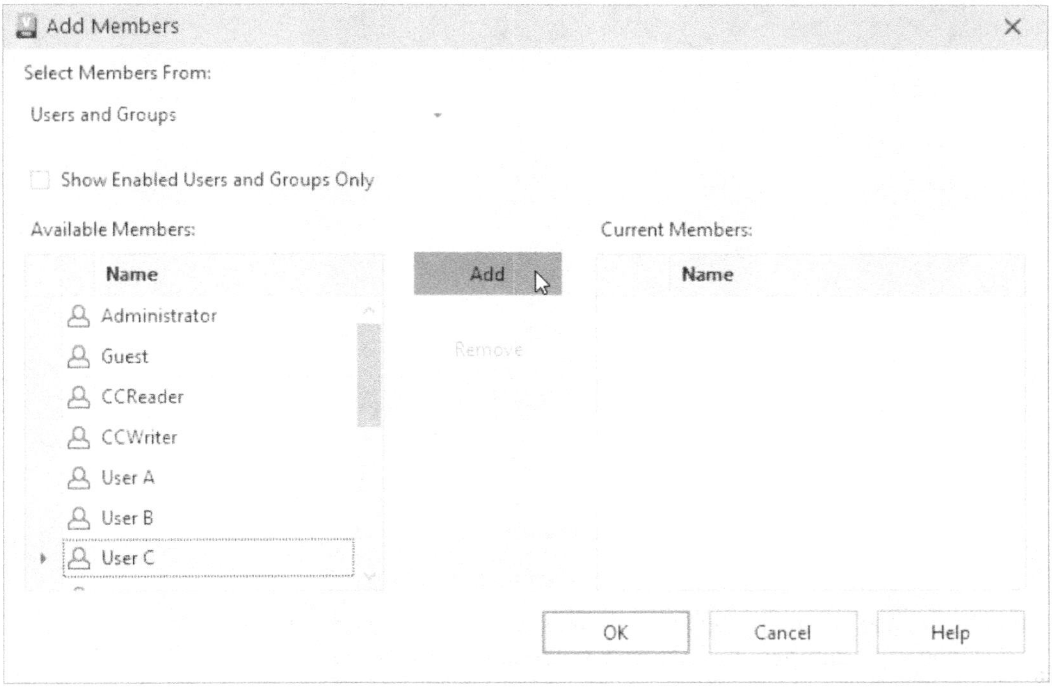


**Figure 4–49**

g. Click **OK** to dismiss the *Add Members* dialog box. Your *New Group Profile* dialog box should look as shown in Figure 4–50.

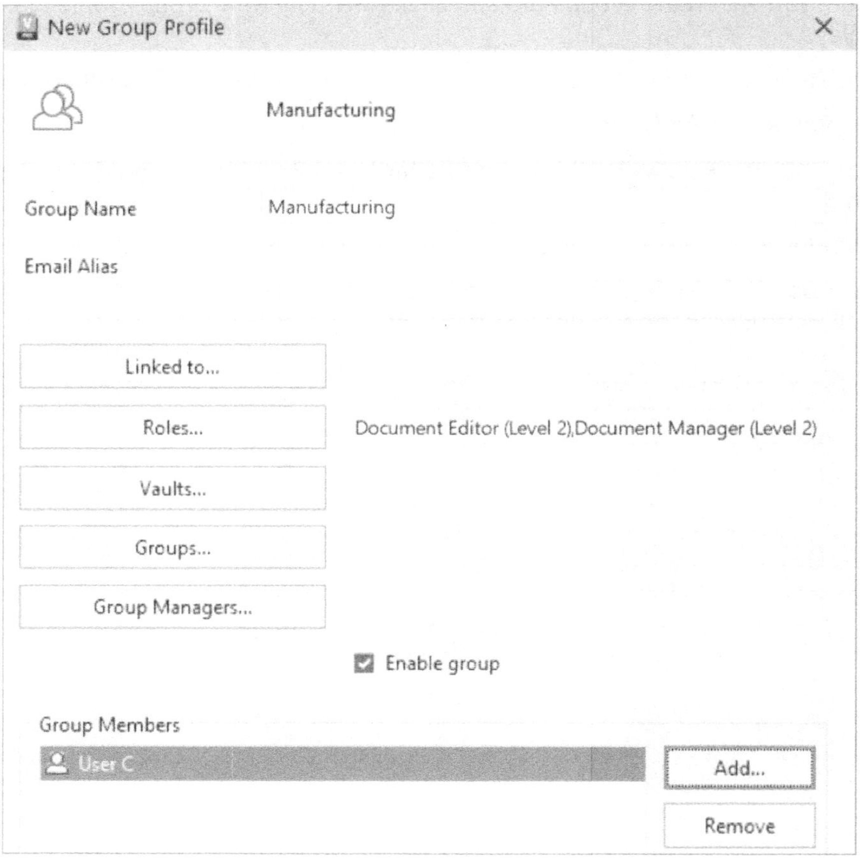


**Figure 4–50**

h. Click **OK** to dismiss the *New Group Profile* dialog box.

6. In this step, you create a group called **Sales** defined with a role of Document Editor Level 2 and Document Manager Level 2 with User D as a member.

   a. Ensure you are on the *Groups* tab and click **New**. The *New Group Profile* dialog box displays.

   b. In the *New Group Profile* dialog box, for the *Group Name*, type **Sales**.

   c. Click **Roles**. The *Add Roles* dialog box displays.

   d. Click the checkbox for **Document Editor Level 2** and **Document Manager Level 2** then click **OK**.

   e. In the *New Group Profile* dialog box, click **Add** to display the *Add Members* dialog box.

   f. Select **User D** from the *Available Members* list then click **Add** to add this user to the *Current Members* list as shown in Figure 4–51.

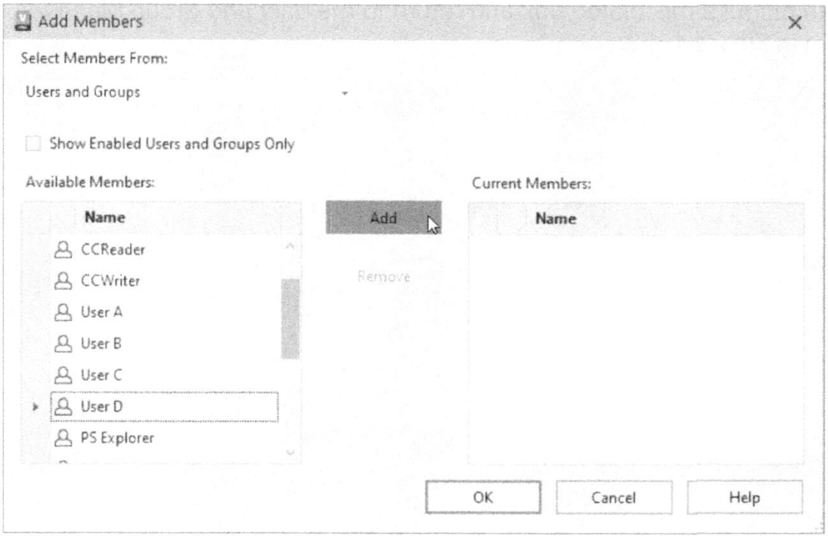


**Figure 4–51**

**g.** Click **OK** to dismiss the *Add Members* dialog box.

***Note:*** *Your New Group Profile dialog box should look as shown in Figure 4–52.*

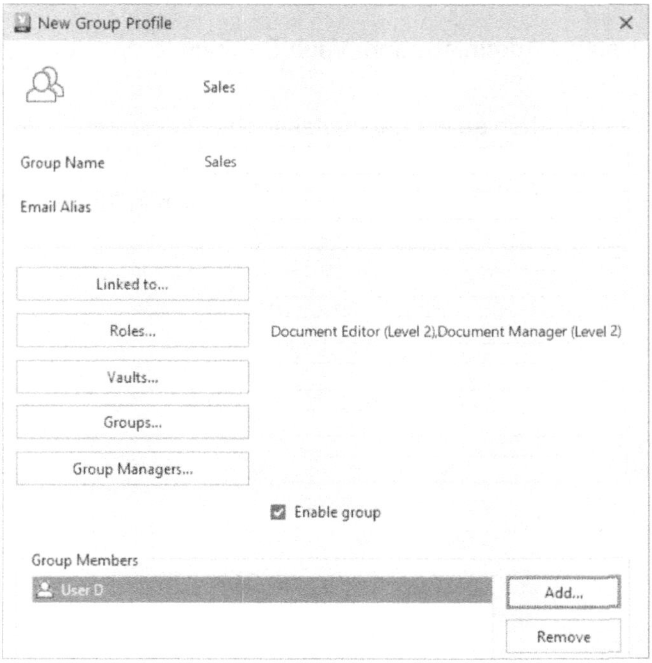


**Figure 4–52**

**h.** Click **OK** to dismiss the *New Group Profile* dialog box.

7. Click **OK** to dismiss this dialog box and return to the *User and Group Management* dialog box shown in Figure 4–53.

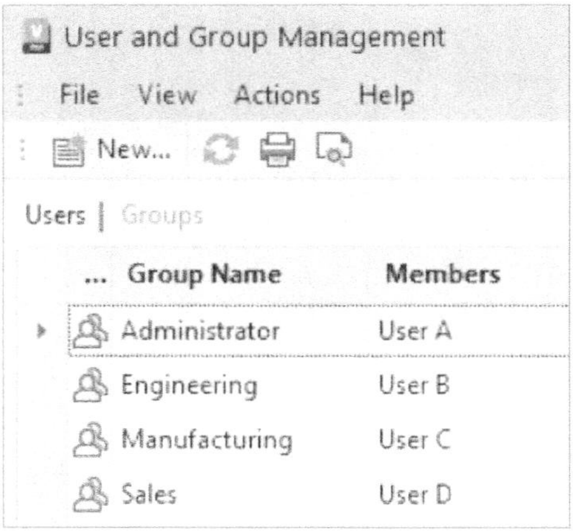


**Figure 4–53**

8. Select **File>Exit** to close this dialog box and return to the *Global Settings* dialog box.
9. Click **Close** to dismiss this dialog box.

## Task 2: Configure lifecycle state: Security.

1. In the *Tools* menu, select **Administration>Vault Settings** to open the *Vault Settings* dialog box.
2. Select the *Behaviors* tab, then select **Lifecycles** in the *Lifecycles and Revisions* section to display the *Lifecycle Definitions* dialog box.
3. Select the lifecycle definition **Standard Process**, as shown in Figure 4–54.

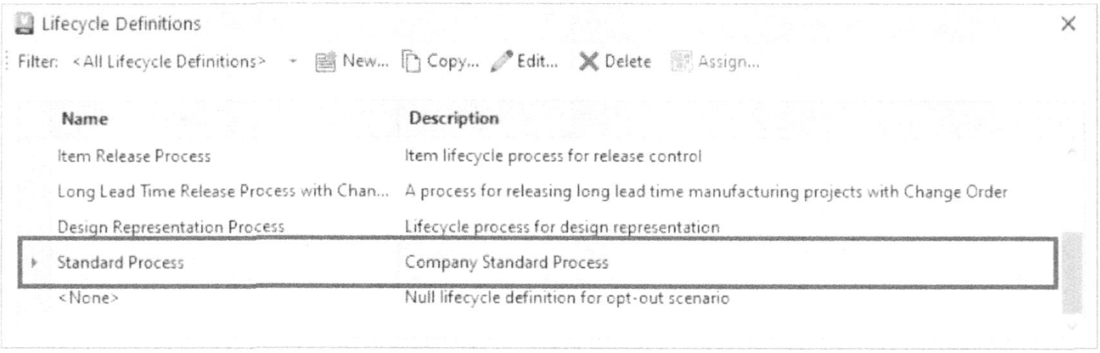


**Figure 4–54**

4. Select **Edit** to display the *Lifecycle Definition - 'Standard Process'* dialog box.

 

5. In the *Lifecycle Details* section, ensure that the **Development** lifecycle state is selected in the list, as shown in Figure 4–55.

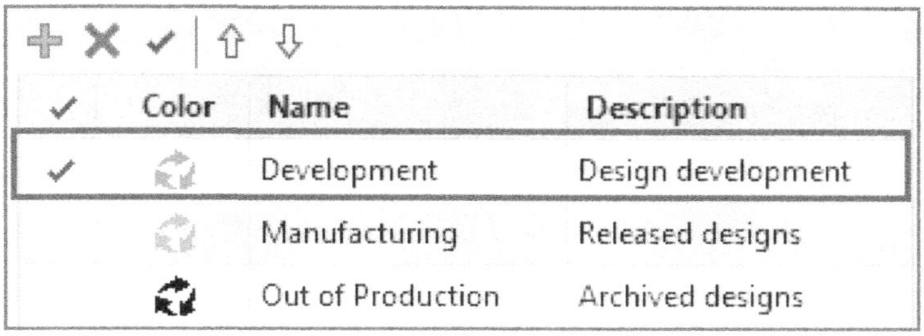


**Figure 4–55**

6. Select the *Security* tab, as shown in Figure 4–56. By default there is no state-based security set.

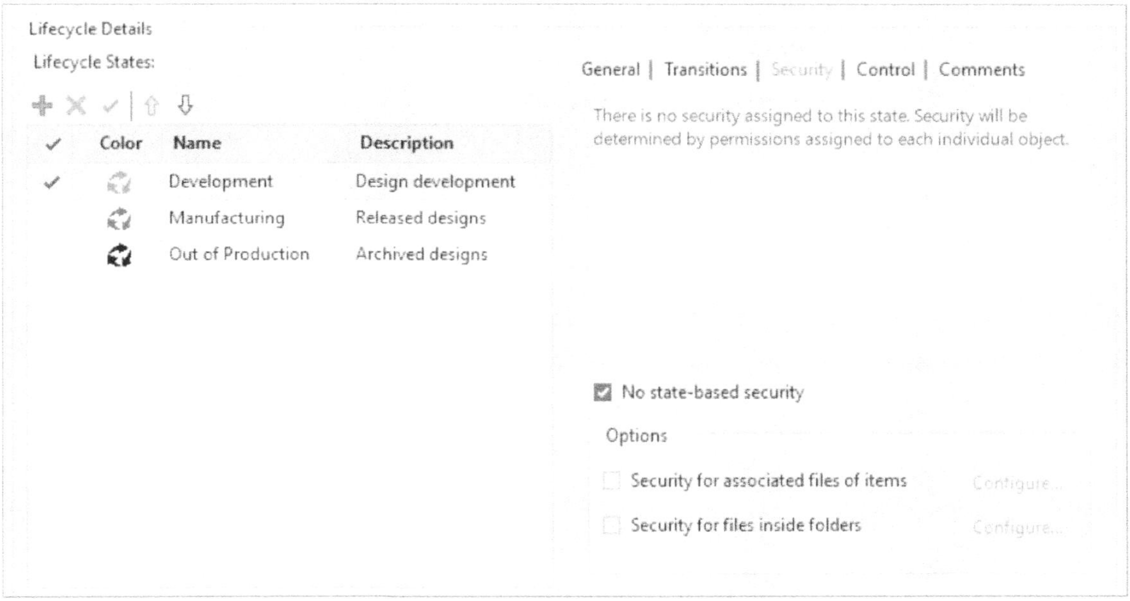


**Figure 4–56**

7. Clear the **No state-based security** checkbox (as shown in Figure 4–57) to enable state-based security.

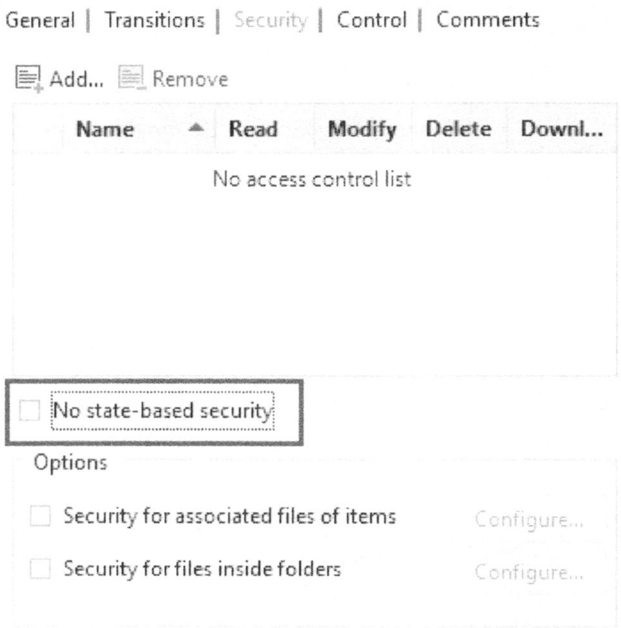


**Figure 4–57**

8. Select **Add** to display the *Add Members* dialog box.
9. In the *Select Members From* drop-down list, select **Groups** as shown in Figure 4–58.

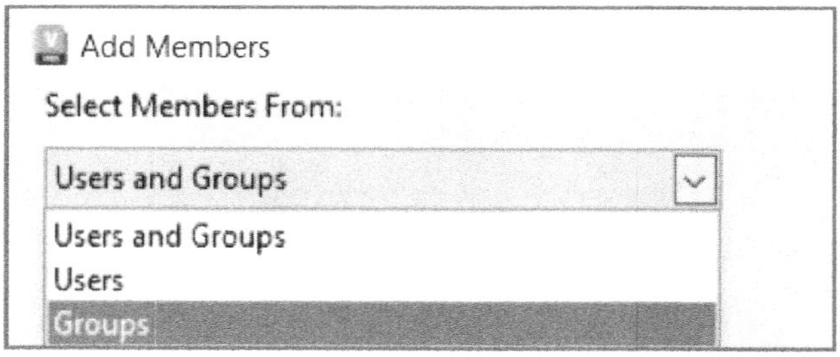


**Figure 4–58**

10. In the *Available Members* list, press <Ctrl> and select the **Administrator**, **Engineering**, **Manufacturing**, and **Sales** groups, and deselect **Everyone** as shown in Figure 4–59.

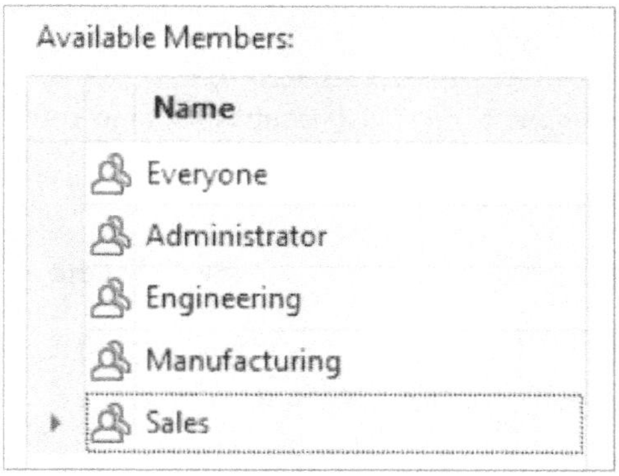


**Figure 4–59**

11. Select **Add** (as shown in Figure 4–60) to add the selection to the *Current Members* list.

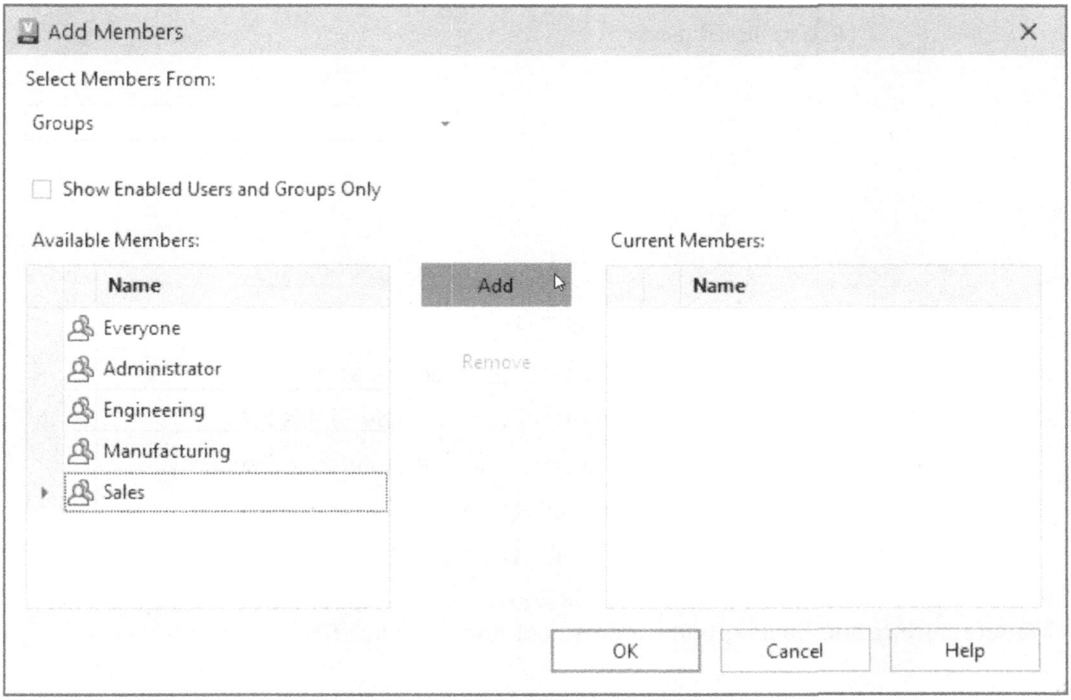


**Figure 4–60**

12. Click **OK** to dismiss this dialog box and return to the *Lifecycle Definition* dialog box.

13. For the **Development** state, make the security selections (i.e., **Allow**, **Deny**, etc.) for **Administrator**, **Engineering**, **Manufacturing**, and **Sales**, as shown in Figure 4–61 by clicking on a cell where the column (i.e., *Read*) and rows (i.e., *Administrator*) intersect to expand the drop-down list.

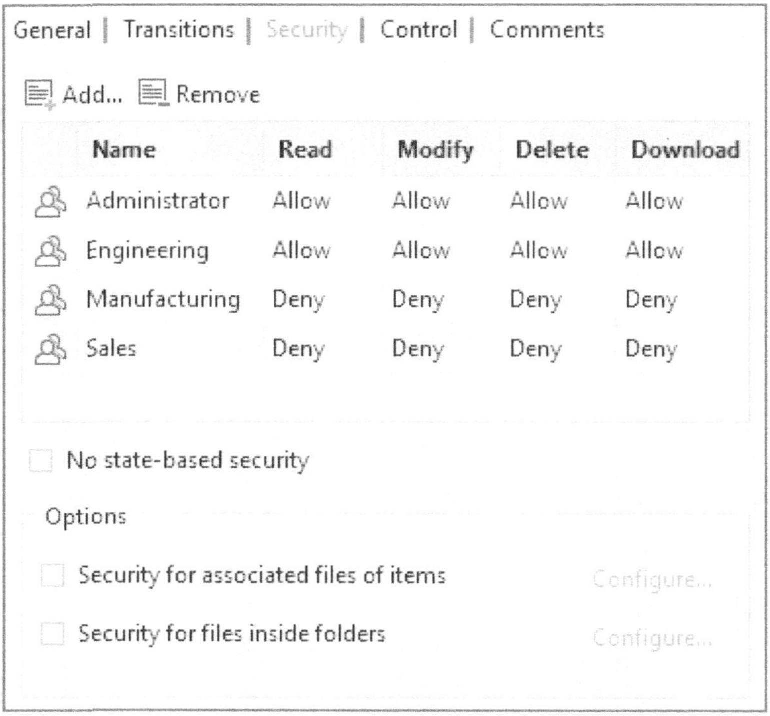


**Figure 4–61**

14. Select **Apply** to apply the settings to the selected lifecycle state.
15. Select the **Manufacturing** lifecycle state from the *Lifecycle States* list.
16. Clear the **No state-based security** checkbox to enable state-based security.
17. Select **Add** to display the *Add Members* dialog box.
18. In the *Select Members From* drop-down list, select **Groups**.
19. In the *Available Members* list, press <Ctrl> and select the **Administrators**, **Engineering**, **Manufacturing**, and **Sales** groups, then select **Add** and click **OK**.

**20.** For the **Manufacturing** state, set the following security settings, as shown in Figure 4–62:

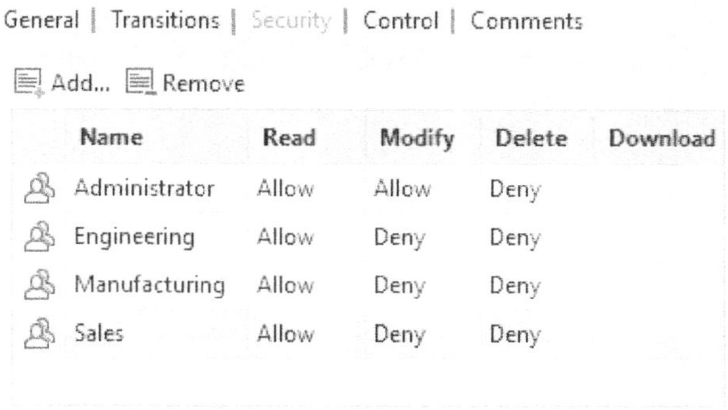


**Figure 4–62**

**21.** Select **Apply** to apply the settings to the selected lifecycle state.

**22.** For the **Out of Production** state, set the following security settings, as shown in Figure 4–63:

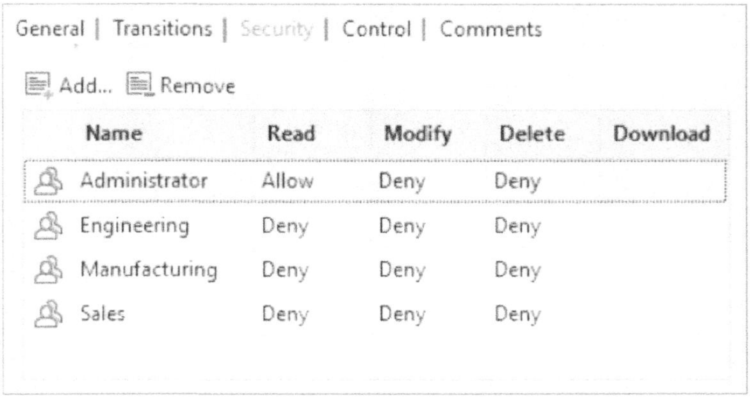


**Figure 4–63**

**23.** Select **Apply** to apply the settings to the selected lifecycle state.

## Task 3: Configure state transitions: Security.

In our example, there are three lifecycle states and six possible transitions that can occur. Some of these transitions are not permitted by anyone and will be configured first.

1. In this step, you will set the Development lifecycle state transition from **Development** to **Out of Production** to remove permissions for all users to perform this operation.
   a. In the *Lifecycle Definition – 'Standard Process'* dialog box, in the *Lifecycle States* list, select the **Development** state.
   b. Select the *Transitions* tab to display a list of possible transitions 'from' and 'to' this state.

c. Select the entry that specifies from **Development** to **Out of Production**, as shown in Figure 4–64.

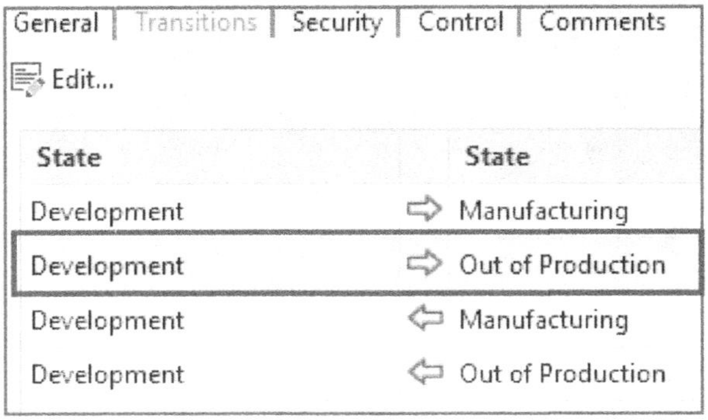


**Figure 4–64**

d. Click **Edit** to display the *Transition* dialog box.

e. Select the *Security* tab and clear the checkbox for the **No restrictions on this transition** option at the bottom of the dialog box, as shown in Figure 4–65.

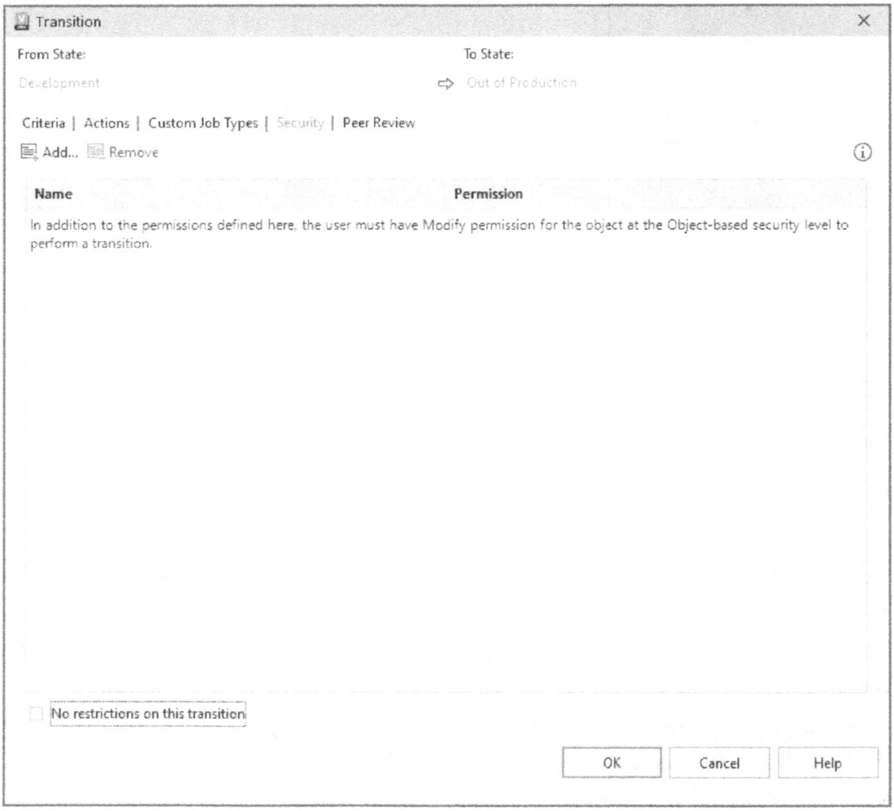


**Figure 4–65**

f. Click **Add** to display the *Add Members* dialog box.

g. In the *Select Members From* drop-down list, select **Groups**.

h. In the *Available Members* list, select **Everyone**.

i. Click **Add** to add the **Everyone** group to the *Current Members* list, as shown in Figure 4–66.

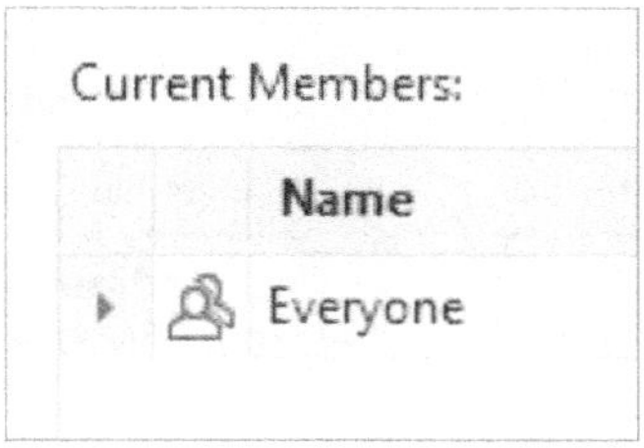


**Figure 4–66**

j. Click **OK** to dismiss the *Add Members* dialog box to return to the *Transition* dialog box.

k. The group **Everyone** has been added to the *Security* list with the default permission **Allow**. Select the default permission cell to expand the drop-down list and select **Deny**, as shown in Figure 4–67.

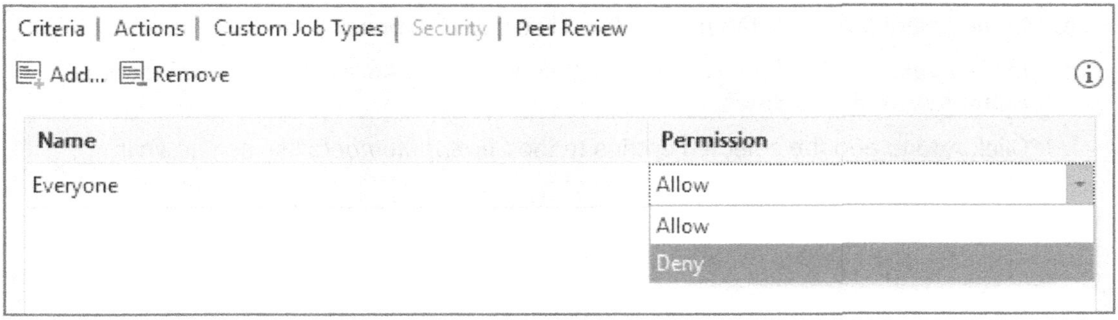


**Figure 4–67**

l. Click **OK** to dismiss the *Transition* dialog box to return to the *Lifecycle Definition – 'Standard Process'* dialog box.

2. In this step, you will set the Development lifecycle state transition from **Manufacturing** to **Development** to remove permissions for the *Manufacturing* and *Sales* groups to perform this operation.

   a. In the *Lifecycle Definition – 'Standard Process'* dialog box, in the *Lifecycle States* list, the **Development** state should still be selected. If not, select it.

   b. Select the *Transitions* tab to display a list of possible transitions from and to this state.

c. Select the entry that specifies from **Manufacturing** to **Development**, as shown in Figure 4–68.

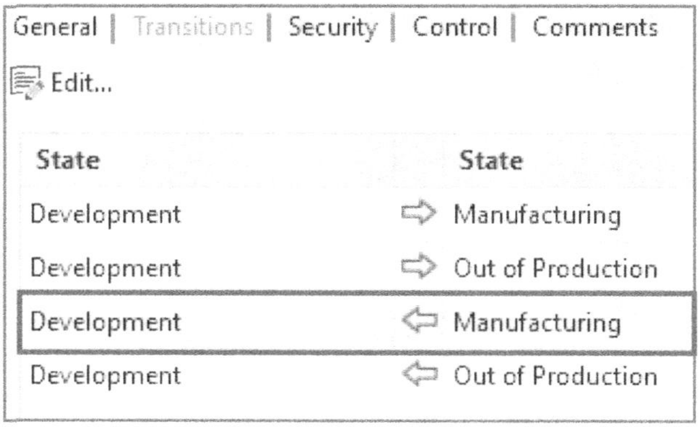


**Figure 4–68**

d. Click **Edit** to display the *Transitions* dialog box.
e. Select the *Security* tab and clear the checkbox for the **No restrictions on this transition** option at the bottom of the dialog box.
f. Click **Add** to display the *Add Members* dialog box.
g. In the *Select Members From* drop-down list, select **Groups**.
h. In the *Available Members* list, press <Ctrl> and select **Administrator**, **Engineering**, **Manufacturing**, and **Sales**.
i. Click **Add** to add the selected entries to the *Current Members* list, as shown in Figure 4–69.

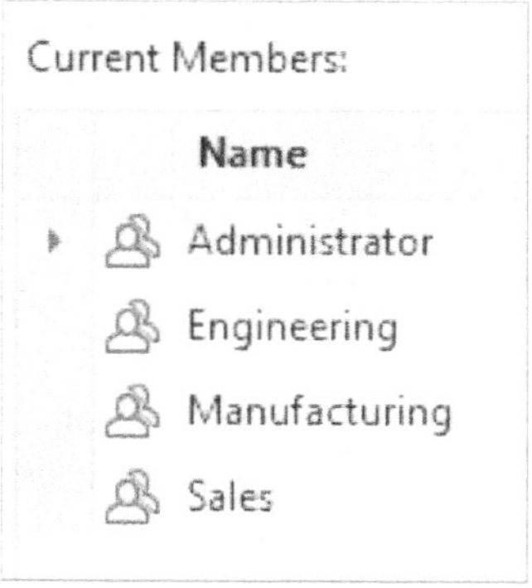


**Figure 4–69**

j. Click **OK** to dismiss the *Add Members* dialog box to return to the *Transition* dialog box.
k. The four groups have been added to the *Security* list with the default permission **Allow**. Select the default permission cell for **Manufacturing** to expand the drop-down list and select **Deny**.

l. Repeat step 2k for the *Sales* group.

m. Click **OK** to dismiss the *Transition* dialog box to return to the *Lifecycle Definition – 'Standard Process'* dialog box.

3. In this step, you will set the Manufacturing lifecycle state transition from **Manufacturing** to **Out of Production** to remove permissions for the *Engineering*, *Manufacturing*, and *Sales* groups to perform this operation.

   a. In the *Lifecycle Definition – 'Standard Process'* dialog box, in the *Lifecycle States* list, select the **Manufacturing** state.

   b. Select the *Transitions* tab to display a list of possible transitions from and to this state.

   c. Select the entry that specifies from **Manufacturing** and to **Out of Production**, as shown in Figure 4–70.

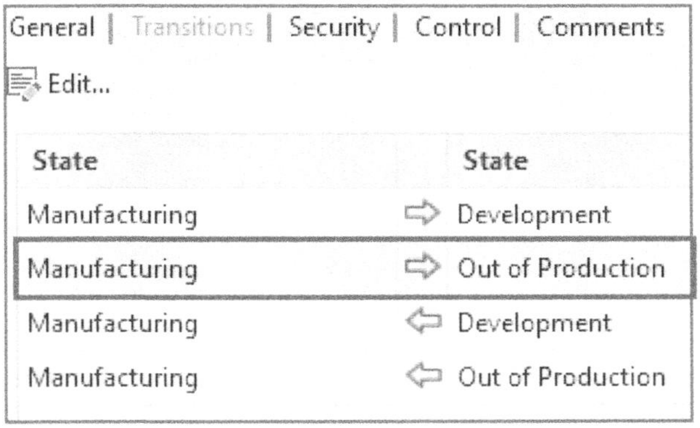


**Figure 4–70**

   d. Click **Edit** to display the *Transitions* dialog box.

   e. Select the *Security* tab and clear the checkbox for the **No restrictions on this transition** option at the bottom of the dialog box.

   f. Click **Add** to display the *Add Members* dialog box.

   g. In the *Select Members From* drop-down list, select **Groups**.

   h. In the *Available Members* list, press <Ctrl> and select **Administrator, Engineering, Manufacturing**, and **Sales**.

   i. Click **Add** to add **Everyone** to the *Current Members* list.

   j. Click **OK** to dismiss the *Add Members* dialog box to return to the *Transition* dialog box.

   k. The four groups have been added to the *Security* list with the default permission **Allow**. Select the default permission cell for **Manufacturing** to expand the drop-down list and select **Deny**.

   l. Repeat step 3k for the *Engineering* and *Sales* group.

   m. Click **OK** to dismiss the *Transition* dialog box to return to the *Lifecycle Definition – 'Standard Process'* dialog box.

4. In this step, you will set the **Out of Production** lifecycle state transition from **Out of Production** to **Manufacturing** to remove permissions for all users to perform this operation.
   a. In the *Lifecycle Definition – 'Standard Process'* dialog box, in the *Lifecycle States* list, select the **Out of Production** state.
   b. Select the *Transitions* tab to display a list of possible transitions from and to this state.
   c. Select the entry that specifies from **Out of Production** and to **Manufacturing**, as shown in Figure 4–71.

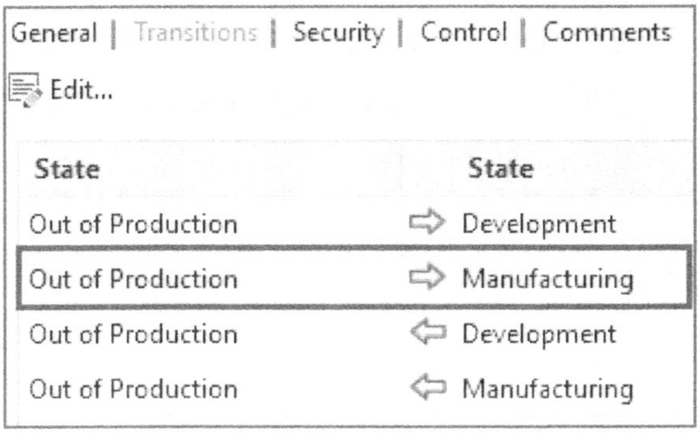


**Figure 4–71**

   d. Click *Edit* to display the *Transitions* dialog box.
   e. Select the *Security* tab and clear the **No restrictions on this transition** checkbox at the bottom of the dialog box.
   f. Click **Add** to display the *Add Members* dialog box.
   g. In the *Select Members From* drop-down list, select **Groups**.
   h. In the *Available Members* list, select **Everyone**.
   i. Click **Add** to add the **Everyone** group to the *Current Members* list, as shown in Figure 4–72.

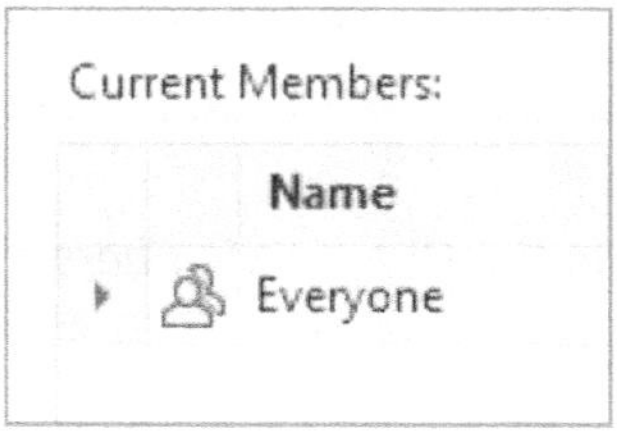


**Figure 4–72**

   j. Click **OK** to dismiss the *Add Members* dialog box to return to the *Transition* dialog box.
   k. The group **Everyone** has been added to the *Security* list with the default permission **Allow**. Select the default permission cell to expand the drop-down list and select **Deny**.

l. Click **OK** to dismiss the *Transition* dialog box to return to the *Lifecycle Definition – 'Standard Process'* dialog box.

## Task 4: Configure state transitions: Criteria.

In our example, there is only one state transition that has criteria. This is from **Development to Manufacturing**.

1. Select the **Manufacturing** lifecycle state in the *Lifecycle States* list. In the *Transitions* tab, select the **Development to Manufacturing** transition, as shown in Figure 4–73.

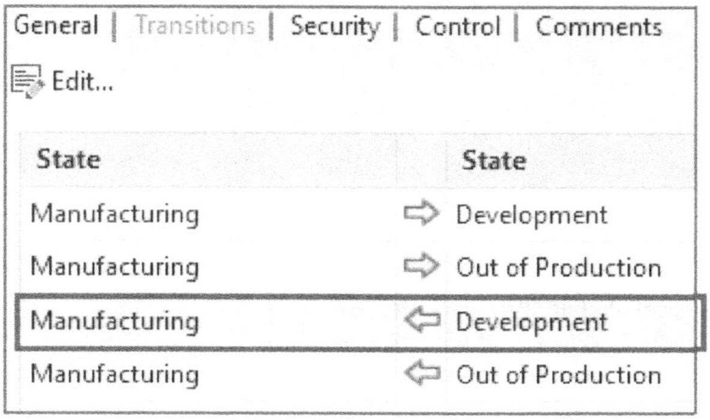


**Figure 4–73**

2. Select **Edit** to display the *Transition* dialog box. The *Criteria* tab should be displayed.
3. In the *Property* drop-down list, select **Property Compliance**.
4. In the *Value* drop-down list, select **Compliant**, as shown in Figure 4–74.

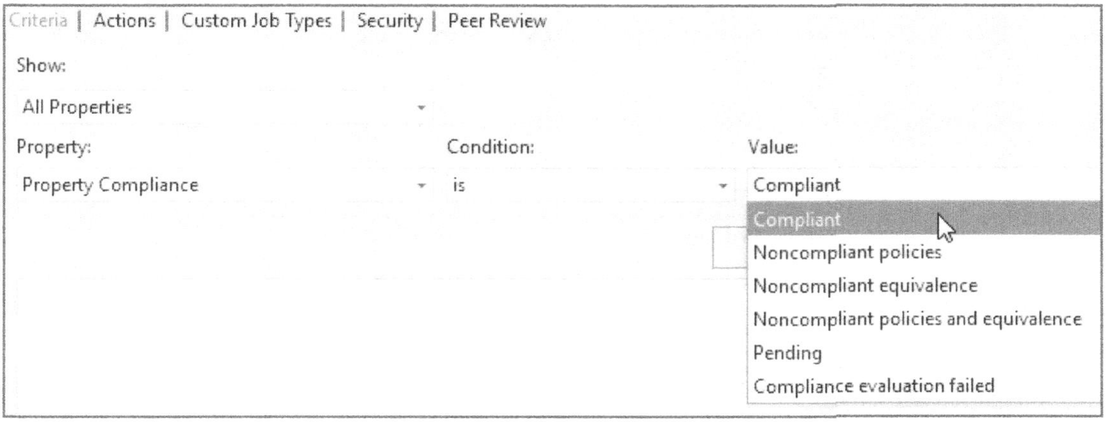


**Figure 4–74**

5. Select **Add** to add it to the list.

## Task 5: Configure state transitions: Actions.

In this case, there are two state transitions that have actions. One action is from **Development to Manufacturing** state transition and the other is from **Manufacturing to Development** state transition. The **Development to Manufacturing** state transition should already be selected.

1. In the *Transition* dialog box, select the *Actions* tab.
2. Select the **Check that dependent child files are "Released"** checkbox, as shown in Figure 4–75.

**Figure 4–75**

3. Click **OK** to dismiss this dialog box and return to the *Lifecycle Definition* dialog box.
4. In the *Transitions* tab, select the **Manufacturing to Development** transition, as shown in Figure 4–76.

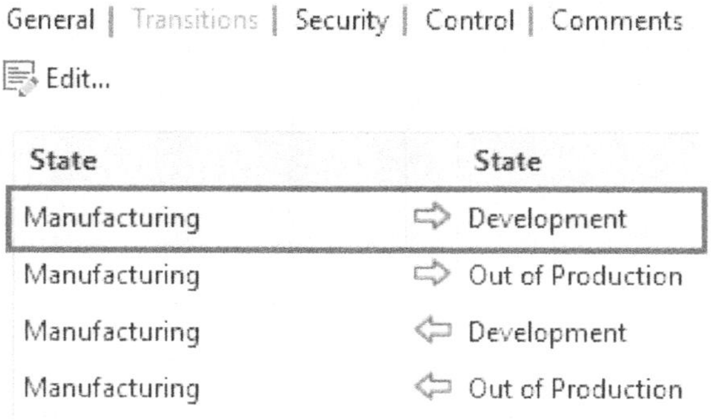


**Figure 4–76**

5. Select **Edit** to display the *Transition* dialog box.
6. Select the *Actions* tab.

7. Select the **Bump primary revision** checkbox, as shown in Figure 4–77.

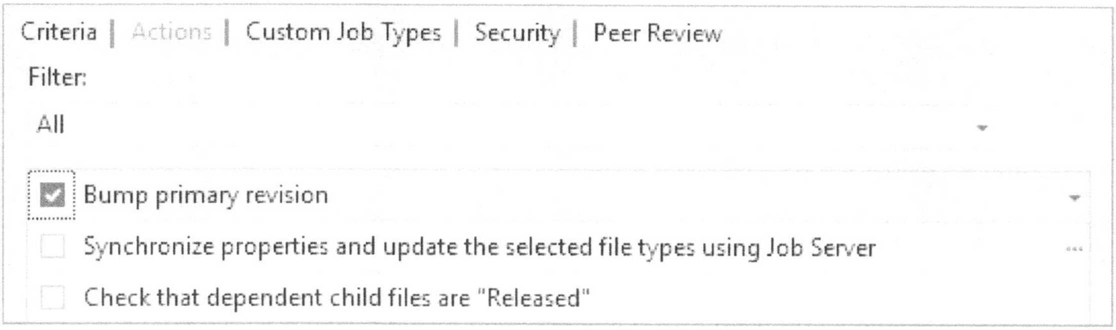


**Figure 4–77**

8. Click **OK** to dismiss this dialog box and return to the *Lifecycle Definition* dialog box for the selected lifecycle definition.

## Task 6: Configure lifecycle state: Control.

The final step is to specify that the *Manufacturing* state is the **Released** state. This is important to check that dependent child files with "Released" criteria know what state to enforce. The **Manufacturing** lifecycle state should still be selected in the *Lifecycle States* list.

1. Select the *Control* tab.
2. Select the checkbox for the **This is a "Released" state** option, as shown in Figure 4–78.

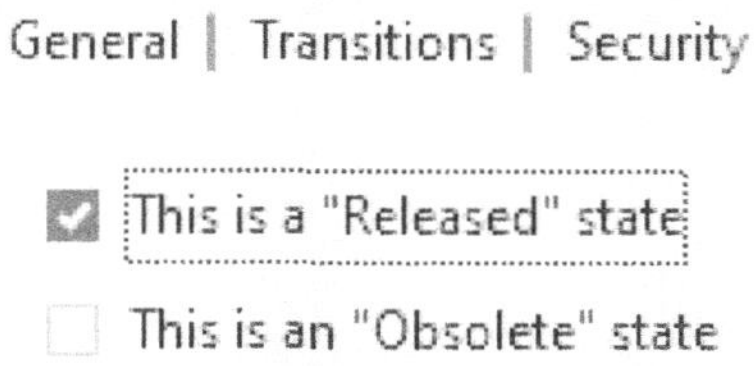


**Figure 4–78**

3. Select **Apply** to apply the change.
4. Click **OK** to dismiss this dialog box and return to the *Vault Settings* dialog box. Close all open dialog boxes.

**End of practice**

# 4.3 Changing Lifecycle States

The *Change State* dialog box changes the state of files, folders, items, and custom objects. Before the state is changed, the criteria, if any, are first checked. The user must have the ability to change the state and any conditions are evaluated. When the state change is performed, any actions specified are then performed. The user has the option of specifying a comment to inform others why the state was changed.

## Change State

There are several ways that a file can change state:

- **Adding a new file to the vault:** New files can be added to the vault using different methods: Manually adding a file, adding a file through the application add-in, migrating from Autodesk Vault to Autodesk Vault Professional and using the Autoloader to add Autodesk Inventor files. In a later section, you will learn how assignment rules and categories can be set up to automatically assign a lifecycle definition and default state to a file.
- **Change category:** Vault Professional enables you to create and assign files to different categories. The action of doing so can also assign a default lifecycle definition and initial state to the file. This will also be covered in a later section.
- **The Change State command:** This is the manual method of changing a state and is based on some significant lifecycle event like revising a set of files that represent products in production or archiving a set of deign files that is no longer in production.

### Change State Command

The **Change State** command is available in three locations:

- Right-click on a file in the main pane
- In the *Actions* menu
- In the *Behaviors* toolbar

This command enables the authorized user to:

- **Specify the lifecycle definition to use:** It is possible to change lifecycle definitions during a state change. This is helpful if the file needs to be managed differently. For example, your organization can manage files in the prototyping phase of product development differently from those that are in production and undergoing revision. Another example could be when one company acquires another and changes the way the company's files are lifecycle managed.
- **Specify the lifecycle state:** Once the definition is chosen, a set of valid lifecycle state transitions is presented. It is up to the user to specify which lifecycle state to change to based on the reason for making the lifecycle change.

- **Select the effected files:** Because the files can have many different relationships, it is possible to select which of the related files will also undergo the state change. This includes parent and children files and attached, library and related documentation.
- **Enter a comment:** It is important to inform other users why the change was made. The lifecycle state transition can be configured to present a list of options or the user can enter their own reason.

**Hint: Change State Dialog Box**

The *Change State* dialog box can change the state of files, folders, items, and custom objects. Multiple instances of any of those entity types can be acted on at one time. However, the *Change State* dialog box does not support more than one entity type at a time. For example, the user cannot change state on a file and folder at the same time.

## How To: Change State

To change the state of a set of related files, do the following:

1. Select the file or group of files from the main pane that are to be changed, as shown in Figure 4–79. If the files are not related, use the <Shift> + select or <Ctrl> + select option to select the files from the list.

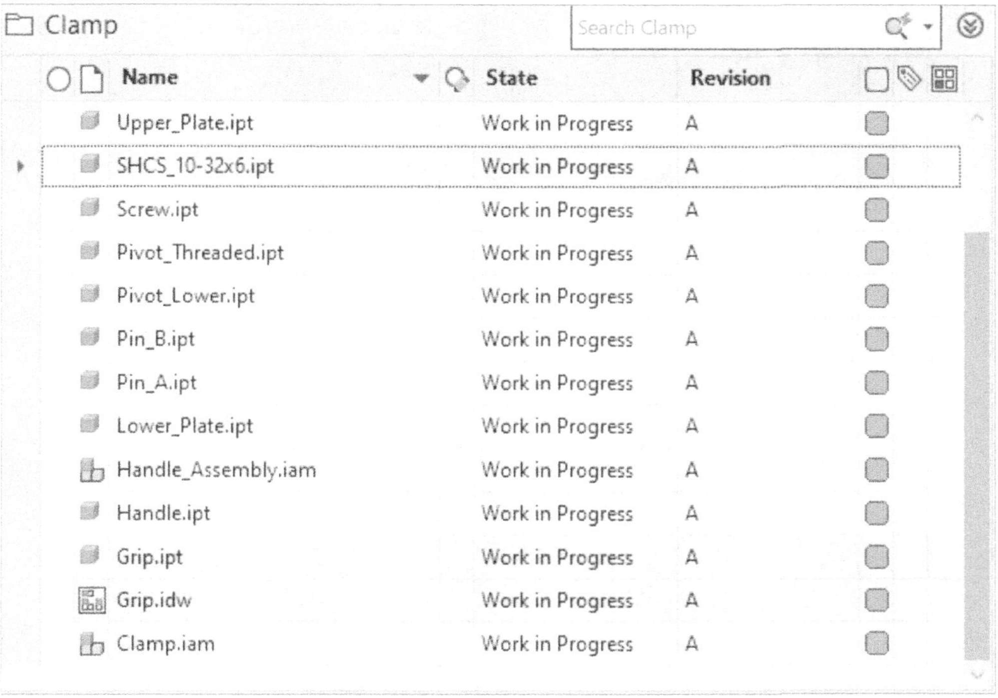


**Figure 4–79**

2. Select **Change State** (as shown in Figure 4–80) in the toolbar to display the *Change State* dialog box.

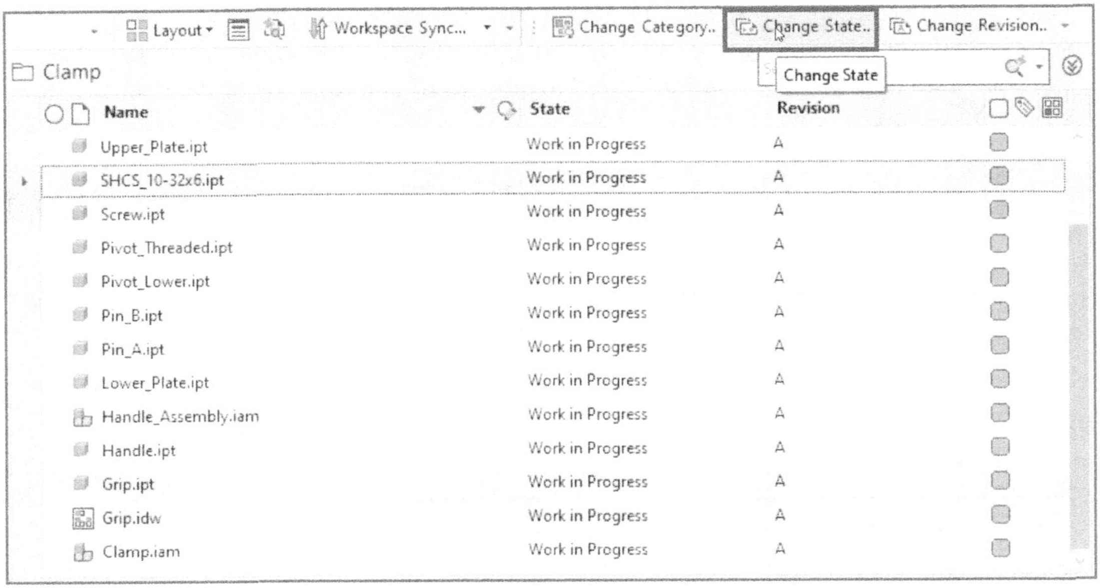


**Figure 4–80**

***Note:*** *You can also change the state by right-clicking on a file and selecting* ***Change State****, as shown in Figure 4–81.*

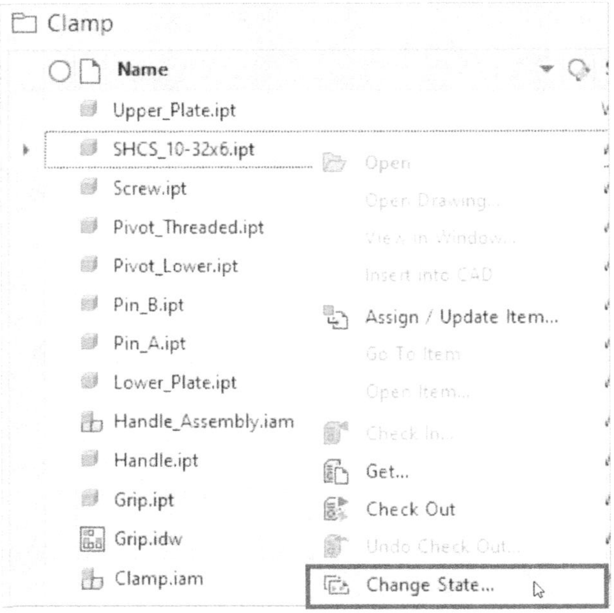


**Figure 4–81**

3. In the *Select a new lifecycle state* section, select the lifecycle definition from the drop-down list, as shown in Figure 4–82.

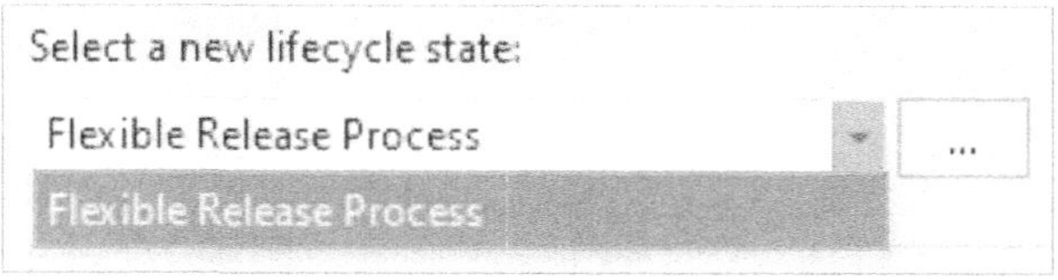


**Figure 4–82**

4. To select a different lifecycle definition, select the button next to the field to display the *Change Lifecycle Definition* dialog box. Select a different lifecycle definition, as shown in Figure 4–83, then click **OK** to dismiss this dialog box.

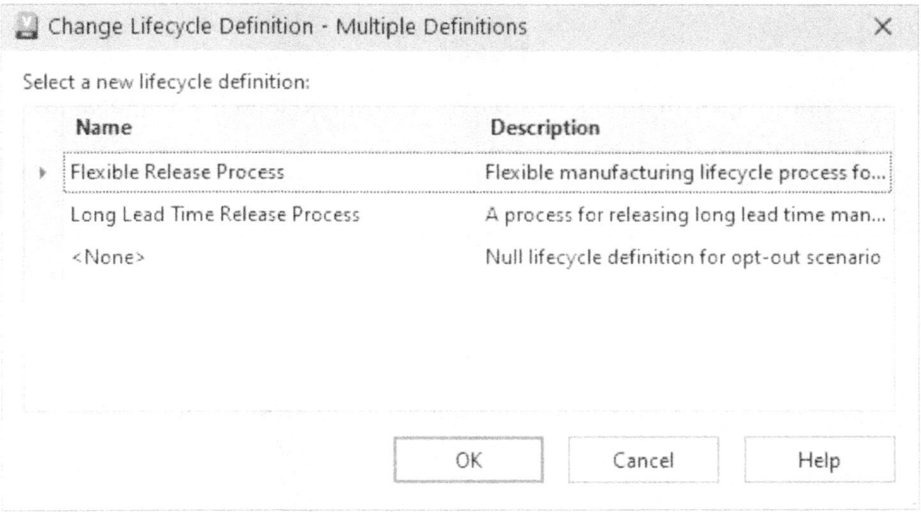


**Figure 4–83**

5. Once the definition is selected, select the state from the drop-down list, as shown in Figure 4–84.

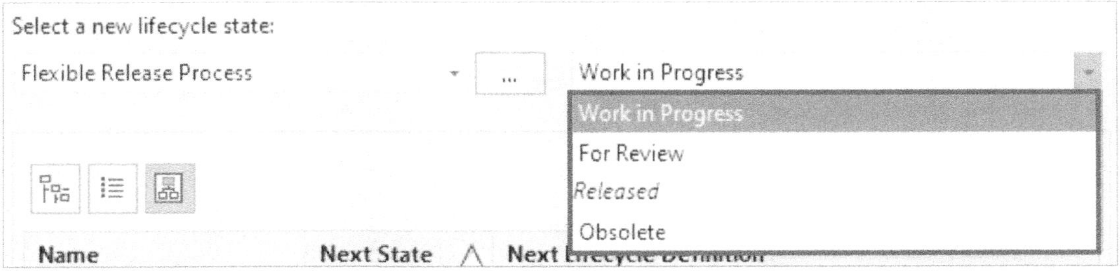


**Figure 4–84**

6. When a new definition or state is chosen, the columns in the file list update to show the new selection, as shown in Figure 4–85.

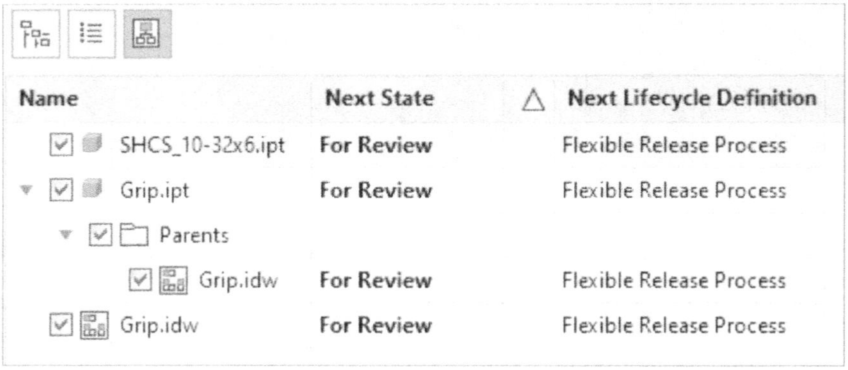


**Figure 4–85**

7. Change the view (as shown in Figure 4–86) to help understand file relationships.

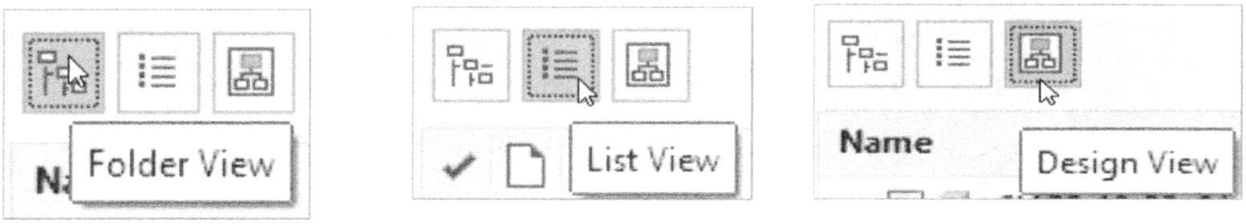


**Figure 4–86**

8. Use the **Parent/Child** selection buttons (as shown in Figure 4–87) to modify the selection.

**Figure 4–87**

9. Select **Settings** to display the *Settings* dialog box shown in Figure 4–88. Here you can refine the selection of related files.

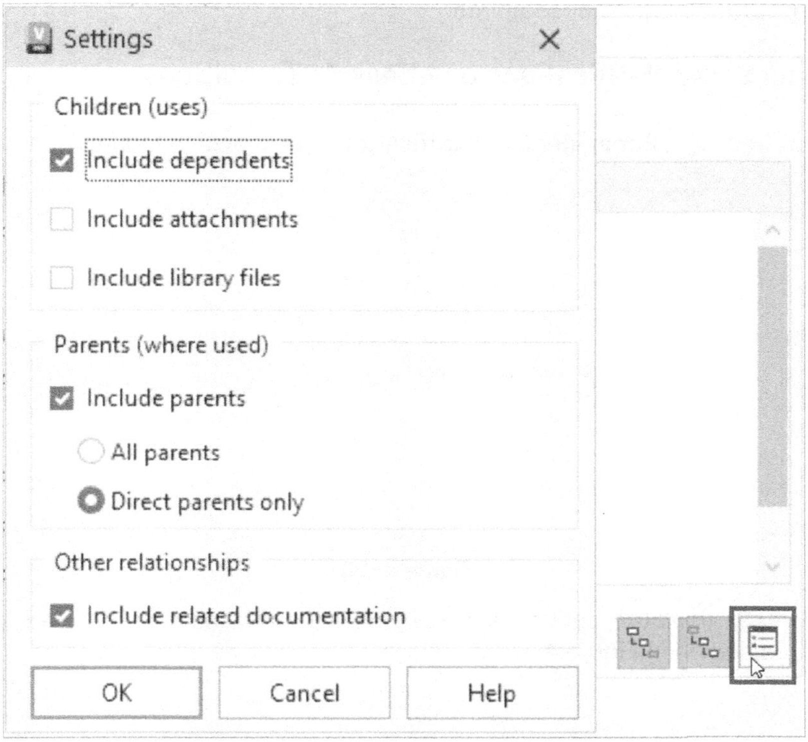


**Figure 4–88**

10. Select the related files that will also change lifecycle state.

11. Enter a comment or select a predefined comment from the drop-down list, as shown in Figure 4–89.

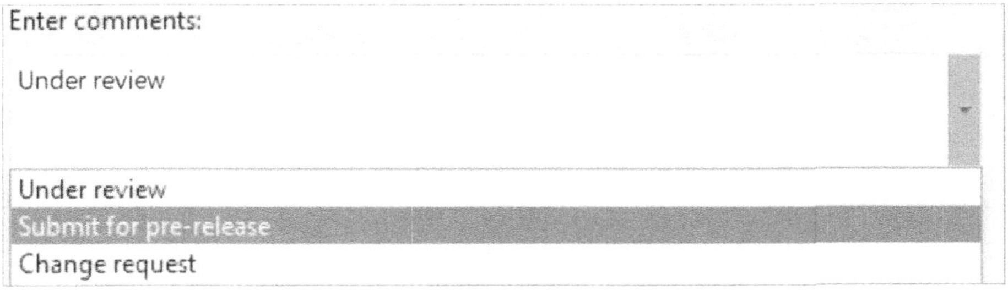


**Figure 4–89**

12. Click **OK** to complete the procedure.

## Email Notifications on Lifecycle Transitions

When lifecycle states move to the next state, selected members can be automatically notified via email using a predefined email template.

## How To: Set up Email Notifications on Lifecycle Transitions

1. Select **Vault Settings>Behaviors tab>Notifications**, as shown in Figure 4–90.

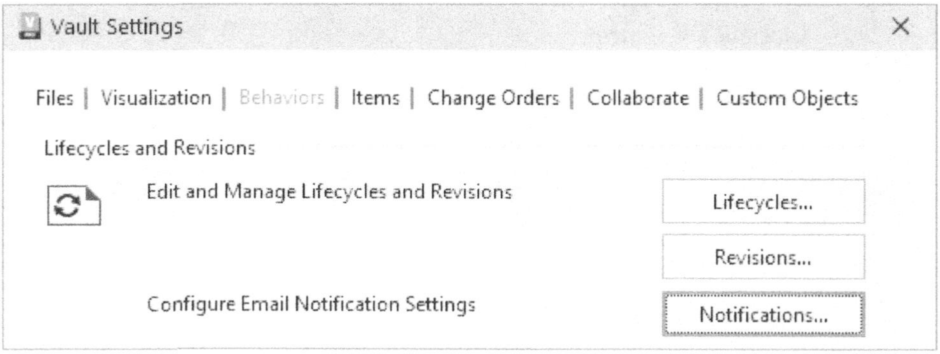


**Figure 4–90**

2. In the *General Settings* tab, set values for *Lifecycle State Transition, Template*, and *Recipients*, as shown in Figure 4–91.

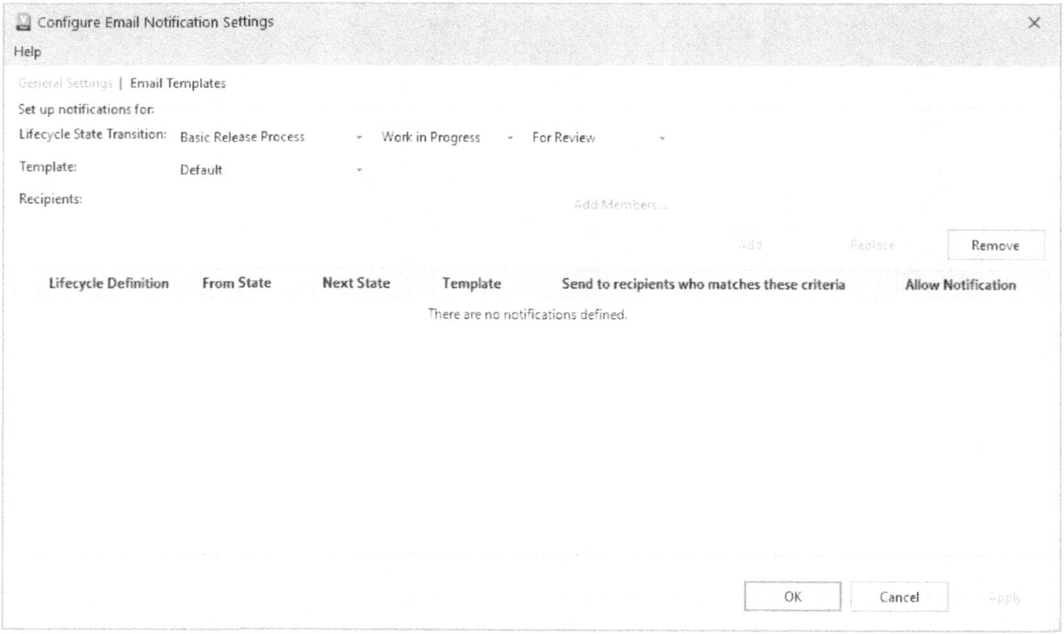


**Figure 4–91**

3. In the *Email Templates* tab, select **Add** to create a new template, as shown in Figure 4–92.

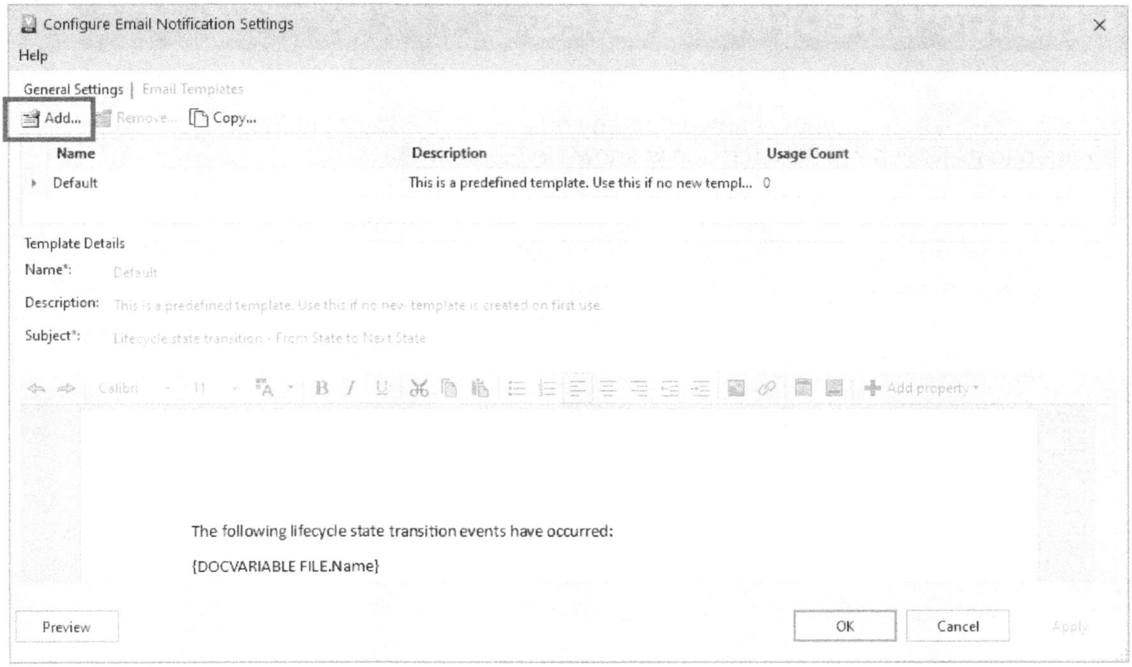


Figure 4–92

# Practice 4c
# Change Lifecycle States

In this practice, you will change the state of the Table files to release them to manufacturing. You will create a new category named **Design** and assign the **Standard Process** lifecycle definition to it. The completed practice is shown in Figure 4–93.

In a later chapter, you will learn how categories can be used to help control your files.

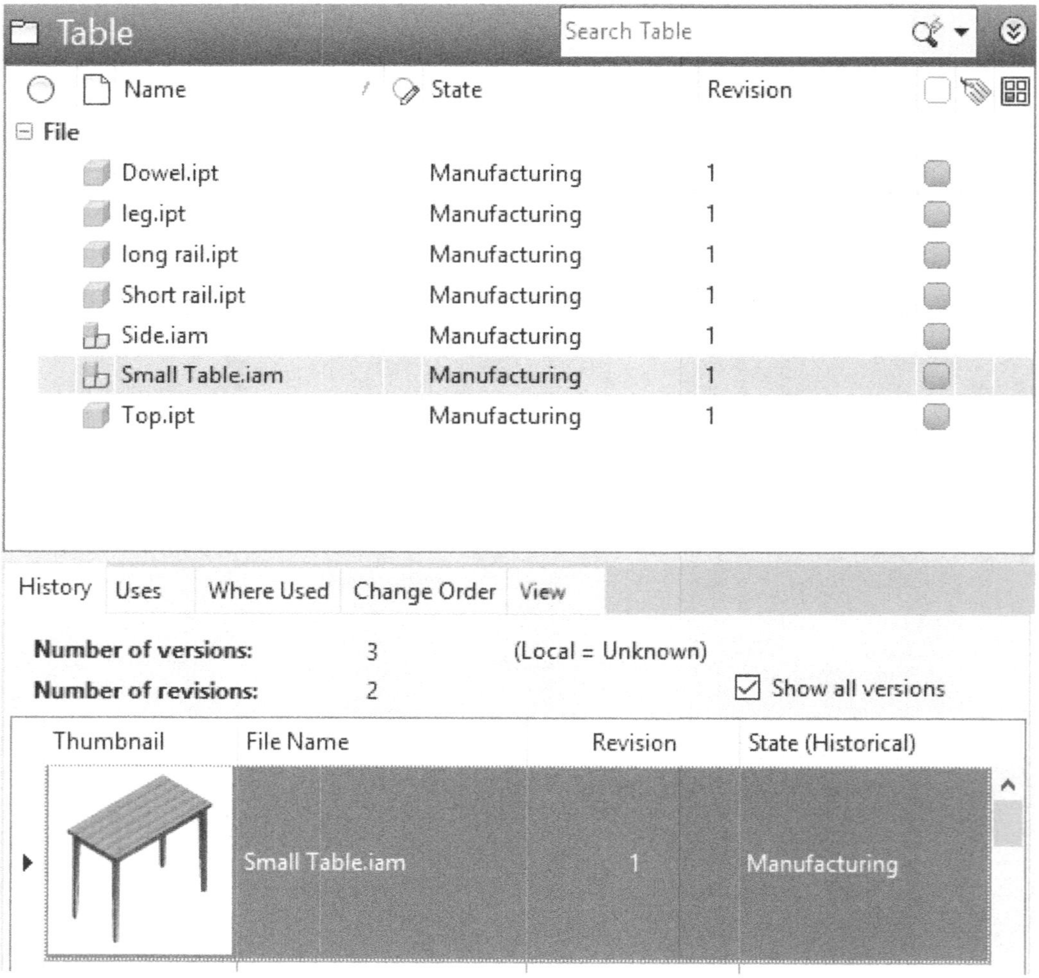


***The completed practice***

**Figure 4–93**

## Task 1: Create a new category.

1. If not already logged in, log in to Vault using the following information:
   - For *User Name*, enter **administrator**.
   - Leave the *Password* field blank.
   - For *Vault*, select **AOTCVault** from the drop-down list.
2. In the *Tools* menu, select **Administration>Vault Settings** to display the *Vault Settings* dialog box.
3. Select the *Behaviors* tab and then select **Categories** in the *Categories* section to display the *Configure Categories* dialog box.
4. Select **File Categories** from the drop-down list, as shown in Figure 4–94.

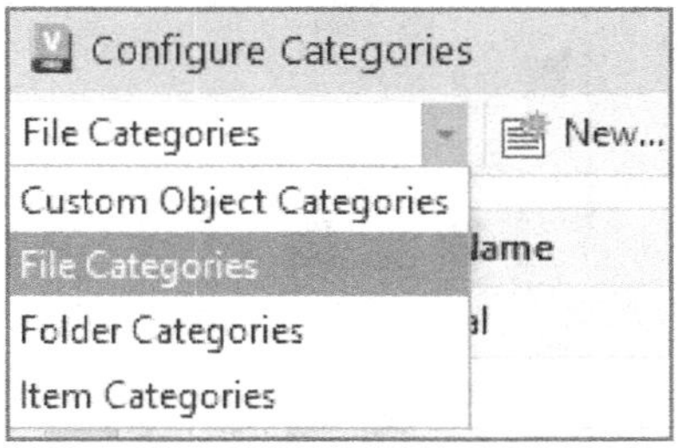


**Figure 4–94**

5. Select **New** in the toolbar to display the *Category Edit* dialog box, as shown in Figure 4–95.

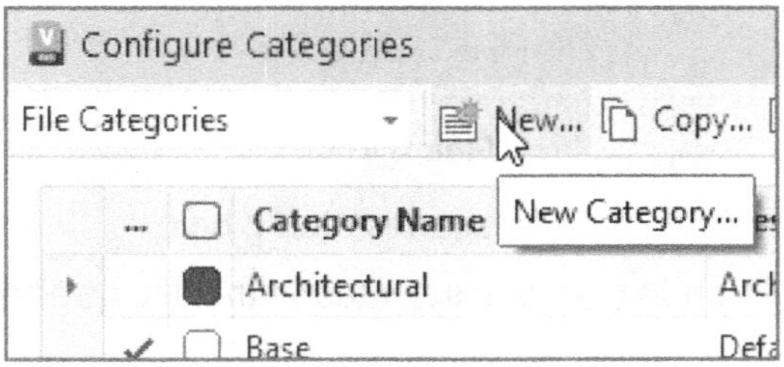


**Figure 4–95**

6. In the *Category Edit* dialog box, enter the following information:
   - For *Name*, enter **Design**.
   - In the *Color* drop-down list, select **Orange**, as shown in Figure 4–96.
   - For *Description*, enter **Design Files**.
   - Ensure that the **Available** checkbox is selected.

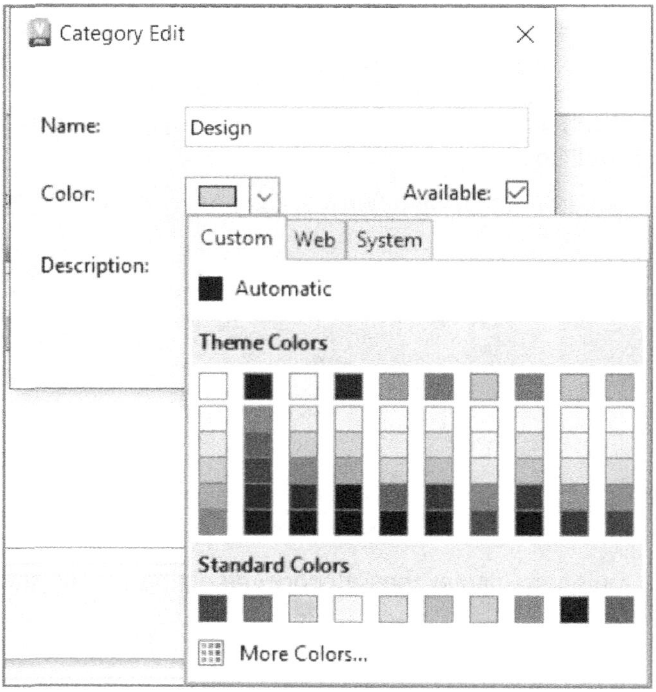


**Figure 4–96**

7. Click **OK** to return to the *Configure Categories* dialog box.
8. Ensure that the new **Design** category is selected in the list, as shown in Figure 4–97.

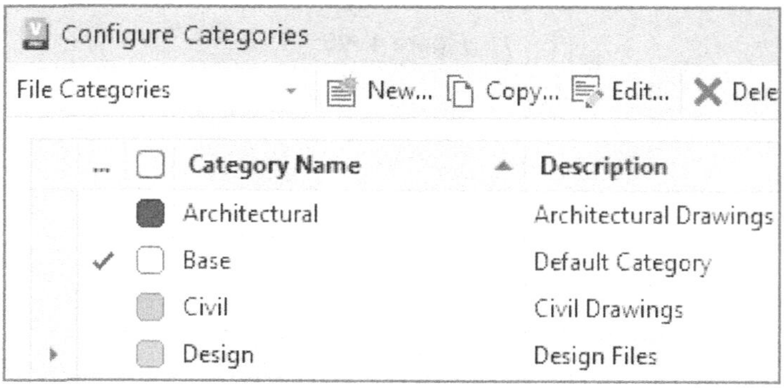


**Figure 4–97**

9. In the *Behaviors* section of the *Configure Categories* dialog box, select the *Lifecycles* tab.
10. In the toolbar, select **Assign**, as shown in Figure 4–98.

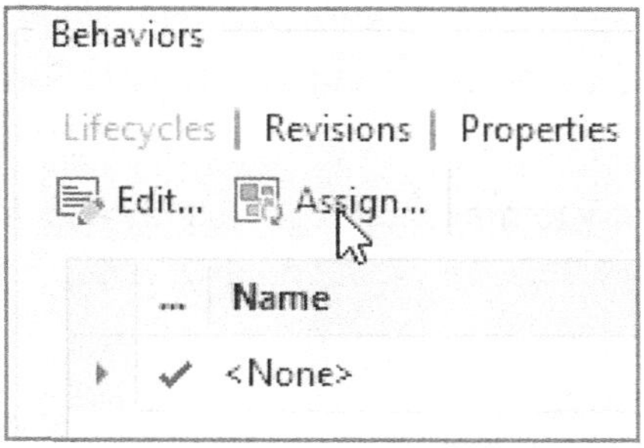


**Figure 4–98**

11. The *Assign Category – Design* dialog box displays.
12. In the *All Lifecycle Definitions* list, select **Standard Process**.
13. Select **Add** to add it to the *Assigned Lifecycle Definitions* list.
14. Double-click on the **Standard Process** entry to make it the default lifecycle definition to use for the Design category, as shown in Figure 4–99.

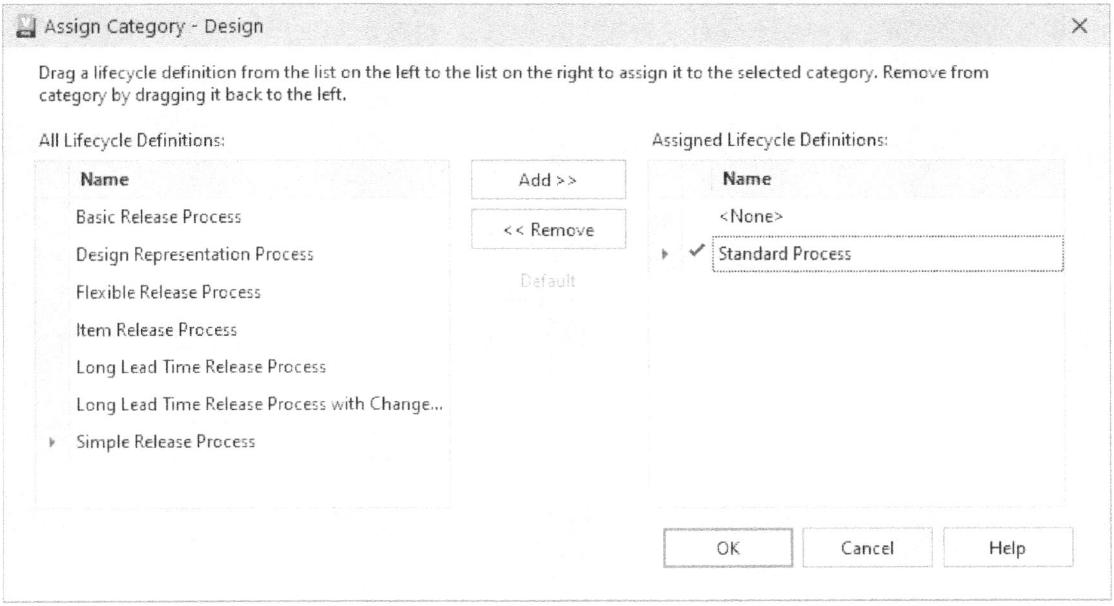


**Figure 4–99**

15. Click **OK** to dismiss this dialog box and return to the *Configure Categories* dialog box.
16. Select the *Revisions* tab in the *Behaviors* section.
17. Select **Assign** to display the *Assign Category – Design* dialog box.
18. In the *All Revision Schemes* list, select **Standard Numeric Format**.
19. Select **Add** to add it to the *Assigned Revision Schemes* list.
20. Double-click on the new entry to make it the default, as shown in Figure 4–100.

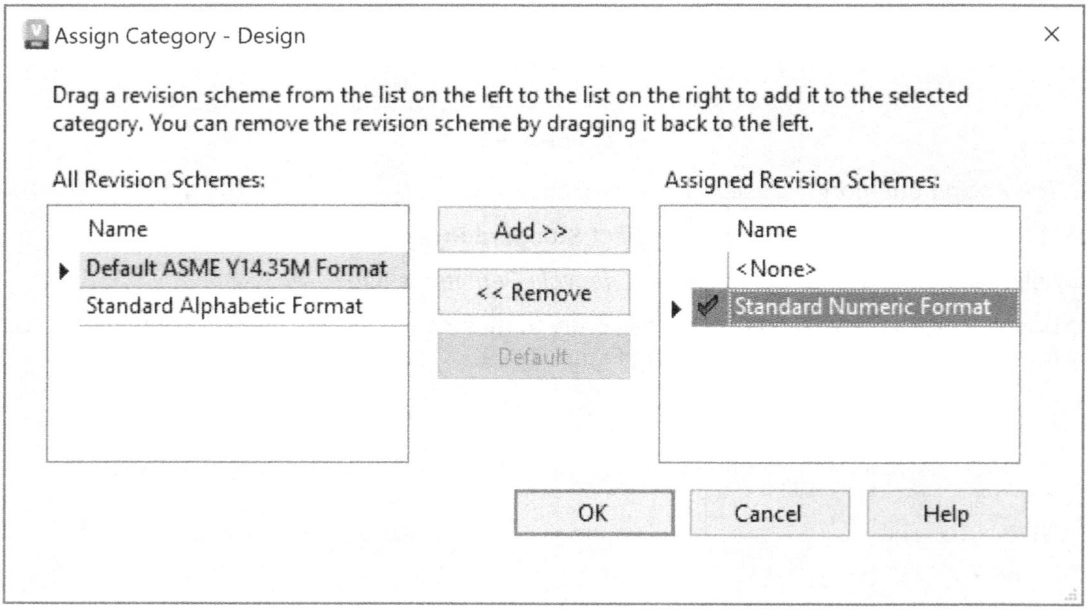


**Figure 4–100**

21. Click **OK** to close the dialog box and return to the *Configure Categories* dialog box.
22. Click **Close** to dismiss this dialog box and return to the *Vault Settings* dialog box. Click **Close** to dismiss this dialog box and return to Vault.
23. Log out of Autodesk Vault.

## Task 2: Use Change Category to change the category on specific files.

1. Log in to Autodesk Vault using the following information:
   - For *User Name*, enter **usera**.
   - For *Password*, enter **vault**.
   - For *Vault*, select **AOTCVault** from the drop-down list.
2. In the *Navigation* pane, expand the *Project Explorer ($)* folder and then expand the *Designs* folder. Double-click on the *Table* folder to display the table assemblies and parts in the main pane, as shown in Figure 4–101.

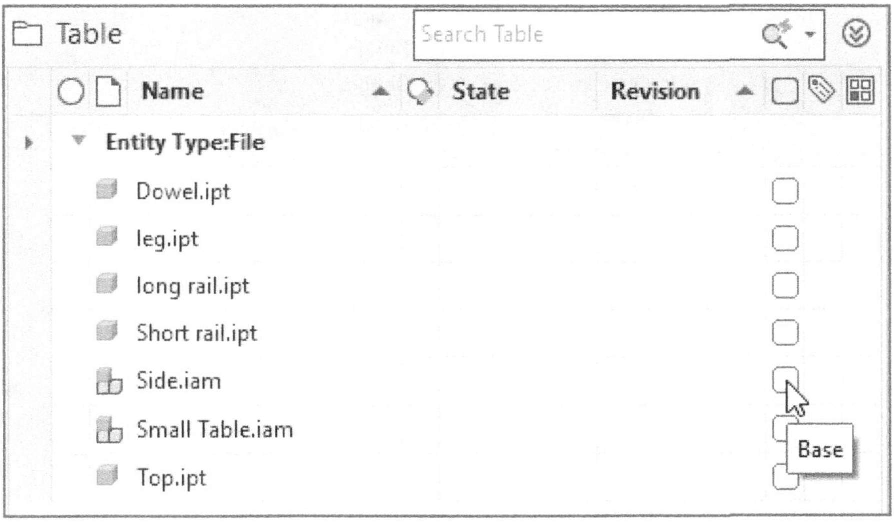


**Figure 4–101**

   - Note that all of the files are assigned to the **Base** category during the migration and have no *Revision* or *State* values.
3. Select **Small Table.iam** and select **Actions>Change Category**.
4. In the dialog box, select **Design** from the Select a new category drop-down list.
5. All of the children for the table should also be selected. If not, select **Include Dependents** in the row of buttons below the file list, as shown in Figure 4–102.

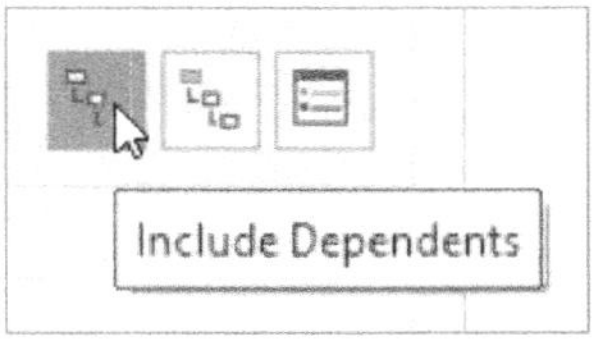


**Figure 4–102**

6. In the *Enter comments* text box, enter the comment **Design files**, as shown in Figure 4–103. Review the dialog box entries. Click **OK** to finish the *Change Category* workflow.

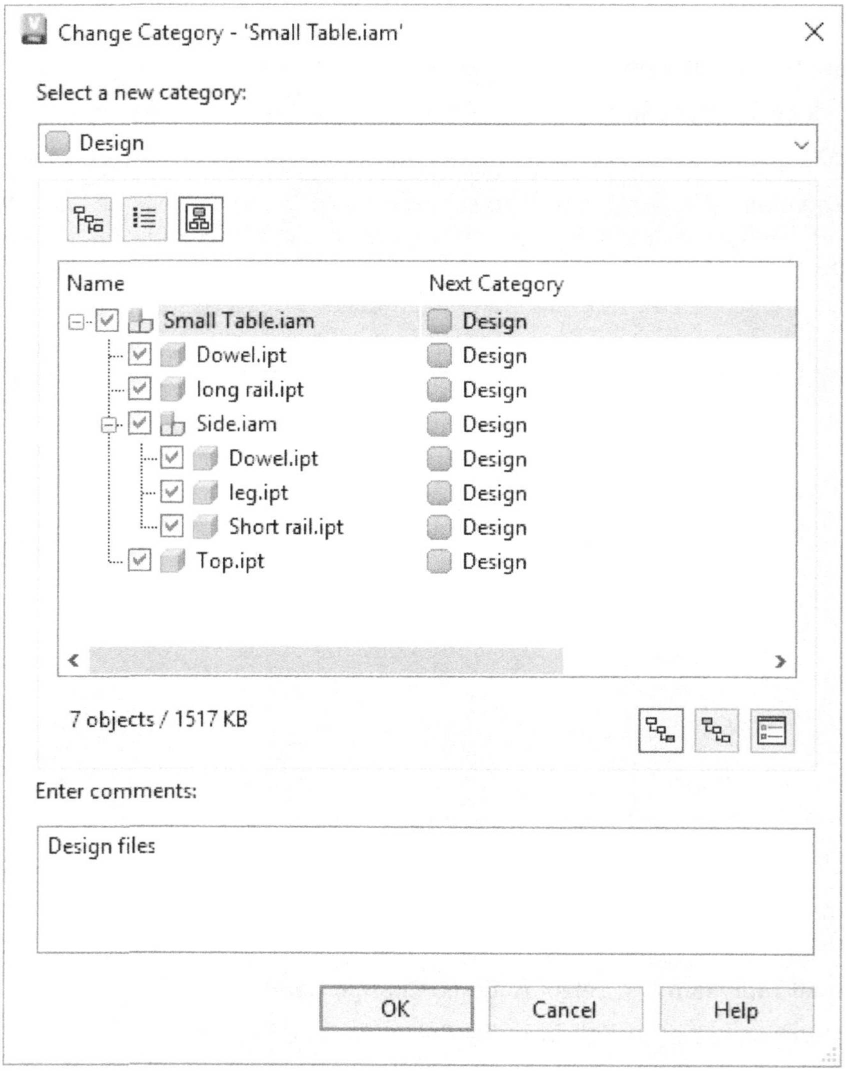


**Figure 4–103**

7. Return to the main pane and review the file list, as shown in Figure 4–104.

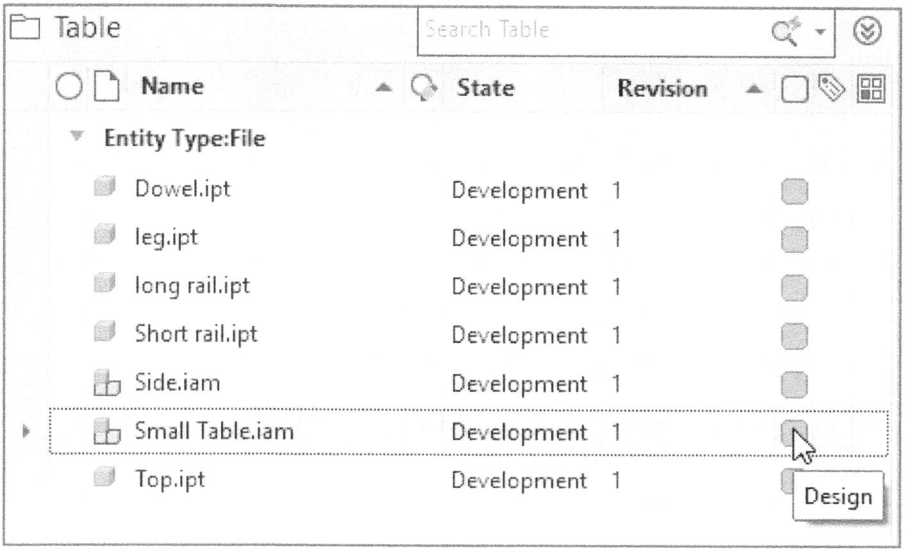


**Figure 4–104**

- The *Category* glyph is now set to **Design**.
- The **Design** category specifies the default lifecycle state for the files to be **Development**, which you can see in the *State* column.
- The rules for changing to the **Development** lifecycle state specify the revision be bumped based on the primary revision with the *Standard Numeric Revision* scheme. The first value in this revision scheme's sequence is **1**, which you can see in the *Revision* column.
- Because a new file version is created when a new revision is made, the files are all at version 2.

8. Log out of Autodesk Vault.
9. Log in to Autodesk Vault using the following information:
   - For *User Name*, enter **userd**.
   - For *Password*, enter **vault**.
   - For *Vault*, select **AOTCVault** from the drop-down list.
10. In the *Navigation* pane, expand the *Project Explorer ($)* folder and then expand the *Designs* folder.

11. Select the *Table* folder, as shown in Figure 4–105. Note that the files are not displayed. In the **Development** lifecycle definition state, the *Sales* group (which userd is a member of) has no *Read*, *Modify*, or *Delete* permissions.

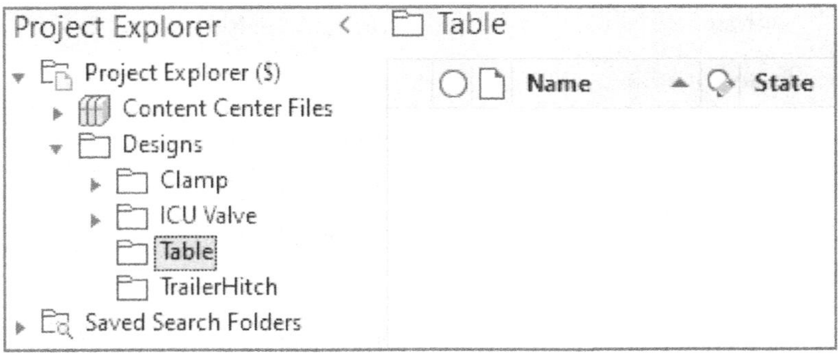


**Figure 4–105**

12. Log out of Vault.
13. Log in to Autodesk Vault using the following information:
    - For *User Name*, enter **userb**.
    - For *Password*, enter **vault**.
    - For *Vault*, select **AOTCVault** from the drop-down list.
14. In the *Navigation* pane, expand the *Project Explorer ($)* folder and then expand the *Designs* folder.
15. Select the *Table* folder. Since userb is part of the *Engineering* group, and this group has *Read* permission in the **Development** state, the files display, as shown in Figure 4–106.

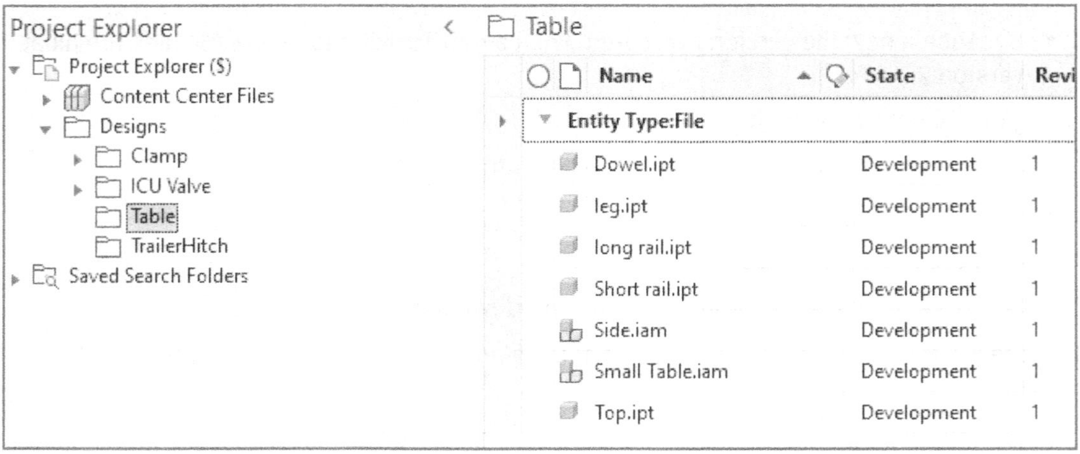


**Figure 4–106**

 

## Task 3: Use Change State to change the lifecycle state on specific files.

1. Select **Small Table.iam**.
2. In the *Behaviors* toolbar, select **Change State**, as shown in Figure 4–107.

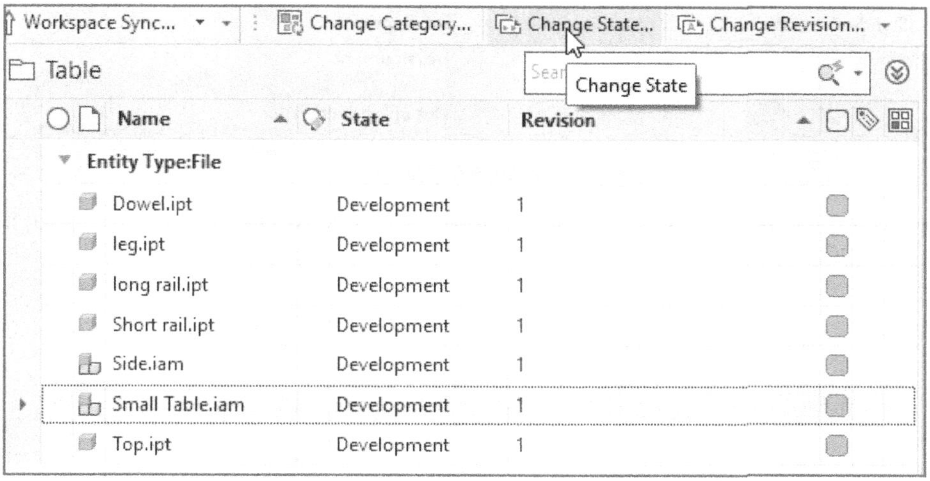


**Figure 4–107**

3. The *Change State – 'Small Table.iam'* dialog box displays. Ensure that only the main assembly **Small Table.iam** is selected, and not any of the children, as shown in Figure 4–108.

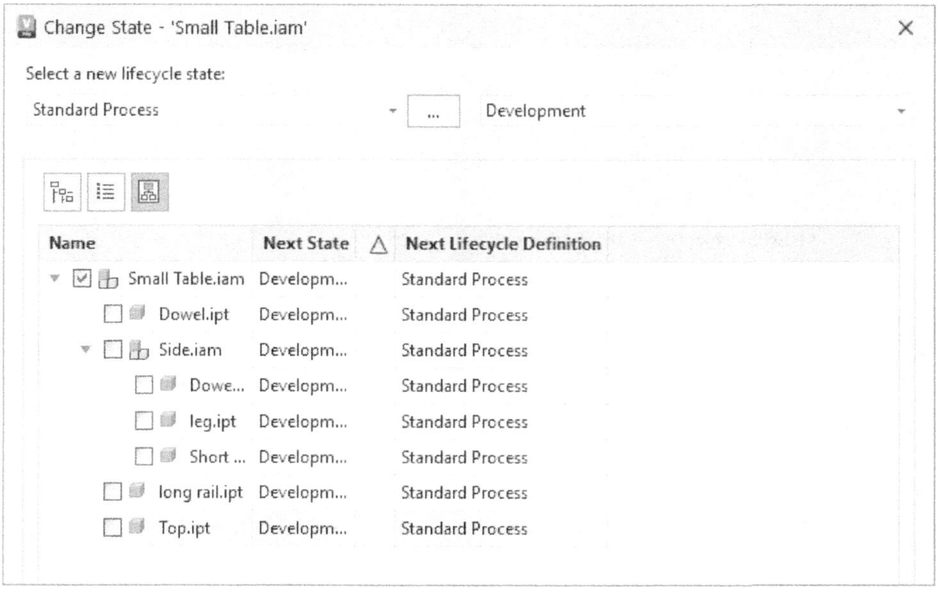


**Figure 4–108**

4. In the *Select a new lifecycle state* field, in the right side drop-down list, select **Manufacturing**, as shown in Figure 4–109.

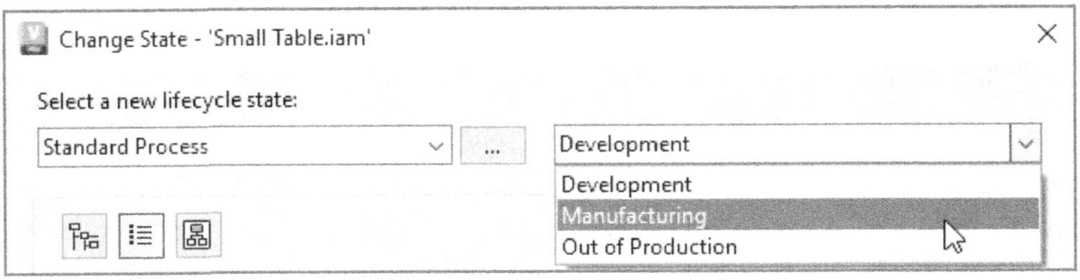


**Figure 4–109**

5. In the *Enter comments* field, enter the comment **Release to production**, as shown in Figure 4–110.

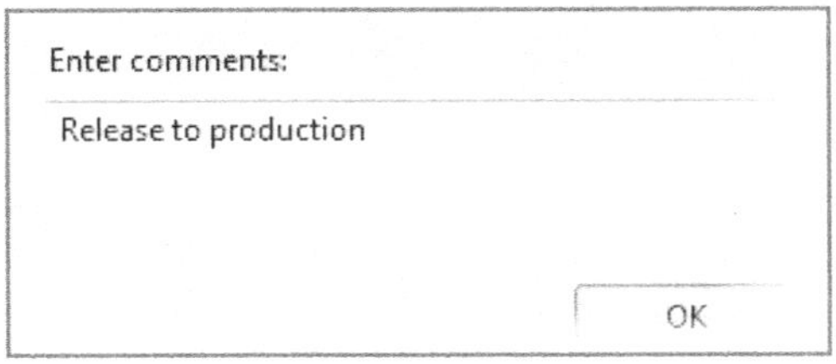


**Figure 4–110**

6. Click **OK** to finish the lifecycle state change.
7. An error message displays. Select **Details** to see the complete error message, as shown in Figure 4–111.

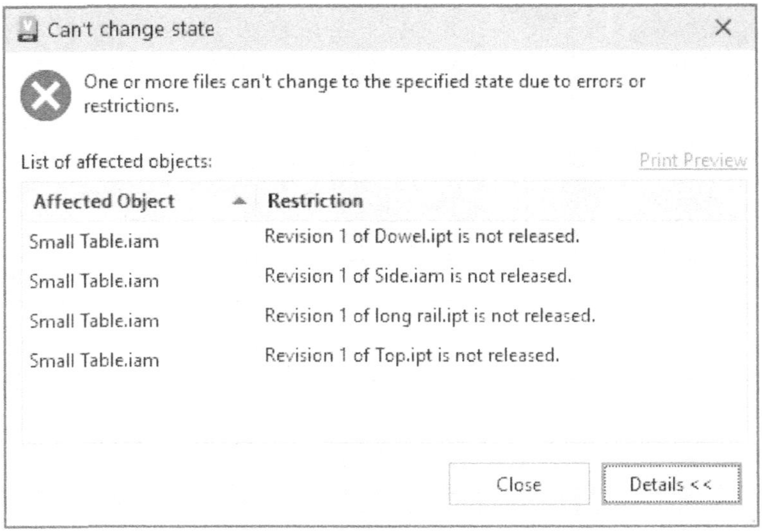


**Figure 4–111**

- In the *Control* setting for the **Manufacturing** state, you specified that the state was a released state. In the transition from **Development to Manufacturing** lifecycle state change, you set the criteria that 'Check that dependent child files are released'. So you must first release the children. To do this, select all the children in the *Change State - 'Small Table.iam'* dialog box.

8. Repeat Step 1 to 6. In the *Change State* dialog box, include dependents to set the new state to **Manufacturing** for all children as well, as shown in Figure 4–112.

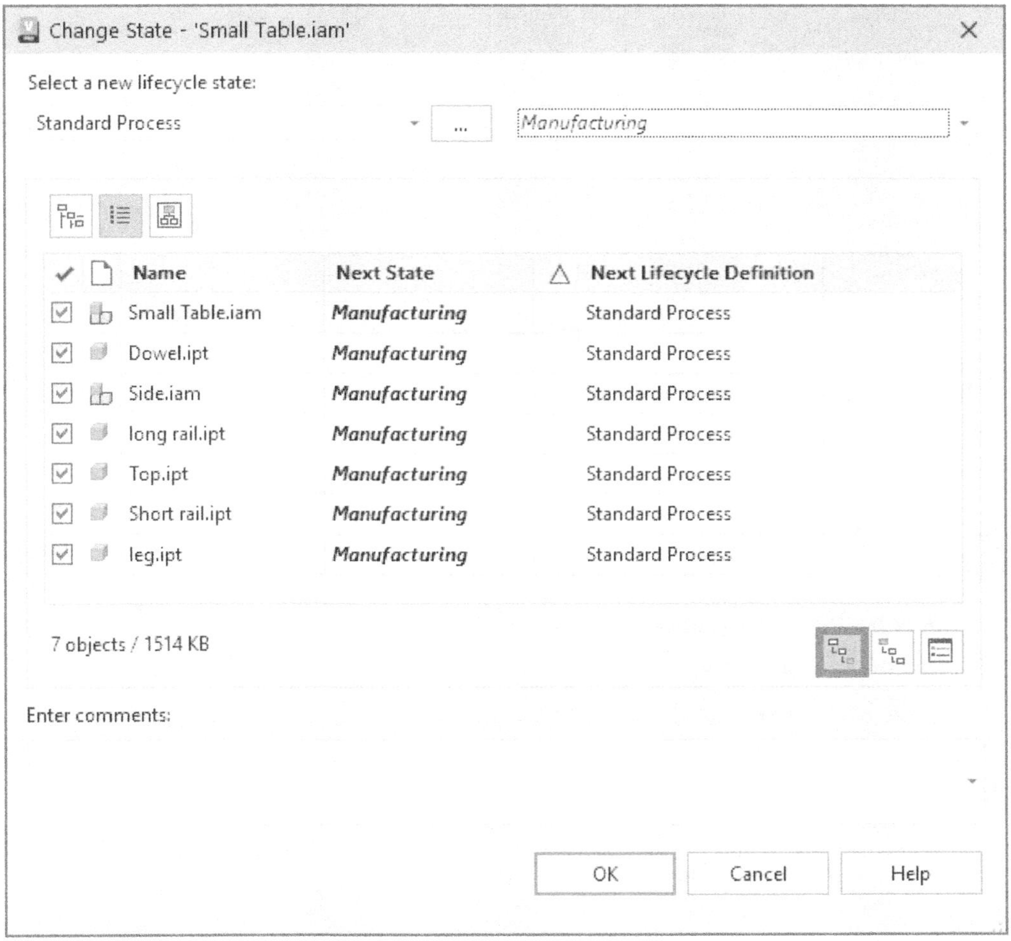


**Figure 4–112**

9. Review the results, as shown in Figure 4–113.

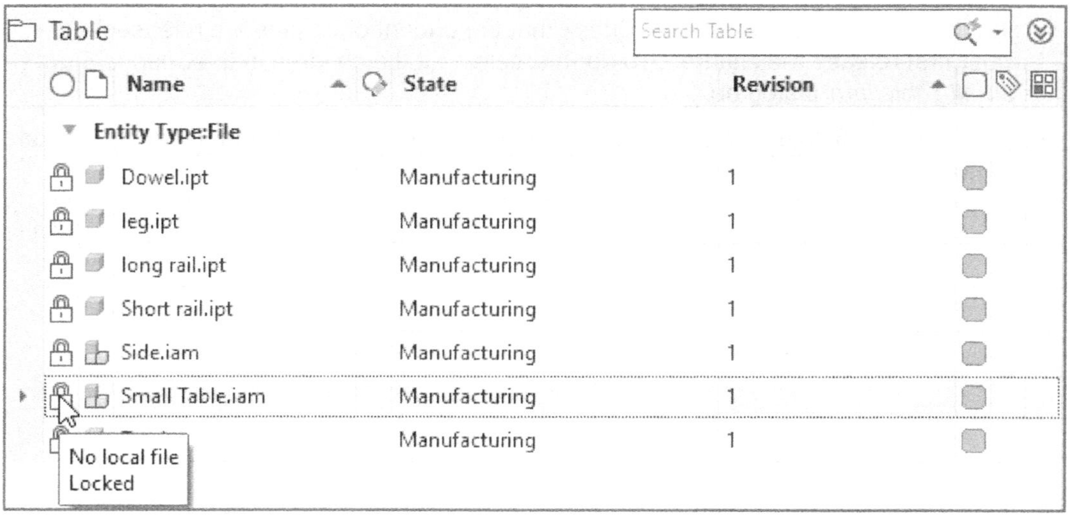


**Figure 4–113**

- The files are locked and cannot be edited.
- The lifecycle state is now set to **Manufacturing**.
- The state change did not create a new revision or version for any of the files.

10. Log out of Autodesk Vault.
11. Log in to Autodesk Vault using the following information:
    - For *User Name*, enter **usera**.
    - For *Password*, enter **vault**.
    - For *Vault*, select **AOTCVault** in the drop-down list.
12. In the *Navigation* pane, expand the *Project Explorer ($)* folder and then expand the *Designs* folder. Select the *Table* folder.

**13.** Review the files, as shown in Figure 4–114.

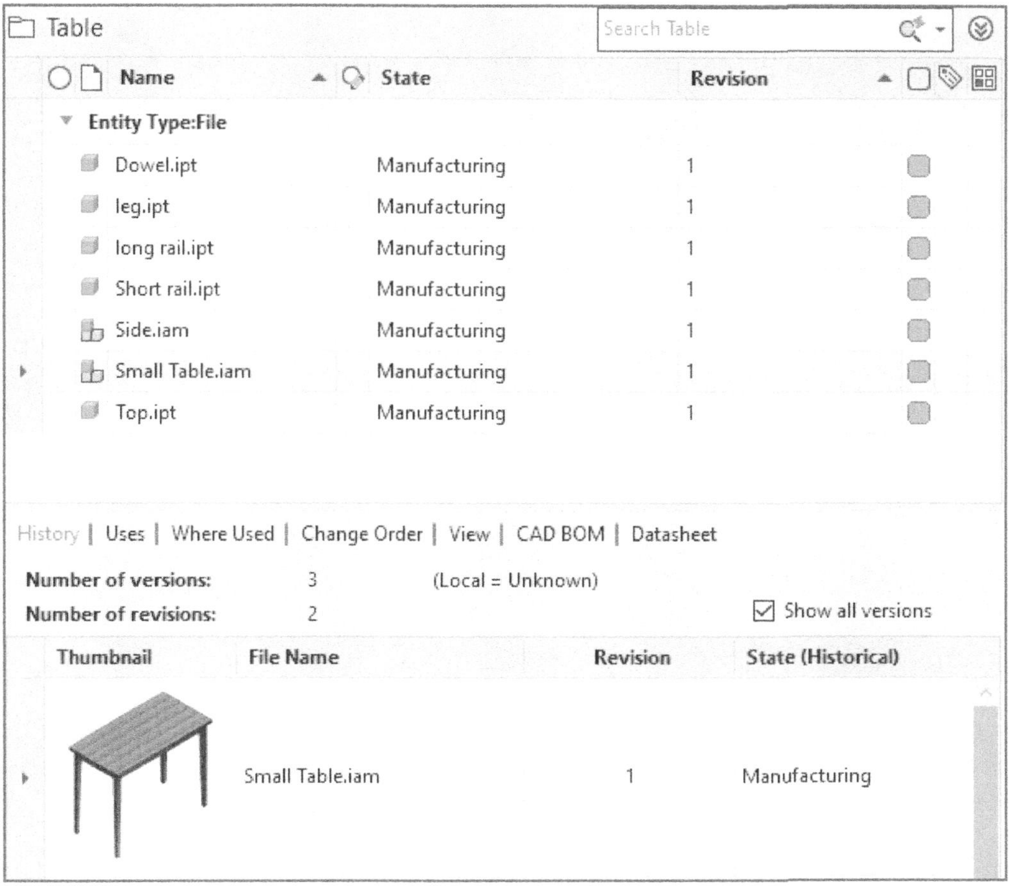


**Figure 4–114**

- The files do not show as being locked. This is because usera is part of the *Administrators* group, which has *Modify* permission in the **Manufacturing (Released)** state. This enables the Administrators to make minor changes to the files without taking them out of production.

**End of practice**

Chapter 5

# Revision Management

Products have defined lifecycles from inception through production. Product development and enhancement introduces changes to the product files. These changes must be tracked and managed to provide a complete history of the changes and modifications as the product develops. Revision management provides consistency throughout the product lifecycle by applying a common definition and behavior to files in a vault.

## Learning Objectives

- Describe the difference between a revision and a version and why both are important.
- Explain what revision schemes and revision scheme formats are.
- Know the details of the default revision schemes and revision scheme formats supplied with the Autodesk® Vault Professional software.
- Modify an existing revision scheme.
- Create new revision scheme.
- Describe the different ways a file or item can be revised.
- Explain the concepts of revision controlled documents and describe what released biased means.
- Use the **Change State** command to automatically revise a group of files or items.
- Use the **Change Revision** command to manually revise a file or item.

# 5.1 Revisions and Versions

Revision management is functionality available in Vault Professional that enables a user to label a significant change or set of changes to a document and its related files. The label itself is the revision and the collection of files affected in that revision are considered a revision level. A revision level can be retrieved later so that a document and the version of the related files associated with that particular revision are preserved.

## Concept

When editing documents in a vault, the changes are saved as versions history on the server using the default file settings. The history has little information that can be used to identify significant events.

The engineering industry has standards used for labeling significant changes to data. This is typically called the document revision. The revision is usually marked with one or more characters, and the document is given a new character string for any significant changes that are done after the document has been released.

The Revision Management feature provides the ability to mark any point in time as a significant change to a document and its related files. A revision level of a document can be retrieved along with the correct revision level of any related documents. When used in combination with lifecycles, a revision level is created automatically during predefined events. The revision will also be marked as '**Released**' when the document is placed into certain lifecycle states identified as released states. During open and download procedures, the user can choose to retrieve released or non-released revisions of the document and its related files.

### Definition: Version

A version is an iteration of a document and its meta-data that has been committed to the system.

Autodesk Vault is designed to help you manage different versions of a file. You can get a previous version or revert to a previous version.

## Definition: Revision

A revision is a collection of file versions rolled up into one object that displays to the user. After a revision is created, document edits are contained in that revision until a new revision is created. This means that as changes are made and committed to the system, the user sees no change to the revision label.

For example, a document is created and assigned the revision level "A". As the user makes changes and those versions are committed, the revision label remains "A". Only when the user performs a revision bumping action will a new revision be created. One way to do this is by using the **Change Revision** command to iterate the revision. This will cause a new revision of the document to be created with the label "B". Any subsequent edits would then be collected in revision "B". The illustration shows the results for a CAD file that is revised four times, a new revision B is created and then revised four more times. The underlined version is the latest version for a given revision.

> ***Note:*** *When you create a new revision of a file, a version of the file is also created. The last file version 4 for revision A in Figure 5–1 is the same as the first file version 5 for revision B.*

**Figure 5–1**

Once the revision objects have been created, any revision can be downloaded or opened. When a revision is downloaded, only one version in that revision is used to represent the revision. If lifecycles are not used, then that version is always the latest version in that revision.

In general, it is up to the user to create a new revision of a file (or set of files) when some milestone is met. As part of a lifecycle transition, actions can be setup to automatically increment the revision based on a set of lifecycle state rules.

For the case of a lifecycle state change, the most common example is when a file that represents a part or component that is being manufactured needs to be changed to address form, fit, or function, problems. In this example, revision A represents the manufactured part before the change is made and revision B represents the revised revision. However, revisions can be used to signify any notable event where it is important to keep a history of the files and its metadata at that point in time.

You can manually create a new revision using the **Change Revision** command. The command enables you to specify the next revision from a specified revision definition and add a comment as to the nature of the revision.

The revision definition is a formula that will automatically calculate the next revision character in a sequence.

Figure 5–2 shows the effect of changing the lifecycle state of the file. The lifecycle rules, as you saw in the last lesson, can be defined to 'bump' (create) a new revision for certain state changes.

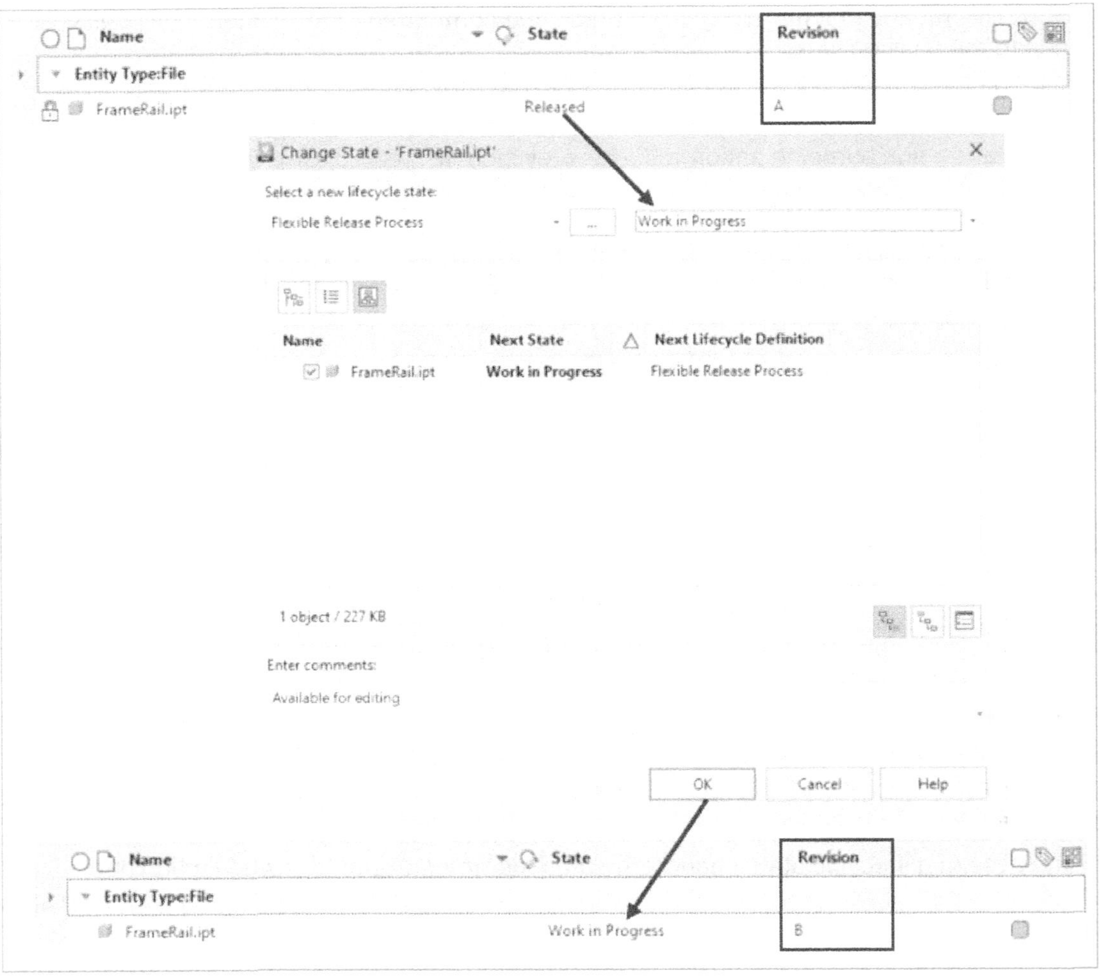


**Figure 5–2**

For both manual and lifecycle-based revision changes, a set of revision schemes with associated revision scheme formats are used to specify the next character or set of characters in the next revision.

 

# Default Revision Schemes and Scheme Formats

## Definition of Terms

The following table defines the terms for revision schemes.

| Term | Description |
|---|---|
| **Revision Scheme** | A formula used to calculate the initial revision characters for a file and the subsequent revision characters as that file is revised. |
| **Revision Scheme Format** | A defined sequence of characters used to create a revision scheme. |
| **Revision Scheme Format Type** | Enables multiple levels of incrementing a revision. The three types are:<br>• Primary Scheme Format<br>• Secondary Scheme Format<br>• Tertiary Scheme Format |
| **Delimiter** | A single character that separates the revision scheme format types. |

There are three default revision scheme formats, ten delimiter characters, and four default revisions scheme definitions included with Autodesk Vault Professional.

## Default Revision Scheme Formats

Autodesk Vault Professional has three predefined revision scheme formats. A format simply specifies the progression of characters as a revision is bumped. They are listed in the following table.

| Name | Description |
|---|---|
| **Alphabetic** | Only alphabetic characters(1) are permitted in the primary format. The first revision is A. |
| **Numeric** | Only numeric characters(2) are permitted in the primary format. The first revision is 1. |
| **Default ASME Y14.35M** | Only alphabetic characters with some characters omitted(3) are permitted in the primary format. The first revision is '-'. |

**Notes:**

1. Alphabetic formats include alphabetic characters starting at A through Z and then AA through ZZ.
2. Numeric formats include the numeric sequence from 1 to 99.
3. Default ASME Y14.35M formats include alphabetic characters starting at A through Y and then AA through YY, excluding any character or combination of characters containing the following letters: I, O, Q, S, X, and Z, as these could be confused with numbers.
   For example, as the primary revision is bumped for the Alphabetic sequence, the progression is A, B, C, D.... For a Numeric format, the progression is 1, 2, 3, 4, 5....

## Default Revision Scheme Definitions

From these three default revision scheme formats, four different revisions schemes are provided.

| Name | Delimiter | Primary | Secondary | Tertiary |
|---|---|---|---|---|
| Standard Alphabetic | Period (.) | Alphabetic | Numeric | Numeric |
| Standard Numeric | Period (.) | Numeric | Numeric | Numeric |
| Default ASME Y14.35M | Period (.) | Default ASME Y14.35M | Numeric | Numeric |
| None | Null Revision Scheme for opt out scenario | | | |

These revision schemes and revision scheme formats are designed to cover a wide range of the revision practices in industry. If either a format or scheme does not meet your needs, new ones can be created.

# 5.2 Creating and Modifying Revision Schemes

The Autodesk Vault Professional software comes with multiple revisions schemes. These represent common revision practices found in a cross section of the manufacturing industry. They can be used with or without modification.

It is possible to modify one of the provided schemes to adapt it to your environment. In some cases, a new revision scheme needs to be created.

## Revision Scheme and Revision Formats

A revision scheme is defined by two basic entities: the delimiter and the revision scheme format. For every revision scheme, there are three revision scheme formats separated by two delimiters. Revision scheme formats can be different but you can only use one type of delimiter per revision scheme.

### Delimiter

This is a character that separates the three revision scheme formats. The permitted characters for delimiters are:

- Single quote (‘)
- Hyphen (-)
- Double quote (“)
- Comma (,)
- Period (.)
- Forward slash (/)
- Colon (:)
- Semi-colon (;)
- Back slash (\)
- Underscore (_).

### Revision Scheme Format

As discussed earlier, these can be alphabetic or numeric sequences. There must be three revision scheme formats for every revision scheme:

- Primary Format
- Secondary Format
- Tertiary Format

## Building a Revision Sequence

The example below shows how the delimiter and the three revision scheme formats are used to build a complete revision scheme.

<Primary Format><Delimiter><Secondary Format><Delimiter><Tertiary Format>

Several examples of revision sequences are shown below using different delimiters and different alphabetic and numeric revision scheme formats.

A, A.1, A.1.1, A.1.2, B...

1, 1/A, 1/B, 1/B/1, 1/B/2, 2...

A, A-A-1, A-A-2, A-B, C...

**Note:** *An organization can use secondary or tertiary formats if they desire, but they must be used in conjunction with a primary format. For each revision scheme, all three formats must be present.*

## Creating a New Revision Scheme

Creating a new revision scheme involves importing a simple text file that has all of the possible characters for the primary revision scheme format. For example, the primary revision scheme format looks like the following sequence:

R1, R1, R3 ...

This is not one of the supplied formats so one will need to be created.

### How To: Create a New Revision Scheme and Format Using Import

The following steps show how a new revision scheme is created:

1. In a plain text editor like Microsoft Notepad, create a file where each row represents a revision character. The first row will be the first character in the sequence, the second row the second character in the sequence and so on.

   **Note:** *You will need to enter as many rows as you expect to use when creating different revisions. If you get to the last character in the sequence then the bump primary revision command will start incrementing the secondary revision and so on with the tertiary until all possible characters are used. This is not likely to happen unless you build all three formats with very few characters.*

2. Save this file (as shown in Figure 5–3) on your local file system.

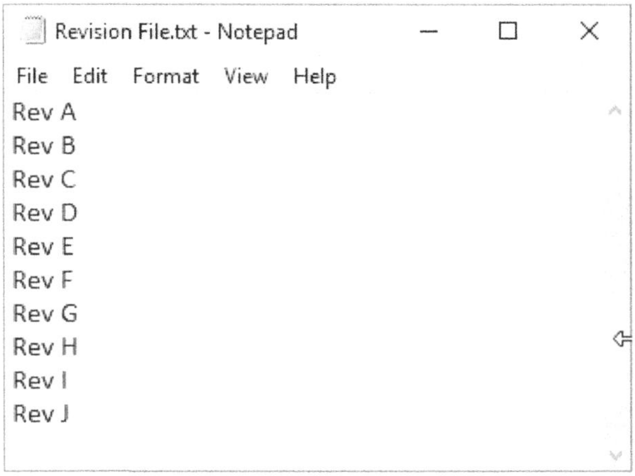


**Figure 5–3**

3. Return to Autodesk Vault Professional logging in as an Administrator. Open the *Vault Settings* dialog box and go to the *Behaviors* tab.
4. Select **Revisions** to open the *Revision Schemes Definitions* dialog box.
5. In the toolbar, click **Import**, as shown in Figure 5–4.

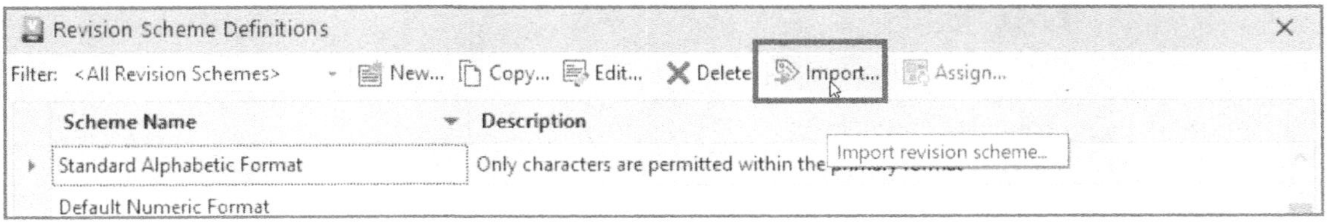


**Figure 5–4**

6. The Import *Revision Scheme Definition* dialog box displays.
7. Select the button next to the *Name* field (shown in Figure 5–5) and browse to the file you created. Select the file from the file browser.

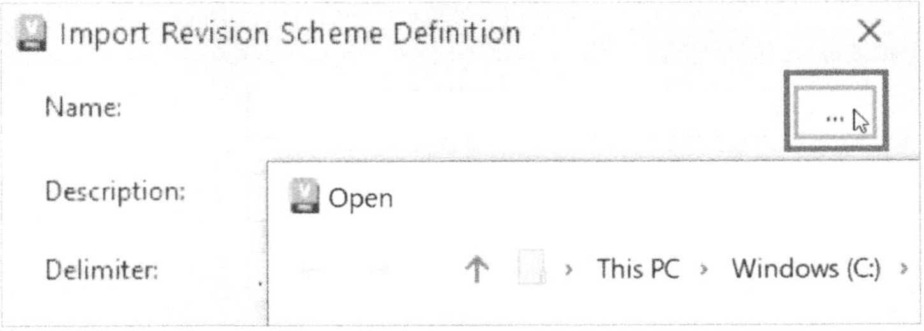


**Figure 5–5**

8. The scheme represented by the values in the file is created. By default, the secondary and tertiary formats are set to the numeric format, as shown in Figure 5–6.

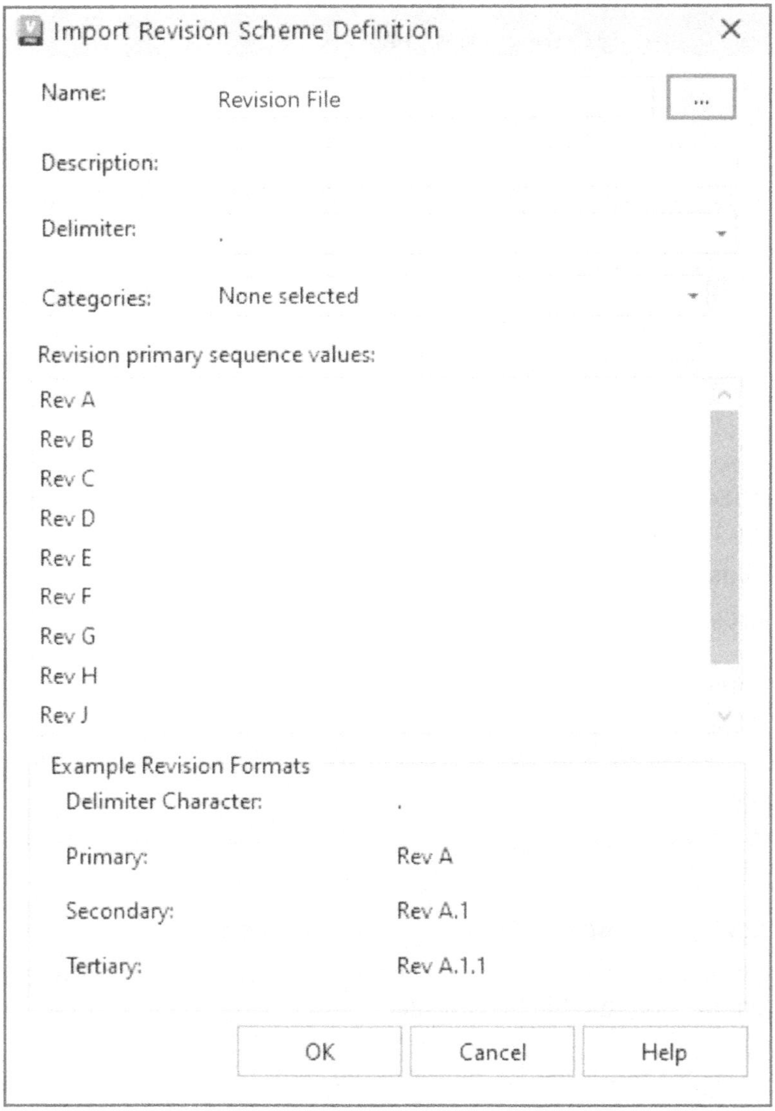


**Figure 5–6**

9. The default name used is the same as the filename. This should be changed to reflect the true name of the new sequence.

**10.** In the *Delimiter* drop-down list, select the delimiter to use, as shown in Figure 5–7.

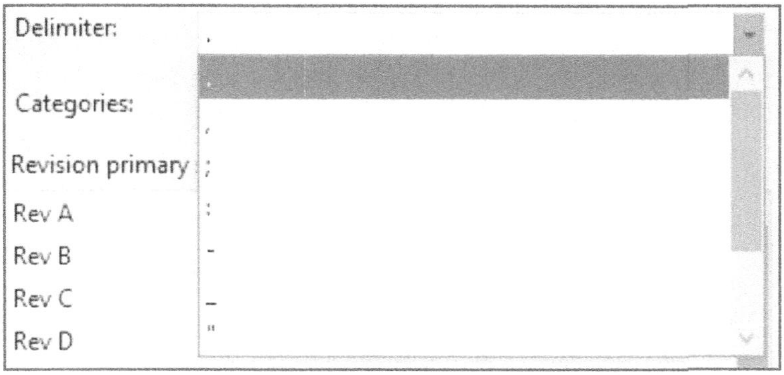


**Figure 5–7**

**11.** Enter a *Description* (as shown in Figure 5–8) and leave the *Category* field blank.

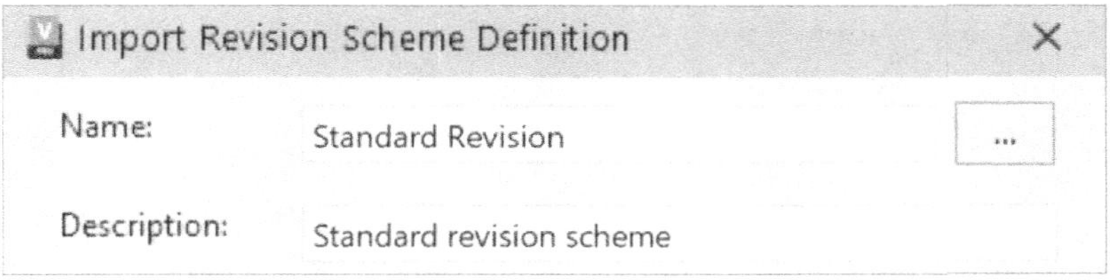


**Figure 5–8**

**12.** Click **OK** to dismiss this dialog box and return to the *Revision Scheme Definitions* dialog box, as shown in Figure 5–9.

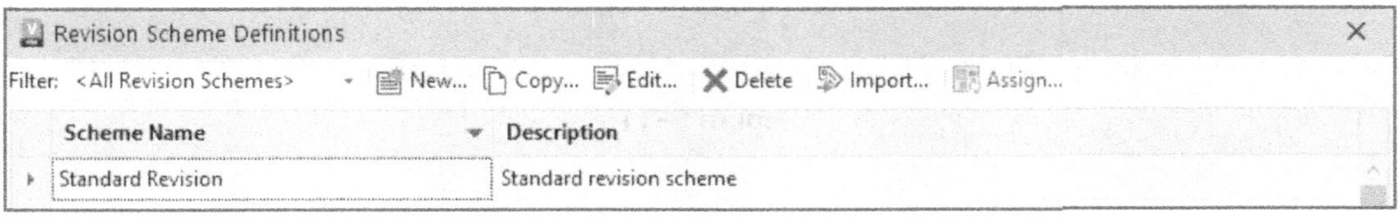


**Figure 5–9**

**13.** Review the new revision scheme. Note the default values for the secondary and tertiary formats. If this is acceptable, click **Close** to dismiss this dialog box.

**14.** To change the secondary or tertiary formats, select **Edit** from the toolbar, as shown in Figure 5–10.

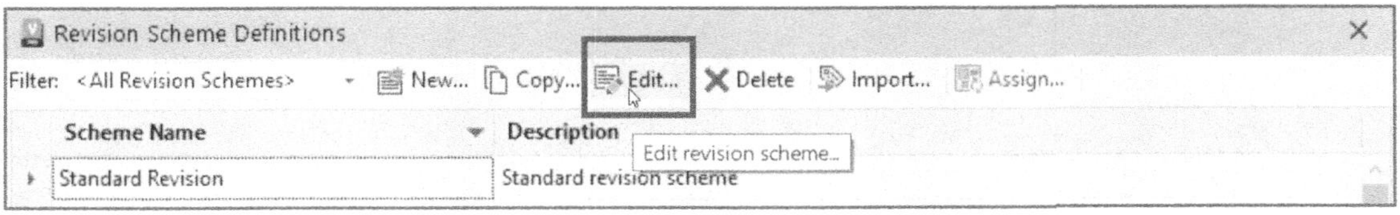


**Figure 5–10**

**15.** The *Revision Scheme Definition* dialog box for the selected sequence displays, as shown in Figure 5–11.

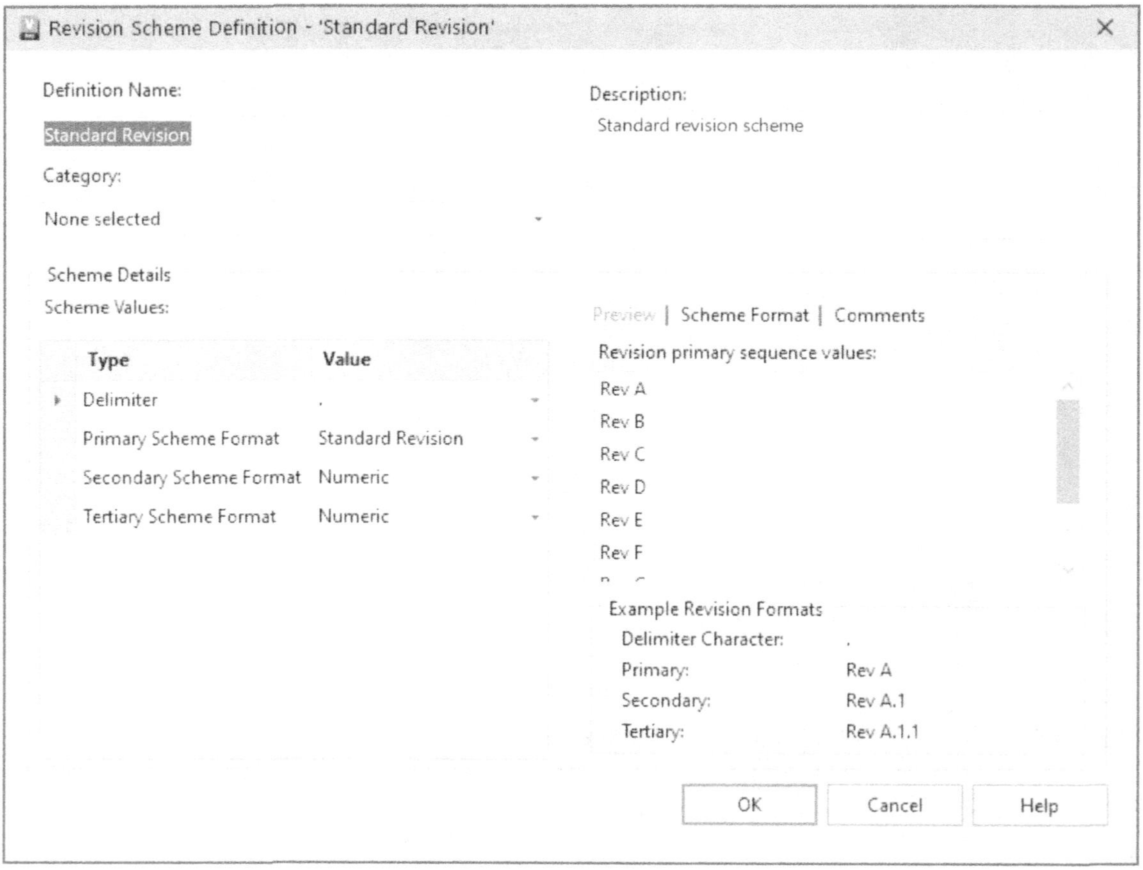


**Figure 5–11**

**16.** In the *Scheme Values* list, select the scheme you want to change, as shown in Figure 5–12. Note that you could also change the primary value at this point.

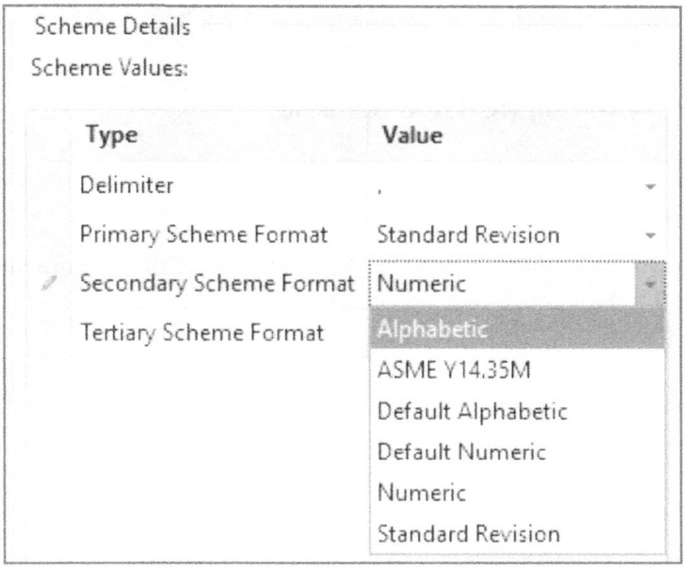


**Figure 5–12**

**17.** Review the examples of the new revision sequence in the *Preview* tab, as shown in Figure 5–13.

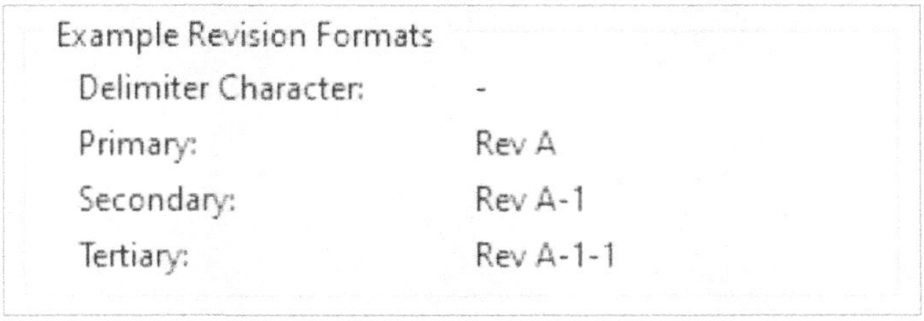


**Figure 5–13**

***Note:*** *In the process of creating a new revision scheme, a revision scheme format was also created. You can use this new revision scheme format in other custom revision schemes you might need.*

**18.** Click **OK** to close the dialog box and return to the *Revision Scheme Definitions* dialog box.

**19.** Click **Close** to return to the *Vault Settings* dialog box.

# Modifying an Existing Revision Scheme

In some cases, modifying an existing revision scheme will enable it to conform to your existing practices or process design.

## How To: Modify an Existing Revision Scheme

The following steps show an example of how an existing revision scheme can be modified:

1. In the *Vault Settings* dialog box, select the *Behaviors* tab.
2. Select **Revisions** in the *Lifecycles and Revisions* section to display the *Revision Scheme Definitions* dialog box.
3. Select **Edit** in the toolbar, as shown in Figure 5–14.

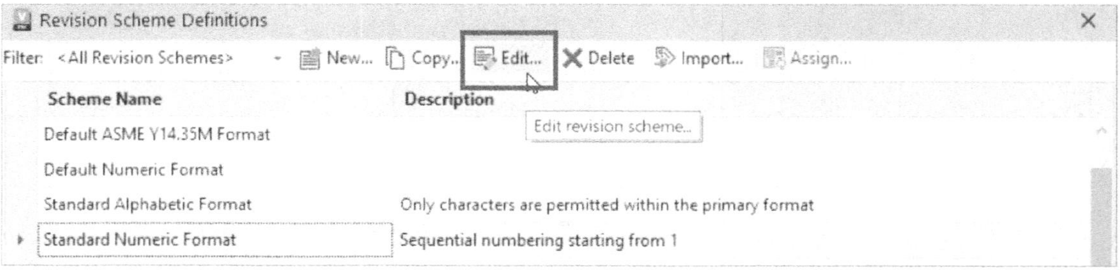


**Figure 5–14**

4. The *Revision Scheme Definition* dialog box for the selected revision scheme displays, as shown in Figure 5–15.

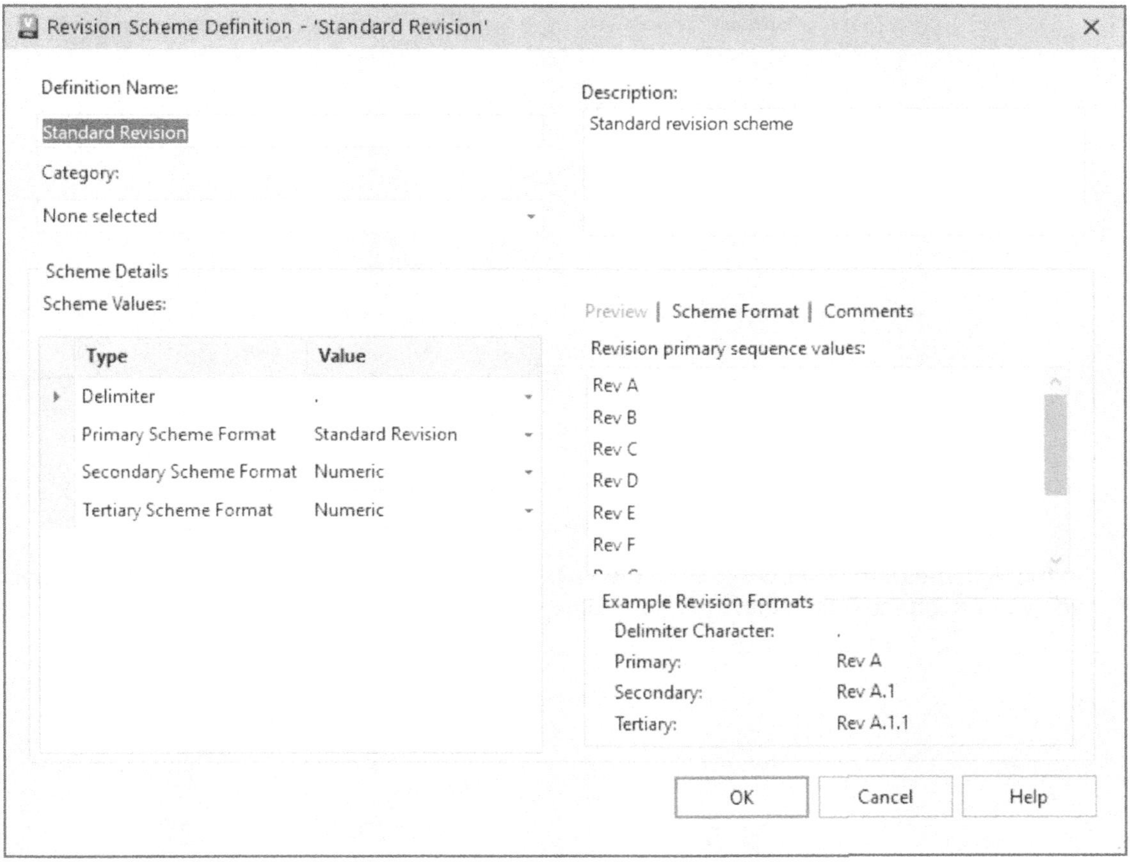


**Figure 5–15**

5. Change the *Definition Name*, *Category*, and *Description* (as shown in Figure 5–16) to better reflect the purpose for this scheme.

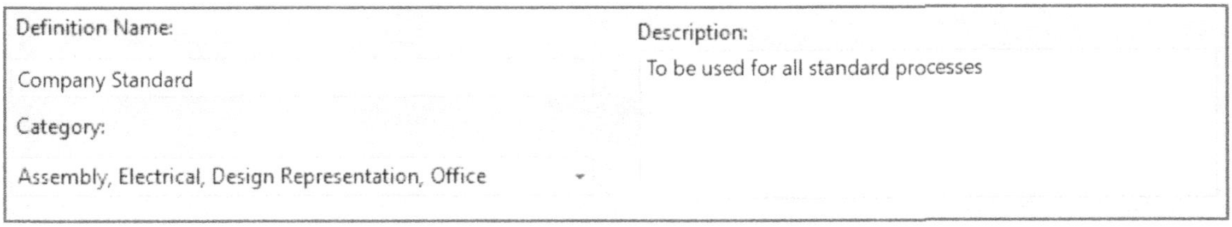


**Figure 5–16**

6. In the *Scheme Details* section, select the *Value* column for the **Delimiter** and select a new value in the drop-down list, as shown in Figure 5–17.

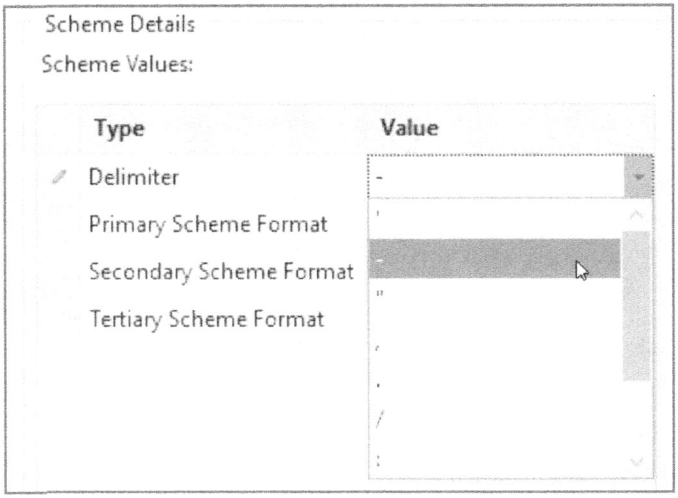


**Figure 5–17**

7. In the *Scheme Details* section, select the *Value* column for the revision scheme format that you want to change and select the new value, as shown in Figure 5–18.

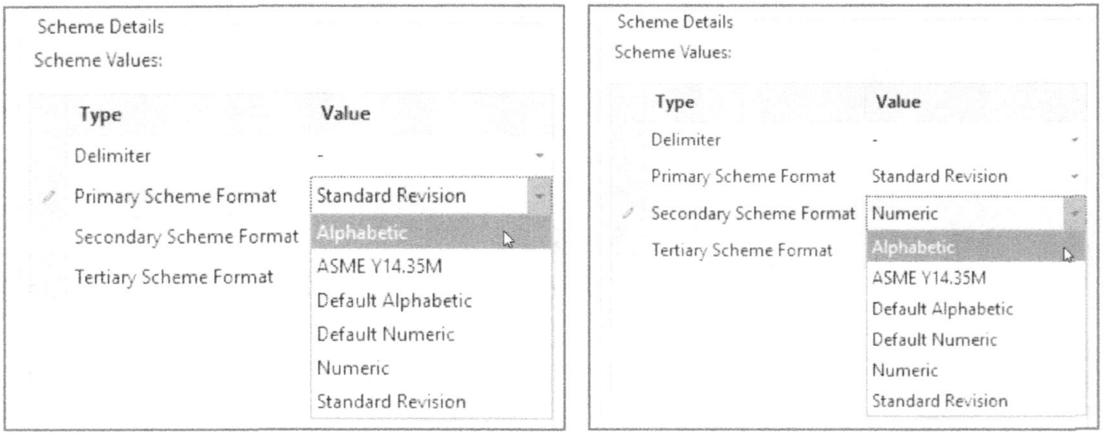


**Figure 5–18**

8. At any point, you can see an example of the changes in the *Preview* tab, as shown in Figure 5–19.

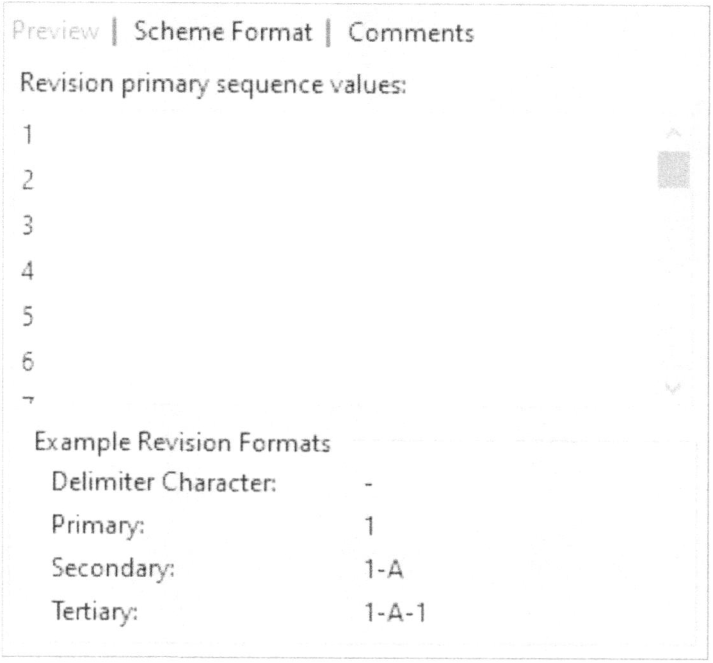


**Figure 5–19**

9. To create a new scheme format to use in this scheme or any other schemes, select the *Scheme Format* tab and select **New**, as shown in Figure 5–20.

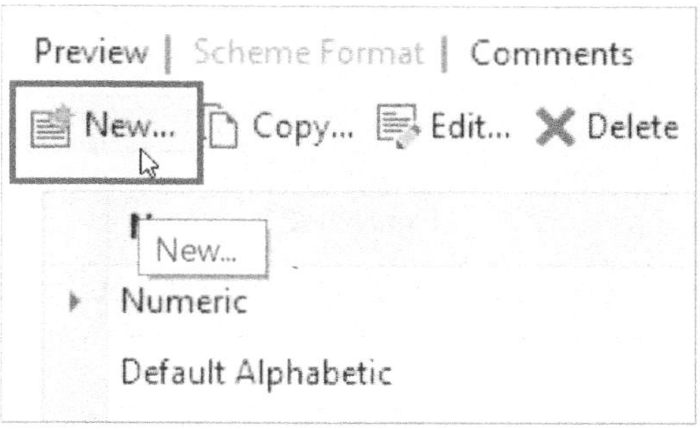


**Figure 5–20**

10. In the *List Scheme Format* dialog box, you can either enter and arrange the values manually or select the button next to the *Scheme Format Name* field (as shown in Figure 5–21), to import a list of values from a plain text (.TXT) file. Click **OK** when done to add the new format to the list.

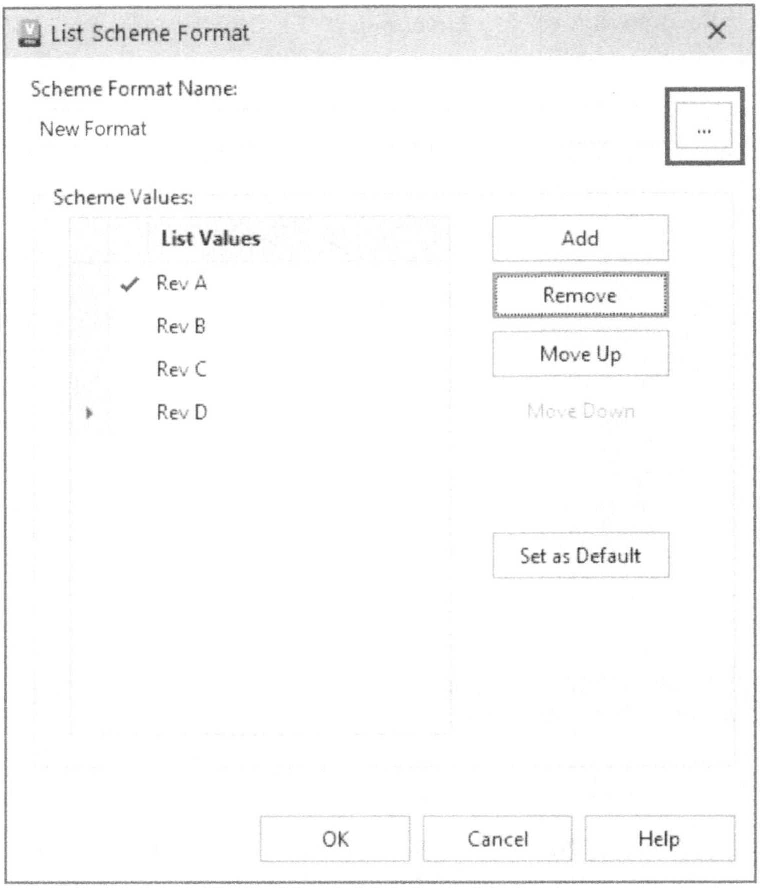


Figure 5–21

11. In the *Comments* tab, you can create one or more comments that will display in the *Revise* dialog box, as shown in Figure 5–22.

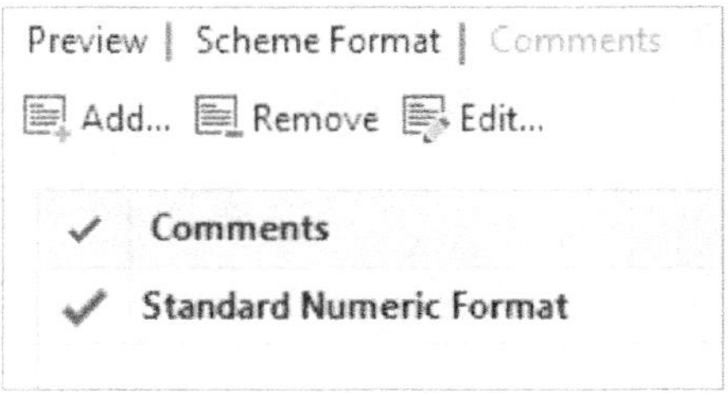


Figure 5–22

12. Select **Add** to add a new comment in the *Comment for* dialog box, as shown in Figure 5–23. Click **OK** to dismiss this dialog box and add the new entry to the list.

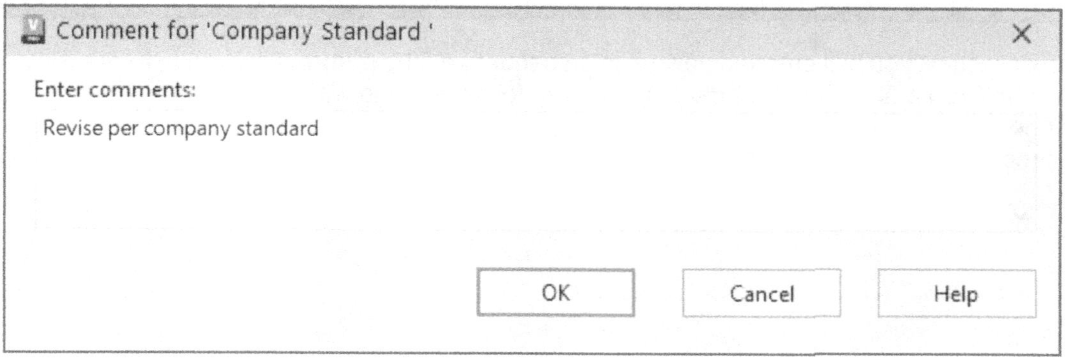


**Figure 5–23**

13. Remove any unwanted comments by first selecting the comment and then selecting **Remove**, as shown in Figure 5–24.

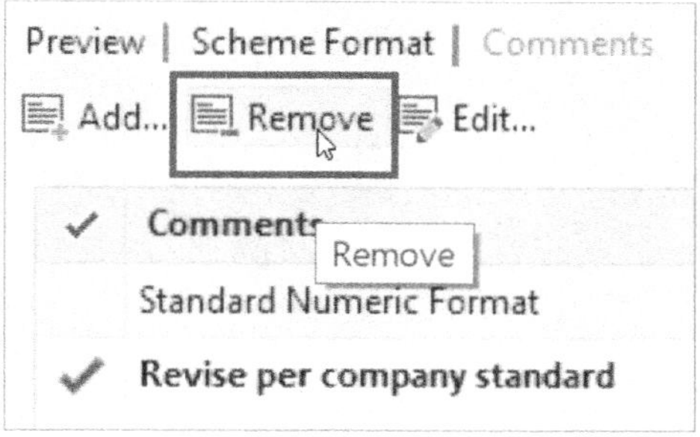


**Figure 5–24**

- Now when the file is revised, the Revision Definition displays in the list of revised files and the comment displays in the *Enter comments* text box.

14. Click **OK** to dismiss the *Revision Scheme Definition* dialog box for this revision scheme.
15. Select **Close** to dismiss the *Revision Scheme Definitions* dialog box and return to the *Vault Settings* dialog box.

# Practice 5a
# Create a Revision Scheme

In this practice, you will create a new revision sequence. The primary revision scheme will be imported from a file. The secondary and tertiary formats along with the delimiter will be configured from the supplied formats. The method used will be a variation on the one shown in the procedure. The completed practice is shown in Figure 5–25.

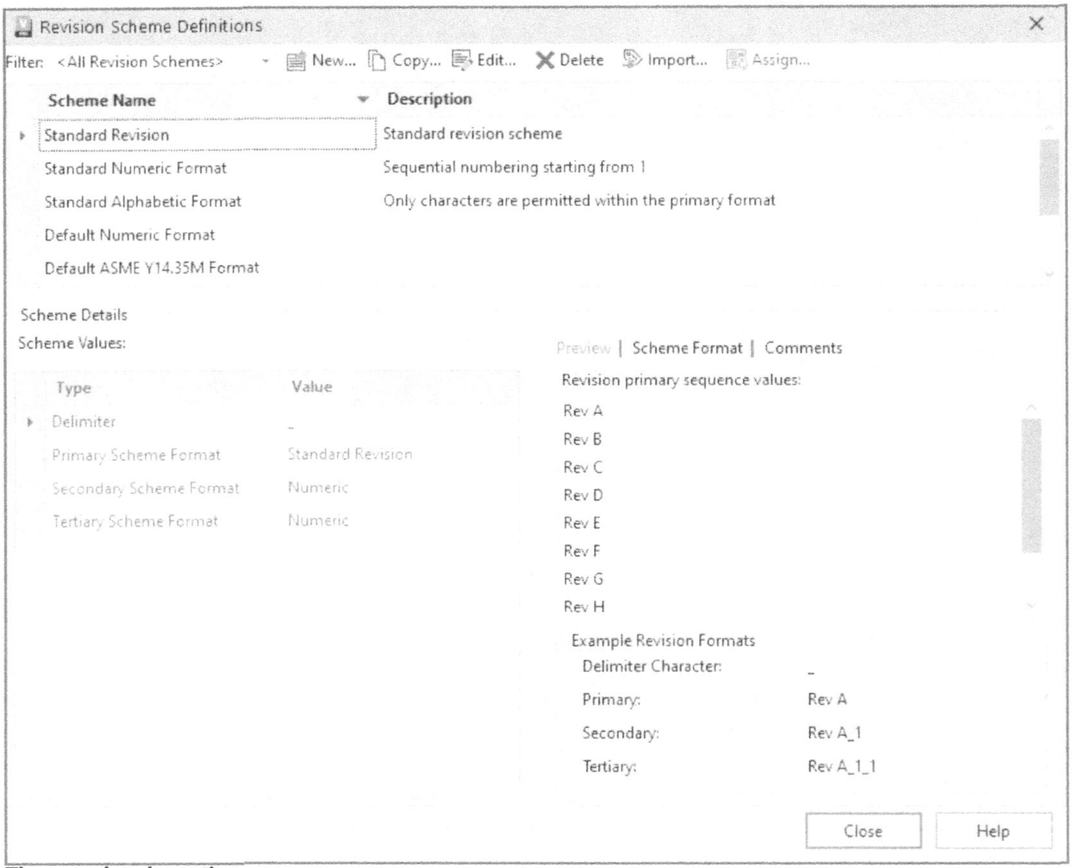


***The completed practice***

**Figure 5–25**

## Task 1: Create the file.

1. Start Microsoft Notepad to create an empty text file.
2. Enter **Rev A** in the first line.

3. Enter nine more lines, each time incrementing the letter. For example, the second line should read **Rev B**.
4. Save the file on your desktop with the name **Revision File.txt**, as shown in Figure 5–26.

**Figure 5–26**

## Task 2: Create the revision scheme.

1. Log in to Autodesk Vault using the following information:
   - For *User Name*, enter **administrator**.
   - Leave the *Password* field blank.
   - For *Vault*, select **AOTCVault** from the drop-down list.
2. In the *Tools* menu, select **Administration>Vault Settings**.
3. In the *Behaviors* tab, select **Revisions** to display the *Revisions Scheme Definitions* dialog box. Click **New**, as shown in Figure 5–27.

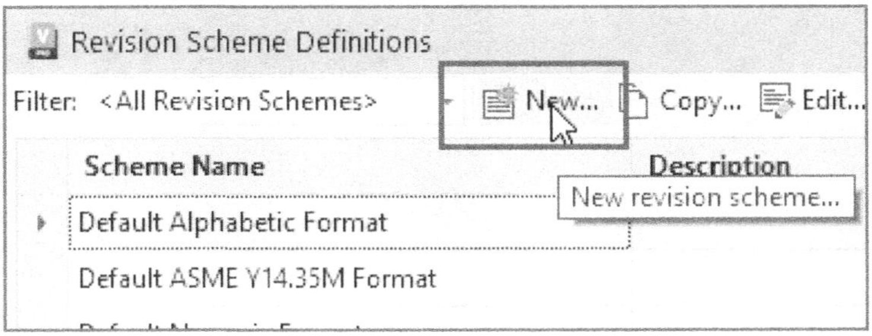


**Figure 5–27**

4. In the *Revision Scheme Definition* dialog box, do the following as shown in Figure 5–28:
    - For the *Definition Name*, enter **Standard Revision**.
    - For the *Description*, enter **Standard revision scheme**.
    - Leave the *Category* drop-down list as **None selected**.

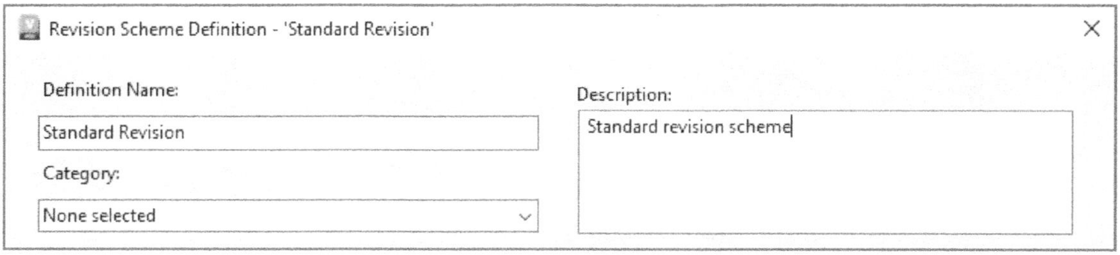


**Figure 5–28**

5. In the *Scheme Details* section, select the **Delimiter** line and then select the *Value* field to display the drop-down list. At the bottom of the list, select the underscore (_), as shown in Figure 5–29.

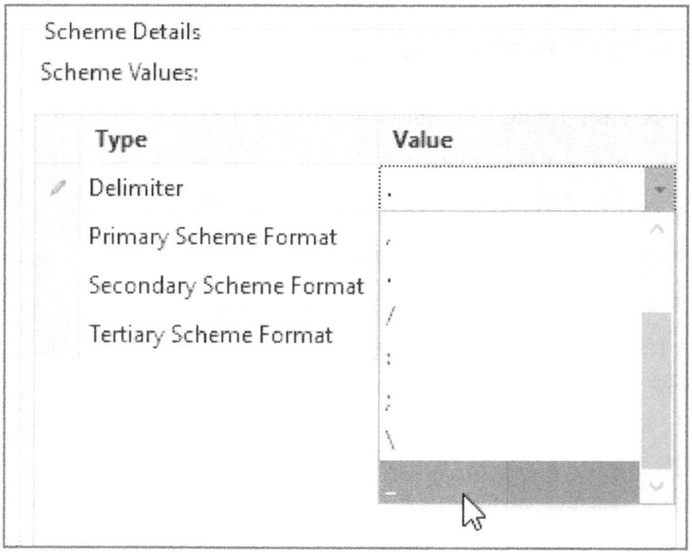


**Figure 5–29**

6. Select the **Primary Scheme Format** line.
7. In the tab section, select the *Scheme Format* tab.
8. Select **New** to display the *List Scheme Format* dialog box, as shown in Figure 5–30.

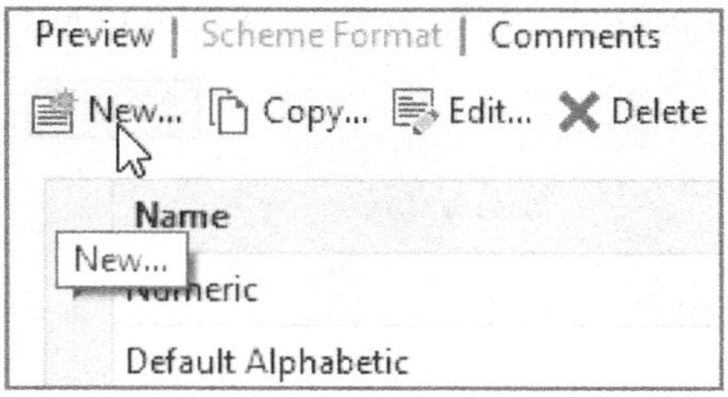


**Figure 5–30**

9. Select the button next to the *Scheme Format Name (*as shown in Figure 5–31) to display an *Open* dialog box. Browse to the file you created at the beginning of the practice and select **Open** to return to the L*ist Scheme Format* dialog box.

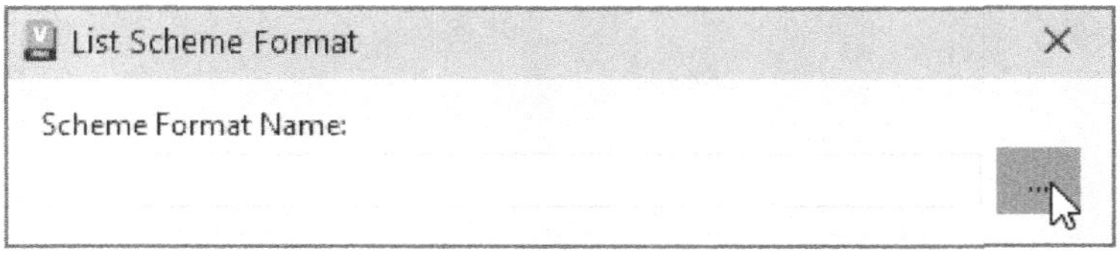


**Figure 5–31**

10. Click **Add** to add a new line to the list, as shown in Figure 5–32.

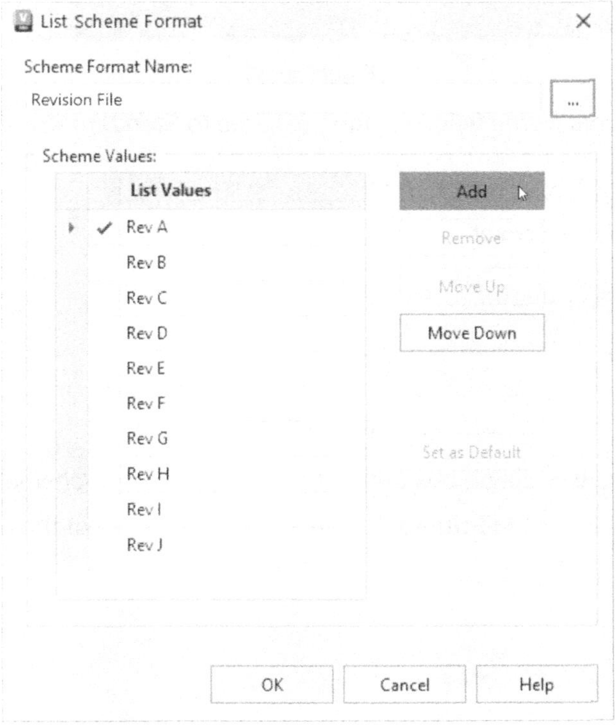


**Figure 5–32**

11. Enter **Rev K**. Move it to the bottom of the list, as shown in Figure 5–33.

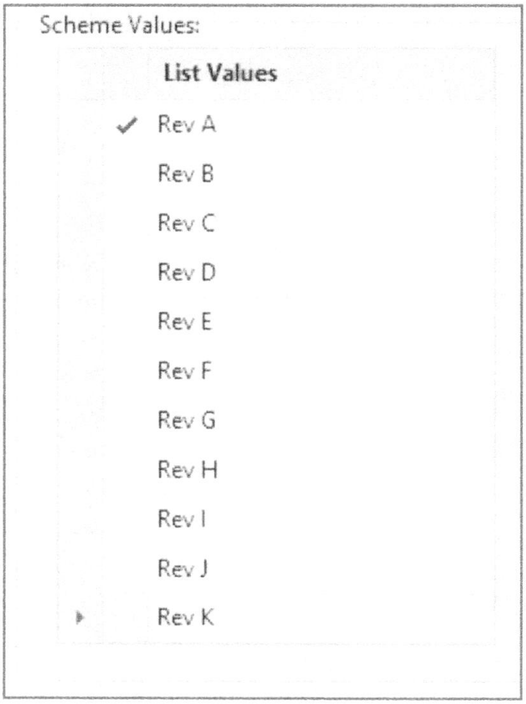


**Figure 5–33**

12. In the *Scheme Format Name* field, change the name to **Standard Primary Format**, as shown in Figure 5–34.

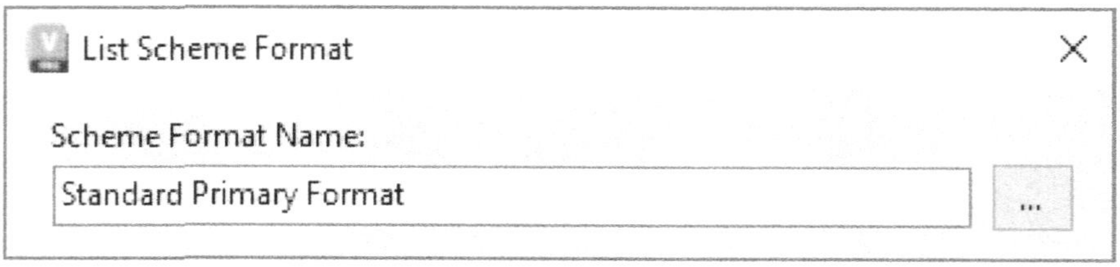


**Figure 5–34**

13. Click **OK** to dismiss this dialog box and return to the *Revision Scheme Definition* dialog box.
14. Select the *Value* field for the **Primary Scheme Format** and select the new format, as shown in Figure 5–35.

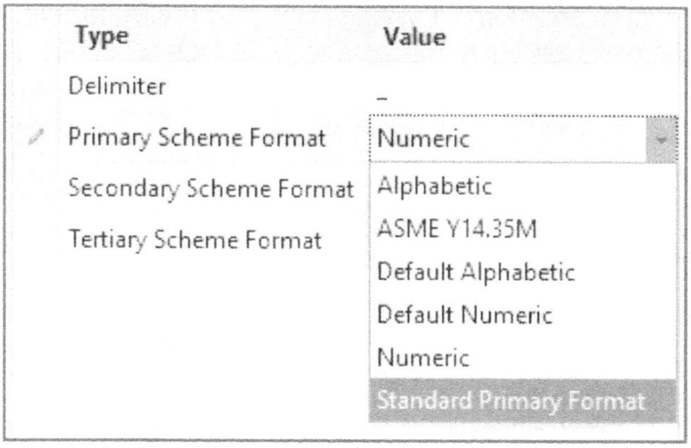


**Figure 5–35**

15. For the **Secondary Scheme Format**, select the *Value* field to display the drop-down list. Select **Alphabetic**.
16. For the **Tertiary Scheme Format**, select the *Value* field to display the drop-down list. Select **Numeric**.
17. Select the *Preview* tab to preview a sample revision character display, as shown in Figure 5–36.

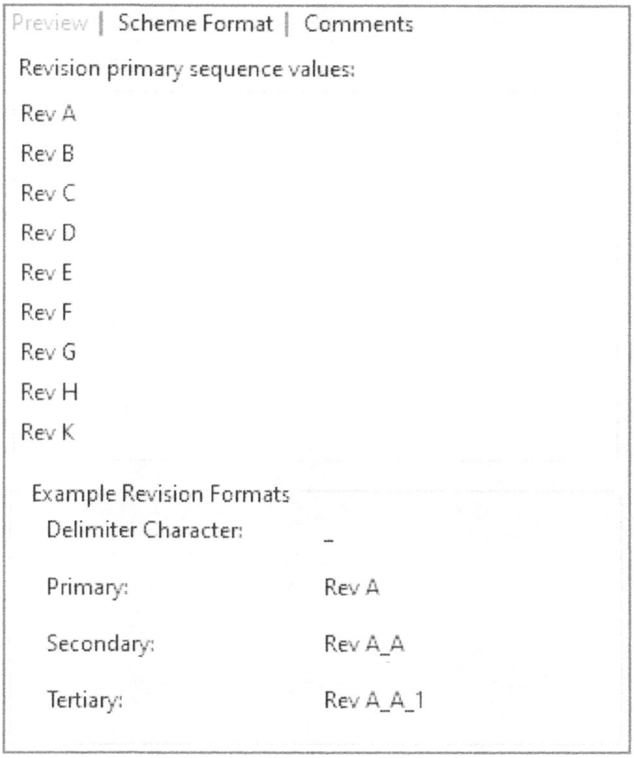


**Figure 5–36**

18. Select the *Comments* tab and then click **Add** to display the *Comment for 'Standard Revision'* dialog box. Enter the text **New Revision**, as shown in Figure 5–37.

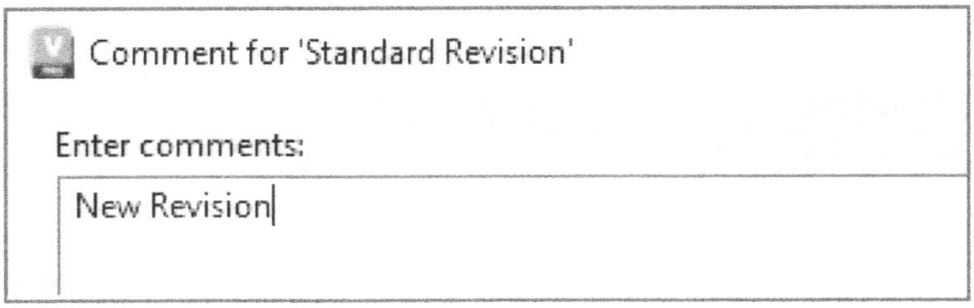


**Figure 5–37**

19. Click **OK** to dismiss the dialog box and return to the *Revision Scheme Definition* dialog box.
20. Click **OK** to dismiss this dialog box and return to the *Revision Scheme Definitions* dialog box that shows all of the schemes, as shown in Figure 5–38.

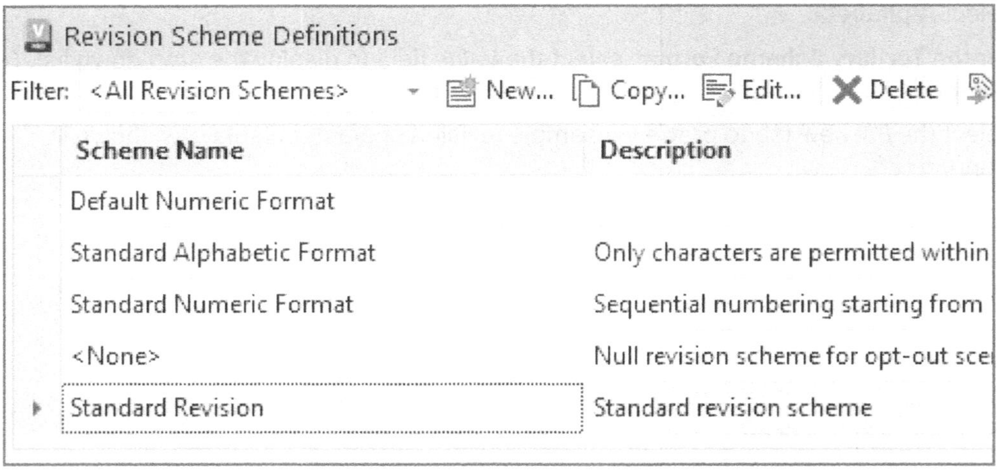


**Figure 5–38**

21. Click **Close** to dismiss this dialog box and return to the *Vault Settings* dialog box.

**End of practice**

# 5.3 Revising Files

The document revision management system in the Autodesk Vault Professional software is very flexible. There are several ways in which a file or item can be revised.

Revisions enable you to label a significant milestone or change to a file or item and all related files. The collection of files affected in a revision are considered a revision level, stored as part of the revision label you assign. A revision level can be stored and retrieved, ensuring that a document, item, and related files associated with that particular revision are preserved.

## Revision Controlled Documents

When using documents that are related to each other, such as an assembly and its referenced components, a relationship is created between the specific revisions of those documents. When an assembly is checked into a vault, the revision of each of its components is recorded so that when that revision is recalled, each related document is retrieved using the recorded revision.

### Editing a Referenced File Without Creating a New Revision

If a document references other files and those files are edited without bumping the revision, the referencing document will consume the edits. For example:

1. Revision A of an assembly references revision B of a part, as shown in Figure 5–39.

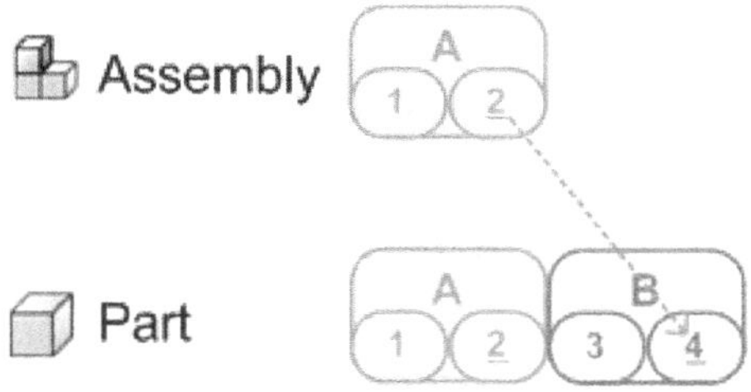


Figure 5–39

2. Changes are made to revision B of the part after revision A of the assembly has been checked in, as shown in Figure 5–40.

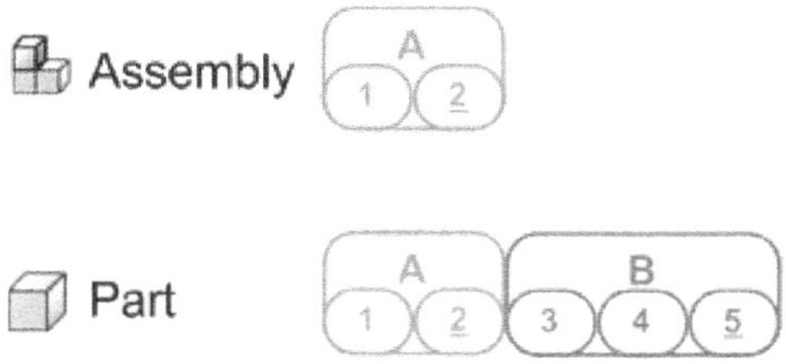


Figure 5–40

 

3. The changes to revision B of the part will show in revision A of the assembly when it is next checked out or opened, as shown in Figure 5–41.

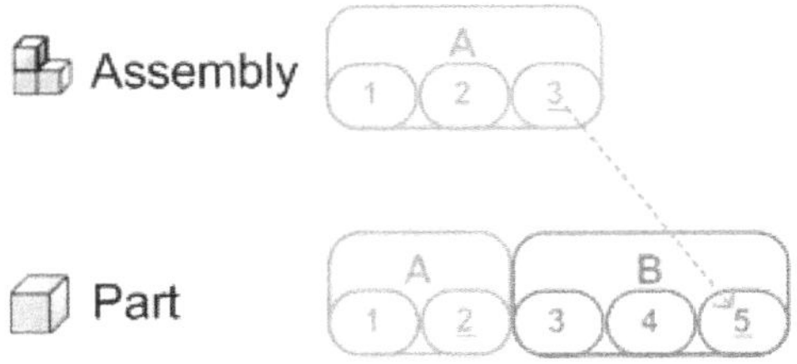


Figure 5–41

## Editing a Referenced File After Creating a New Revision

If a document references other files and a new revision is created for one of those files, the referencing document still maintains a relationship with the original revision. For example:

1. Revision A of an assembly references revision B of a part, as shown in Figure 5–42.

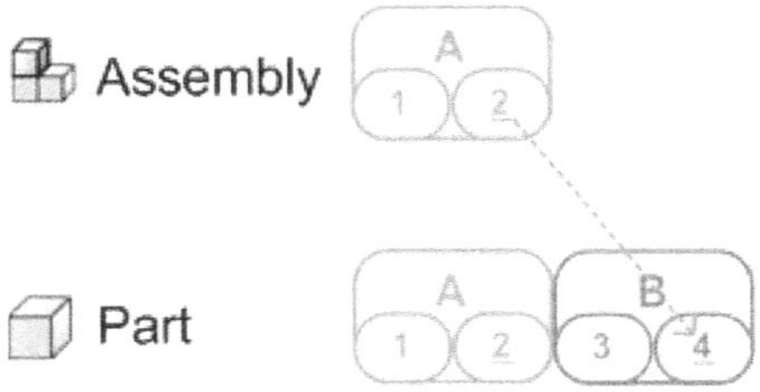


Figure 5–42

2. A new revision of the part is created and labeled C.
3. Edits are made to revision C of the part, as shown in Figure 5–43.

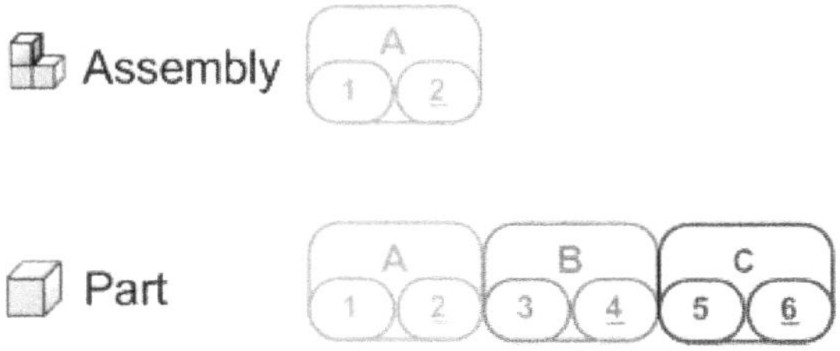


Figure 5–43

4. The changes to revision C of the part will show in revision A of the assembly if the Revision in the Get/Check Out dialog box for the assembly is set to **Latest**.

# Revisions and Lifecycles

Using revisions and lifecycles together provides significantly more flexibility than revisions alone can provide. For example, a given revision of a component can be edited and released out of context of any referencing assemblies, and the released changes will be used when the assembly is opened.

## What Does It Mean When a Revision Is Marked as Released?

When a version in a revision is marked as released, it is given priority over newer versions and will represent the revision. This prioritization is known as a released bias and is an option that can be toggled off in several of the dialog boxes.

> ***Note:*** *Versions marked as released can never be purged from the system and can only be deleted by an administrator.*

## What Does Released Biased Mean?

Released biased is an option in several of the dialog boxes indicating that released data should take priority over non-released data. This will help to ensure that new, non-released revisions of parts are not consumed unintentionally. This option can be toggled off.

> ***Note:*** *Released bias is enabled by default.*

## Example 1: Released Biased Options

In Figure 5–44, **Assembly1.iam** is in a *Released* state at Revision A. It uses two parts. **Part1.ipt** is in a *Work in Progress* state at Revision C. **Part2.ipt** is in a *Released* state at Revision A.

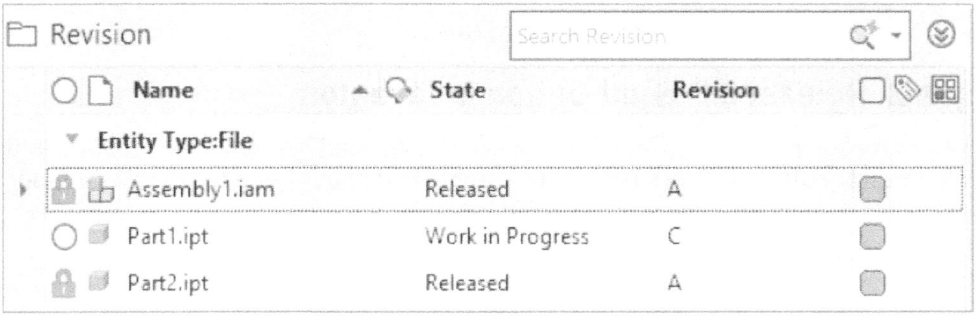


**Figure 5–44**

The *Uses* tab of **Assembly1.aim** is shown in Figure 5–45. By default, the view is **Released Biased**. The Released revision of **Part1.ipt** is shown.

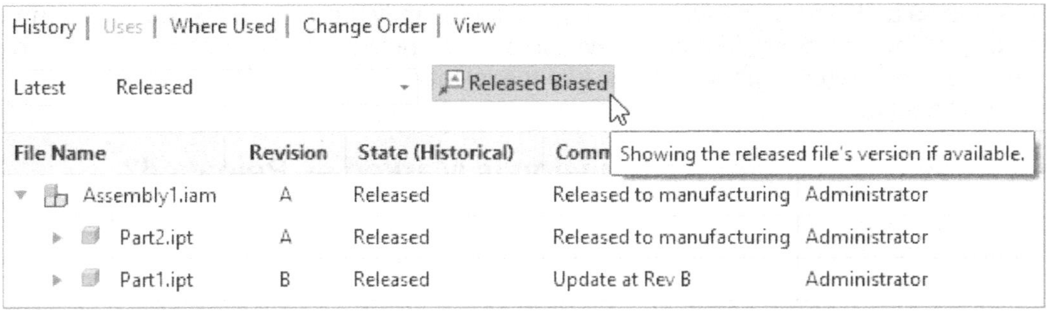


Figure 5–45

In Figure 5–46, the **Released Biased** option is toggled off. In this case, the *Uses* tab shows that the assembly uses the **Work in Progress** Revision C of **Part1.ipt**.

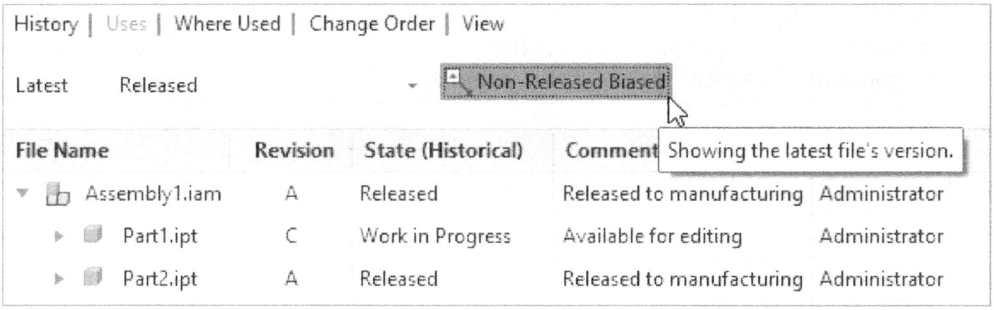


Figure 5–46

## Example 2: Released Biased Option in Inventor

Using the parts shown in the previous example, a new **Assembly2.iam** file is created in the Autodesk Inventor software. The **Place From Vault** command is used to place an instance of **Part1.ipt** in the new assembly, as shown in Figure 5–47.

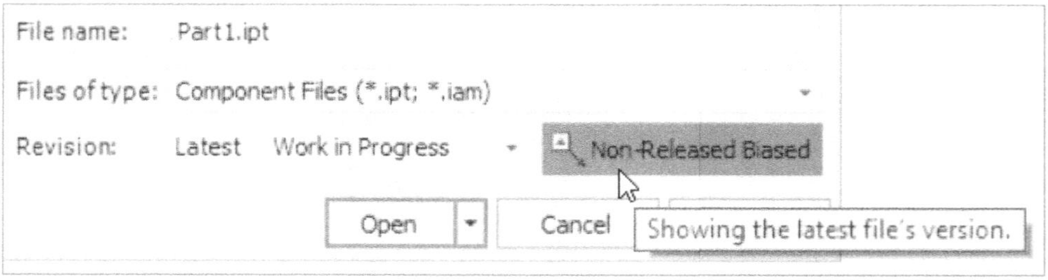


Figure 5–47

The default in Autodesk Inventor is to use **Non-Released Biased** revisions. If the part were placed and the assembly checked in, the results in the *Uses* tab of **Assembly2.iam** will be as shown in Figure 5–48.

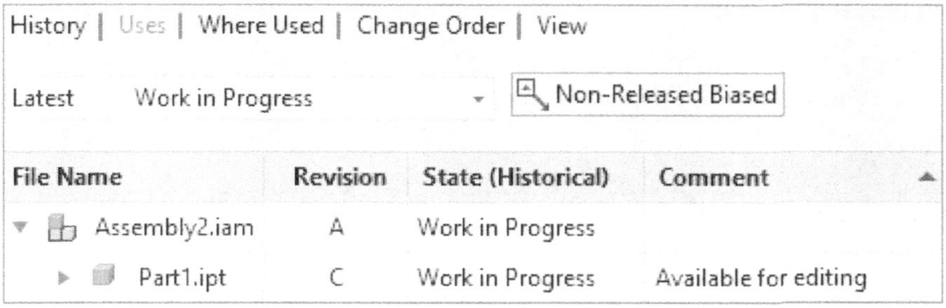


**Figure 5–48**

Another **Assembly3.iam** file is created. The **Place From Vault** command opens the *Select From Vault* dialog box. This time, the user specifies to use the Released version of **Part1.ipt**. Note in Figure 5–49 how the **Released Biased** indicator now shows that the released data will be used.

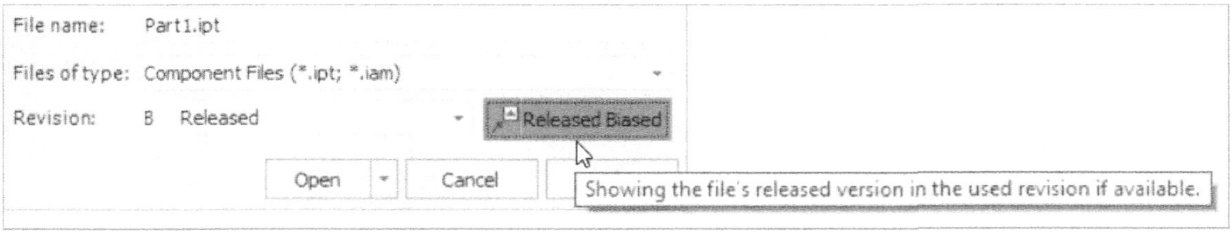


**Figure 5–49**

When this new assembly is checked in, the *Uses* tab shows that the Released revision of **Part1.ipt** is used.

## What Does Leading Mean When Referring to a Version or Revision?

The leading version is always the latest version of a file, even if Released Bias is enabled. The leading revision is always the latest version of the latest revision of a file (as shown in Figure 5–50), even if Released Bias is enabled.

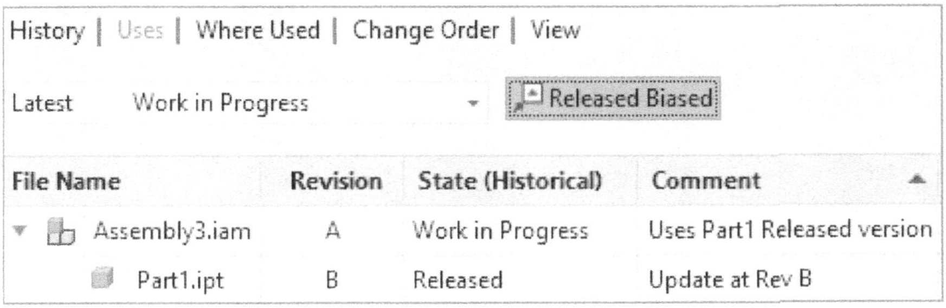


**Figure 5–50**

# Change Revision Command

The **Change Revision** command is used to manually create a new revision of a file or item and is available in the *Actions* menu.

> ***Note:*** *You can also change the revision in the Autodesk Inventor software by selecting Revise in the Vault tab>Control panel or in the shortcut menu in the Autodesk Vault Browser.*

## How To: Revise a File or Item

To create a file revision using the **Change Revision** command, do the following:

1. Select the file or group of files from the main pane that are to be changed. If you need to change a set of related files, you can use the options in the dialog box (shown in Figure 5–51) to select these for you. If the files are not related, use the <Shift> + select or <Ctrl> + select option to select the files from the list.

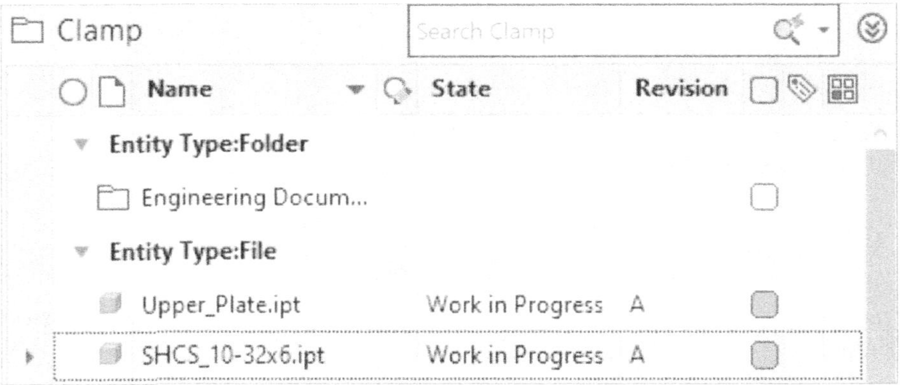


**Figure 5–51**

2. Select **Change Revision** in the *Actions* menu.

3. The *Change Revision* dialog box displays with the selected file(s), as shown in Figure 5–52.

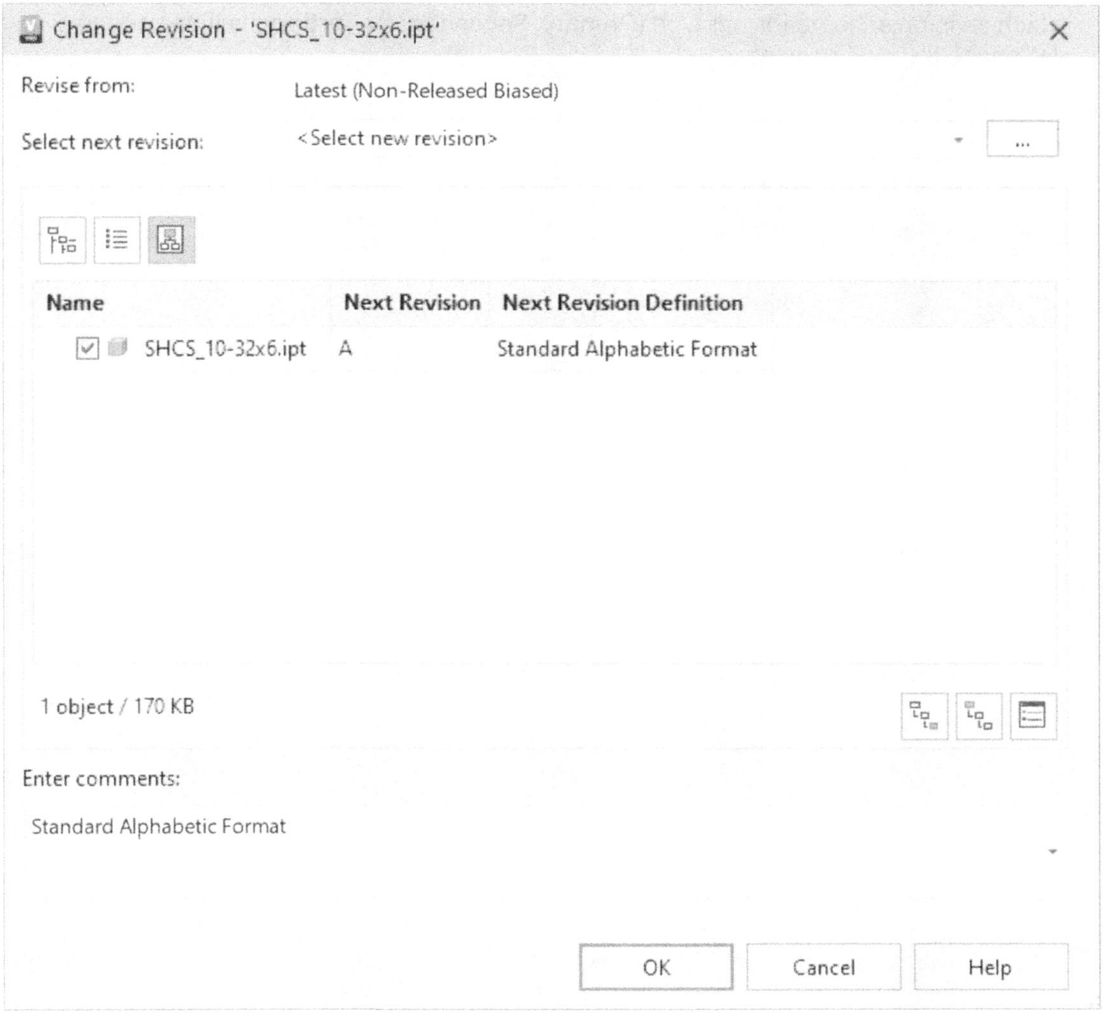


**Figure 5–52**

***Note:*** *You can also specify that the value of a user-defined property can be used to create the next revision. In a later lesson, you will learn how you can map a file property value to a user-defined value. This is especially useful when the authoring application controls the revision. For example, you might want to use the Autodesk Inventor Rev Number file property to control the revision.*

4. The dialog box indicates that the **Latest (Non-Released Biased)** revision will be copied to the new revision. In the *Select next revision* drop-down list (shown in Figure 5–53), indicate which revision scheme format type (**Primary**, **Secondary**, or **Tertiary**) will be used to determine the next revision.

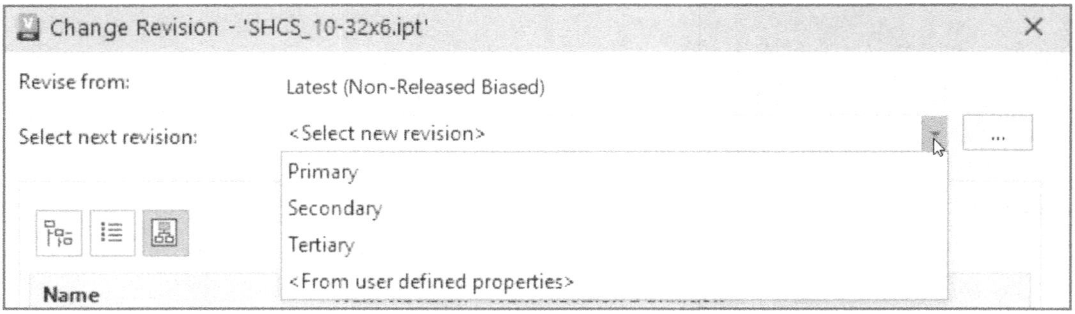


**Figure 5–53**

5. To change the revision scheme definition to use to generate the next revision, select the button next to the drop-down list to display the *Change Revision Definition* dialog box. Select the new revision scheme definition from the list, as shown in Figure 5–54. Click **OK** to dismiss the dialog box and return to the *Change Revision* dialog box.

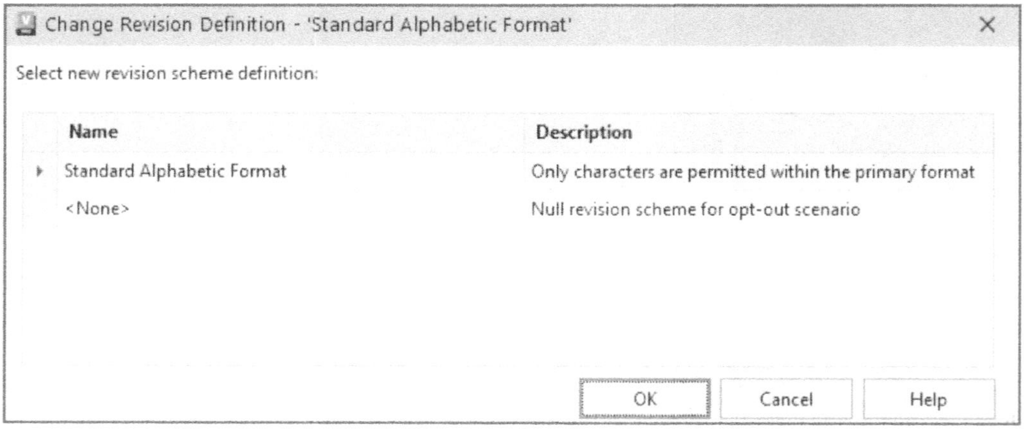


**Figure 5–54**

6. Use the **View** buttons (shown in Figure 5–55) to change the view to help understand file relationships.

**Figure 5–55**

7. Use the **Parent/Child** selection buttons (shown in Figure 5–56) to modify the selection.

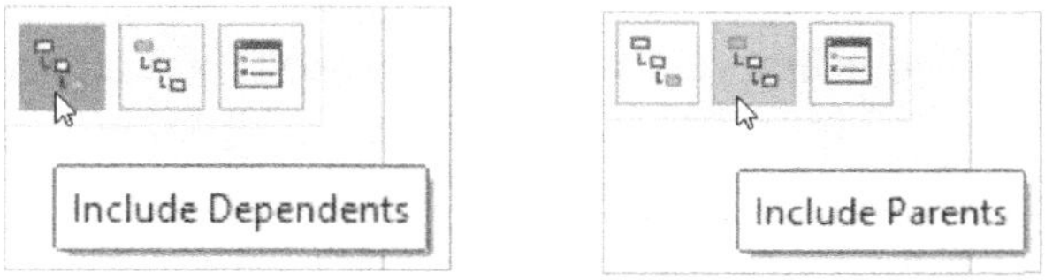


**Figure 5–56**

8. Select **Settings** to display the *Settings* dialog box, as shown in Figure 5–57. Here you can refine the selection of related files.

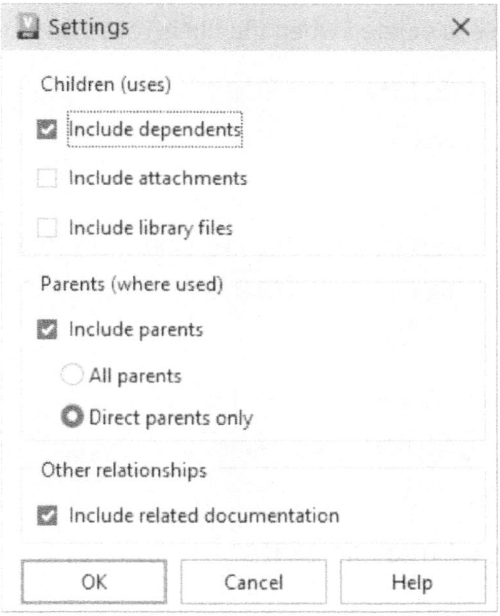


**Figure 5–57**

9. Select a comment from the drop-down list (if configured) or enter a custom comment, as shown in Figure 5–58.

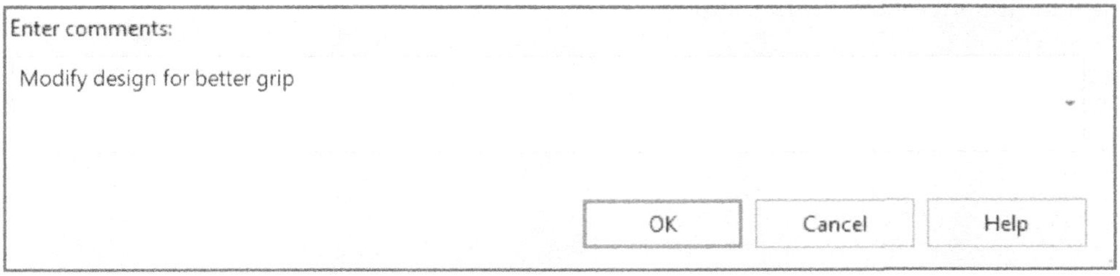


**Figure 5–58**

10. Click **OK** to complete the procedure.

# Roll Back the Lifecycle State of a File

Return a file or files to a previous lifecycle state with the **Roll Back Lifecycle State Change** command.

When a file is rolled back, it:

- returns to the file version associated with the rolled-back state.
- returns to the security, lifecycle definition, and revision scheme associated with the rolled-back state.
- retains any property definitions associated with the current version.

The current version of the file is deleted when the file is rolled back to a previous state.

## Rules for Rolling Back a File Lifecycle State

The lifecycle of a file can be rolled back if:

- the file is currently checked in.
- no parent versions consume the current child version that you want to roll back.
- the previous lifecycle state has not been deleted.
- the file is not in <null> definition.
- there is no label on the current version of the file.
- the administrator has not enabled the **Restrict File and Item Lifecycle State Changes to Change Orders** option.

## How To: Roll Back a File's Lifecycle State

You must be a Document Manager Level 2 or Administrator to roll back a file's lifecycle state.

1. Select one or more files in the main view and select **Actions>Roll Back Lifecycle State Change**.
2. A dialog box displays describing to which state the file will be rolled back. Click **Continue** to complete the lifecycle state rollback.

Chapter 6

# Managing Properties

Streamline your vault environment by managing property values for easier indexing and searching. Use the mapping feature to automatically update property values based on other file input, establishing property constraints to ensure that values meet your specifications.

## Learning Objectives

- Differentiate between system-defined properties and user-defined properties.
- Manage user-defined properties (create new, edit, add, or remove properties).
- Work with the Properties Grid in Autodesk® Vault and edit property values.
- Configure property constraints.
- Map properties.

# 6.1 System-Defined Properties vs. User-Defined Properties

Properties are attributes associated with a file. Autodesk Vault recognizes two types of property definitions: system-defined properties and user-defined properties (UDPs). System-defined properties are those properties that are derived from the vault. Autodesk Vault has a global set of properties that are applied to files in the vault. User-defined properties are created using the administrative tools.

## Terms, Data Types, and Attributes

Before working with properties, it is important to become familiar with the terms, data types, and attributes associated with the Autodesk Vault properties system.

The following table contains terms commonly used with properties.

| Term | Definition |
|---|---|
| **Associations** | Attribute that determines whether the property is associated with a file, folder, item, or change order. |
| **Compliant** | The status of a property that meets all property policies and equivalence evaluations. |
| **Data Type** | The type of data accepted for the property value. This type can be text, number, Boolean, or date. |
| **Database Property** | Any property in the database, either user-defined or system. |
| **Entity** | An entity is the system class with which a file can be associated. Entities are files, items, or change orders. |
| **Equivalent** | The status of a mapped property when its value matches the source value. |
| **File Property** | A property associated with a file. |
| **Mapped Property** | A property from which the propriety being defined gets its value. For example, a UDP can get its value from several different file properties. A file property can get its value from a system property. |
| **Mapping** | A set of relationships between the property being defined and a property from which it receives its value. There can be multiple mappings for a given property definition. |
| **Master** | The property from which a mapped property gets its value. The master property writes its value to the subordinate property. |
| **Non-compliant** | The status of a property when it has failed to meet one or more property policies or its equivalence evaluation. |
| **Non-equivalent** | The status of a mapped property when its value does not match the source value. |

 

| Term | Definition |
|---|---|
| **Property Definition** | All attributes and constraints about the property including its name, data type, initial value, mapping, minimum and maximum values, case values, in-use value, and basic search value.<br>The name used in the GUI (graphical user interface) to identify the property. |
| **Property Name** | The name used in the GUI (graphical user interface) to identify the property. |
| **Property Policy** | Depending on the data type, the property policy specifies certain constraints that must be met. The constraints can include a value range, a value type, or a value format must be met. For example, a property policy can be described as follows: the property must have a value and that value must be in the range of 1 to 10.<br>When a property fails to meet its property policies, it is considered non-compliant. |
| **Property Value** | The literal content of a property attribute for a specific file version. |
| **Override** | Determines whether the property value is overridden by the policy defined by its category. |
| **Subordinate** | The mapped property that receives its value from the master property. |
| **System-Defined Property** | A property in the database created by the system, which is then assigned to a file. |
| **User-Defined Property (UDP)** | A property in the database created by an administrator. The property can be applied to a file when it is added to a vault. |

Every property value has a data type that determines how that value is read and processed.

| Data Type Name | Description |
|---|---|
| **Boolean** | True or False |
| **Date Type** | Can be a specific date or date range expressed by a beginning and end date |
| **Number** | Numbers only |
| **Text** | Letters, numbers, and punctuation |

Properties have attributes that determine how the property is described and the constraints for its value.

| Attribute Name | Description |
|---|---|
| **Basic Search** | A constraint that determines whether or not the property should be included in basic searches. |
| **Case Sensitivity** | A constraint that applies to text data types. This constraint can be set to none, UPPER CASE, lower case, Name Case, or Sentence case. |
| **Enforce List of Values** | A constraint that determines whether the property must have a value from a list. |
| **Initial Value** | An attribute that specifies the initial property value when one is not specified.<br>Note the initial values are best used with write mappings. If an initial value is set on a regular read mapping, that read mapping has higher priority and will overwrite the initial value. The only case in which an initial value will not be overwritten by a read mapping is if the value it maps to is blank. |
| **List Values** | Displays the *List Type* dialog box from which you can enter and order values for a list. At least one item must display in the list. |
| **Minimum Length** | The minimum number of characters a property value can have. |
| **Maximum Length** | The maximum number of characters a property value can have. |
| **Requires Value** | A constraint which determines whether the property must have a value to be compliant. |
| **State** | The state of a property definition specifies whether it is enabled or disabled in the vault. A disabled property is not displayed or searched and cannot be used to store a value for a given file. |
| **Usage** | Indicates the number of files currently using the property. Use this information to determine which properties are used more than others, to help decide which properties can be removed from the vault. |

The main view in the vault client has a *Property Compliance* column that lists various status icons. The icons in this column indicate whether a property associated with the file is compliant, non-compliant, pending, or has failed the equivalence evaluation.

| Icon | Value | Definition |
|---|---|---|
| No icon | Compliant | All properties meet policy requirements and equivalence. |
|  | Non-compliant | One or more properties do not meet property policy requirements or equivalence.<br>Hover the cursor over the icon to learn more about why one or more properties failed compliance. |
|  | Not calculated | There has been a change to one or more properties but equivalence and policy have not been verified yet. |
|  | Pending | Properties are currently being evaluated for equivalence. |
|  | Evaluation failed | The equivalence evaluation failed. This is a rare situation and can result when the processor enters an evaluation loop.<br>**Note:** In the *Find* dialog box, an evaluation failed value is added. This enables you to search for any files for which the evaluation failed. |

# Introduction to the Property Definitions Dialog Box

When files are checked into the vault, only the properties that are set enabled are automatically extracted and indexed by default. All the extracted properties being tracked by the vault can be managed using the *Property Definitions* dialog box. The *Property Definitions* dialog box lists:

| | |
|---|---|
| **Property Name** | The name of the property as it displays in the interface. The display name can be edited by the vault administrator. |
| **Data Type** | The type of data represented by the property. The data types are: text, number, date, and Boolean. |
| **Usage** | Indicates the number of files currently using the property. Use this information to determine which properties are used more than others, to help decide which properties can be removed from the vault. |
| **State** | Indicates whether or not the property is enabled for indexing and visible to the user.<br>• **Enabled:** If a property is set to **Enabled**, the property is indexed and extracted from files when they are added or checked into the vault.<br>• **Disabled:** If a property is set to **Disabled**, it is not indexed and it is not extracted from files when they are added or checked in to the vault. Administrators can clean up unwanted properties by marking them **Disabled**. |
| **Associations** | Lists the entity class that can use the property. Classes are files, folders, items, change orders, and custom objects. |

| | |
|---|---|
| **Folder Categories** | If the property is associated with a folder category, the category name displays. Category values will override property values if the property **Override** attribute is enabled. |
| **File Categories** | If the property is associated with a file category, the category name displays. Category values will override property values if the property **Override** attribute is enabled. |
| **Item Categories** | If the property is associated with an item category, the category name displays. Category values will override property values if the property **Override** attribute is enabled. |
| **Basic Search** | Indicates if a string property is searched when using the basic search feature. The possible values are:<br>• **Searched:** The property is included in the basic search.<br>• **Not Searched:** The property is excluded from the basic search.<br>• **Not Allowed:** The property is not a string value and therefore cannot be included in the basic search. |

**Important**: When a new user-defined property is created, it does not have to be associated with any categories. However, even if the property is associated with an entity (e.g., file, folder, change order, item, or custom object), if it is not associated with any categories, it will not display in the properties grid for that entity.

When migrating an existing vault database, all existing properties set to **Enabled** are migrated. However, any new properties default to **Disabled**. To improve indexing performance, all properties without mappings are not created unless specified by the administrator.

## How To: Rename a Property

The display name of a property can be edited to make it more meaningful. Both system-defined and user-defined names can be changed by selecting Edit in the *Property Definitions* dialog box.

1. Select **Tools>Administration>Vault Settings**.
2. In the *Vault Settings* dialog box, select the *Behaviors* tab.
3. In the *Properties* section, select **Properties**.

4. The *Property Definition* dialog box opens, as shown in Figure 6–1. Here you can rename the selected Property using the **Edit** command.

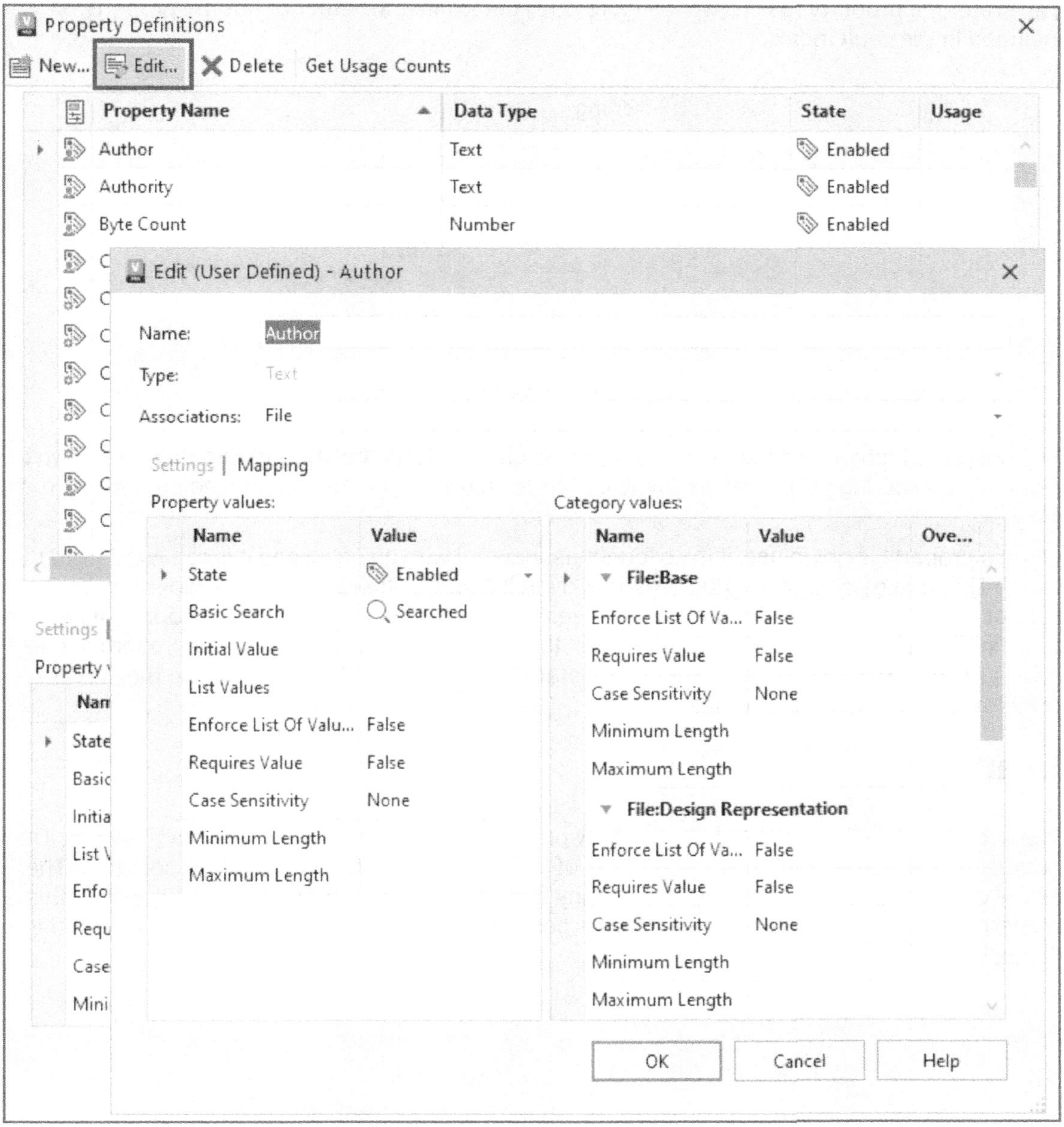


**Figure 6–1**

# Change the State

The state of a property (as shown in Figure 6–2) determines whether or not the property is included in the vault index.

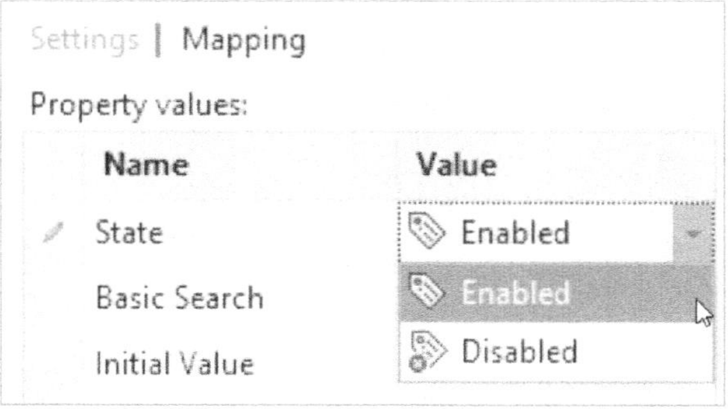


**Figure 6–2**

You specify which properties to include in the vault by setting the state to **Enabled**, as shown in Figure 6–2. Marking properties as **Disabled** lets administrators remove unused properties from view.

When a property is not in use, it is no longer associated with any files and it is removed from the index. This makes searching more efficient overall because there are fewer properties. You cannot search on a property that is not in use. You cannot display an unused property as a column in a grid. You cannot map properties to unused file properties. Unused properties can be re-associated with files by changing the state back to **Enabled** and then using the server console to re-index the properties.

# Examining Usage Count

The usage count of a property tells you how prevalent the property is throughout the vault. The number in the *Usage* column is the number of files with which the property is associated. The usage count of a property tells you how many files have a value associated with them for this property. You will find the **Get Usage Counts** command in the menu pane of *Property Definitions* dialog box, as shown in Figure 6–3.

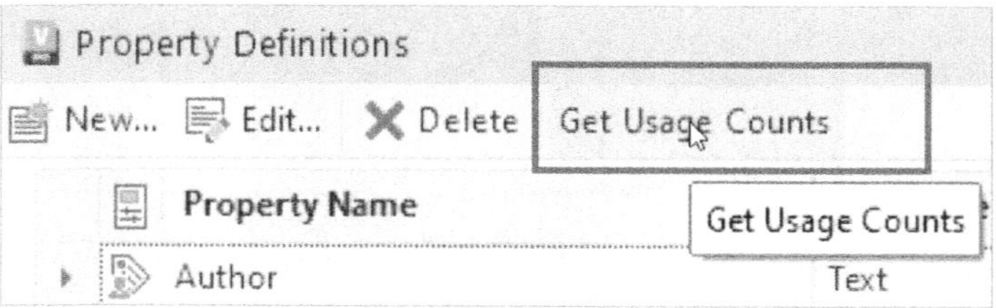


**Figure 6–3**

# Specifying Searchable Properties

The Basic Search setting for a property determines whether or not that file property is available for searching when a basic search is performed. The Basic Search setting applies only to the basic search and not to searches using the query builder or the *Find* dialog box. Only string type file properties can be set to **Searched**.

String type file properties that are set to **Searched** (as shown in Figure 6–4) are available for the basic search. Properties set to **Not Searched** are not currently available for the basic search. By setting unused file properties to **Not Searched**, you can increase search performance. Properties set to **Not Allowed** are not string type properties and are not available for the basic search. A property set to **Not Allowed** cannot be changed to any other setting.

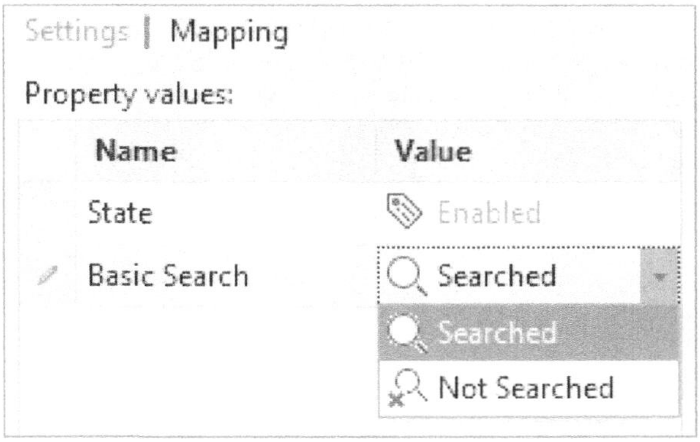


**Figure 6–4**

When the state of a property is set to **Disabled**, the basic search setting is automatically set to **Not Searched**. If that property is later set to **Enabled**, the basic search setting remains **Not Searched**. In order for the property to be available for searching, the administrator must manually set the property to **Searched**.

# Initial Value

The *Initial Value* (as shown in Figure 6–5) is applied once when the property is initially associated with an object. The initial value is only applied in the absence of a user-supplied or a mapped value.

The initial association occurs in three circumstances: 1) object is created (e.g., adding a file or creating an item); 2) assignment to a category that automatically attaches the property; and 3) manual property attachment.

There are two types of initial value: **static** and **mapped**. The static value is a fixed value and can be any value that is valid for the selected data type. An initial mapped value copies the value from a file or BOM property.

Initial values should NOT be used on properties where all regular mappings read the value from a file or BOM. A blank value in the mapped file or BOM field takes precedence over the initial value. This can appear as if the initial value is not applied when in fact the mapped value of 'blank' takes precedence.

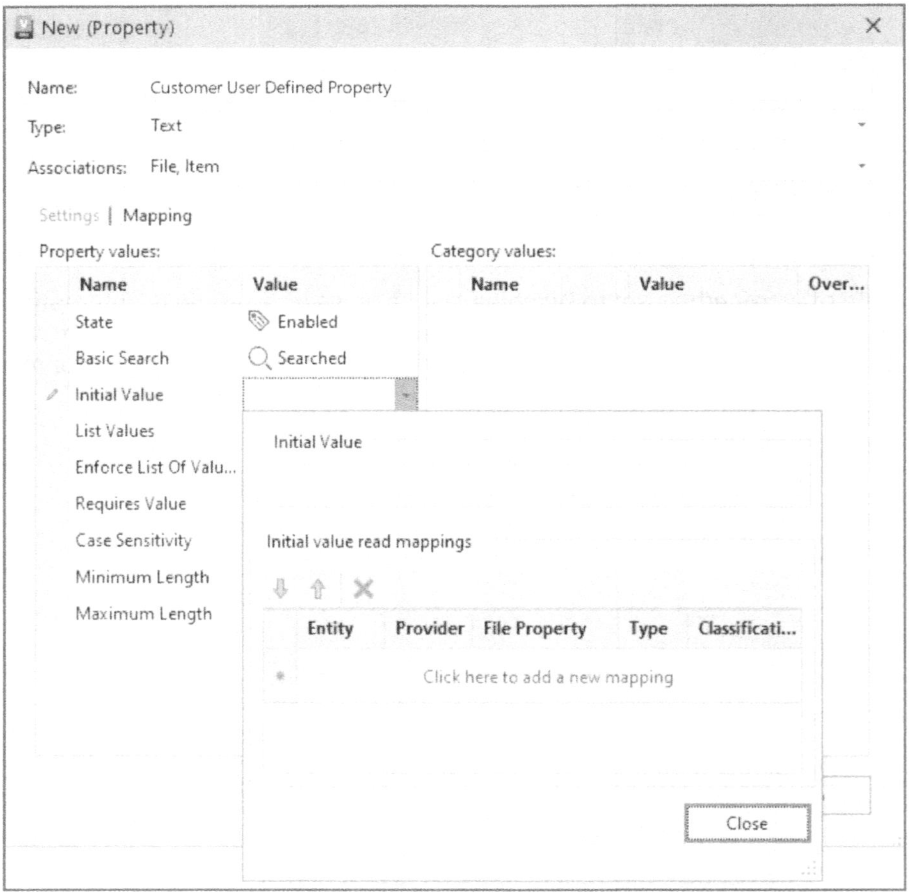


**Figure 6–5**

# List Values

Properties of type *Text* and *Number* can provide a list of values for user selection and searching. The administrator can add or remove values from the list at any time. Removal of a value from the list does not remove the value from any property where that value has been applied. When specifying the value for this property, the user can choose from the list of values. Entering values that are not on the list is permitted. If this property is mapped to read a value from a file or BOM, the imported value is not required to be on the list.

## Enforce List Values

When enabled, the **Enforce List Values** option provides a warning symbol adjacent to this property if the value is not on the list. When a value is in violation of this policy, the default configuration for lifecycle transitions will not permit for a file or item to be released.

# Add or Remove a User-Defined Property

A user-defined property (UDP) can be added to a file or removed from a file. When a new version of the file is created, the change to the property assignment is shown. You must have administrative access to perform these tasks. To use the **Add or Remove Property** command, you cannot have the file checked out for edit.

### How To: Add or Remove a Property

1. From the main file list, select one or more files.
2. Select **Actions>Add or Remove Property**.
3. In the *Add or Remove Property* dialog box, select the property from the *Property* list.

4. For the *Action* value of the property, select **Add** or **Remove** from the drop-down list, as shown in Figure 6–6.
   - **Add:** The property is added to the selected file or files using the default value. If the property is already assigned to a selected file, no action is taken for that file.
   - **Remove:** The property is removed from the selected file or files. If the property is not assigned to a selected file, no action is taken for that file.

   ***Note:*** *If a property is assigned by means of a category, it cannot be removed from a file.*

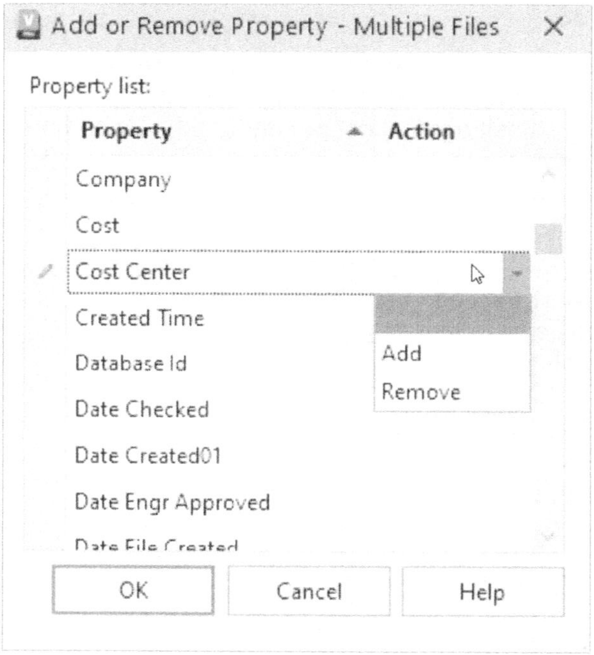


**Figure 6–6**

5. Click **OK**.

   ***Note:*** *If any restrictions occur with a selected file, the property is neither added nor removed and an error message displays.*

# Practice 6a
# Create a New User-Defined Property

In this practice, you will create a new user-defined property (UDP). After the new property is created, you will edit some settings and finally add this property to a selection of files.

## Task 1: Create a new UDP.

1. In the *Tools* menu, select **Administration>Vault Settings**.
2. In the *Vault Settings* dialog box, select the *Behaviors* tab and select **Properties**, as shown in Figure 6–7.

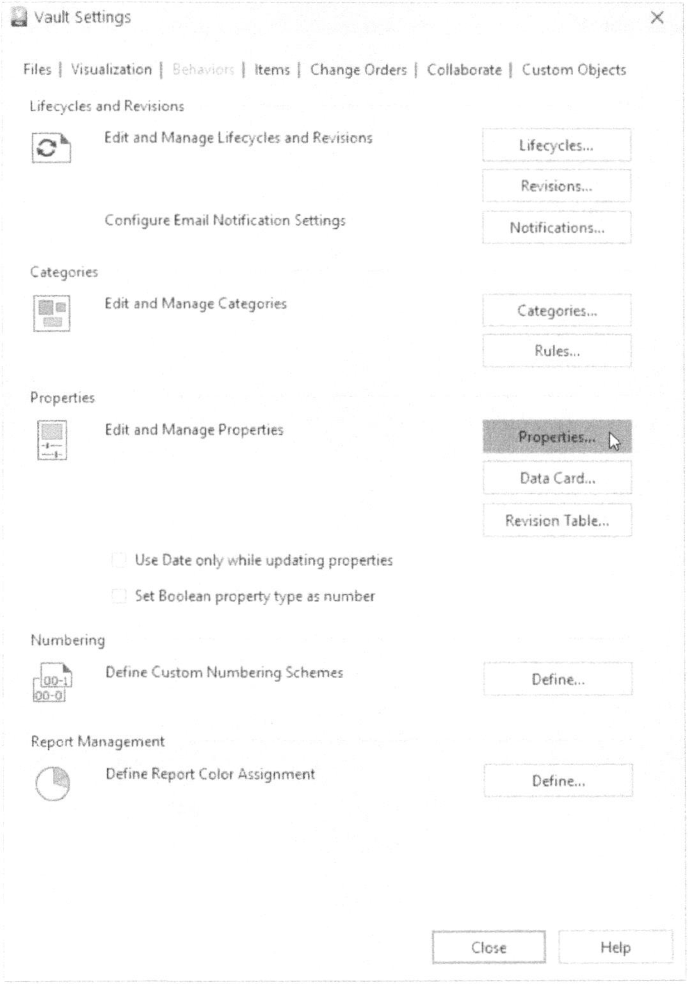


Figure 6–7

3. In the *Property Definitions* dialog box, click **New**.
4. In the *New Property* dialog box, enter: **MyNewProperty**.
5. In the *Type* list, select the **Text** property type.
6. Assign the UDP to one or more categories of your choice by selecting the category checkboxes in the *Associations* drop-down list shown in Figure 6–8. Categories can be preselected in this list based on the filter previously selected in the *Property Definitions* dialog box. You can select or clear categories as required. Click **Close**, then click **OK** to return to the *Property Definitions* dialog box. Click **Close** again to return to the *Vault Settings* dialog box.

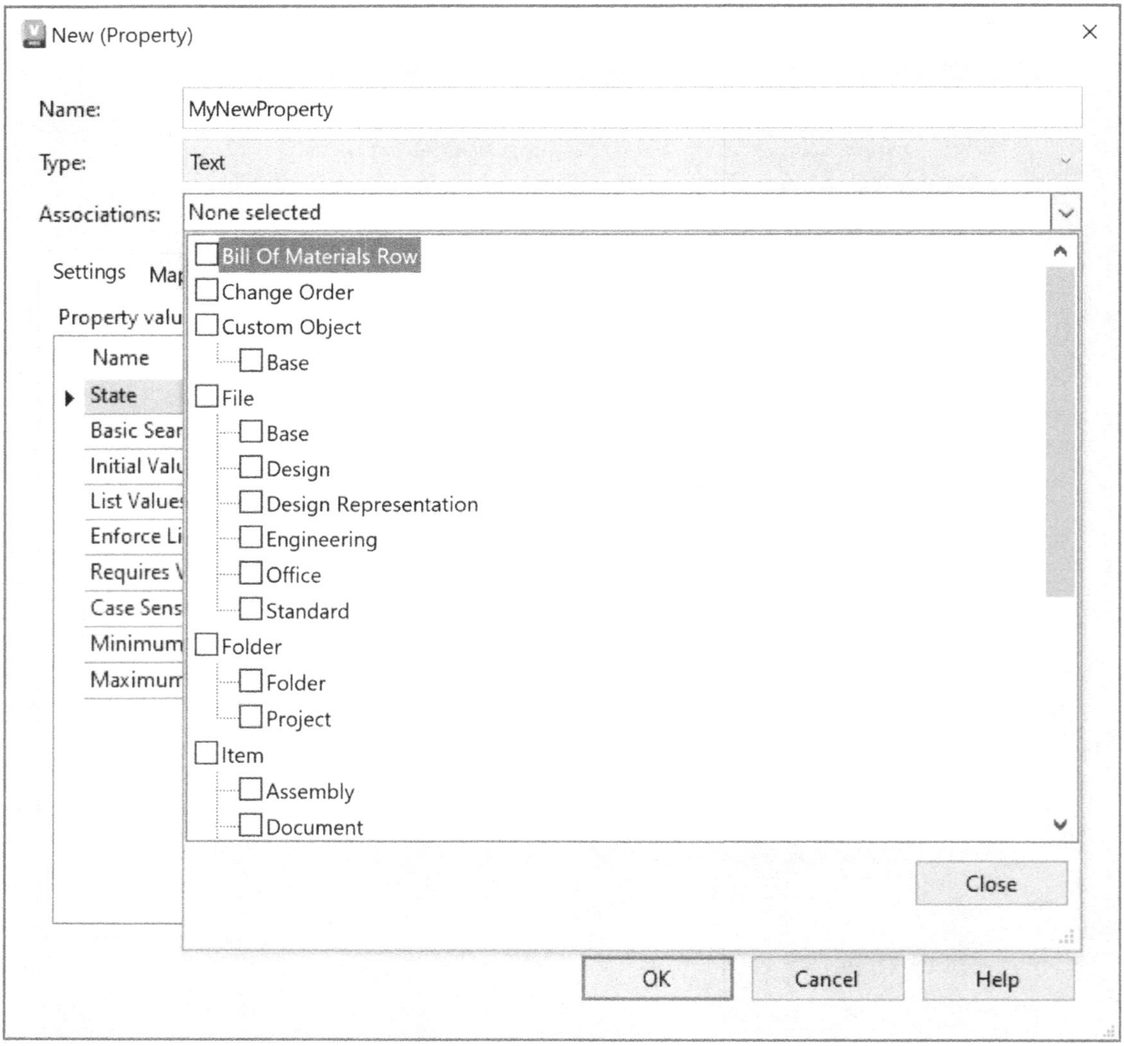


Figure 6–8

## Task 2: Edit the new property.

1. In the *Vault Settings* dialog box, select the *Behaviors* tab and select **Properties**.
2. In the *Properties Definitions* dialog box, select **MyNewProperty** and select **Edit**, as shown in Figure 6–9.

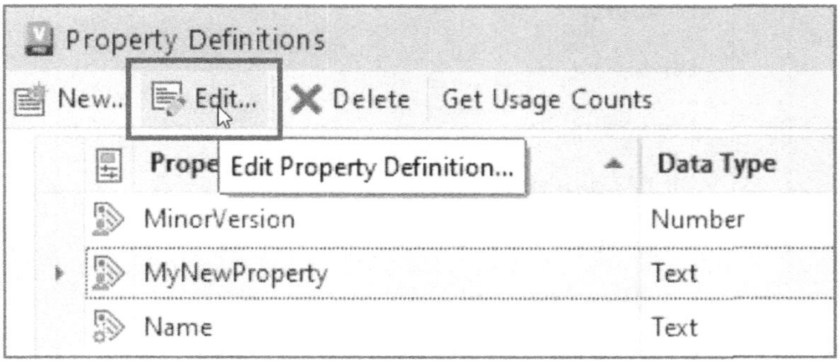


**Figure 6–9**

3. Rename your new property (e.g., change from **MyNewProperty** to **MyEditedProperty**).
4. Modify some other settings like Basic Search, other property values, etc.
5. Click **OK** to save the changes, then click **Close** twice to close the open dialog boxes.

## Task 3: Add/remove properties to files.

1. Select one or more non-released files you want to add the new property to.
2. Select **Actions>Add or Remove Property**.
3. In the *Add or Remove Property* dialog box, search for the new property named **MyEditedProperty**.

4. In the *Action* column, you can select **Add** or **Remove** to add and remove properties, as shown in Figure 6–10.

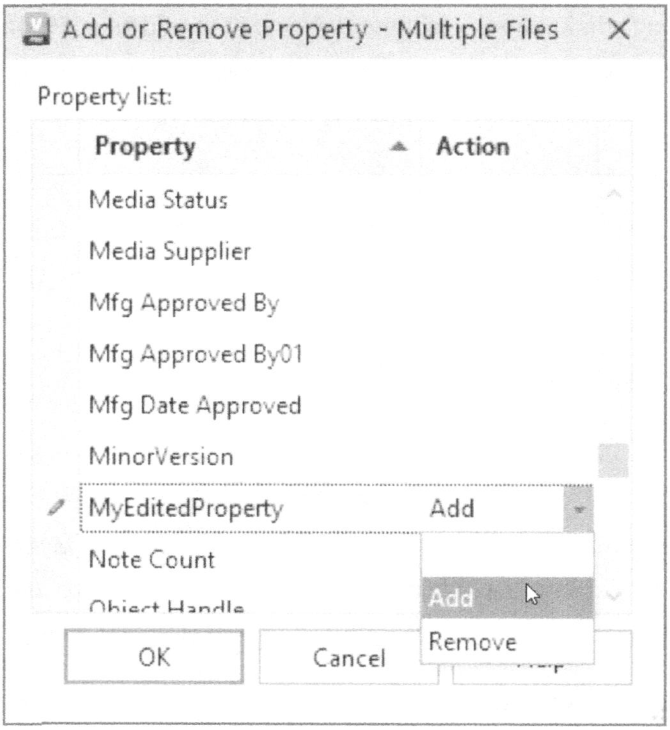


**Figure 6–10**

5. Click **OK** to confirm and save these settings.

**End of practice**

# 6.2 The Properties Grid

You can customize the files in the vault by creating, adding, and removing properties, and modifying property values. The *Properties* grid lists all properties for a selected file. The tab for the *Properties* grid displays at the bottom of the right pane when a file is selected from the file list.

Properties are separated based on whether they are system-defined or user-defined. Collapse or expand each group to review the properties for those definitions.

The *Properties* grid displays the name and value of each property associated with the selected file, as shown in Figure 6–11. You can configure the *Properties* grid to show only certain properties.

> ***Note:*** *System-defined property values cannot be modified. You can only modify values of user-defined properties.*

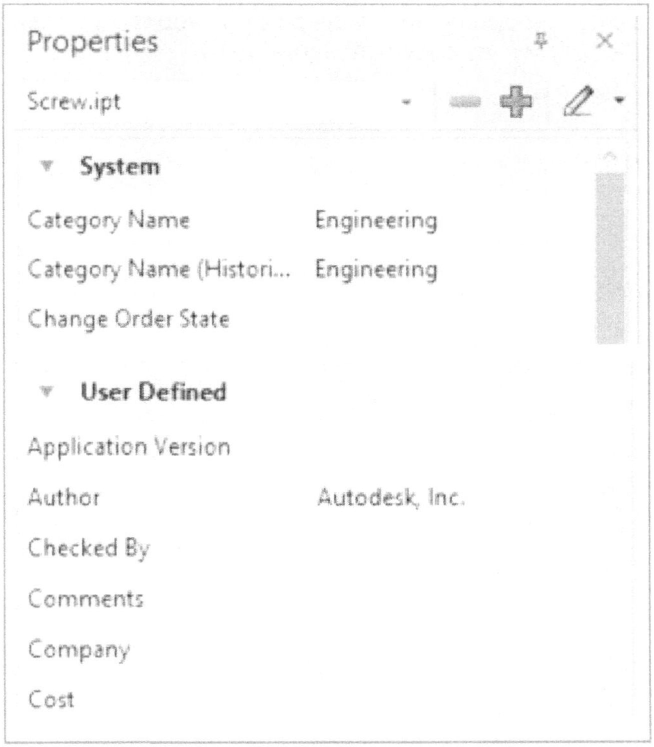


**Figure 6–11**

# Hide/Restore Properties

To hide and restore properties from the grid, there are two buttons in the upper-right corner in grid, as shown in Figure 6–12.

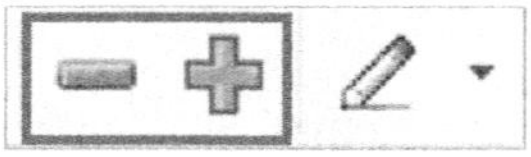

Figure 6–12

## How To: Hide/Restore Properties from the Properties Grid

1. Select a property that should disappear from the grid list. By clicking on the minus symbol (Hide Properties), the property is hidden and can be restored by clicking the plus symbol (Restore Properties).
2. A *Property Filter* dialog box opens. Select the property you want to restore and select **Restore Selected Properties**, as shown in Figure 6–13.
3. All selected properties are restored and available in the grid.

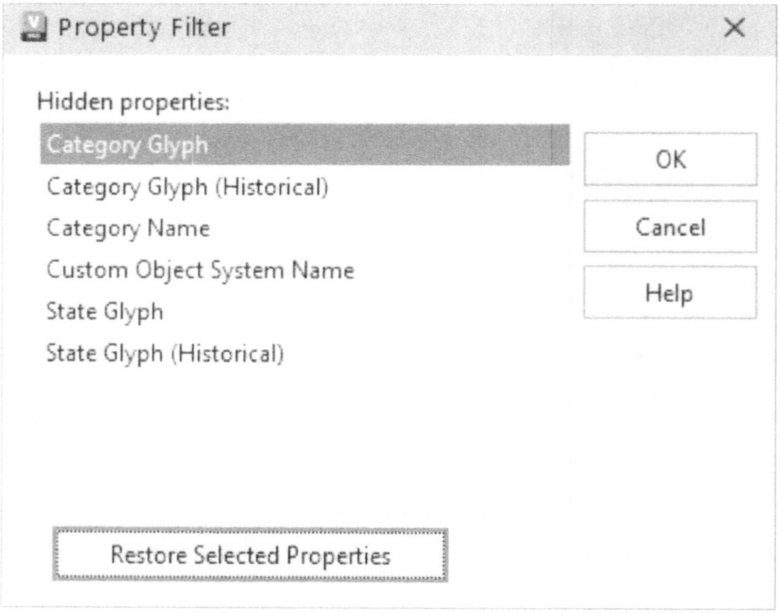


Figure 6–13

- You can make selections on one or more properties and hide/restore them by one click. Conform to the Windows shortcut standards (press <Shift> or <Ctrl> for selection).

 

# Edit Properties from the Grid

User-defined properties in a vault can be edited using the Property Editing wizard. The wizard enables you to select any number of files, regardless of type, and edit their properties. The selected files are checked out, the properties are updated, and then the files are checked back in to the vault.

> ***Note:*** *You must be assigned the role of either Editor or Administrator to perform this action. Contact your vault administrator to verify your role. The files must also be checked in and unlocked.*

Files can be selected from the main pane, the Properties grid, or while in the property editor to have properties edited. You can select multiple files at once to edit properties. For example, you can select an Inventor assembly and all of its children from the *Uses* tab and then use the Property Editing wizard to edit all the properties for the entire design.

For Autodesk Inventor files, including Inventor .DWG files, and Microsoft Office documents, all user-defined properties are available for editing. If a property is missing a value, you can fill it in and it will be added to the file. If the file does not contain the property as a predefined object, then a custom property can be created containing the value.

> ***Note:*** *If using Autodesk Vault Professional, items and change orders can also be selected along with other files for editing their properties in a heterogeneous view.*

## How To: Edit Properties from the Properties Grid

1. Select multiple files (e.g., Autodesk Inventor .IPT files) and open the Properties grid.
2. Select the property (or multiple properties) you want to edit.

3. Selecting the **Edit Selected Properties** command (as shown in Figure 6–14) to open the *Property Edit* dialog box, which enable you to edit the selected properties of the selected files.

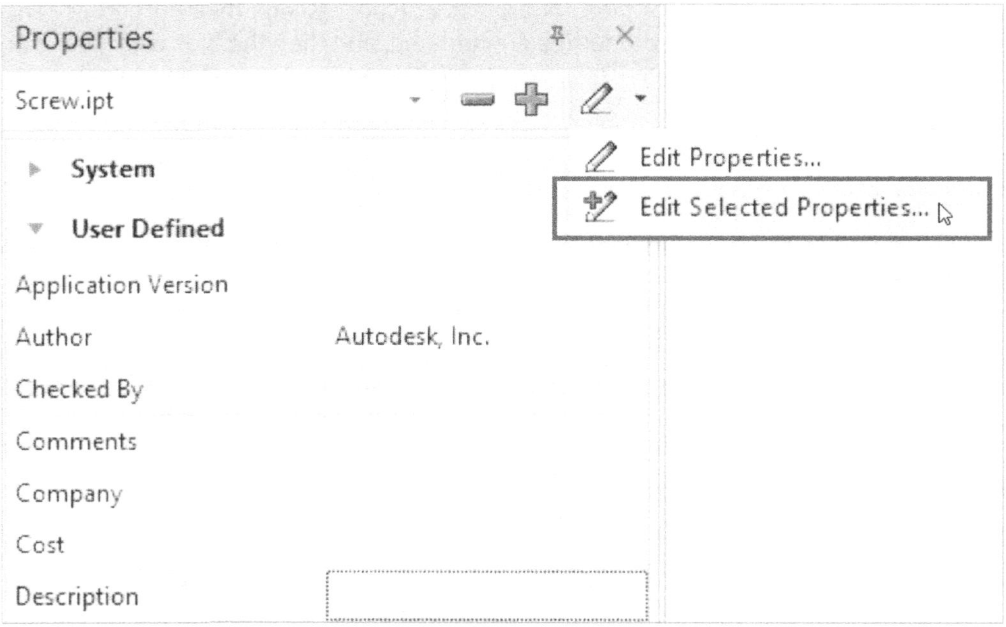


**Figure 6–14**

4. You can edit the properties (as shown in Figure 6–15), then confirm the changes by clicking **OK**.

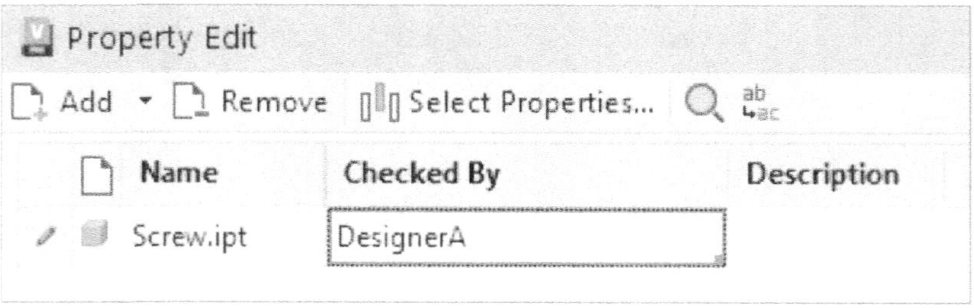


**Figure 6–15**

5. The property values are saved and you will get a confirmation dialog box with the results, as shown in Figure 6–16.

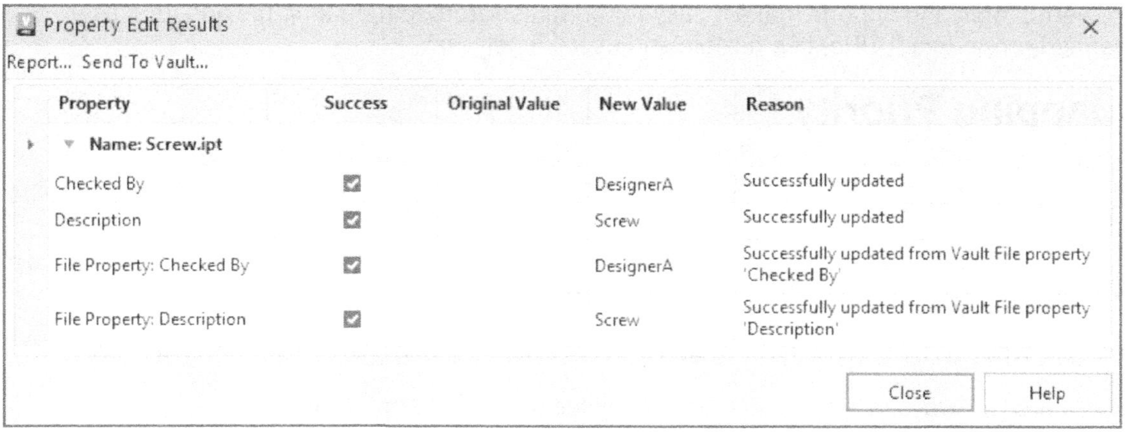


**Figure 6–16**

# 6.3 Mapping Properties

Powerful tools and options make it easy for administrators to map their file and item user-defined properties (UDPs) in a flexible and user-friendly way.

## Mapping Priority

Mapping priority determines the order in which properties are written to a file. If more than one property writes to a particular file, the highest ranking property takes precedence.

You can map properties to a user-defined property so that values from the master file, such as a file property, are written to the subordinate UDP.

### Importing and Exporting Values Between Vault and File Properties

There are two ways in which a file property value is added to the vault:

- Certain file property definitions come with the client and are already included in the vault.
- Adding a file to the vault only captures the values based on the existing mappings. In the case of a mapping that writes to the file, it will only write if the file property field exists, or if the write setting is set to 'create' for a custom property. Otherwise, only property definitions already defined in the vault will be created for the file to reduce extraneous property definitions or duplicates.

## Mapping

To create a property mapping, the administrator must first choose which object group is to be mapped. In Figure 6–17, this is specified under the first column titled *Entity*. The available choices are based on the value of the *Associations* field. Several content providers are included, but in most cases it is best to leave the selection on **All Files (*.*)**. Vault will automatically select the most appropriate content provider based on the file format. Next, select a file that contains the property or BOM field to be mapped. The image below shows the file properties available for mapping in the file **manifold_block.ipt**.

The *Type* column shows the data type of the source property. Mapping can be done across data types. However, there are special considerations that are detailed in the next section. The mapping direction by default will choose bi-directional unless the file or BOM property does not support the input of values. When this occurs, the mapping option will be limited to **Read only**. Read-only mappings should be used sparingly because any UDP that contains only read-only mappings cannot be modified in Vault.

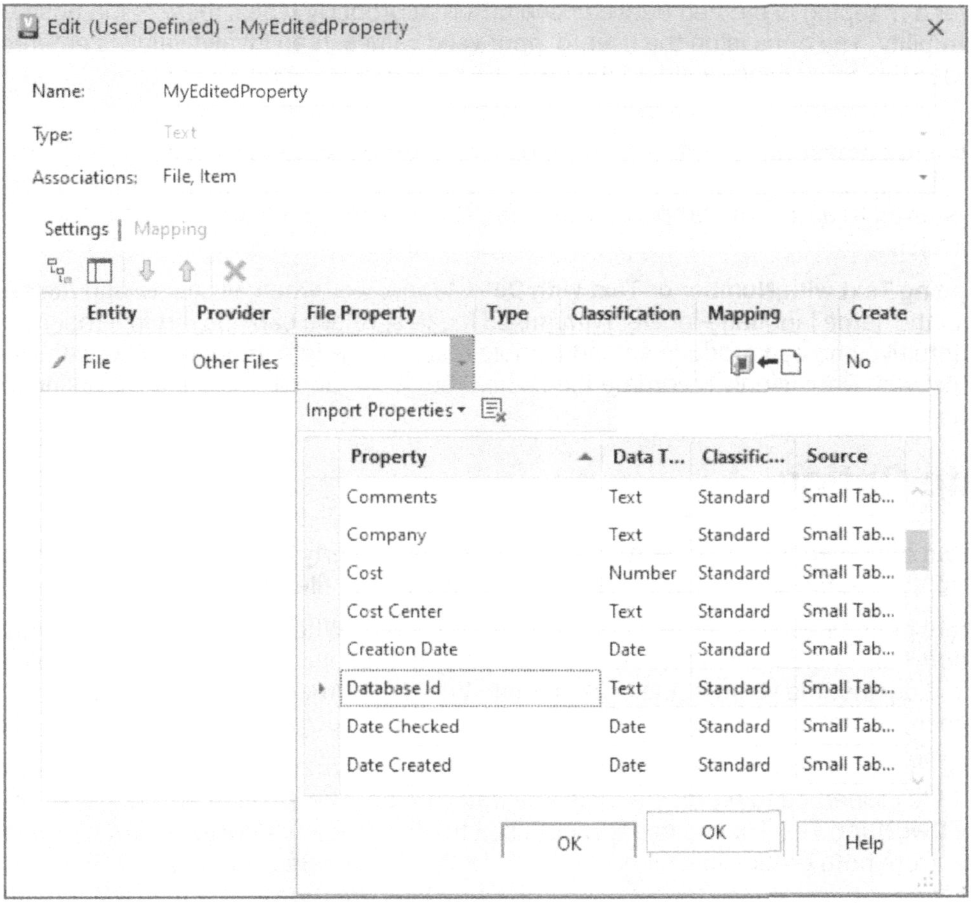


**Figure 6–17**

# Mapping Across Data Types

There are four property types: **Text**, **Number**, **Boolean**, and **Date**. The following matrix defines valid property mappings.

| | **Source Property (File or BOM)** | | | | |
|---|---|---|---|---|---|
| | | Text | Number | Boolean | Date |
| | Text | Yes | Yes(2) | Yes(1) | Yes(2) |
| | Number | Yes(2) | Yes | Yes | No |
| | Boolean | Yes(1) | Yes | Yes | No |
| **UDP** | Date | Yes(2) | No | No | Yes |

Whenever a mapping is created between two different property types, there is the possibility of incompatibility. The onus is on the user to input valid values. If an invalid value is entered, in most cases the equivalence will flag the property as non-equivalent. The exceptions are listed below.

1. **Mapping Boolean with Text:** The supported valid text values are: Yes/No, True/False and 1/0. These values are localized. A string like 'Autodesk' entered in a Text property cannot be transferred to a Boolean property. This property mapping would be flagged as not equivalent.
2. **Mapping Text with Number or Text with Date:** Works well when all clients and the server are in the same language-locale. With mixed locales, values can convert in a manner that is not intuitive and can produce an undesirable result. Therefore, mapping Text with Number or Text with Date is only recommended when the server and all clients are working in the same locale.

# Create Option

The **Create** option applies to write mappings. If the file property does not exist when a value is pushed to the file, the administrator can choose whether the file property is created or not.

The **Create** option has another function that is not obvious. When enabled, the equivalence calculation will consider the absence of the property definition in the file as a blank value and compare it against the value of the UDP in Vault. When the **Create** option is disabled, equivalence will be set to 'Good' when the mapped property definition does not exist in the file.

Example: I have two departments in my organization that both create .DWG files but they use different file properties to represent the same information. The R&D department uses the file property **DwgNum**. The Tooling department uses the file property **DrwNo**. I want to manage all drawings from both groups in a single Vault and with one **Drawing Number** UDP. The correct configuration is to create bidirectional mappings and set the **Create** option to **Off** for both mappings. The result is that a modification of the Drawing Number UDP will write its value back to whichever property exists and it will not create an extra property. , as shown in Figure 6–18

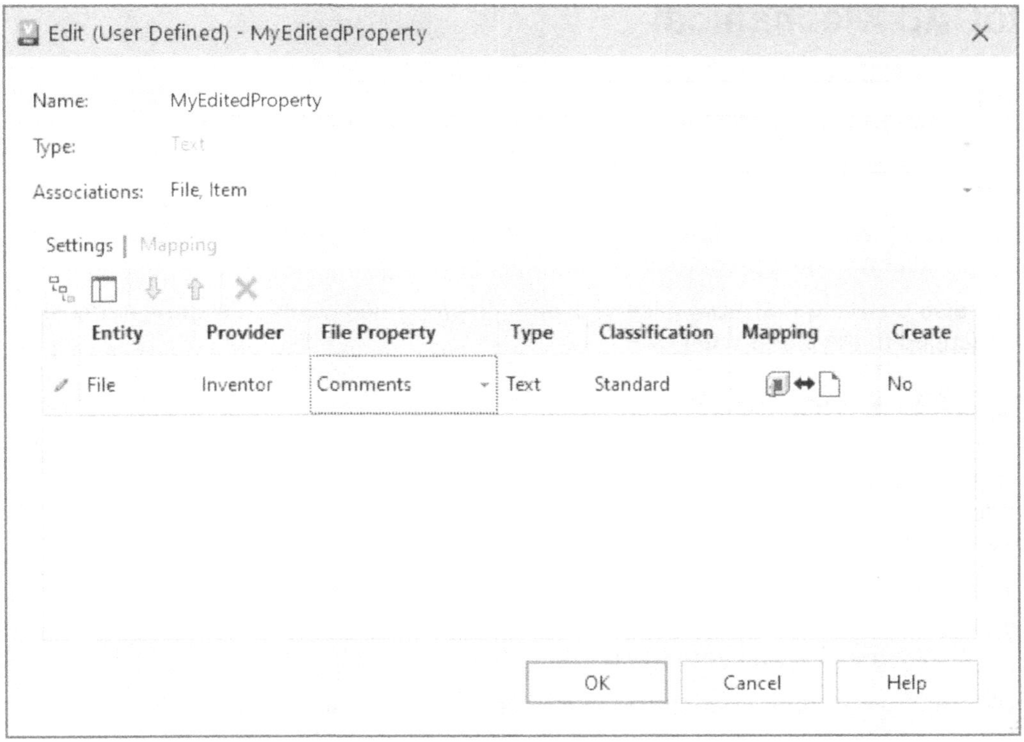


**Figure 6–18**

# Mapping AutoCAD Block Attributes

Autodesk AutoCAD® block attribute mapping requires configuration on the ADMS. Select **Index Block Attributes** from the *Tools* menu in Autodesk Data Management Server Console. Enter the AutoCAD block names from which to extract attributes. Note that the block names are case sensitive. After this is done, it is possible to map a UDP to an attribute using the mapping process described above. Configured mappings enable the system to read and/or write values between the UDP and the attribute.

Usage of attribute mapping is intended for single instances of a block or when all block instances have the same attribute values. It is not possible for multiple block instances to be mapped to separate UDPs. Many companies have one instance of a title block in a given .DWG files. Occasionally, there are companies that use multiple instances of a title block in a single file. In these cases, the attributes often share the same values. An example is a drawing file that contains three borders of different size. Each border uses the same title block with attributes.

The attributes for *Customer Name*, *Engineer*, *Project Number*, etc. will share the same value for all instances. Such attributes that share the same value can be mapped to a UDP. Attributes like *Border Size* will have a unique value for each block instance. Therefore, *Border Size* should not be mapped to a UDP in Vault.

 

# AutoCAD Mechanical

Autodesk AutoCAD Mechanical (ACM) supports three distinct sets of properties, all of which can be mapped to Vault UDPs. The three ACM property sets are file, assembly, and component. See the ACM documentation for details about the intended use and differences between these properties.

Vault file properties can map to ACM file properties and Vault item properties can map to ACM assembly and component properties.

It should also be noted that ACM assembly and file properties having the same name should not be mapped to the same Vault UDP.

# AutoCAD Electrical

Autodesk AutoCAD Electrical (ACE) supports both file and BOM properties. ACE BOM properties can be mapped to Item properties. ACE uses properties located in .DWGs, .WDPs, and associated databases. ACE properties are exposed to Vault in four ways:

- Ordinary DWG™ file properties and block attributes can be mapped to Vault File objects. The majority of these mappings support bi-directional mapping. Creation of these mappings is described in the Mapping section of this document.
- WDP properties support mapping to Item properties. They also support bi-directional mapping. Creating a mapping with WDP properties requires the AutoCAD Electrical Content Source Provider. The provider is specified in the second column of the image at the right. This provider is automatically set when a file of type **.WDP** is selected (as shown in Figure 6–19) under the *File Property* column. If an associated .WDL file has been created, both the line number and the alternate property name will automatically display in the list for selection. You can select the line number or the alternate display name to create the mapping. All WDL properties will display in the list of selectable properties; it does not matter if a value is present.

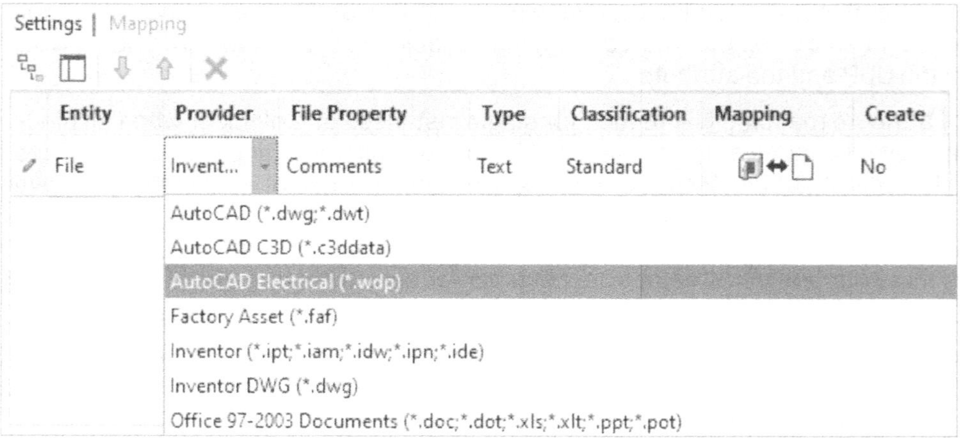


**Figure 6–19**

- Component BOM properties can be mapped to Item properties. This includes properties such as *Catalog Number, Component Name, Component Type, Electrical Type, Equivalence Value, Manufacturer*, etc.
    - To create a mapping to a component BOM property, create a new UDP and associate it to Items. Then, in the *Mapping* tab, create a new mapping, ensuring that the first column *Entity* is set to **Item**. Under the *File Property* column, browse and select any file that contains the property to which you will create the mapping. Some properties require that a value exist or the property is not available for selection in the list.
    - **Reminder:** When creating new properties it is best to associate them to a category, which will automatically associate them to the files and/or items where the property should display. If this is not done, the property will have to be manually associated to the file or item.
- Reference Designator properties, when mapped, will display in Vault as optional data on an Item BOM. There are eighteen Reference Designator properties available: INST, LOC, TAG, DESC1...3, RATING1...12. These properties can be mapped to an Item BOM using the DWG content source provider.
    - To create a mapping to a Reference Designator, create a new UDP and associate it to Reference Designator. Then, in the *Mapping* tab, create a new mapping, ensure that the first column *Entity* is set to **Reference Designator**. Under the *File Property* column, select the DWG containing the Reference Designator to which the mapping needs to be created. All Reference Designators are available for selection in the list without requiring a value.

# Practice 6b
# Map Properties

In this practice, you will learn how to map your newly created user-defined property (UDP).

## Task 1: Create a user-defined property and map it with a file property.

1. In the *Tools* menu, select **Administration>Vault Settings**.
2. In the *Vault Settings* dialog box, select the *Behaviors* tab and select **Properties**. The *Property Definitions* dialog box displays.
3. In this example, the customer is working with SAP as the ERP system. The Inventor file property *Part Number* should be mapped with a new user-defined property called **SAP-ID**. Therefore, create a new UDP with name **SAP-ID**. Click **New** to display the *New (Property)* dialog box and enter the information, as shown in Figure 6–20. Ensure that your *Type* is set to **Number**.

**Figure 6–20**

4. Select the *Mapping* tab.
5. Click in the * **Click here to add a new mapping** field, as shown in Figure 6–21.

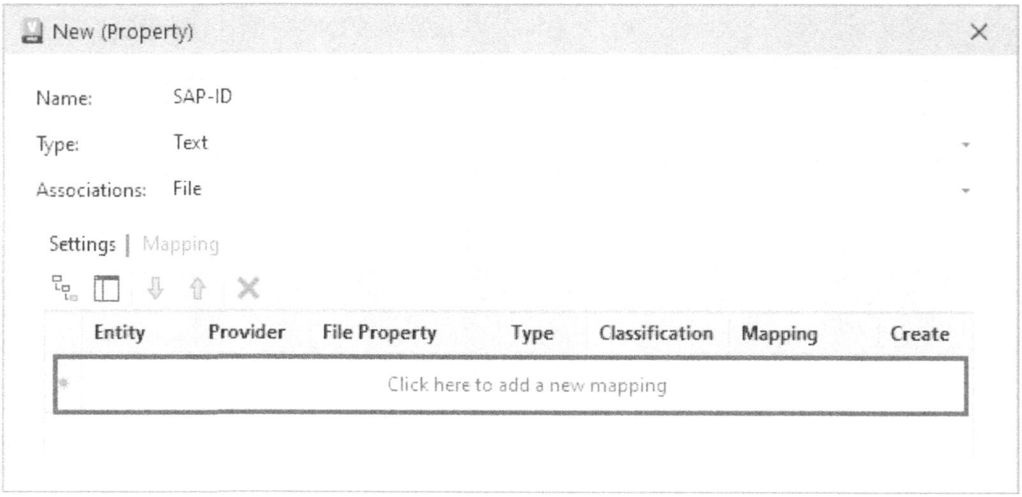


**Figure 6–21**

6. The *Entity* field might auto populate to **File**. If it does not, expand the list and select **File**.
7. The *Provider* field might auto populate to **Other Files**. If it does not, expand the list and select **Other Files**.
8. Click in the field under *File Property* and select **Import Properties**, as shown in Figure 6–22.

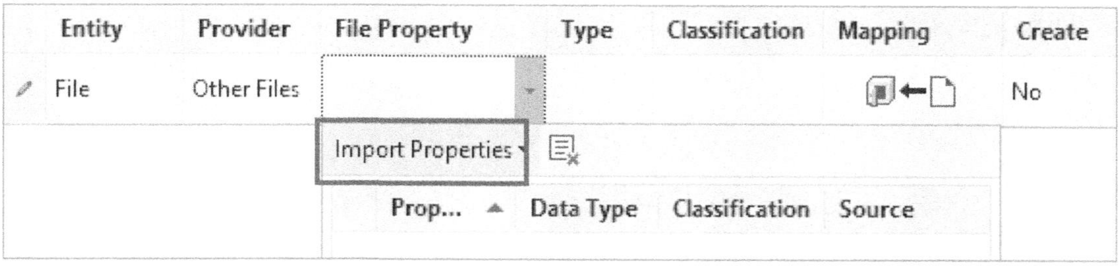


**Figure 6–22**

9. Select **Import From Vault**, as shown in Figure 6–23.

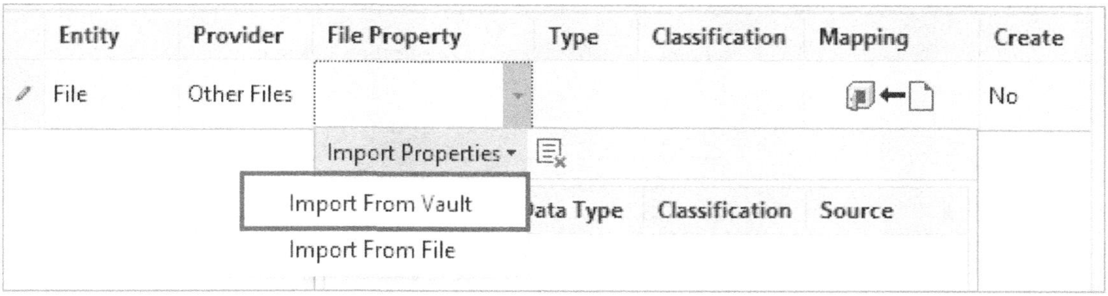


**Figure 6–23**

10. In the *Select File* dialog box, navigate to the *Designs/Clamp* folder. Then select **Clamp.iam** and click **Open**.

11. The *Import Properties* list is updated with the properties available for import from the specified file, **Clamp.iam**. Select **Part Number** from the list, as shown in Figure 6–24.

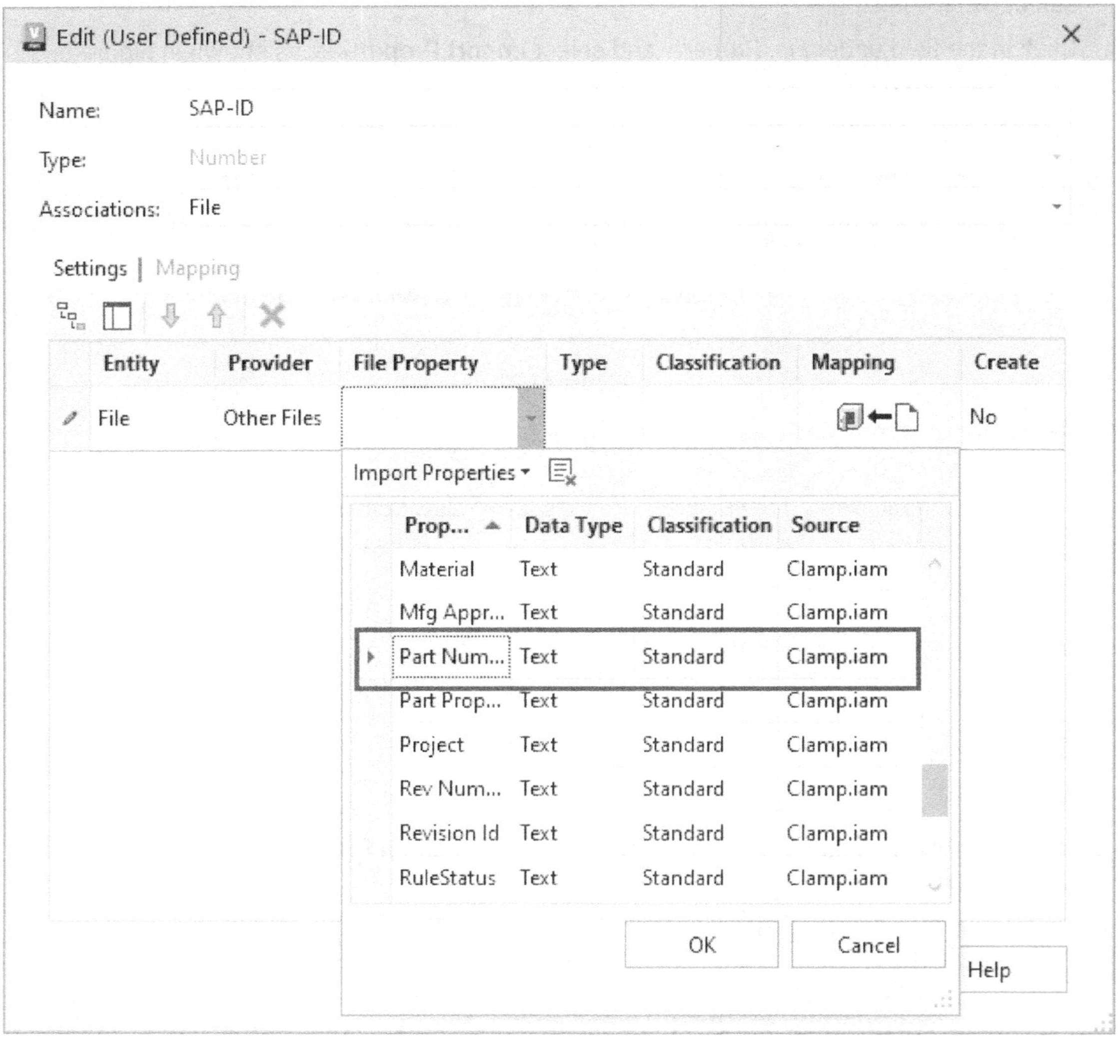


**Figure 6–24**

12. Click **OK** to save the imported property list and create the mapping. The Provider will automatically update to show the provider of **Inventor**, as shown in Figure 6–25.

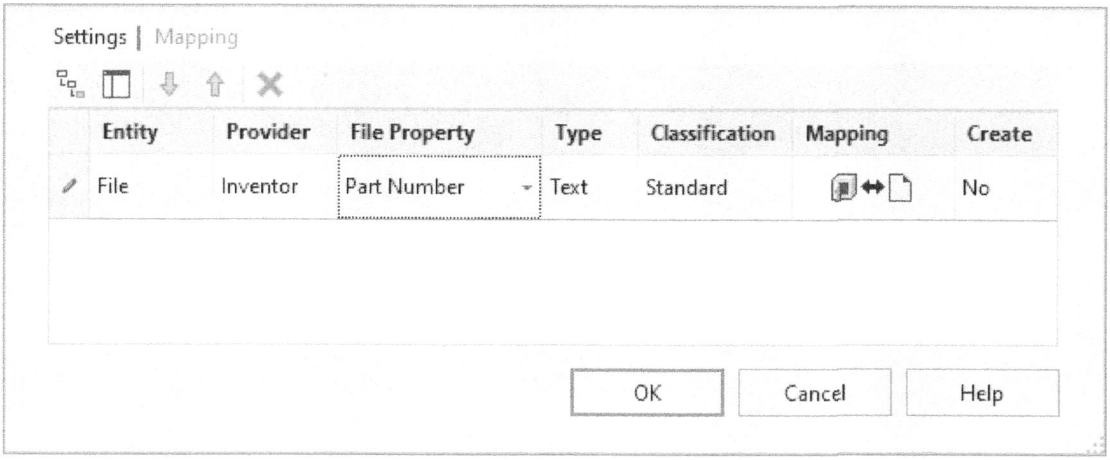


**Figure 6–25**

13. Click **OK**.

*Note: To remove a mapping, select the mapping then click the (Delete) icon.*

14. Optional, create another mapping for the new **SAP-ID** property. Properties at the top of the list take precedence over those lower on the list. You can reorganize the list using the **Move Up** and **Move Down** arrow icons in the *Mapping* tab.

Chapter 7

# Automatic File Naming in Autodesk Vault Professional

The **Automatic File Naming** feature lets you configure how files and items are named when they are added to the vault. You can select from two existing schemes, Mapped and Sequential, or you can create custom numbering schemes using one or more parameters. In this chapter, you will learn how to use and configure automatic file numbering schemes.

## Learning Objective

- Create, edit, and delete custom numbering schemes that automatically create a filename or number on save.

# 7.1 Creating Custom Numbering Schemes

In the Autodesk® Vault Professional software, it is possible to assign a numbering scheme that gives the ability to apply an automatic file naming or numbering on save from a new file created from a template inside of Autodesk® Inventor® or AutoCAD®.

## Define Numbering Schemes

You can select from several existing schemes (Mapped, Sequential, ECO) or you can create custom numbering schemes using one or more parameters.

| | |
|---|---|
| **Mapped** | Numbers are generated based on the user-defined properties mapped to the file or item in the *Map Properties* dialog box. |
| **Sequential** | Numbers are generated sequentially. This is the default number scheme and cannot be edited or deleted. |
| **ECO (if using Autodesk Vault Professional)** | Change order names are generated based on a defined fixed text, a delimiter, and an auto-generated number. |
| **Custom** | Numbers are generated based on a custom design. This feature provides the flexibility to create a numbering scheme where the number carries information about the file. |

## How To: Define the Numbering Schemes for Auto File Naming

1. In the *Tools* menu, select **Administration>Vault Settings**.
2. In the *Vault Settings* dialog box, click the *Behaviors* tab.
3. In the *Numbering* section, select **Define**.The *Numbering Schemes* dialog box is displayed, as shown in Figure 7–1.

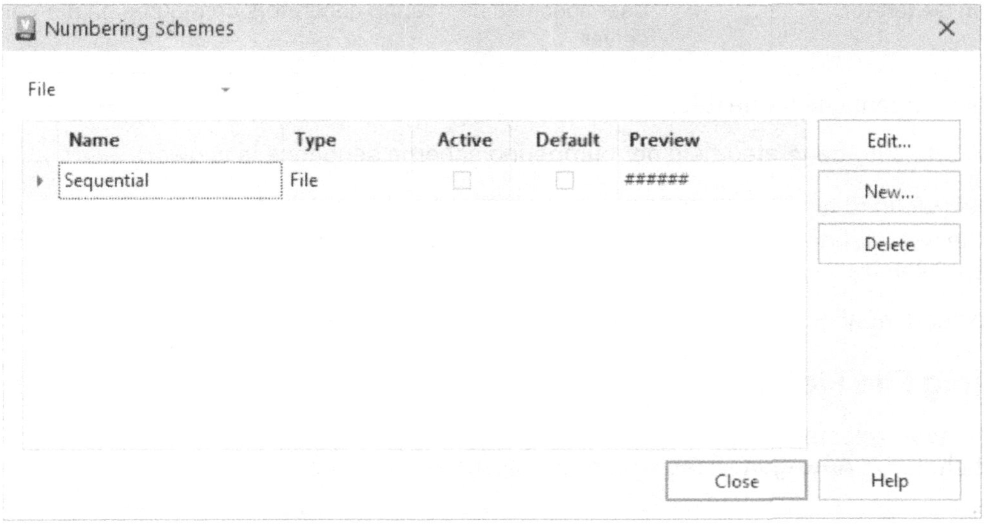


**Figure 7–1**

# Numbering Field Essentials

Each separate part in a file number is called a field. There are six basic fields:

| | Example | Description |
|---|---|---|
| **Autogenerated** | 1001, 1002, 1003 | Creates a sequential file number automatically each time a file is created. No user input is required. |
| **Delimiter** | - | A single character, such as a dash that separates each field. |
| **FixedText** | 2004 | Use this for a value you do not want changed and want to have in each file number. |
| **FreeText** | prototype | Creates a free form field so users can enter additional information. |
| **PredefinedList** | blue, yellow, green | Provides a list of choices to the user each time a file is created. |
| **Workgroup Label** | WG1 | The workgroup ID for the workgroup in which the number is generated. |

## Numbering Generator

There are three types of number generators:

| | |
|---|---|
| **Simple Number Generator** | It produces numbers based on the other information provided in the numbering scheme. |
| **Centralized Number Generator** | It avoids duplicated generated number at the same time in a replicated environment. |
| **Custom Generator** | User-specified numbering generators configured on the Vault server. |

General numbering scheme rules:

- Only one auto-generated field per numbering scheme sequence is allowed.
- A user-defined numbering scheme can only be edited or deleted when it is not in use. That is, the user-defined numbering scheme has not been used or all the objects using it have been deleted.
- The sequential numbering scheme cannot be edited or deleted.

## Defining File Fields

The field type selected in the *Add Field* dialog box determines the available field settings. The default choice is **Auto-generated sequence**, as shown in Figure 7–2.

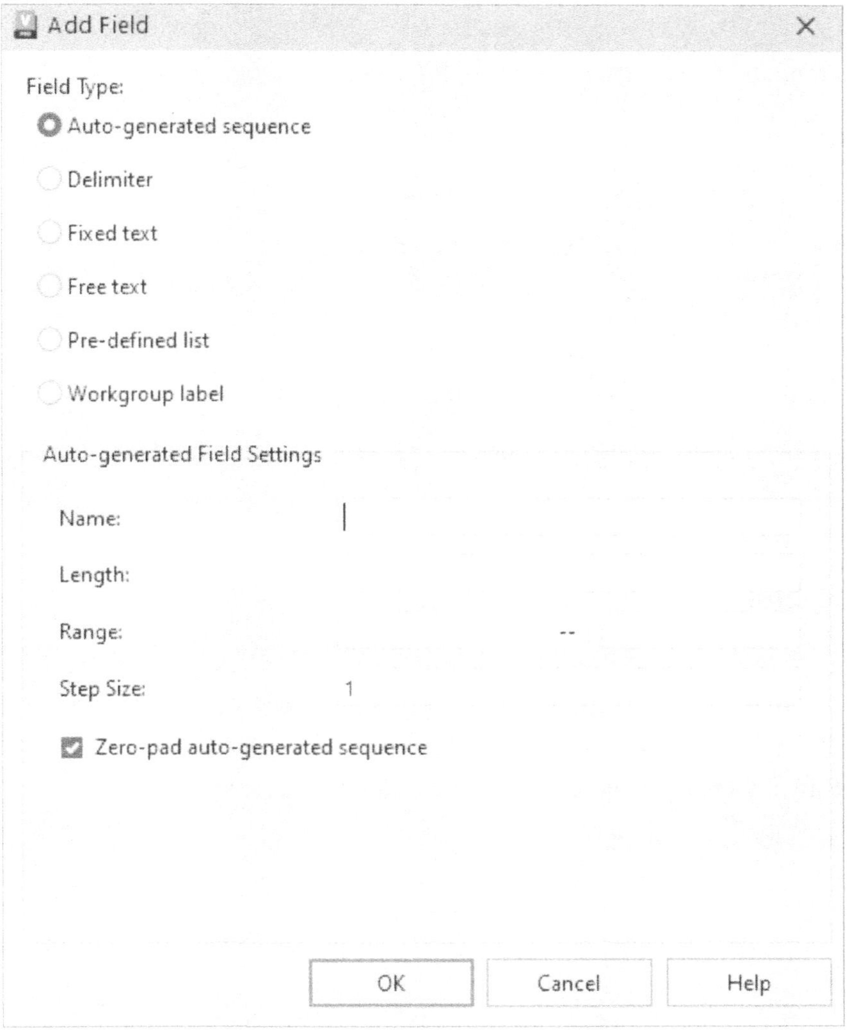


**Figure 7–2**

## Auto-generated Field Settings

- Use the *Name* text box to give a name to the auto-generated field.
- The *Length* determines the number of characters of the *Range* field, and must be a positive value.
- The *Range* specifies the beginning and end of the auto generated number.

  ***Note:*** *The lower limit must be less than the upper limit.*

- *Step Size* controls how the auto-generated number is incremented.

## Delimiter

- The value **must be a character**. The delimiter is used to separate fields.

## Fixed Text

- Use the *Name* text box to give a name to the fixed text field.
- The value entered in the *Fixed Text* field always displays in the file number and cannot be modified by the user.

## Free Text

- Use the *Name* text box to give a name to the free text field.
- *Max Length* controls the maximum number of characters permitted for this field.
- **Max Length required** forces user to enter the number of characters specified in the *Max Length* field. The number length cannot be over 50.

## Predefined List

- Use the *Name* text box to give a name to the predefined list field.
- Specify a list of values in the *Code* field. You can optionally enter a description for each of the values.
- Use **Move up** and **Move down** to change the order of the values.
- Use **Delete** to remove a value.

## Workgroup Label

Selecting this option automatically assigns the workgroup label as a fixed value in the numbering scheme, as shown in Figure 7–3.

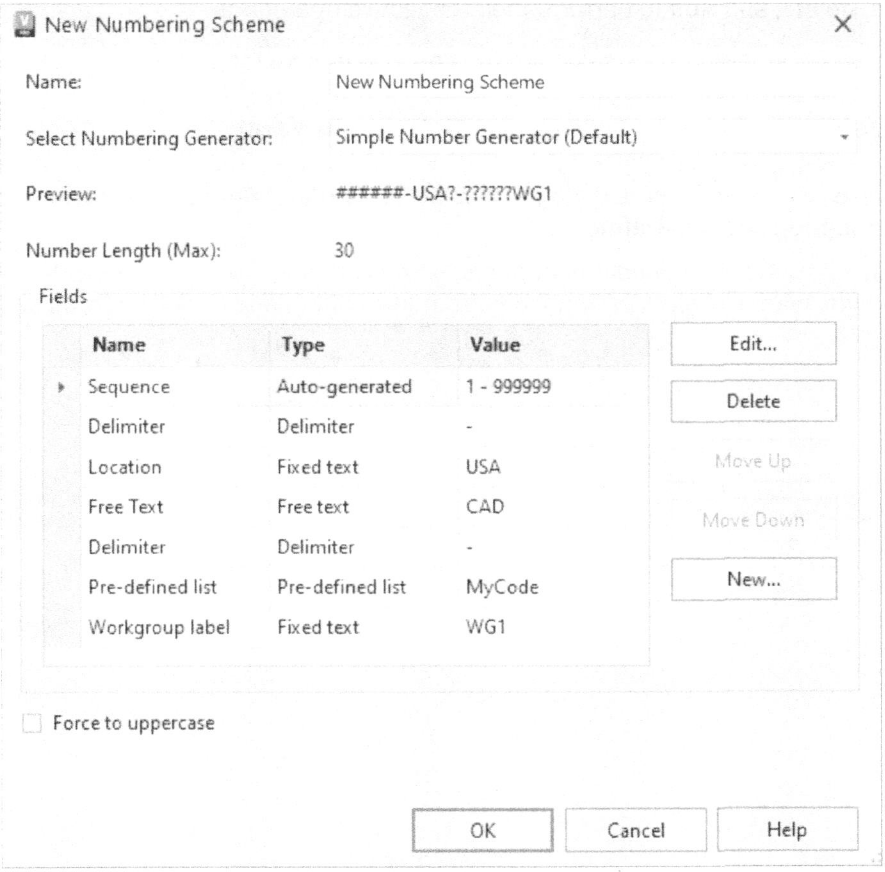


**Figure 7–3**

## Preview and Edit Numbering Schemes

The *New Numbering Scheme* dialog box and the Edit Numbering Scheme dialog box enable you to review and edit a numbering scheme.

- The name displays in the *Name* field. The name of the numbering scheme cannot be modified.
- The *Preview* field displays all fields defined. A field requiring user input displays as a question mark (?). Auto-generated fields display as a pound sign (#).
- The *Number of Digits* field shows the maximum possible file number length.

- The **Append workgroup label** checkbox lets you add the workgroup label to the file or item name. This label is useful in differentiating files between workgroups.
- Use **Move Up** and **Move Down** to change the order of the values.
- Use **Edit**, **Delete**, and **Add** to perform their respective operations.
- Force letters to uppercase by selecting the **Force to uppercase** checkbox.

## How To: Delete an Existing Numbering Scheme in Vault

1. Open the *Numbering Scheme* dialog box using **Tools>Vault Settings>Behaviors tab>Numbering section>Define**.
2. Now you can view all defined numbering schemes in Vault. To delete, select the numbering scheme you want to delete permanently from the system and click **Delete**, as shown in Figure 7–4.

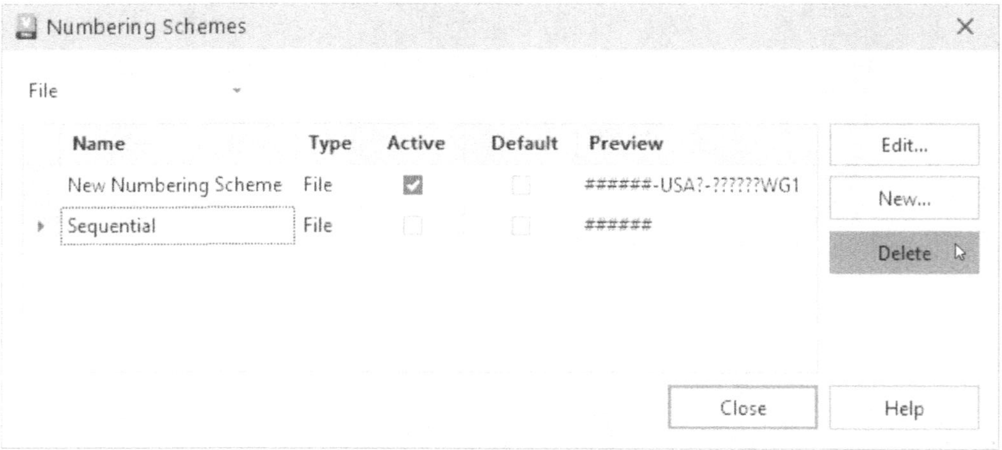


**Figure 7–4**

3. A dialog box opens to confirm the deletion. Click **OK** to delete the scheme permanently.

**Hint: General Numbering Scheme Rules**

- Only one auto-generated field per numbering scheme sequence is permitted.
- A user-defined numbering scheme can only be edited or deleted when it is not in use. That is, the user-defined numbering scheme has not been used or all the files using it have been deleted.
- The sequential numbering scheme cannot be edited or deleted.

# Practice 7a
# Define a Custom Numbering Scheme

In this practice, you will learn how to use numbering schemes. You will manage existing numbering schemes, create and edit new ones, and finally delete the created scheme.

## Task 1: Manage numbering schemes.

1. In the *Tools* menu, select **Administration>Vault Settings**.
2. In the *Vault Settings* dialog box, select the *Behaviors* tab.
3. In the *Numbering* section, select **Define**.

   ***Note:*** *The Numbering Schemes dialog box lists the available numbering schemes. The default numbering scheme is indicated with a checkmark. You can also create new schemes, edit existing schemes, and set the default scheme.*

4. Select whether you want to view **File**, **Item**, **Change Order**, or **All numbering schemes** from the *Filter* drop-down list. Select **File**, as shown in Figure 7–5.

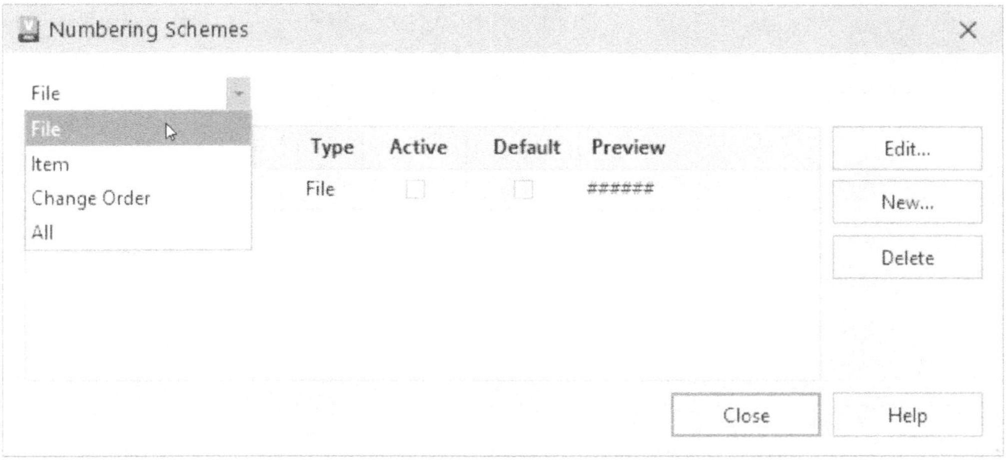


**Figure 7–5**

## Task 2: Create a new numbering scheme.

1. Click **New**.
2. In the *New Numbering Scheme* dialog box, enter the scheme name, as shown in Figure 7–6.

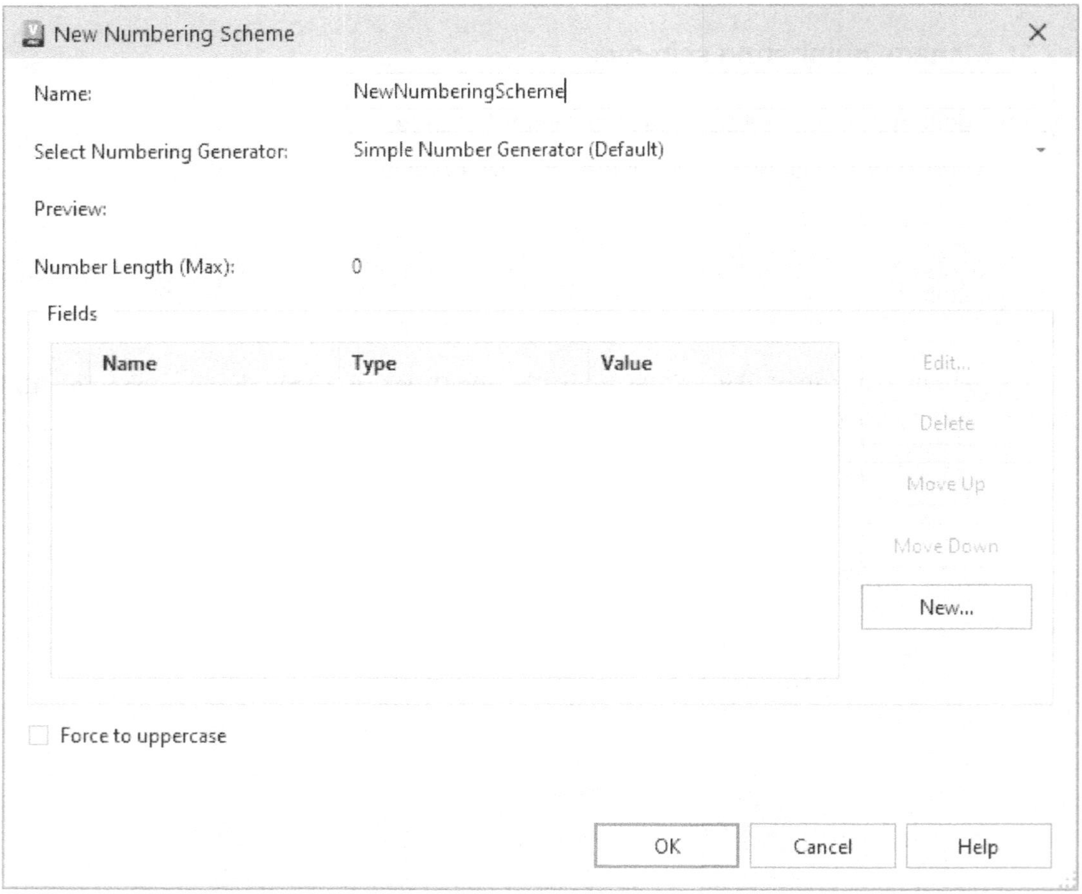


**Figure 7–6**

3. In this step, you will add an *Auto-generated sequence* field to the new number scheme.
    a. In the *New Numbering Scheme* dialog box, click **New**. The *Add Field* dialog box displays.
    b. Click on **Auto-generated sequence**.
    c. In the *Auto-generated Field Settings* area, fill out the information, as shown in Figure 7–7.

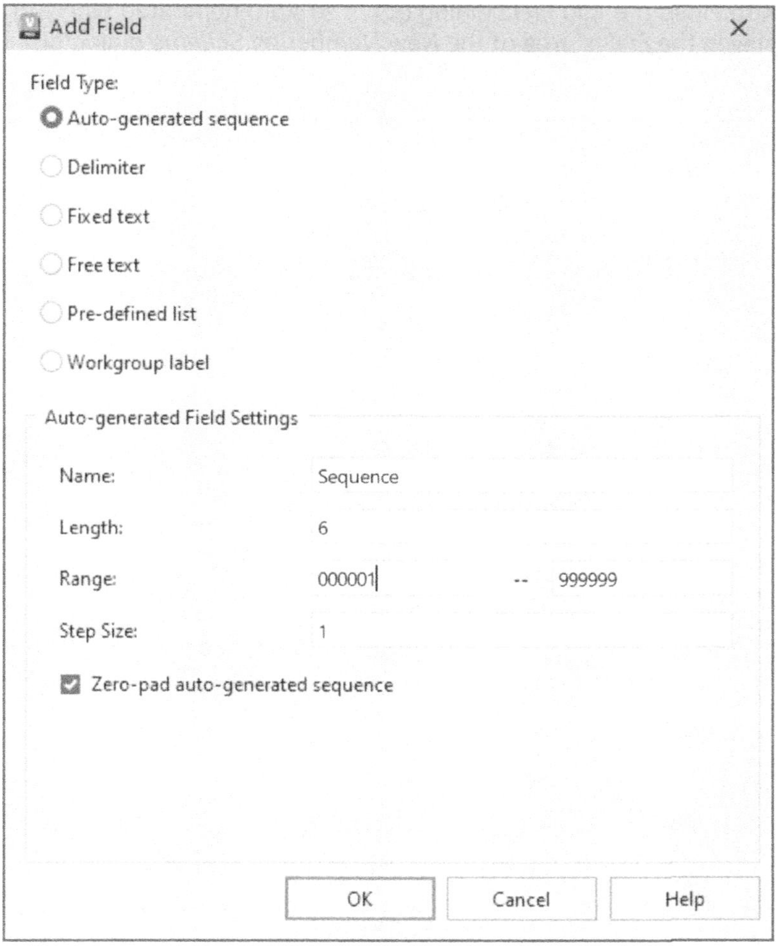


**Figure 7–7**

***Note:***

- The Length must be a positive number.
- The Step Size must be at least 1.
- The auto generated sequence is zero padded by default. To remove zero padding, clear the checkbox. An example of zero padded number is 00001, 000002, 000003.
- There can only be one auto-generated number in the scheme. The *Auto-generated sequence* type will be grayed out in the *Add Field* dialog box once one has been applied to the numbering scheme.

 

**d.** Click **OK** to close the *Add Field* dialog box. The Auto-generated type you just created will display in the *Fields* area of the *New Numbering Scheme* dialog box, as shown in Figure 7–8.

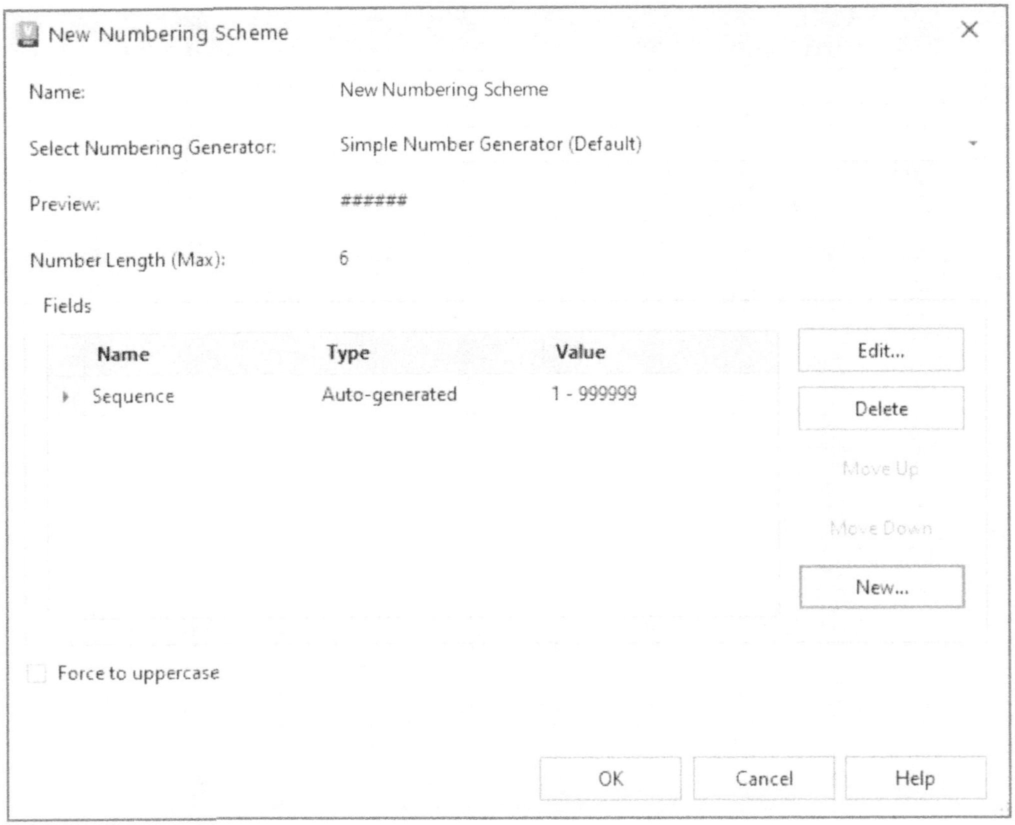


**Figure 7–8**

 

**4.** In this step, you will add a *Delimiter* field to the new number scheme.

**a.** In the *New Numbering Scheme* dialog box, click **New**. The *Add Field* dialog box displays.

**b.** Click **Delimiter**.

**c.** In the *Delimiter Field Settings* area, for *Delimiter Value*, enter: **–** (hyphen), as shown in Figure 7–9.

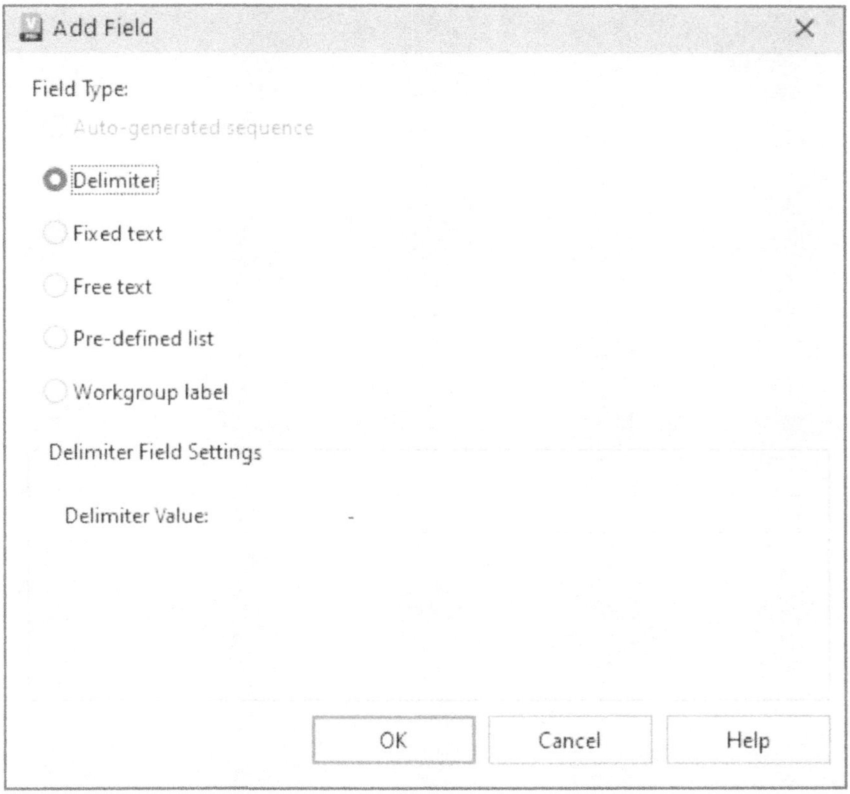


**Figure 7–9**

***Note:*** *The delimiter must be a character, such as hyphen or underscore, to separate the fields.*

**d.** Click **OK** to close the *Add Field* dialog box.

5. In this step, you will add a *Fixed text* field to the new number scheme.
    a. In the *New Numbering Scheme* dialog box, click **New**. The *Add Field* dialog box displays.
    b. Click **Fixed text**.
    c. In the *Fixed Text Field Settings* area, fill out the information, as shown in Figure 7–10.

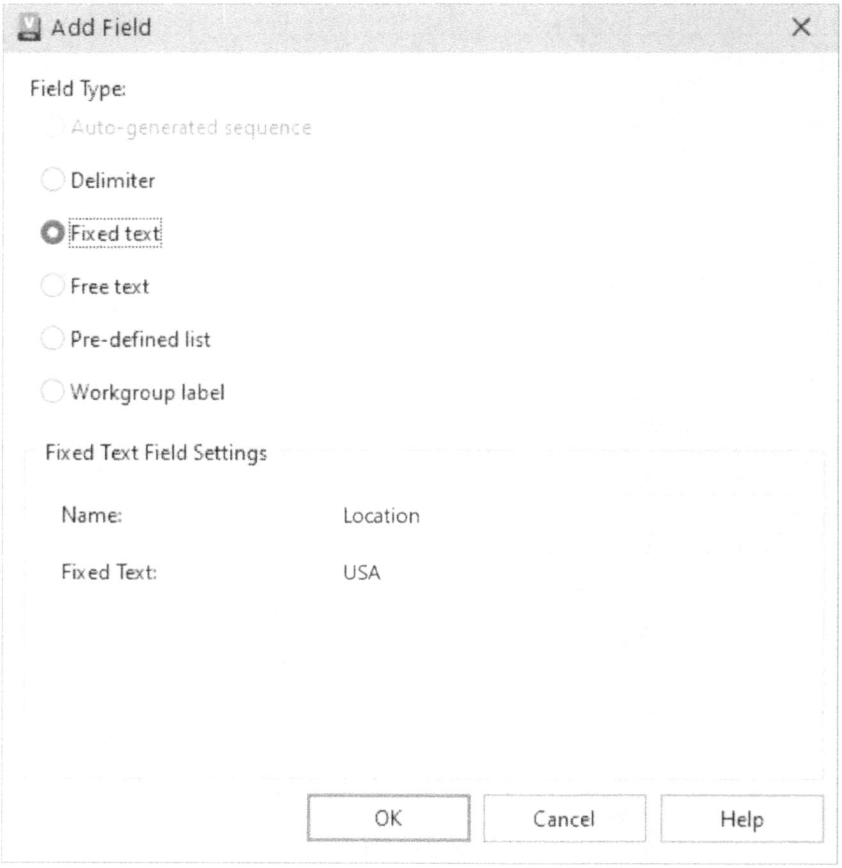


**Figure 7–10**

*Note:*

- The value entered in the *Fixed Text* field is constant and cannot be edited.
- The value cannot exceed 50 characters.

    d. Click **OK** to close the *Add Field* dialog box.

6. In this step, you will add a *Free text* field to the new number scheme.
    a. In the *New Numbering Scheme* dialog box, click **New**. The *Add Field* dialog box displays.
    b. Click **Free text**.

c. In the *Free Text Field Settings* area, fill out the information, as shown in Figure 7–11.

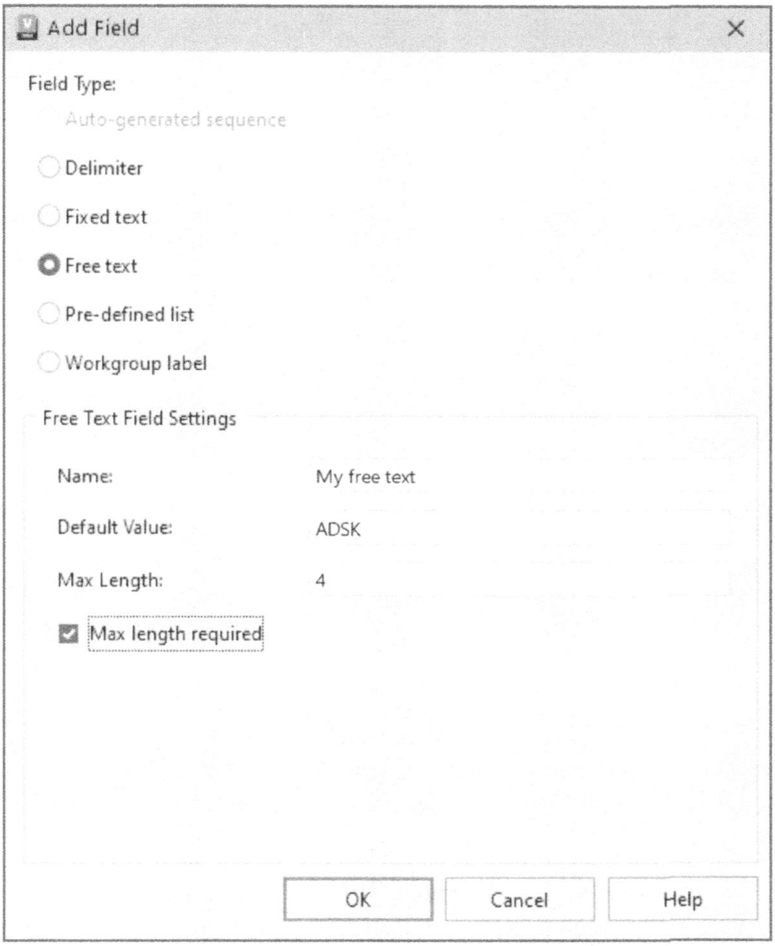


**Figure 7–11**

***Note:***

- The *Default Value* is what will be automatically populated when a user applies this numbering scheme.
- Select the **Max length required** checkbox to fix the length of the field to the value specified in the *Max Length* field.

d. Click **OK** to close the *Add Field* dialog box.

7. In this step, you will add another *Delimiter* field to the new number scheme.

a. In the *New Numbering Scheme* dialog box, click **New**. The *Add Field* dialog box displays.

b. Click **Delimiter**.

c. In the *Delimiter Field Settings* area, in the *Delimiter Value* field, enter: **–** (hyphen), as shown in Figure 7–12.

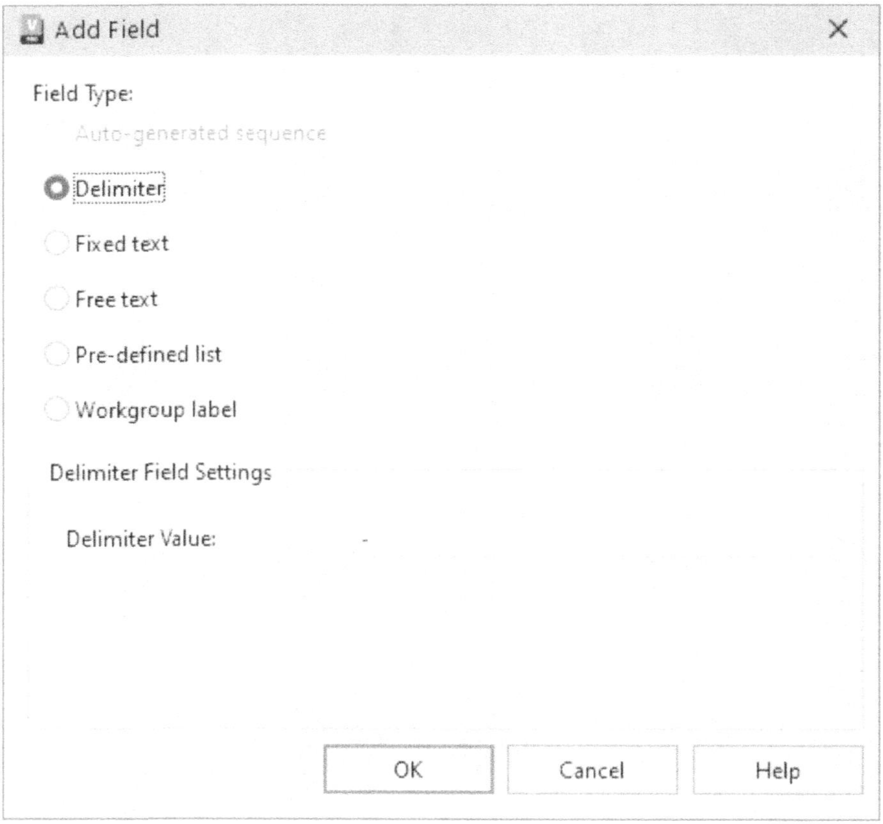


**Figure 7–12**

d. Click **OK** to close the *Add Field* dialog box.

8. In this step, you will add a *Predefined list* field to the new number scheme.
   a. In the *New Numbering Scheme* dialog box, click **New**. The *Add Field* dialog box displays.
   b. Click **Pre-defined list**.
   c. In the *Name* field, enter: **Pre-defined List**.
   d. In the *Predefined List Field Settings* area, click in the *Code* field and *Description* field to fill out the information, as shown in Figure 7–13.

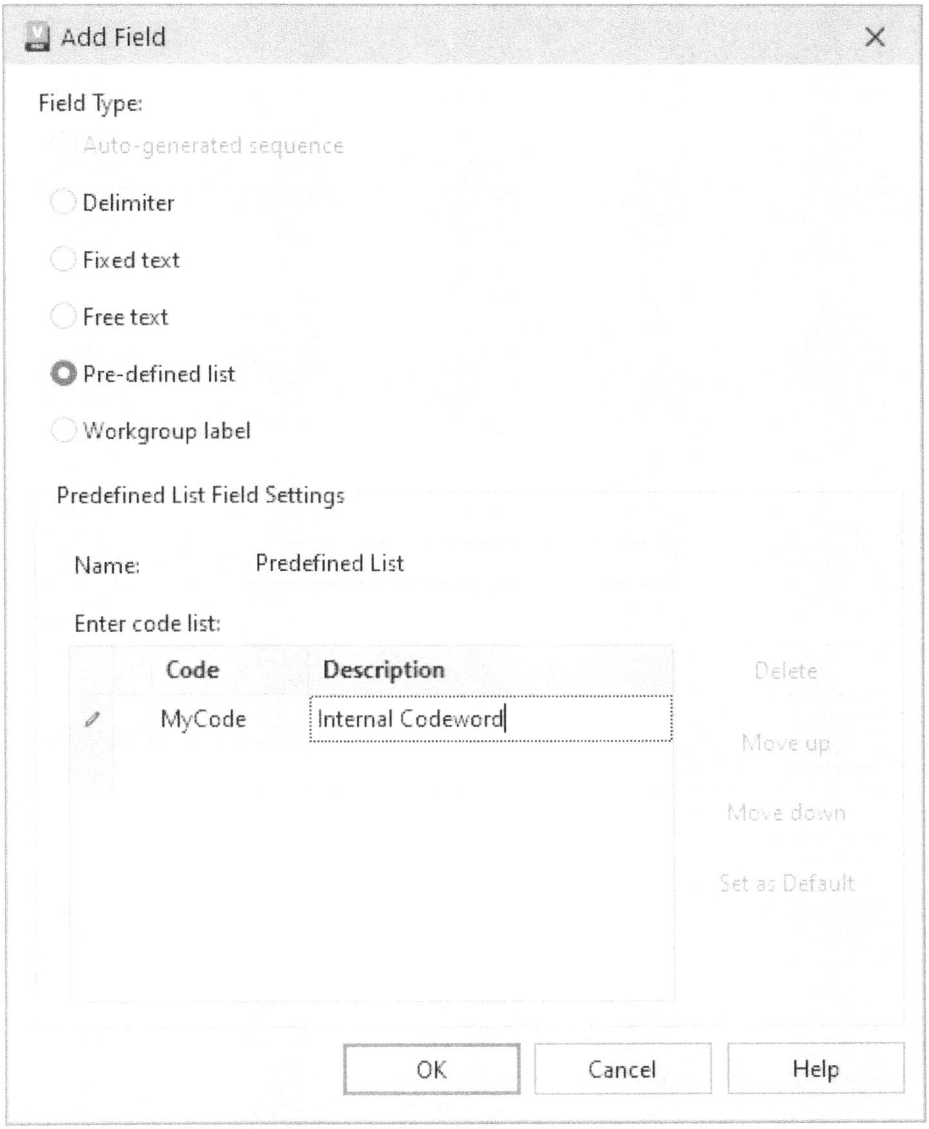


**Figure 7–13**

e. Press <Enter> then select the *MyCode* row and click **Set as Default**. A checkmark displays next to the *MyCode* row, as shown in Figure 7–14.

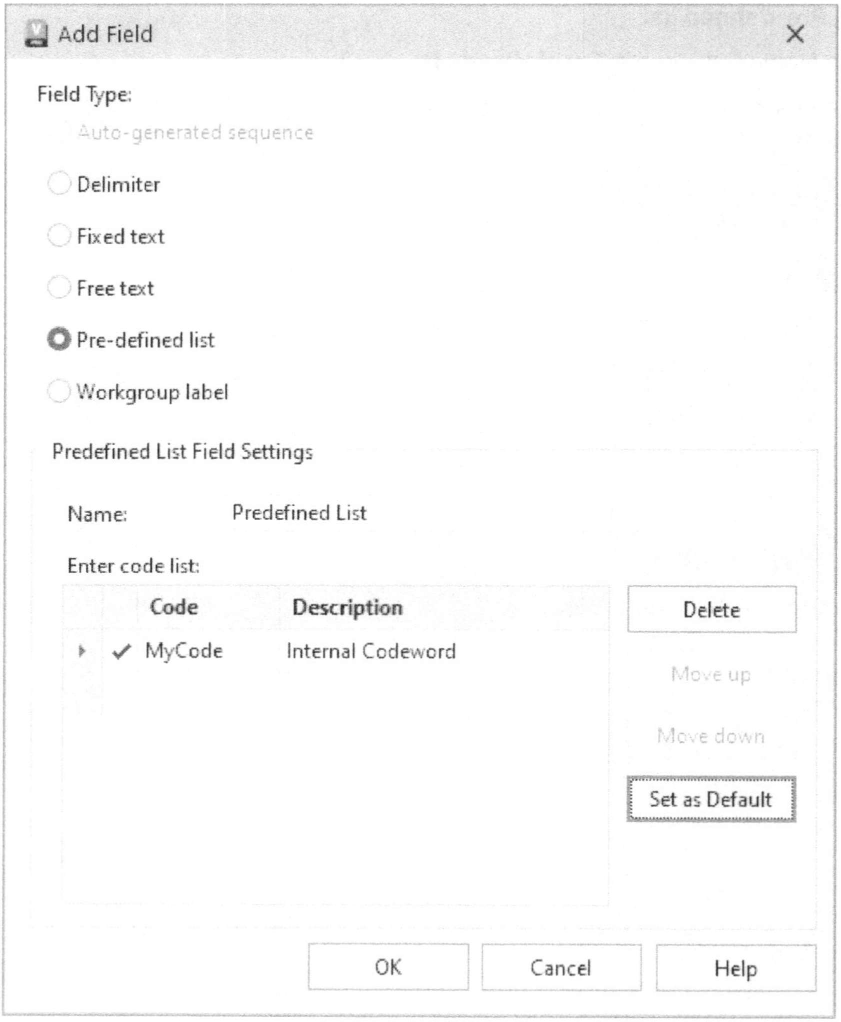


**Figure 7–14**

f. Click **OK**.

***Note:***

- If you have more than one code list, you can highlight the value you want to reorder and click **Move up** or **Move down** to change the order.
- To delete an entry, highlight a value and click **Delete**.

g. Click **OK** to close the *Add Field* dialog box.

9. In this step, you will add another *Delimiter* field to the new number scheme.
   a. In the *New Numbering Scheme* dialog box, click **New**. The *Add Field* dialog box displays.
   b. Click **Delimiter**.
   c. In the *Delimiter Field Settings* area, in the *Delimiter Value* field, enter: **–** (hyphen), as shown in Figure 7–15.

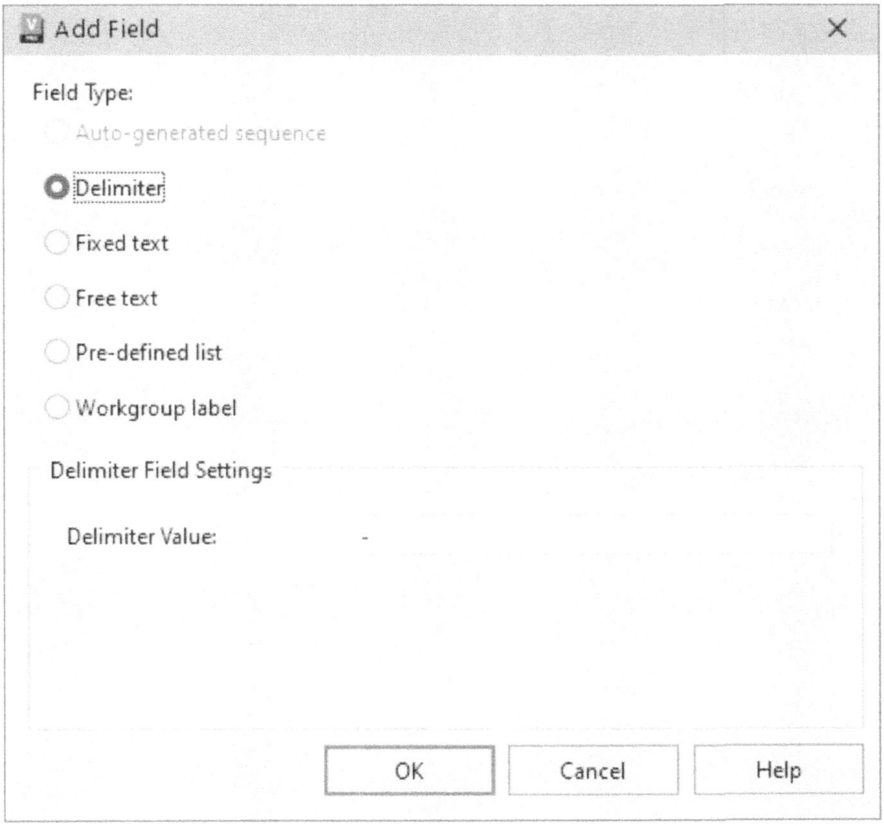


**Figure 7–15**

   d. Click **OK** to close the *Add Field* dialog box.

**10.** In this step, you will add a *Workgroup label* field to the new number scheme.

a. In the *New Numbering Scheme* dialog box, click **New**. The *Add Field* dialog box displays.

b. Click *Workgroup* label.

c. In the Workgroup label Settings area, the information is automatically populated, as shown in Figure 7–16.

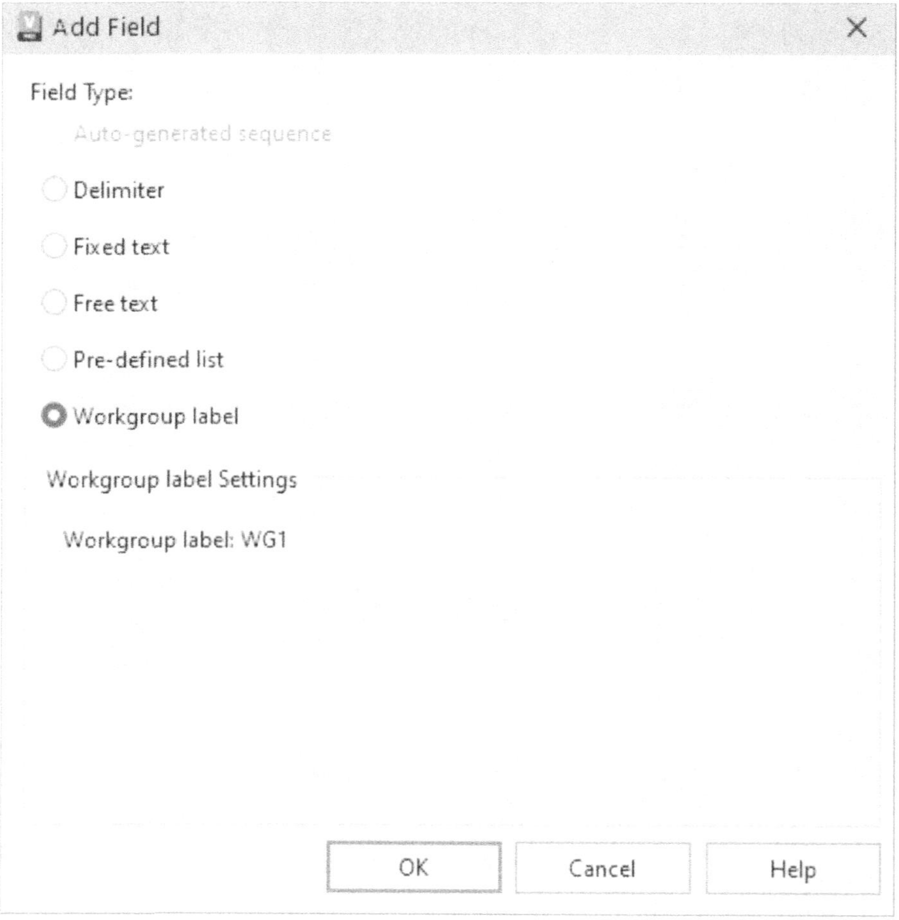


**Figure 7–16**

d. Click **OK** to close the *Add Field* dialog box.

**11.** Review the fields in the *New Numbering Scheme* dialog box. It should look like as in Figure 7–17.

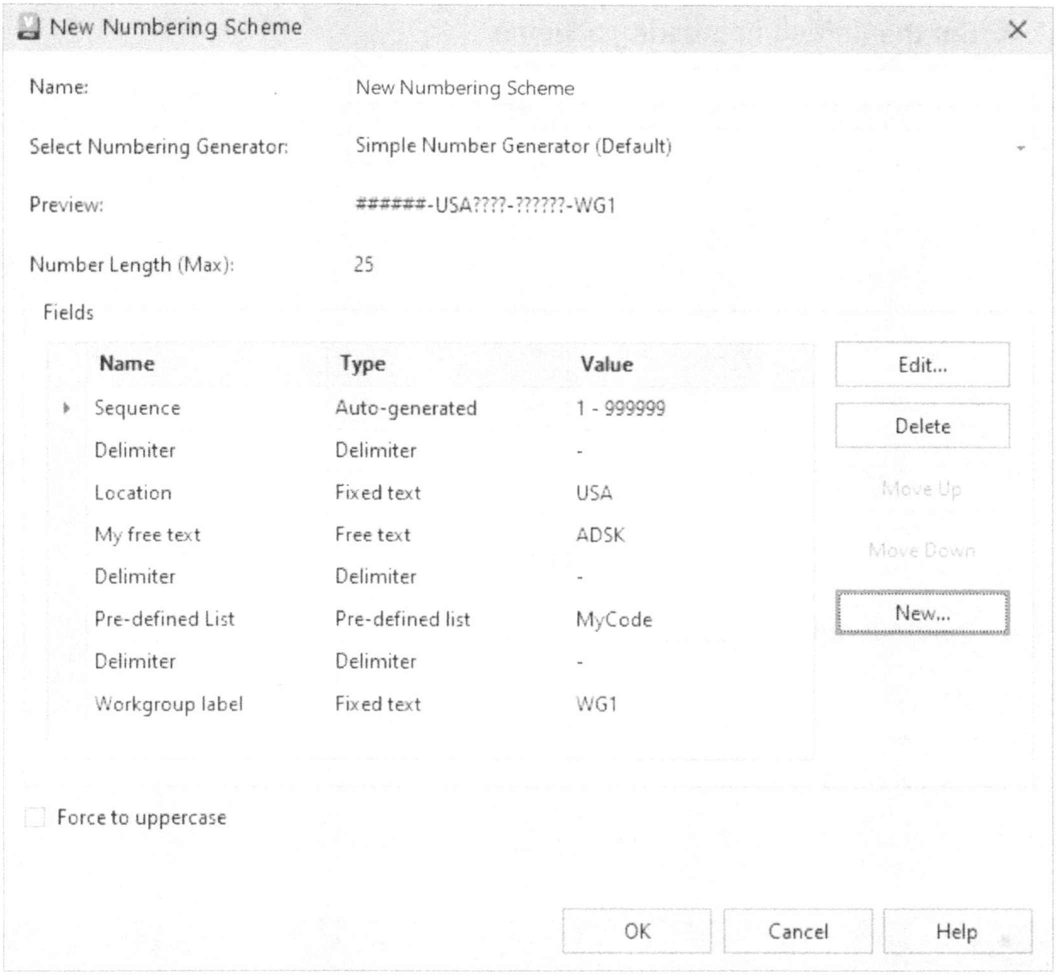


**Figure 7–17**

12. Click **OK** to close the *New Numbering Scheme* dialog box and return to the *Numbering Schemes* dialog box.

## Task 3: Edit an existing numbering scheme.

Only numbering schemes that have not been used by a file can be edited, with the exception that in-use schemes can have their ranges increased.

1. Select a numbering scheme from the list.
2. Click **Edit**.
3. In the *Edit Numbering Scheme* dialog box, change the values for the selected numbering scheme.
4. Click **OK**.

## Task 4: Set the default numbering scheme.

1. Select the numbering scheme you just created from the list.
2. Click the **Default** and **Active** checkbox, as shown in Figure 7–18.

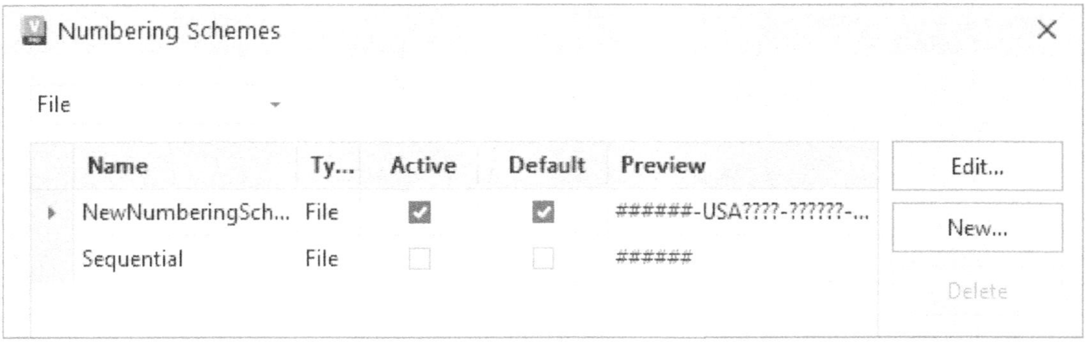


**Figure 7–18**

## Task 5: Delete a numbering scheme.

Only schemes that are not in use can be deleted.

1. Select a numbering scheme from the list.
2. Click **Delete**.

   ***Note:*** *You cannot delete a default scheme. Select another scheme to be the default before deleting it.*

**End of practice**

 

# Practice 7b
# Create a New Autodesk Inventor File Numbering Scheme

In this practice, you will create a new Autodesk Inventor part and save it from within the Autodesk Inventor software to the Autodesk Vault software. The new part will be created with the new numbering scheme you created.

## Task 1: Create a number scheme.

1. Complete the steps in *Practice 7a: Define a Custom Numbering Scheme* to create a default numbering scheme.

## Task 2: Create an Inventor component and save it to Vault.

1. Open Autodesk Inventor.
2. In the *Vault* tab > *Access* panel, click **Log in**.
3. In the *Log In* dialog box, do the following:
    - For User Name, enter: **administrator**
    - For Password, keep it blank
    - For Vault, select **AOTCVault** from the drop-down list, or click on the ellipses to access a list.
    - Click **OK** to login.
4. Set the project file.
    a. In Inventor, access the *Projects* dialog box (Quick Access toolbar or Home page).
    b. In the *Projects* dialog box, click **Browse**.
    c. In the *Choose project file* dialog box, navigate to *C:\Vault Professional Admin\Working Folder* and double-click on **Designs.ipj**.
    d. Click **Done** to close the *Projects* dialog box.
5. Create an Inventor part file.
    a. Click **New** in the Quick Access toolbar.
    b. In the *Create New file* dialog box, select the **Standard.ipt** file template.
    c. Start a 2D sketch and select a plane.
    d. Draw a circle and extrude it.

6. Save the file (<Ctrl>+S). The *Generate File Number* dialog box displays automatically as shown in Figure 7–19.

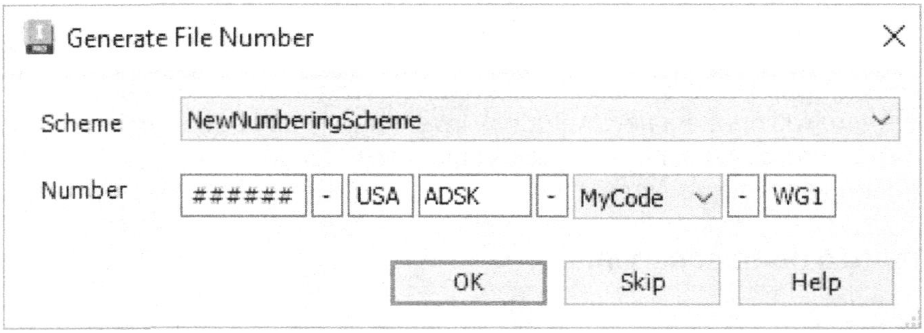


**Figure 7–19**

*Note: The **New Numbering Scheme** is the default scheme listed.*

7. Click **OK** to accept the default. The *Save As* dialog box displays with the *Designs* folder as the *Save In* location and the File Name will be auto populated with the numbering scheme format.
8. Click **Save**.
9. In the Vault Browser, right-click, and select **Check In** as shown in Figure 7–20.

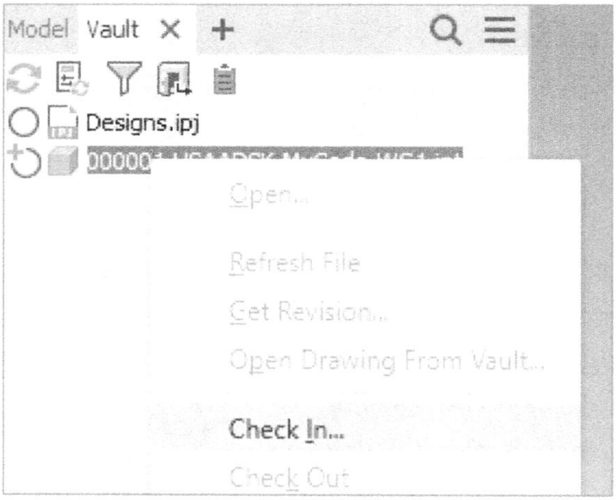


**Figure 7–20**

**10.** Open Vault, navigate to the Project Explorer and then the *Designs* folder and the new file should display, as shown in Figure 7–21.

**Figure 7–21**

**End of practice**

Chapter

8

# Working with Items

This chapter describes how to create and manage items in Autodesk® Vault Professional. You can assign items to CAD files in the vault or create new items for products not specifically modeled in CAD.

Items are used to represent the design data, but a large collection of items can be difficult to manage in the vault. By using customized views and filters, you can sort or filter the item list based on item properties to manage the items effectively.

## Learning Objectives

- Create, modify, and delete items, use filters to view items, and add and remove file attachments.
- Create, modify, and delete custom views, use filters to view items, and find items.
- Work with default item properties and user-defined properties, including item numbers.
- Export item data.

# 8.1 Creating Items

In this section, you learn how to create, modify, and delete items, use filters to view items, and add and remove file attachments.

Use items to help manage your vault data and make that data available to the extended design team. Figure 8–1 displays the *Item Master*.

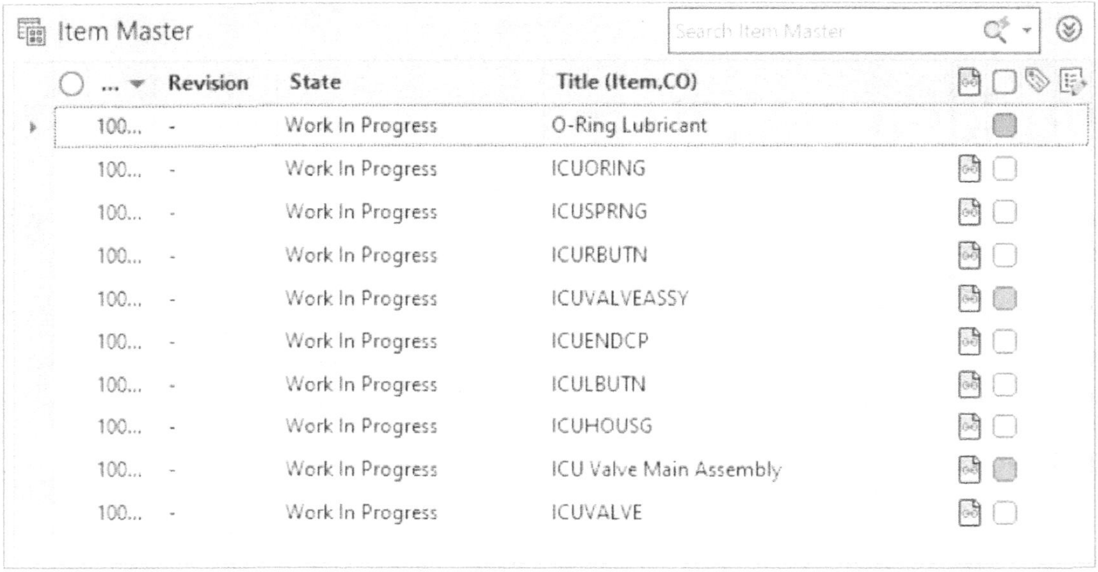


**Figure 8–1**

## About Items

Working with items is a crucial part of automating the data management process and maintaining control of your design data. When a new design is added to the vault, each part or assembly can be assigned an item so it can be clearly identified.

You create items by assigning them to design data from the vault or by creating a new item directly in the *Item Master*.

 

## Definition of Items

Items represent physical elements that a company uses to produce the products it manufactures. Common items include parts and assemblies, documents, consumable goods such as grease, paint, fluids, and lubricants, and even artwork. Some items are purchased while others are manufactured by the company.

An item is identified by a unique identifier (the item number). This number is used to identify the item in change orders, product lists, bills of materials, and ERP systems. Figure 8–2 displays items with their unique identifier (*Number*).

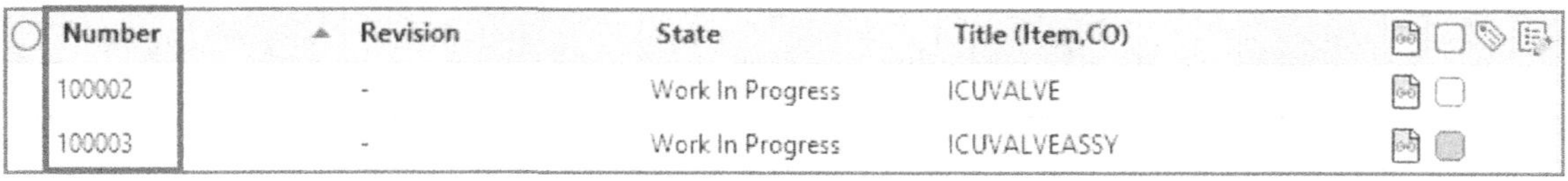


**Figure 8–2**

### Example of Assigning Items

As part of a new design, a new part is added to the vault. You assign an item to the part. The new item has a unique item number, which can be as simple as a six number sequence (Part 100352) or a complex set of text and numbers (Part RD-100-0152).

This item number normally follows company standards and is used to help identify the item. The application uses this number to track the item through its lifecycle.

# Item Master

To manage and track the lifecycle of items used in product development, users are required to access a list of items where they can preview, create, modify, and delete items as required. The *Item Master* is where this list of items is found.

## About the Item Master

The *Item Master* contains a complete list of all items in the Vault. These items usually represent design data in the vault. Items in the *Item Master* are identified by unique identifiers (item numbers). Each item has a number of system and user-defined properties, as shown in Figure 8–3.

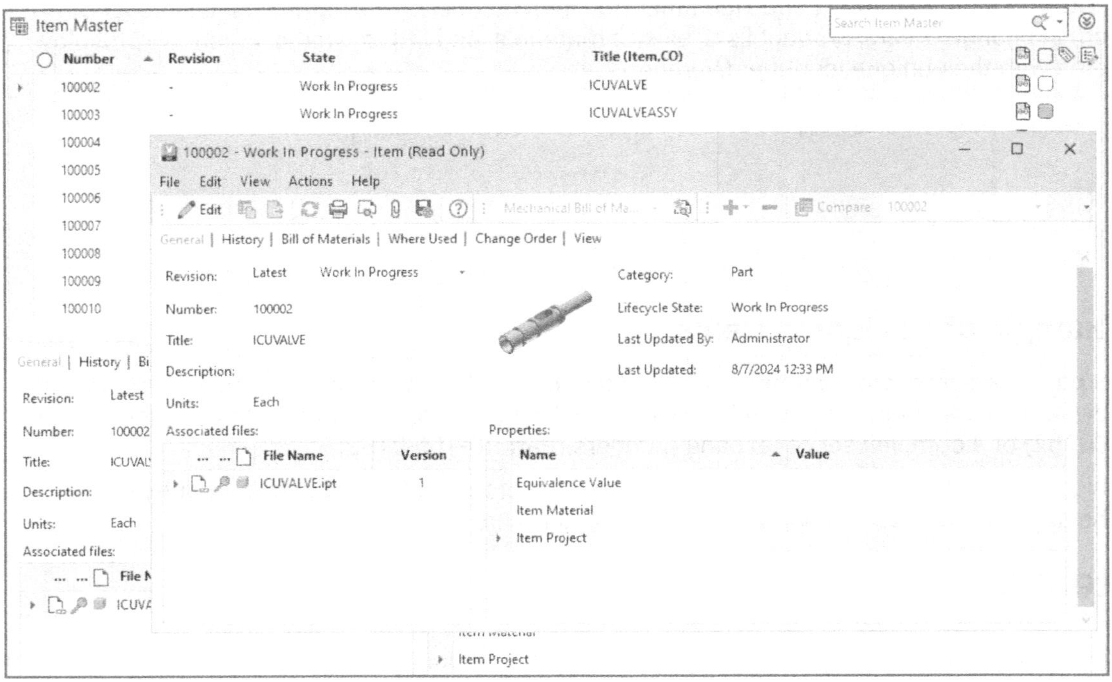


**Figure 8–3**

## Using the Item Master

Using the *Item Master*, you can:

- List all items in the system and define custom views to filter the list.
- Add or remove columns (fields) in the list, change column order and width, and sort by any column.
- Group items by column headings.
- Preview comments automatically.
- Go to a specific item.
- Find an item or items, and optionally save the search.
- Change column text alignment.

- Create new items.
- Edit items.
- Preview items in the *Preview* pane.

## Example of the Item Master

As new designs are added to the vault and assigned items, the *Item Master* list grows, as shown in Figure 8–4.

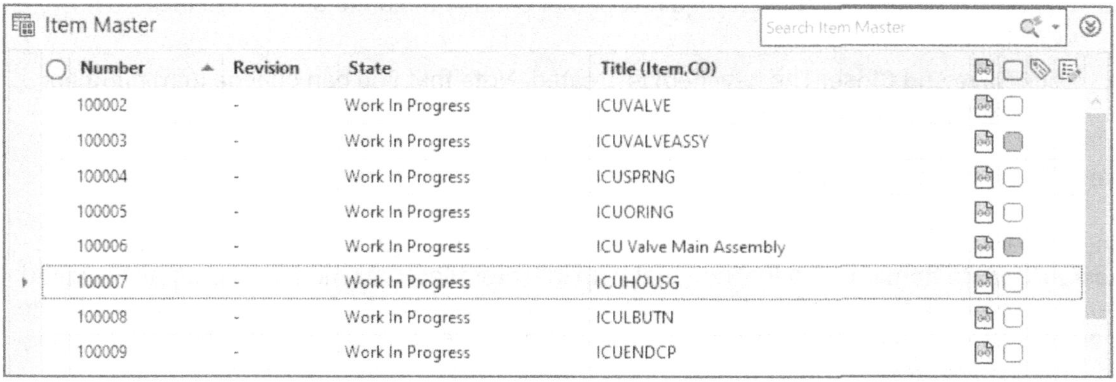


**Figure 8–4**

# Creating Items

Typically when you create items you assign them to data files in the vault. In some cases, you need to create an item that is not modeled in the design. Examples include purchased items or items that are typically not modeled such as lubricants, paint, artwork, or packaging. You can include these items in the *Item Master* by creating new items. Another example would be when you follow a "BOM first" workflow. You create a list of items in the *Item Master* based on what you know about the BOM structure and then fill it in with CAD data at a later time.

Items can be created in the following ways:

- Use the **New Item** command in the *Item Master* to create an item from scratch.
- Assign an item to a file using the **Assign Item** command.
- Drag and drop files into the *Item Master* tab.
- Drag and drop files into the **Item Master** node in the browser.

If an item is in read-only mode, you can use **File>Save As** to copy the item's properties, BOM rows, and attachments to a new item. The new item is automatically added to the *Item Master* and opened in read-only mode. Note that file links are not copied to the new item. For this reason, CAD rows are copied over as manual rows.

## How To: Create New Items

The following steps describe how to create new items using the **New Item** command.

1. Select **Item Master**.
2. In the *Standard* toolbar, click **New**.
3. If the administrator has granted you permission to assign item categories, select a category and click **OK** to continue to the new item record.
4. Review the item properties. If required, add or change the units and add a title and description.
5. Click **Save and Close**. The new item is created. Note that you can change item numbers using **Actions>Change Number**.

## How To: Assign Items to Files in Vault

The following steps describe how to assign items to files in Vault Professional using the **Assign/Update Item** command. Note that with Inventor files, only models should be assigned items. Inventor drawings will automatically be associated to items via their relationship to the models. AutoCAD drawings can be assigned items, as they do not make use of model files.

1. Ensure that all files to which you want to assign an item are checked in to the vault.
2. Select **Project Explorer**.
3. In the main pane, right-click on one or more files and select **Assign/Update Item**. A new item is created for each of the files selected and for the related files.
4. If you assign an item to a single file, the item record automatically opens for editing. Begin making changes, if required.
5. If you select multiple files and assign an item, an item icon displays in the *Item* column. However, you must right-click on a file and select **Open Item** to view the item record. Select **Edit** on the item record toolbar to begin editing. **Note:** Item numbering is automatically applied based on the default numbering scheme. However, if the numbering scheme requires user input, the *Item Number* dialog box opens. Enter the required values and click **OK** to continue.
6. Click **Save and Close** when you are finished.
7. The *Item Master* is updated with the new items. If items were assigned to Autodesk Inventor assembly files, any associated drawing (.IDW) and presentation (.IPN) files are linked to the items. If items were assigned to Inventor part files, the associated drawing (.IDW) files are linked to the items.

   ***Note:*** *When you assign an item to an assembly file, all parts and subassemblies in that assembly must have items assigned as well. Items are assigned automatically to all the required files if they do not have items assigned already.*

 

# Attaching and Detaching Files

When you create an item from a file in the vault, the vault file is automatically attached to the item. You can manually attach additional supporting files such as documents or images. You can add attachments such as drawings for a purchased part, product specification sheets, assembly instructions, regulatory documents, material safety data sheets, rendered images of the product, and so on.

You attach and detach files by editing items. By default, the latest version of an attached file displays when an item is updated.

File attachment links are represented in three ways: a primary associated file (displays a blue key), a secondary association (displays a gray key), or a general/automatic attachment (no key shown).

In some cases, you might want to maintain a specific version of an attached file by pinning the attached file. When pinned, the version of the file specified when the file was originally attached remains when the file or item is updated. This is useful in legacy data where an older part might be specified by a previous version of a now updated specification.

## How To: Manage File Attachments

The following steps describe how to attach files to items or detach files from items.

1. Right-click on an item and select **Attachments**. The current attachments for the item display in the *Attachments* dialog box.
2. To manually attach files, click **Attach** and browse to the location of the file or click **Search** to find files in the vault. Select one or more files and click **Open**. The most recent version of the attached file displays in the *Attachments* dialog box. An additional method to attach files to an item is to open an item and change to edit mode, then drag and drop a file from Vault into the item's attachments window. **Note:** The item must be in a **Work in Progress** state to modify attachments.
3. Modify the way an **Item Update** operates on the attached files. By default, attached files update to the most recent version each time the item is updated. You can pin a particular version of the file to the item so that it references that version instead of the newest version during item updates.
4. Select the *Version Number* field and select the version of the file you want to pin from the drop-down list.
5. Select the **Pin** checkbox to pin the file to the specified version. During an update, the file version specified at the time of attachment remains attached to the item and the item is updated with the most current information from that file version.
6. To detach a file, select the file and click **Detach**.
7. Click **OK** to save your changes and close the dialog box.

# Automatic Attachments

Some files are associated automatically with the primary associated file when it is promoted to an item.

## Definition of Automatic Attachments

When you add CAD files to a vault, the relationships and links between files are maintained. For example, the links between an assembly file and its part and subassembly files are maintained by the vault. These linked files are automatically promoted to items when the assembly is promoted. In a similar way, cross-reference links between drawings in AutoCAD®, AutoCAD® Mechanical, AutoCAD® Electrical, or Autodesk® Civil 3D® are also maintained in Vault.

## Example of Automatic Attachments

An Inventor drawing is created from an Inventor part, and both are checked in to the vault. In Project Explorer, the two files are visible, as shown in Figure 8–5.

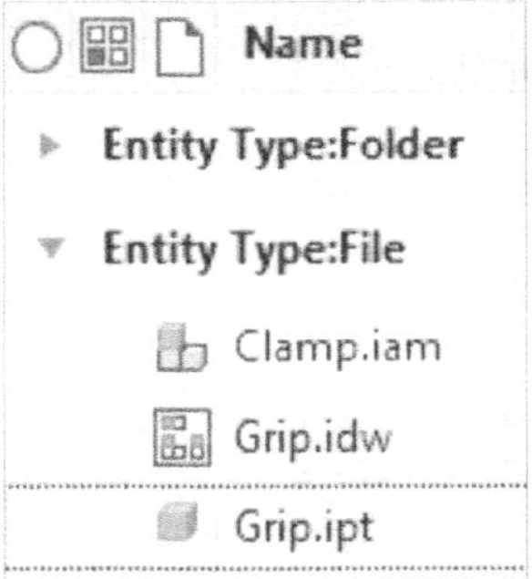


**Figure 8–5**

After assigning an item to the **Grip.ipt** part, the **Grip.idw** file also shows a link to an item in Project Explorer, as shown in Figure 8–6.

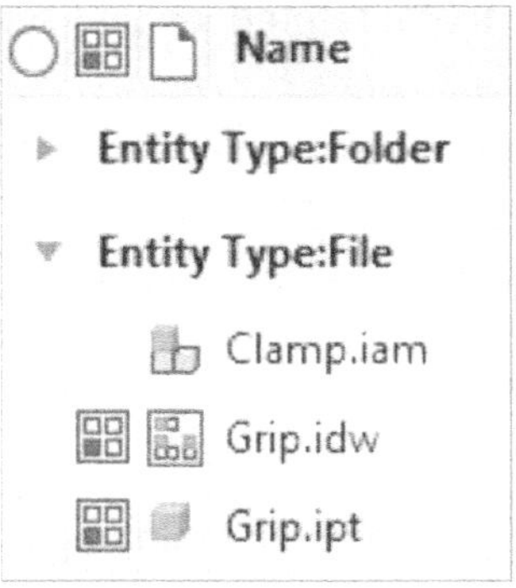


**Figure 8–6**

After assigning an item to the Grip.ipt part, the item also shows a link to both the files in the *Associated files* list on the *General* tab. Note that the key icon (shown in Figure 8–7) indicates the item's primary associated file.

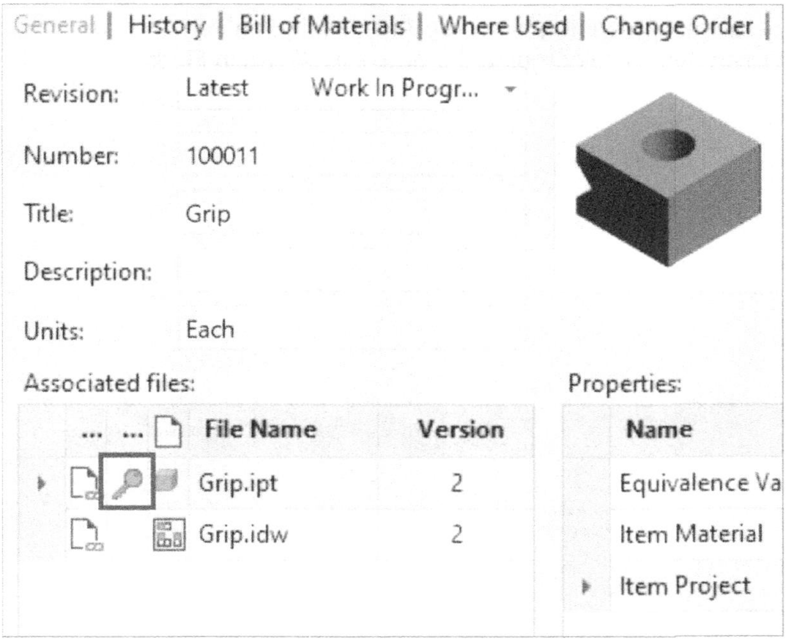


**Figure 8–7**

# Practice 8a
# Assign Items to Vault Files

In this practice, you create a custom view for Vault, assign an item to a part and an assembly, and attach files to an item. The completed practice is shown in Figure 8–8.

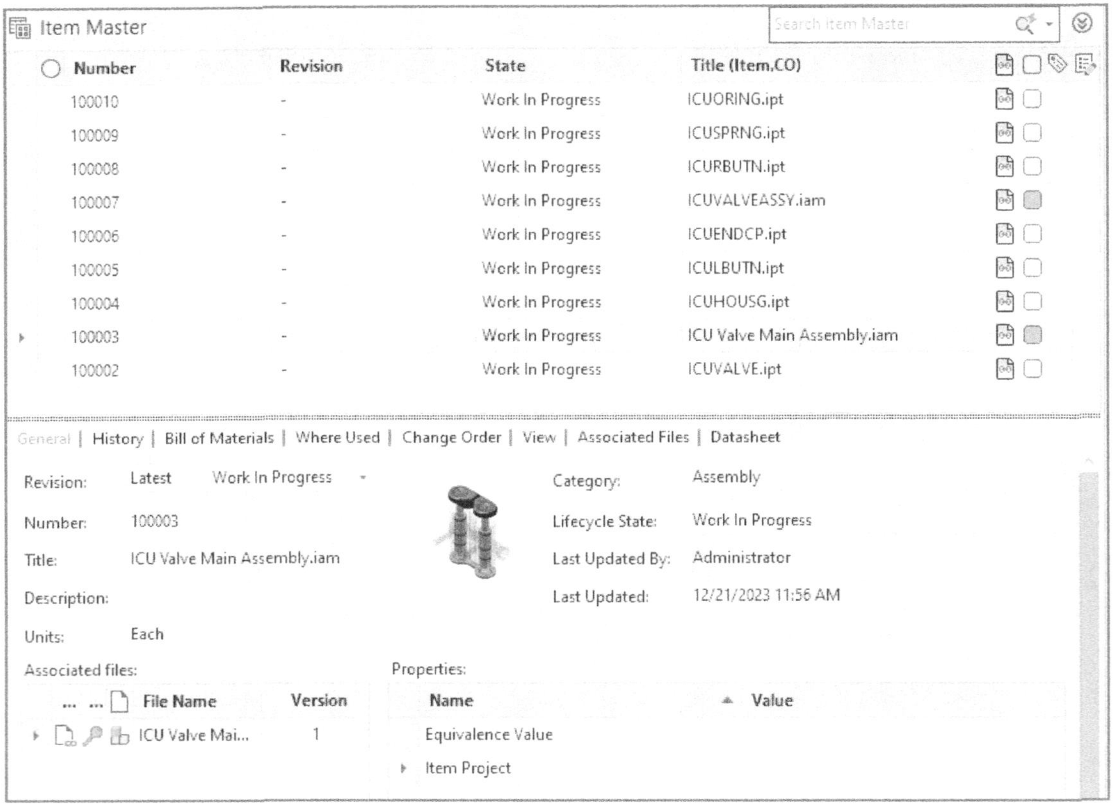


***The completed practice***

**Figure 8–8**

## Task 1: Assign an item.

1. Start Autodesk Vault Professional. Log in using the following information:
   - For *User Name*, enter **administrator**.
   - Leave the *Password* field blank.
   - For *Vault*, select **AOTCVault**.
2. In the *Navigation* pane, click **Home** and expand **AOTCVault**. Expand **Project Explorer**.

3. Navigate to the *Designs\ICU Valve* folder, as shown in Figure 8–9.

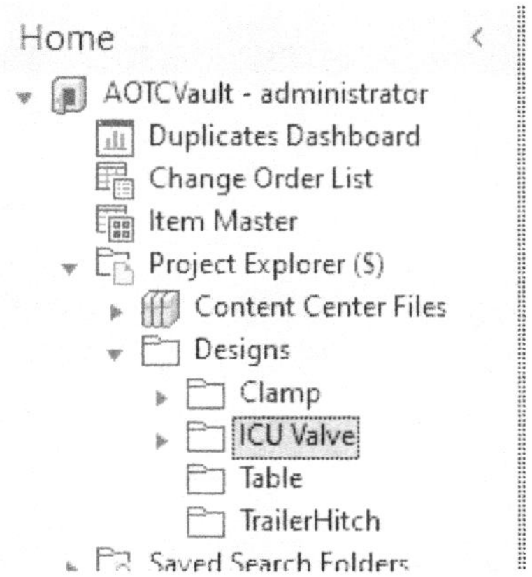


Figure 8–9

4. In the main pane, right-click on **ICUVALVE.ipt**.
5. Select **Assign/Update Item**, as shown in Figure 8–10 and Figure 8–11.

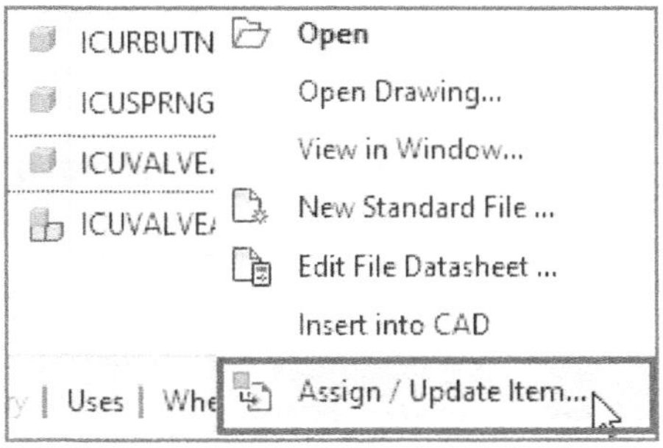


Figure 8–10

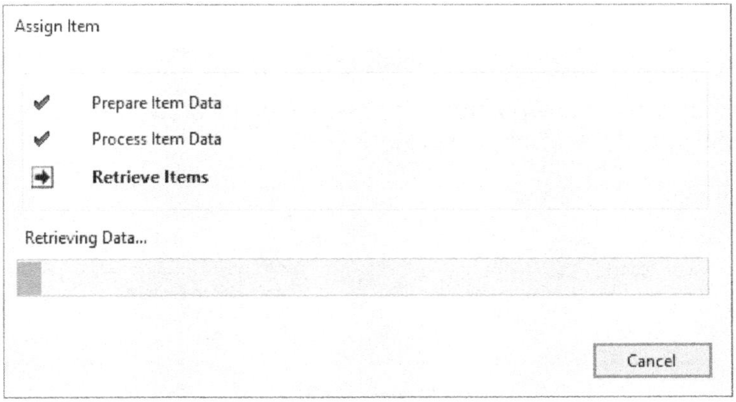


Figure 8–11

6. The item is created for **ICUVALVE.ipt**, displaying the *General* tab information, as shown in Figure 8–12.

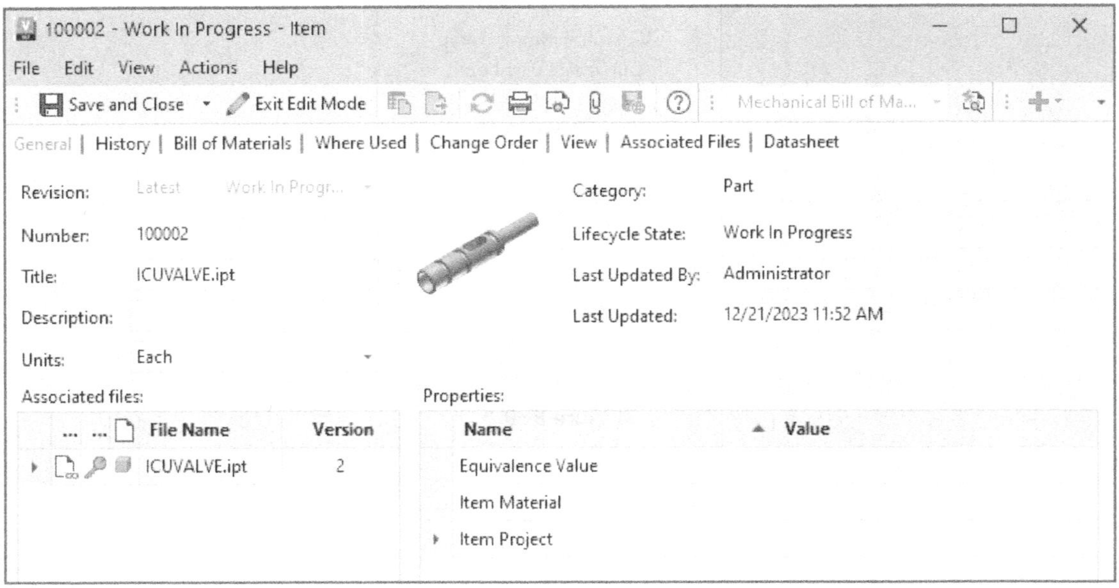


**Figure 8–12**

7. In the toolbar, click **Save and Close** to save the item and close the window, as shown in Figure 8–13.

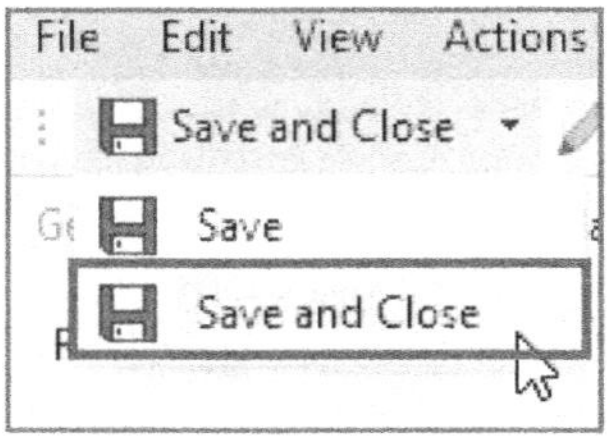


**Figure 8–13**

8. In the main window, place the pointer on the item icon located in the last grid column. The *Go to Item* tooltip displays, as shown in Figure 8–14.

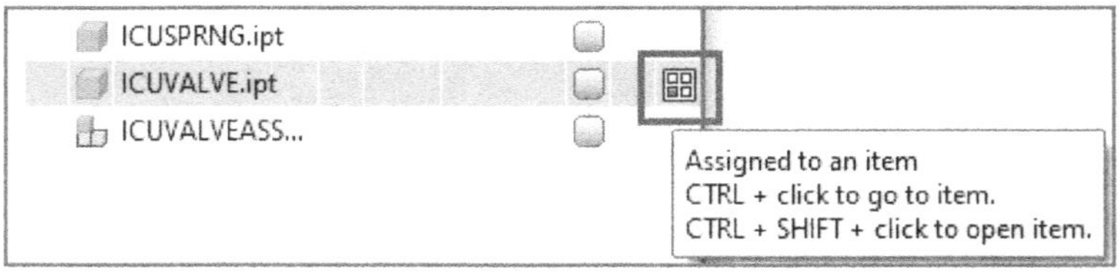


**Figure 8–14**

9. Hold <Ctrl> and click the item icon to display the item. Note the tabs in the *Preview* pane.

 

10. In the *Navigation* pane, click **Home** and then navigate to *Project Explorer>Designs>ICU Valve*.
11. In the main pane, select **ICU Valve Main Assembly.iam** and drag it onto the **Item Master** node in the *Navigation* pane. A new Item is created for the assembly, as shown in Figure 8–15.

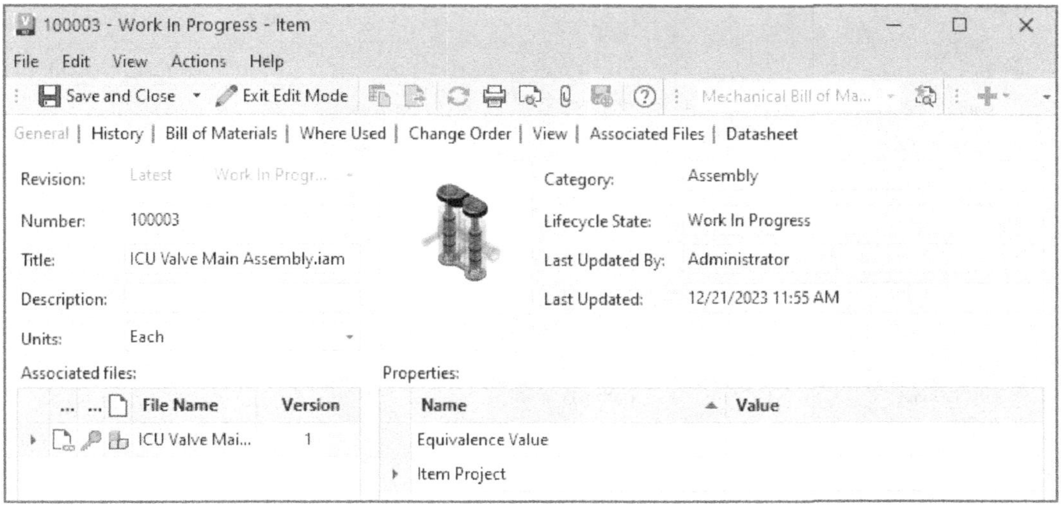


**Figure 8–15**

12. In the toolbar, click **Save and Close**.
13. An item icon displays next to all files in the *ICU Valve* folder, as shown in Figure 8–16.

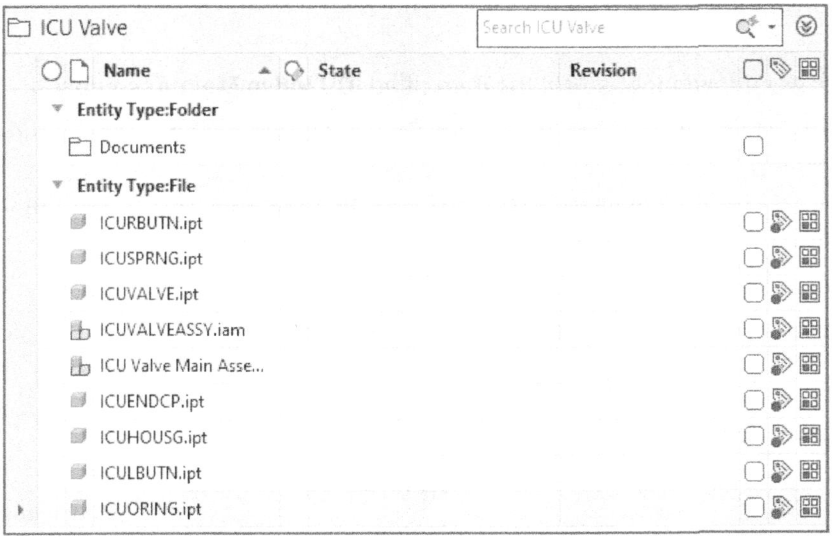


**Figure 8–16**

- Note that when you assign an item to an assembly file, it automatically assigns items to all subassemblies and parts used in the assembly. Without these extra items, the bill of materials is incomplete.

14. In the *Navigation* pane, in *Home*, select **Item Master**. If required, in the *Advanced* toolbar drop-down list, select **All Items**. The list is updated with the new items, as shown in Figure 8–17.

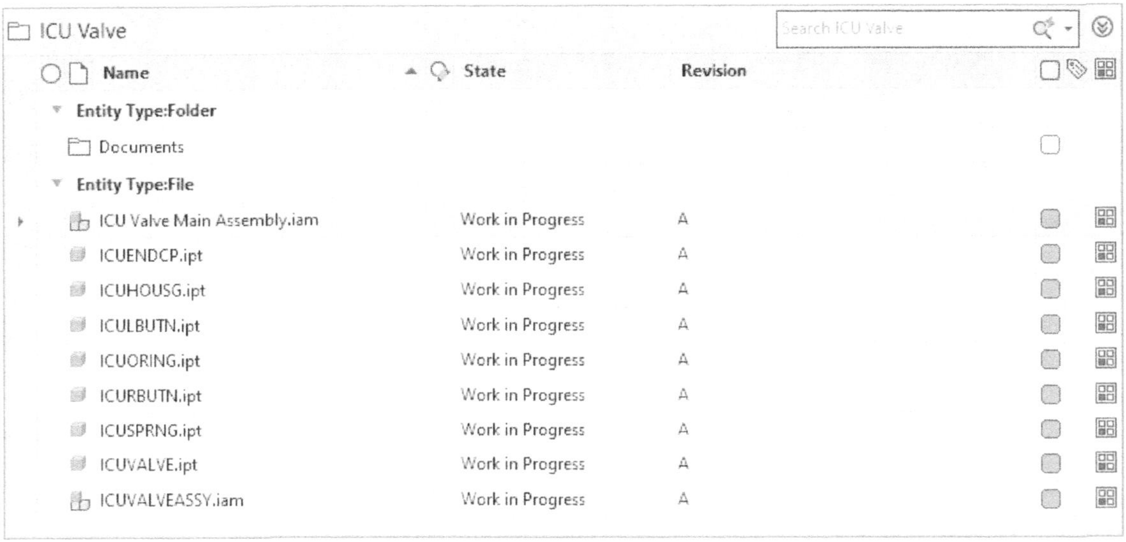


**Figure 8–17**

## Task 2: Attach files to an item.

1. In the *Item Master* window, select the item titled **ICU Valve Main Assembly**.
2. In the *Preview* pane, select the *General* tab. Only one file is associated with the item in the main assembly.
3. In the *Item Master*, double-click the **ICU Valve Main Assembly** item to open the *Item Master* dialog box.
4. Click **Edit** to edit the item.
5. In the toolbar, click **Attachments**, as shown in Figure 8–18.

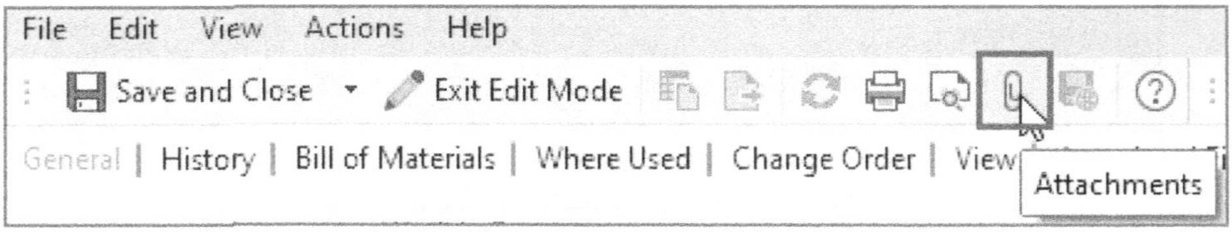


**Figure 8–18**

 

6. In the *Attachments for Item* dialog box, click **Attach**. The *Select File to Attach* dialog box displays.
7. Navigate to the *Designs\ICU Valve\Documents* folder. Select **ICU Valve Rendering.png** and click **Open**.
8. In the *Attachments for Item* dialog box, click **OK**. The attached files are listed under the Associated files area of the *Item* dialog box.
9. In the toolbar, click **Save and Close**.

**End of practice**

# Practice 8b
# Create New Items

In this practice, you will create new items to represent physical objects not modeled in the vault. The completed practice is shown in Figure 8–19.

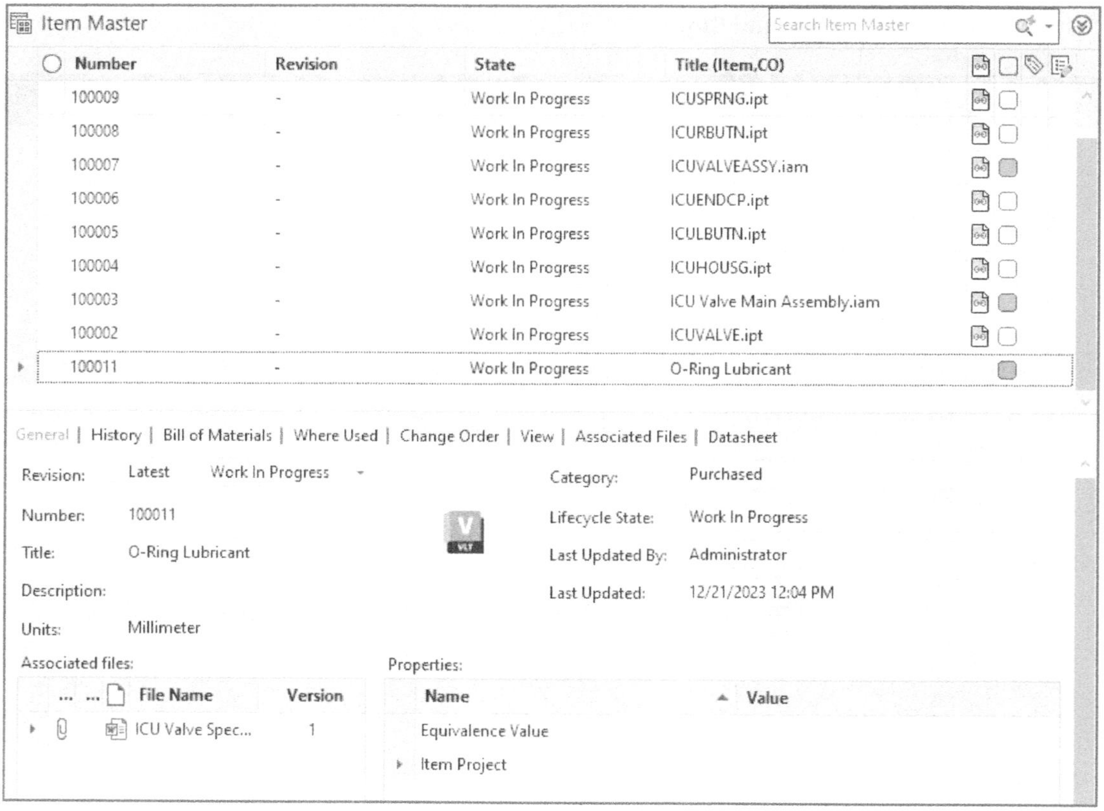


***The completed practice***

**Figure 8–19**

1. Start Autodesk Vault Professional. Log in using the following information:
   - For *User Name*, enter **administrator**.
   - Leave the *Password* field blank.
   - For *Vault*, select **AOTCVault**.
2. In the *Navigation* pane, click **Home**, then click **Item Master**.

3. Right-click on **Item Master** and select **New Item**, as shown in Figure 8–20.

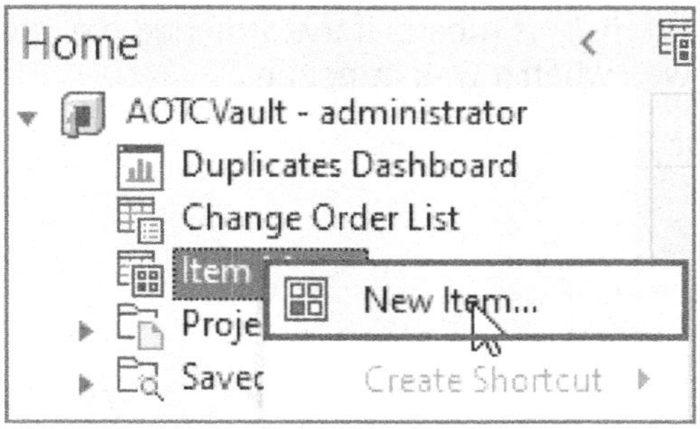


**Figure 8–20**

4. In the *New Item – Select Category* dialog box, select **Purchased** and click **OK**, as shown in Figure 8–21.

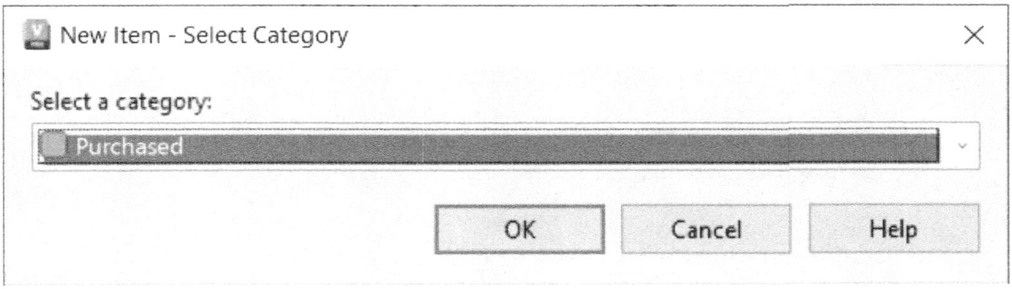


**Figure 8–21**

5. In the *Edit Item* dialog box, do the following:
   - For *Title*, enter **O-Ring Lubricant.**
   - For *Units*, expand the drop-down list and select **Milliliter**.
   - Click **Save and Close**.
6. The new item displays in the *Item Master* in the main pane.
7. In the *Item Master*, right-click on the **O-Ring Lubricant** and select **Attachments**.
8. In the *Attachments* dialog box, click **Attach**.
9. Navigate to the *Designs\ICU Valve\Documents* folder. Select **ICU Valve Specification Sheet - Grease.doc** and click **Open**.

**10.** In the document row, in the Pinned icon column, select the checkbox shown in Figure 8–22.
**Note:** When an attachment is pinned, the file version specified at the time of attachment remains attached to the item. This means if the attached file updates, the attachment will remain at the version it was when it was attached.

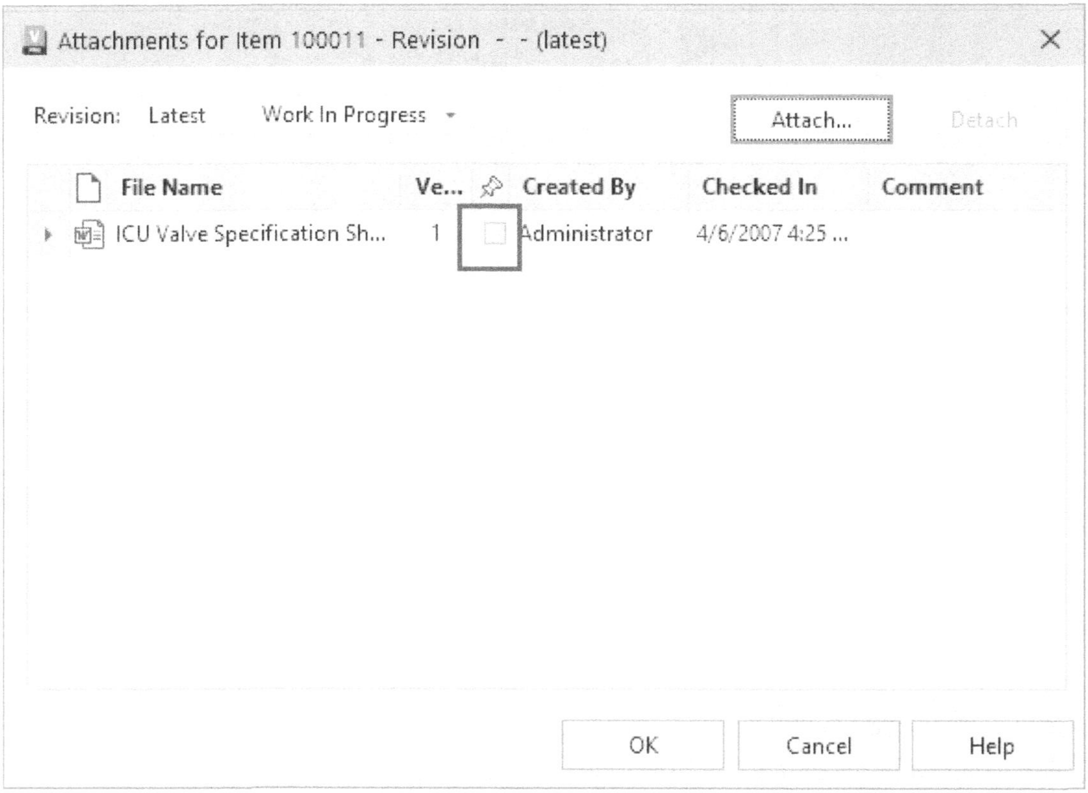


**Figure 8–22**

**11.** Click **OK**.

**End of practice**

# 8.2 Working with Items

In this section, you learn how to create, modify, and delete customized views, use filters to view items, and work with item properties shown in Figure 8–23. You can also export items for use with other applications or to create reports.

You can use items to index and manage products in manufacturing. You also use items in the creation of bills of materials (BOMs) in Autodesk Vault Professional and in tracking change orders.

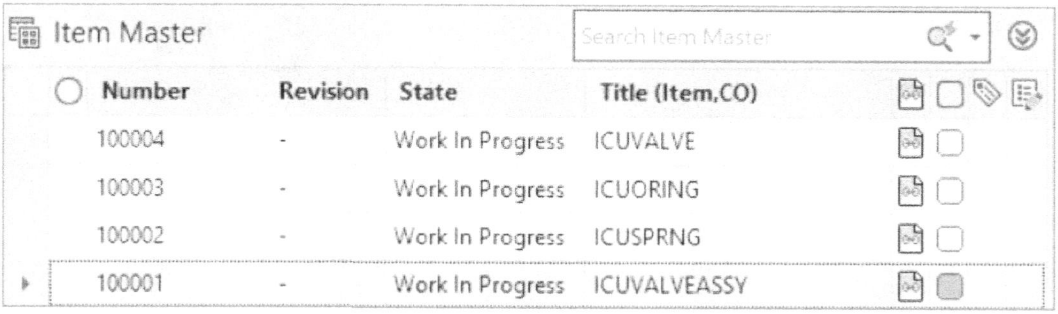


**Figure 8–23**

## Using the Item Preview Pane to View Items

The extended design team requires access to design data. Because many team members outside the engineering team do not use CAD, items cannot be viewed directly in the native CAD application.

Visualization files are the main tools used for viewing items. Visualization files can be of different file formats but the most common are DWF and DWFx files. Visualization files can be published automatically when files are checked in to the vault, thereby making viewing items in the vault easier and faster. With 3D visualization files, users can pan, zoom, and orbit 3D Autodesk Inventor models. Individual components in an assembly can be shown, hidden, or isolated. With 2D visualization files, users can print and view drawings and mark them up to provide feedback.

Use the *View* tab in the *Preview* pane to view an item's associated vault files, as shown in Figure 8–24.

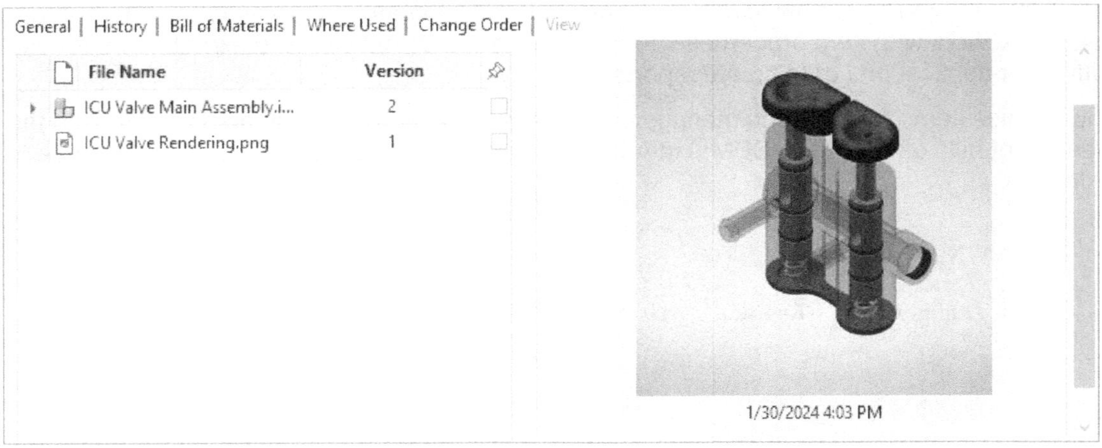


**Figure 8–24**

## Viewing Revision History

You can view revisions on the *History* tab. Vault Professional provides thumbnail images of the different revisions to the file, as shown in Figure 8–25.

**Figure 8–25**

## How To: View an Item

The following steps describe how to view an item's associated files:

1. In the *Item Master* window, select the item.
2. In the *Preview* pane, click the *View* tab.
3. Select the file in the *Attached Files* list.

## How To: View Data in a Separate Dialog Box

The following steps describe how to view data that opens in a separate dialog box:

1. In the *Item Master* window, select the item.
2. In the *Preview* pane, click the *View* tab.
3. Select the file in the *Attached Files* list and click on the thumbnail to display the file in the *Preview* pane.
4. Click **View** to open the file in a separate window.
5. Click **Maximize** in the upper-right corner to view in full screen mode.

# Using the Where Used Tab

With the *Where Used* tab in the *Preview* pane, you can analyze where items are included in the vault. By detecting dependencies before making changes, you can avoid costly mistakes.

## Example of Using the Where Used Tab

In Figure 8–26, the *Where Used* tab shows that the **ICUVALVE** part is used in the **ICUVALVEASSY** assembly. In turn, the assembly is used in the **ICU Valve Main Assembly** file. The part is used directly in one assembly (it has one direct parent) and is used in a total of two assemblies (total number of parents).

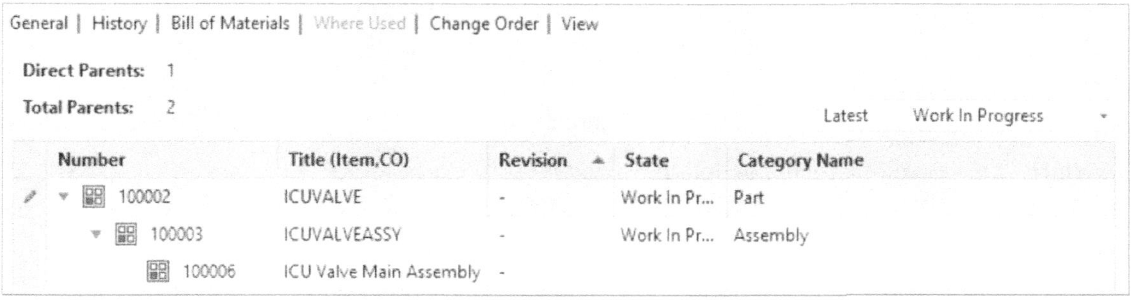


Figure 8–26

# Define Custom Filters to View Items

The number of items in the system can grow quite rapidly, and finding items in the list can be difficult. Many methods are available to filter the item list. By default, a custom view is already applied to the *Item Master*, which shows the items that have been updated in the last seven days. The default custom view displays in the *Advanced* toolbar, as shown in Figure 8–27.

**Figure 8–27**

It is strongly recommended that you create custom views to filter your data. Customizing helps speed up the display of item lists because only filtered item data is retrieved from the server rather than the entire item list.

## How To: Define a Custom Filter in the Item Master

The following steps describe how to define a custom filter in the *Item Master*:

1. In the *Item Master* list, right-click on the heading of a column and select **Customize View**.
2. In the *Customize View* dialog box, select **Custom Filters**.
3. In the *Custom Filters* dialog box, select an item property, condition, and value required.
4. Click **Add**.
5. If required, select additional properties, conditions, and values then add them to the criteria list.
6. Click **OK**. The *Item Master* list is filtered. A small filter symbol displays on the right side of the *Item Master* title bar, as shown in Figure 8–28.

**Figure 8–28**

*__Note:__ If the Item Master list is not displaying items you expect to see, check the filter settings and ensure that it is displaying the required content.*

## How To: Save Custom Views

The following steps describe how to save custom views:

1. In the *Advanced* toolbar, from the *Views* list, select **Define custom views**, as shown in Figure 8–29.

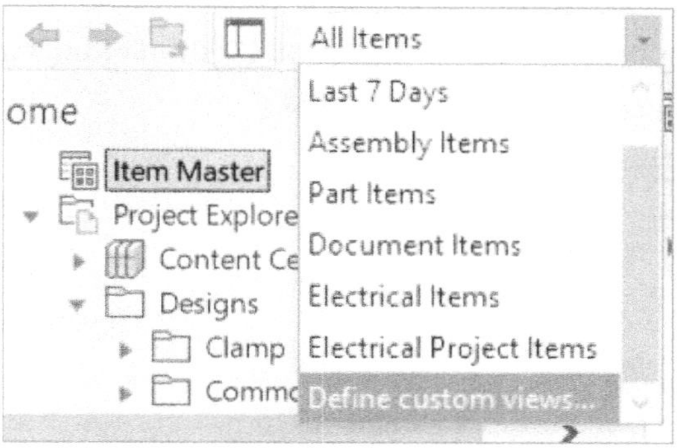


**Figure 8–29**

2. In the *Manage Custom Views* dialog box, click **New**.
3. In the *Create Custom View* dialog box, enter the required view name. Click **OK**.

   ***Note:*** *If a custom filter already exists (the filter icon displays on the Item Master title bar), then you might not want to edit the filter again. Skip the next four steps.*

4. Click **Modify**.
5. In the *Customize View* dialog box, select **Custom Filters**.
6. In the *Customize Filters* dialog box, add the filter criteria.
7. Click **OK** to exit the *Custom Filters* dialog box. Click **Close** to exit the *Customize View* dialog box.
8. Click **Close** to exit the *Manage Custom Views* dialog box.

## How To: Manage Custom Views

The following steps describe how to manage custom views:

1. In the *Advanced* toolbar, from the Views list, select **Define custom views**.
2. In the *Manage Custom Views* dialog box, select the required view name.

   ***Note:*** *You cannot rename or delete the default custom views (e.g., All Items, Last 7 Days, etc.). Although not recommended, it is possible to add additional custom filter criteria to these two custom views.*

3. Click **Modify**, **Copy**, **Rename**, or **Delete**, as required.

4. Close all dialog boxes.

   **Note:** *Use the Custom View list in the Advanced toolbar to switch between custom views.*

## How To: Clear Custom Filters

The following steps describe how to clear custom filters:

1. In the *Item Master* window title bar, right-click on **Custom Filter Applied**.
2. Select **Clear Custom Filters**, as shown in Figure 8–30.

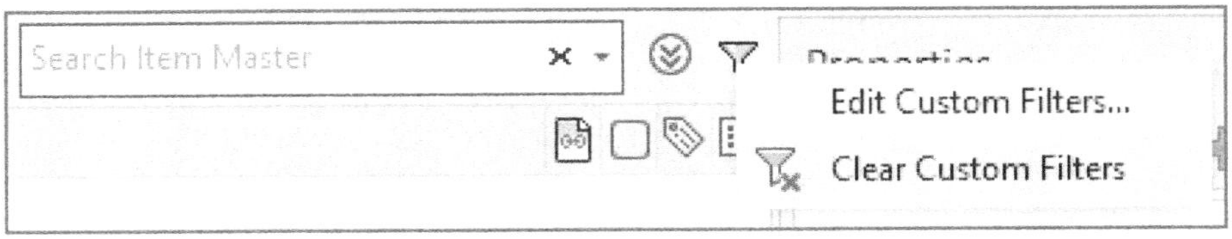


**Figure 8–30**

## How To: Enable Filtering by Column

The following steps describe how to enable filtering by column:

1. On the right side of the column heading, click the **Column Filter** icon.

   **Note:** *Hover over the column you want to filter and the Column Filter icon will appear in the top right of the column.*

2. Select either the *Values* tab or *Text Filters* tab shown in Figure 8–31.

**Figure 8–31**

3. To create a filter from column values, in the *Values* tab, select checkboxes next to the files whose data you would like displayed. Click **Close** when finished.
4. To create a filter using text filters, in the *Text Filters* tab, select an operator from the drop-down list. Click **Close** when finished.
5. To create a custom filter, select the *Text Filters* tab and select **Custom Filter**, then define criteria.

 

# Customize Column Display in the Item Master

Columns in the *Item Master* list represent item properties. Many item properties are available, and you can filter the number of columns (properties) displayed in the list.

In this procedure, you customize the *Item Master* view by working with the list columns.

## How To: Remove Columns in the Item Master

The following steps describe how to remove a column in the list:

1. In the *Item Master* list, right-click on the column header you want to remove.
2. Select **Remove This Column**.

## How To: Add, Remove, and Rearrange Columns in the Item Master

The following steps describe how to add, remove, and reorder columns:

1. In the *Item Master* list, right-click on a column header and select **Customize View**.
2. In the *Customize View* dialog box, click **Fields**.
3. In the *Customize Fields* dialog box, add and remove fields as required.
4. Customize the order of the fields by moving them up and down the list.

   ***Note:*** *If you want to customize only the order of the fields (columns), drag the column headers to rearrange them in the Item Master list.*

## How To: Group Items by Column Header

The following steps describe how to group items by column header:

1. In the *Advanced* toolbar, click **Group By Box**, as shown in Figure 8–32.

**Figure 8–32**

2. In the *Item Master*, drag a column header to the location indicated. The items in the list are automatically listed in groups based on the column header value. In Figure 8–33, the items are grouped by state.

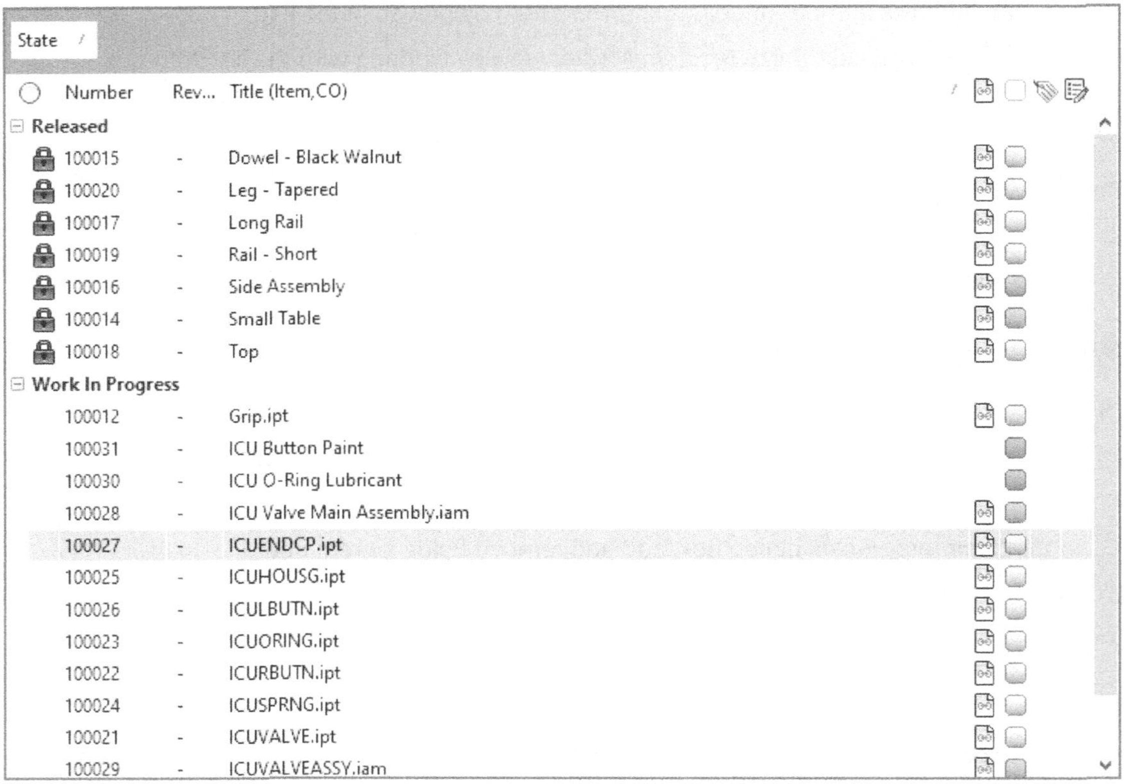


**Figure 8–33**

**Hint: Grouping by Column Header Value**

Grouping by column header value can be useful when you work on a number of projects.

- Add a project name property to each item in the *Item Master*.
- Customize the view to show the item project field, then group the items by this field.

## How To: Toggle Off the Group By Box Display

The following steps describe how to toggle off the Group By Box display:

1. In the Advanced toolbar, ensure that **Group By Box** is selected.
2. Drag the column header back to the header row.
3. In the Advanced toolbar, click **Group By Box** to disable the utility.

# Find Items

In this procedure, you find items by using the item number, using shortcuts, and searching for items.

## Search Tips

- Use **Go To** and go directly to an item.
- Use **My Shortcuts** to go to items.
- Search for items using **Find**.

### How To: Go to a Specific Item by Item Number

The following steps describe how to go to a specific item by item number:

1. In the toolbar, click in the *Go to* box, as shown in Figure 8–34.

**Figure 8–34**

2. Enter an item number and press <Enter>.

### How To: Create and Use Shortcuts to Navigate in the Item Master

The following steps describe how to create and use shortcuts to navigate in the *Item Master*:

1. In the *Item Master*, drag an item to the *My Shortcuts* window in the *Navigation* pane, as shown in Figure 8–35.

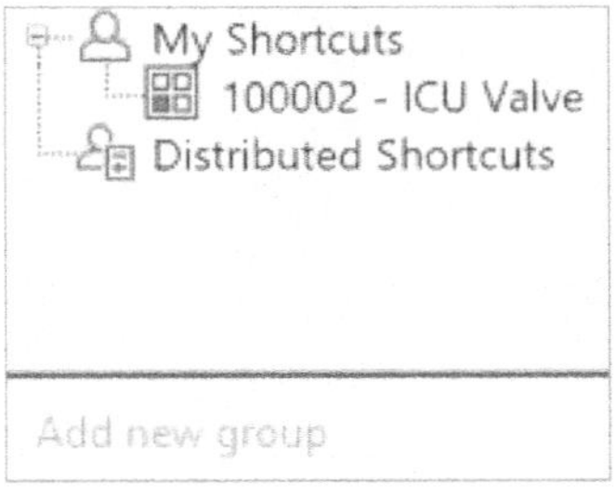


**Figure 8–35**

2. Under *My Shortcuts*, you can also add new groups (folders) to organize the shortcuts.
3. To go to an item, click the item shortcut.

## How To: Search Items

The following steps describe how to search for an item or items and how to save the search:

1. In the search box, enter the search text, as shown in Figure 8–36.

**Figure 8–36**

2. Click **Search**. The items containing the search string display in the main table.
3. To save the search, do the following:
   - In the search bar, click **Show search options** menu.
   - Click **Save Search**.
   - Enter a search name and click **OK**, as shown on the right in Figure 8–37.

**Figure 8–37**

   - The saved search displays in the *Navigation* pane under *My Search Folders*.

# Practice 8c
# Work with Items

In this practice, you will create a custom view, shortcuts, and a saved search for the project. You will also learn how to link the ICU Button Paint item to the ICU buttons, how to delete items, and how to export the *Item Master* view. The complete practice is shown in Figure 8–38.

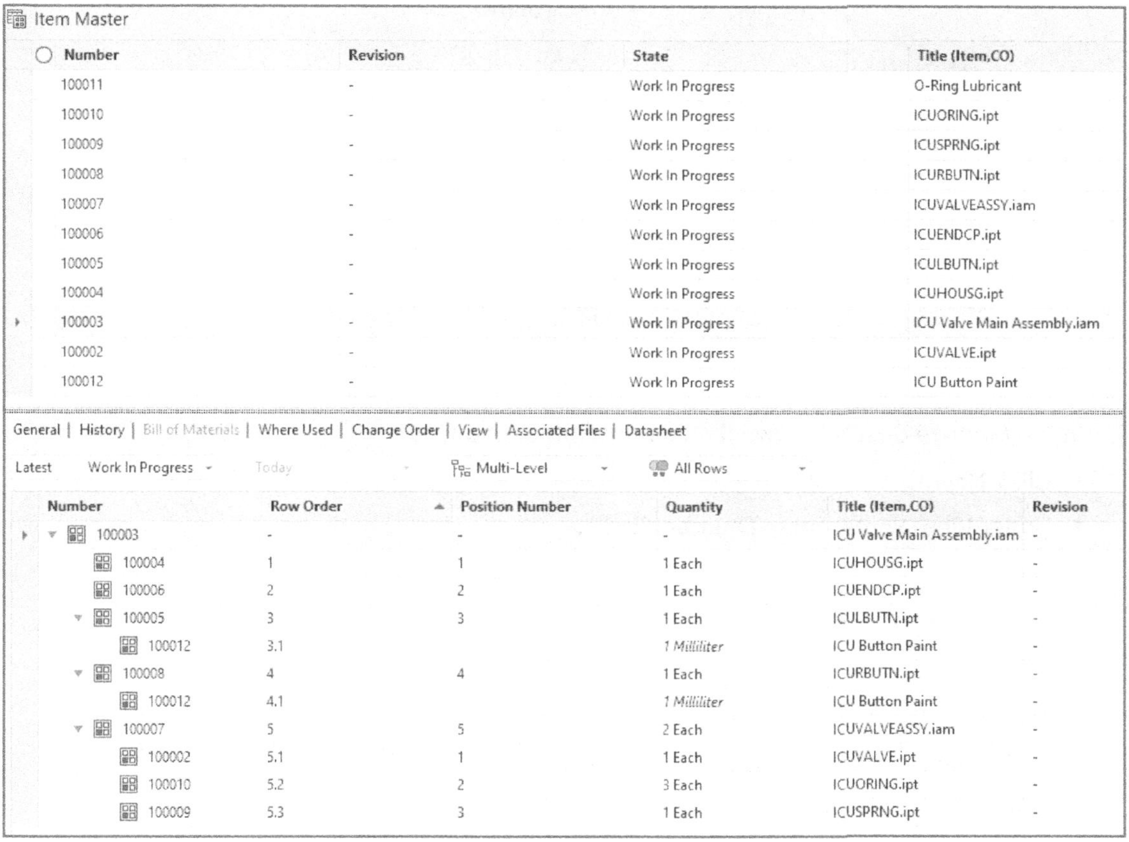

Item Master

| Number | Revision | State | Title (Item,CO) |
|---|---|---|---|
| 100011 | - | Work In Progress | O-Ring Lubricant |
| 100010 | - | Work In Progress | ICUORING.ipt |
| 100009 | - | Work In Progress | ICUSPRNG.ipt |
| 100008 | - | Work In Progress | ICURBUTN.ipt |
| 100007 | - | Work In Progress | ICUVALVEASSY.iam |
| 100006 | - | Work In Progress | ICUENDCP.ipt |
| 100005 | - | Work In Progress | ICULBUTN.ipt |
| 100004 | - | Work In Progress | ICUHOUSG.ipt |
| 100003 | - | Work In Progress | ICU Valve Main Assembly.iam |
| 100002 | - | Work In Progress | ICUVALVE.ipt |
| 100012 | - | Work In Progress | ICU Button Paint |

General | History | Bill of Materials | Where Used | Change Order | View | Associated Files | Datasheet

Latest Work In Progress Today Multi-Level All Rows

| Number | Row Order | Position Number | Quantity | Title (Item,CO) | Revision |
|---|---|---|---|---|---|
| 100003 | - | - | - | ICU Valve Main Assembly.iam | - |
| 100004 | 1 | 1 | 1 Each | ICUHOUSG.ipt | - |
| 100006 | 2 | 2 | 1 Each | ICUENDCP.ipt | - |
| 100005 | 3 | 3 | 1 Each | ICULBUTN.ipt | - |
| 100012 | 3.1 | | 1 Milliliter | ICU Button Paint | - |
| 100008 | 4 | 4 | 1 Each | ICURBUTN.ipt | - |
| 100012 | 4.1 | | 1 Milliliter | ICU Button Paint | - |
| 100007 | 5 | 5 | 2 Each | ICUVALVEASSY.iam | - |
| 100002 | 5.1 | 1 | 1 Each | ICUVALVE.ipt | - |
| 100010 | 5.2 | 2 | 3 Each | ICUORING.ipt | - |
| 100009 | 5.3 | 3 | 1 Each | ICUSPRNG.ipt | - |

***The completed practice***

**Figure 8–38**

## Task 1: Create a custom view for items.

1. Start Autodesk Vault Professional. Log in using the following information:
   - For *User Name*, enter **administrator**.
   - Leave the *Password* field blank.
   - For *Vault*, select **AOTCVault**.

2. In the *Navigation* pane, click **Home** and select **Item Master**.
3. In the *Advanced* toolbar, select **Define custom views** from the toolbar drop-down list, as shown in Figure 8–39.

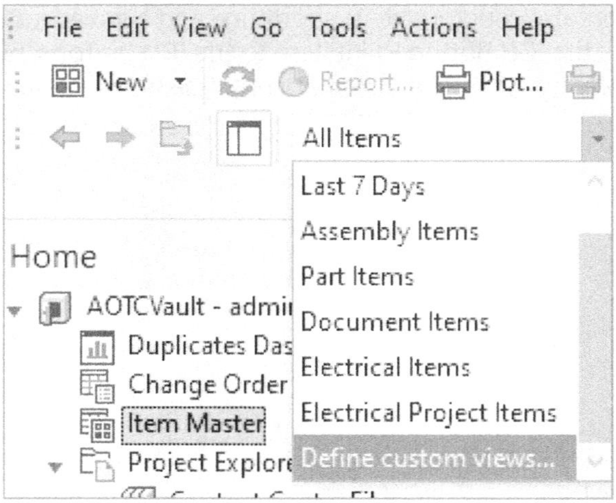


**Figure 8–39**

4. In the *Manage Custom Views* dialog box, do the following:
   - Click **New**.
   - Under *View Name*, enter **Thumbnails**.
   - Click **OK**.
5. In the *Manage Custom Views* dialog box, select the **Thumbnails** view. Click **Modify**.
6. Click **Fields**.
7. In the *Customize Fields* dialog box, do the following:
   - In the *Select available fields from* drop-down list, select **Items**.
   - In the *Available fields* list, select **Thumbnail**. Click **Add**.

 

- Under *Show these fields in this order*, select **Thumbnail**. Click **Move Up** until Thumbnail displays above Number. Order the fields as shown in Figure 8–40.

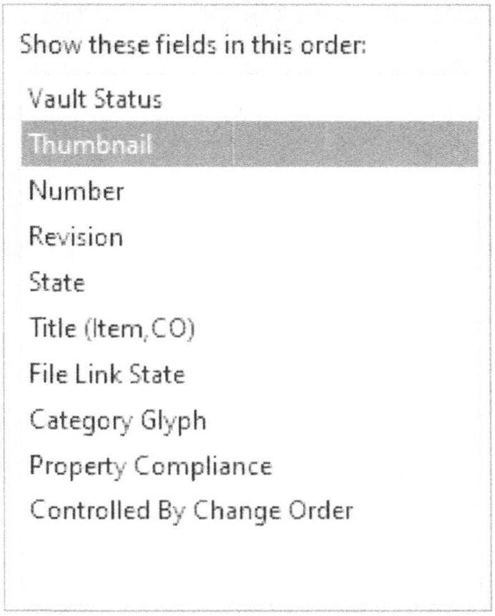


**Figure 8–40**

- Click **OK**.

8. Click **Close** and **Done** to close the other dialog boxes. The main pane displays thumbnails (generated from the visualization files), as shown in Figure 8–41.

**Figure 8–41**

9. To adjust the size of the thumbnails, resize the *Thumbnail* column.

## Task 2: Create shortcuts.

1. Under *Saved Shortcuts*, right-click on **My Shortcuts** and select **New Group**.
2. Enter **ICU Valve**. Press <Enter>.
3. In the *Item Master* main pane, drag the **ICU Valve Main Assembly.iam** item to the *ICU Valve* shortcut group.
4. Expand the *ICU Valve* shortcut group.
5. Right-click on the shortcut to the **ICU Valve Main Assembly.iam** item and select **Rename**, as shown in Figure 8–42.

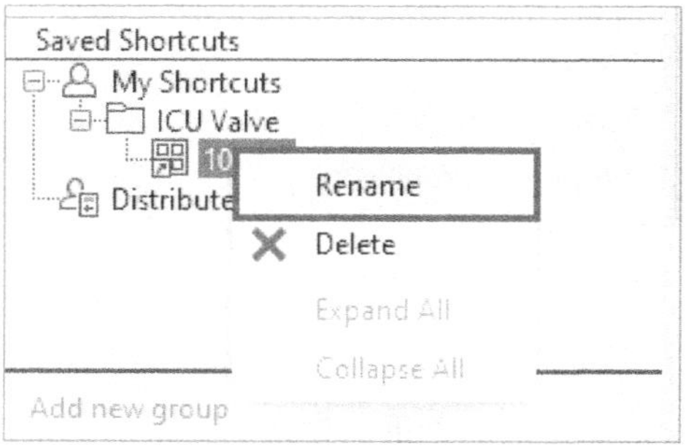


**Figure 8–42**

6. Enter **- Main Assembly** after the item number.
7. Press <Enter>. Note that your item number might differ than the one shown in Figure 8–43.

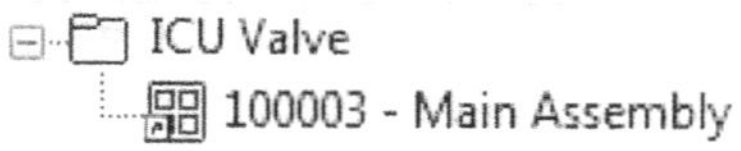


**Figure 8–43**

8. In the standard toolbar, click **Find**.
9. On the *Basic* tab, for the search text, enter ***BUTN** and press <Enter>.
10. Select **File>Save Search**.
11. In the *Save Search* dialog box, for *Search Name*, enter **Buttons**. Click **OK**. Close the *Find* dialog box.
12. View the saved search that displays under *Saved Search Folders>My Searches*, as shown in Figure 8–44.

**Figure 8–44**

13. Select the **Buttons** saved search to view the results, as shown in Figure 8–45.

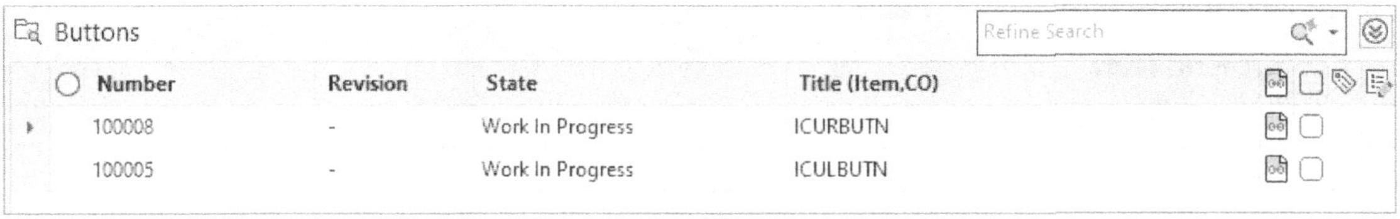


Figure 8–45

## Task 3: Link items.

1. In *Home*, right-click on **Item Master** and select **New Item**.
2. In the *New Item – Select Category* dialog box, select **Purchased** and click **OK**.
3. In the *Edit Item* dialog box, do the following:
    - For *Title*, enter **ICU Button Paint**.
    - For *Description*, enter **Paint**.
    - Set *Units* to **Milliliter**.
    - Click **Save and Close**.
4. Under *My Search Folders*, click **Buttons**.
5. Right-click on the **ICURBUTN** item and click **Update** to edit it.
6. Select the *Bill of Materials* tab.
7. Right-click on the row and select **Add Row>From Existing Item**, as shown in Figure 8–46.

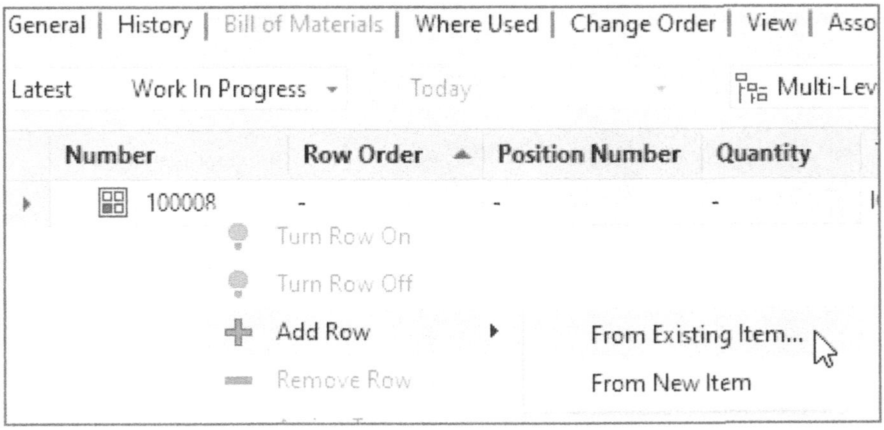


Figure 8–46

8. In the *Find* dialog box, select the *Basic* tab if it is not selected already. Do the following:
   - For the search text, enter **Paint**.
   - Click **Find Now**.
   - Select the row displayed.
   - Click **OK**.
   - The ICU Button Paint item is linked to the **ICURBUTN.ipt** item, as shown in Figure 8–47.

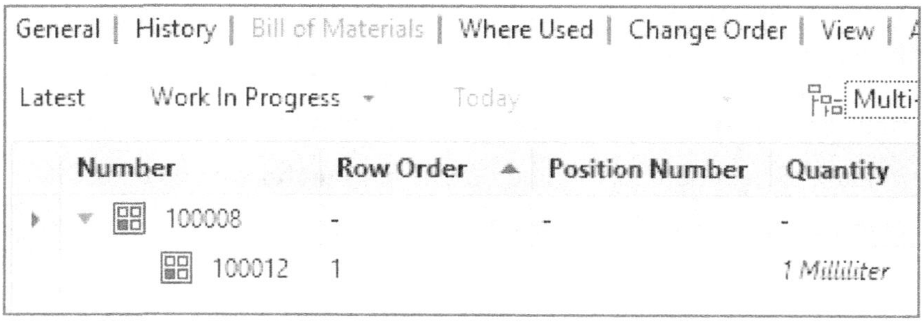


**Figure 8–47**

9. Click **Save and Close**. Repeat the previous steps to link the **ICU Button Paint** item to the **Left button (ICULBUTN.ipt)** item.
10. In the *ICU Valve* shortcut group, click the shortcut to the **Main Assembly**.
11. In the *Preview* pane, click the *Bill of Materials* tab. Verify that the **ICU Button Paint** item is listed twice, under the ICU buttons (as shown in Figure 8–48).

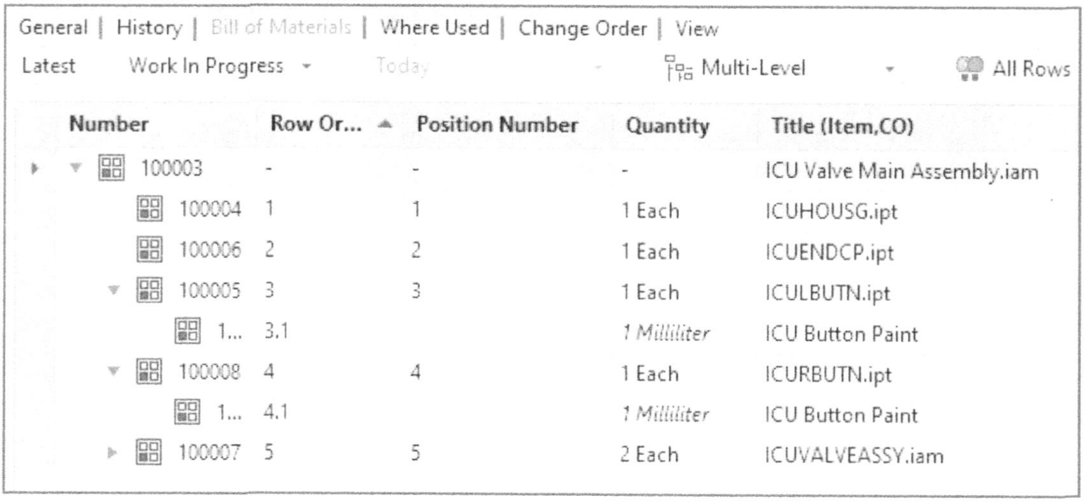


**Figure 8–48**

12. Select **Listing by Project** in the *Custom Views* list. The *Item Master* list now displays the *Item Project* column.

## Task 4: Delete items.

1. In the *Item Master*, right-click on the **O-Ring Lubricant** item and select **Change State**.
2. In the *Select Lifecycle* dialog box, select **Obsolete**.
3. Click **OK**.
4. In the *Item Master*, right-click on the **O-Ring Lubricant** item again and select **Delete**.

   ***Note:*** *You can delete an item only if its lifecycle state is set to Obsolete.*

5. Click **Yes** to confirm the item deletion.

**End of practice**

# 8.3 Item Properties

In this section, you will learn how to use item properties to search for and sort items, organize items, and filter the *Item Master* list, as shown in Figure 8–49. You use item properties to manage items.

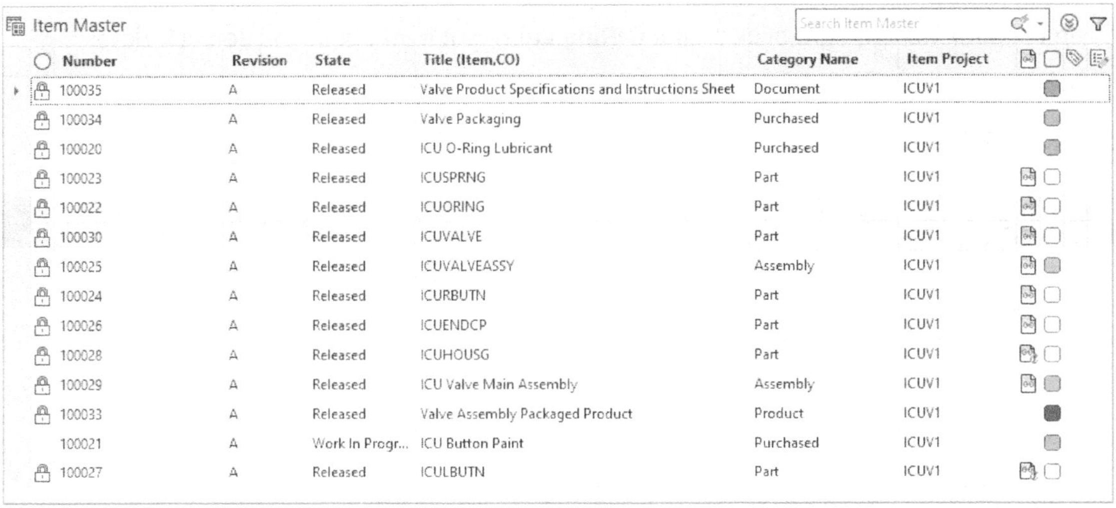

Item Master

| Number | Revision | State | Title (Item,CO) | Category Name | Item Project |
|---|---|---|---|---|---|
| 100035 | A | Released | Valve Product Specifications and Instructions Sheet | Document | ICUV1 |
| 100034 | A | Released | Valve Packaging | Purchased | ICUV1 |
| 100020 | A | Released | ICU O-Ring Lubricant | Purchased | ICUV1 |
| 100023 | A | Released | ICUSPRNG | Part | ICUV1 |
| 100022 | A | Released | ICUORING | Part | ICUV1 |
| 100030 | A | Released | ICUVALVE | Part | ICUV1 |
| 100025 | A | Released | ICUVALVEASSY | Assembly | ICUV1 |
| 100024 | A | Released | ICURBUTN | Part | ICUV1 |
| 100026 | A | Released | ICUENDCP | Part | ICUV1 |
| 100028 | A | Released | ICUHOUSG | Part | ICUV1 |
| 100029 | A | Released | ICU Valve Main Assembly | Assembly | ICUV1 |
| 100033 | A | Released | Valve Assembly Packaged Product | Product | ICUV1 |
| 100021 | A | Work In Progr... | ICU Button Paint | Purchased | ICUV1 |
| 100027 | A | Released | ICULBUTN | Part | ICUV1 |

**Figure 8–49**

# Default Item Properties

By default, each item has several properties that store and manage its number, revision, lifecycle, and other associated data.

## Definition of Default Item Properties

Items have properties that apply to all items by default, called system properties. In some cases, the properties are marked (Item, CO) to denote that they are unique to items and change orders.

The following list describes the main properties that display on the *General* tab:

| Property Name | Description | Comment or Example |
|---|---|---|
| **Number** | Unique item identifier | Normally a numerical sequence |
| **Category** | Categorization of the item. | "Part," "assembly," or "purchased" |
| **Title** | Brief description of item or change order | Up to 128 characters |
| **Description** | Secondary description of item or change order | Up to 128 characters |
| **Units** | Quantity | Select from a list |
| **Lifecycle State** | Item lifecycle state | "Work in Progress" or "Released" |
| **Revision** | Item revision | String or character |
| **Last Updated By** | Name of user who last updated item | Read-only, assigned by system |
| **Last Updated** | Date the item was last updated | Read-only, assigned by system |

## Example of Specifying Default Item Properties

When an item is assigned to a file, the item is given a number of default properties.

The new item has a unique item number, which can be as simple as a six- number sequence (Part 100010) or as complex as a set of text sequences (Part BRD-200-0012). You can change the item number after it is assigned if required. The *Title* and *Description* can be used to help distinguish the item later on. The *Units* are specific to the item – for the most part the unit is 'each' but for consumables, it can specify how much (volume, weight, etc.) of the item is used in the product.

The final set of properties is controlled by the system. The *Lifecycle State* designates the position in the product development process. You can change the lifecycle state to **Released**, signifying it is ready for production, or **Work in Progress**, denoting that it is being edited. As designs evolve, they are given *Revisions* to denote major milestones in a product development lifecycle. For example, a part can be released to manufacturing at Revision A, but later be modified based on warranty reports to Revision B to correct a defect noted by customers. The updates are tagged with the user that last updated the item (*Last Updated By*) and the time the update was done (*Last Updated*).

# User-Defined Item Properties

In addition to the system properties, there are a number of predefined user-defined properties that are assigned to items as they are created. These are based on common file properties associated with the different authoring applications. For example, the property *Material* (designating what property the item is made of) can be set from a file property in Autodesk Inventor.

Additionally, you might want to specify some properties that are unique to your company. For example, you can have different *Business Units* that produce designs that you might want to identify or search on.

## Best Practices for Working with User-Defined Properties

The administrator can define additional item properties to add company-specific properties to items. You can use these properties to help arrange or find items in the vault.

It is recommended that:

- You attach user-defined properties to items or remove them from items in the vault. Properties are created and managed by the administrator using the *Property Definitions* dialog box (found under **Tools>Administration>Vault Settings>Behaviors>Properties**).
- The administrator maps item properties to read values from CAD files in the vault if possible. For example, the property *Material* (designating what material the item is made of) can be set from a file property in Autodesk Inventor.
- You begin all user-defined properties with Item (or an acceptable prefix), as shown in Figure 8–50. This will avoid confusion with properties in the vault or in another application. You can also scroll to the right to view the *Association* column, which displays the entity class of the property.

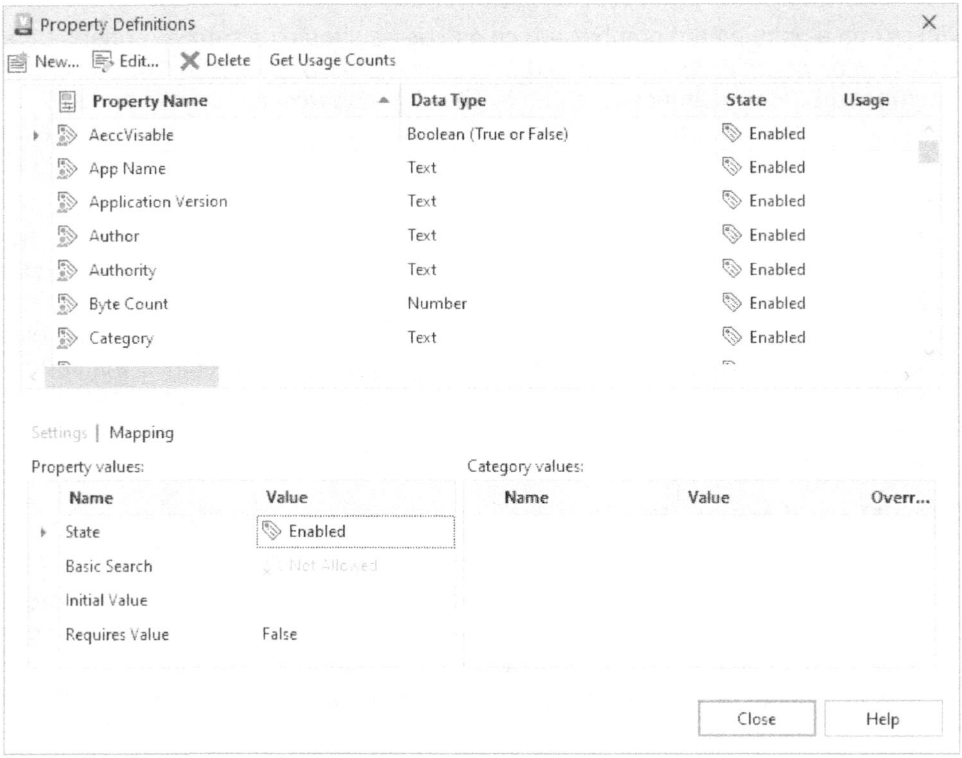


**Figure 8–50**

 

## Example of Using a User-Defined Item Property

You create an *Item Project* property value for a predefined item user-defined property so that you can sort by that property or use it to search for items, as shown in Figure 8–51.

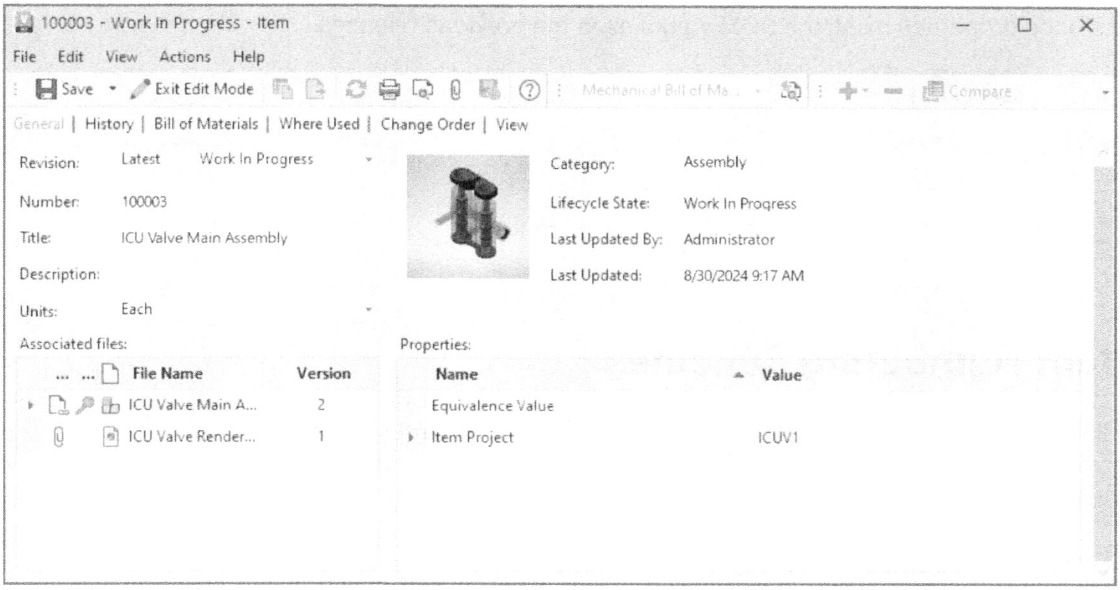


**Figure 8–51**

You can ask the administrator to map the user-defined item property to properties in the vault files.

- You can attach or detach properties per item by right-clicking in the *Properties* field and selecting **Add or Remove Property**.
- You can edit the properties of more than one item at a time by selecting multiple items and then selecting **Edit Properties** (<Ctrl>+<E>).

## Inventor Instance Properties

You can also assign properties to individual component instances. Instance properties work the same way as item property occurrences within the Vault bill of materials (BOM). Items with the same part number are grouped by the instance property value as shown in Figure 8–52. If no instance properties exist, the BOM works as in the previous releases.

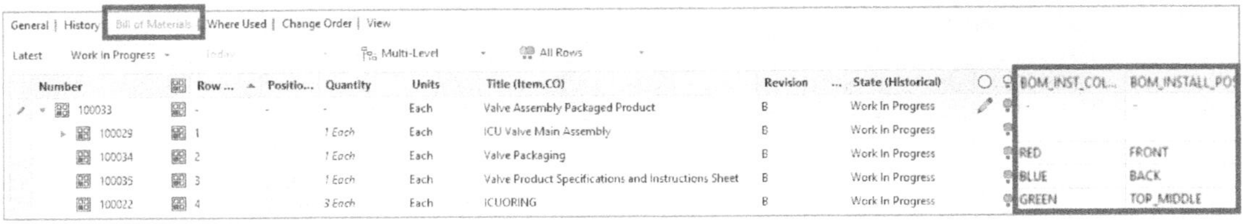


Figure 8–52

# Item Numbering Schemes

All items have unique item numbers that you can use to identify and track the items in different operations. These item numbers are assigned based on a numbering scheme that is created by the administrator.

## Guidelines for Item Numbers

There are two predefined numbering schemes shipped with Vault Professional. It is recommended that you use customized numbering schemes created by the administrator.

The two predefined schemes are shipped with the software by default.

- **Sequential numbering:** This scheme creates item numbers in sequence and is the default. This is a simple numbering scheme that starts with 100001 and goes to 999999.
- **Mapped numbering:** This scheme is selected automatically when a file property is mapped to the item number. You can choose the numbering scheme when you add new items to the vault. It can be any value up to 50 characters long.

## Custom Numbering Schemes

If you choose to use a custom numbering scheme, the scheme can follow company standards or use any identifier. It is recommended that you make this identifier as simple as possible. A six-digit numbering scheme starting with 100000 is ideal.

## Example of Using Item Numbers

Figure 8–53 shows the use of a custom sequential scheme. Note that parts, assemblies, and purchased items are numbered from 100033 to 100043.

Item Master

| Number | Revision | State | Title (Item,CO) | Category Name | Units |
|---|---|---|---|---|---|
| 100033 | A | Work In Progress | ICUVALVE.ipt | Part | Each |
| 100034 | B | Released | ICU O Ring Lubricant | Purchased | Milliliter |
| 100035 | B | Released | ICU Button Paint | Purchased | Milliliter |
| 100036 | A | Work In Progress | ICU Valve Main Assembly.iam | Assembly | Each |
| 100037 | B | Released | ICULBUTN | Part | Each |
| 100038 | A | Released | ICUHOUSG.ipt | Part | Each |
| 100039 | A | Released | ICUSPRNG.ipt | Part | Each |
| 100040 | A | Released | ICUENDCP.ipt | Part | Each |
| 100041 | C | Work In Progress | ICURBUTN | Part | Each |
| 100042 | A | Work In Progress | ICUORING.ipt | Part | Each |
| 100043 | A | Work In Progress | ICUVALVEASSY.iam | Assembly | Each |

**Figure 8–53**

Numbering schemes can include such things as company initials, a type sequence, a numeric sequence, and a manufacturing process code, as in BRD-PRT-10051-P. However, a scheme like this might be needlessly complex and require too much work to set up and use.

It is recommended that you start the item numbering with a digit other than zero since some spreadsheets eliminate the leading zeros when data is imported.

For example, Figure 8–54 shows the use of the sequential scheme. Note that parts, assemblies, and purchased items are numbered from 000012 to 000022.

Item Master

| Number | Revision | State | Title (Item,CO) | Category Name | Units |
|---|---|---|---|---|---|
| 000012 | A | Work In Progress | ICUVALVE.ipt | Part | Each |
| 000013 | C | Work In Progress | ICU O Ring Lubricant | Purchased | Milliliter |
| 000014 | C | Work In Progress | ICU Button Paint | Purchased | Milliliter |
| 000015 | A | Work In Progress | ICU Valve Main Assembly.iam | Assembly | Each |
| 000016 | C | Work In Progress | ICULBUTN | Part | Each |
| 000017 | B | Work In Progress | ICUHOUSG.ipt | Part | Each |
| 000018 | B | Work In Progress | ICUSPRNG.ipt | Part | Each |
| 000019 | B | Work In Progress | ICUENDCP.ipt | Part | Each |
| 000020 | C | Work In Progress | ICURBUTN | Part | Each |
| 000021 | A | Work In Progress | ICUORING.ipt | Part | Each |
| 000022 | A | Work In Progress | ICUVALVEASSY.iam | Assembly | Each |

**Figure 8–54**

This is poor practice. Many software programs such as spreadsheets import the item numbers without the leading zeros, so item number "000020" displays as "20", which might be undesirable when creating a report.

## How To: Change Item Numbers

1. Right-click on one or more items in the *Item Master* or BOM view and select **Change Number**.
2. Select a numbering scheme from the drop-down list. **Use Property Mapping** uses mapped properties to generate the item number.
3. If a field requires user input, enter text as required.
4. Click **Precheck** to verify the new item number. Make any changes, if required.
5. If more than one item is in the list and you want to remove one, select the item and click **Remove**.
6. Click **OK** to accept the new item number.

 

# Practice 8d
# Work with Item Properties

In this practice, you add a new item with user-defined properties, link the item to the ICU valve assembly, display the user-defined property in the *Item Master* view, add a customized view for the current project, change the item project property, group the *Item Master* list by project, customize the view by box, and renumber items. The completed practice is shown in Figure 8–55.

Item Master

| Number | Revision | State | Title (Item,CO) | Item Project |
|---|---|---|---|---|
| 100020 | - | Work In Progress | ICU O-Ring Lubricant | ICUV1 |
| 100021 | - | Work In Progress | ICU Button Paint | ICUV1 |
| 100022 | - | Work In Progress | ICUORING | ICUV1 |
| 100023 | - | Work In Progress | ICUSPRNG | ICUV1 |
| 100024 | - | Work In Progress | ICURBUTN | ICUV1 |
| 100025 | - | Work In Progress | ICUVALVEASSY | ICUV1 |
| 100026 | - | Work In Progress | ICUENDCP | ICUV1 |
| 100027 | - | Work In Progress | ICULBUTN | ICUV1 |
| 100028 | - | Work In Progress | ICUHOUSG | ICUV1 |
| 100029 | - | Work In Progress | ICU Valve Main Assembly | ICUV1 |
| 100030 | - | Work In Progress | ICUVALVE | ICUV1 |

***The completed practice***

**Figure 8–55**

## Task 1: Add a new item.

1. If not already started, start Autodesk Vault Professional. Log in using the following information:
   - For *User Name*, enter **usera**.
   - For *Password*, enter **vault**.
   - For *Vault*, select **AOTCVault**.
2. In the *Navigation* pane, click **Home**, then click **Item Master** to display items for the ICU valve. Right-click on **Item Master** in the *Navigation* pane and select **New Item**. The New *Item - Select Category* dialog box displays.
3. In the *New item – Select Category* dialog box, expand the drop-down list and select **Purchased** then click **OK**.

4. In the *Edit Item* dialog box, set the following, as shown in Figure 8–56:
   - For *Title*, enter **ICU O-Ring Lubricant**.
   - For *Description*, enter **Grease for subassembly**.
   - For *Units*, select **Milliliter**.

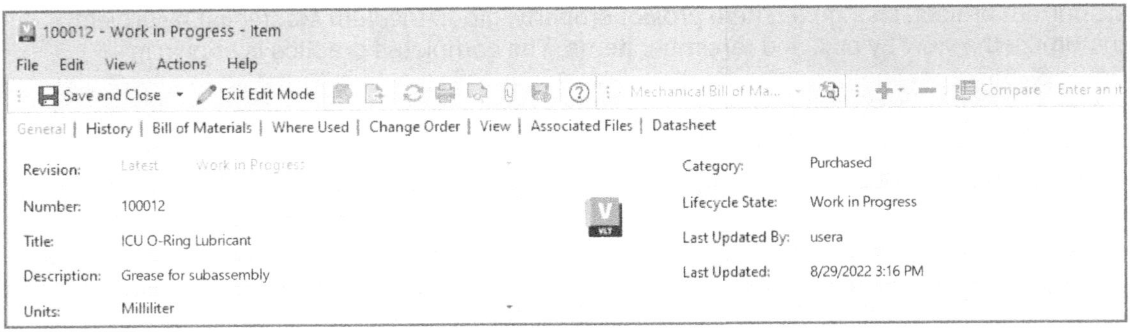


Figure 8–56

5. In the *Properties* area, if the *Item Project* user- defined item is visible, skip to Step 8.
6. In the *Properties* area, right-click anywhere and select **Add or Remove Property**. The *Add or Remove Property* dialog box displays.
7. In the *Add or Remove Property* dialog box, do the following:
   - Select **Item Project**.
   - Select **Add** from the *Action* drop-down list.
   - Click **OK**.
8. In the *Properties* area, click the *Value* field next to **Item Project**. Enter **ICUV1**as shown in Figure 8–57.

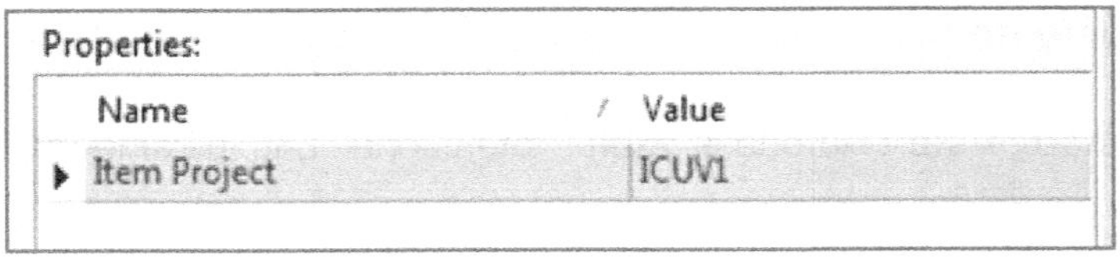


Figure 8–57

 

9. In the standard toolbar, click **Attachments**, as shown in Figure 8–58. Click **Yes** to save. The *Attachments for Item* dialog box displays.

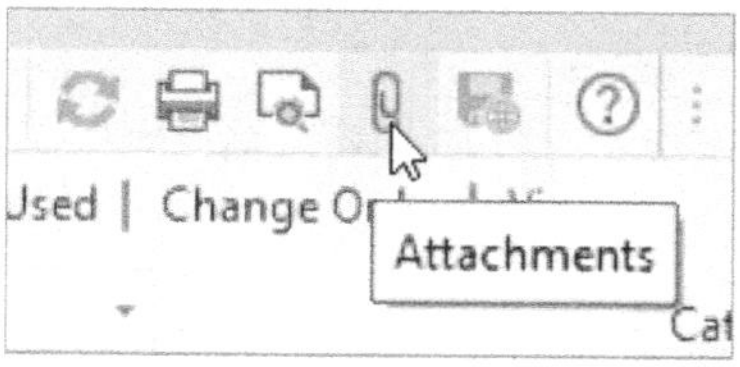


**Figure 8–58**

10. In the *Attachments for Item* dialog box, click **Attach**.
11. Navigate to the *Designs\ICU Valve\Documents* folder.
    - Select **ICU Valve Specification Sheet - Grease.doc**.
    - Click **Open**.
    - Click **OK**.
12. Close the *Item* dialog box. The new item displays in the *Item Master* list.

## Task 2: Link item to the assembly.

1. Double-click the **ICUVALVEASSY.iam** item to open it.
2. In the standard toolbar, click **Edit**.
3. Select the *Bill of Materials* tab. Right-click on the top row and select **Add Row>From Existing Item**.
4. In the *Find* dialog box, click the *Basic* tab if it is not selected already.
5. Enter **Grease** as the search text. Click **Find Now**.
6. Select the row displayed. Click **OK**. The ICU O-Ring Lubricant item is now linked to the ICUVALVEASSY.iam item. (Your item numbers might be different.)
7. Click **Save and Close**.

## Task 3: Display the user-defined property.

1. In the Advanced toolbar, select **All Items** from the *Custom Views* list.
2. In the Advanced toolbar, select **Define Custom Views** from the *Custom Views* list.
3. In the *Manage Custom Views* dialog box, click **New**.
4. In the *Create Custom View* dialog box, for *View Name*, enter **Listing by Project**. Click **OK**.
5. Select **Listing by Project** and click **Modify**.
6. In the *Customize View* dialog box, click **Fields**.
7. In the *Customize Fields* dialog box, for *Select available fields from*, select **Items** from the list.

8. In the *Available fields* list, select **Item Project**.
9. Click **Add** to add **Item Project** to the list on the right after **Title (Item, CO)**, as shown in Figure 8–59.

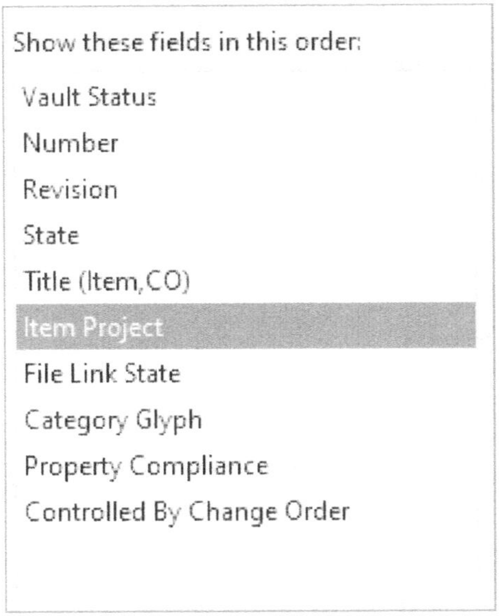


**Figure 8–59**

10. Click **OK**.
11. Close the remaining dialog boxes.
12. The *Item Master* list now shows the *Item Project* column.

***Note:*** *The new customized view you just created lists all items in the Item Master. Because this list can be very long, you create another custom view that is based on it, but that adds a custom filter to search for "ICUV1" in the Item Project property.*

## Task 4: Add a customized view.

1. In the *Advanced* toolbar, select **Define Custom Views** from the *Custom Views* list.
2. In the *Manage Custom Views* dialog box, with **Listing by Project** selected, select the *Modify* drop-down list then click **Copy**.
3. In the *Create Custom View* dialog box, for *View Name*, enter **ICU Valve 1 Project**. Click **OK**.
4. With **ICU Valve 1 Project** selected, select the *Copy* drop-down list then click **Modify**.
5. Click **Custom Filters**.

 

6. In the *Custom Filters* dialog box, do the following:
    - For *Property*, select **Item Project**.
    - For *Condition*, select **contains**.
    - For *Value*, enter **ICUV1**.
    - Click **Add**.
    - Click **OK** to close the *Custom Filters* dialog box.
7. Close the remaining dialog boxes.

## Task 5: Change Item Project property.

1. In the *Advanced* toolbar, select **Listing by Project** from the *Custom Views* list.
2. In the *Item Master*, double-click the **ICUVALVE.ipt** item. Click **Edit**.
3. Under *Properties*, click the value next to *Item Project*. Enter **ICUV1** and click **Save and Close**.
4. Select all ICU Valve Items and then click the **Edit Properties** icon in the *Properties* pane to add the *Item Project* property. Edit all values to be **ICUV1**. In *Home*, expand **Project Explorer**, **Designs**, and **Table**.
5. In the *Table* list, right-click on **Small Table.iam** and select **Assign/Update Item**.
6. Click **Save and Close**.
7. In *Home*, click **Item Master**.
8. Edit each of the seven items belonging to the Table project, and enter **Table1** in the *Item Project* property, as shown in Figure 8–60.

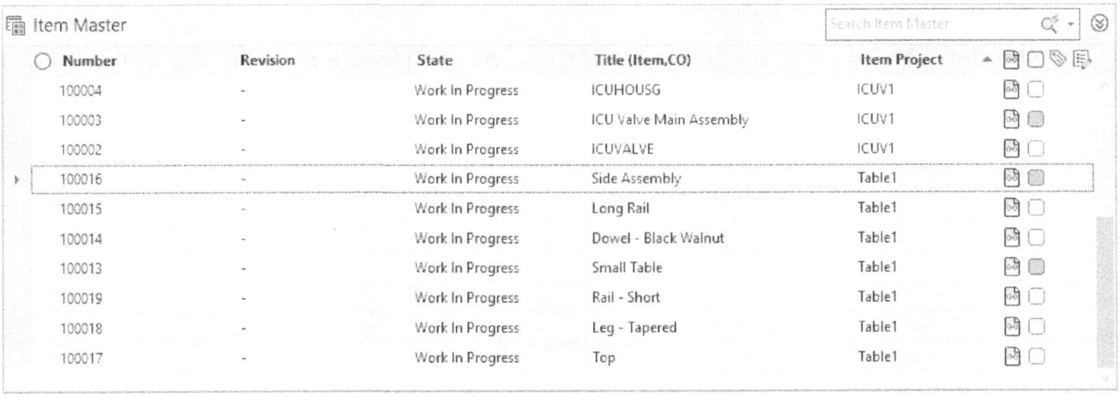
Item Master

| Number | Revision | State | Title (Item,CO) | Item Project |
|---|---|---|---|---|
| 100004 | - | Work In Progress | ICUHOUSG | ICUV1 |
| 100003 | - | Work In Progress | ICU Valve Main Assembly | ICUV1 |
| 100002 | - | Work In Progress | ICUVALVE | ICUV1 |
| 100016 | - | Work In Progress | Side Assembly | Table1 |
| 100015 | - | Work In Progress | Long Rail | Table1 |
| 100014 | - | Work In Progress | Dowel - Black Walnut | Table1 |
| 100013 | - | Work In Progress | Small Table | Table1 |
| 100019 | - | Work In Progress | Rail - Short | Table1 |
| 100018 | - | Work In Progress | Leg - Tapered | Table1 |
| 100017 | - | Work In Progress | Top | Table1 |

**Figure 8–60**

9. In the *Advanced* toolbar, for Custom Views, select **ICU Valve 1 Project** from the list. Only the ICUV1 project items display.

10. For practice, search for the **Table1** *Item Project* using the custom filters and add a new custom view called **Table 1 Project** (which is based on the ICU Valve1 project). The custom filter is shown in Figure 8–61.

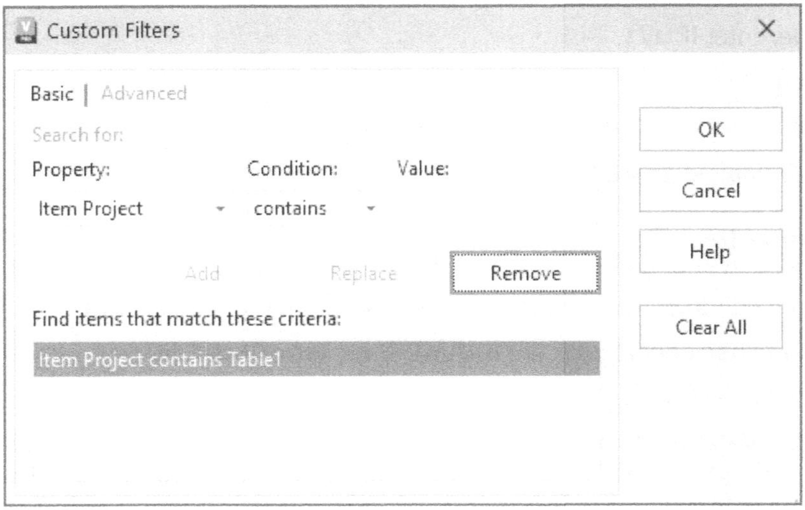


Figure 8–61

## Task 6: Group the listing by project.

1. In the *Advanced* toolbar, select **Listing by Project** from the Custom Views list.
2. In the *Item Master*, right-click on the *Item Project* header and select **Group by This Field**.
3. In the *View* menu, select **Refresh**.
4. In the *Advanced* toolbar, click **Group By Box** (as shown in Figure 8–62) to toggle it off. The listed items are grouped and boxed by project. You can expand or collapse each project as you work.

Figure 8–62

**Hint: Group by Box View**

The *Group by Box* view does not display as expected for items that are used in more than one project. For example, an item that is used in the Table1 and ICUV1 projects might have an *Item Project* property of "ICUV1, Table1." This shared item lists correctly using the ICU Valve 1 Project custom view and the Table 1 custom view, but does not list correctly under the *Group by Box Listing by Project View*.

## Task 7: Renumber items.

1. In the *Advanced* toolbar, from the *Custom Views* list, select **ICU Valve 1 Project**. Make a note of which items are assemblies and which are purchased.

   ***Note:*** *You can add the Category Name column to your view (as shown in Figure 8–63) to make it easier to see which are assemblies and which are purchased.*

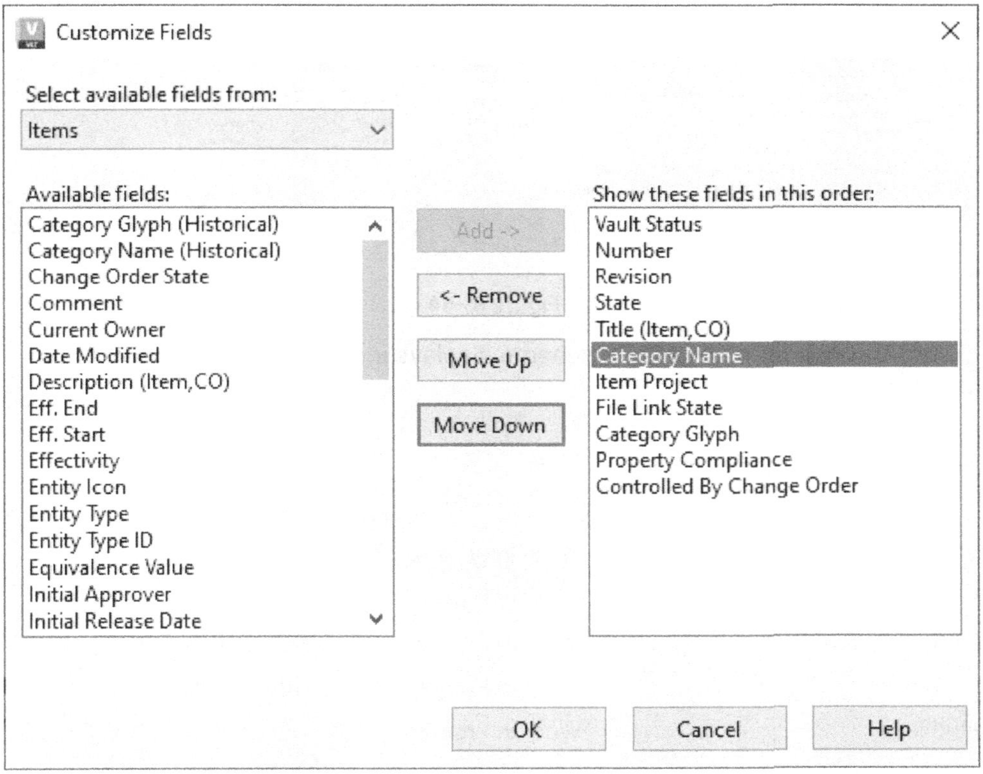


**Figure 8–63**

2. In the *Item Master*, do the following:
   - Select the first item in the list.
   - Press <Shift> and select the last item in the list.
   - Right-click anywhere over the selected items and select **Change Number**.
3. In the *Change Item Number* dialog box, from the *Select a Numbering Scheme* list, select **AOTC-Complex**.

4. In the *Change Item Number* dialog box, do the following, as shown in Figure 8–64:
   - For *Type*, select **200** to change the assembly item numbers.
   - For *Type*, select **300** to change the purchased item numbers.
   - For *Type*, select **100** to change the part item numbers.

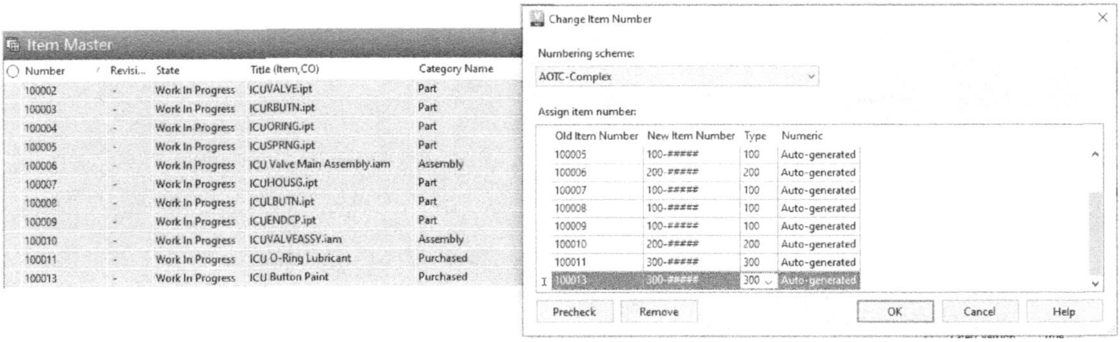


**Figure 8–64**

5. Click **OK**. The new item numbering scheme displays in the *Item Master*, as shown in Figure 8–65.

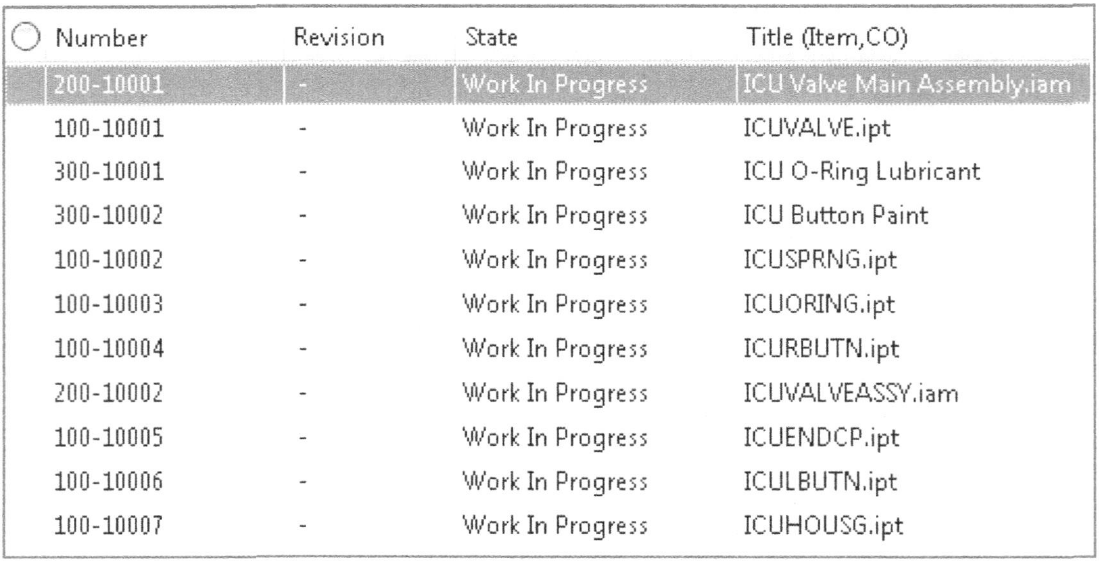

| Number | Revision | State | Title (Item,CO) |
|---|---|---|---|
| 200-10001 | - | Work In Progress | ICU Valve Main Assembly.iam |
| 100-10001 | - | Work In Progress | ICUVALVE.ipt |
| 300-10001 | - | Work In Progress | ICU O-Ring Lubricant |
| 300-10002 | - | Work In Progress | ICU Button Paint |
| 100-10002 | - | Work In Progress | ICUSPRNG.ipt |
| 100-10003 | - | Work In Progress | ICUORING.ipt |
| 100-10004 | - | Work In Progress | ICURBUTN.ipt |
| 200-10002 | - | Work In Progress | ICUVALVEASSY.iam |
| 100-10005 | - | Work In Progress | ICUENDCP.ipt |
| 100-10006 | - | Work In Progress | ICULBUTN.ipt |
| 100-10007 | - | Work In Progress | ICUHOUSG.ipt |

**Figure 8–65**

6. In the *Advanced* toolbar, select **All Items** from the *Custom Views* list.
7. In the *Advanced* toolbar, select **ICU Valve 1 Project** from the *Custom Views* list.

8. In the *Item Master,* do the following:
    - Select the first item in the list.
    - Press <Shift> and select the last item in the list.
    - Right-click anywhere over the selected items and select **Change Number**.
9. In the *Change Item Number* dialog box, from the *Select a Numbering Scheme* list, select **AOTC-Numeric**. Click **OK**. Note that the item numbers differ from the ones at the start of the practice. To avoid confusion, old item numbers are not reused.

**End of practice**

# 8.4 Exporting Items

Other data management and analysis applications are often used along with Autodesk Vault Professional. You can export Vault Professional item properties in a range of file formats to provide engineering and product data to other applications.

## Export Items from Vault Professional

You can export item data from Autodesk Vault Professional to a variety of file formats.

### How To: Export Items

The following steps describe how to export items to a file:

1. Log in to Autodesk Vault Professional as a user assigned the ERP Manager role.
2. In the *Item Master*, select all the items to export. It might be useful to filter the items or export from a saved search to restrict the items to those required.
3. Select **File>Export Items**.
4. Select the **Released and Obsolete items only** checkbox to only show items in this state.
5. Items that are checked (as shown in Figure 8–66) are exported. If you do not want to export an item that is checked, toggle off the checkbox next to that item.

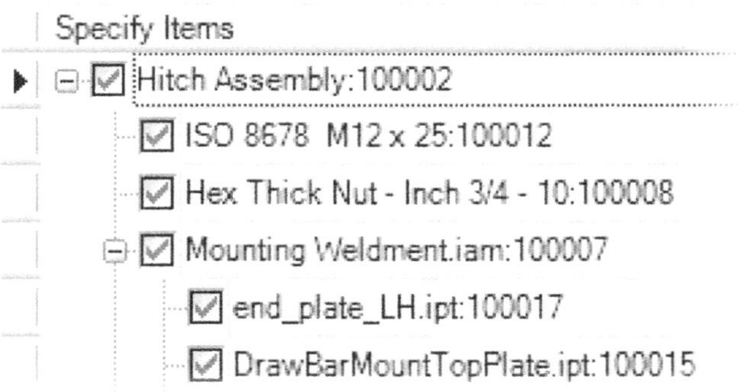


**Figure 8–66**

*__Note:__ If you export an assembly, its child components are automatically selected for export.*

6. Click **Next**.

 

7. On the *Specify File* pane, under *File types*, click **CSV (Comma Separated Values .CSV)**, as shown in Figure 8–67.

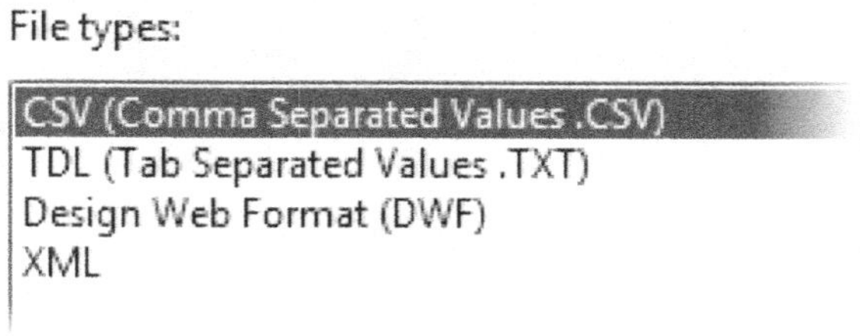


**Figure 8–67**

8. Under *BOM Indicator*, click **Level numbers**.

   ***Note:*** *If you select Parent Item for the BOM indicator, each exported item, other than the top-level items, includes the item number of its parent item.*

The exported file includes a numeric indicator of the hierarchical position of the file in the item structure, as shown in Figure 8–68. For example, if the first subassembly was assigned Level 1, the first child part in the subassembly is assigned Level 1.1, the second part 1.2, and so on.

| | A | B | C | D |
|---|---|---|---|---|
| 1 | Level | Number | Title (Item,CO) | Quan |
| 2 | 1 | 100002 | Hitch Assembly | |
| 3 | 1.1 | 100012 | ISO 8678 M12 x 25 | |
| 4 | 1.2 | 100008 | Hex Thick Nut - Inch 3/4 - 10 | |
| 5 | 1.3 | 100007 | Mounting Weldment.iam | |
| 6 | 1.3.1 | 100017 | end_plate_LH.ipt | |
| 7 | 1.3.2 | 100015 | DrawBarMountTopPlate.ipt | |
| 8 | | | | |

**Figure 8–68**

9. Click **Browse**. Browse to your export folder. Enter the filename. Click **Save**.

10. Click **Next**. In the *Specify Attributes* pane, drag field names from the *Attributes* list to the *Export file* list, as shown in Figure 8–69. To remove a field from the *Export file* list, drag it outside the list. Click **Clear Mapping** to remove all fields except **Level**.

    ***Note:*** *If you select Level Numbers as the BOM indicator, you must include the Number attribute in the Export File list.*

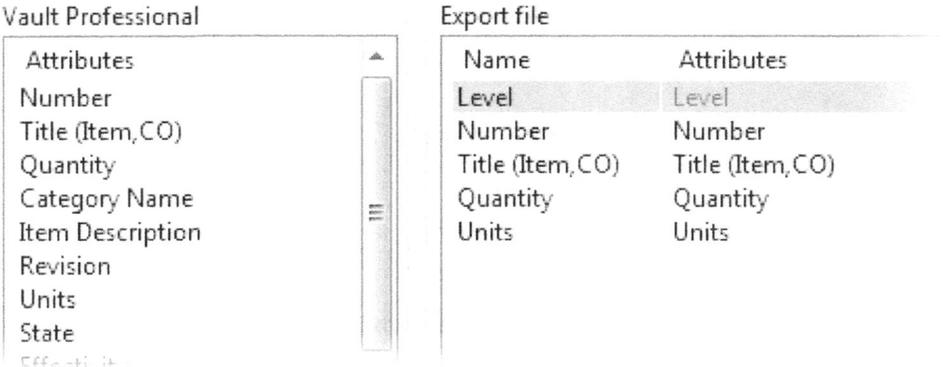


**Figure 8–69**

11. Click **Export**. An export summary displays. In the *Summary* pane, you can print the report or distribute it by email.
12. Click **Finish**. The exported file is available for import into an ERP system or other software. An example CSV export file is shown in Figure 8–70.

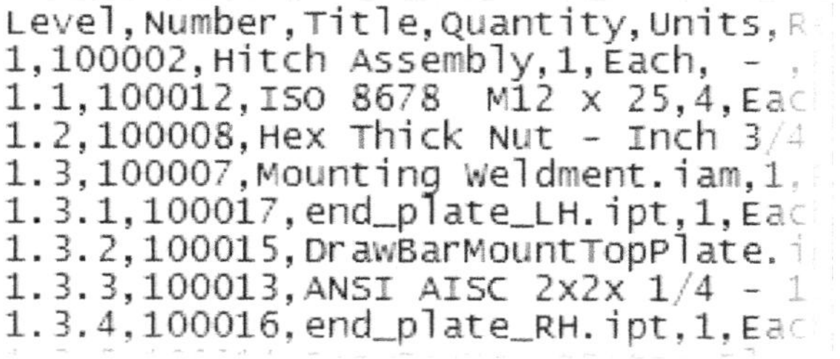


**Figure 8–70**

# Practice 8e
# Export Items from Vault Professional

In this practice, you change an assembly and its components to a **Released** lifecycle state, then export properties of the items to a .CSV file.

1. Start Autodesk Vault Professional. Log in using the following information:
   - For *User Name*, enter **administrator**.
   - Leave the *Password* field blank.
   - For *Vault*, select **AOTCVault**.

   ***Note:*** *To export items, you must be logged in as a user with at least ERP Manager role permissions.*

2. In *Home*, click **Item Master** to display the list of items in the vault.
3. In the *Advanced* toolbar, select **Assembly Items** from the Custom Views list.
4. In the main pane, right-click on the **Small Table** assembly item and select **Change State**.
5. In the *Select Lifecycle* dialog box, click **Released**, as shown in Figure 8–71. Ensure that **Include dependents** is selected in the *Change State* dialog box and click **OK**.

**Figure 8–71**

   - The lifecycle state of the table assembly and each of its components is set to **Released**.

6. In the main pane, select the **Small Table** assembly item.
7. Click **File>Export Items**.

8. For *Specify File*, do the following:
    - Click **Next**.
    - Select **CSV**.
    - Browse to the Desktop folder.
    - For *File Name*, enter **Small Table Items**.
    - Click **Save**.
    - Click **Next**.
    - Drag a few field names from the *Vault Professional* list to the *Export file* list.
    - Click **Export**.
9. Click **Finish** and open the file in Microsoft Excel and review the data.

**End of practice**

Chapter 9

# Managing Change

Vault Professional provides control over how new designs or design changes are released, eliminating the issues commonly involved with manual processes. Creating a change order enables you to describe the changes to a design and manage the progression of that change order as it is reviewed, approved, or rejected.

## Learning Objectives

- Create and change item lifecycles manually.
- Define and control lifecycle states.
- Create and approve change orders.

# 9.1 Revision Control

In this section, you learn how to use revision control to manually control lifecycle states and how different workflows affect revision control.

In design and manufacturing, a part can go through many design iterations. Lifecycle states control the revisions of a part or assembly in this process, as shown in Figure 9–1.

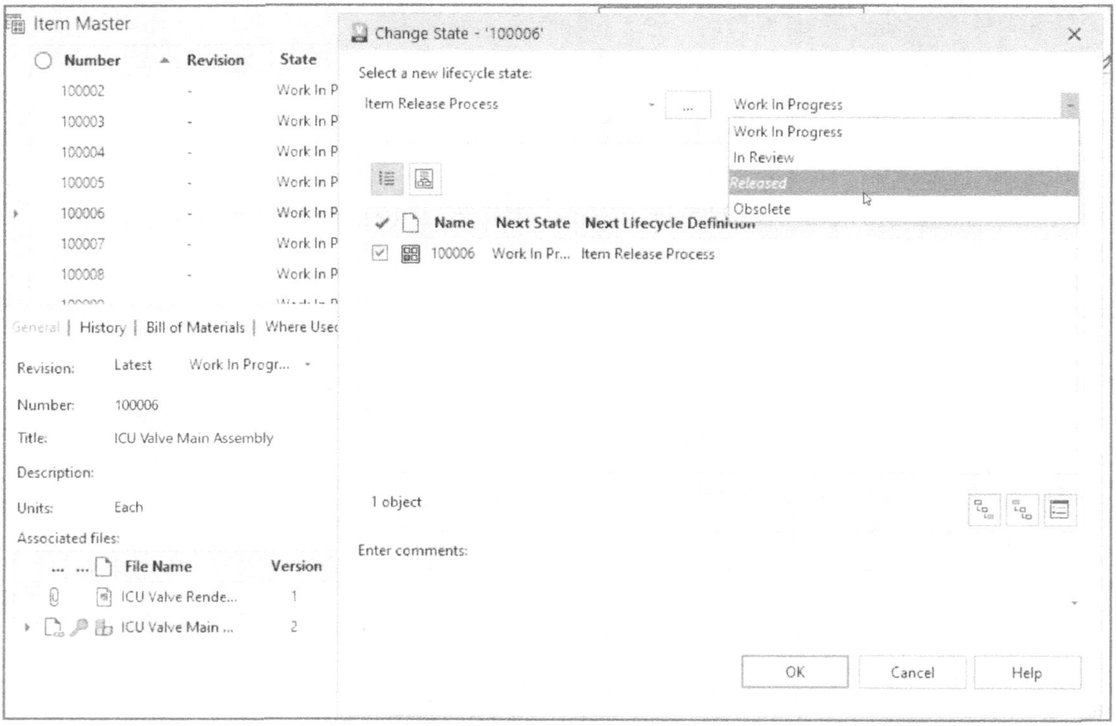


**Figure 9–1**

 

# Item Lifecycle States

To manage design data, you must control the various stages from design to manufacturing. To do this, you mark an item using one of the lifecycle states, as shown in Figure 9–2.

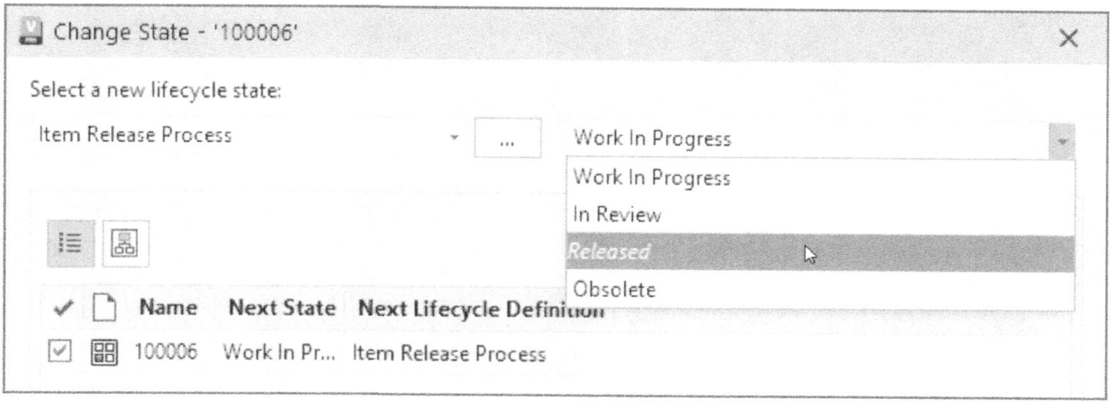


**Figure 9–2**

## Definition of Lifecycle States

> ***Note:*** *The actual names of the lifecycle states can be changed to reflect those used in your organization. This will be covered in a later section.*

The lifecycle state of an item indicates where it is in the design and manufacturing process. The following table describes the default states:

| Lifecycle State | Description |
|---|---|
| **Work in Progress** | The item is available for editing. Files associated with the item can be checked out and edited. The item can be updated to the latest file versions. New items are automatically assigned **Work in Progress** status. |
| **In Review** | The item is being reviewed prior to release to production. The item and its associated files cannot be edited or updated. |
| **Released** | The item is available for production. The item cannot be edited or updated. |
| **Obsolete** | The item is no longer used in production and cannot be updated. Items in the **Obsolete** state can be deleted. |

## Manually Changing a State

To change a state, right-click on the item in the *Item Master* and select **Change State**. The *Change State* dialog box displays the states available based on the current state of the item.

In Figure 9–3, the item is set to **Work in Progress**. You can select **In Review**, **Released**, or **Obsolete**.

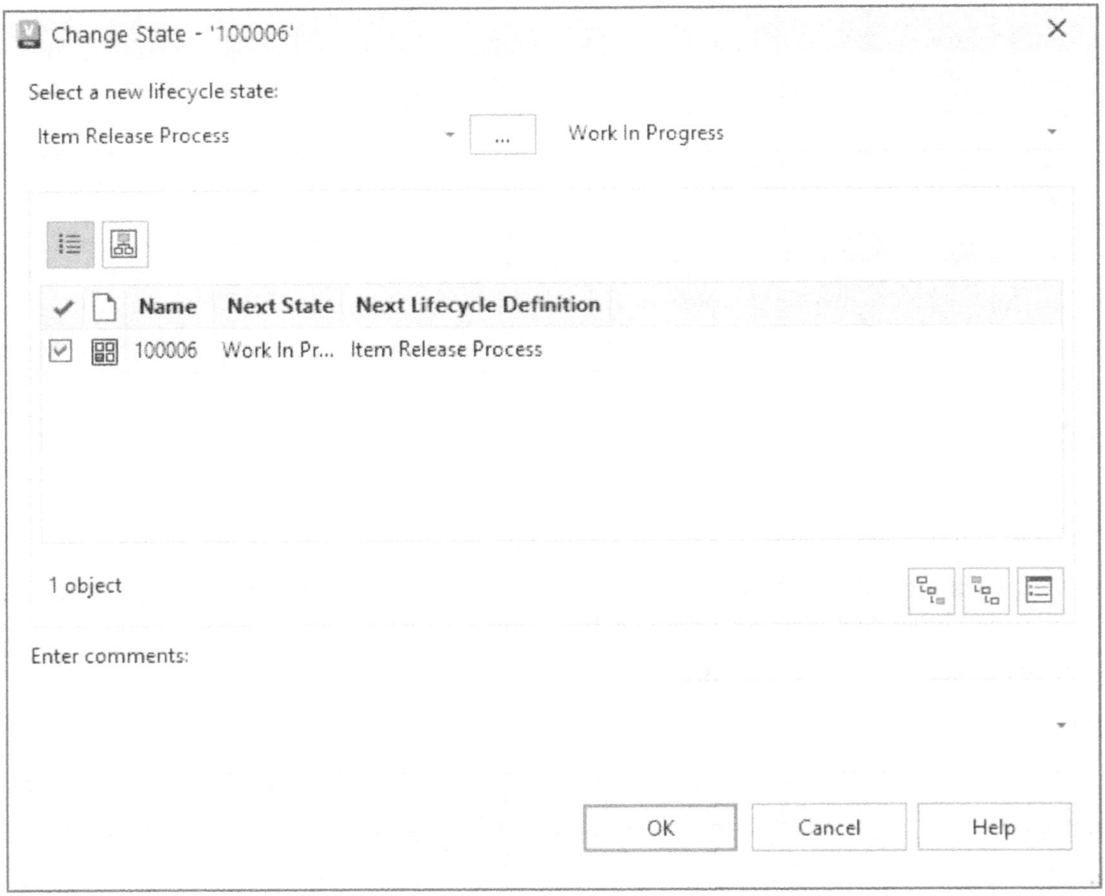


**Figure 9–3**

## Example of a Manual State Change

The design team has determined that a part is ready for manufacturing. During the design phase, the part has a **Work in Progress (WIP)** lifecycle state. You set the lifecycle state to **Released** to indicate that the part is ready for manufacturing and distribution.

## Revisions and Lifecycle State

By default, when you change an item's state from **Released** to **WIP**, the revision automatically bumps using the primary revision bump action.

The following state changes do not bump the revision status of an item:

- WIP to Obsolete
- WIP to Released
- WIP to In Review
- Released to Obsolete
- In Review to Obsolete
- In Review to Released
- In Review to WIP
- Obsolete to In Review
- Obsolete to WIP

***Note:*** *Depending on your company's configuration, not all of these state changes will be available.*

## Revision Formats

A user with an administrator or Item Editor (Level 2) role sets the revision sequence and can either specify one of the formats shown in Figure 9–4 or create a custom revision scheme.

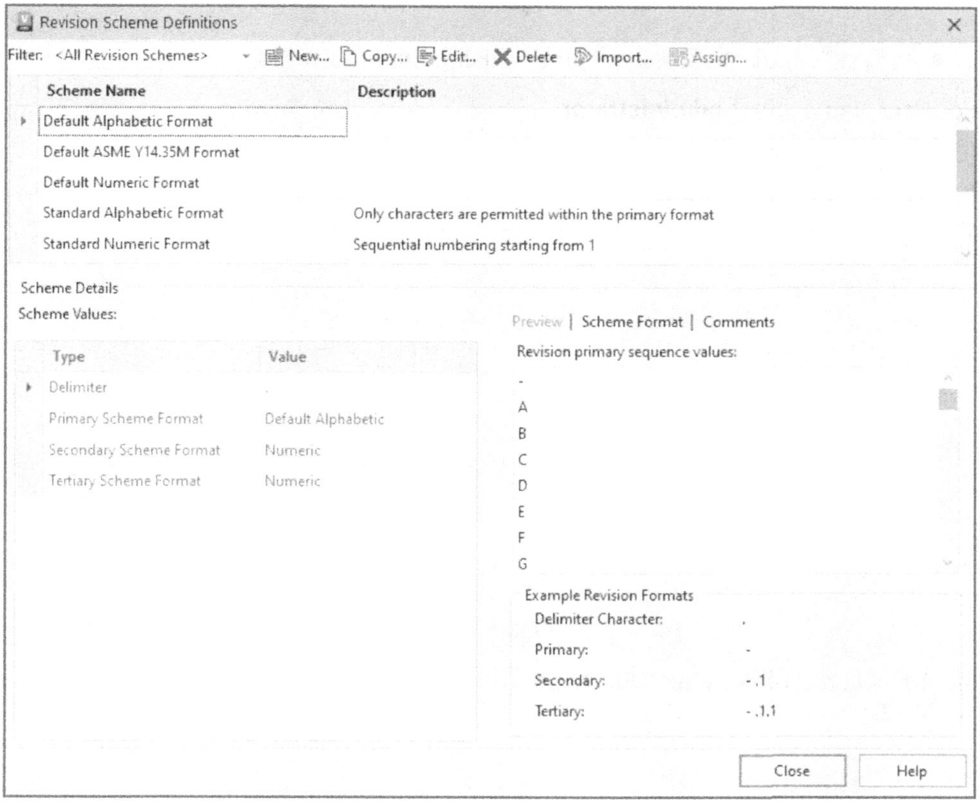


**Figure 9–4**

Examples of the revision format display in the *Preview* tab of the *Revision Scheme Definitions* dialog box.

# Practice 9a
# Change Lifecycle States Manually

In this practice, you create an item and manually change the lifecycle state. The completed practice is shown in Figure 9–5.

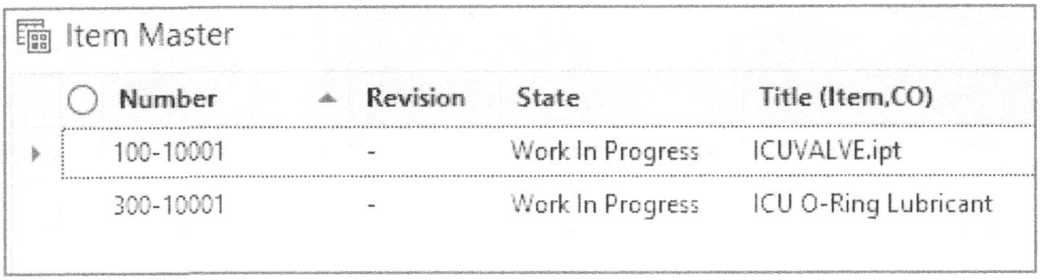


***The completed practice***

**Figure 9–5**

1. Start Autodesk® Vault Professional. Log in using the following information:
   - For *User Name*, enter **administrator**.
   - Leave the *Password* field blank.
   - For *Vault*, select **AOTCVault**.
2. In the *Go* menu, select **Item Master**, as shown in Figure 9–6.

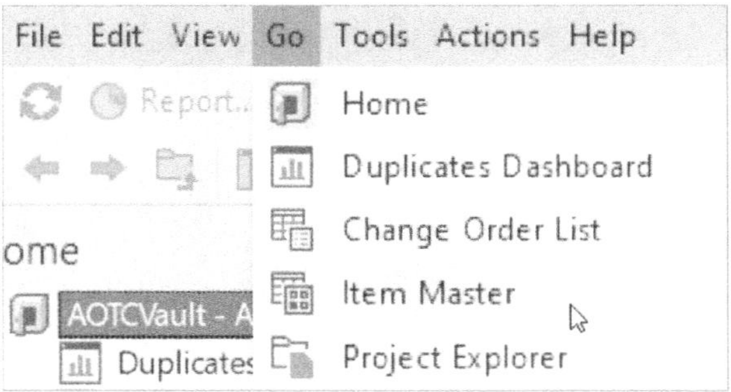


**Figure 9–6**

3. In the *Advanced* toolbar, select **All Items** from the *Custom Views* list, as shown in Figure 9–7.

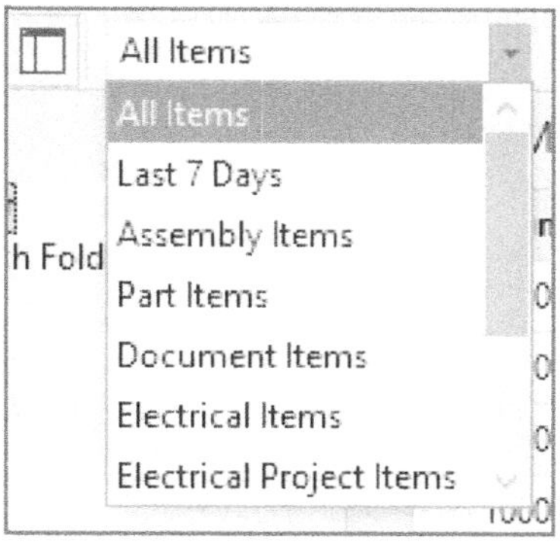


**Figure 9–7**

4. In the *Go* menu, select **Project Explorer**.
5. Expand the *Designs* folder. Click the *Clamp* folder, as shown in Figure 9–8.

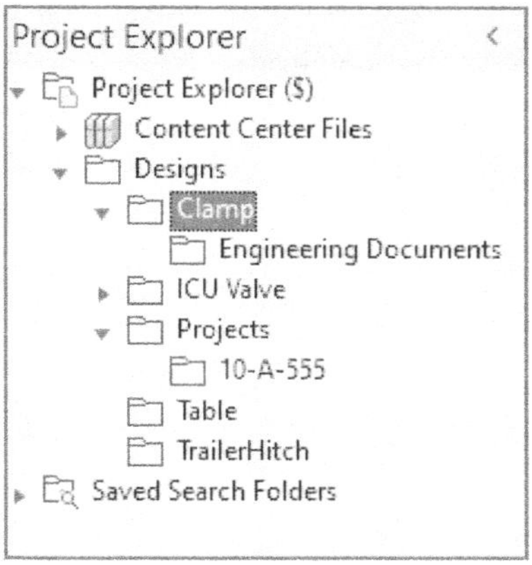


**Figure 9–8**

6. Right-click on **Handle.ipt** and select **Assign/Update Item**, as shown in Figure 9–9.

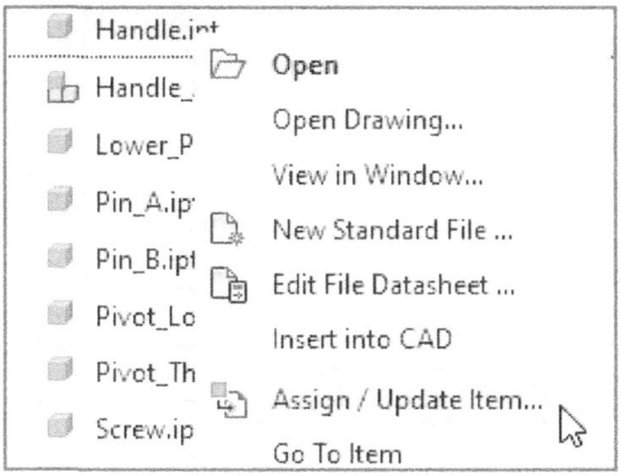


**Figure 9–9**

7. In the *Edit Item* window, click **Save and Close**. An item icon displays next to the file name, as shown in Figure 9–10.

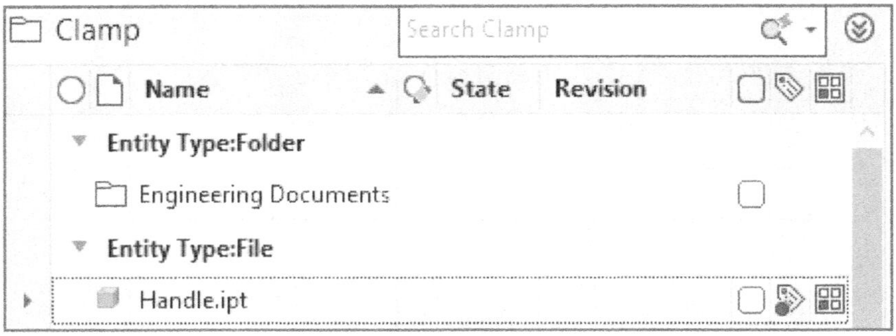


Figure 9–10

8. In the *Go* menu, select **Item Master**.
9. In the *Item Master*, click the *Number* column to sort the item numbers in descending order.
10. In the *Item Master*, right-click on the new item.

*Note: Your item number might differ from the illustrations shown in this practice. Your item should be the highest number. In this example, it is 100021.*

11. Select **Change State**, as shown in Figure 9–11.

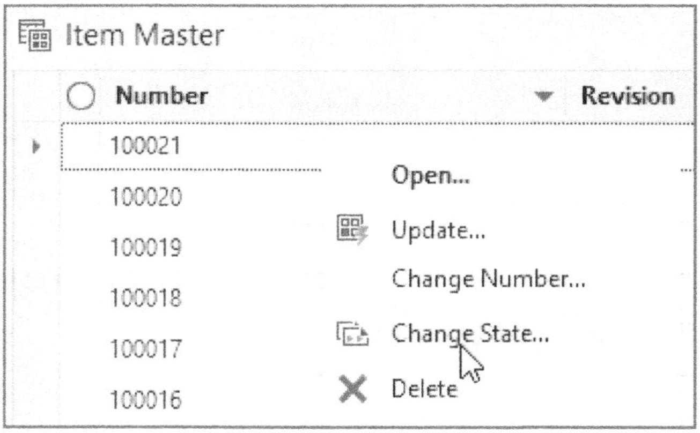


Figure 9–11

12. In the *Select Lifecycle* dialog box, select **Released**.

13. Click **OK**. Note that the *Revision* is a dash (-) and the lifecycle state is changed to **Released**. A lock symbol is placed beside the item, as shown in Figure 9–12.

**Figure 9–12**

14. In the *Go* menu, select **Project Explorer**.
15. Review the part. Note the lock symbol (shown in Figure 9–13) beside the part here as well.

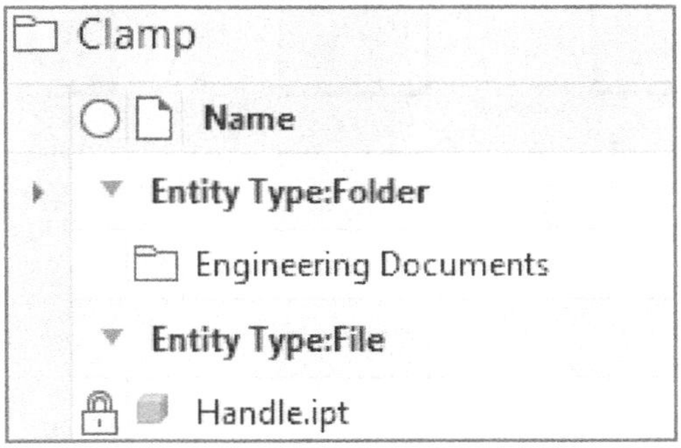


**Figure 9–13**

16. In the *Go* menu, select **Item Master**.
17. Right-click on the item and select **Change State**.
18. Select **Work In Progress** and click **OK**.
19. Review the status of the part. The *Revision* is now set to **A**, as shown in Figure 9–14. Note that the lock icon is removed from the item.

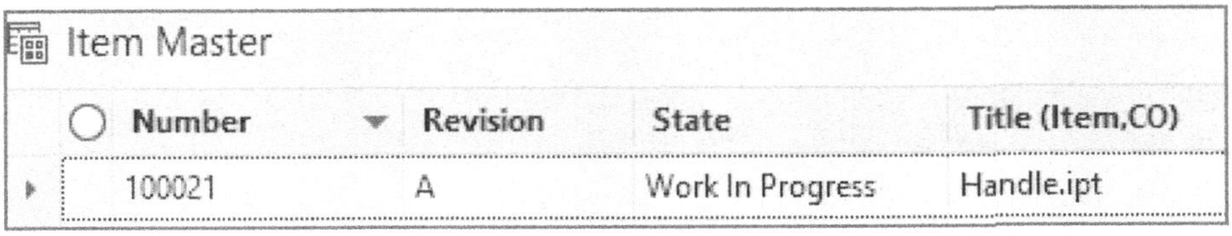


**Figure 9–14**

**End of practice**

# 9.2 Change Orders

This section describes how to create change orders to control the release of new designs or changes to those designs.

The Change Order Editor role provides permissions to create or participate in a change order. In addition, the administrator defines appropriate change order permissions for each participant in the change order process. (shown in Figure 9–15)

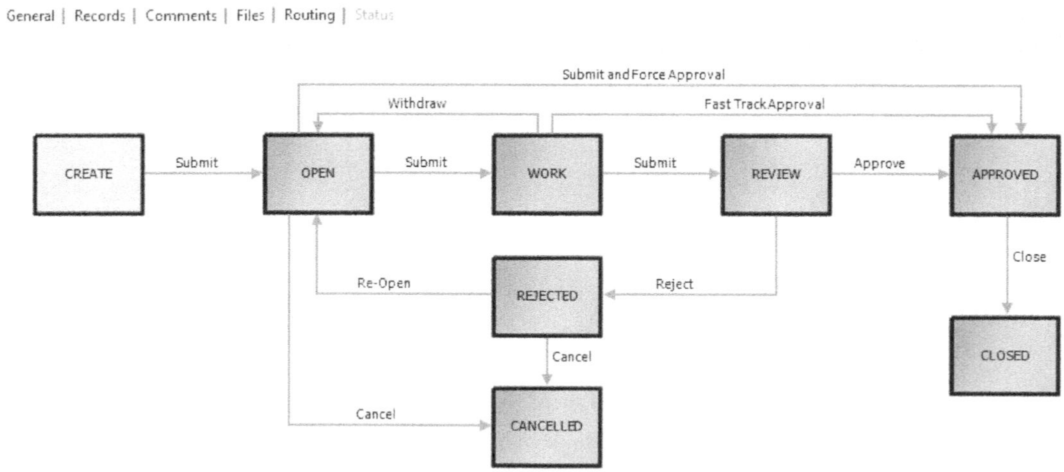


**Figure 9–15**

# Introduction to Change Orders

When you create a revision, design changes are made and the changes are then approved by one or more people. Using the change order process, when you (the change requestor) modify files or items, the change is routed to the correct members in the design team before being released to production. When the change order reaches the **Closed** state (as shown in Figure 9–16), it will display a dialog box with the associated items and files that enables the user to manually change the states.

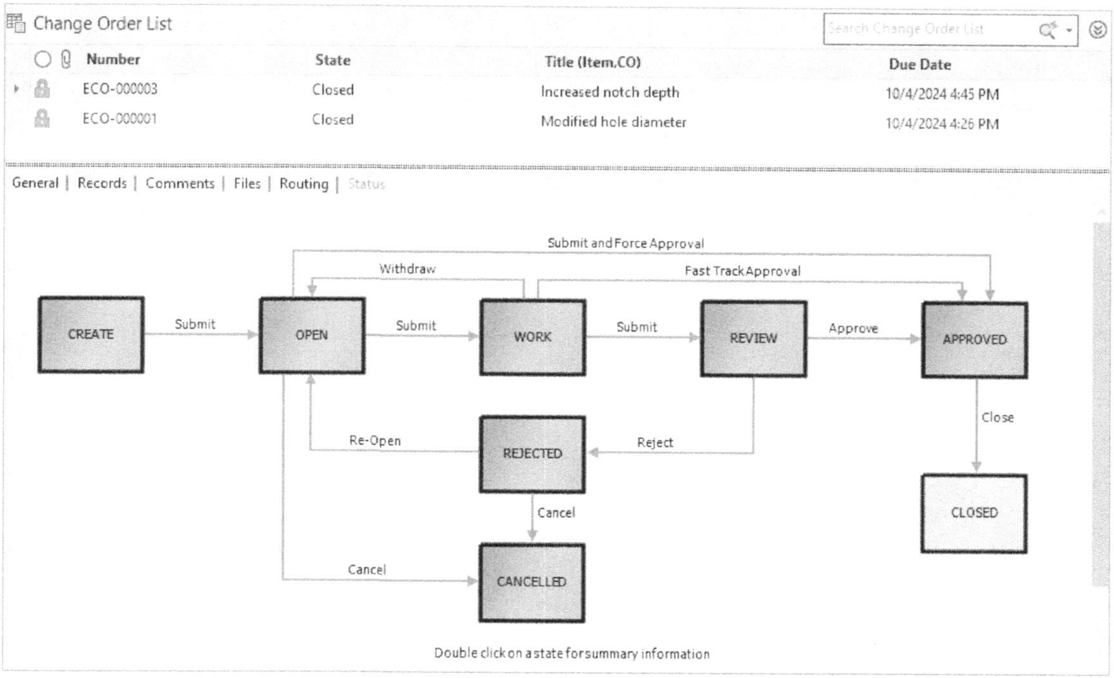


**Figure 9–16**

## Definition of Change Orders

You can use change orders to both describe the changes made to a design and to manage the progress of those changes through review, approval, rejection, and release to production. The *Change Order* dialog box (shown in Figure 9–17) provides a historical record of why, how, and when changes were made.

Figure 9–17

# Description of Change Order Workflow

The *Status* tab in the *Change Order* dialog box (shown in Figure 9–18) displays a workflow chart of all possible combinations of state progressions.

> **Note:** *Some companies include a Check state between Work and Review.*

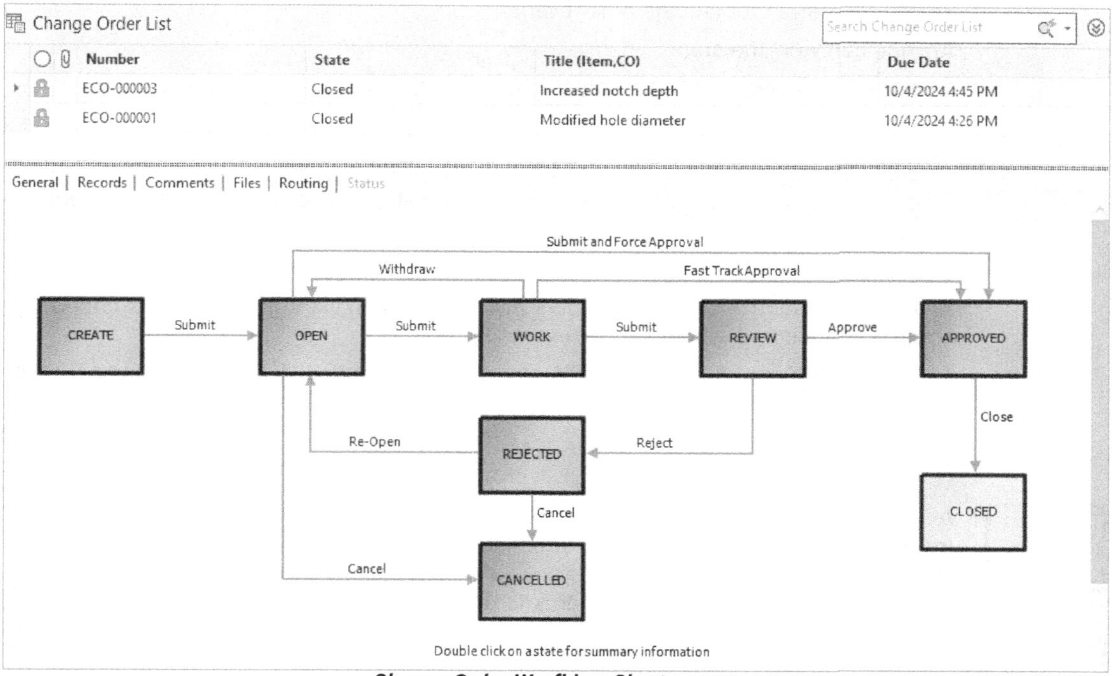


***Change Order Worfklow Chart***

**Figure 9–18**

You can also visually identify the current status of the change order by clicking the *Status* tab on the respective *Change Order* dialog box. Double-clicking a state gives you summary information about that state.

| State | Description |
|---|---|
|  | After a user has created and submitted the change order, the change order enters the **Open** state. In the **Open** state, the Change Administrator can edit the title, edit the value of a user-defined property, and change the attachments.<br>The Change Administrator can perform the same editing tasks in the **Open** state as in the state when the change order is first being created with one exception: The specified numbering scheme cannot be changed.<br>Change the lifecycle state of an item by using the change state command in the context menu of a selected item. |

| State | Description |
|---|---|
| WORK | As soon as the change order enters the Work state, the Responsible Engineer is notified that there is a change order requiring attention, then the following occurs:<br>The change order number is added to each participant's work list.<br>An email message is sent to each person on the routing list if they have subscribed to email notification for change order events.<br>Anyone can view the status.<br>A reviewer can view, add, and reply to change order comments.<br>The Responsible Engineer can edit the change order, make any required revisions, and then submit the change order for review. |
| REVIEW | As soon as the change order enters the Review state, routing participants are notified that there is a change order requiring attention, then the following occurs:<br>The change order number is added to each participant's work list.<br>An email message is sent to each person on the routing list if they have subscribed to email notification for change order events.<br>A reviewer can view, add, and reply to change order comments. Approvers can approve or reject the changes. Unanimous approval requires that all approvers must approve the changes.<br>Anyone can view the status. |
| APPROVED | A participant with approver status can approve a change order. The Approvers approve in the **Review** state. If the Change Administrator submits the approved change order to the **Closed** state, a records dialog box displays that enables the Change Administrator change the state of the attached items to release them. |
| REJECTED | When a participant with Approver status rejects a change order, the change order enters into the **Rejected** state.<br>As a Change Administrator, you can do the following:<br>• Cancel the change order.<br>• Reopen the change order. |
| CANCELLED | In the **Cancelled** state, no action can be taken by anyone. |
| CLOSED | In the **Closed** state, no action can be taken by anyone. |

# 9.3 Creating Change Orders

Use the *Change Order* dialog box (shown in Figure 9–19) to create change orders. A change requestor initiates the process and adds comments, attaches files, and selects a routing template (a predefined list of participants).

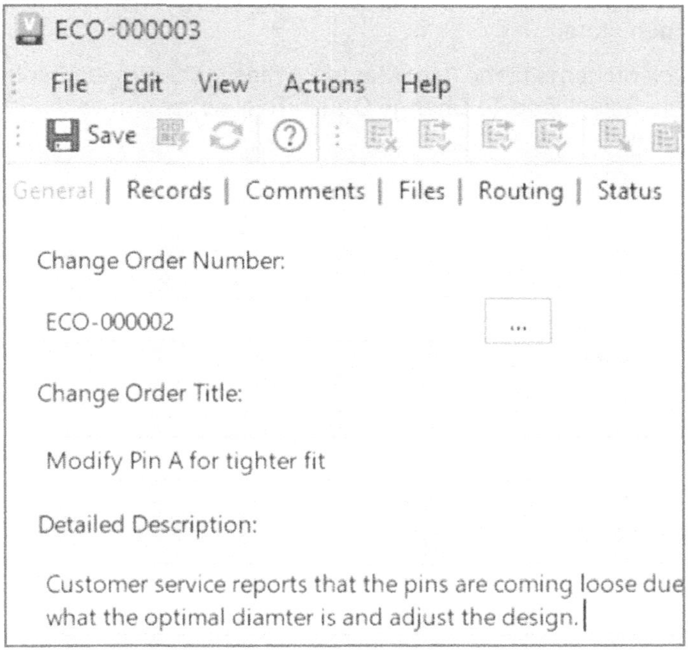


**Figure 9–19**

## Change Order Options

The tab functions in the *Change Order* dialog box are described in the following table.

| Options | Description |
|---|---|
| **General** | Contains the change order attributes. |
| **Records** | Displays the list of files and items associated with the change order. The record details for each file or item include a title, description, revision, and state. |
| **Comments** | Summarizes the decisions for the change order in the form of comments. The *Comments* tab collects all actions taken on the change order or comments submitted for the change order. |
| **Files** | Lists all files for the change order. Attachments and markups are also listed. |
| **Routing** | Lists the participants involved with the current change order. |
| **Status** | Contains a graphical representation of the current status of the change order. |

## How To: Create a Change Order

The following steps describe how to create a change order. You must have Administrator or Change Order Editor permissions to create or participate in a change order. **Note:** You should not save the change order until you have selected a routing template. After the change order is saved, the change requestor cannot change the routing list, but the change administrator can change this in the **Open** state.

1. You can right-click on items in the *Item Master* or files in the Project Explorer view to display the context menu. Select **Add To Change Order>To New**, as shown in Figure 9–20.

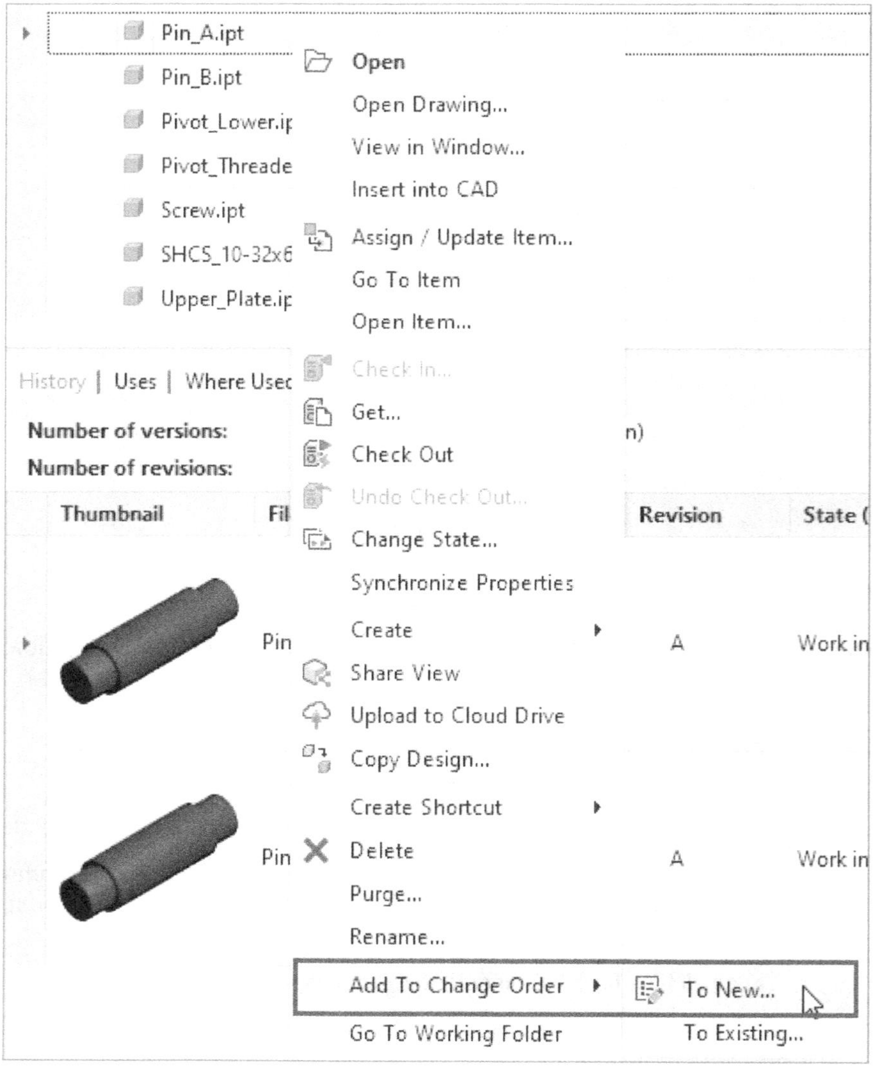


**Figure 9–20**

2. The *Change Order* dialog box displays, as shown in Figure 9–21.

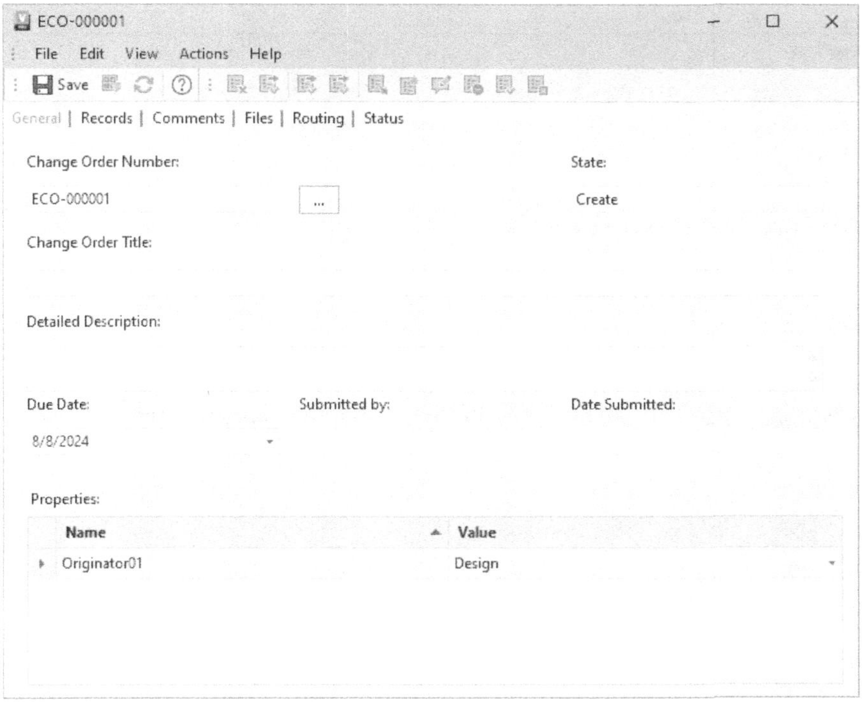


**Figure 9–21**

3. The Change Order Number is automatically generated and populated by the system. If desired, you can change the generated number. If there is only one *Change Order Numbering Scheme* active in the system, the number will increment to the next available number. If there is more than one *Changer Order Numbering Scheme* active in the system, the *Change Order Numbering Schemes* dialog box will display. Click on the drop-down list and select the desired scheme (as shown in Figure 9–22), and the system will follow that protocol.

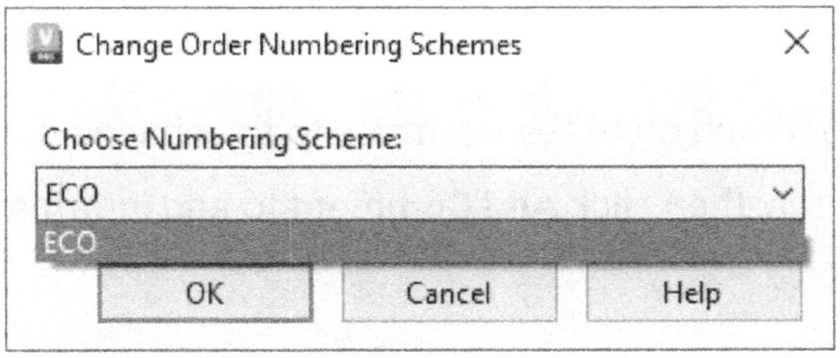


**Figure 9–22**

***Note:*** *The numbering scheme cannot be changed by the change requestor after the change order has been saved, but the change administrator can change the number in the* ***Open*** *state.*

4. Enter a title under *Change Order Title* and enter a detailed description, as shown in Figure 9–23. Under *Due Date*, select a date when the change order is to be completed.

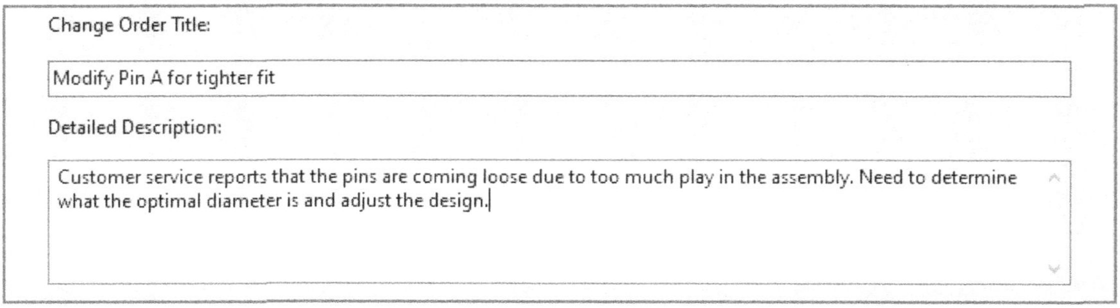


**Figure 9–23**

5. Click the *Records* tab. The file selected in Step 1 displays, as shown in Figure 9–24.

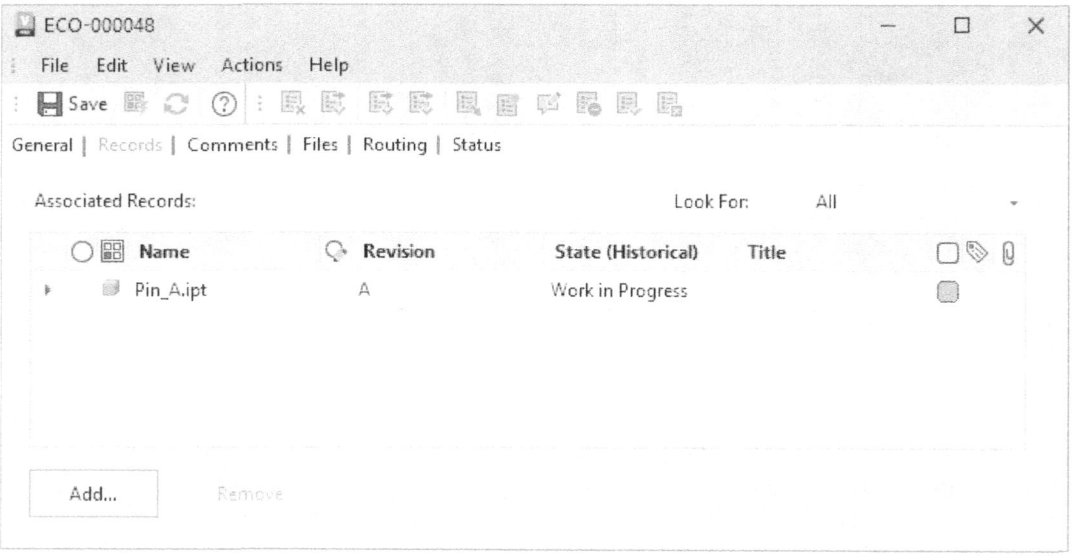


**Figure 9–24**

- You can use **Add** to attach other files or items to the change order.

6. Select the *Comments* tab, then click **Add Comment** to add information about the required design change, etc, as shown in Figure 9–25.

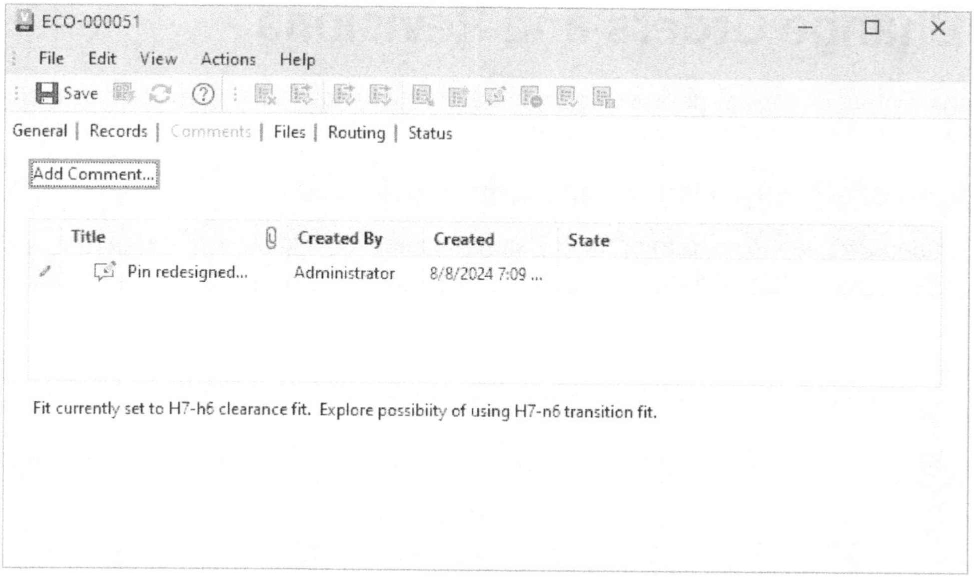


**Figure 9–25**

7. Click the *Routing* tab. Select a routing list, as shown in Figure 9–26.

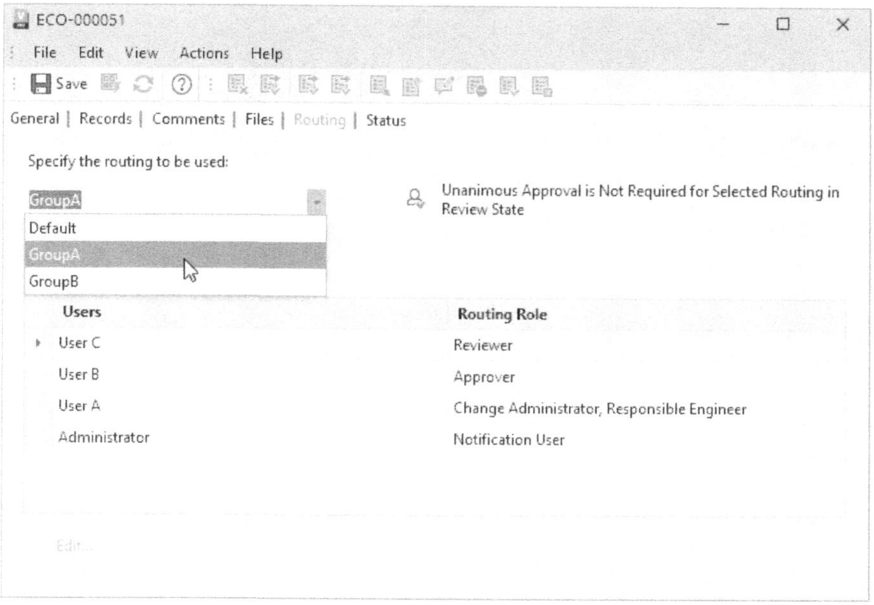


**Figure 9–26**

- An example of a routing list and what it represents is shown in the *Example of Change Order Routing* section.

8. Click **Save** to create the change order.

# 9.4 Change Orders and Revisions

The lifecycle state change generates a primary revision change to the items or files included in a change order. A qualified user can manually change the revision for any item or file.

## Definition of Change Orders and Item Revisions

You can manually change an item or file revision (as shown in Figure 9–27) regardless of its participation in a change order.

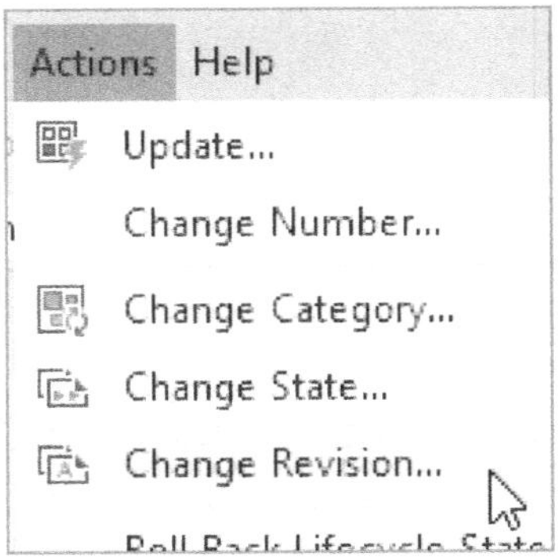


**Figure 9–27**

For example, if a part is currently a work in progress, a department can create a secondary revision to indicate a design change, as shown in Figure 9–28.

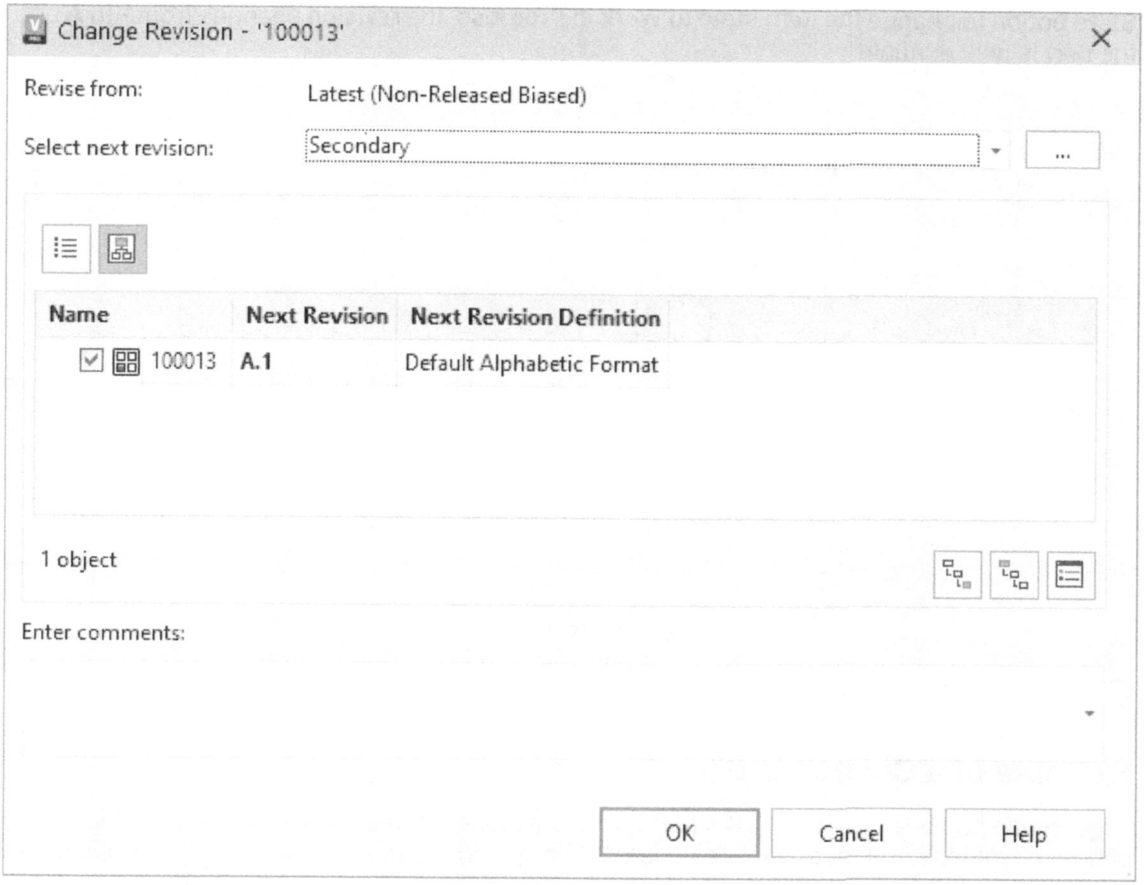


**Figure 9–28**

By default, items associated with a change order are locked for state changes and only the Change Administrator or Responsible Engineer can make them editable in the **Open** or **Work** states. If an item in the **Released** state is added to a change order and editing is enabled, the item's state changes to **Work in Progress**. A new revision is automatically created unless the bump revision action is set to **None** in the *Lifecycle Rules* dialog box.

## Example of a Revision Change

In Figure 9–29, the part file **Grip.ipt** is released and has a revision -. When you use the **Change State** option to change the item state to **Work in Progress,** the revision changes from - to **A** and the part is now editable.

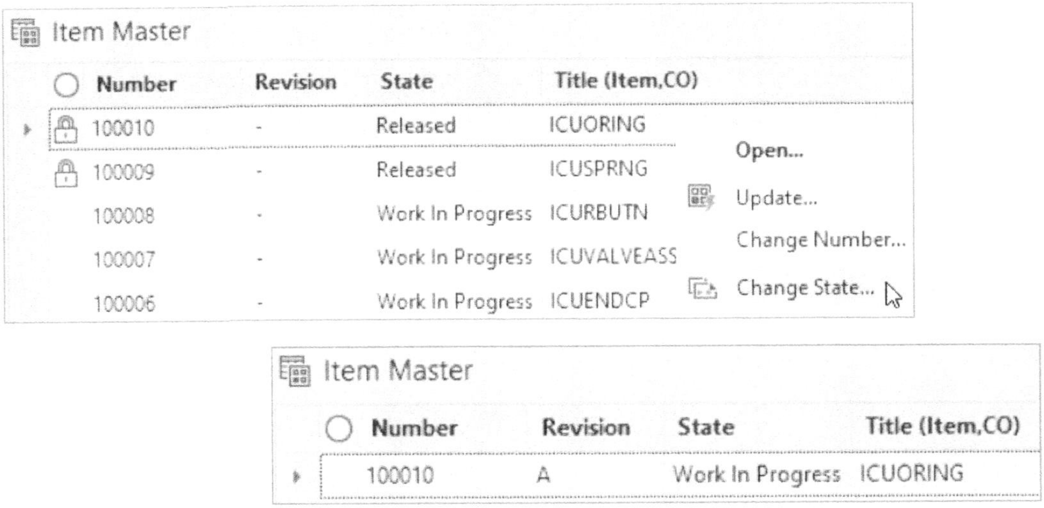


Figure 9–29

# Change Orders and Lifecycle States

## Example of a Change Order

Engineering has been notified that a part has had a higher-than-expected failure rate under certain conditions and must be redesigned. When you create the change order for the existing item, the part can be modified and the change routed through the design team for approval.

When the item is not included in an active change order, you can manually change the state of the item, as shown in Figure 9–30.

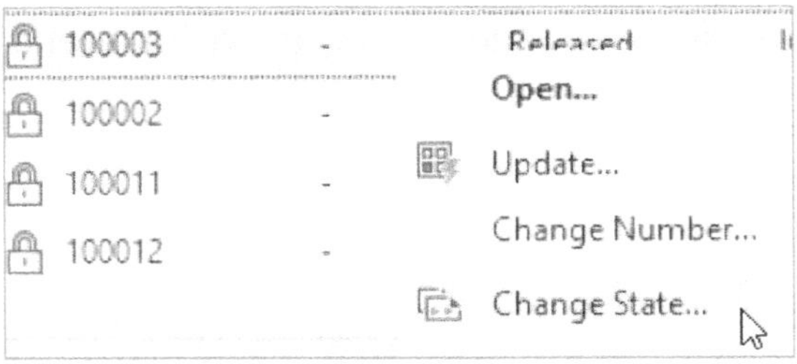


Figure 9–30

When an item is attached to a change order, the functionality is disabled at the item level and transferred into the change order while in the edit mode.

## Rules for Using Change Orders with Files

### General Rules

- Only users with Administrator or Change Order Editor security permissions can affect change orders.
- A file can only be associated with one active change order at a time. Once a change order has been closed or cancelled, the file can be associated with a new or a currently active change order.
- Change orders do not drive file state changes. However, a change order will prevent certain lifecycle state changes for the file depending on the change order's state and if linked to change order is added as a criteria in the file's lifecycle transition.

### Rules for Closing a Change Order

- The change order must be in the **Approved** state.

### Rules for Releasing Files with Relationships

- Releasing an assembly on a change order that has unreleased children (not on a change order) releases the children. Effectivity is immediate.
- If a previously unreleased child is on another change order, the change order containing the parent item cannot be closed until the change order associated with the child item is either closed or canceled.

### Best Practices

- As a best practice, you should add all affected children to a change order with an assembly. Reviewers and Approvers are notified of all affected files.
- In general, you should add all files affected by a design change to the change order. For example, in Autodesk Inventor, changing a part also changes the parent assembly.

## Rules for Using Change Orders with Items

Certain rules apply to using change orders with items and lifecycle states, closing a change order, or releasing items with relationships. Follow these rules and best practices for using change orders with items.

## General Rules

- To alter change orders, you must have Administrator or Change Order Editor security permissions. A change order may not be editable when in a particular state where a user has no responsibilities in that state on that change order.
- An item can only be associated with one active change order at a time. Once a change order has been closed or cancelled, the item can be associated with a new or active change order.
- The Change Administrator can make an item editable in all states except **Canceled** and **Closed**. The Responsible Engineer can make an item editable in the Work state, changing the lifecycle state.
- When an item is in the **Work in Progress** state and associated with a change order, an Item Editor Level 2 can edit the item, but cannot use the following commands:
    - Change State
    - New Change Order

## Rules for Using Change Orders with Items and Lifecycle States

- If a released item is added to a change order and the Change Administrator changes the state of the item to **Work in Progress**, the item changes to **Work in Progress** and a new revision is created according to the bump revision action specified in the *Lifecycles Rules* dialog box. If the bump revision action is set to **None**, a new revision is created but will display the same revision level.
- The state of an item does not change when it is attached to a change order, except at the closure of the change order. The Change Administrator is presented with a dialog box showing the attached items, which enables the Change Administrator to release the affected items.
- After a new revision is created, the Change Administrator can change the lifecycle state of the item to make the item editable or non-editable. To do this, use the **Change State** command available from the context menu.

## Rules for Closing a Change Order

- In order to close a change order, it must be in the **Approved** state.
- When you close a change order, a *Change State* dialog displays asking whether you want to change the state for associated items. You can modify the item states before closing the change order, or simply close the change order without making any changes.

## Rules for Releasing Items with Relationships

- Releasing an assembly on a change order that has unreleased children (not on a change order) releases the children. Effectivity is immediate.

- If a previously unreleased child is on another change order, the change order containing the parent item cannot be closed until the change order associated with the child item is either closed or cancelled.

### Best Practices

- As a best practice, you should add all children to a change order with an assembly. Reviewers and Approvers are notified of all affected items.
- In general, you should add all items affected by a design change to the change order. For example, in Autodesk Inventor, changing a part also changes the parent assembly.

# Roll Back the Lifecycle State of a File

Return a file to a previous lifecycle state with the **Roll Back Lifecycle State Change** command. When a file is rolled back, it:

- Returns to the file version associated with the rolled-back state.
- Returns to the security, lifecycle definition, and revisions scheme associated with the rolled-back state.
- All file properties are reset to the values of the previous version.
- Deletes the current version of the file.

## Rules for Rolling Back a File Lifecycle State

The lifecycle of a file can be rolled back if:

- The file is currently checked in.
- No parent versions consume the current child version that you want to roll back.
- The previous lifecycle state has not been deleted.
- The file is not in <null> definition.
- There is no label on the current version of the file.
- The administrator has not enabled the **Restrict File and Item Lifecycle State Changes to Change Orders** option. Files should never be rolled back past the last released state. Only roll files back to **Released** in the **Work in Progress** or **In Review** states.

### How To: Roll Back a File's Lifecycle State

You must be a Document Manager Level 2 or Administrator to roll back a file's lifecycle state.

1. Select a file in the main view and select **Actions>Roll Back Lifecycle State Change**.
2. A dialog box displays describing to which state the file will be rolled back.
3. Click **Continue** to complete the lifecycle state rollback.

# Roll Back the Lifecycle State of an Item

Return an item to a previous lifecycle state with the **Roll Back Lifecycle State Change** command.

When an item is rolled back, it:

- Returns to the item version associated with the rolled-back state.
- Returns to the security, lifecycle definition, and revisions scheme associated with the rolled-back state.
- All item properties are reset to the values of the previous version.
- Deletes the current version of the item.

## Rules for Rolling Back an Item Lifecycle State

You can roll back an item from any state to another state as long as:

- The rolled-back state has not been deleted.
- The current lifecycle state is not <null> and the rolled-back state is not <null>.
- The rolled-back state is not controlled by purge settings.
- There are no ECO restrictions on state change.
- The rolled-back state did not exist before the ECO was created.
- The ECO is not closed.

  ***Note:*** *If the ECO was canceled, you can still roll back to the last state in the ECO. Items should never be rolled back past the last released state. Only roll items back to* ***Released*** *in the* ***Work in Progress*** *or* ***In Review*** *states.*

- There are no component link restrictions. For example, if rolling back to the previous state would link the item to a component that is only permitted one link and the component is already linked to another item, then the rollback is not permitted.

Only users with Item Editor Level 2, ERP Manager, or Administrator roles can change the state on an item.

### How To: Roll Back the Lifecycle State of an Item

1. Select an item in the *Item Master*, and then select **Actions>Roll Back Lifecycle State Change**.
2. Click **Continue** to complete the lifecycle state rollback.

# Clear Item and Change Order Locks

Occasionally, it is required to remove the item and change order locks reserved to you. Use the **Clear Item and CO Locks** command to clear all of the locked items and change orders and return them to read-only mode.

> ***Note:*** *This command releases locks for items and change orders that are reserved to the user performing the command. Changes to the items or change orders are not saved.*

## How To: Clear Item and Change Order Locks

1. In the Vault Client, select **Actions>Clear Item and CO Locks**.
2. Verify that you want to clear the locks.
3. All locked items and change orders are returned to read-only state. Changes are not saved.

# Identifying Change Order Participants

When you create a change order, you specify a routing list of participants with predefined roles and specific permissions and responsibilities. Participants are notified that a change order requires their attention. All roles, except the Reviewer and Notification User, control the progression of the change order (within the state that the role controls). For example, the Responsible Engineer has control over the **Work** state only. Change Administrators have some level of control over almost all states, but principally the **Open, Rejected,** and **Approved** states. The Reviewer role (as shown in Figure 9–31) can add markups, view, add, and reply to comments.

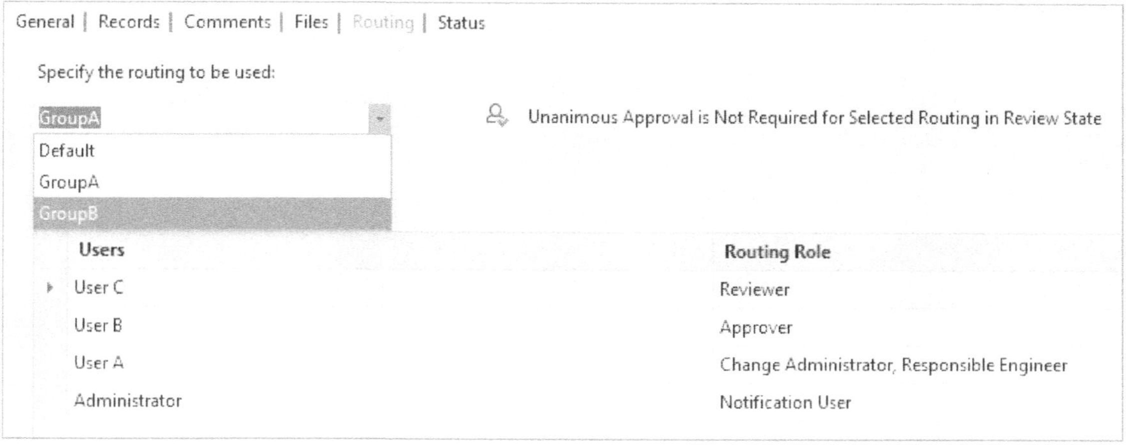


**Figure 9–31**

## Example of Change Order Routing

The administrator creates routing participant lists in the *Global Settings* dialog box (**Tools>Administration>Global Settings>***Change Orders* tab), as shown in Figure 9–32.

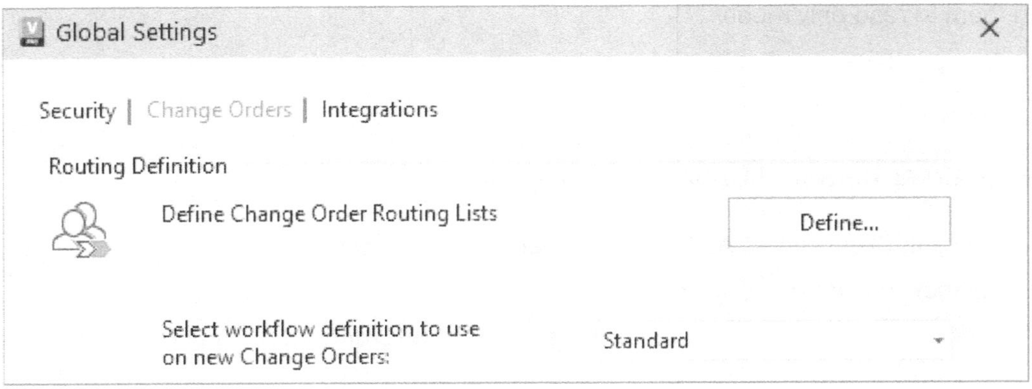


**Figure 9–32**

Lists can contain any number of users, but you must specify at least one Approver, one Responsible Engineer, and one Change Administrator in order to create a routing list, as shown in Figure 9–33. A Checker must also be included if the **Check** state is enabled.

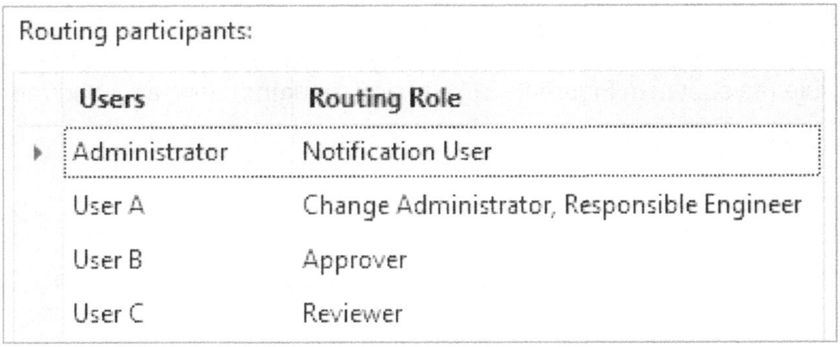


**Figure 9–33**

To set the routing, the administrator can select **Unanimous approval for Review state required** in the *Routing Settings* dialog box, as shown in Figure 9–34.

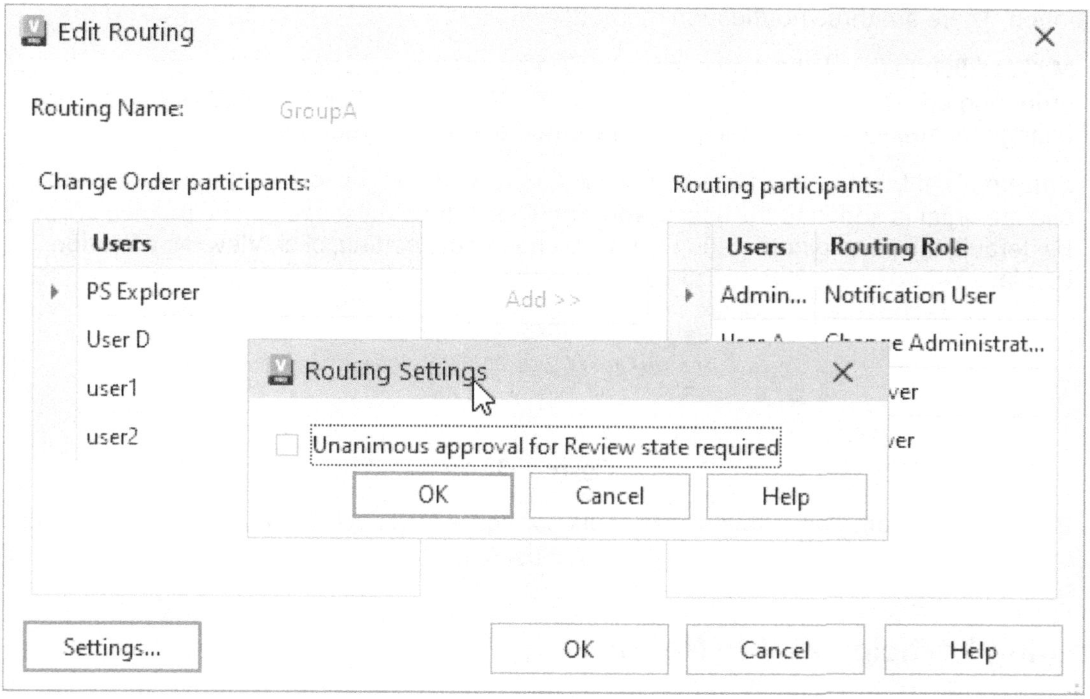


**Figure 9–34**

## Routing Editing Rules

The following rules apply to editing the routing after the change order has been created:

- Depending on the state of the change order, anyone on the routing can add another reviewer, except for the Notification User.
- The Change Administrator can add or remove Approvers, Change Administrators, and Responsible Engineers. In the *Work* state, the Responsible Engineer can only add another user as a Responsible Engineer, Reviewer, or Notification User.
- Only the Administrator, Change Administrator, and Responsible Engineer can remove a Reviewer.
- Change order activities can only be performed by the routing participants.

## Notification

A user on the routing list is notified when the change order enters a state that requires their attention. There are three notification methods:

- **My Worklist:** In the *Navigation* pane, when *Home* or *Change Order List* displays, the change order number and due date display on this list. Clicking on a change order in this list will change the main pane to Change Orders with that change order selected.
- **Pop-up alert:** Displays briefly (as shown in Figure 9–35) in the lower right corner, when a change order is added to the user's work list. This pop-up message can be toggled off or on. By default, the pop-up notification is on. To change the setting, click **View>Notification Display**.

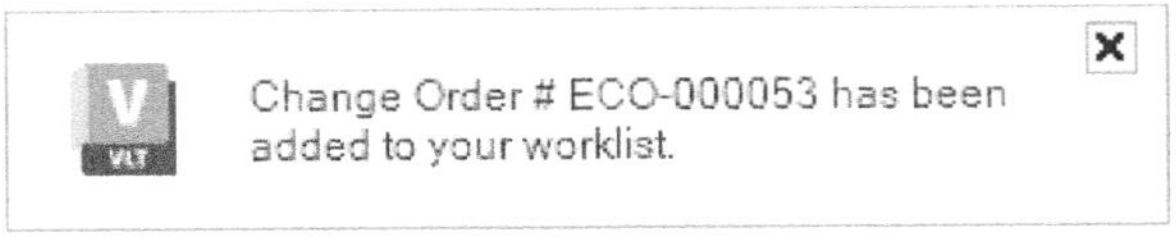


Figure 9–35

- **Email notification:** The administrator must configure Autodesk Data Management Server for email notification and Vault Professional users must have valid email addresses in their user profiles.

## Routing Participants Are Notified

- The change order number displays on each routing participant's *My Worklist* depending on the state of the change order. For example, the Responsible Engineer is notified when the change order enters the **Work** state, but the Approver does not get notified until it enters the **Review** state.
- Following the same logic, an email message is sent to each person on the routing list depending on the state of the change order. For example, the Reviewer is notified by email when the change order enters the **Review** state.
- Vault Professional includes a role called Notification Users in the *ECO Routing* tab. This user is notified when a change order is closed, usually indicating that a new revision of items or documents is now available.
- If Vault Professional is running but inactive, a pop-up alert displays momentarily on the user's screen in the lower-right corner when the change order is added to their work list.

## Participants and Change Order Roles

The following steps describe the typical workflow for creating a change order as well as the roles of participants at each step in the process:

1. A user creates a change order. This user can be any member of the design team as long as they have a Change Order Editor role. The following actions occur:
   - They are added to the routing list as a Change Requestor.
   - The change order enters the **Create** state.
   - The Change Requestor adds information in the properties and can add any additional files or items to the change.
   - The Change Requestor or the Change Administrator submits to the **Open** state.
   - The Change Administrator is notified if the change order is submitted to the **Open** state.
2. In the **Open** state, the Change Administrator reviews the order and determines whether to add comments, markups, or additional properties. In the **Open** state, it is the Change Administrator's task to determine whether the change order should be processed. It can be canceled for a request that is unfulfillable.
   - The Change Administrator selects the items in the *Records* tab of the change order and changes state to put them in **Work In Progress**. They can also add additional files or items if affected by the change.
   - The Change Administrator submits the change order to the **Work** state.
   - The Responsible Engineer is notified. Reviewers are also notified in the **Work** state, so that they can offer comments during the modifications.
3. If the Change Administrator did not put the items into the **Work in Progress** state, the Responsible Engineer can at this point. The Responsible Engineer checks out the files from the vault and modifies them with regards to the change order. The files are checked back in to the vault and the items are updated and the state is changed to **In Review**.
4. The Responsible Engineer submits the change order and it enters the **Review** state. If the **Check** state is enabled, the Checker is notified of the change order. They can review the changes, reject the change order back to the **Work** state for further changes, or approve the work to send the change order onto the **Review** state.
5. The Reviewers and Approvers are notified. They can review the design changes and add comments and markups. The Approvers can, at any time, approve the change order. If the administrator has selected the **Unanimous approval for Review state required** option in the *Routing Settings* dialog box, all Approvers must review and submit their acceptance of the change order. The change order is now set to **Approved**.
6. The Change Administrator is once again notified. Any **Work in Progress** or **In Review** items on the change order must be set to **Released**.
7. The change order is now closed. All Notification Users are notified by email (if configured), indicating new items are ready for production.

# Practice 9b
# Create and Approve Change Orders

In this practice, you will create two change orders. You will submit and approve the first. For the second, three routing participants must approve the change order because unanimous approval is required. The completed practice is shown in Figure 9–36.

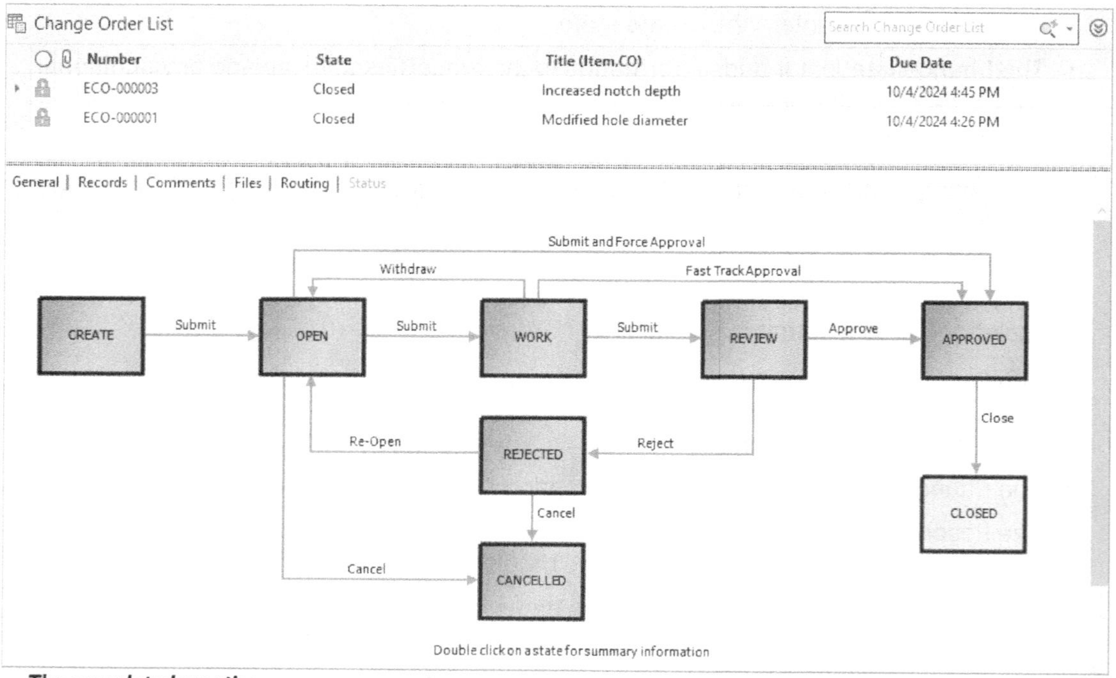


*The completed practice*

**Figure 9–36**

## Task 1: Create and approve change orders.

1. Start Autodesk Vault Professional. Log in using the following information:
   - For *User Name*, enter **administrator**.
   - Leave the *Password* field blank.
   - For *Vault*, select **AOTCVault**.
2. In Project Explorer, expand the *Designs* folder.
3. Click the **Clamp** folder, as shown in Figure 9–37.

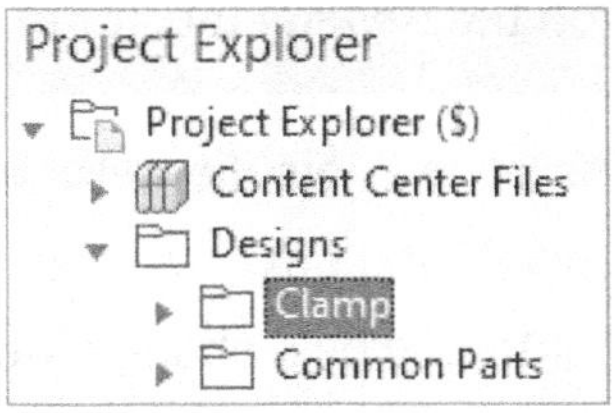


Figure 9–37

4. Right-click on **Grip.ipt** and select **Assign/Update Item**.
5. In the *Edit Item* window, select **Save and Close**.
   - An icon displays next to the part name and the associated drawing, as shown in Figure 9–38. After the item has been created, it is recommended to right-click on the file and select **Go To Item** to quickly change to the *Item Master* view with the particular item selected.

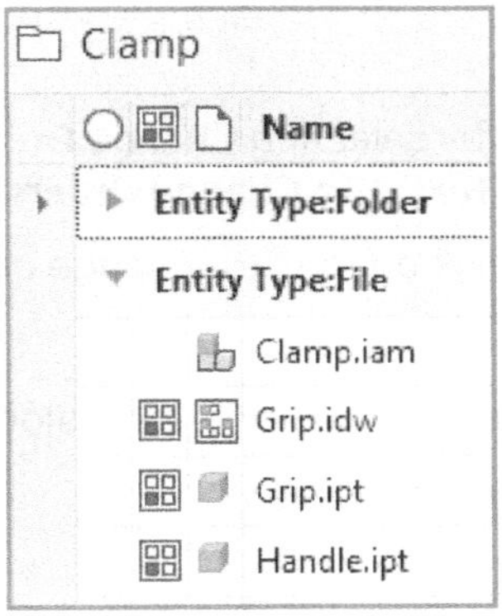


Figure 9–38

6. Switch to the *Item Master*. Right-click on the new item and select **Add To Change Order>To New**, as shown in Figure 9–39.

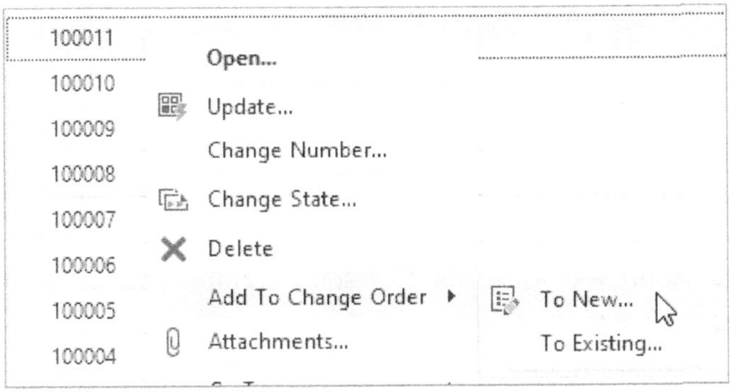


Figure 9–39

7. In the *Change Order* dialog box, on the *General* tab, for *Change Order Title*, enter **Modified hole diameter**.
8. For *Detailed Description*, enter **Increased hole diameter to 7.92 mm**.
9. Click **Save**. Close the *Change Order* dialog box.
10. An icon displays next to items controlled by a change order, as shown in Figure 9–40.

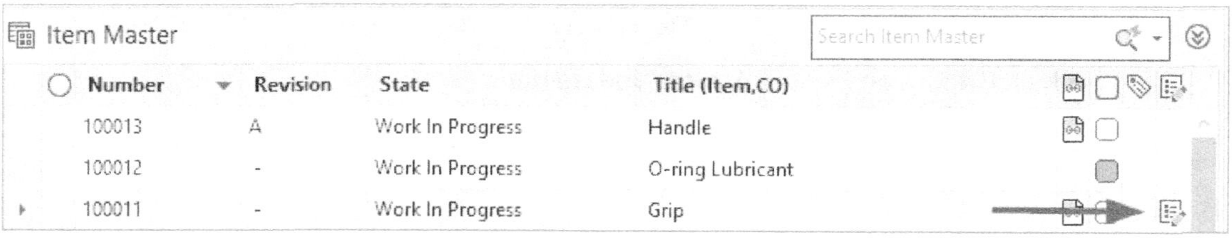


**Figure 9–40**

***Note:*** *Your item and change order numbers might differ from the illustrations in this practice.*

11. Switch to the *Change Order List* by selecting **Change Order List**. It is recommended to right-click on the item and select **Go To>Go To Change Order**.
12. In the *Change Order List*, right-click on the new change order. Do the following:
    - Select **Respond>Submit**.
    - Click **OK** to dismiss the *Submit – Add Comment* dialog box.

    The status of the change order is set to **Open**.
13. Log in using the following information:
    - *User Name*: **usera**
    - *Password:* **vault**
14. In the *Change Order List*, right-click on the new change order. Do the following:
    - Select **Respond>Submit and Force Approval**.
    - Click **OK**.

    ***Note:*** *usera is a Change Administrator and can force the approval of a change order.*
15. In the *Status* tab, the status of the change order is set to **Approved**. Do the following, as shown in Figure 9–41:
    - Double-click the **Approved** state icon to display summary information about the state.
    - Close the *Summary* dialog box.

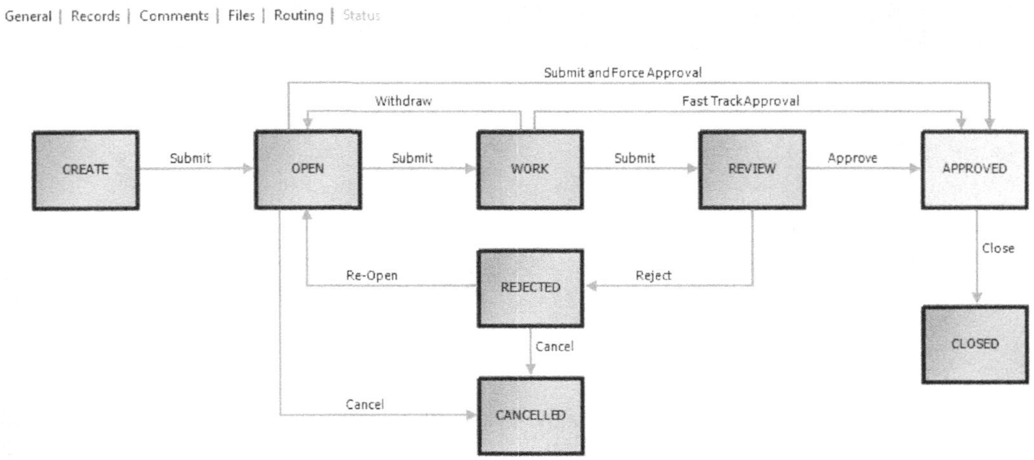


**Figure 9–41**

16. In the *Change Order List*, right-click on the new change order. Do the following:
    - Select **Respond>Close Change Order**.
    - Click **OK**.
    - Select **Released**.
    - Click **OK**.
17. Review the status. Because the effectivity was set to immediate, the status is now **Closed**, as shown in Figure 9–42.

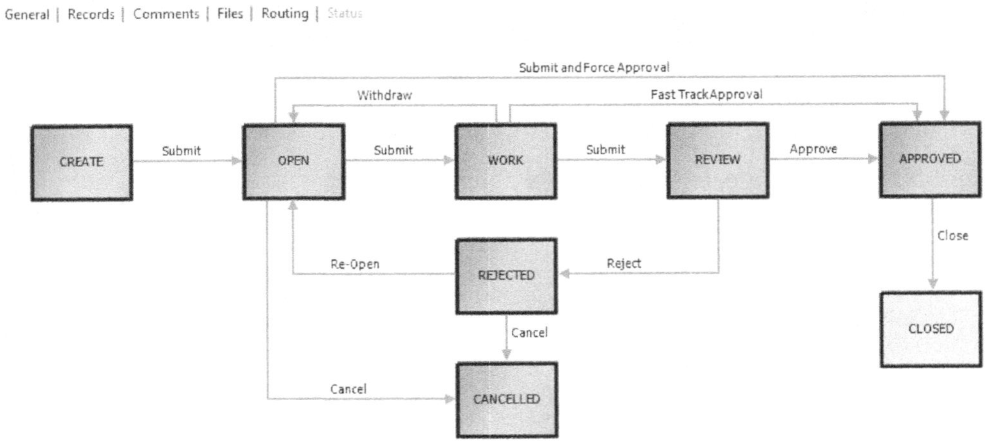


**Figure 9–42**

18. Switch to the *Item Master*.
19. Select the item.

20. In the *Preview* pane, note that the lifecycle state is set to **Released**, as shown in Figure 9–43.

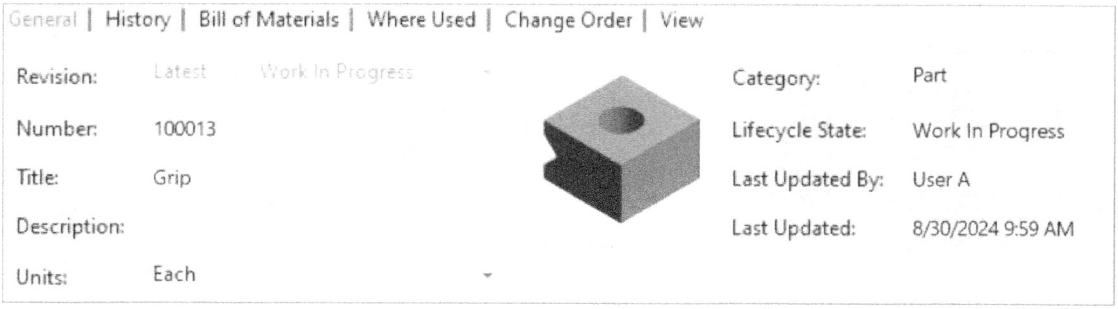


Figure 9–43

## Task 2: Create a new change order.

1. In the *Item Master*, right-click on the item created in the previous task. Do the following:
   - Select **Change State>Work in Progress**.
   - Click **OK**.

   A new revision is created, as shown in Figure 9–44.

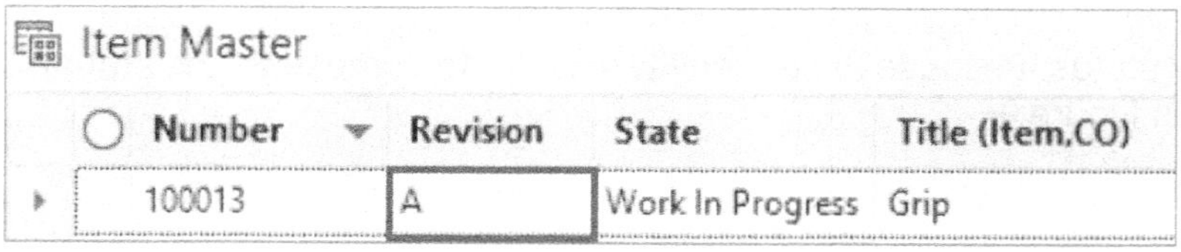


Figure 9–44

2. Right-click on the item, then select **Add to Change Order>To New**. Do the following:
   - For *Change Order Title*, enter **Increased notch depth**.
   - For *Detailed Description*, enter **Notch depth increased to 3.18 mm**.

 

3. In the *Properties* area, in the *Value* column, click **Design**. Select **Manufacturing** from the list, as shown in Figure 9–45.

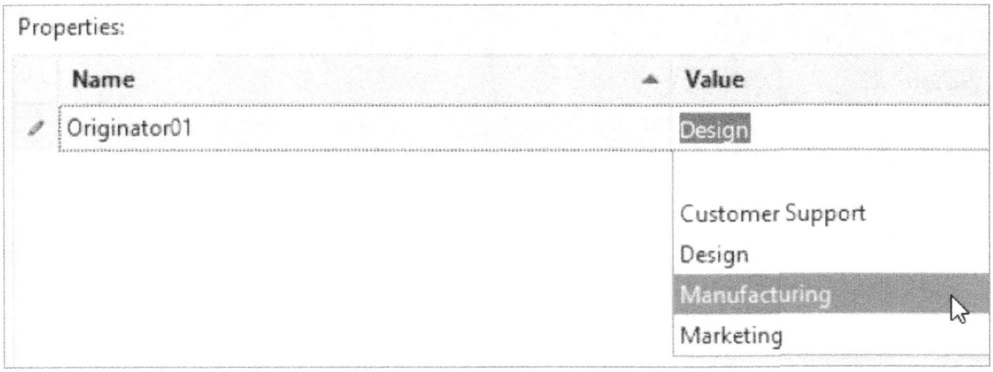


**Figure 9–45**

4. Select the *Files* tab at the top of the dialog box. In the *Attached Files* list, select **Grip.idw**, as shown in Figure 9–46.

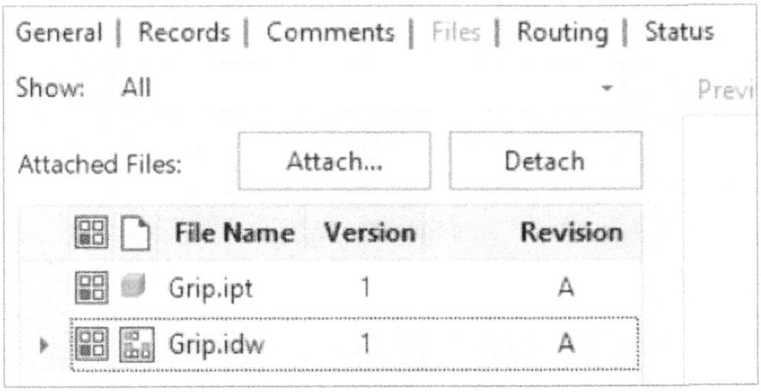


**Figure 9–46**

5. In the *Preview* tab, select the drawing thumbnail, as shown in Figure 9–47.

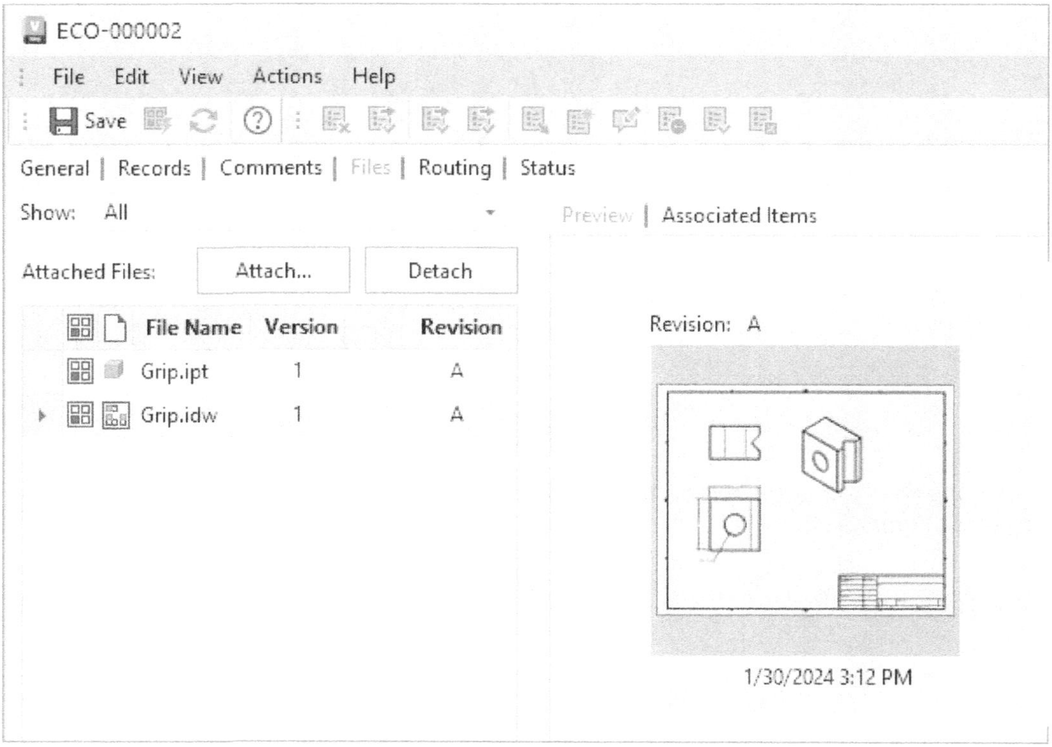


**Figure 9–47**

6. The drawing displays in the Autodesk Viewer. Click the Markup icon.
7. Click **Create New**, as shown in Figure 9–48.

**Figure 9–48**

8. Click **Clear** to clear the canvas, if prompted.

9. Do the following to create a markup, as shown in Figure 9–49:
   - On the top view, zoom in to the notch feature.
   - Click the Cloud icon and click and drag to create a markup around the notch.
   - Click the Callout icon to create a callout with the text of **Notch depth increased to 3.18 mm**.

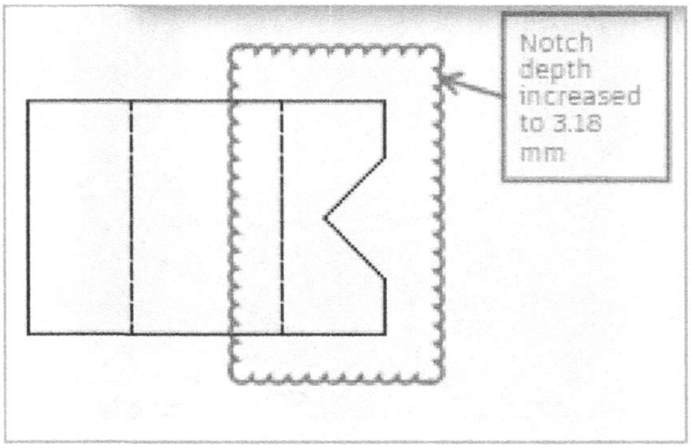


Figure 9–49

10. Click **Save** and from the drop-down list, select **As screenshot** shown in Figure 9–50.

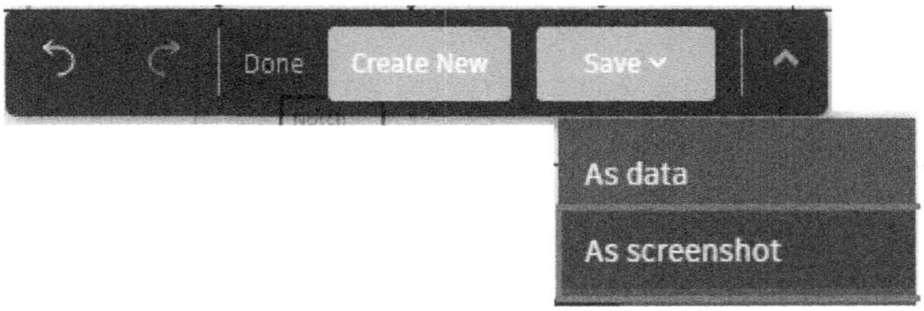


Figure 9–50

11. Enter the file name - **Note.png**, then click **Save**, as shown in Figure 9–51.

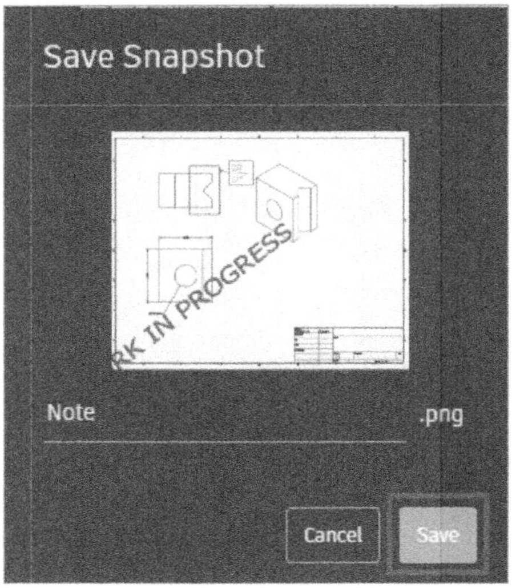


**Figure 9–51**

12. Save **Note.png** to the working folder as prompted (*C:\Vault Professional Admin\Working Folder*). Then add the file to the vault *Designs>Clamp>Engineering Documents* folder.
13. In the *Files* tab, click **Attach**, as shown in Figure 9–52.

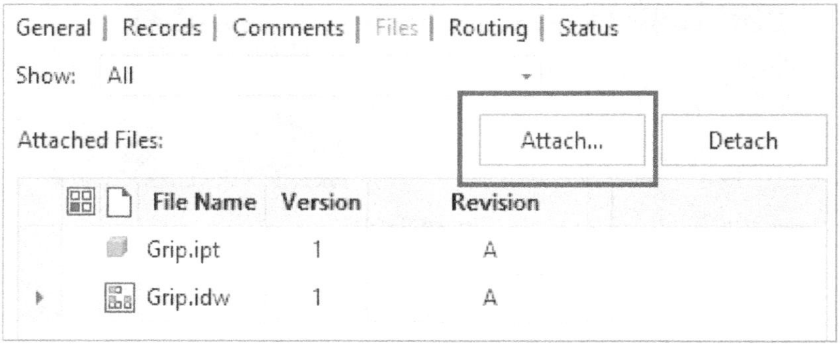


**Figure 9–52**

14. Select **Note.png** from the vault *Designs>Clamp>Engineering Documents* folder.
15. Select **Note.png** to view the markup in the *Preview* tab, as shown in Figure 9–53.

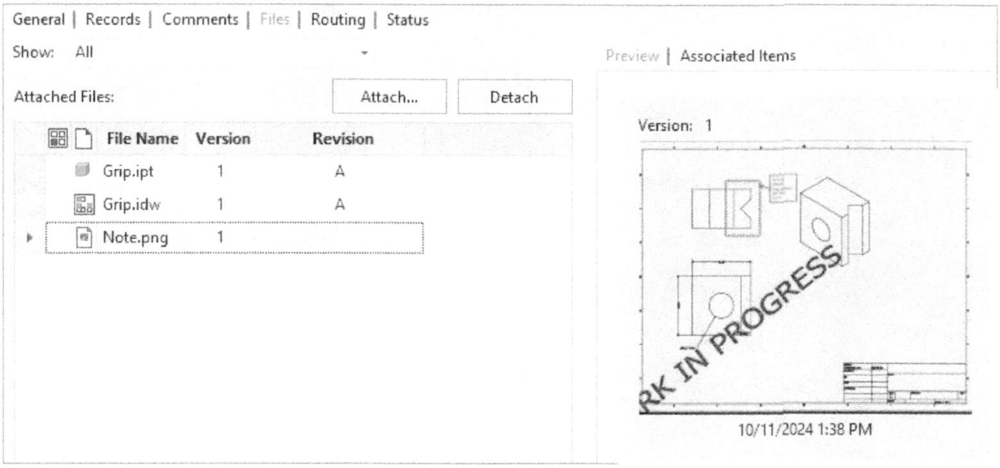


Figure 9–53

16. Select the *Comments* tab. Select **Add Comment**. In the *Add Comment* dialog box, do the following (as shown in Figure 9–54):
    - For *Title*, enter **Notch depth increased to 3.18 mm**.
    - For *Comments*, enter **Due to a number of failures in the field, the notch depth has been increased**.
    - Click **OK**.

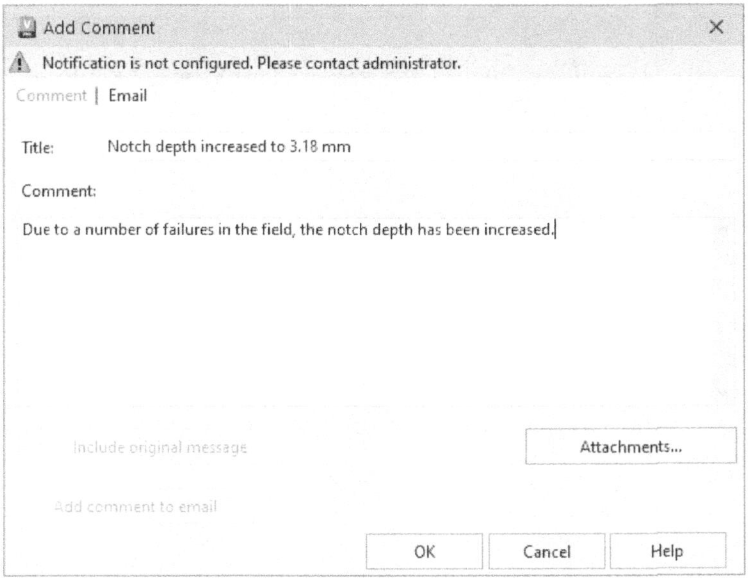


Figure 9–54

***Note:*** *You can also add attachments to comments by clicking the Attachments button in the Add Comment dialog box.*

17. In the *Change Order* dialog box, select the *Routing* tab. From the list, select **GroupB**, as shown in Figure 9–55.

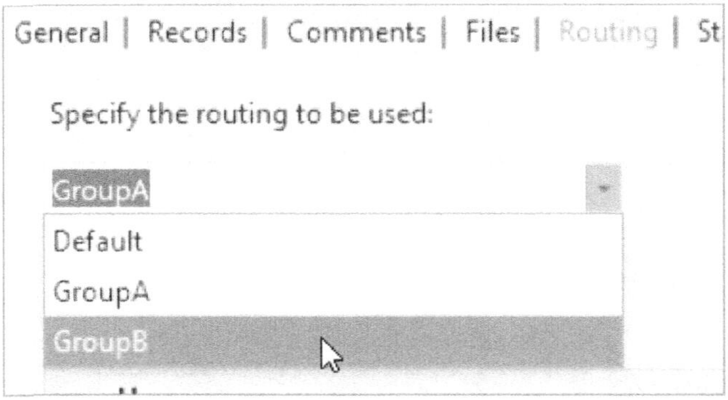


**Figure 9–55**

18. Review the routing participants. usera, userb, and userc are part of this group.
    - User A is the Change Administrator. Since User A is creating the change order, they will also be the Change Requestor for this change order.
    - User B is an Approver and the Responsible Engineer.
    - User C is an Approver.

    Figure 9–56 shows that the administrator created this list with unanimous approval required for a change order.

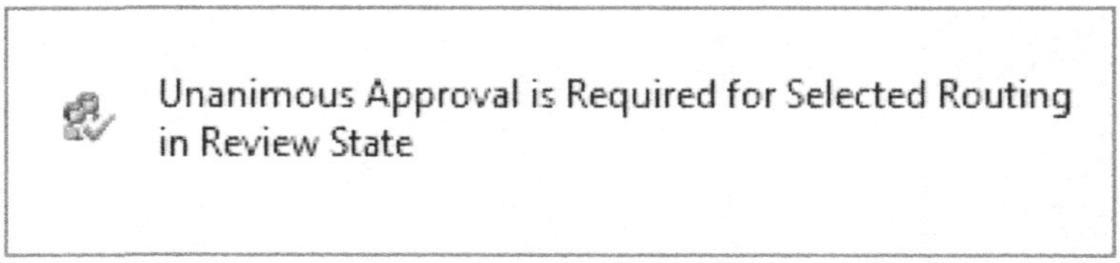


**Figure 9–56**

**19.** Select the *Status* tab. The workflow chart (in Figure 9–57) shows that the change order is set to **Create**.

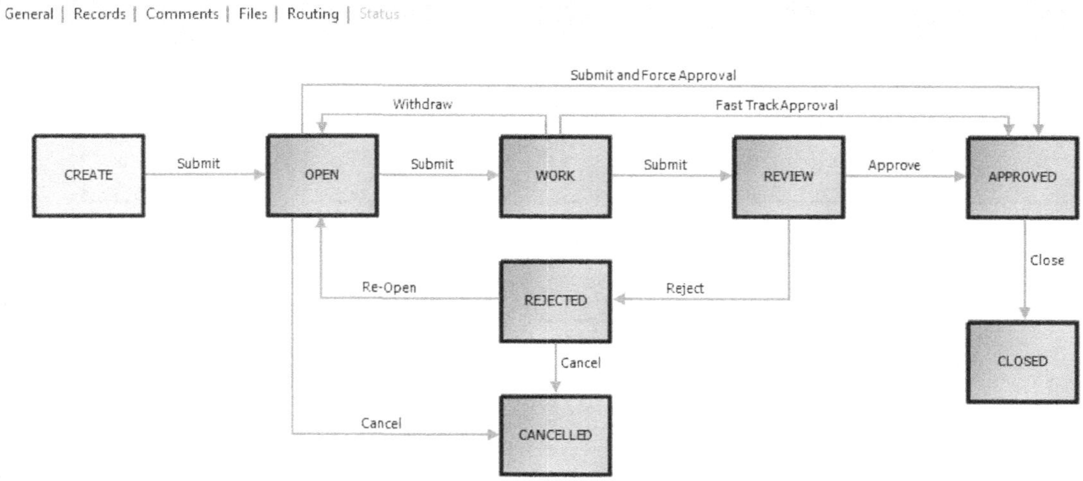


**Figure 9–57**

**20.** Click **Save**. Close the *Change Order* dialog box. It is recommended to NOT save the change order until this step. Saving beforehand will remove the user's ability to set the routing choice as shown in the earlier step.

## Task 3: Submit new change order to OPEN state.

1. In the *Change Order List* dialog box, right-click on the new change order. Do the following (as shown in Figure 9–58):
   - Select **Respond>Submit**.
   - Click **OK** to dismiss the *Submit – Add Comment* dialog box. Note that by default a title is entered indicating the ECO is submitted to the **Open** state.

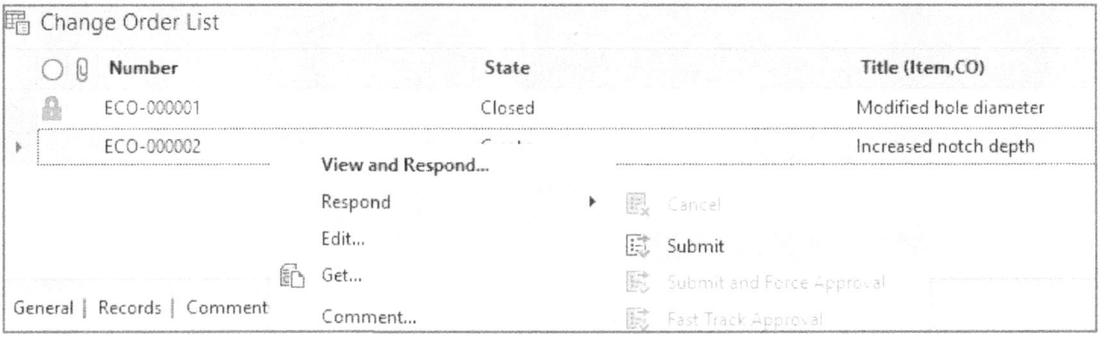


**Figure 9–58**

2. In the *Change Order List*, select the new change order. Select the *Status* tab to display the workflow chart, as shown in Figure 9–59.

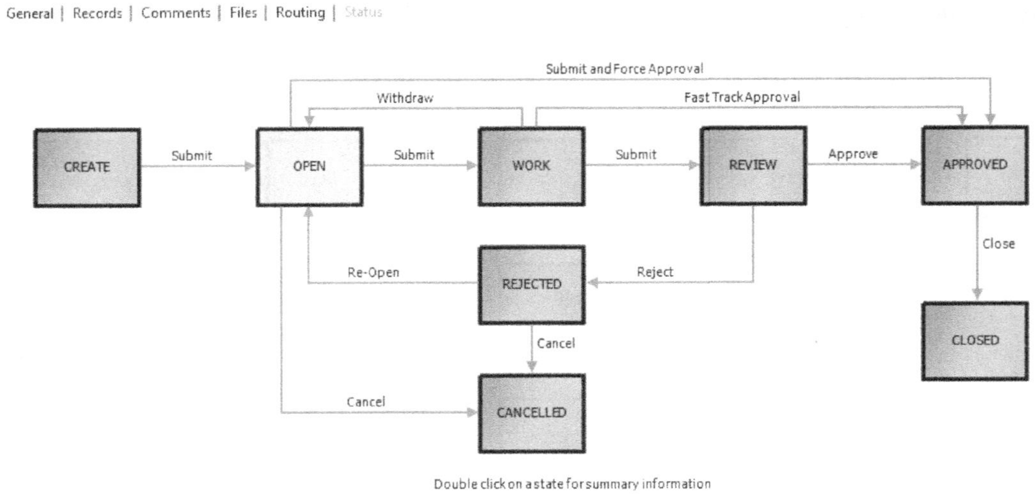


**Figure 9–59**

3. In the status diagram, double-click the **Open** state to display the summary information about the state, as shown in Figure 9–60. Close the *Summary* dialog box.

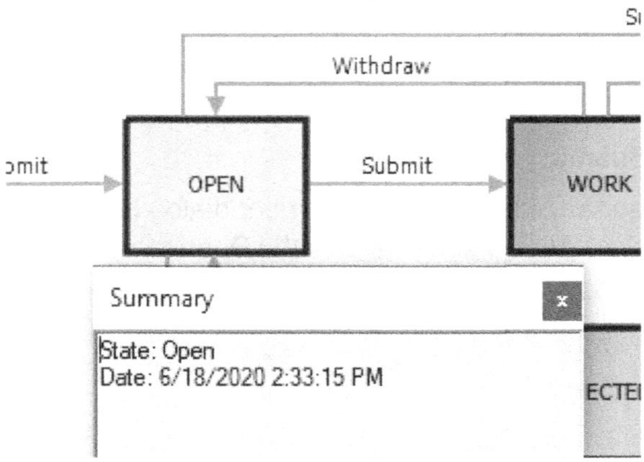


**Figure 9–60**

You are currently logged in as usera. Usera submits the change order again to change the status to Work.

4. In the *Change Order List*, right-click on the new change order. Do the following as shown in Figure 9–61:
   - Select **Respond>Submit**.
   - Click **OK** in the *Submit – Add Comment* dialog box, again accepting the default comment.
   - Note the new state of the change order in the *Status* tab.

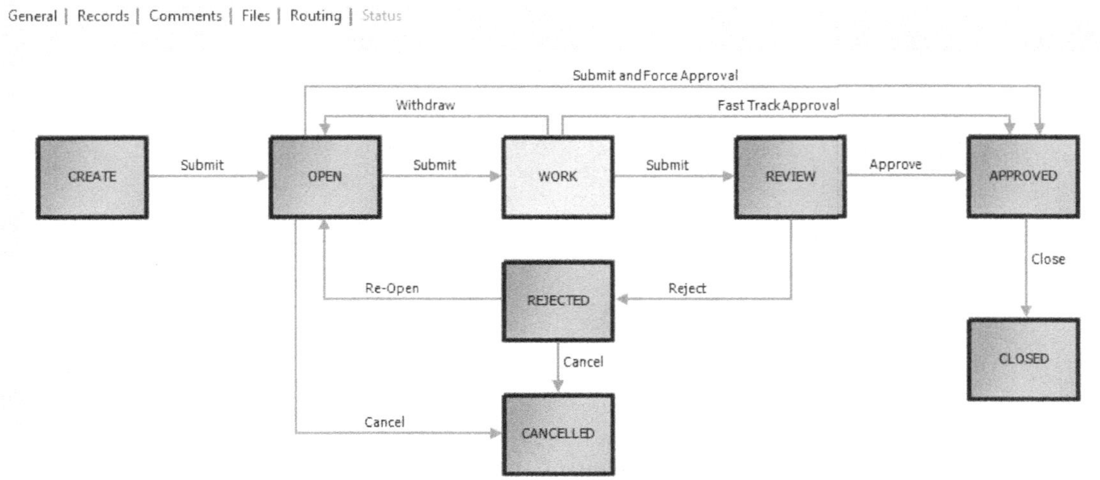


**Figure 9–61**

You now log in as userb, the Responsible Engineer.

## Task 4: Submit new change order to REVIEW state.

1. Select **File>Log Out**. The *Log Out* dialog box displays.
2. Select **Log In**. The *Log In* dialog box displays.
3. Log in using the following information:
   - *User Name*: **userb**
   - *Password:* **vault**
   - *Vault:* **AOTCVault**
4. Review **My Worklist**. The ECO is listed, as shown in Figure 9–62.

**Figure 9–62**

- Clicking on the ECO in your worklist will take you directly to the *Change Order List* with the change order selected.

5. In the *Preview* pane, select the *Comments* tab. Review the comments. Note that the details in the comment titled **Notch depth increased to 3.18mm**.
6. Select the *Files* tab and click the attached markup file **Note.png** in the *Attached Files* list to view the markup, as shown in Figure 9–63.

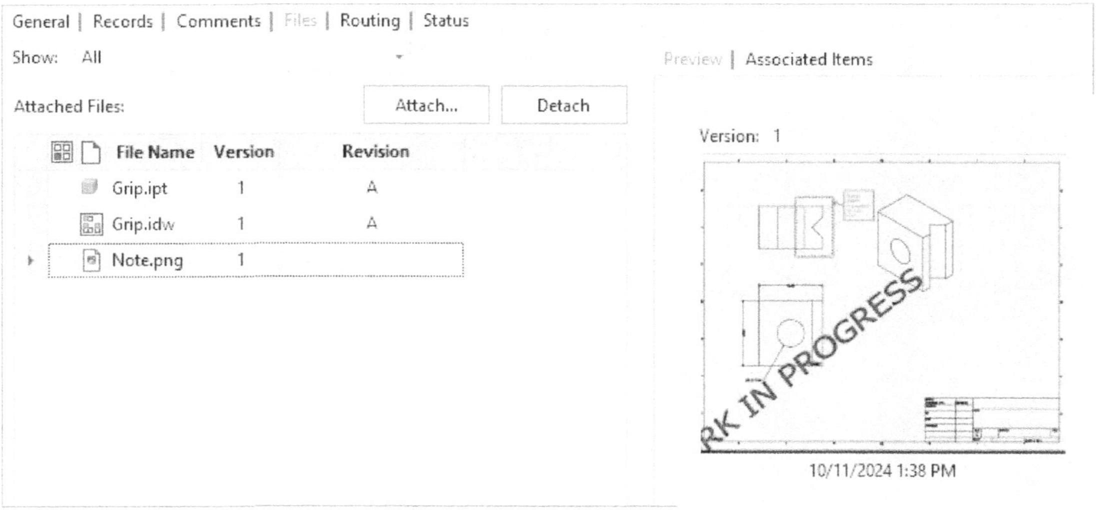


**Figure 9–63**

## Task 5: Submit new change order to APPROVED state.

1. In the *Change Order List*, right-click on the new change order. Do the following, as shown in Figure 9–64:
   - Select **Respond>Submit**. This will move the change order to the **Review** state.
   - The *Submit – Add Comment* dialog box displays. In the *Comments* field, enter **Reviewed by the responsible engineer. The new design is correct.**
   - Click **OK**.

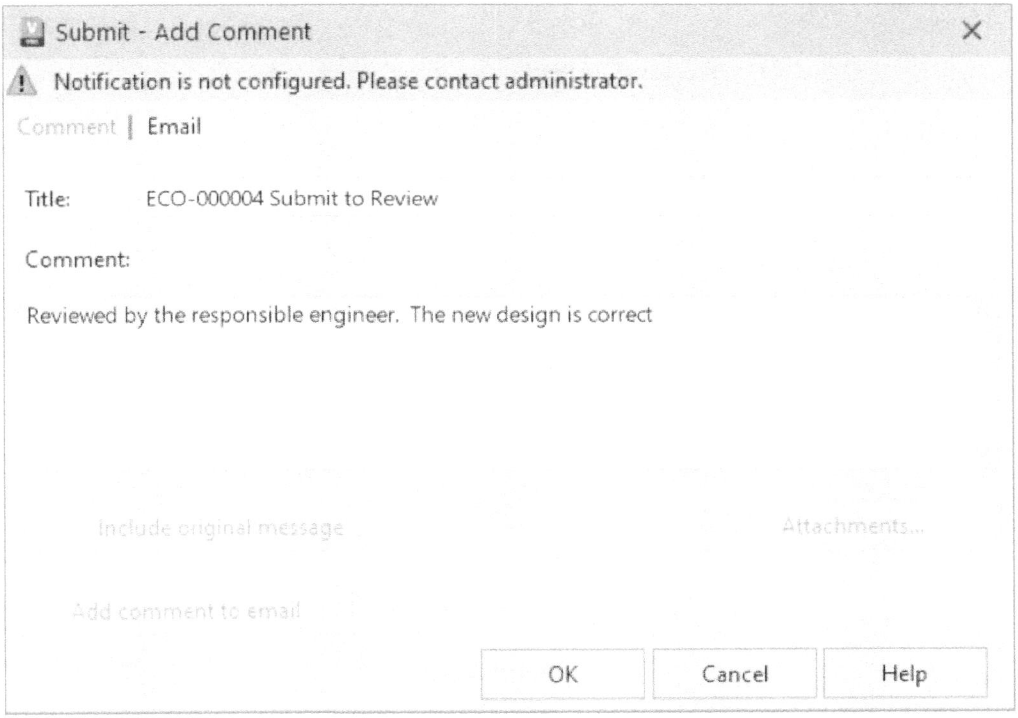


**Figure 9–64**

2. Note that the change order still displays in *My Worklist*. The change order requires unanimous approval from all reviewers. In addition to being the Responsible Engineer, userb is also a Reviewer. userb must also approve the change order.

3. In the *Change Order* list, right-click on the new change order. Do the following, as shown in Figure 9–65:
   - Select **Respond>Approve**.
   - In the *Approve – Add Comment* dialog box, enter **The design is approved.**
   - Click **OK**.

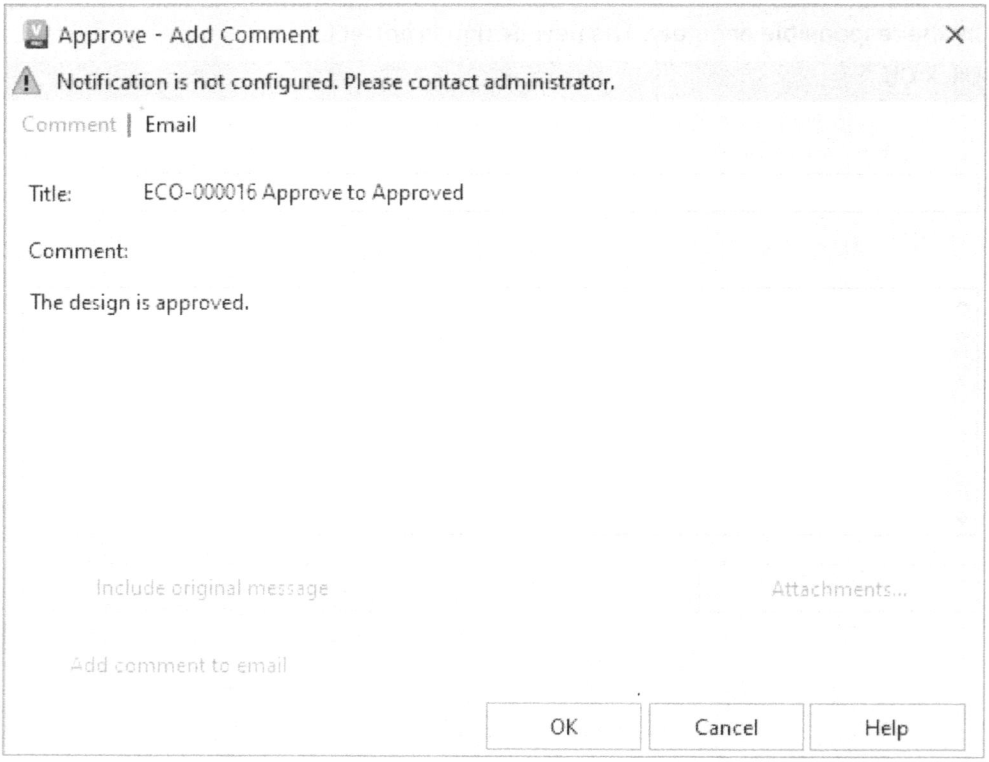


**Figure 9–65**

4. Select the *Status* tab. Note that the change order state is still **Review**. Double-click on the state to review the status, as shown in Figure 9–66. The change order requires unanimous approval from all reviewers.

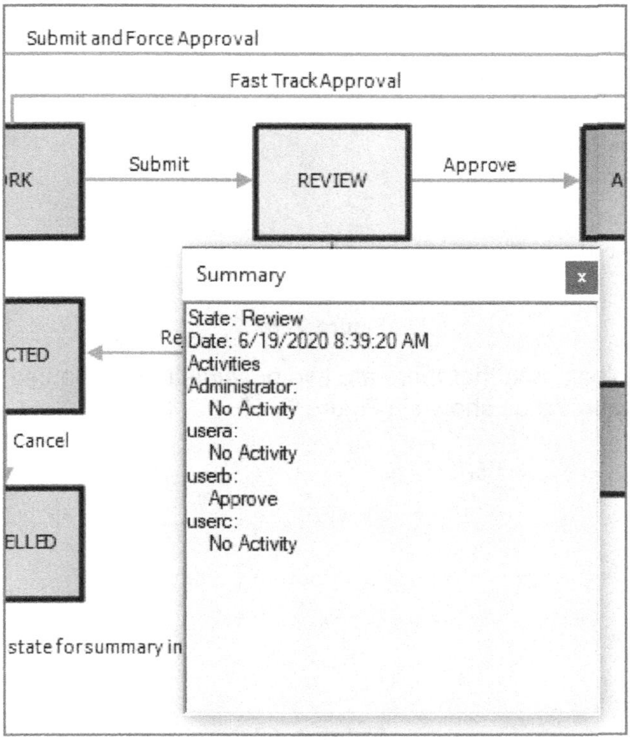


**Figure 9–66**

*Note: userc must also approve the change order.*

5. Select **File>Log Out**.
6. Select **Log In**.
7. Log in using the following information:
   - *User Name:* **userc**
   - *Password:* **vault**
   - *Vault:* **AOTCVault**
8. Note that the change order is in *My Worklist*. Select on the change order to switch to the *Change Order List* with the change order selected.
9. Double-click on the change order to open it for review.

10. Select the *Comments* tab and review the comments, as shown in Figure 9–67.

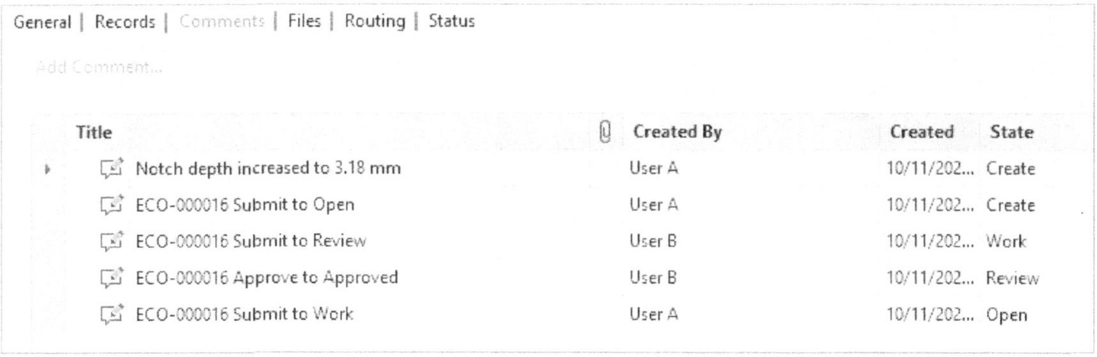


**Figure 9–67**

11. In the *Respond* toolbar, note that there are two possible icons enabled – **Reject** and **Approve**. Select **Approve**, as shown in Figure 9–68.

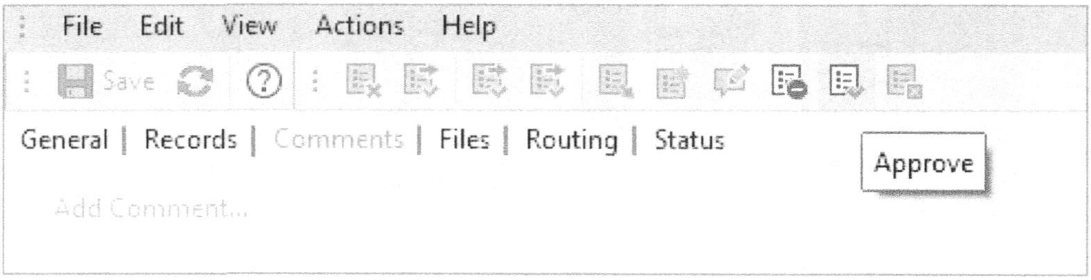


**Figure 9–68**

12. In the *Approve – Add Comments* dialog box, in the *Comment* section, enter **Approved – ready for immediate release.**
13. Click **OK** to exit the dialog box.

**14.** Select the *Status* tab. Because the two Approvers, userb (User B) and userc (User C), have approved the change, the state is set to **Approved**, as shown in Figure 9–69.

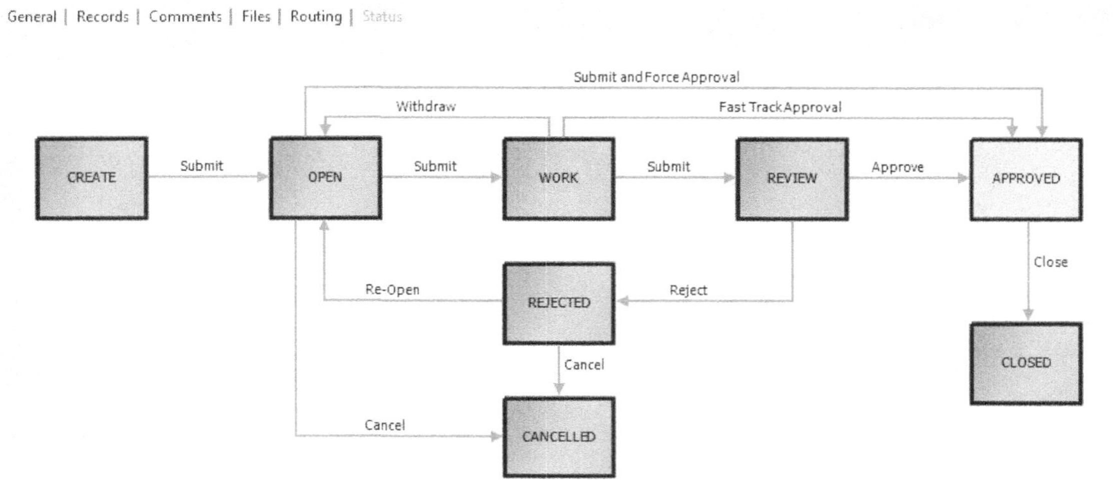


**Figure 9–69**

The Change Administrator is responsible for closing the change order by setting the effectivity of the items on the change order. In this scenario, usera is the Change Administrator.

**15.** Close the *Change Order* dialog box.

## Task 6: Close the new change order.

1. Log in as **usera** using the data provided earlier in this practice.
2. Note once again that the change order displays in *My Worklist*. Select it to go to the change order.
3. In the *Change Order List*, right-click on the new change order. Do the following:
   - Select **Respond>Close Change Order**.
   - Click **OK**.
   - Select **Released**.
   - Click **OK**.

4. In the *Change Order List*, review the status of the change order. Note that it is now **Closed**, as shown in Figure 9–70.

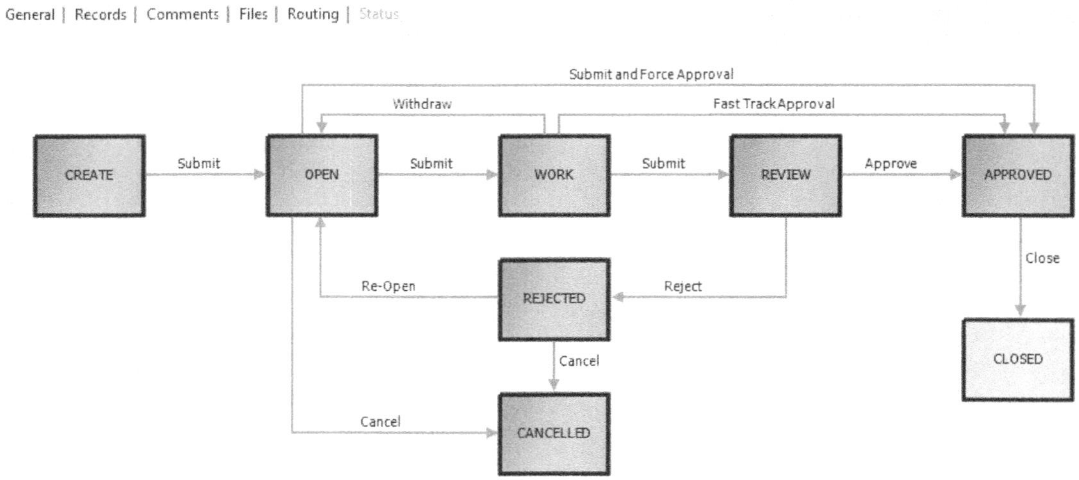


**Figure 9–70**

5. Select the *Records* tab and note the *Revision* and *State (Historical)* of the item. It has been now released at Revision **A**, as shown in Figure 9–71.

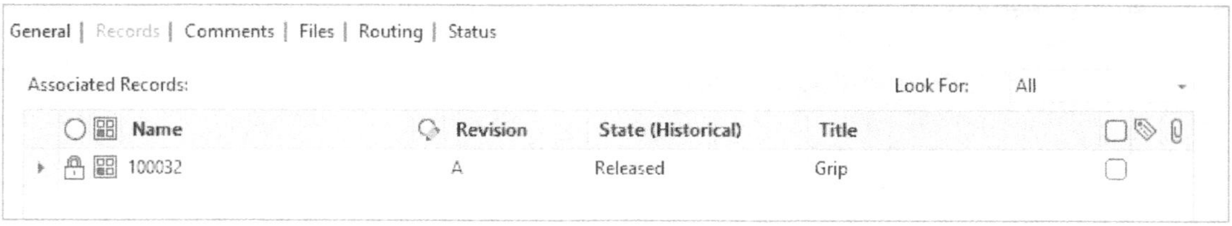


**Figure 9–71**

**End of practice**

Chapter 10

# Creating Reports

Autodesk® Vault Professional software provide the ability to generate formatted reports representing data contained in a vault. You can generate reports for files, items,and change orders, and organize the report based on specific properties. For example, a report can display files grouped by a category, show the distribution of lifecycle states across a model, and summarize currently open change orders, or show the distribution of lifecycle states across a model. Reports can display the data in a variety of ways, including charts, tables, and data sheets. You can also format data using dozens of predefined operators.

In this chapter, you learn how to create and modify report templates so that you can customize Vault reports that contain information relevant to your business, in a format that suits your needs.

## Learning Objectives

- Create reports from an advanced search and configure how the data displays.
- Identify the different out-of-the box report templates and the information they are formatted to display.
- Create new report templates using the Autodesk Template Utility (for advanced users).
- Create project reports, also known as folder reports or folder dashboards.

# 10.1 Creating Reports

In this section, you learn how to create a report from an advanced search (as shown in Figure 10–1) and configure how the report data displays.

Use search reports to illustrate details about files stored in the vault by using charts, tables, and data sheets.

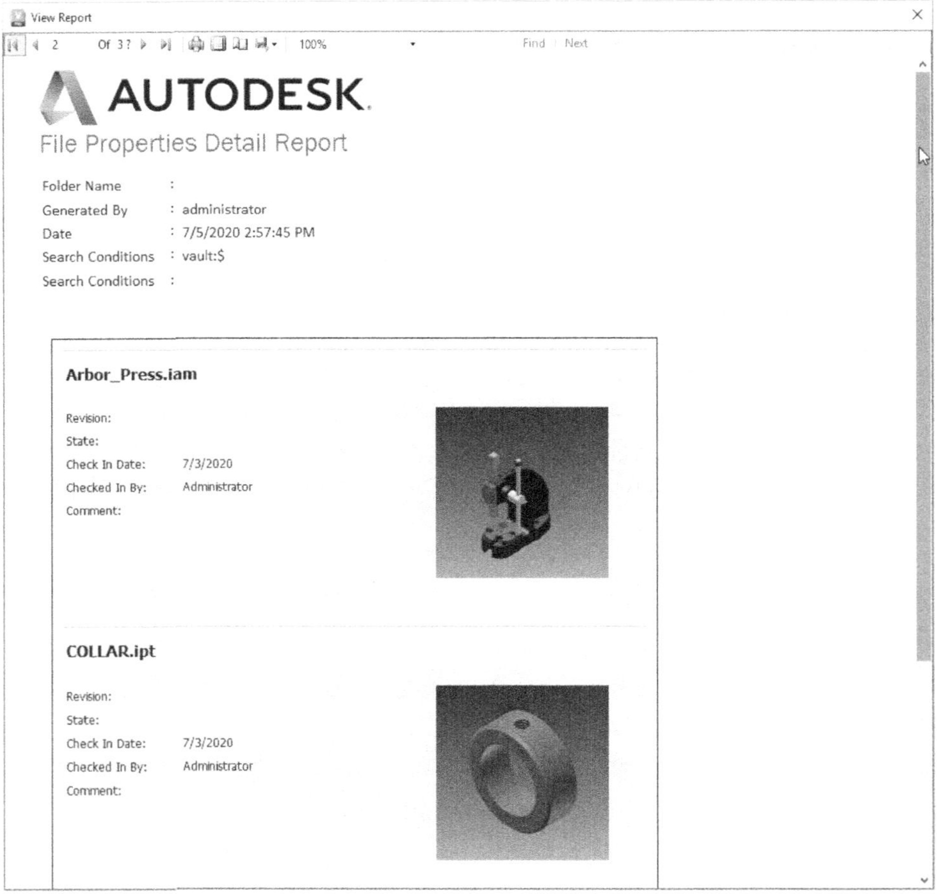


**Figure 10–1**

## About Reports

Working with reports is a way of illustrating file details for those who do not have direct access to the vault. Reports can be organized to suit the needs of your business and to illustrate certain file details.

Search options specified in the *Advanced Find* dialog box determine which vault objects display in a report. The properties displayed in the report and the report layout are specified in a report template file (as shown in Figure 10–2), which is selected during the report generation. Through the report template, you have complete control of the report content, layout, and format.

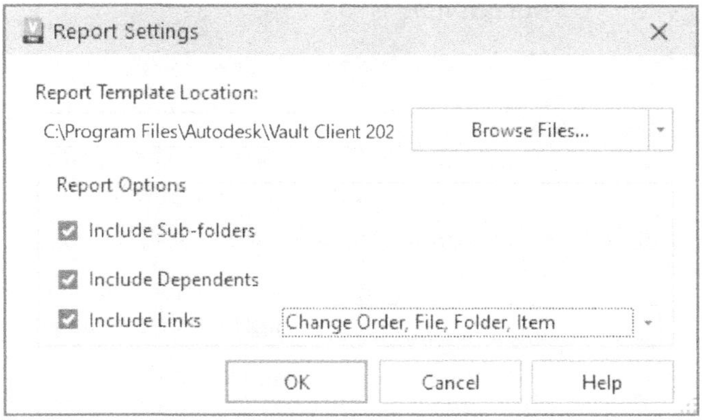


**Figure 10–2**

You generate reports by creating an advanced search with specified parameters and then clicking **Report**. After selecting a template for the report, the information displays in a window for viewing.

You can also generate and view reports from the *Reports* tab, built into the *Preview* pane of a folder. These reports are known as folder reports or vault project reports and are based on data contained in the selected folder. You can also include data from subfolders, dependents, and links in these reports.

## Example of Creating a Report

A report must be generated to determine which files in a vault have been released for manufacturing. You create an advanced search with the condition that the search return files only with the lifecycle state of **Released**. Once the search is complete, you generate a report and choose the template that shows the details of each file listed. Once the report is generated, you save a copy to the vault and email a copy to the project manager for review.

# Report Templates

Report descriptions for Autodesk Vault reports are contained in RDLC files stored on the Vault client machine. These report description files are referred to as report templates. Autodesk Vault report templates are fully RDLC compliant, but Autodesk Vault requires certain naming conventions in the <DataSet> section of the template for integrating Vault data into the report.

A report template authoring utility is installed with the vault client to help you create simple client report definition files (.RDLC) for storing search data. This utility provides only a raw template structure for categorization purposes. A more sophisticated template authoring tool is required for custom visual layouts.

 

## Pre-existing Report Templates

When the Autodesk Vault Client is installed, several pre-existing report templates are provided. The following table describes some of these templates:

| Template Name | Description |
|---|---|
| **ECO Average Close Rate** | Displays the average number of days it takes to close an ECO. |
| **ECO By State** | Displays the ECOs in groups based on ECO state. |
| **ECO Detail** | Displays the ECO Number, Change Order Properties, State, Due Date, and submission information without table formatting. |
| **ECO Status Created on Month** | Displays the number of ECOs per State. |
| **ECO Table** | Displays the ECO Number, Change Order Properties, State, Due Date, and submission information in table format. |
| **File by Category** | Displays the filename, revision, state, comments, and check-in information in a pie-chart organized by category. |
| **File Detail** | Displays the filename, revision, state, check-in information, and comments without table formatting. |
| **File Table** | Displays the filename, revision, state, check-in information, and comments in a table format. |
| **File Transmittal** | Displays the filename, revision, state, vault folder location, and date the version was created for each file. |
| **File by Lifecycle State** | Displays the filename, revision, state, comments, and check-in information in a graph by lifecycle state. |
| **File Checked Out By** | Displays checked out information in a graph. |
| **Item By State** | Displays the item information in groups based on state. |
| **Item Detail** | Displays the item name, revision, state, type, units, modification information, compliance status, and description without table formatting. |
| **Item Table** | Displays the item name, revision, state, type, units, modification information, compliance status, and description in a table. |
| **Project Dashboard** | Displays project data in graphical format, including graphs for Lifecycle State Distribution by Category, Category Distribution, Lifecycle State Distribution, and Checked-Out Files Distribution by Users. |
| **Vault Professional In-CAD** | Displays check out information, lifecycle state, category, designer, and other In-CAD data displayed in pie-charts. |
| **BOM - First-Level** | Displays the BOM First Level details. |
| **BOM - Multi-Level** | Displays the BOM Multi-Level details. |

| Template Name | Description |
|---|---|
| **BOM - Parts-Only** | Displays the BOM Parts Only details. |

# Microsoft Report Viewer

Autodesk Vault uses the Microsoft Report Viewer to generate and display reports, as shown in Figure 10–3. Microsoft Report Viewer contains a full-featured, highly customizable reporting engine to display reports for SQL Server Reporting Services. However, the report viewer can also be run in "local mode" - enabling applications like Vault to provide data for report rendering without requiring the overhead of SQL Server Reporting Services. Autodesk Vault runs the report viewer in local mode. Report descriptions for Vault reports are contained in RDLC files stored on the Vault client machine.

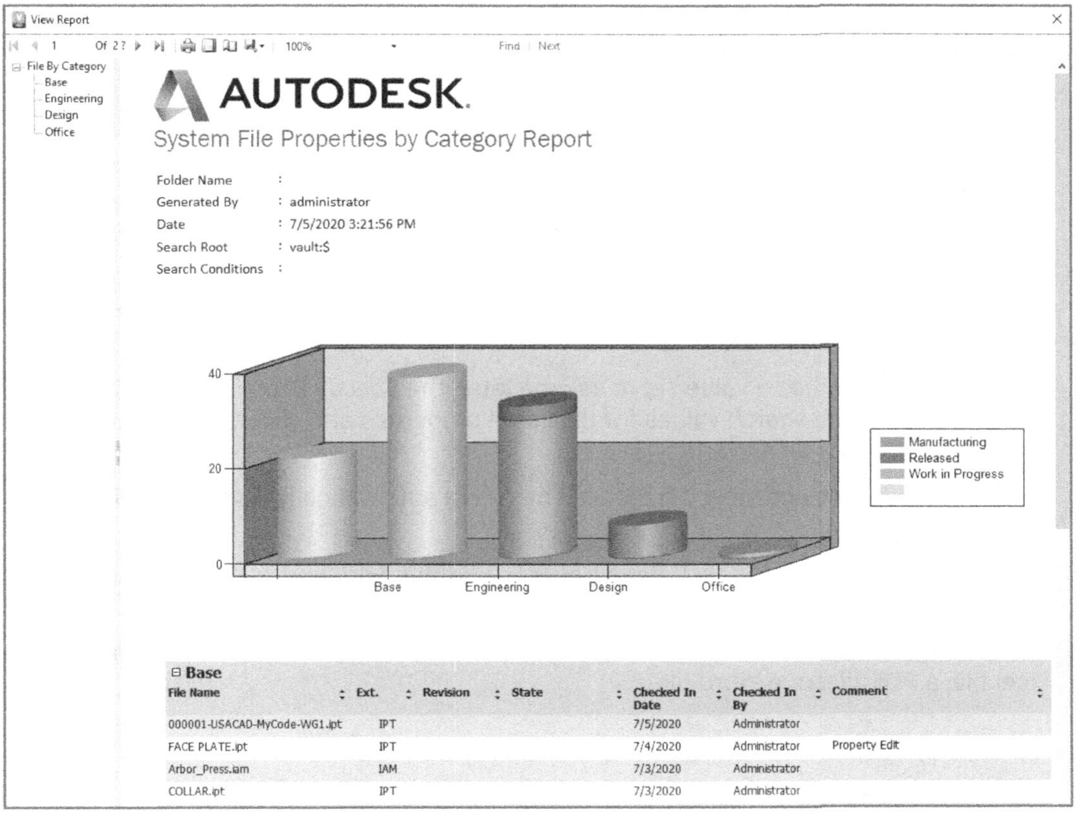


**Figure 10–3**

# Creating Search Reports

To create a search report, you must be familiar with how to generate searches with conditions. Familiarize yourself with the template you intend to use before creating the search. Once you understand which file properties will be displayed, you can specify search conditions to return the required vault objects for the report.

Report templates can be stored in a local folder or in a vault. During installation, the pre-existing report templates are placed in a local folder at *C:\Program Files\Autodesk\Vault <edition> <year>\ Explorer\Report Templates*.

## How To: Create a New Report

The following steps describe how to create a new search report:

1. Click **Find**. The *Find* dialog box displays.
2. Select the *Basic* tab or the *Advanced* tab depending on the type of criteria for which you want to search.
3. Specify the search criteria for this report.
4. Click **Report**. The *Select Report Template* dialog box displays.
5. Enter the path of a template that you would like to use or click **Browse** to navigate to the required template. The last selected report template displays by default.
6. Click **OK** to generate a report. If none of the search criteria is set to **ask me later**, the report is created and displayed automatically.
7. If any of the criteria has a value set to **ask me later**, the *Specify Search Values* dialog box displays. Specify the search values for the listed properties and click **OK**. The *Select Report Template* dialog box displays.
8. Click **OK** to generate and view the report. The report automatically displays in Microsoft Report Viewer.
9. In Microsoft Report Viewer, click **Page Setup** to configure printing preferences and to print the report.
10. To export the report, click the **Export** icon and select whether to export the report as an Excel file, a PDF file, or a Word file.

# Creating Autodesk Vault Project Reports

To create a vault project report, also known as a folder report, ensure that all objects (files, subfolders, items, or change orders) or links to the objects that are being reported on are in one project folder.

## How To: Create a Vault Project Report

The following steps describe how to create a vault project report:

1. Select a project folder in the main pane.
2. Select the *Reports* tab in the *Preview* pane and select **Configure**.
3. In the *Report Settings* dialog box, select **Browse Files** to navigate to the required template. The last selected report template displays by default.
4. Select the required report template and click **Open**.
5. Select one or more report options if required.
6. Click **OK** to generate and view the report. The report automatically displays in the *Preview* pane.

# Practice 10a
# Create a Search Report

In this practice, you create a search report using a pre-existing template and save the report to Autodesk Vault. The completed practice is shown in Figure 10–4.

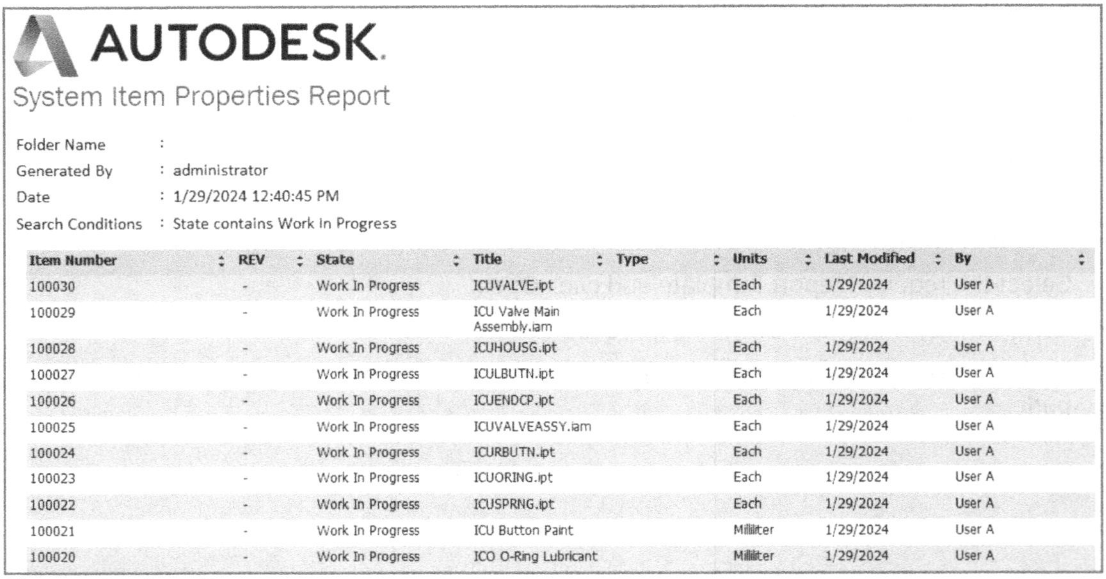

AUTODESK.

System Item Properties Report

Folder Name :
Generated By : administrator
Date : 1/29/2024 12:40:45 PM
Search Conditions : State contains Work In Progress

| Item Number | REV | State | Title | Type | Units | Last Modified | By |
|---|---|---|---|---|---|---|---|
| 100030 | - | Work In Progress | ICUVALVE.ipt | | Each | 1/29/2024 | User A |
| 100029 | - | Work In Progress | ICU Valve Main Assembly.iam | | Each | 1/29/2024 | User A |
| 100028 | - | Work In Progress | ICUHOUSG.ipt | | Each | 1/29/2024 | User A |
| 100027 | - | Work In Progress | ICULBUTN.ipt | | Each | 1/29/2024 | User A |
| 100026 | - | Work In Progress | ICUENDCP.ipt | | Each | 1/29/2024 | User A |
| 100025 | - | Work In Progress | ICUVALVEASSY.iam | | Each | 1/29/2024 | User A |
| 100024 | - | Work In Progress | ICURBUTN.ipt | | Each | 1/29/2024 | User A |
| 100023 | - | Work In Progress | ICUORING.ipt | | Each | 1/29/2024 | User A |
| 100022 | - | Work In Progress | ICUSPRNG.ipt | | Each | 1/29/2024 | User A |
| 100021 | - | Work In Progress | ICU Button Paint | | Milliter | 1/29/2024 | User A |
| 100020 | - | Work In Progress | ICO O-Ring Lubricant | | Milliter | 1/29/2024 | User A |

***The completed practice***

**Figure 10–4**

## Task 1: Create a search report.

1. Start Autodesk Vault. Log in using the following information:
   - For *User Name*, enter **administrator**.
   - Leave the *Password* field blank.
   - For *Vault*, select **AOTCVault**.
2. In the *Navigation* pane, click **Project Explorer ($)**.
3. Click **Find** in the toolbar.

4. In the *Find* dialog box, select the *Advanced* tab, as shown in Figure 10–5.

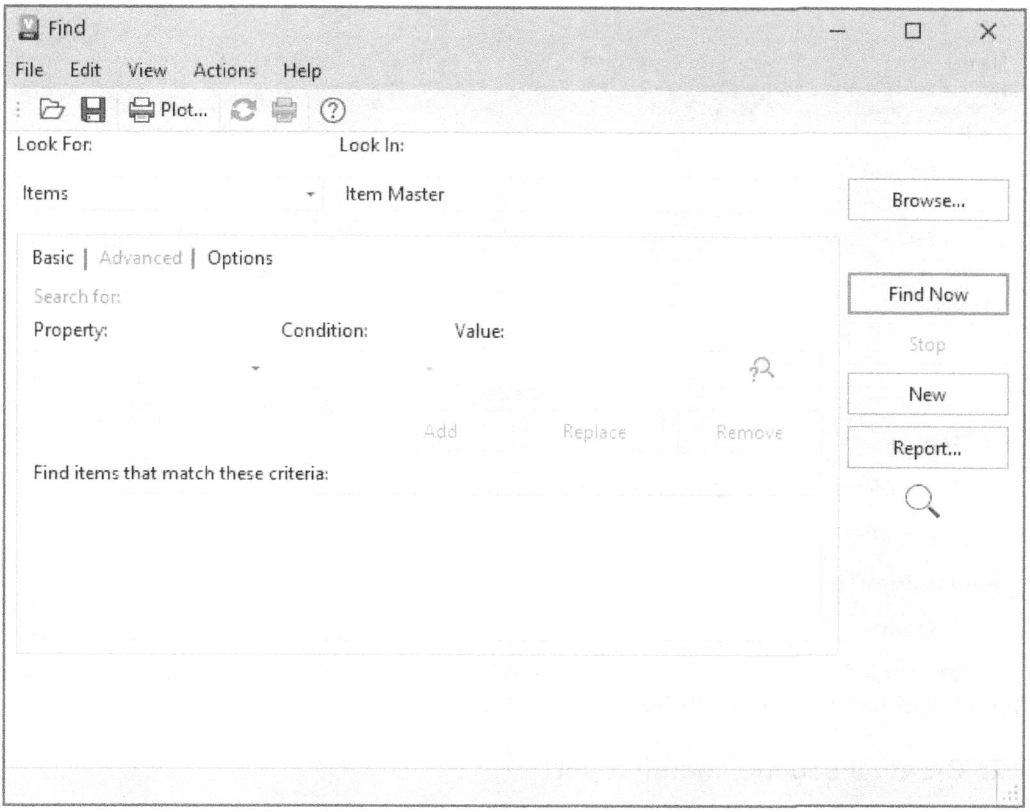


**Figure 10–5**

5. In the *Advanced* tab, do the following to create a search criteria:
   - Select **State** from the *Property* drop-down list.
   - Select **contains** from the *Condition* drop-down list.
   - Enter **Work in Progress** in the *Value* field.
   - Click **Add**.

   The resulting search criteria displays as shown in Figure 10–6.

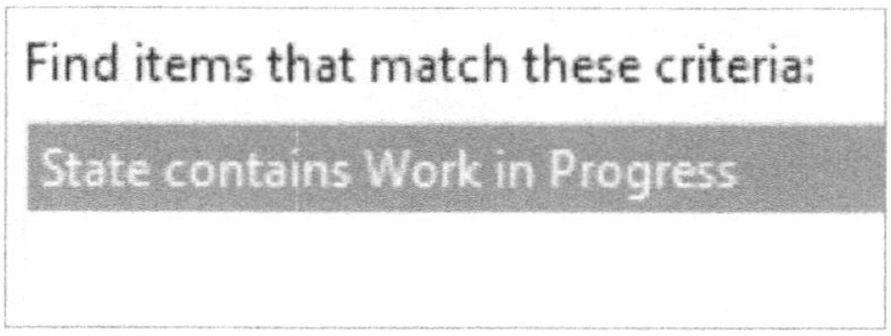


**Figure 10–6**

6. Click **Find Now**. All of the files in a **Work in Progress** state are listed, as shown in Figure 10–7.

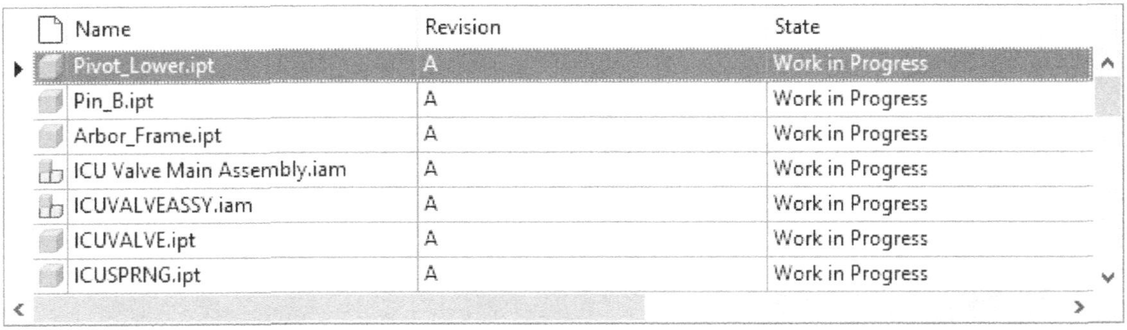

| Name | Revision | State |
|---|---|---|
| Pivot_Lower.ipt | A | Work in Progress |
| Pin_B.ipt | A | Work in Progress |
| Arbor_Frame.ipt | A | Work in Progress |
| ICU Valve Main Assembly.iam | A | Work in Progress |
| ICUVALVEASSY.iam | A | Work in Progress |
| ICUVALVE.ipt | A | Work in Progress |
| ICUSPRNG.ipt | A | Work in Progress |

**Figure 10–7**

7. Click **Report**.
8. In the *Select Report Template* dialog box, do the following:
   - Click the ellipsis (...) button.
   - Select **Item Table.rdlc**.
   - Click **Open**.
9. Click **OK** in the *Select Report Template* dialog box. The report is generated and immediately launched in Microsoft Report Viewer. Close the Viewer.

## Task 2: Create a second search report.

1. In the *Navigation* pane, select **Home**.
2. Select the *Item Master* list. Alternatively, you can click **Item Master**.
3. Click **Find** in the toolbar.

4. In the *Find* dialog box (as shown in Figure 10–8), select the *Advanced* tab.

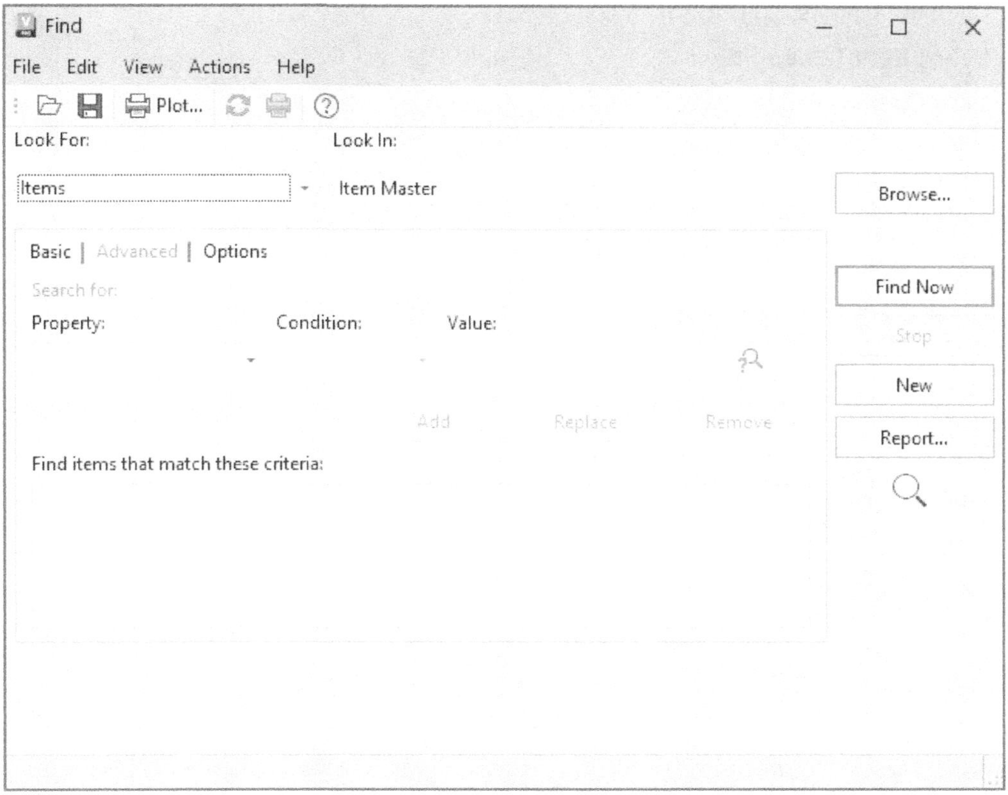


**Figure 10–8**

5. On the *Advanced* tab, do the following, as shown in Figure 10–9:
    - Select **State** from the *Property* drop-down list.
    - Select **does not contain** from the *Condition* drop-down list.
    - Enter **Obsolete** in the *Value* field.
    - Click **Add**.

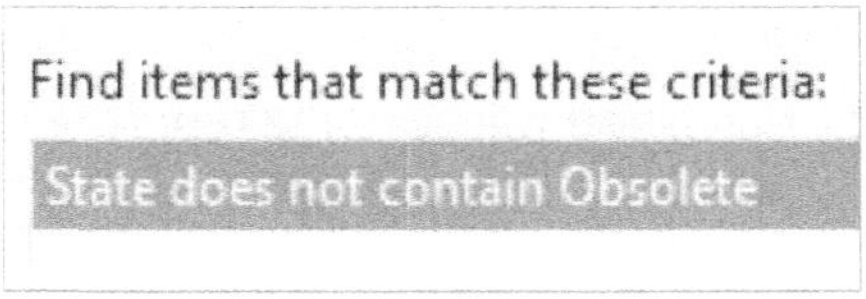


**Figure 10–9**

6. Click **Find Now**. All of the items that are not in an **Obsolete** state are listed in the report.
7. Click **Report**.

8. In the *Select Report Template* dialog box, do the following:
   - Click the ellipsis (...) button.
   - Select **Item Table.rdlc**.
   - Click **Open**.
9. Click **OK** in the *Select Report Template* dialog box. The report is generated and immediately launched in Microsoft Report Viewer, as shown in Figure 10–10. The generated report might vary slightly depending on the files in your database.

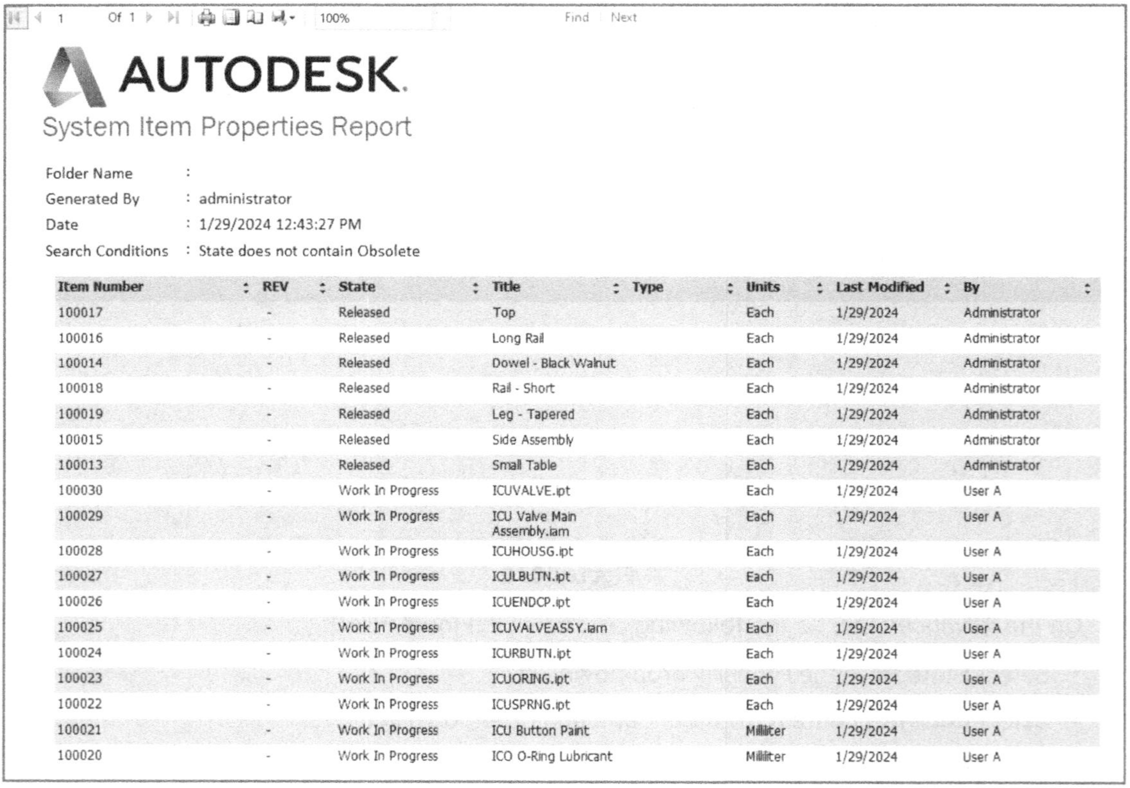

1 Of 1 100% Find | Next

AUTODESK.

System Item Properties Report

Folder Name :
Generated By : administrator
Date : 1/29/2024 12:43:27 PM
Search Conditions : State does not contain Obsolete

| Item Number | REV | State | Title | Type | Units | Last Modified | By |
|---|---|---|---|---|---|---|---|
| 100017 | - | Released | Top | | Each | 1/29/2024 | Administrator |
| 100016 | - | Released | Long Rail | | Each | 1/29/2024 | Administrator |
| 100014 | - | Released | Dowel - Black Walnut | | Each | 1/29/2024 | Administrator |
| 100018 | - | Released | Rail - Short | | Each | 1/29/2024 | Administrator |
| 100019 | - | Released | Leg - Tapered | | Each | 1/29/2024 | Administrator |
| 100015 | - | Released | Side Assembly | | Each | 1/29/2024 | Administrator |
| 100013 | - | Released | Small Table | | Each | 1/29/2024 | Administrator |
| 100030 | - | Work In Progress | ICUVALVE.ipt | | Each | 1/29/2024 | User A |
| 100029 | - | Work In Progress | ICU Valve Main Assembly.iam | | Each | 1/29/2024 | User A |
| 100028 | - | Work In Progress | ICUHOUSG.ipt | | Each | 1/29/2024 | User A |
| 100027 | - | Work In Progress | ICULBUTN.ipt | | Each | 1/29/2024 | User A |
| 100026 | - | Work In Progress | ICUENDCP.ipt | | Each | 1/29/2024 | User A |
| 100025 | - | Work In Progress | ICUVALVEASSY.iam | | Each | 1/29/2024 | User A |
| 100024 | - | Work In Progress | ICURBUTN.ipt | | Each | 1/29/2024 | User A |
| 100023 | - | Work In Progress | ICUORING.ipt | | Each | 1/29/2024 | User A |
| 100022 | - | Work In Progress | ICUSPRNG.ipt | | Each | 1/29/2024 | User A |
| 100021 | - | Work In Progress | ICU Button Paint | | Milliliter | 1/29/2024 | User A |
| 100020 | - | Work In Progress | ICO O-Ring Lubricant | | Milliliter | 1/29/2024 | User A |

**Figure 10–10**

10. Click **Export** in the View Report toolbar.
11. Select **PDF** as the format in which you will save the report.
12. In the *Save As* dialog box, navigate to the desktop.
13. Name the report and click **Save** to store it on your desktop.
14. Close the *View Report* and *Find* dialog boxes.

## Task 3: Create a Vault project report.

1. Select **Project Explorer**.
2. Right-click on **Project Explorer ($)** and select **New Folder**, as shown in Figure 10–11.

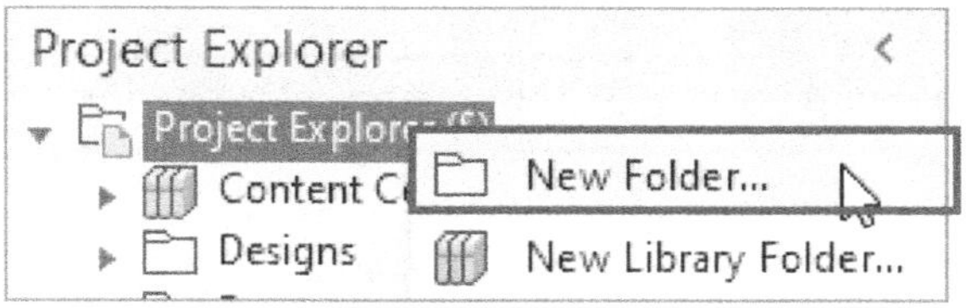


**Figure 10–11**

3. Create a new folder called **Projects**.
4. Right-click on **Projects** and select **New Folder** to create a new folder called **10-A-555**, as shown in Figure 10–12. Click **OK**.

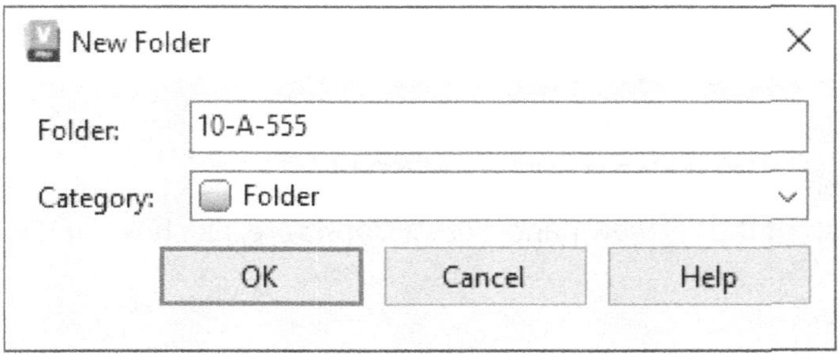


**Figure 10–12**

5. Select **Designs\TrailerHitch**, as shown in Figure 10–13.

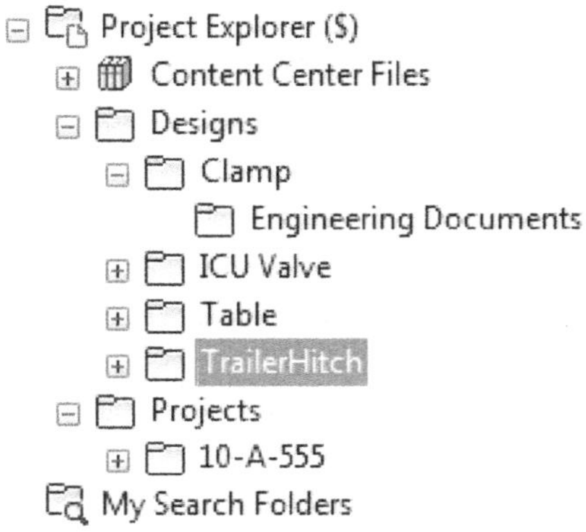


**Figure 10–13**

6. Select all of the folder's files using <Ctrl>+<A>.
7. In the *Edit* menu, select **Copy**, as shown in Figure 10–14.

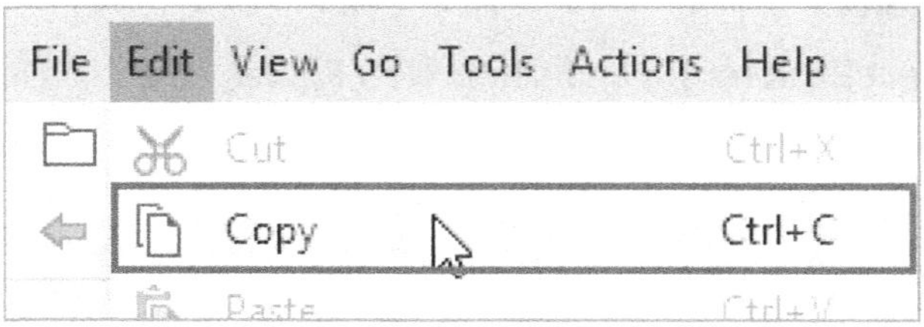


**Figure 10–14**

8. Navigate to the *10-A-555* project folder.
9. In the *Edit* menu, select **Paste as link**.
10. Select **Item Master**.
11. Select all of the items using <Ctrl>+<A>.
12. In the *Edit* menu, select **Copy**.
13. Navigate to the *10-A-555* project folder.
14. In the *Edit* menu, select **Paste as link**.
15. In the main pane, select the **10-A-555** project folder.
16. In the *Reports* tab of the *Preview* pane, select **Configure**, as shown in Figure 10–15.

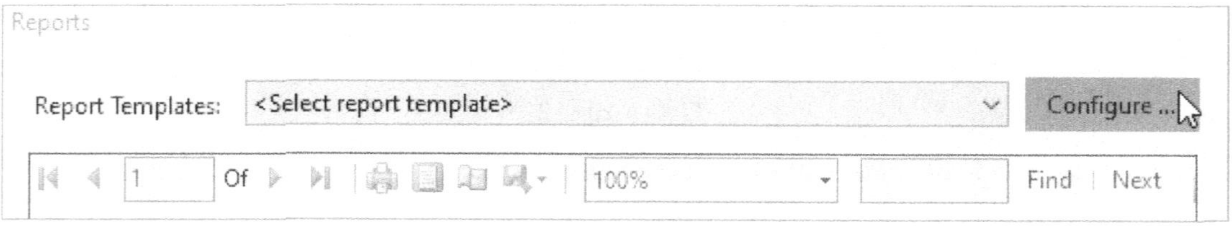


**Figure 10–15**

17. In the *Report Settings* dialog box, ensure all *Report Options* are selected and click **Browse Files**, as shown in Figure 10–16.

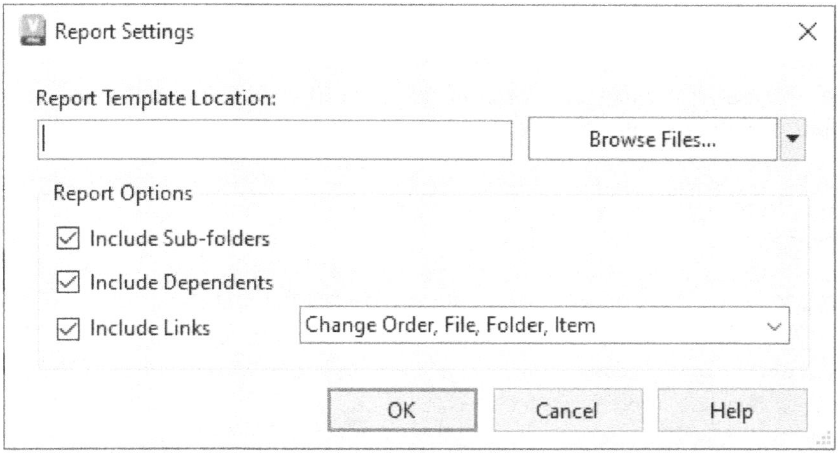


Figure 10–16

18. Select the **Project Dashboard.rdlc** template and click **Open**.
19. Click **OK**. The report is automatically displayed in the *Preview* pane, as shown in Figure 10–17. The generated report might vary slightly depending on the files in your database.

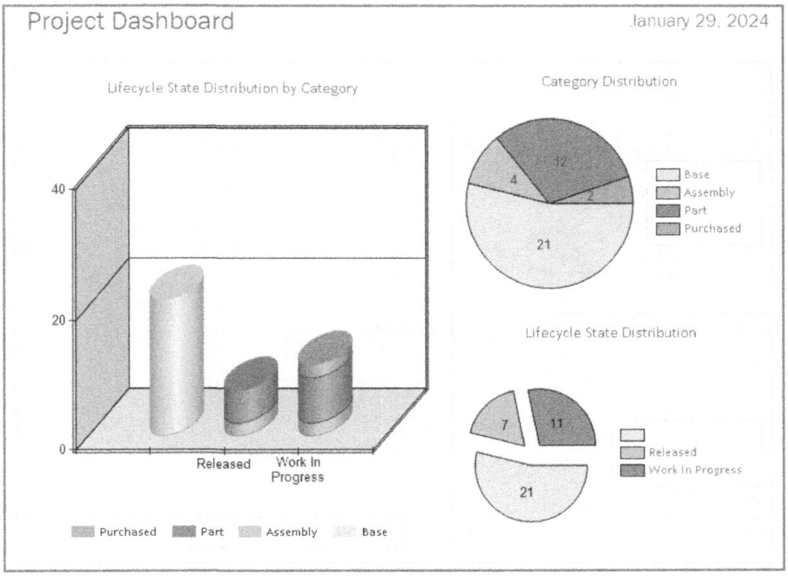


Figure 10–17

**End of practice**

# 10.2 Creating Custom Report Templates

In this section, you learn how to create and modify custom report templates using the Autodesk Report Template Utility and Microsoft Visual Studio.

> ***Note:*** *The Autodesk Report Template Utility is intended for advanced users who are familiar with XML and RDLC authoring applications. You must have Microsoft Visual Studio installed to complete this lesson.*

Use custom report templates (as shown in Figure 10–18) to illustrate your vault data in a way that suits your business needs.

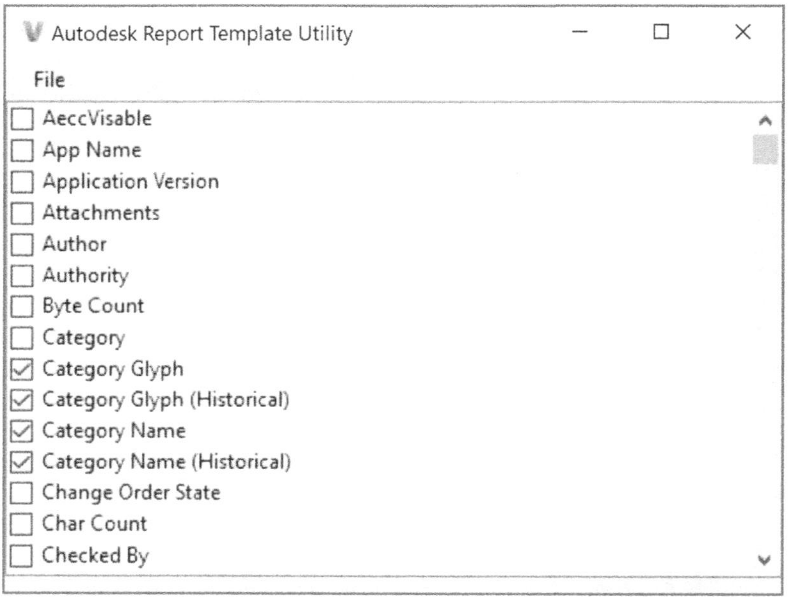


**Figure 10–18**

# Introduction to the Autodesk Report Template Utility

The Autodesk Report Template Utility (shown in Figure 10–19) is a software used to create an initial RDLC report template that contains all of the required Vault data binding information, but no formatting. You can open the RDLC file created by the Autodesk Report Template Utility in Visual Studio to specify the layout and formatting.

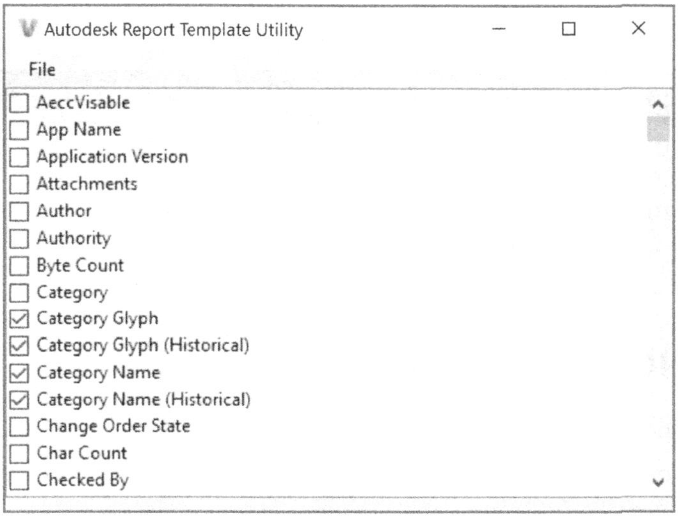


**Figure 10–19**

The **ReportTemplateAuthoritingUtility.exe** file is located in the *C:\Program Files\Autodesk\ <Autodesk Vault edition> <year>\Explorer* folder, where <Autodesk Vault edition> is the name of the Autodesk Vault edition you are using (such as Autodesk Vault Professional) and <year> is the release year.

## Report Template Authoring

Report Viewer uses the Microsoft-proposed standard Report Definition Language (RDL) to describe the format of the report. RDL is an XML schema that can contain:

- Formatting descriptions for tables, charts, images, headers, footers, and so on
- Data field definitions
- Report parameters

There are two types of RDL files supported by Report Viewer – one each for the server and local report processing mode. Vault uses the local processing mode, so you will be using the local types of RDL file – which, by convention, is stored in files with the .RDLC extension. RDL and RDLC files have the same XML schema, but RDLC files do not contain database connection information since the client application (in this case Vault) provides the data.

Although RDLC files contain XML, no knowledge of XML is required to create and edit them.

 

### How To: Access the Autodesk Report Template Utility

The following steps describe how to access the Autodesk Report Template Utility:

1. Open File Explorer.
2. Navigate to the *C:\Program Files\Autodesk\<Autodesk Vault edition><year>\Explorer* folder, where <Audodesk Vault edition> is the name of the Autodesk Vault edition you are using (such as Autodesk Vault Professional) and <year> is the release year.

**Hint: Editing RDL Files**

Detailed information on the editing of RDL files is outside the scope of this lesson, but Microsoft provides a good overview here: http://msdn.microsoft.com/en-us/library/ms159267.aspx, and a tutorial here: http://msdn.microsoft.com/en-us/library/ms167305.aspx.

There are also a number of books available on the subject of SQL Server Reporting Services that have sections covering RDLC report template creation and editing.

# Creating a New Report Template

You create a new report template in three steps:

1. Create a preliminary template in the Autodesk Report Template Utility with the properties you want to show in the report
2. Customize the template layout using Microsoft Visual Studio.
3. Test the template by generating a sample report.

## Example of Using the Autodesk Report Template Utility

Your manager asks you to print a comprehensive report about files in all existing projects that have been released. She requests that the report include the file's state, revision ID, originator, and relative project. With these properties in mind, you open the Autodesk Report Template Utility and generate a preliminary template that meets your manager's criteria.

Then, using Microsoft Visual Studio, you modify the layout of the template to show the files in a bar chart based on project. Afterward, you create a search that returns all released files across all projects and then run the report using the newly created template.

## How To: Create a Preliminary Report Template

The following steps describe how to create a custom report template:

1. Open File Explorer.
2. Navigate to the *C:\Program Files\Autodesk\<Autodesk Vault edition><year>\Explorer* folder, where <Audodesk Vault edition> is the name of the Autodesk Vault edition you are using (such as Autodesk Vault Professional) and <year> is the release year.
3. Launch the **ReportTemplateAuthoringUtility.exe** file. The *Login* dialog box displays.
4. Enter your login data and click **OK**. The *Autodesk Report Template Utility* dialog box displays.
5. Select **File>New**.
6. Select the type of report template that you want to create from the *Report Type* drop-down list.
7. Select the report properties that you want to include in your report template from the *Report Properties* list.
8. Select **File>Save As**. The *Save Template* dialog box displays.
9. Navigate to the local folder or vault folder where you want the report template file to be saved and enter a filename in the *File name* field.
10. Click **Save** to save the file.

    ***Note:*** *The report template is blank as the Autodesk Report Template Utility did not add any layout or format information to the RDLC file.*

## How To: Customize the Layout of a New Report Template

The following steps describe how to create a custom report template:

1. Open Visual Studio and load the RDLC file you created using the Autodesk Report Template Utility, as shown in Figure 10–20.

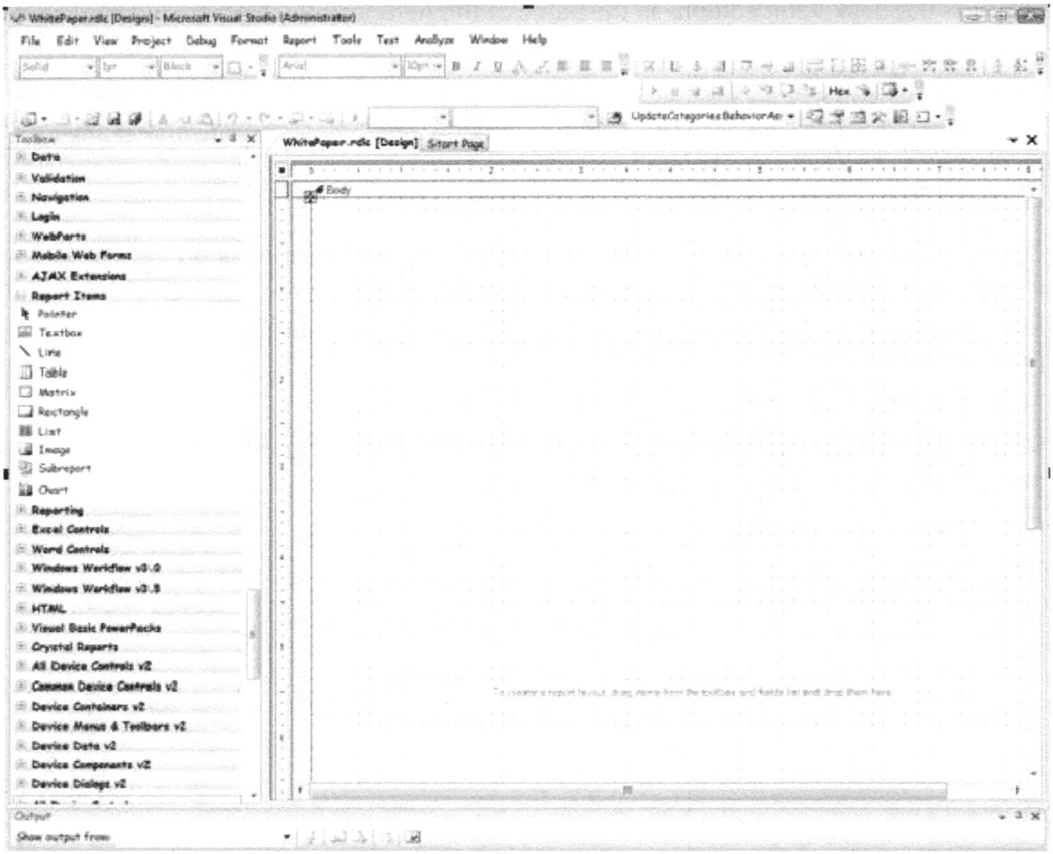


**Figure 10–20**

2. Add controls from the toolbox to the report template.
3. Once a control is placed in a report template, the control can be configured to display the value of a Vault property. Right-click on the control and select **Expression** in the context menu. In the *Expression* dialog box, select **Fields** from the *Category* list, as shown in Figure 10–21. Double-click on a property name to fill in the expression text box. Click **OK**.

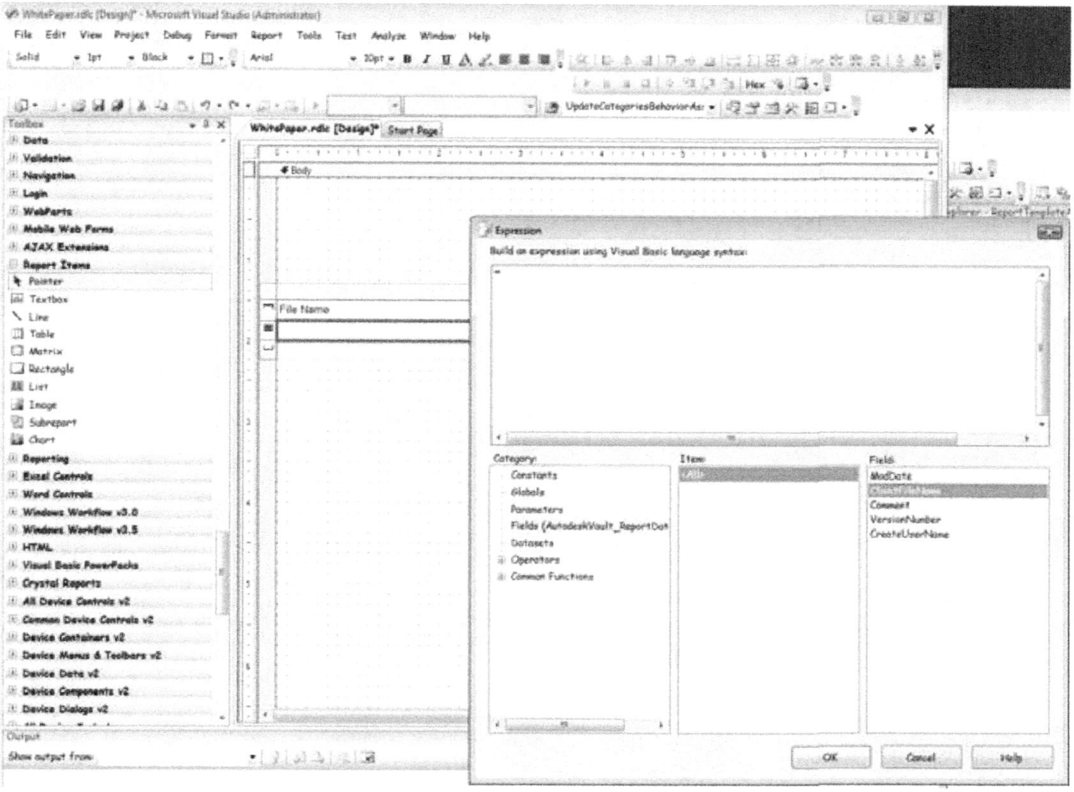


**Figure 10–21**

The field expression is now associated with the report control. When the report is generated, this control will be filled with the specified property for each Vault object processed, as shown in Figure 10–22.

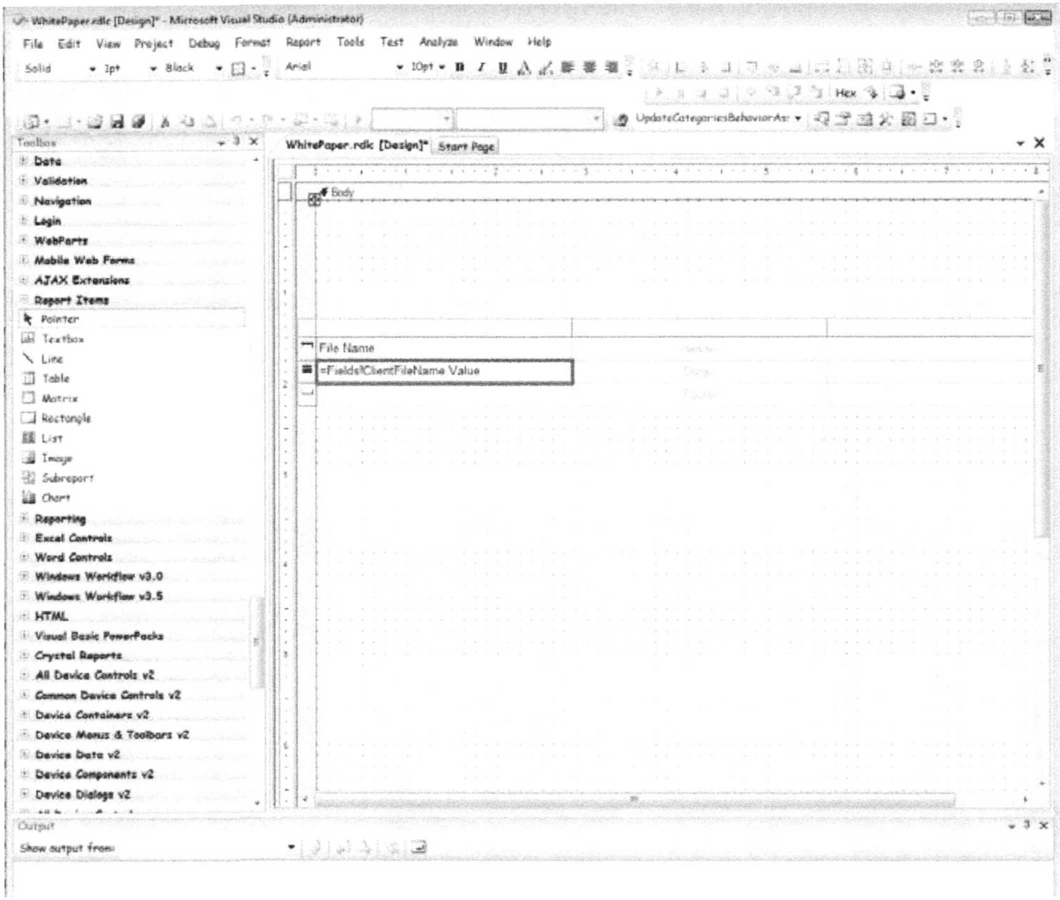

**Figure 10–22**

4. Save the template as an .RDLC file.

## How To: Test the Report Template in Vault

1. Without exiting Visual Studio, start Vault and then run a report.
2. Specify the newly created template in the *Report Template* dialog box.
3. View the results.
4. Modify the template in Visual Studio, as required.
5. Save the template.
6. Repeat, as required.

 

# Including Non-Property Vault Data in a Report

There is information relevant to a report that is not stored as properties in Autodesk Vault. To display this information in a report, a number of RDL-defined parameters must be supplied with values by the Vault prior to report processing. This process enables the template author to place and format these values in a report.

The following report parameters are supplied with values by Vault:

| Template Parameter Name | Value |
|---|---|
| **Vault_UserName** | The name of the Vault user who generated the report. |
| **Vault_VaultName** | The name of the vault that provided data for the report. This is the vault that the user who generates the report is logged into. |
| **Vault_SearchRoot** | The name of the folder(s) specified in the Look in control located in the *Find* dialog box in Autodesk Vault. |
| **Vault_LatestVersionOnly** | The state of the **Find latest versions only** checkbox in the *Options* tab of the *Find* dialog box in Autodesk Vault. |
| **Vault_SearchSubFolders** | The state of the **Search Subfolders** checkbox in the *Options* tab of the *Find* dialog box in Autodesk Vault. |
| **Vault_SearchFileContent** | The state of the **Search file content** checkbox in the *Basic* tab of the *Find* dialog box in Autodesk Vault. |
| **Vault_SearchConditions** | A string representation of the search conditions specified in the *Advanced* tab of the *Find* dialog box in Autodesk Vault. |

## Creating Reports with Non-Property Vault Data

To use one or more of these parameters in your report, create a parameter of the same name in your template by loading the template in Visual Studio, right-clicking outside of the report template, and selecting **Report Parameters**, as shown in Figure 10–23.

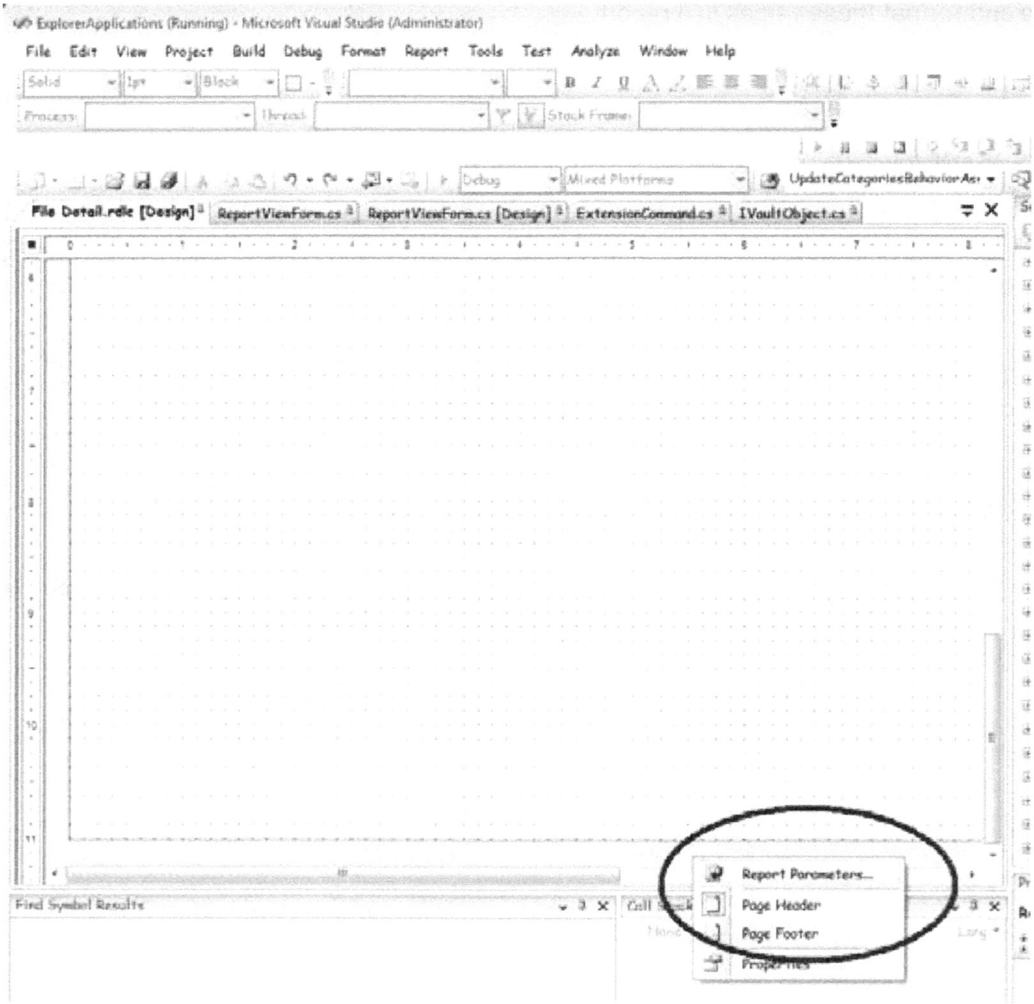


**Figure 10–23**

In the *Report Parameters* dialog box, you specify the parameters you want to include in your report. If you specify any of the reserved report parameter names listed above, the Vault reporting engine will supply a value for that parameter at runtime. Reserved parameter names must be spelled exactly as displayed in the table for the report engine to find them. Parameter names are case sensitive. The remainder of the fields in the *Report Parameters* dialog box can retain their default values, as shown in Figure 10–24.

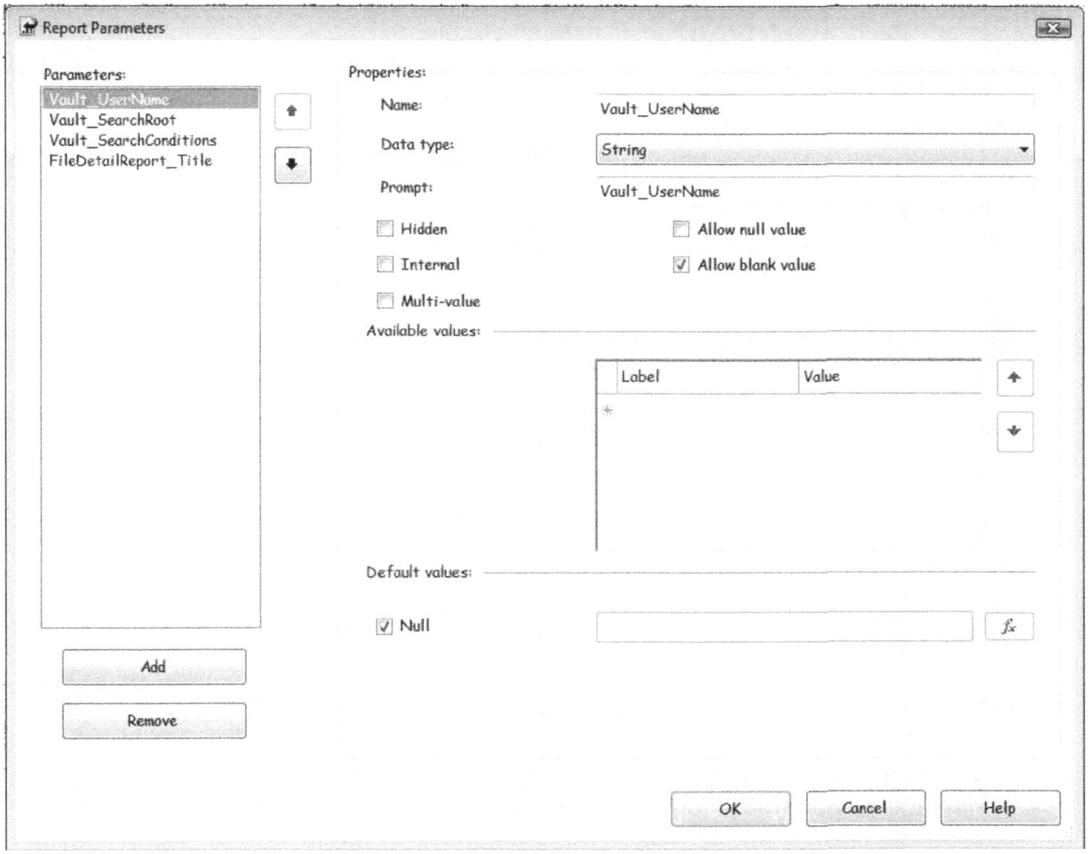


**Figure 10–24**

Placing a parameter value in a report is similar to placing property values: right-click on a control and then select **Expression** in the context menu. In the *Expression* dialog box, double-click on a property name to specify the parameter value to be used for this control, as shown in Figure 10–25.

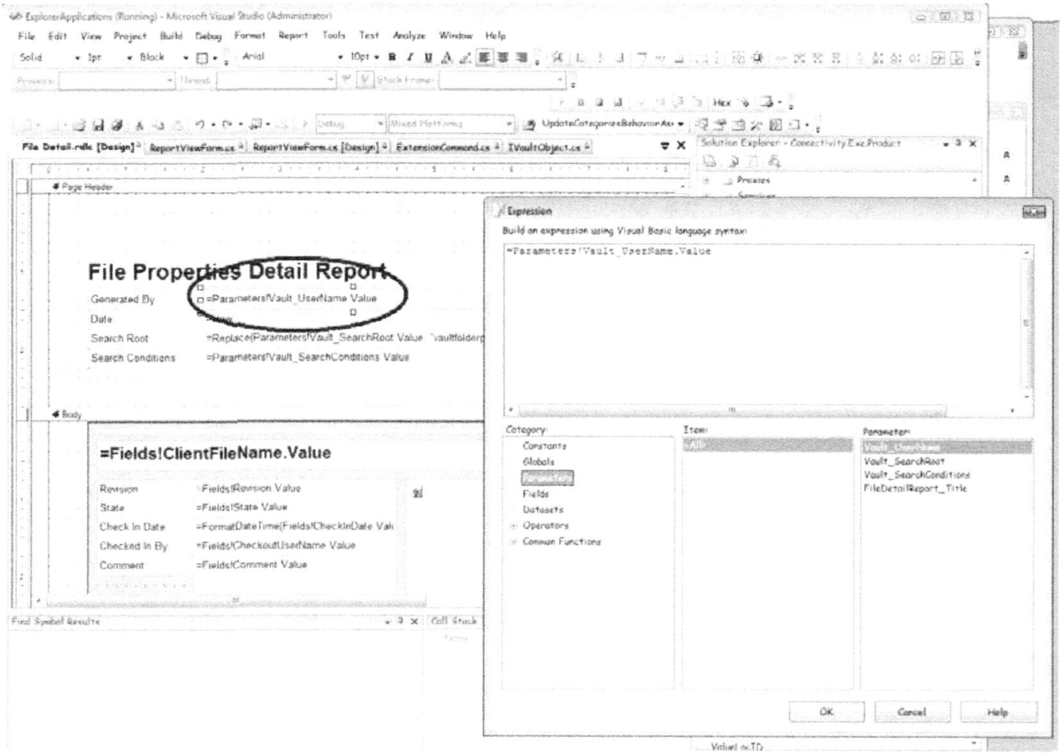


**Figure 10–25**

You can use parameter values in expressions just like field value. All of the sample templates included with Vault do parameter formatting in this way.

Chapter 11

# Working with Bills of Materials

This chapter describes how to use bills of materials (BOMs) in Autodesk® Vault Professional. You learn how these BOMs are integrated with other applications, including Autodesk® Inventor® and Autodesk® Vault.

## Learning Objectives

- Manage bills of materials.
- View and edit part BOMs to change item quantities, and print and export BOMs.
- Describe the integration of Inventor, Vault, and Vault Professional and the relationship between an Inventor BOM and the associated Vault Professional item BOM.

# 11.1 Bills of Materials

This section describes how to manage and use bills of materials (BOMs).

As an essential element in the design or manufacture of products, a BOM, in its simplest form, can be a list of components and the quantity of each required. It can, however, describe much more. BOMs can indicate which parts are manufactured and which are purchased, the materials, part numbers, and stock numbers of each part, and how the parts are structured and assembled.

Use the *Bill of Materials* tab in the *Edit Item Record* dialog box or in the *Preview* pane to work with the items BOM. The *Bill of Materials* tab is shown in Figure 11–1.

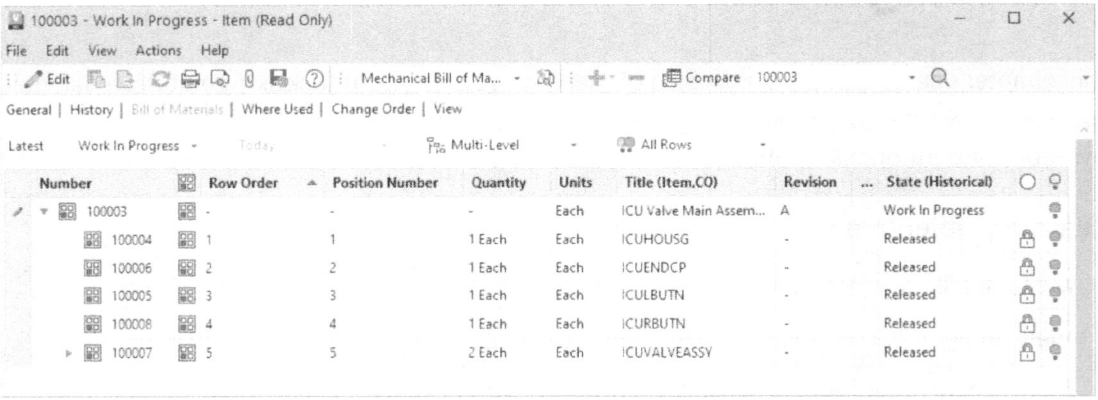

**Figure 11–1**

## About Bill of Materials

You can manage and track components of an assembly by using a BOM that lists all its parts and subassemblies. When you link purchased items to an assembly, the items become part of the BOM list as well. Although you typically associate a BOM with an assembly, all items have a bill of materials. You can view the BOM for any item by clicking the *Bill of Materials* tab.

### Part and Assembly Bill of Materials

A part BOM contains information related to a single item. The item can represent an Autodesk Inventor part, a purchased part, or another item added to the *Item Master*. If the item is linked to other items as part of a larger group, you might not be able to edit some of its properties, such as the quantity. You can add rows of other items to a part BOM. For example, you can include an existing document item that provides process or materials information on the part.

Unlike a part BOM, an assembly BOM contains multiple rows of item data that are linked directly or indirectly to the assembly item. Because these linked items are required for an assembly, some industries refer to this list as a recipe or formula. An assembly BOM does not require an actual modeled assembly. You can create a new item for non-modeled assemblies and add rows of other items to this new item's BOM.

## Examples of Part Bill of Materials

Figure 11–2 shows a BOM for an ICUSPRNG part. Standard modeled parts are usually measured in units of one (each). Note that the quantity field for this item is edited in its parent BOM.

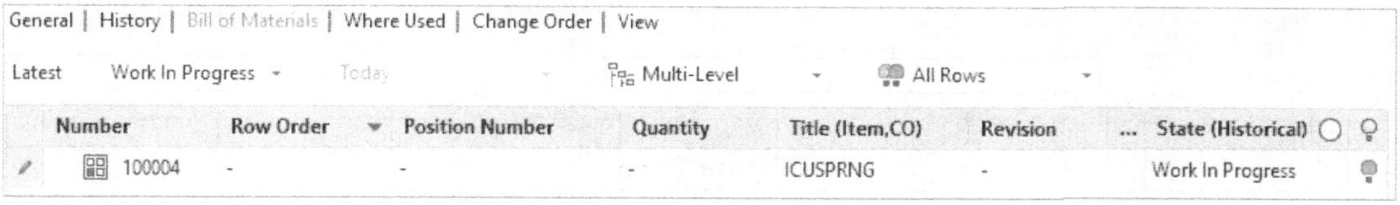


**Figure 11–2**

Figure 11–3 shows a BOM listing for a non-modeled part (lubricant). Its unit of measurement is set to milliliter.

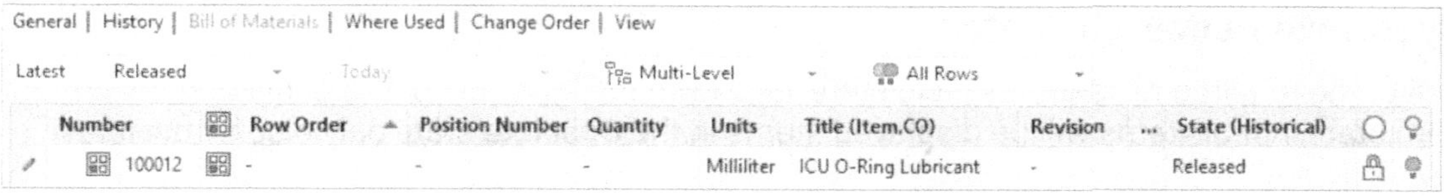


**Figure 11–3**

## Examples of Assembly Bill of Materials

Figure 11–4 shows the BOM for an ICU valve main assembly, including parts, subassemblies, and non-modeled items such as paint and lubricant.

Note that when viewing the BOM in Vault Professional, the *Row Order* column indicates the order of the items. Each subassembly listed in the BOM displays its own numbering scheme, starting at 1. The parent rows increment by one and the children rows increment by tenths. For example, if a parent row is 4, then the first child starts with 4.1.

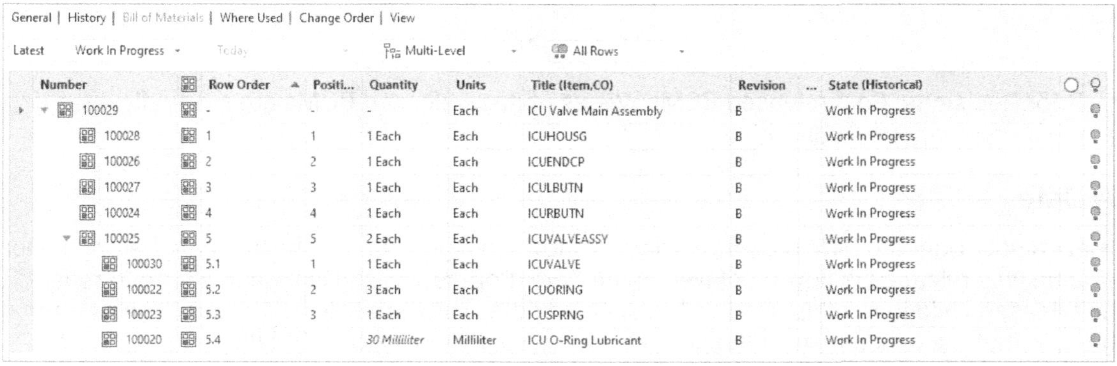


**Figure 11–4**

 

Figure 11–5 shows the BOM for an ICU valve left button. Note that another item (button paint) is linked to the button part, making it an assembly.

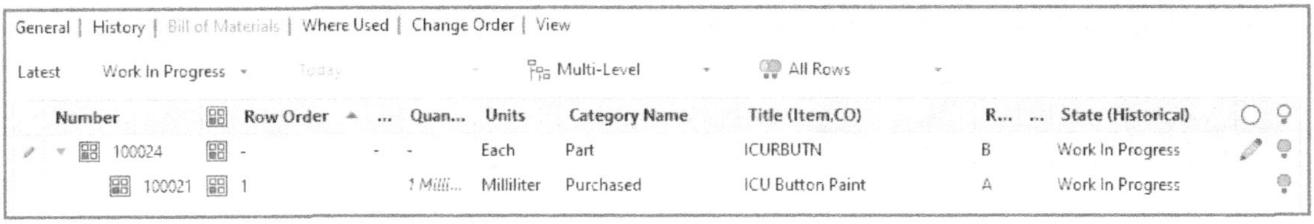


**Figure 11–5**

## Viewing a Bill of Materials

You can change your view of an item's bill of materials based on item revision/lifecycle state, date, BOM structure, or BOM row on/off status.

### By Revision/Lifecycle State

Select the required revision/lifecycle state, as shown in Figure 11–6. Depending on the current item state, not all items will be displayed. Items in the **Obsolete** state only display the latest revision.

- **Latest:** The current BOM. There can be items in any state in the BOM.

**Figure 11–6**

- **Prior Revisions:** Past released BOMs. Views of past released BOMs are read-only, even if the item record is in edit mode.

### By Date

Select a date from the *Date* drop-down list, as shown in Figure 11–7. The last date before a later revision was released is now displayed in the *Date* drop-down list. Change this date to reflect the released child item revisions for that specific date. The date selected must be on or after the date that the revision was released. The selected child revision BOM displays as of the selected date.

**Figure 11–7**

## By Bill of Materials Structure

You can select from the three types of BOM structures shown in Figure 11–8:

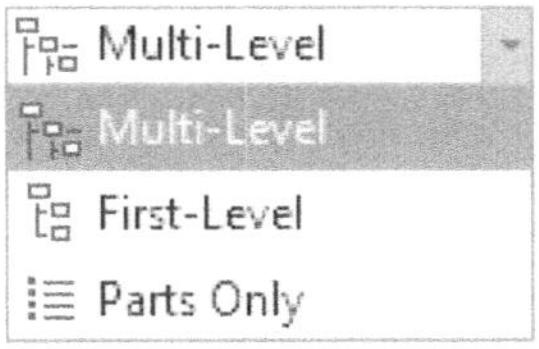


**Figure 11–8**

- **Multi-Level**: A hierarchical list of all child items in the current BOM. BOM rows can only be modified when the BOM is in **Multi-Level** view.
- **First-Level:** This displays only the top-level child items of the current item.
- **Parts Only:** Items for parts only. The BOM is flattened to a single level. No subassembly items display.

## By Bill of Materials Row Display

You can filter whether all BOM rows are displayed, or only those rows that are toggled on or toggled off using the *BOM Rows* drop-down list.

- **All Rows:** All BOM rows display regardless of whether they are toggled on for the BOM.
- **On Rows Only:** Only rows that have been toggled on for the BOM display.
- **Off Rows Only:** Only rows that are toggled off display.

*Note: When the **Parts Only** view is selected, the row filter is automatically set to **On Rows Only** and cannot be changed.*

# Editing a Bill of Materials

You can view an item's BOM on the *Bill of Materials* tab in the *Item Master*. You must use the *Item Editor* to make changes to the BOM. The item must be in a **Work in Progress** state.

To edit an item, double-click it in the *Item Master* and select **Edit** from the toolbar. The *Edit Item* dialog box displays, as shown in Figure 11–9.

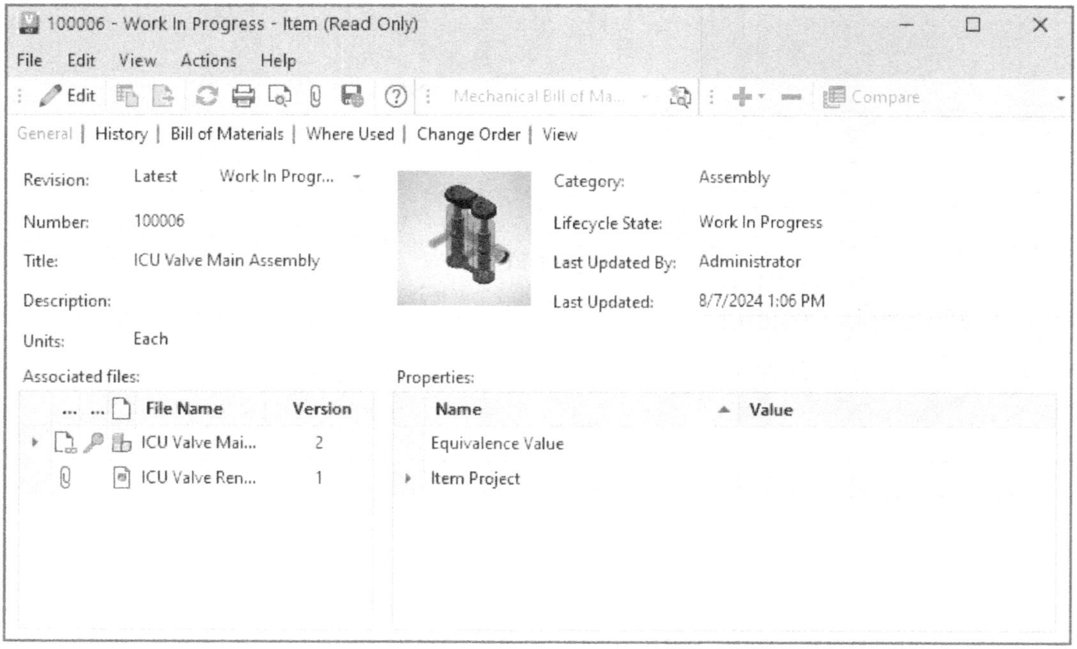


**Figure 11–9**

Click the *Bill of Materials* tab to access the BOM data, as shown in Figure 11–10.

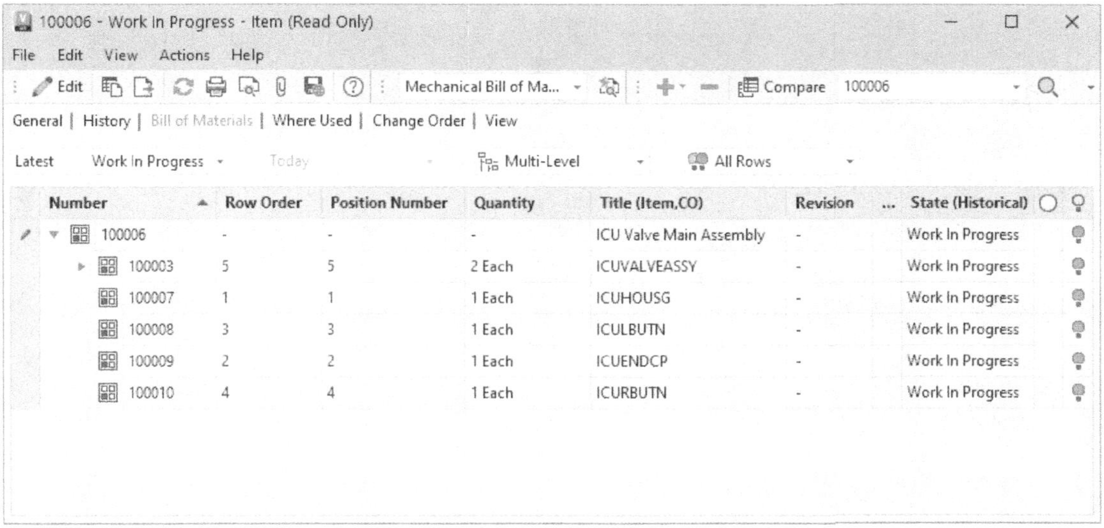

Figure 11–10

## How To: Add Item Rows to an Item Bill of Materials

The following steps describe how to add item rows to an item BOM:

1. In the *Item Master* window, select the *Bill of Materials* tab. Right-click on the top row of the BOM.
2. Select **Add Row>From Existing Item** (or **From New Item**), as shown in Figure 11–11.

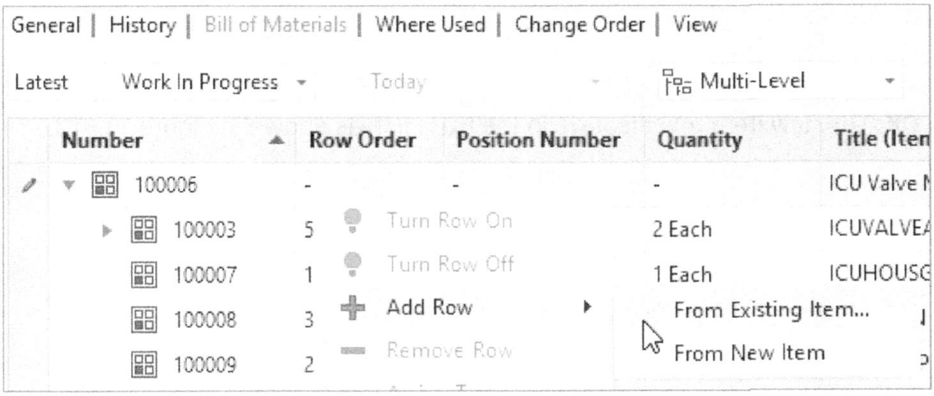

Figure 11–11

3. If you selected **From Existing Item**, enter the item number or search for the item in the list, as shown in Figure 11–12.

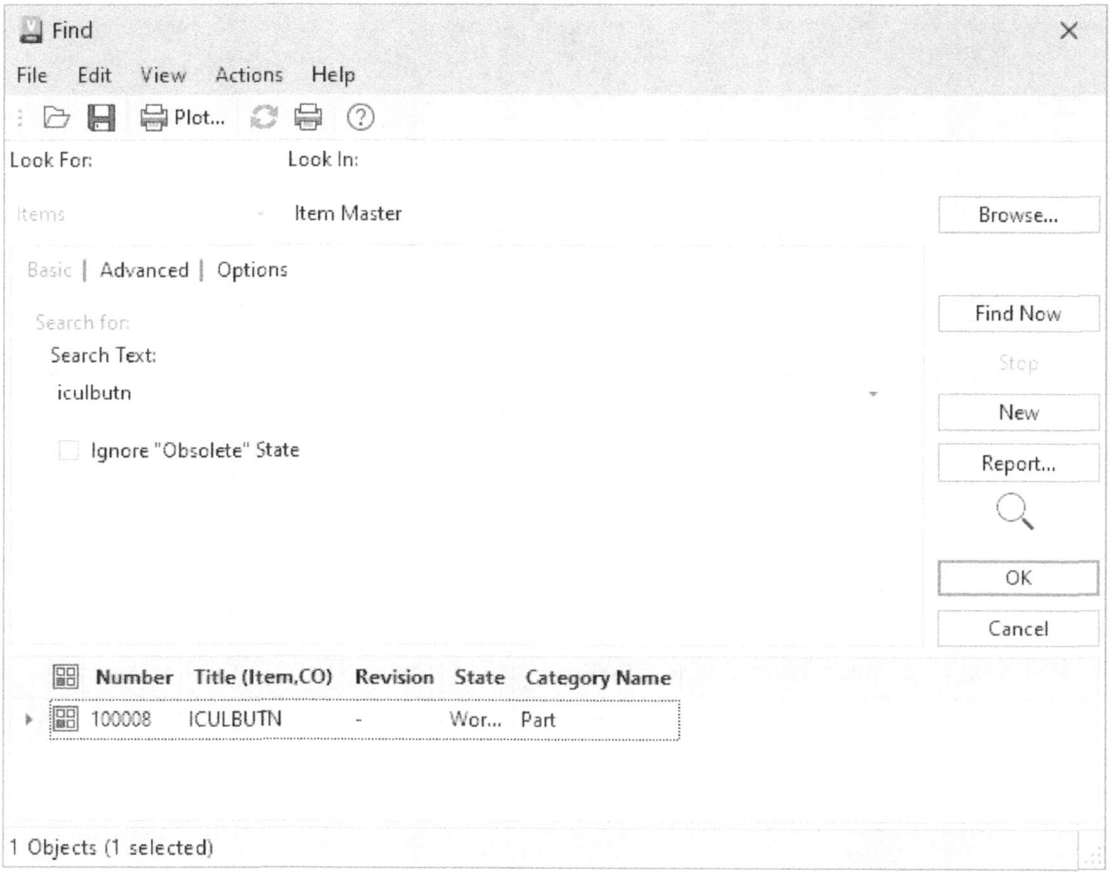


**Figure 11–12**

4. Click **OK**. The new item row displays in the BOM list, as shown in Figure 11–13.

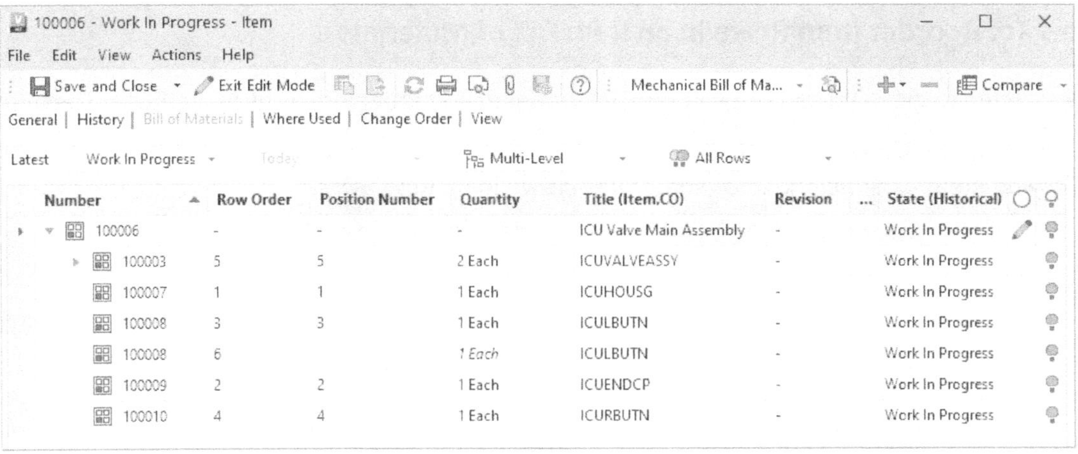


**Figure 11–13**

5. If you selected **From New Item**, new items added to the BOM in Vault Professional are appended to the end of the order. New items added to the BOM from a CAD add-in are appended to the end of the order when an update is performed.

**Hint: Editing BOMs**

You can edit a BOM only if it displays in the **Multi-Level** view (BOM tree view) that shows the relationships between the items. You cannot edit a BOM if it displays in the **First-Level** or **Parts Only** list views (the flat BOM view). Any row that you add to the top-level item becomes a first-level child item of the top-level item. To add items to a subassembly, you edit that item and add the item rows there.

## How To: Delete Item Rows from an Item Bill of Materials

The following steps describe how to delete item rows from an item BOM. When you delete an item from a BOM, it is not removed from the *Item Master*, but rather it is removed from the Item BOM.

1. In the *Item Master*, select the *Bill of Materials* tab. Right-click on the item row to be removed.
2. Select **Remove Row**. The item row is removed. When an item is removed from the BOM, a gap occurs in the numbering sequence. To update the order, drag and drop rows to reset the numbers. Only the top-level children in an item's BOM can be renumbered.

 

## How To: Reorder Item Rows in an Item Bill of Materials

Items listed in the BOM can be reordered by dragging and dropping items in the BOM. The items can be returned to the last saved order by clicking  (Restore Saved Order) in the toolbar. The following steps describe how to reorder item rows in an item BOM:

1. In the *Item Master*, double-click the item to edit and click the *Bill of Materials* tab.
2. Click **Edit**.
3. Click on the *Row Order* column to sort by the current order. Note: The BOM must be sorted by the *Row Order* column to reorder rows.
4. Select a row and drag and drop it to the new location, as shown in Figure 11–14.
**Note:** Rows can be dragged and dropped within the current parent. They cannot be dragged outside of the parent.

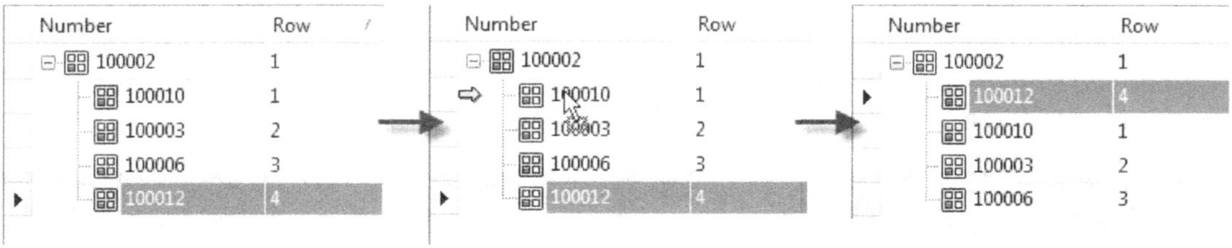


**Figure 11–14**

5. In the *BOM Item* toolbar, click **Save and Close** to save the changed order, or select **File>Exit** to close the item record without saving the new BOM order.

*Note: You can also reorder the BOM based on the values in a specific column. Click a BOM column header to sort the rows based on the values in that column. Click the same header to reverse the sort order.*

6. To restore the previous saved BOM order, select **Restore Saved Order** from the *Edit* toolbar, as shown in Figure 11–15.

**Figure 11–15**

## Changing Bill of Materials Item Quantities

The correct quantities of modeled items are calculated by default. Vault Professional works with the Inventor BOM structure, uses the same units of measure, and automatically adjusts for phantom, reference, or inseparable assemblies.

The quantity of any item can be changed in the BOM. For example, you can change the quantity of items that were added to the BOM from scratch, or of parts that are modeled once but are reused throughout the design (such as bolts). When adding non-CAD items to a BOM, you must include a quantity because there is no CAD data to determine the quantity automatically. Item quantity can only be edited on the *Bill of Materials* tab in an item record.

The BOM can only be edited when it is in **Multi-Level** view.

The item quantity can be either **Static** or **Calculated**. A calculated quantity is derived from the source CAD file and updates accordingly. A static quantity overrides the quantity specified in the linked CAD file, which means that the original quantity contained in the CAD design is no longer reflected in the BOM.

A different font is used to identify whether a quantity is static or calculated. An italic font is used for static quantities.

### How To: Change Item Quantites in the Bill of Materials

You can change any quantity in the BOM, including calculated numbers. The following steps describe how to change BOM item quantities:

1. In the Item record, click **Edit** and select the *Bill of Materials* tab.
2. Select a row in the BOM.
3. Click the quantity for the row.
4. Enter a new number for the quantity.
5. Press <Enter>.

   ***Note:*** *When you change the quantity of an item, you override the quantity derived from the linked CAD file by default. The original quantity contained in the CAD design is no longer reflected in the BOM, and the BOM does not update if the quantity is changed in the source file.*

## Override the Current Quantity

Right-click on the quantity and select **Static Quantity**, as shown in Figure 11–16. The quantity no longer reflects the value in the linked CAD file and does not update when the quantity is changed in the source file.

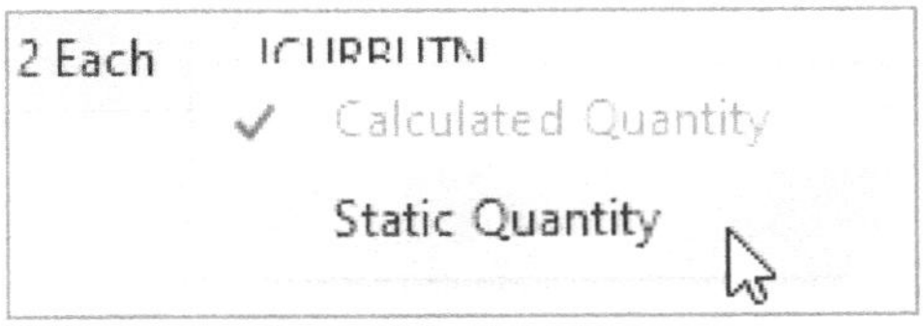


**Figure 11–16**

## Revert the Quantity to the CAD Value

Right-click on the quantity and select **Calculated Quantity**, as shown in Figure 11–17. The quantity reflects the value in the linked CAD file.

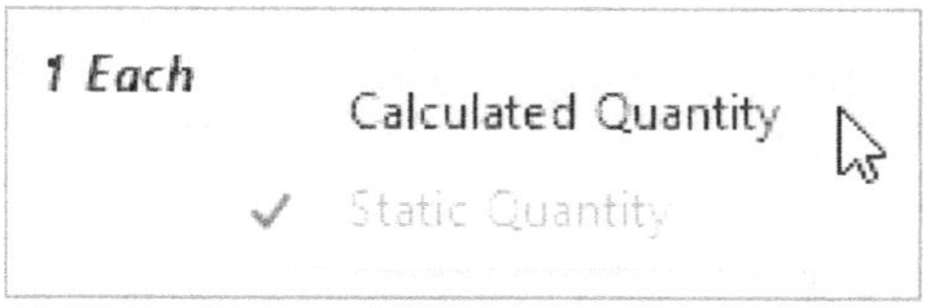


**Figure 11–17**

# Bill of Materials Output

You can view item BOMs in either tree or list view. Both views can be printed or exported to a Microsoft Excel spreadsheet, a tab-delimited text file, or an HTML page.

You can customize the setup for printing BOMs from the *File* menu or the toolbar in the *Edit Item Record* dialog box.

Figure 11–18 shows the use of **Print Preview** to display the form to be printed.

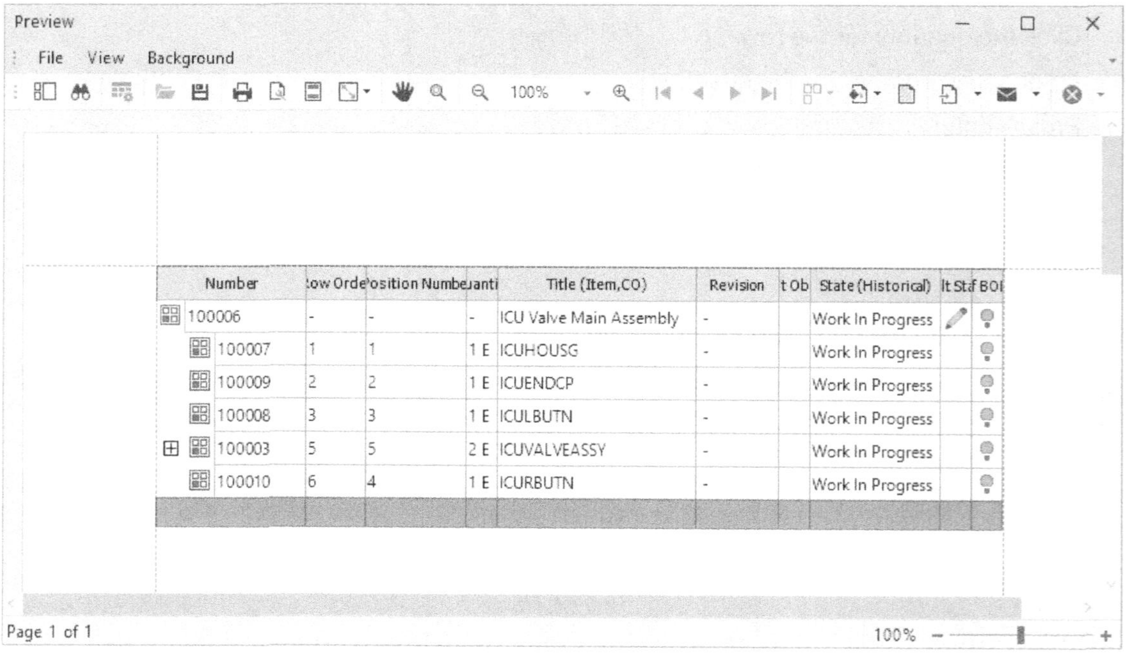


**Figure 11–18**

## How To: Format and Print a Bill of Materials

The following steps outline how to prepare and print a bill of materials:

1. In the *Open* or *Edit Item* dialog box, or in the *Preview* pane, select the *Bill of Materials* tab, as shown in Figure 11–19.

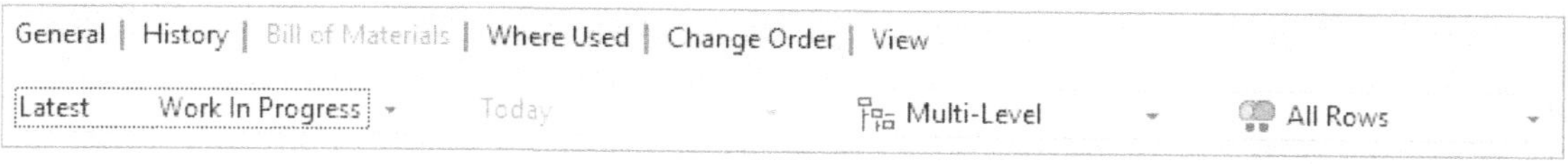


**Figure 11–19**

2. Select the BOM *Revision* or *Lifecycle State* for the selected item, as shown in Figure 11–20.

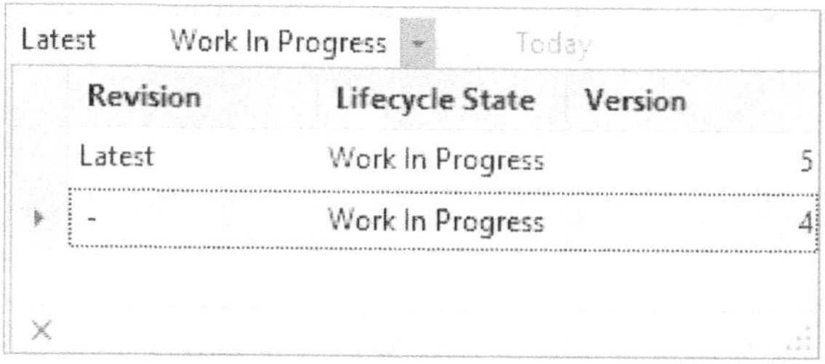


**Figure 11–20**

3. Select the BOM format from the *Structure* list, as shown in Figure 11–21.

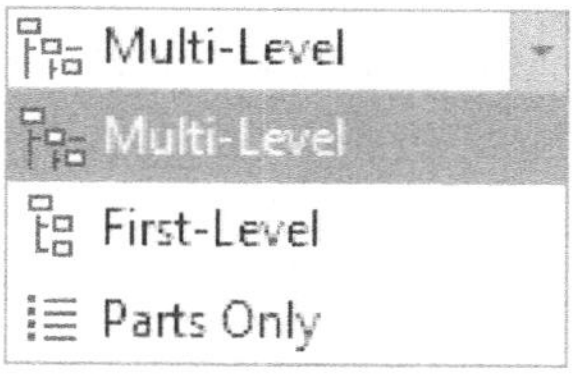


**Figure 11–21**

4. Click **File>Print Preview** or click the **Print Preview** icon, as shown in Figure 11–22.

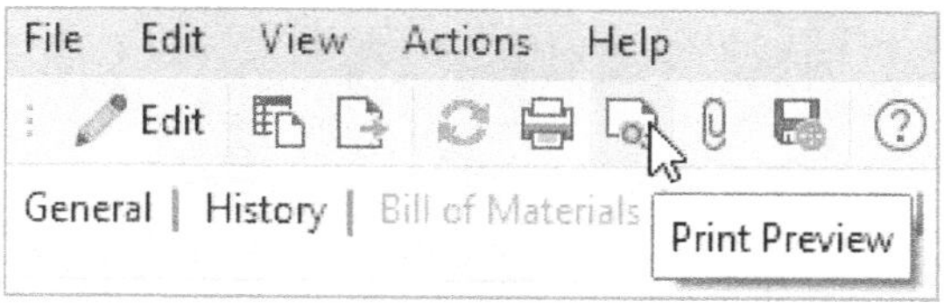


**Figure 11–22**

5. In the *Preview* dialog box, click **Customize**, as shown in Figure 11–23.

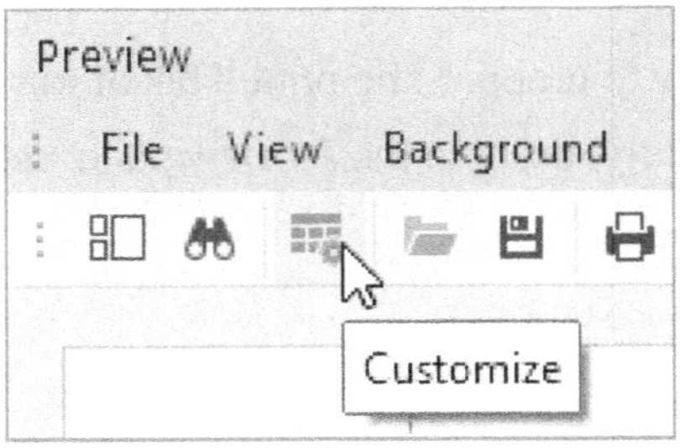


**Figure 11–23**

6. In the *Printable Component Editor*, select format and behavior settings to customize the print out. Click **OK**, as shown in Figure 11–24.

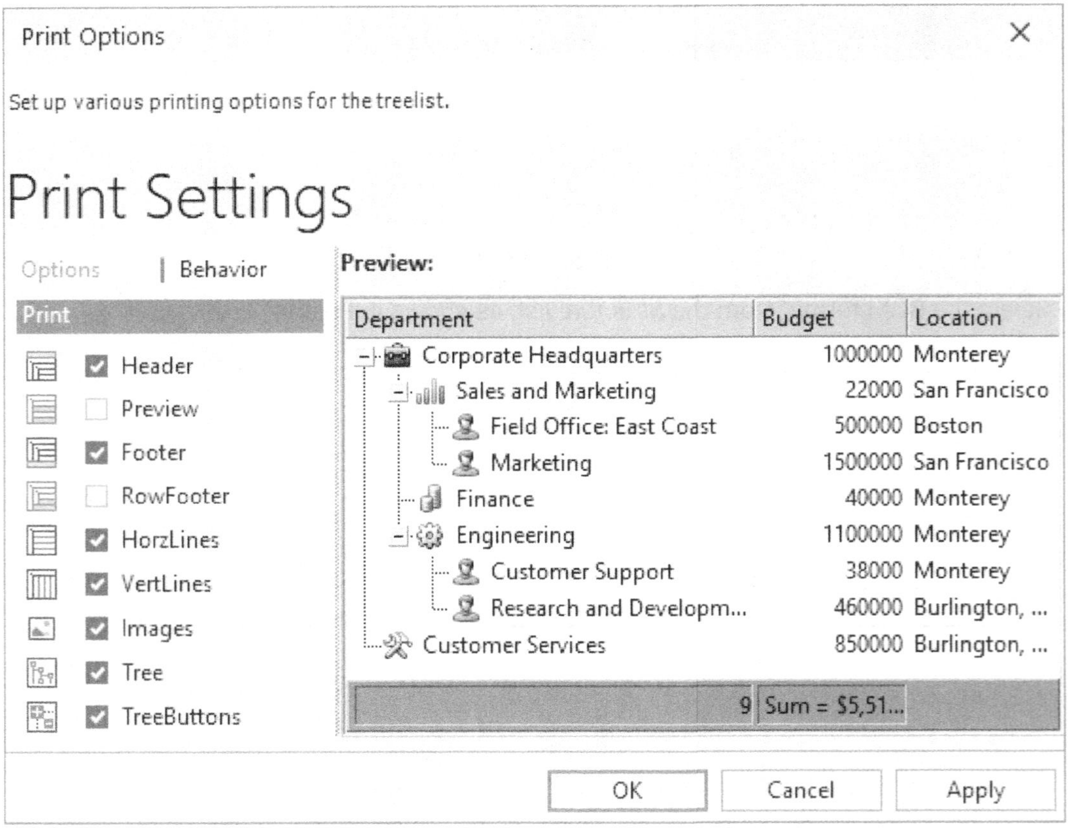


**Figure 11–24**

7. In the *Preview* dialog box, on the toolbar, click **Header And Footer** or **Page Setup** to further customize the report, as shown in Figure 11–25.

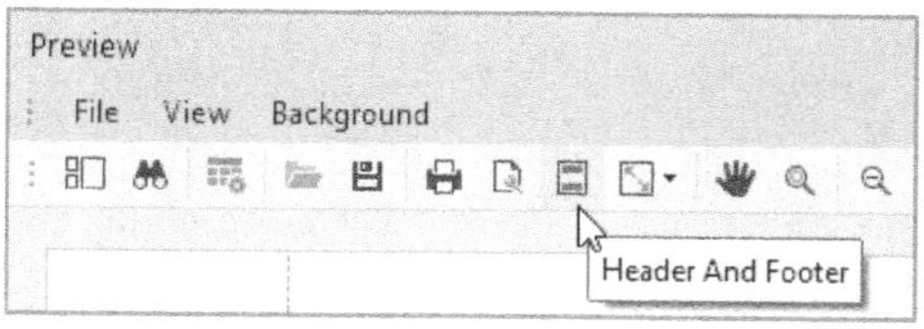


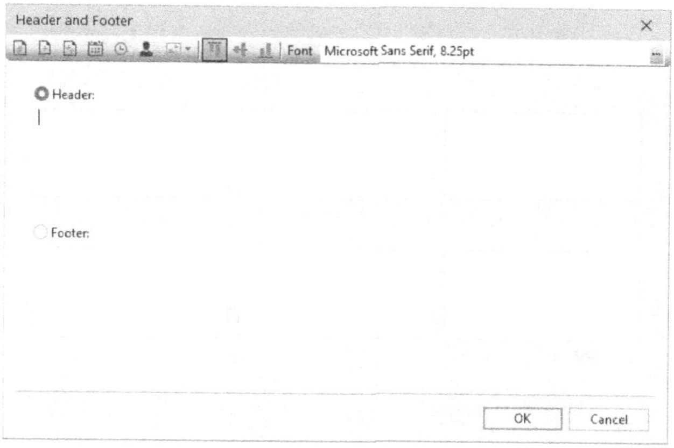


**Figure 11–25**

8. Click **Print** or **Print Direct**, as shown in Figure 11–26.

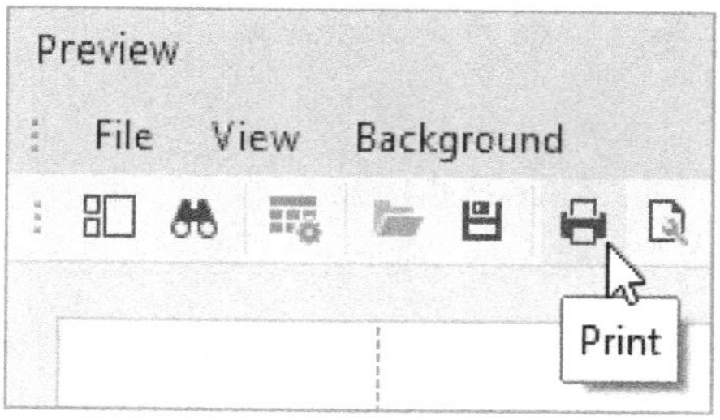


**Figure 11–26**

## How To: Export a Bill of Materials

The following steps outline how to export a BOM in a variety of file formats:

1. In the *Item Master* window, right-click on an item and select **Open**, as shown in Figure 11–27.

**Figure 11–27**

2. In the *Item Record* dialog box, click **Edit** and select the *Bill of Materials* tab.

3. Select the BOM format from the *Structure* list. In this example (shown in Figure 11–28), print the **Parts Only** list of the BOM.

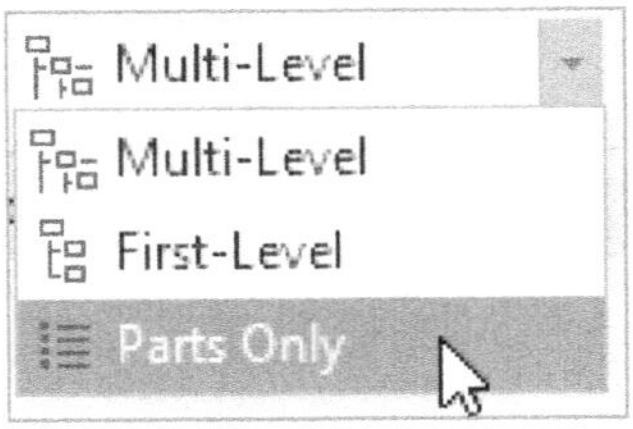


**Figure 11–28**

4. In the *File* menu, select **Save BOM View** (as shown in Figure 11–29), or click the **Save BOM View** icon in the Standard toolbar.

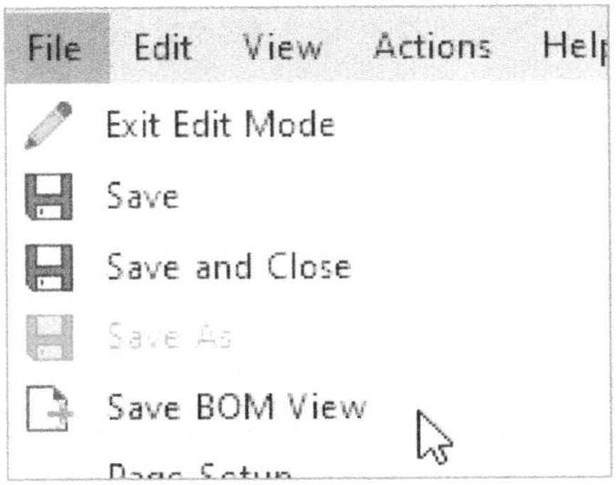


**Figure 11–29**

5. Select the file format for the export, as shown in Figure 11–30. Enter a filename. Click **Save** to save the BOM to a file.

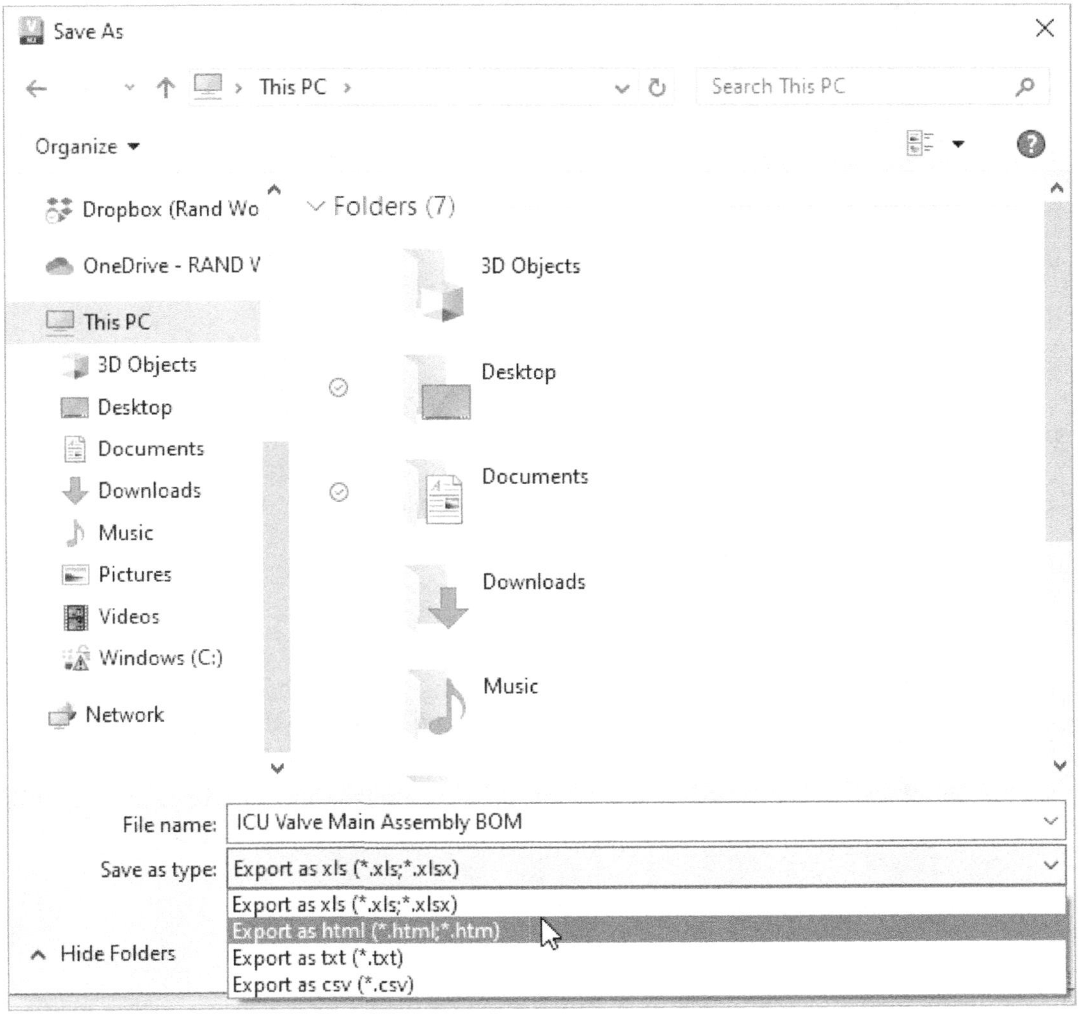


**Figure 11–30**

# Practice 11a
# Work with an Assembly Bill of Materials

In this practice, you manage and edit a product's BOM. You learn to:

- Change BOM quantities.
- Add new items and link items in the BOM.
- Reorder BOM rows.
- View BOMs.
- Redesign the Valve Assembly Packaged Product.
- Save the BOM view.

## Task 1: Change BOM quantities.

1. Start Autodesk Vault Professional. Log in using the following information:
   - For *User Name*, enter **administrator**.
   - Leave the *Password* field blank.
   - For *Vault*, select **AOTCVault**.
2. Navigate to the *Item Master* so that it is active and displaying in the main pane. Ensure that the view is set to **All Items**. Double-click the item titled *ICUValveAssy* to display the *Item Master* dialog box. Select **Edit** in the toolbar. Select the *Bill of Materials* tab.
3. On the *Bill of Materials* tab, right-click on one of the column headers and select **Customize View**, as shown in Figure 11–31. The *Customize View* dialog box will display.

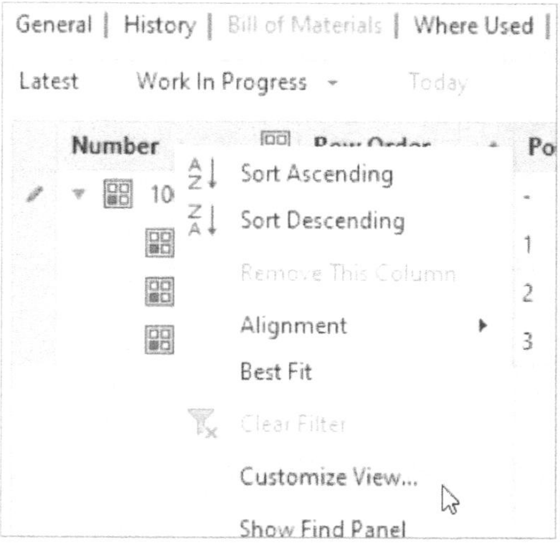


**Figure 11–31**

4. Click **Reset**, and then click **System default** to reset the fields to their default state.
5. In the *Customize View* dialog box, click **Fields**. The *Customize Fields* dialog box displays.
6. In the *Customize Fields* dialog box, do the following as shown in Figure 11–32:
   - For *Select available fields from*, expand the list and select **Item Fields**.
   - Under *Available fields*, press and hold <Ctrl> and select **Entity Icon** and **Units**. Click **Add** to move them to the *Show these fields in this order list*.
   - Under *Show these fields in this order*, select **Units**.
   - Click **Move Up** until it displays below **Quantity**.
   - Move **Entity Icon** below **Number**.
   - Click **OK** to close the *Customize Fields* dialog box.

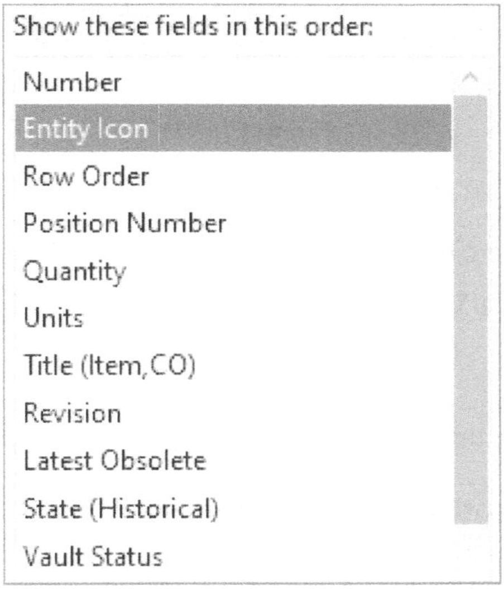


**Figure 11–32**

7. In the *Customize View* dialog box, click **Close** to return to the *Item* dialog box.

8. On the *Bill of Materials* tab, select the **ICU O-Ring Lubricant** item. Do the following as shown in Figure 11–33:
   - For *Quantity*, enter **30**.
   - Press <Enter>.
   - Click **Save and Close**.

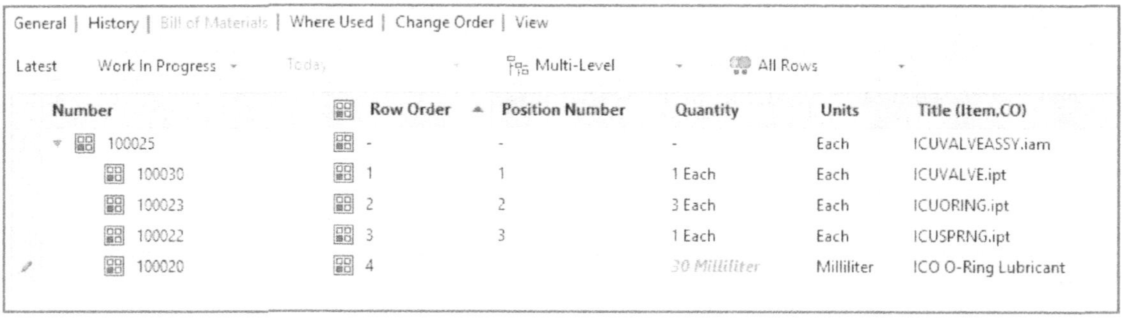


**Figure 11–33**

*Note: These steps can also be performed from the top-level BOM.*

9. In the *Item Master*, double-click the **ICULBUTN.ipt** item and click **Edit** in the toolbar.
10. On the *Bill of Materials* tab, for the quantity of the **ICU Button Paint**, enter **20** then press <Enter>.
11. Click **Save and Close**.
12. Repeat the previous two steps for the **ICURBUTN.ipt** item.

## Task 2: Add new items and link items in the BOM.

1. In *Home*, right-click on **Item Master** and select **New Item**, as shown in Figure 11–34.

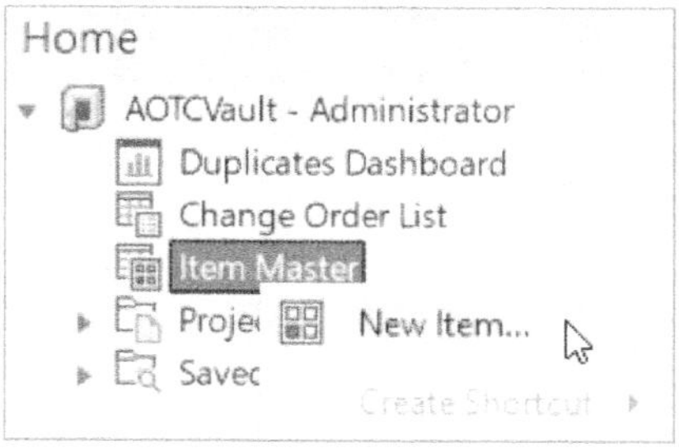


**Figure 11–34**

2. For *Category*, select **Product**.
3. For *Title*, enter **Valve Assembly Packaged Product**.

4. To complete the information for the new item, do the following:
   - For *Units*, verify that **Each** is selected.
   - Under *Item Properties*, select the **Item Project** row.
   - For *Value*, enter **ICUV1**.
   - Click **Save and Close**.
5. In *Home*, right-click on **Item Master** and select **New Item**.
6. For *Category*, select **Purchased**.
7. Enter the following information for the new item:
   - For *Title*, enter **Valve Packaging.**
   - For *Description*, enter **Product Box**.
8. To complete the information for the new item, do the following, as shown in Figure 11–35:
   - For *Units*, verify that **Each** is selected.
   - Under *Properties*, select the **Item Project** row.
   - For *Value*, enter **ICUV1**.
   - Click **Save and Close**.

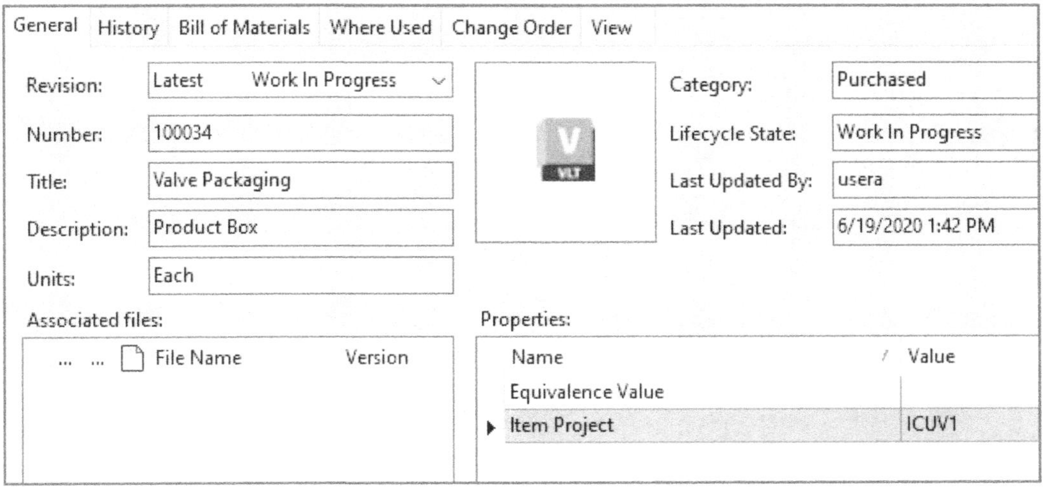


**Figure 11–35**

9. In *Home*, right-click on **Item Master** and select **New Item**.
10. For *Category*, select **Document**.
11. Enter the following information for the new item:
    - For *Title*, enter **Valve Product Specifications and Instructions Sheet**.
    - For *Description*, enter **Product Spec**.

12. To complete the information for the new item, do the following:
    - For *Units*, verify that **Each** is selected.
    - Under *Properties*, select the **Item Project** row.
    - For *Value*, enter **ICUV1**.
    - Click **Save and Close**.
13. In the *Item Master*, double-click the **Valve Assembly Packaged Product** item and click **Edit**. Select the *Bill of Materials* tab.
14. Right-click on **Valve Assembly Packaged Product** and select **Add Row>From Existing Item**.
15. In the *Find* dialog box, select the *Basic* tab if it is not selected already. Do the following:
    - Under *Search Text*, enter **valve**.
    - Click **Find Now**.
16. Select the following items in the *Found* list (shown in Figure 11–36) and click **OK**.
    - **ICU Valve Main Assembly.iam**
    - **Valve Product Specification and Instructions Sheet**
    - **Valve Packaging**

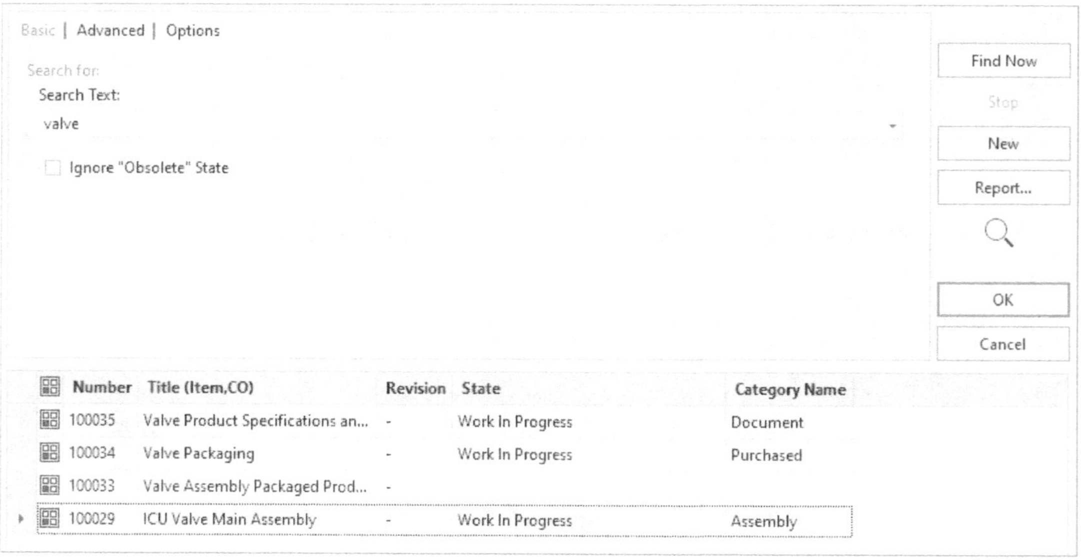


**Figure 11–36**

17. In the Bill of Materials, select the **ICU Valve Main Assembly** row, right-click, and select **Expand All**. Your BOM should look like the one in Figure 11–37.

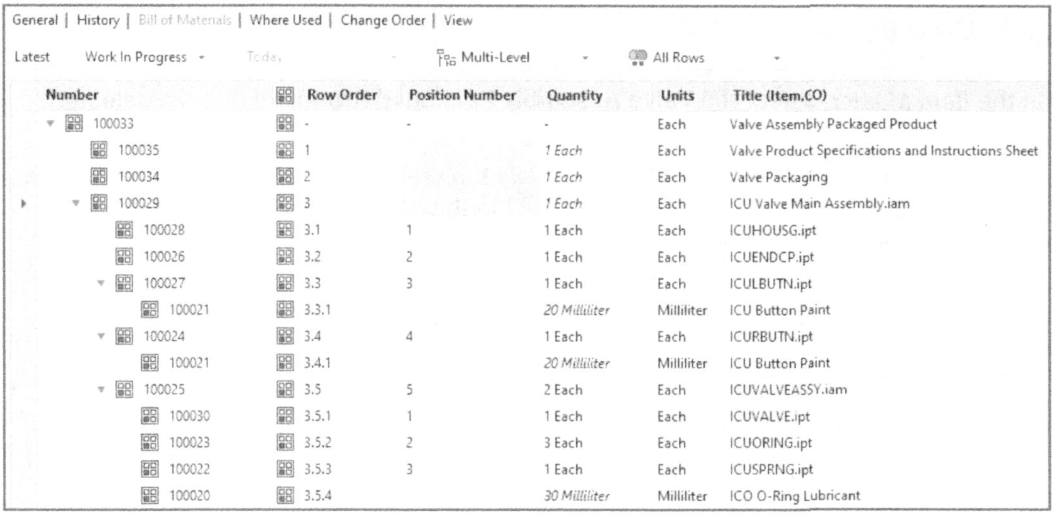


| Number | Row Order | Position Number | Quantity | Units | Title (Item,CO) |
|---|---|---|---|---|---|
| 100033 | - | - | - | Each | Valve Assembly Packaged Product |
| 100035 | 1 | | 1 Each | Each | Valve Product Specifications and Instructions Sheet |
| 100034 | 2 | | 1 Each | Each | Valve Packaging |
| 100029 | 3 | | 1 Each | Each | ICU Valve Main Assembly.iam |
| 100028 | 3.1 | 1 | 1 Each | Each | ICUHOUSG.ipt |
| 100026 | 3.2 | 2 | 1 Each | Each | ICUENDCP.ipt |
| 100027 | 3.3 | 3 | 1 Each | Each | ICULBUTN.ipt |
| 100021 | 3.3.1 | | 20 Milliliter | Milliliter | ICU Button Paint |
| 100024 | 3.4 | 4 | 1 Each | Each | ICURBUTN.ipt |
| 100021 | 3.4.1 | | 20 Milliliter | Milliliter | ICU Button Paint |
| 100025 | 3.5 | 5 | 2 Each | Each | ICUVALVEASSY.iam |
| 100030 | 3.5.1 | 1 | 1 Each | Each | ICUVALVE.ipt |
| 100023 | 3.5.2 | 2 | 3 Each | Each | ICUORING.ipt |
| 100022 | 3.5.3 | 3 | 1 Each | Each | ICUSPRNG.ipt |
| 100020 | 3.5.4 | | 30 Milliliter | Milliliter | ICO O-Ring Lubricant |

**Figure 11–37**

## Task 3: Reorder BOM rows.

1. Review the rows in the BOM. Company policy requires the packaging to be the last item in the BOM.
2. Click the down arrow symbol to close the **ICU Valve Main Assembly.iam** tree view.
3. Drag the **Valve Packaging** row to the bottom of the list if required.
4. Drag the **Valve Product Specifications and Instructions Sheet** down to the last row, as shown in Figure 11–38.

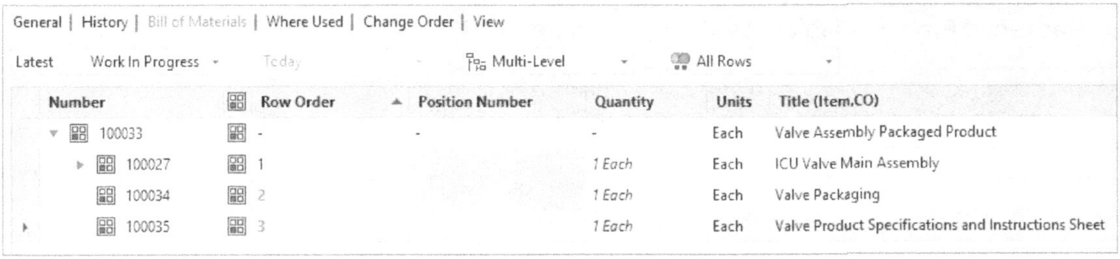


| Number | Row Order | Position Number | Quantity | Units | Title (Item,CO) |
|---|---|---|---|---|---|
| 100033 | - | - | - | Each | Valve Assembly Packaged Product |
| 100027 | 1 | | 1 Each | Each | ICU Valve Main Assembly |
| 100034 | 2 | | 1 Each | Each | Valve Packaging |
| 100035 | 3 | | 1 Each | Each | Valve Product Specifications and Instructions Sheet |

**Figure 11–38**

5. Click **Save and Close**. The Valve Assembly Package is complete.
6. In the *Item Master*, right-click on **Valve Assembly Packaged Product** and select **Change State**.
7. In the *Select Lifecycle* dialog box, select **Released**. Click **OK**.
   - Note that all the children (the components) of the Valve Assembly Package were also released.

## Task 4: View BOMs.

1. In the *Item Master*, select the **Valve Assembly Packaged Product** if it is not selected already.
2. In the *Preview* pane, select the *Bill of Materials* tab. Review the BOM rows. Note that the quantity of the O-ring lubricant is 30 milliliters in the ICUVALVEASSY item, as shown in Figure 11–39. (There are two ICUVALVEASSY items.)

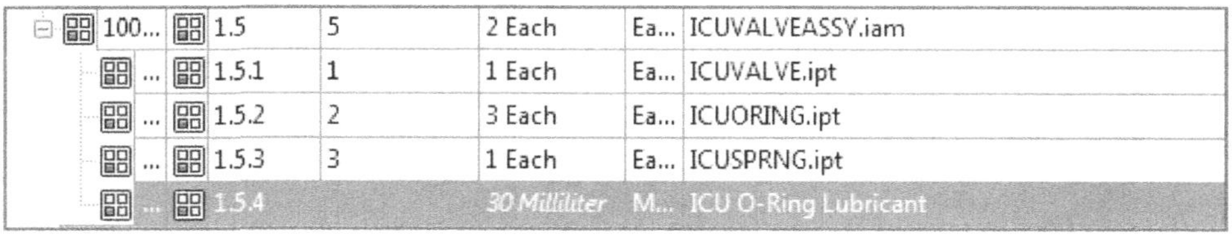


**Figure 11–39**

3. For Structure, select **Parts Only**. Note the quantity of the ICU O-ring lubricant (60 milliliters), as shown in Figure 11–40. This value is the correct total because there are two ICUVALVEASSY items with 30 milliliters of lubricant each.

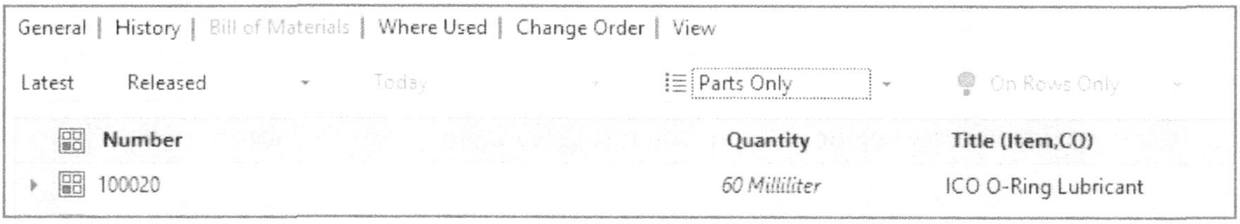


**Figure 11–40**

4. For Structure, select **First Level**. The three items you linked to the Valve Assembly Packaged Product display, as shown in Figure 11–41.

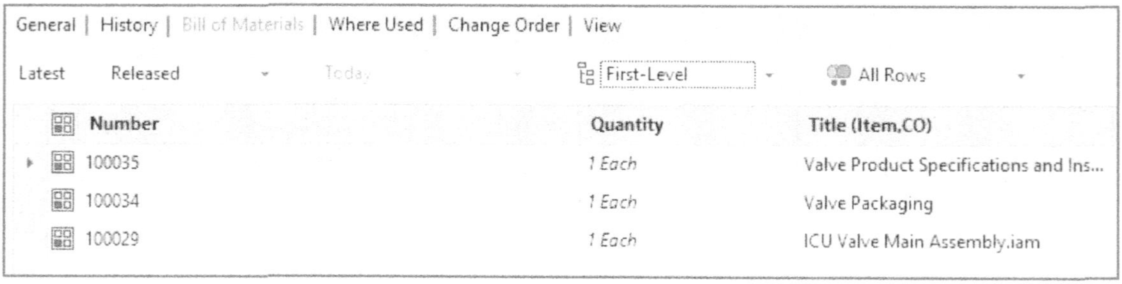


**Figure 11–41**

5. For Structure, select **Multi-Level** to return to the structured BOM list.

## Task 5: Redesign the valve assembly package.

1. In the *Item Master*, right-click on the **ICULBUTN.ipt** item and select **Change State**.
2. In the *Select Lifecycle* dialog box, select **Work in Progress**. Click **OK**.
3. Repeat Steps 1 and 2 to change the lifecycle state to **Work in Progress** for the **ICURBUTN.ipt**, **ICUVALVEASSY.iam**, and **Valve Assembly Packaged Product items**.
4. Double-click the **ICURBUTN.ipt** item and click **Edit**. On the *Bill of Materials* tab, select the **ICU Button Paint** row, right-click, and select **Remove Row**, as shown in Figure 11–42. Click **Save and Close**.

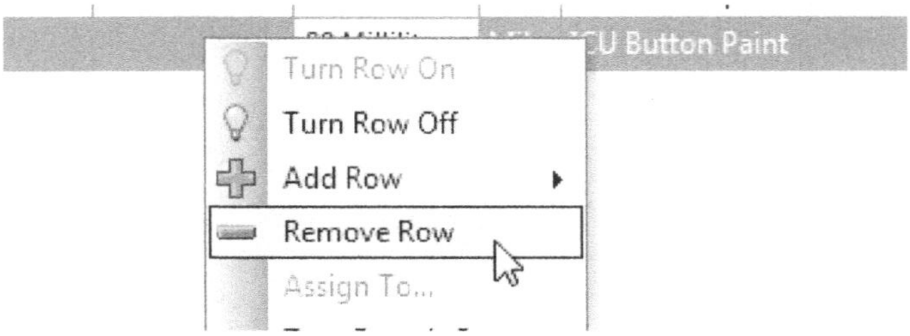


**Figure 11–42**

5. Repeat the previous step to remove the **ICU Button Paint** row from the **ICULBUTN.ipt** item.
6. In the *Item Master*, double-click the **Valve Assembly Packaged Product** item and click **Edit**. Select the *Bill of Materials* tab.
7. Select and right-click on the top row. Select **Add Row>From Existing Item**.

8. In the *Find* dialog box, do the following, as shown in Figure 11–43:
    - Select the *Basic* tab if it is not selected already.
    - Under *Search Text*, enter **ICU*.**
    - Click **Find Now**. A number of items are returned in the search results.
    - Select the **ICUORING.ipt** row.
    - Click **OK**.

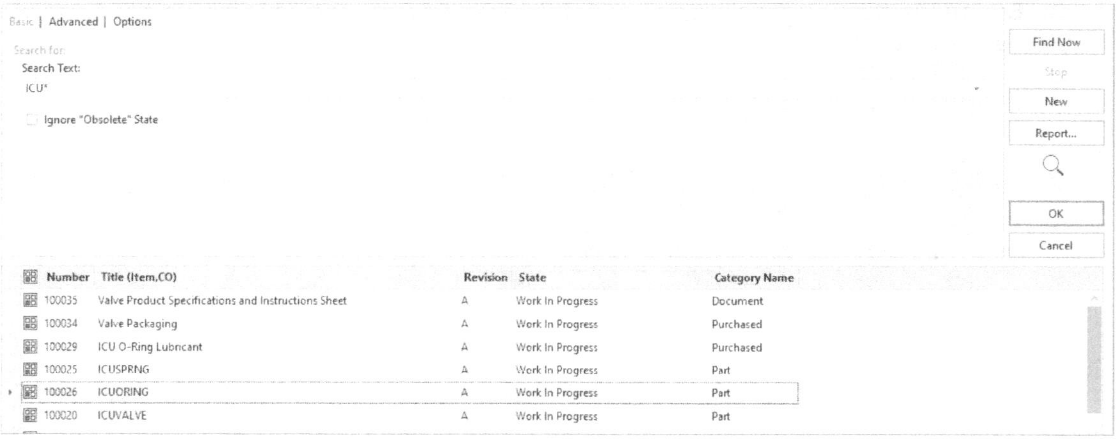


**Figure 11–43**

9. The ICUORING.ipt item is added to the BOM. Do the following, as shown in Figure 11–44:
    - Change its quantity to **3**.
    - Click **Save and Close**.

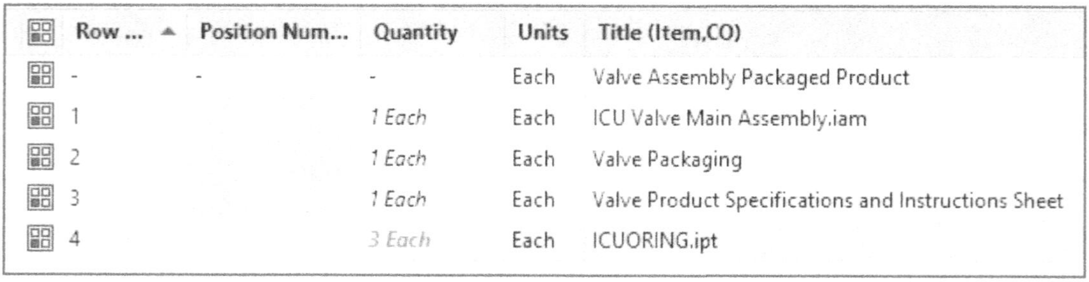

| Row ... | Position Num... | Quantity | Units | Title (Item,CO) |
|---|---|---|---|---|
| - | - | - | Each | Valve Assembly Packaged Product |
| 1 | | 1 Each | Each | ICU Valve Main Assembly.iam |
| 2 | | 1 Each | Each | Valve Packaging |
| 3 | | 1 Each | Each | Valve Product Specifications and Instructions Sheet |
| 4 | | 3 Each | Each | ICUORING.ipt |

**Figure 11–44**

10. In the *Item Master*, change the lifecycle state of the **Valve Assembly Packaged Product** item to **Released**. If prompted to confirm the state change for children, click **Yes**.

## Task 6: Save BOM view.

1. In the *Item Master,* double-click the **Valve Assembly Packaged Product** item. Select the *Bill of Materials* tab and select **File>Save BOM View**, as shown in Figure 11–45.

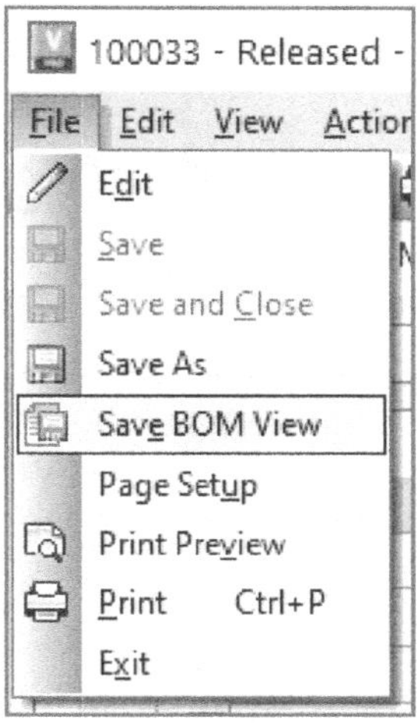


Figure 11–45

2. For *File name*, enter **ICU Product BOM - Rev A**. Click **Save**.

3. Open Microsoft Excel. Open **ICU Product BOM - Rev A.XLS**, as shown in Figure 11–46.

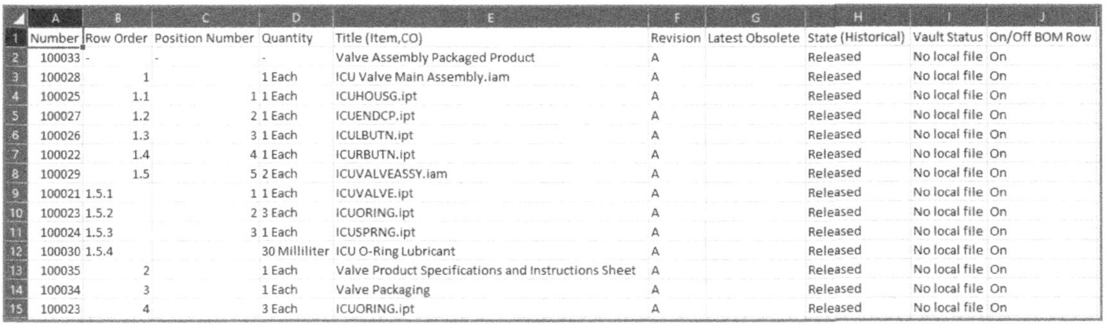

| Number | Row Order | Position Number | Quantity | Title (Item,CO) | Revision | Latest Obsolete | State (Historical) | Vault Status | On/Off BOM Row |
|---|---|---|---|---|---|---|---|---|---|
| 100033 | - | - | - | Valve Assembly Packaged Product | A | | Released | No local file | On |
| 100028 | 1 | | 1 Each | ICU Valve Main Assembly.iam | A | | Released | No local file | On |
| 100025 | 1.1 | 1 | 1 Each | ICUHOUSG.ipt | A | | Released | No local file | On |
| 100027 | 1.2 | 2 | 1 Each | ICUENDCP.ipt | A | | Released | No local file | On |
| 100026 | 1.3 | 3 | 1 Each | ICULBUTN.ipt | A | | Released | No local file | On |
| 100022 | 1.4 | 4 | 1 Each | ICURBUTN.ipt | A | | Released | No local file | On |
| 100029 | 1.5 | 5 | 2 Each | ICUVALVEASSY.iam | A | | Released | No local file | On |
| 100021 | 1.5.1 | 1 | 1 Each | ICUVALVE.ipt | A | | Released | No local file | On |
| 100023 | 1.5.2 | 2 | 3 Each | ICUORING.ipt | A | | Released | No local file | On |
| 100024 | 1.5.3 | 3 | 1 Each | ICUSPRNG.ipt | A | | Released | No local file | On |
| 100030 | 1.5.4 | | 30 Milliliter | ICU O-Ring Lubricant | A | | Released | No local file | On |
| 100035 | 2 | | 1 Each | Valve Product Specifications and Instructions Sheet | A | | Released | No local file | On |
| 100034 | 3 | | 1 Each | Valve Packaging | A | | Released | No local file | On |
| 100023 | 4 | | 3 Each | ICUORING.ipt | A | | Released | No local file | On |

Figure 11–46

4. Close Vault Professional and Excel.

**End of practice**

# 11.2 Integration with Autodesk Inventor

This section describes how to use Autodesk Vault Professional with other applications. The primary focus is the relationship between Autodesk Inventor and Vault Professional BOMs. The lesson also covers working with Vault Professional and Autodesk Vault, AutoCAD®, AutoCAD® Mechanical, and AutoCAD® Electrical.

## About Autodesk Inventor and Integration with Vault Professional

Autodesk Vault integrates with Autodesk Inventor software using an Autodesk Inventor add-in. Users can use Vault Professional to assign item numbers to vaulted parts and assemblies. You can edit assembly BOMs in both Autodesk Inventor and Vault Professional, and coordinate property information between Autodesk Inventor, Autodesk Vault, and Autodesk Vault Professional, as shown in Figure 11–47.

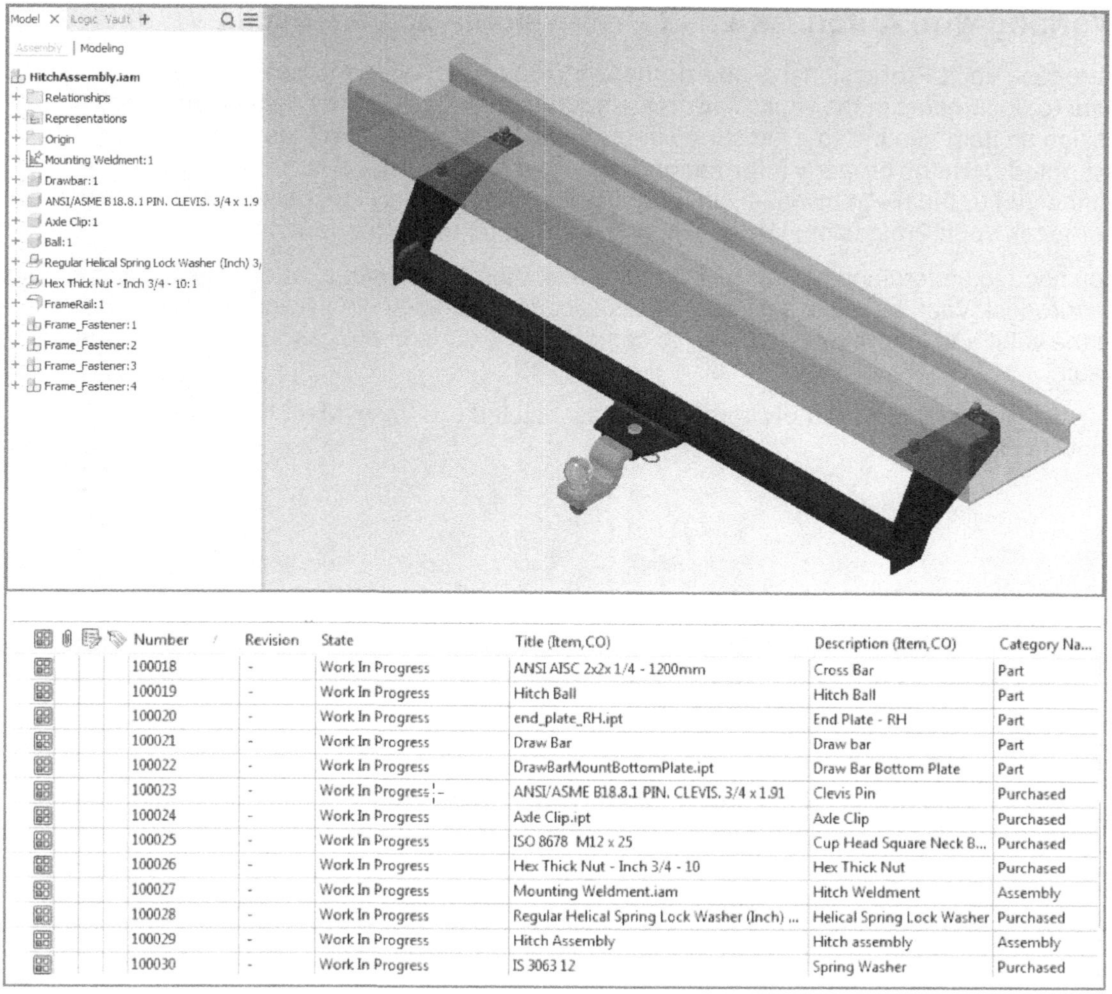


| Number | Revision | State | Title (Item,CO) | Description (Item,CO) | Category Na... |
|---|---|---|---|---|---|
| 100018 | - | Work In Progress | ANSI AISC 2x2x 1/4 - 1200mm | Cross Bar | Part |
| 100019 | - | Work In Progress | Hitch Ball | Hitch Ball | Part |
| 100020 | - | Work In Progress | end_plate_RH.ipt | End Plate - RH | Part |
| 100021 | - | Work In Progress | Draw Bar | Draw bar | Part |
| 100022 | - | Work In Progress | DrawBarMountBottomPlate.ipt | Draw Bar Bottom Plate | Part |
| 100023 | - | Work In Progress | ANSI/ASME B18.8.1 PIN, CLEVIS, 3/4 x 1.91 | Clevis Pin | Purchased |
| 100024 | - | Work In Progress | Axle Clip.ipt | Axle Clip | Purchased |
| 100025 | - | Work In Progress | ISO 8678 M12 x 25 | Cup Head Square Neck B... | Purchased |
| 100026 | - | Work In Progress | Hex Thick Nut - Inch 3/4 - 10 | Hex Thick Nut | Purchased |
| 100027 | - | Work In Progress | Mounting Weldment.iam | Hitch Weldment | Assembly |
| 100028 | - | Work In Progress | Regular Helical Spring Lock Washer (Inch) ... | Helical Spring Lock Washer | Purchased |
| 100029 | - | Work In Progress | Hitch Assembly | Hitch assembly | Assembly |
| 100030 | - | Work In Progress | IS 3063 12 | Spring Washer | Purchased |

**Figure 11–47**

## Application Overviews

Autodesk Inventor is a 3D parametric CAD application. You can combine individual part models in a hierarchy of assemblies to create a complete digital design. You supply values for intrinsic document properties and can add custom properties to any part or assembly.

Use Autodesk Vault to provide work-in-progress version control for Inventor models and other documents. A vault stores versions of documents, file relationships between documents, and property data associated with each version. You check files out of the vault to modify them in Inventor and check in the new versions to share with your design team.

When you use Autodesk Vault Professional to assign items to these files, users outside the engineering department can also access property and bill of materials data from the files stored in a vault.

# Working with Autodesk Vault Professional and Autodesk Vault

Autodesk Vault Professional is an external application that adds manufacturing and release data to documents in the vault. You create an Autodesk Vault Professional item when you assign an item number to a file stored in the vault. Initial property values for the item are extracted from the property information stored in the vault. After it is created, the item is connected to the file in the vault, but property values are largely independent. You can add Autodesk Vault Professional items without associating them to a vault file.

You need to understand how actions in Autodesk Vault Professional affect the associated files in Autodesk Vault because a number of tasks can be completed only when files are checked in to the vault and lifecycle state changes can affect the state of the associated files in Autodesk Vault.

The ICU Valve Main Assembly item and the associated ICU Valve Main Assembly.iam file is show in Figure 11–48.

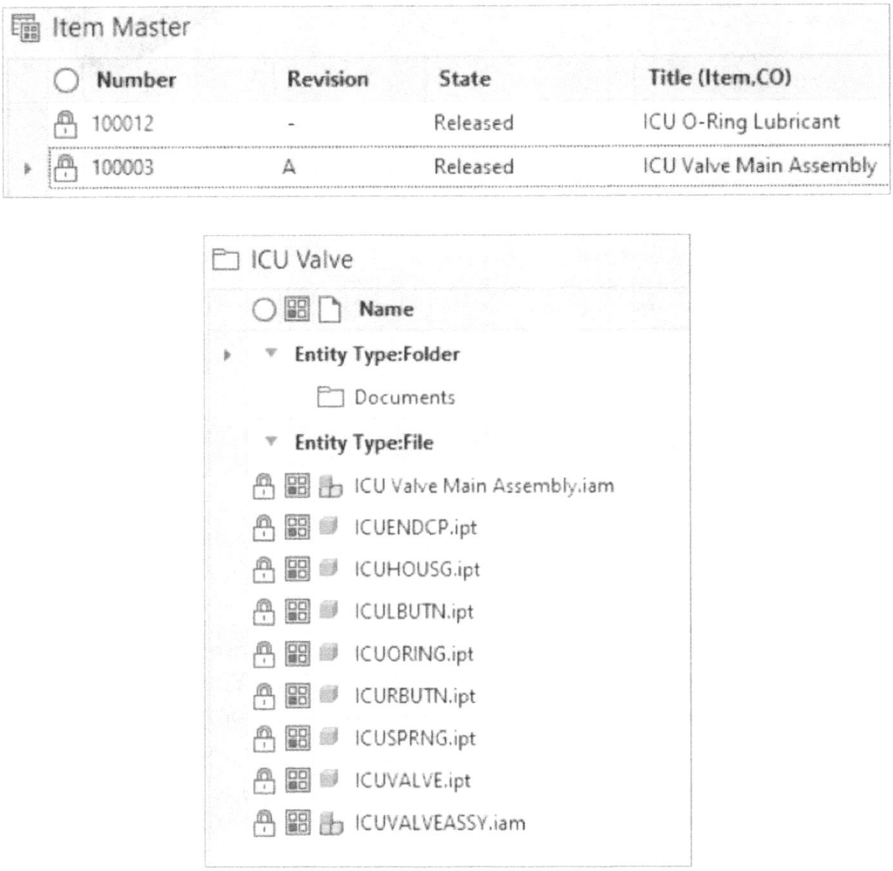


**Figure 11–48**

All of the associated files of a released item in Vault Professional are locked in the vault.

## Working with Autodesk Vault Professional and Autodesk Inventor

When you create an item from a part or assembly stored in a vault, Autodesk Vault Professional extracts property information from Autodesk Vault. The property values are typically assigned in Autodesk Inventor, but you can edit values for existing properties in Autodesk Vault. Item properties can be mapped back to the properties in the associated Autodesk Inventor part or assembly document. If you understand the relationship between properties in all three applications, you can effectively integrate Autodesk Vault Professional into an Autodesk Inventor design environment.

An Autodesk Inventor assembly BOM maps information to the BOM in the associated item in Autodesk Vault Professional (shown in Figure 11–49). Your understanding of this process helps to ensure its accuracy.

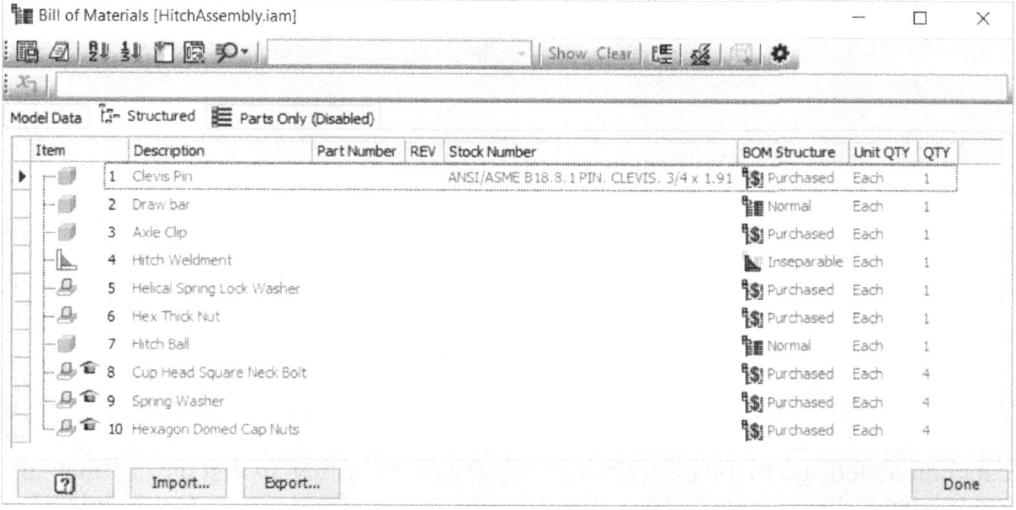


| Item | Description | Part Number | REV | Stock Number | BOM Structure | Unit QTY | QTY |
|---|---|---|---|---|---|---|---|
| 1 | Clevis Pin | | | ANSI/ASME B18.8.1 PIN, CLEVIS, 3/4 x 1.91 | Purchased | Each | 1 |
| 2 | Draw bar | | | | Normal | Each | 1 |
| 3 | Axle Clip | | | | Purchased | Each | 1 |
| 4 | Hitch Weldment | | | | Inseparable | Each | 1 |
| 5 | Helical Spring Lock Washer | | | | Purchased | Each | 1 |
| 6 | Hex Thick Nut | | | | Purchased | Each | 1 |
| 7 | Hitch Ball | | | | Normal | Each | 1 |
| 8 | Cup Head Square Neck Bolt | | | | Purchased | Each | 4 |
| 9 | Spring Washer | | | | Purchased | Each | 4 |
| 10 | Hexagon Domed Cap Nuts | | | | Purchased | Each | 4 |

***Autodesk Inventor Bill of Materials***

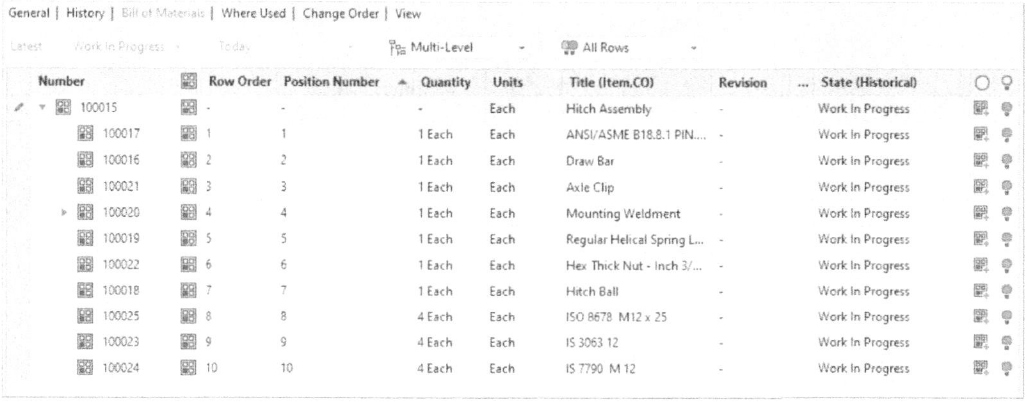


| Number | Row Order | Position Number | Quantity | Units | Title (Item,CO) | Revision | State (Historical) |
|---|---|---|---|---|---|---|---|
| 100015 | - | - | - | Each | Hitch Assembly | - | Work In Progress |
| 100017 | 1 | 1 | 1 Each | Each | ANSI/ASME B18.8.1 PIN.... | - | Work In Progress |
| 100016 | 2 | 2 | 1 Each | Each | Draw Bar | - | Work In Progress |
| 100021 | 3 | 3 | 1 Each | Each | Axle Clip | - | Work In Progress |
| 100020 | 4 | 4 | 1 Each | Each | Mounting Weldment | - | Work In Progress |
| 100019 | 5 | 5 | 1 Each | Each | Regular Helical Spring L... | - | Work In Progress |
| 100022 | 6 | 6 | 1 Each | Each | Hex Thick Nut - Inch 3/... | - | Work In Progress |
| 100018 | 7 | 7 | 1 Each | Each | Hitch Ball | - | Work In Progress |
| 100025 | 8 | 8 | 4 Each | Each | ISO 8678 M12 x 25 | - | Work In Progress |
| 100023 | 9 | 9 | 4 Each | Each | IS 3063 12 | - | Work In Progress |
| 100024 | 10 | 10 | 4 Each | Each | IS 7790 M 12 | - | Work In Progress |

***Autodesk Vault Professional Bill of Materials***

**Figure 11–49**

## Example of Application Integration

The following example shows a workflow for a change order performed on a Released item. The associated file in the vault is locked when the item is in a **Released** state.

1. A Vault Professional user creates a new change order for a released part or assembly item, as shown in Figure 11–50. On submittal of the change order, the Change Administrator or Responsible Engineer changes the item status to **Work in Progress** creating a new item revision. This action unlocks the part or assembly the vault.

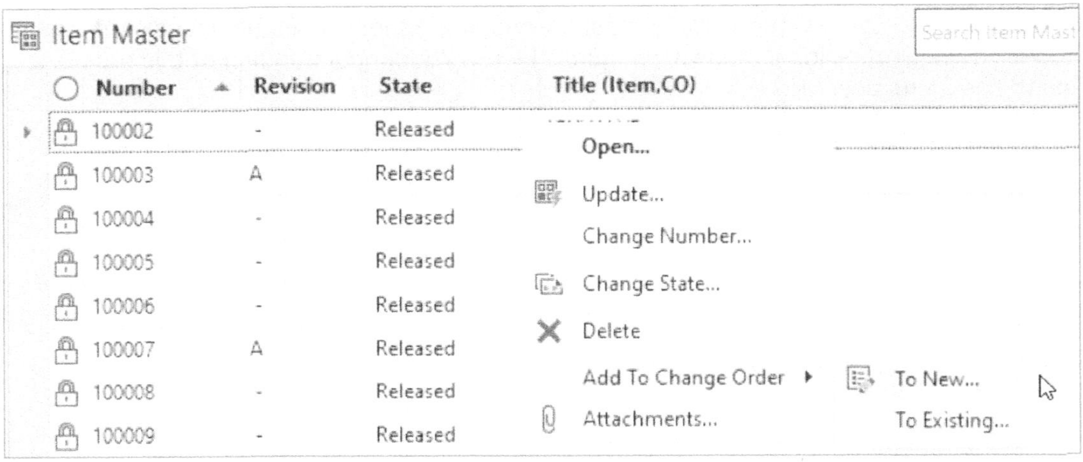


Figure 11–50

2. When the Responsible Engineer works on the change order, they can open the change order and examine the items associated with it. The items are on the *Records* tab. From here, the user can directly go to the item, as shown in Figure 11–51. Note that having an item associated to the change order on the *Records* tab causes the files associated to the item to be displayed on the *Files* tab. In the **Work** state, the Responsible Engineer can open a file directly from the *Files* tab and can check the file out at that time.

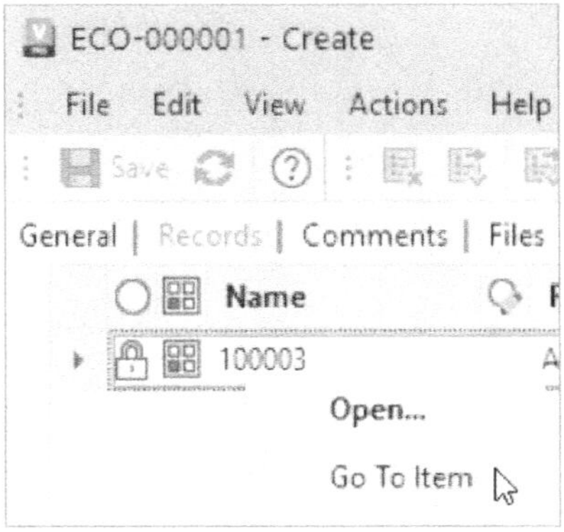


Figure 11–51

3. Looking at the item, the user can see which file is associated with what requires work and go directly to the vault folder containing the file, as shown in Figure 11–52.

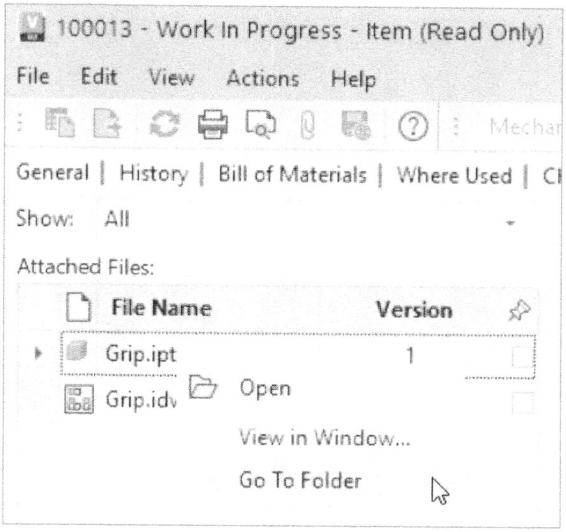


**Figure 11–52**

4. The user can open a file by right-clicking on it and selecting **Open** (as shown in Figure 11–53) and check out the file by clicking **Yes** in the *Open File* dialog (as shown in Figure 11–54).

**Figure 11–53**

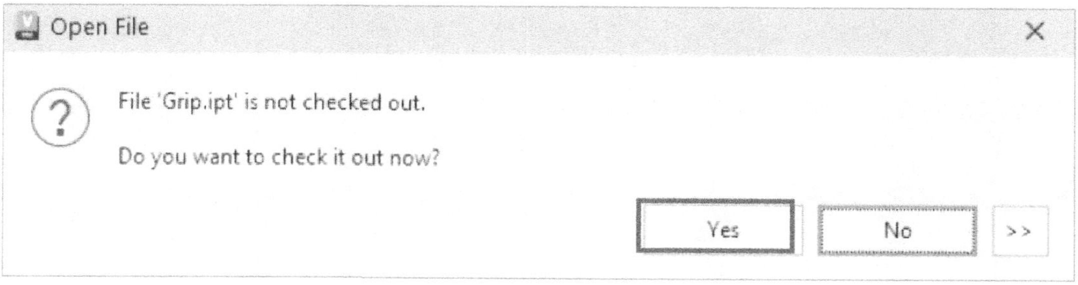


**Figure 11–54**

5. The Autodesk Inventor user edits the file and checks them back in to the vault, as shown in Figure 11–55.

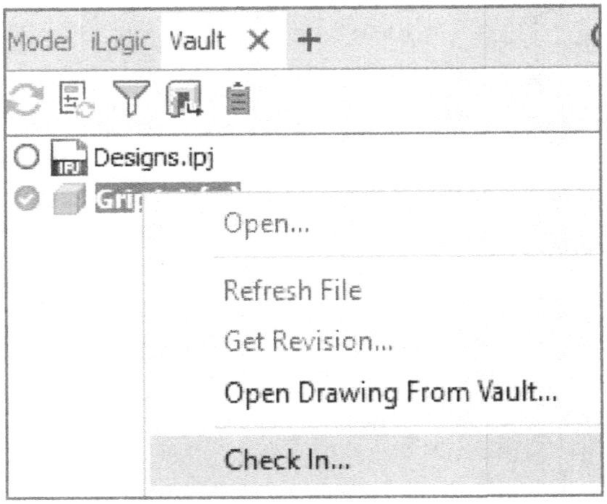


**Figure 11–55**

6. The Vault Professional user then updates the item to update the link to the new file version., as shown in Figure 11–56.

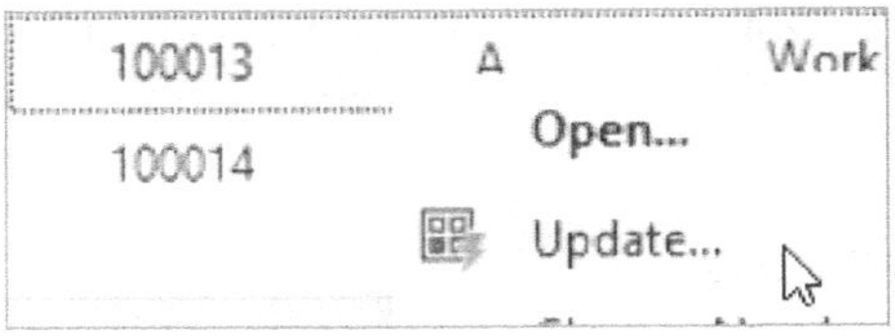


**Figure 11–56**

7. Finally, the change order is completed, returning the item to a **Released** state. The files are again locked in the vault, as shown in Figure 11–57.

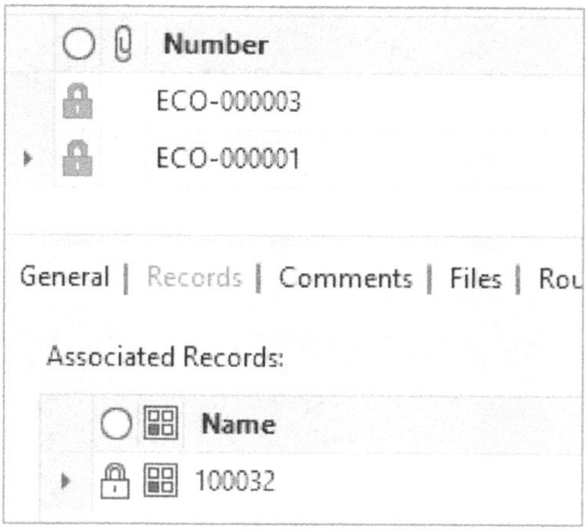


**Figure 11–57**

***Note:*** *When you check out, edit, and check in a component, you must update the associated item in Autodesk Vault Professional before you can change the lifecycle state of the item. Each item revision is associated with a specific version of the component in the vault. The change order cannot be completed unless the items have been updated.*

# Autodesk Inventor BOMs

Information in Autodesk Inventor assembly BOMs is translated into the BOMs of the associated Autodesk Vault Professional items. Autodesk Inventor assembly BOMs contain information about their hierarchy of parts, subassemblies, and virtual components, and are usually displayed as structured lists of components, as shown in Figure 11–58.

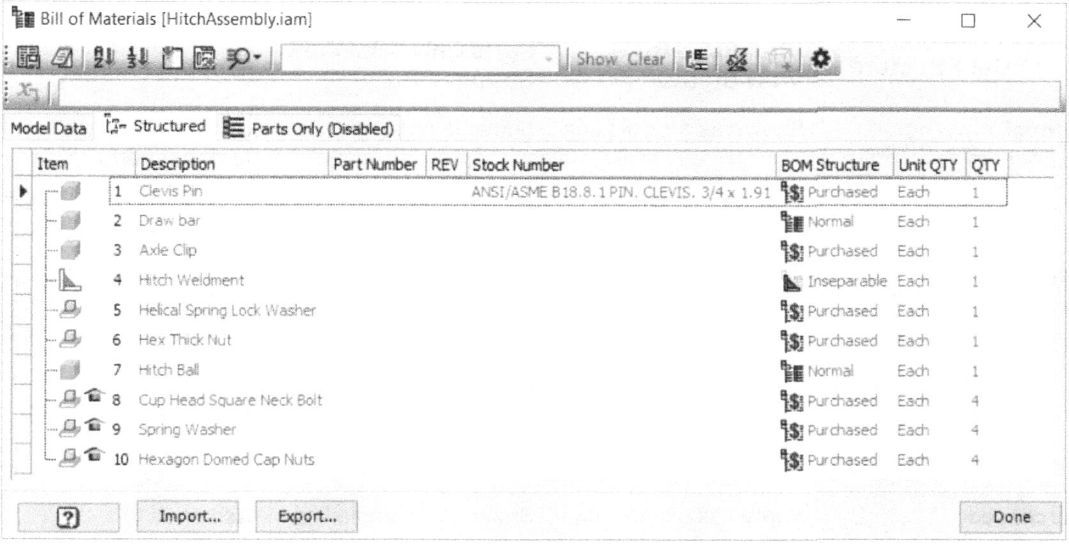


**Figure 11–58**

## Parts Only BOM

You can select a **Parts Only** view that flattens the BOM to a single level and aggregates all parts in the assembly hierarchy, as shown in Figure 11–59:

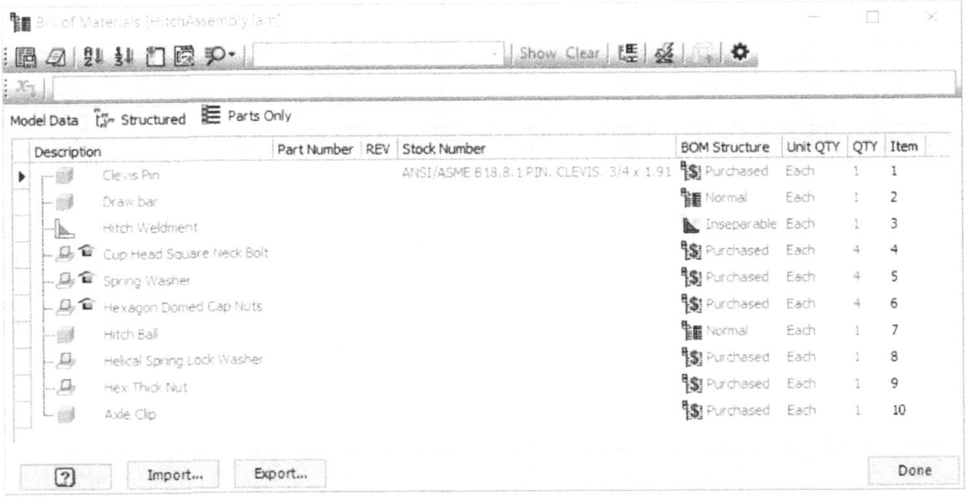


**Figure 11–59**

## BOM Structure

Each part, subassembly, and virtual component in the assembly is assigned a BOM structure that determines the status of the component in the assembly BOM.

The following table explains the display status of individual parts assigned different BOM structure types.

| Part BOM Structure | Structured BOM View Status | Parts Only BOM View Status | Notes/Example |
|---|---|---|---|
| **Normal** | Shown as a single line | Shown as a single line | Default BOM structure for most parts<br>Quantity can be affected by parent BOM structure |
| **Reference** | Excluded from view | Excluded from view | Typically assigned to parts that provide reference for the current design |
| **Phantom** | Excluded from view | Excluded from view | Skeleton model parts are often assigned a Phantom structure |
| **Purchased** | Shown as a single line | Shown as a single line | Assigned to components that are not fabricated |

| Part BOM Structure | Structured BOM View Status | Parts Only BOM View Status | Notes/Example |
|---|---|---|---|
| **Inseparable** | Not normally assigned to parts | Not normally assigned to parts | |

The following table outlines the display status of a subassembly and its child components when it is assigned different BOM structure types.

| Subassembly BOM Structure | Structured BOM View Status | Parts Only BOM View Status | Notes/Example |
|---|---|---|---|
| **Normal** | Shown as a single line<br>Child components displayed as subcomponents in the assembly BOM | Excluded from view | Default BOM structure for most subassemblies |
| **Reference** | Components and all children excluded from view | Excluded from view | Typically assigned to parts or assemblies that provide reference for the current design |
| **Phantom** | Excluded from view<br>Child components promoted to Phantom subassembly level<br>Quantity of Phantom component affects quantity of promoted children | Excluded from view | A Phantom assembly that groups a bolt, nut, and washers and can reduce model complexity |
| **Purchased** | Shown as a single line<br>Child components displayed as subcomponents (often not shown in parts list) | Shown as a single line (treated as a part)<br>Child components excluded from view | Assigned to assemblies that are not fabricated |
| **Inseparable** | Shown as a single line<br>Child components displayed as subcomponents (often not shown in parts list) | Shown as a single line<br>(treated as a part)<br>Purchased child components promoted and shown<br>Other child components excluded from view | Assigned to assemblies that are not easily disassembled<br>Weldments and riveted assemblies are examples of Inseparable assemblies |

A component's BOM structure also determines how the corresponding item displays in an Autodesk Vault Professional BOM.

 

## Assigning a BOM Structure

Subassemblies retain their current BOM structure when you place them in a higher-level assembly. Parts are assigned the Normal BOM structure when placed in an assembly. Figure 11–60 shows how you select the BOM structure in the *Create In-Place Component* dialog box.

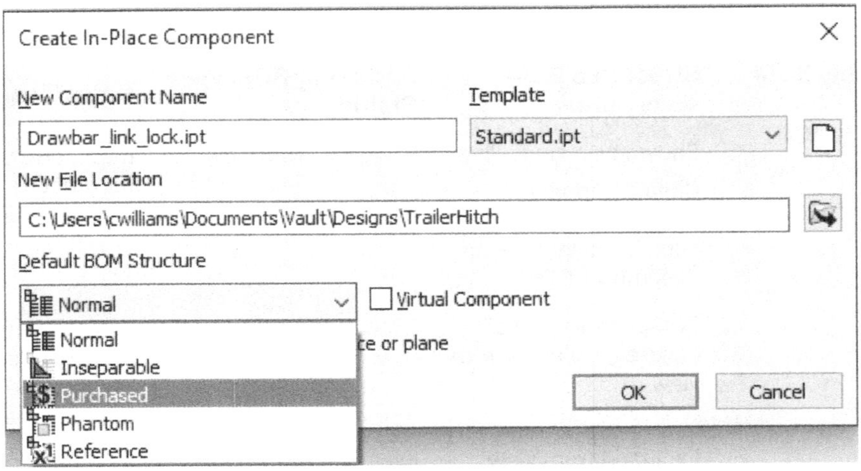


**Figure 11–60**

## Editing a BOM Structure

You can change the BOM structure of a component from its default setting to Reference by right-clicking the component in the browser and selecting **BOM Structure>Reference**. You can restore the default BOM structure using the same steps.

Figure 11–61 shows how you can select any BOM structure for a component in the *Bill of Materials* dialog box. These options are not available from the browser shortcut menu.

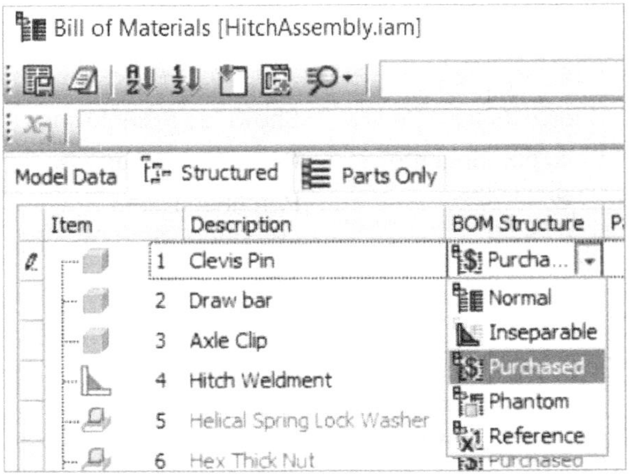


**Figure 11–61**

## Example of BOM Structure

You can assign the Inseparable BOM structure to the welded frame assembly, as shown in Figure 11–62. The assembly itself can contain a skeleton part model (Phantom BOM structure), multiple frame members (Normal BOM structure), and purchased components, such as lifting shackles (Normal or Purchased BOM structure).

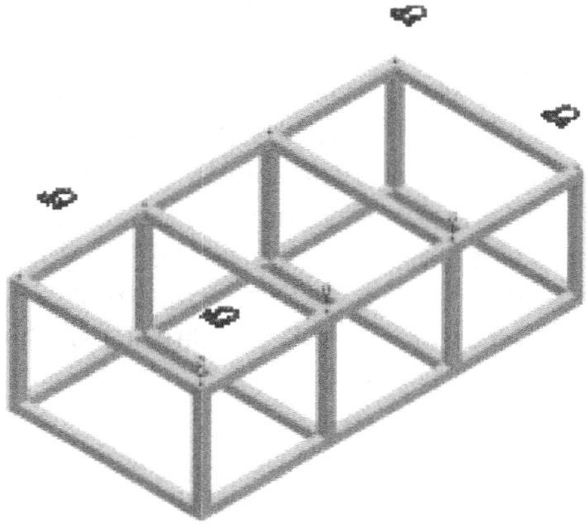

**Figure 11–62**

# Virtual Components

You add virtual (non-geometric) components to assemblies to represent engineering components that cannot be easily modeled, as shown in Figure 11–63.

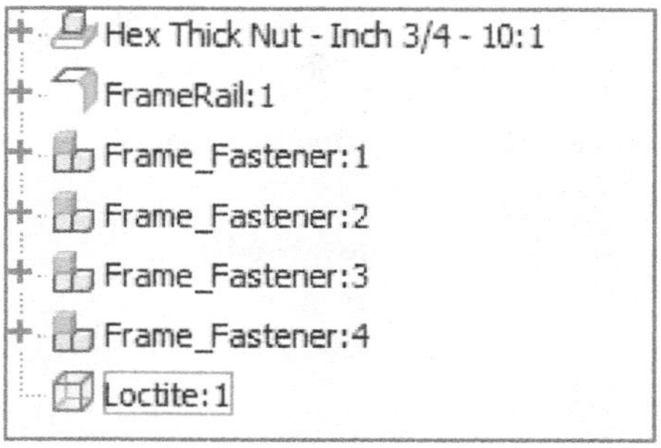


**Figure 11–63**

## Definition of Virtual Components

You create virtual components in place in Inventor assemblies. They have no geometry and are not saved as separate files when you save the parent assemblies. Lubricants, glue, and other engineering materials are often represented by virtual parts. You can add any number of virtual components to an assembly.

## Virtual Components and Autodesk Vault Professional Items

From a BOM perspective, virtual components are similar to user-created items in Vault Professional. You can add a user-created item to the BOM of another item. Similarly, when you add a virtual component to an assembly, it is automatically added to the BOM of the assembly.

When you assign item numbers to an assembly containing virtual components in Autodesk Vault Professional, each virtual component with Normal, Purchase, or Inseparable BOM structure is assigned a separate item number.

Your company's practices determine whether you should represent something as a virtual component in Inventor, or ignore it in Inventor and add a user-defined item in Vault Professional. You can add key engineering components to Inventor assemblies in the engineering environment. You can add common non-modeled components as items in Vault Professional. As with other items in a Vault Professional BOM, you can override quantity and other values for the item you create from the virtual component. The Autodesk Inventor BOM with virtual component is shown in Figure 11–64. The Autodesk Vault Professional BOM with virtual component is shown in Figure 11–65.

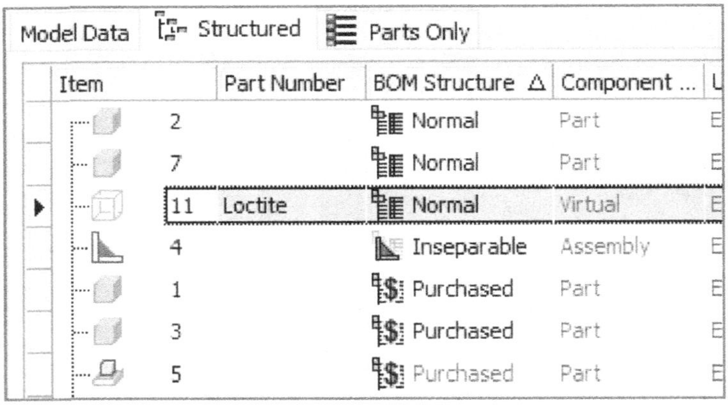


***Autodesk Inventor BOM with virtual component***

**Figure 11–64**

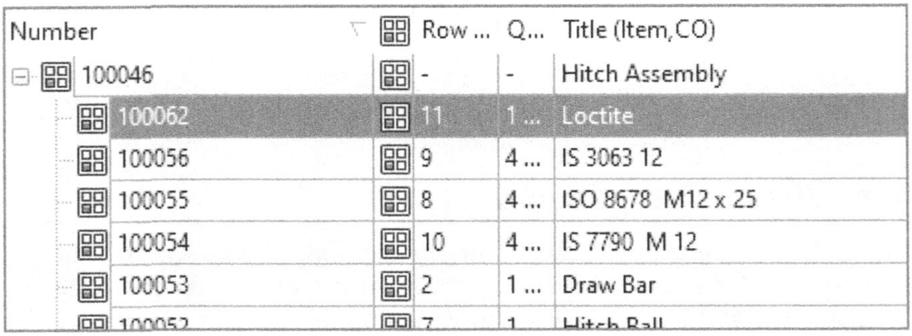


***Autodesk Vault Professional BOM with virtual component***

**Figure 11–65**

## How To: Create Virtual Components

You must create virtual components in place in an assembly. The following steps describe how to create virtual components:

1. In the *Assemble* panel, click **Create Component**.
2. In the *Create In-Place Component* dialog box, select the **Virtual Component** checkbox.
3. Under *New Component Name*, enter a name for the virtual component, as shown in Figure 11–66.
4. Under *Default BOM Structure*, select a BOM structure from the list.

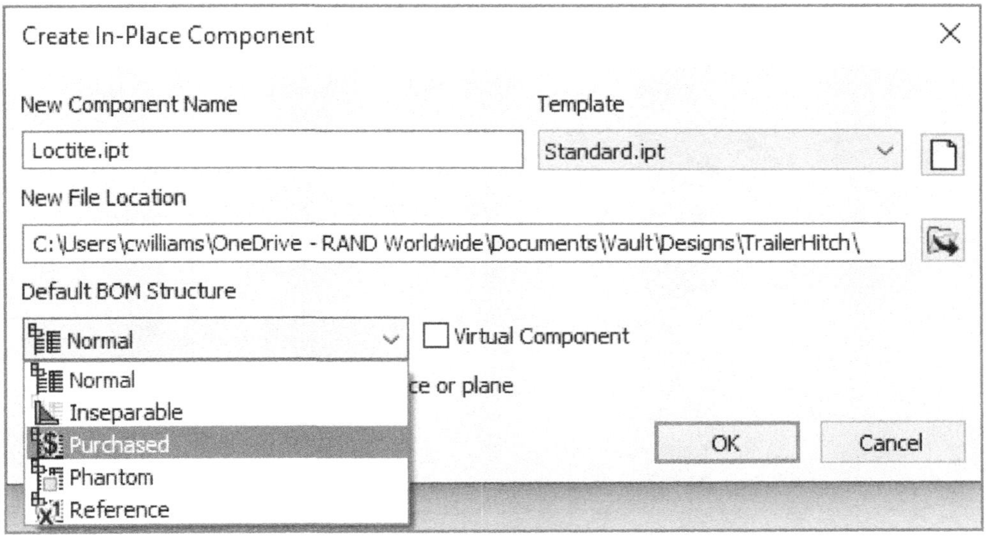


**Figure 11–66**

5. Click **OK**.

6. The virtual component is listed in the *Assembly* tab of the *Model* browser, as shown in Figure 11–67.

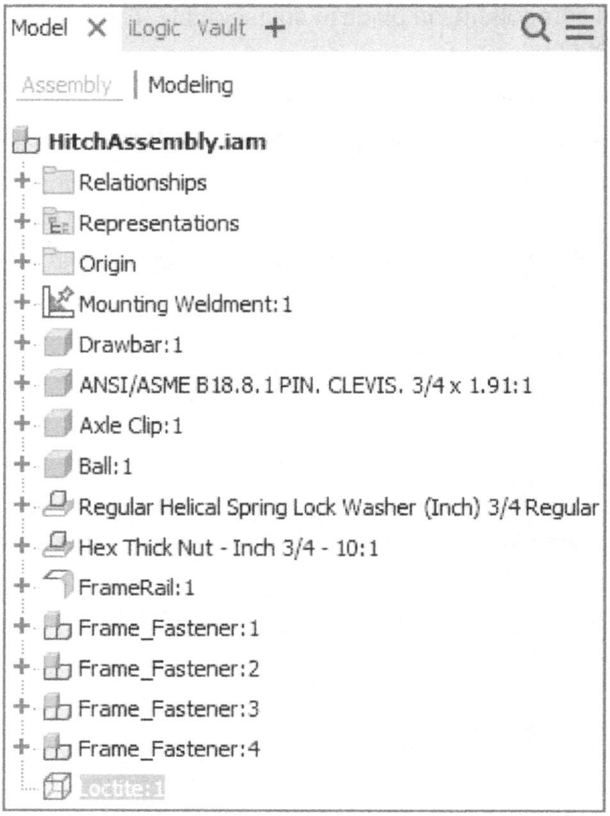


**Figure 11–67**

## Editing Virtual Components

Virtual components are not separate files but they contain the same properties present in other Inventor documents. You can edit both their properties and their BOM structure. You can change this setting to better reflect the component in the assembly BOM.

### How To: Edit a Virtual Component

The following steps describe how to change the units and quantity for a virtual component:

1. In the *Model* browser, right-click on the virtual component and select **Component Settings**, as shown in Figure 11–68.

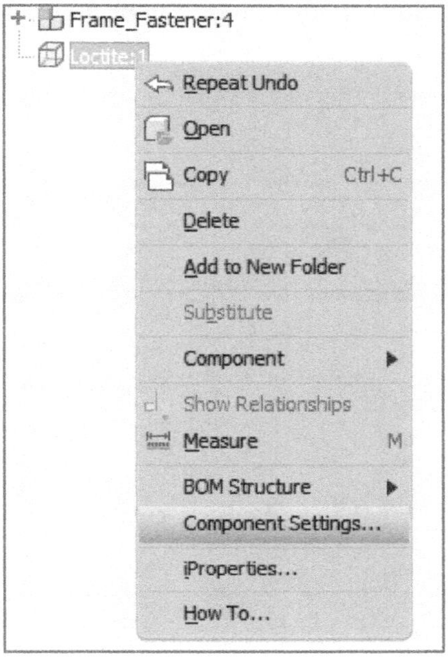


**Figure 11–68**

2. In the *Component Settings* dialog box, click the *Base Quantity* drop-down list and scroll until you find the appropriate value, as shown in Figure 11–69. Click **OK**.

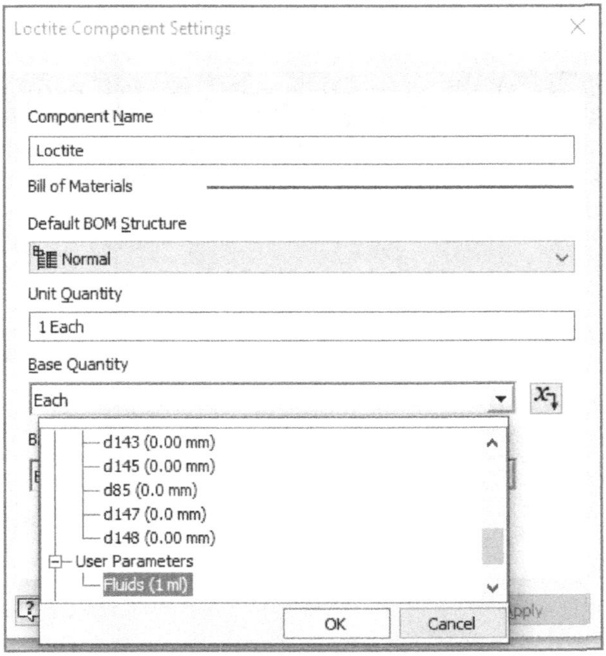


**Figure 11–69**

3. In the *Bill of Materials* dialog box, in the *Unit QTY* field, enter the appropriate value, as shown in Figure 11–70.

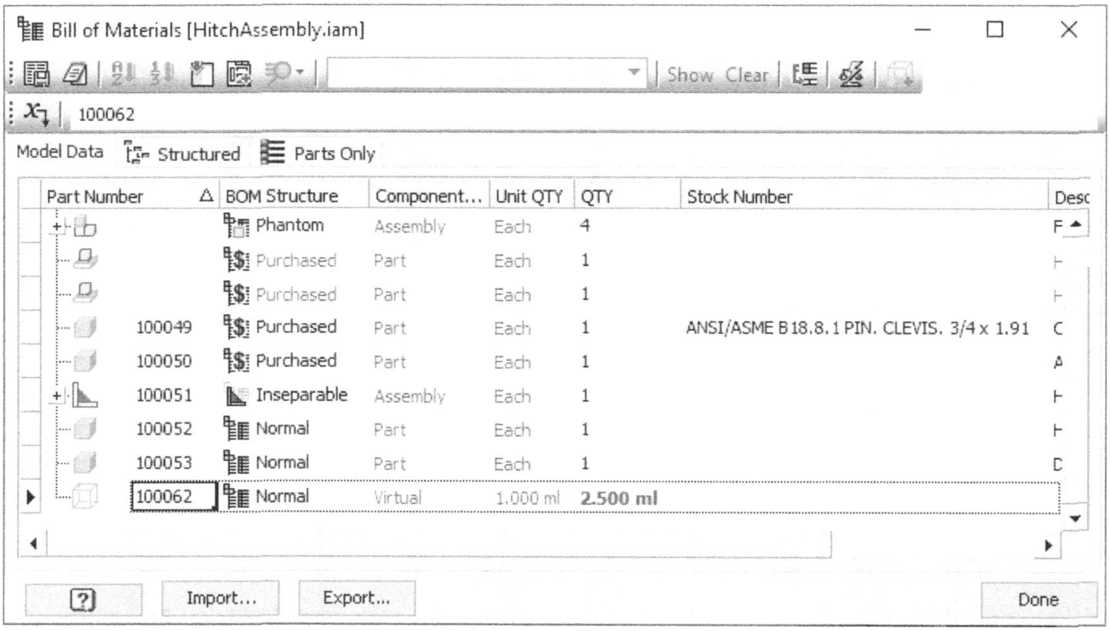


**Figure 11–70**

4. Override the quantity for the virtual part in the assembly BOM.

**Hint: Base Quantity Value**

If the Base Quantity value is not in the list, it can be created by editing the Parameters table and entering a new user-defined parameter. The units associated with the user parameter are assigned to the base quantity field for virtual part.

## Guidelines for Virtual Components

- Develop a company or departmental strategy for implementing virtual parts, user-created items, or combination of both.
- Virtual components are not saved as separate files, but rather are contained in assemblies.
- Virtual components with Normal, Purchased, or Inseparable BOM structures are assigned separate item numbers when their parent assemblies are assigned item numbers.
- Virtual components have the same properties as other Autodesk Inventor documents.

# Modifying Content Center Component Properties

You can customize Content Center library components to integrate them into Vault Professional, as shown in Figure 11–71.

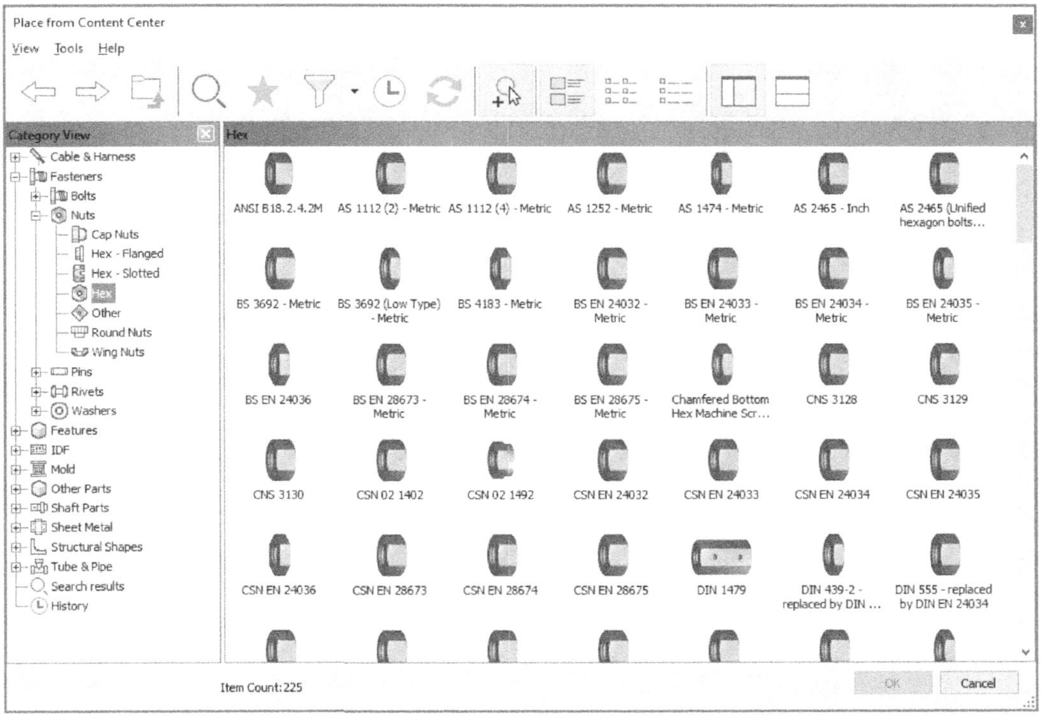


**Figure 11–71**

# Content Center Library Components

Many Autodesk Inventor assemblies contain components from the Content Center libraries that ship with Autodesk Inventor. These libraries contain a large number of common engineering components from a variety of standards, including ANSI, ISO, JIS, and others. You copy data from the read-only default libraries to a custom read/write library where you can customize the property information in the component family. When you assign an item to an Autodesk Inventor assembly that contains library components, those components are also assigned items.

Figure 11–72 shows a custom read-write library added to the Content Center libraries.

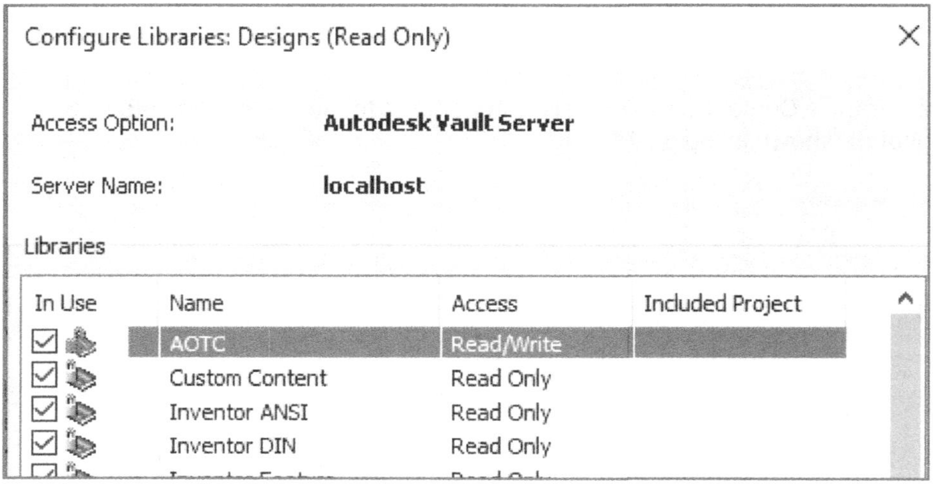


**Figure 11–72**

You can also publish your own components to a custom library by creating an iPart factory that includes a table to define the variations in the part. You can include model properties as columns in the table and assign default values for each variation of the part. After you publish the iPart factory to a custom Content Center library, you can place the different versions in assemblies. Each variation retains the property values defined in the original iPart table.

See "iParts" and "Content Center" in the Autodesk Inventor Help for more information on working with and publishing your own library parts.

Figure 11–73 shows an iPart Factory part and the iPart Author table that you use to create the different iPart member definitions.

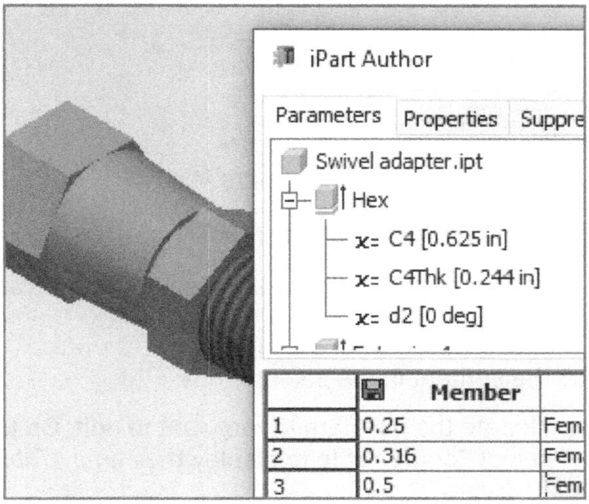


**Figure 11–73**

## How To: Modify Properties of Content Center Components

The following steps describe how to copy data from a default read-only library to a custom read-write library and edit the properties in the library table:

1. Log in to the Autodesk Data Management Server Console as a user with at least Content Center Editor permission.
2. Expand the folders and select **Libraries**. Right-click and select **Create Library**.
3. Enter the *Display Name* and select a *Partition* based on the Inventor version you are using for the library, as shown in Figure 11–74.
4. Click **OK** to create the library.

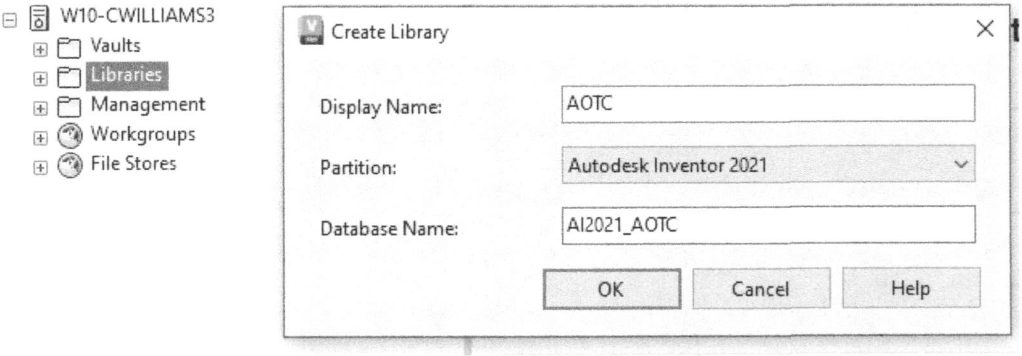


**Figure 11–74**

5. In Autodesk Inventor, open any assembly. On the *Manage* tab, select **Editor** in the *Content Center* section, as shown in Figure 11–75. User requires a Content Center Editor role.

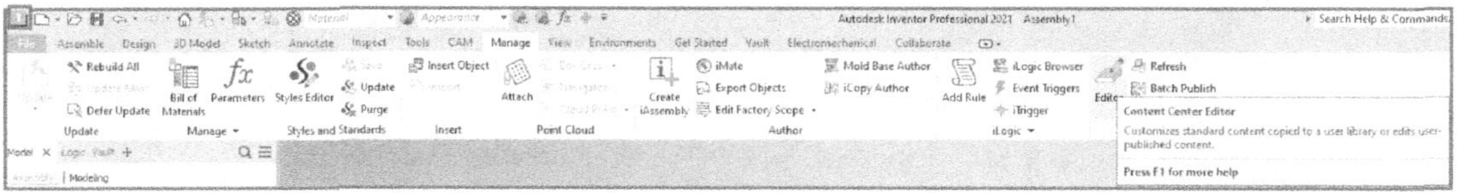

**Figure 11–75**

6. In the *Content Center Editor* dialog box, do the following:
   - Right-click on the category or family to copy and select **Copy To**.
   - Click the name of a read-write library.
   - Click **Yes** to refresh the content in the server.
7. In the read-write library, locate the part family you want to edit. On the *List* panel, right-click on the part family and select **Family Table** to display the *Family Table* dialog box.
8. In the *Family Table* dialog box, display the *iProperties* columns only. Add a new column.
9. In the *Column Properties* dialog box, enter a column name and column caption. Select a data type for the property.
10. Under *Map to Inventor Property*, select the Autodesk Inventor property to populate with the value from the new column.
11. Select the **Expression** checkbox. Enter a constant string or use a combination of strings and parameter names to populate the cells based on other values in the table. Click **OK**.
12. If required, repeat Steps 5 to 8 to add other columns.
13. Optionally, delete or suppress rows in the table that are not used in your designs. You can also add rows or edit parameter values to create custom versions of the library part.

    ***Note:*** *Any component placed from the Content Center has a default Purchased BOM structure. You can edit this structure in the Bill of Materials dialog box.*

When you place parts from the table into subsequent assemblies, the property values in the library part reflect the values in the columns mapped to Inventor properties.

 

# Working with DWG Files

You can use Autodesk Vault Professional with drawing (DWG) files created in the AutoCAD software products, such as AutoCAD, AutoCAD Mechanical, AutoCAD Electrical, and Autodesk Inventor. A DWG file is shown in Figure 11–76.

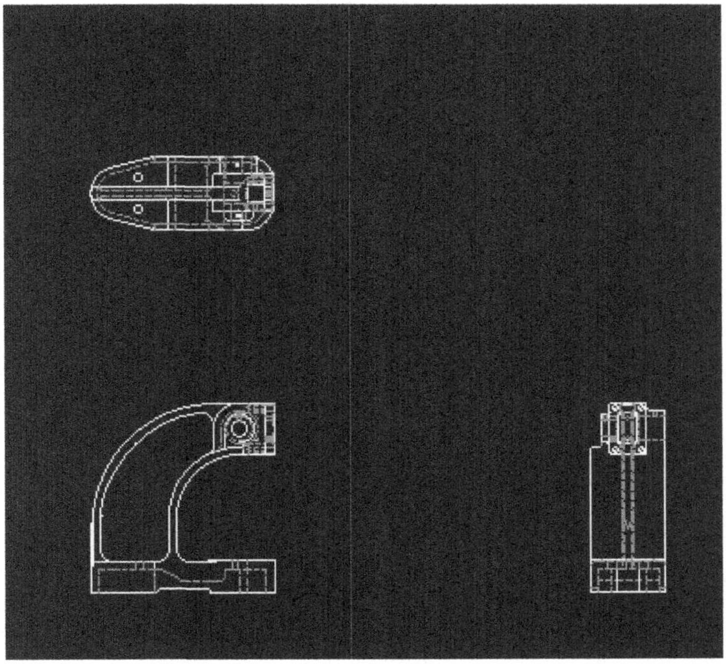

Figure 11–76

## DWG Files, Autodesk Vault, and Autodesk Vault Professional

Many companies work with a variety of Autodesk CAD software applications. Although a focus of Autodesk Vault and Autodesk Vault Professional is to work with data from Autodesk Inventor, you can manage versions and assign items to drawing files in Autodesk Vault.

Always check out and check in drawing files using the Vault ARX application inside your AutoCAD-based software. AutoCAD Electrical users must check out and check in all files in a project at the same time.

When you have checked drawing files into the vault, you can assign items to them using the same technique you use to assign items to Inventor parts and assemblies. Figure 11–77 shows an AutoCAD Mechanical file being checked in to the vault.

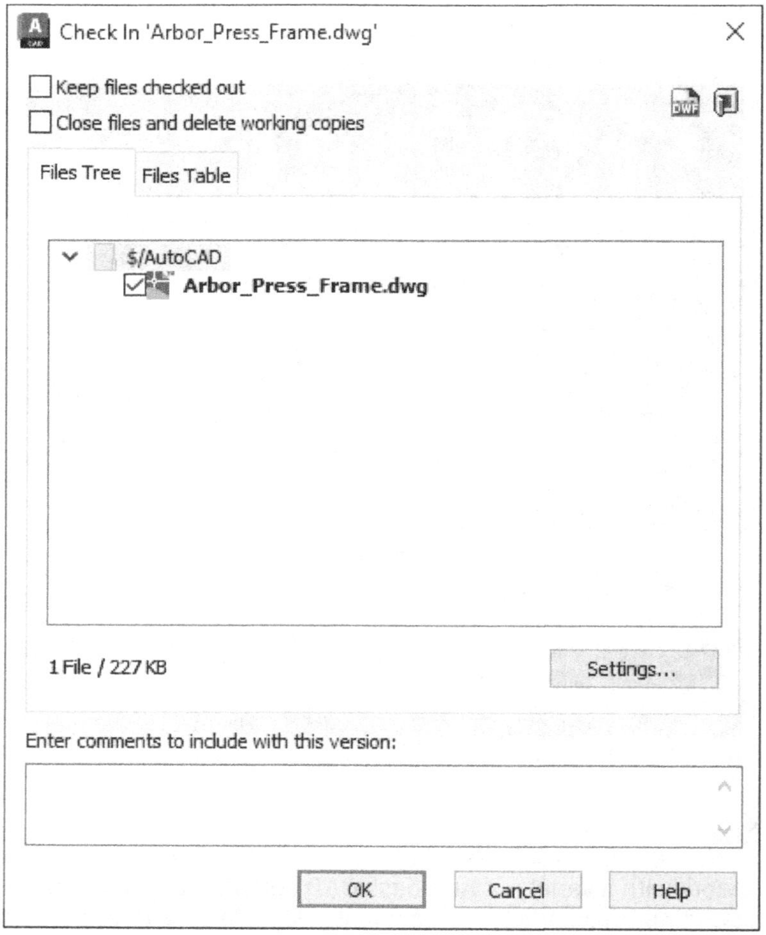


**Figure 11–77**

When you work with drawing files in Autodesk Vault Professional, consider the following:

- AutoCAD Mechanical BOM data is used to determine category. Assembly drawing file BOM data is translated into the item BOM.
- When you assign an item to a drawing file, any externally referenced files (Xrefs) are added as attachments to the item in Autodesk Vault Professional. Always check in the drawing containing the Xrefs to maintain the file relationships.
- Property extraction and mapping between Autodesk Vault Professional and drawing files is not as robust as it is with Inventor documents. No provision exists for writing item property values back to the properties in a drawing file.

- You can control lifecycle status and changes to drawing files with Autodesk Vault Professional engineering change orders. If the vault is set to enforce file locking, you cannot check out a drawing file from the vault unless its lifecycle state is set to **Work in Progress**.

You can generate 2D drawings in Autodesk Inventor in either Autodesk Inventor's native format (IDW) or DWG format. You can assign items to both of these file formats. If a drawing file does not exist in the vault when you assign an item to its associated part or assembly, you must manually attach the drawing item to its part or assembly item when the drawing is added to vault and assigned an item.

## Example of AutoCAD Files and Autodesk Vault Professional

Your design team uses AutoCAD or AutoCAD Electrical in combination with Inventor. An AutoCAD drawing contains a 2D reference layout for your Inventor assembly. AutoCAD Electrical drawing files detail electrical requirements for your design and provide pin and wire information for a harness assembly in Autodesk Inventor Professional.

You add the AutoCAD drawing file to the vault. You then attach it to your top-level Inventor assembly file and assign an item to the Inventor assembly. You add the AutoCAD Electrical drawings to the vault. You assign items to the AutoCAD Electrical drawings and use their Vault Professional bills of materials to aid the design.

# Practice 11b
# Work with Inventor Assemblies and BOMs

In this practice, you will examine an Inventor assembly BOM and how various BOM structure settings affect Vault Professional item creation. You will work with components having Normal, Reference, Phantom, Purchased, and Inseparable BOM structures. You will add a component to the assembly after assigning an item number to the assembly and examine how the new component is added to the *Item Master*, as shown in Figure 11–78.

| Number | Row Order | Pos... | Quantity | Units | Title (Item,CO) |
|---|---|---|---|---|---|
| 100038 | - | - | - | Each | HitchAssembly |
| 100042 | 1 | 1 | 1 | Each | ANSI/ASME B18.8.1 PIN. |
| 100039 | 2 | 2 | 1 | Each | Drawbar |
| 100045 | 3 | 4 | 1 | Each | Mounting Weldment |
| 100047 | 4 | 8 | 4 | Each | ISO 8678 M12 x 25 |
| 100048 | 5 | 9 | 4 | Each | IS 3063 12 |
| 100046 | 6 | 10 | 4 | Each | IS 7790 M 12 |
| 100043 | 7 | 7 | 1 | Each | Ball |
| 100041 | 8 | 5 | 1 | Each | Regular Helical Spring L |
| 100040 | 9 | 6 | 1 | Each | Hex Thick Nut - Inch 3/4 |
| 100044 | 10 | 3 | 1 | Each | Axle Clip |
| Safety Bracket | 11 | 11 | 1 | Each | Safety Bracket.ipt |

**Figure 11–78**

## Task 1: Set up the vault.

1. Start Autodesk Vault Professional. Log in using the following information:
   - For *User Name*, enter **administrator**.
   - Leave the *Password* field blank.
   - For *Vault*, select **AOTCVault**.

2. Select **Go>Project Explorer**, as shown in Figure 11–79. This will display the Project Explorer in the *Navigation* pane.

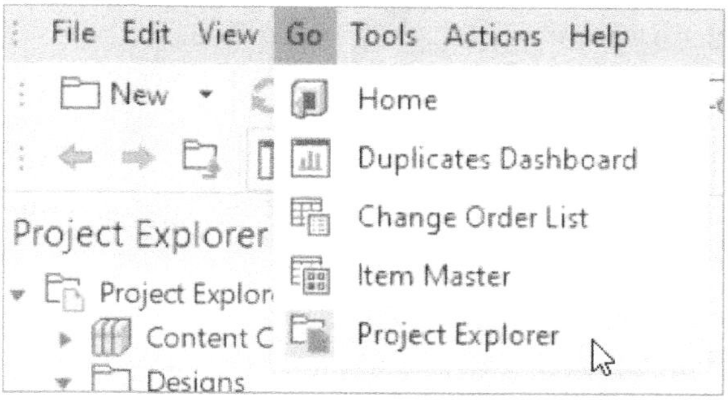


**Figure 11–79**

3. Right-click on the *Project Explorer ($)* folder. Do the following:
   - Click **Details**. The Details for "$" dialog box displays.
   - Confirm that the working folder is set to *C:\Vault Professional Admin\WorkingFolder*.
   - Click **OK**.
4. The Title property needs to be remapped in order for the item Title property to be displayed correctly. Do this:
   a. Select **Tools>Administration>Vault Settings** to display the *Vault Settings* dialog box.
   b. Select the *Behaviors* tab and select **Properties** from the *Properties* area. The *Property Definitions* dialog box displays.
   c. In the *Property Name* column, find the system property **Title (Item, CO)** and click on it to select it.
   d. In the *Property Definitions* toolbar, select **Edit**. The *Edit (System)* dialog box displays.
   e. Select the *Mapping* tab.
   f. Scroll the list to find the entry for **Provider: Inventor** and select the file property **Component Name**.
   g. Select the up arrow in the *Mapping* toolbar to move this entry to the top of the list.
   h. Click **OK** to dismiss the *Edit* dialog box.
   i. Click **Close** to dismiss the *Property Definitions* dialog box.
5. Start Autodesk Inventor.
6. Select **File>Manage>Projects**.

7. In the *Projects* dialog box, click **Browse**. Do the following:
   - Browse to *C:\Vault Professional Admin\VaultWorking Folder*.
   - Select **Designs.ipj**.
   - Click **Open**.
   - Click **Done**.
8. Select the *Vault* tab, then select **Log In** from the *Access* group. Log in using the following information:
   - *User Name:* **administrator**
   - Leave *Password* field blank
   - *Database:* **AOTCVault**

   **Note:** *If you have installed Inventor with separate log-ins for Vaults and Content Center libraries, select Vault Log In.*

## Task 2: Work with Autodesk Inventor assemblies and BOMs.

1. Select the *Vault* tab, then select **Open** from the *Access* group. Do the following:
   - Navigate to the *Designs\TrailerHitch* folder.
   - Click **HitchAssembly.iam**.
   - Click **Open**.
2. If prompted to check out the assembly, click **No**. If prompted to get files from the vault, click **Yes to All**. The assembly displays as shown in Figure 11–80.

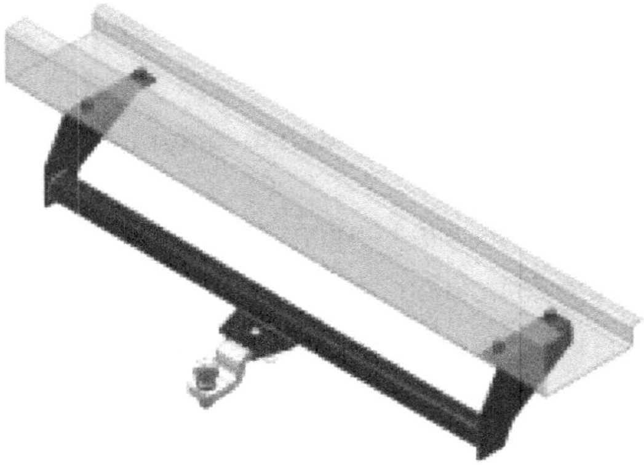

**Figure 11–80**

3. Examine the *Model* browser. The *Model* browser is a hierarchical list of the assembly components, as shown in Figure 11–81.
   - The **Mounting Weldment** subassembly contains the black components that make up the welded portion of the hitch assembly.
   - Each instance of the **Frame_Fastener** subassembly contains one bolt, one washer, and one nut.

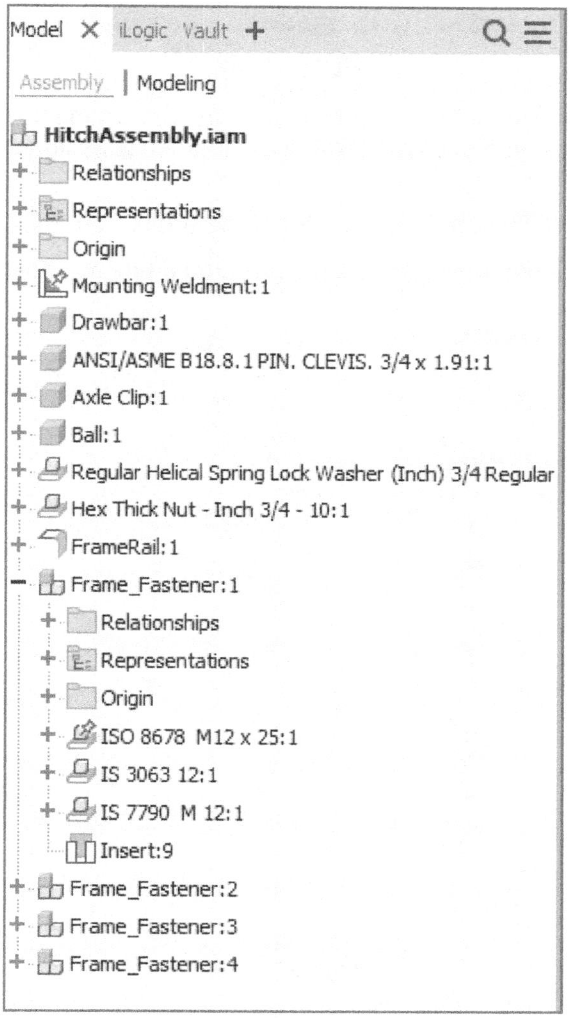


**Figure 11–81**

4. In the *Model* browser, right-click on **Frame_Fastener:1**.

5. Place the cursor over BOM Structure to display the assigned structure of the Phantom assembly, as shown in Figure 11–82.

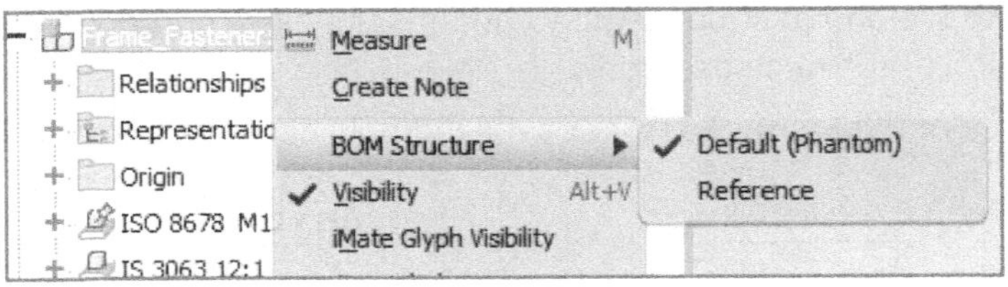


**Figure 11–82**

6. In the *Model* browser, repeat the two previous steps to examine the BOM structure of other components. (For example, the **FrameRail:1** component is assigned a Reference BOM structure.)
7. In the *Assemble* tab of the ribbon, select **Bill of Materials** from the *Manage* panel.
8. In the *Bill of Materials* dialog box, select the *Structured* tab, as shown in Figure 11–83.

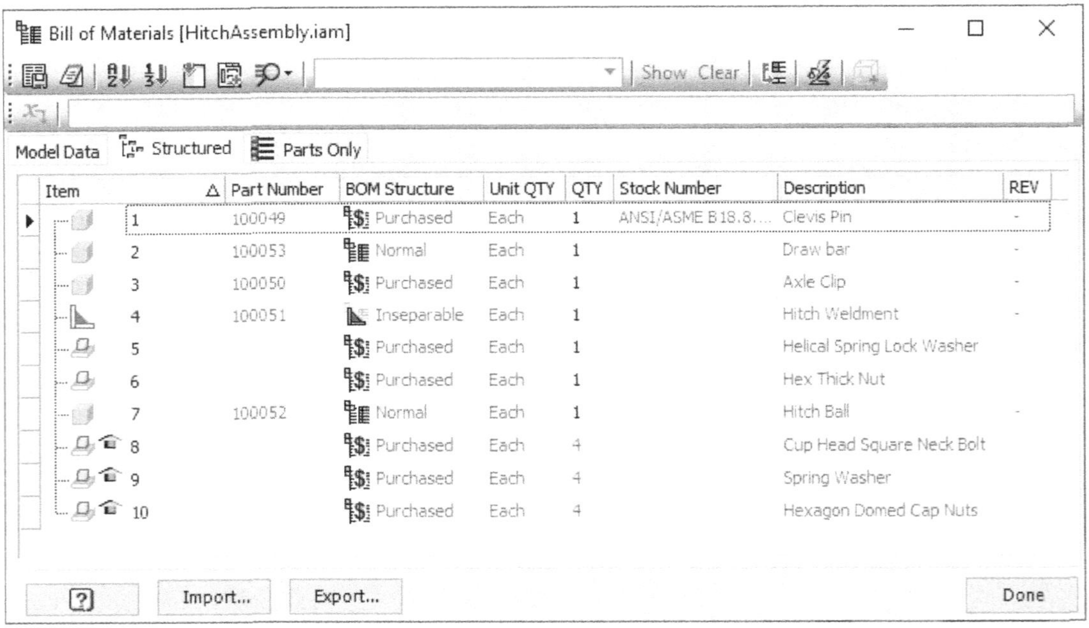


**Figure 11–83**

- The Phantom Frame_Fastener subassemblies are not listed in the BOM. The three child components from the Frame_Fastener subassembly display as promoted items in the BOM as items 8 - 10. The *QTY* column displays the number of components in one subassembly (1) multiplied by the number of phantom subassemblies (4).

9. If a column is not visible, do the following:
   - In the BOM, right-click on a column header.
   - Click **Runtime Column Customization**.
   - Drag the required column from the *Customization* dialog box to the required location on the display.
10. Add the *Filename* column to the display if it is not visible.
11. All items display unavailable because they are not checked out of the vault.

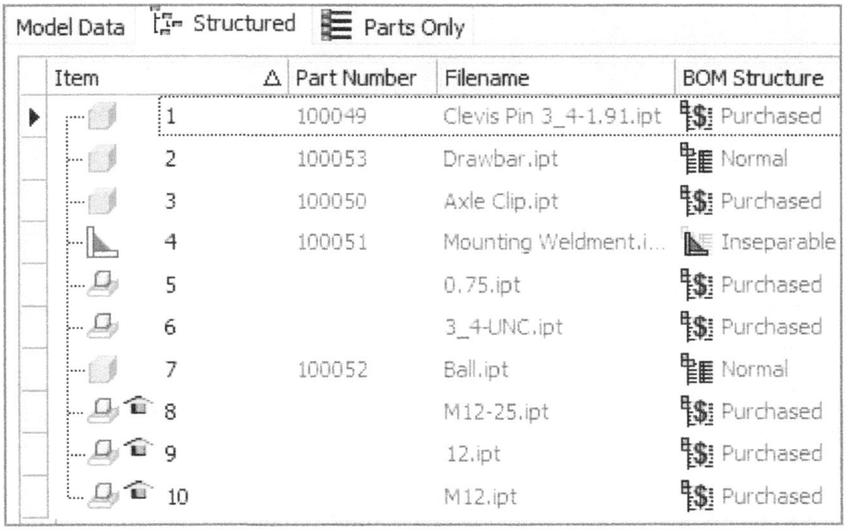


**Figure 11–84**

- The *BOM Structure* column displays the assigned BOM structure for each component. The library components are shown as **Purchased**, as shown in Figure 11–84. The Drawbar and Ball components are Normal. The Mounting Weldment assembly is shown as Inseparable.

12. In the *Bill of Materials* dialog box, click **Done**. If you get prompted to check out the files, select **No to All**.

## Task 3: Assign an item to the assembly.

1. Switch to Autodesk Vault Professional.
2. In the *Go* menu, select **Project Explorer**. Expand the *Designs* and *TrailerHitch* folders.

   ***Note:*** *The components with the Reference and Phantom BOM structures are included in the vault. The BOM structure affects only items in Vault Professional*

3. Right-click on **HitchAssembly.iam** and select **Assign/Update Item**. If the assembly is checked out, select **Undo Check Out** first.

4. In the item record window, select the *Bill of Materials* tab.
   - The **Inseparable Weldment** assembly and all its child items are included in the default tree view. The **Reference FrameRail** part and the **Phantom Frame_Fastener** assembly are not included in the list. The child components in the **Phantom Frame_Fastener** assembly are assigned item numbers.

| Number | Row Order | Position Number | Quantity | Units | Title (Item,CO) |
|---|---|---|---|---|---|
| 100015 | - | - | - | Each | Hitch Assembly |
| 100017 | 1 | 1 | 1 Each | Each | ANSI/ASME B18.8.1 PIN.... |
| 100016 | 2 | 2 | 1 Each | Each | Draw Bar |
| 100021 | 3 | 3 | 1 Each | Each | Axle Clip |
| 100020 | 4 | 4 | 1 Each | Each | Mounting Weldment |
| 100026 | 4.1 | 1 | 47.244 Inch | Inch | ANSI AISC 2x2x 1/4 - 12... |
| 100028 | 4.2 | 2 | 1 Each | Each | end_plate_RH |
| 100029 | 4.3 | 3 | 1 Each | Each | end_plate_LH |
| 100030 | 4.4 | 4 | 1 Each | Each | DrawBarMountTopPlate |
| 100027 | 4.5 | 5 | 1 Each | Each | DrawBarMountBottomP... |
| 100019 | 5 | 5 | 1 Each | Each | Regular Helical Spring L... |
| 100022 | 6 | 6 | 1 Each | Each | Hex Thick Nut - Inch 3/... |
| 100018 | 7 | 7 | 1 Each | Each | Hitch Ball |
| 100025 | 8 | 8 | 4 Each | Each | ISO 8678 M12 x 25 |
| 100023 | 9 | 9 | 4 Each | Each | IS 3063 12 |
| 100024 | 10 | 10 | 4 Each | Each | IS 7790 M 12 |

**Figure 11–85**

***Note:** Your item numbers and column organization might not match Figure 11–85.*

5. Select **First-Level** from the *Structure* drop-down list, as shown in Figure 11–86.
   - The child items of the **Inseparable Weldment** assembly are not displayed.

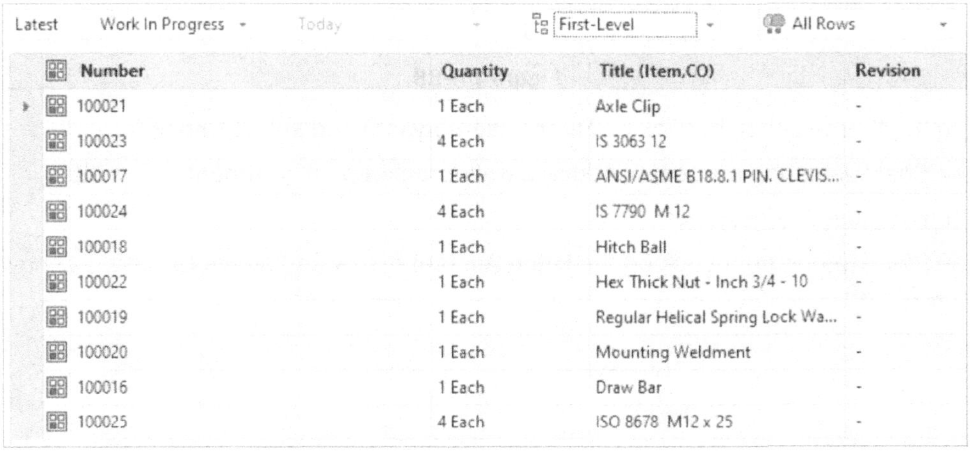


| Number | Quantity | Title (Item,CO) | Revision |
|---|---|---|---|
| 100021 | 1 Each | Axle Clip | - |
| 100023 | 4 Each | IS 3063 12 | - |
| 100017 | 1 Each | ANSI/ASME B18.8.1 PIN, CLEVIS... | - |
| 100024 | 4 Each | IS 7790 M 12 | - |
| 100018 | 1 Each | Hitch Ball | - |
| 100022 | 1 Each | Hex Thick Nut - Inch 3/4 - 10 | - |
| 100019 | 1 Each | Regular Helical Spring Lock Wa... | - |
| 100020 | 1 Each | Mounting Weldment | - |
| 100016 | 1 Each | Draw Bar | - |
| 100025 | 4 Each | ISO 8678 M12 x 25 | - |

**Figure 11–86**

6. For Structure, select **Multi-Level**.
7. Click **Save and Close**.
8. Switch to Autodesk Inventor.
9. On the *Vault* tab, select **Place** in the *Access* panel.
10. In the *Select File from Vault* dialog box, navigate to the *$\Designs\TrailerHitch* folder. Do the following:
    - Select **Safety Bracket.ipt**.
    - Click **Open**.
    - Click in the graphics window background.
11. Right-click, then click **OK**.

    ***Note:*** *You typically position the bracket in the assembly with assembly constraints. You are not required to apply the constraints in this practice.*

12. Save the assembly, as shown in Figure 11–87. In the *Save* dialog box, click **OK**.

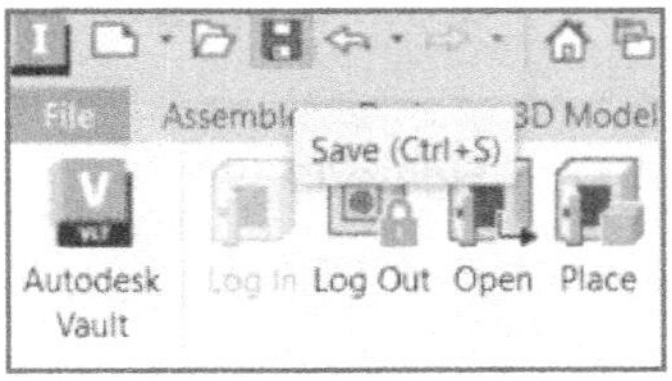


**Figure 11–87**

**13.** In the browser title bar, select **Vault**, as shown in Figure 11–88.

**Figure 11–88**

**14.** In the Vault browser, right-click on **HitchAssembly.iam** and select **Check In**.

**15.** In the *Check In* dialog box, enter **Added safety bracket** as a comment. Click **OK**.

**16.** Switch to Vault Professional.

**17.** In the *Item Master*, right-click on the **Hitch Assembly** row and select **Update**, as shown in Figure 11–89.

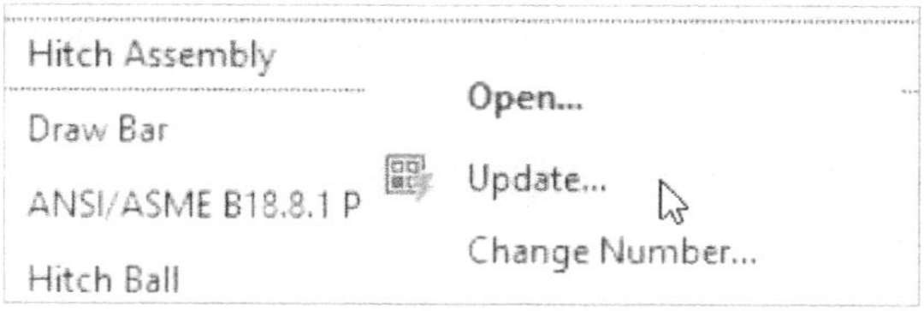


**Figure 11–89**

**18.** In the *Item record* window, select the *Bill of Materials* tab. Note that the safety bracket part is automatically added, as shown in Figure 11–90.

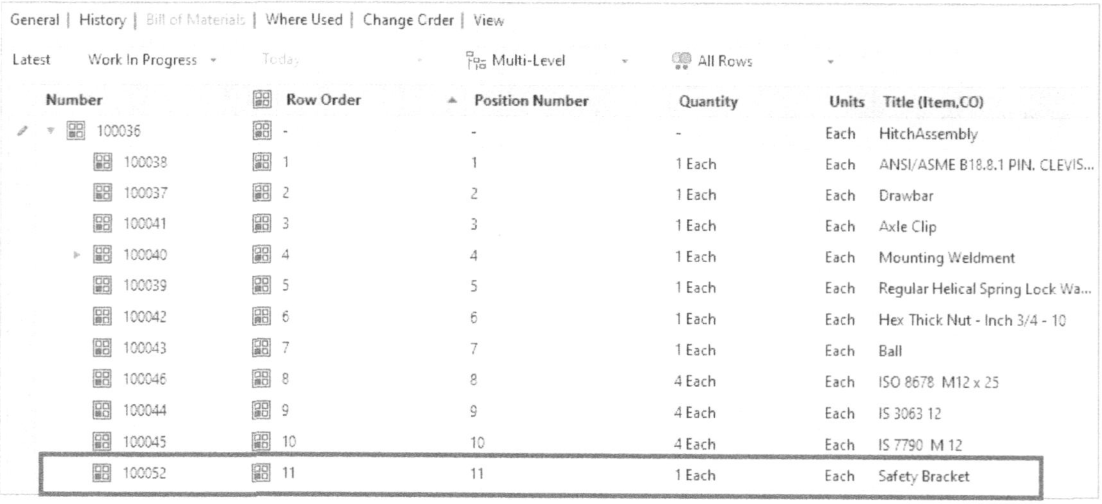


**Figure 11–90**

***Note:*** *The item numbers do not match the item numbers in the previous illustration.*

**End of practice**

Chapter 12

# Autodesk Inventor In-CAD Data Management

You can manage and evaluate your vault file data from within the Autodesk® Inventor® software by using the **Data Cards** and **Data Mapping** features. Data Cards lets you examine pertinent vault details about a model and modify property information for individual or multiple files. Data Mapping lets you generate report data for a model and publish the results as a chart. You can also map the report results onto the open model to better evaluate your design.

Both of these features give you an advantage in understanding and managing your design without ever having to leave the Autodesk Inventor software.

In this chapter, you learn how to view data cards, modify properties using data cards, generate reports, and map report data to your model.

## Learning Objectives

- Enable and access both data card views.
- Build and navigate a data card deck, isolate a card, and remove a card from a card deck.
- Edit properties and track changes with data cards.
- Generate a report based on an open model.
- Map data in a report to the open model.

# 12.1 Working with Data Cards

Data cards provide convenient summaries of the metadata assigned to a file or group of files through a single point of access. With data cards, you can determine a file's vault status, see a thumbnail of the file, and review and modify property information without leaving the Inventor application.

In this section, you learn how to enable the **Data Cards** feature and view file properties in fingertip view and full data card view. You also learn how to build and manage a card deck, and use single or multiple data cards to manage file properties. A data card example is shown in Figure 12–1.

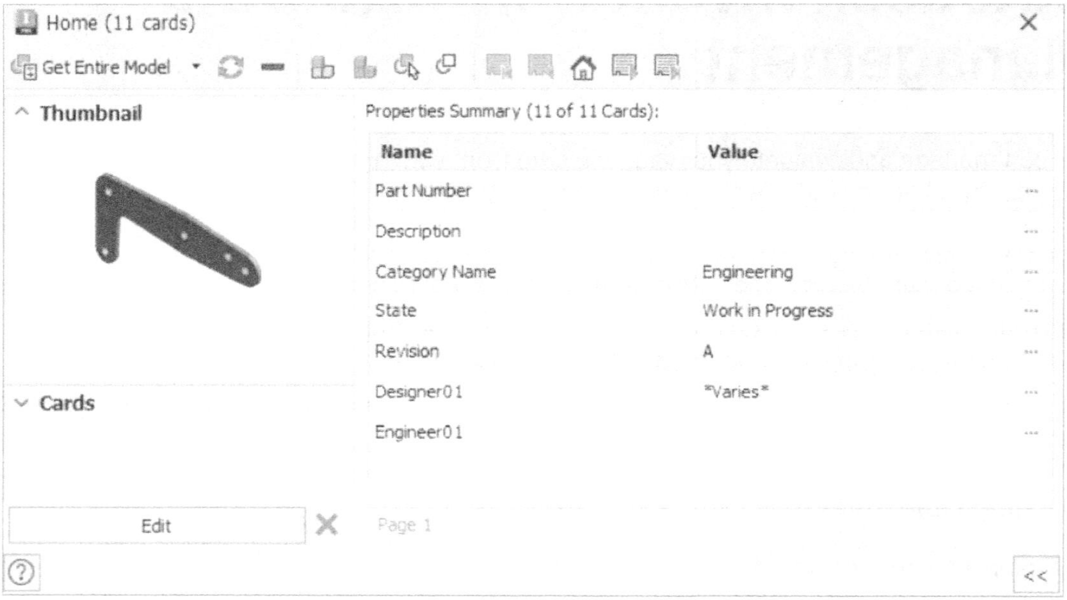


**Figure 12–1**

## About Data Card Views

Data cards let you view pertinent vault details and properties for specified files. This insight into the statuses and properties of your model files makes it easier to manage the files throughout the lifecycle of the model.

Whenever a part is selected on the CAD canvas or in the Model or Vault browser list, the part is highlighted on the canvas and in the list, and the data card automatically updates to show the relevant information for that part.

Data cards can be displayed in two different ways: the fingertip view and the full data card view.

Access the Data Cards feature by clicking **Data Cards** in the Autodesk Vault ribbon.

## Fingertip View

The fingertip view is the default view for Data Cards. This view (shown in Figure 12–2) is a collapsed, read-only version of the full data card.

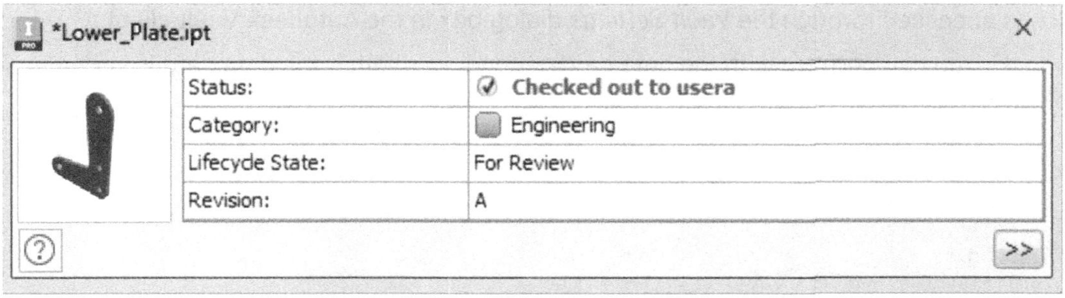


**Figure 12–2**

When a file is selected and the **Data Cards** feature enabled, the fingertip displays the following information:

- Thumbnail
- Component name
- Status
- Category
- Lifecycle State
- Revision

Click **>>** (Expand) to switch from fingertip view to full data card view.

## Full Data Card View

The fingertip can be expanded into a full data card, which displays all of the information in the fingertip view and certain property information, as shown in Figure 12–3. The CAD administrator can determine which properties display in the *Configure Data Card* dialog box, which is accessed through the *Vault Settings* dialog box in the Autodesk Vault client.

The tasks you can perform with the data card depend on whether the data card is in read-only mode or edit mode.

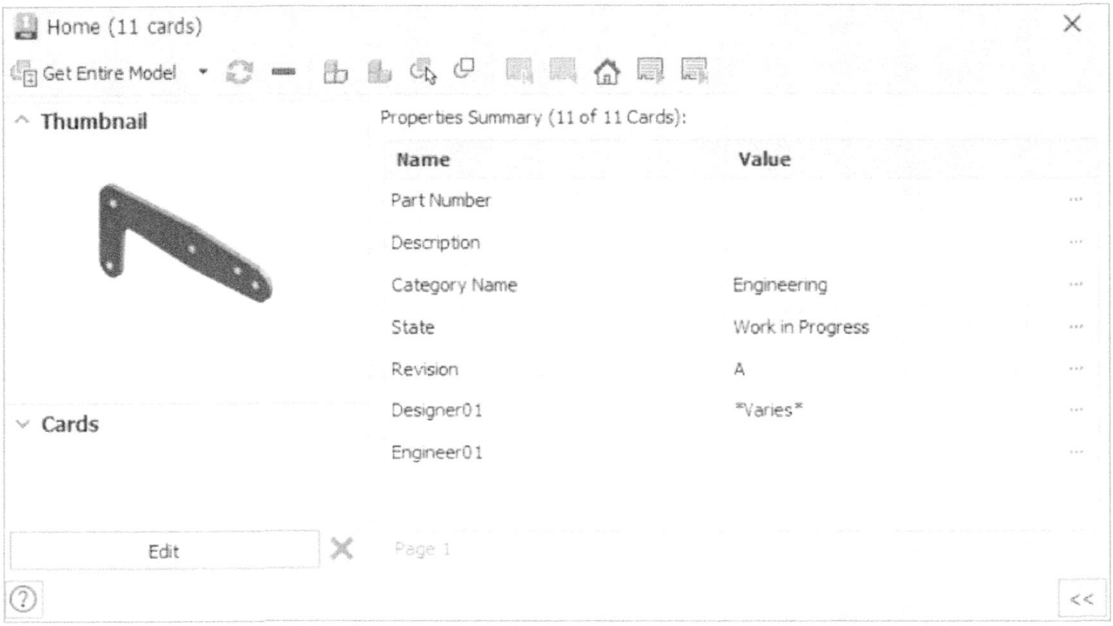


**Figure 12–3**

### Read-Only Mode

The read-only mode is the default mode for viewing the full data card. This mode enables you to compare selected files and to filter the property values based on your needs.

When a data card opens for a selected file or when a **Refresh** command is performed, the values for the properties are grabbed from the server and displayed. A pending icon displays next to the property name when the retrieval is in process. The pending icon disappears once the value is received for that property.

### Edit Mode

The property grid can be changed to edit mode by clicking **Edit**. When in edit mode, the file is automatically checked out of the vault and you can edit the displayed property values. When you are finished editing, the new values are written to the local file and to the server file. These edits are made permanent when the file is checked into the vault. All actions performed on an individual card affect only the component associated with the card.

 

## Example of Using a Data Card to Examine File Information

You just found out that one of the parts you are working with in your model has been set from **Released** back to **Work in Progress**. You need to find out who last checked in the part so that you can talk to that person about the changes they made.

You select the part in the model and then click **Data Cards** to enable the fingertip view for that part. You can see the lifecycle state is set to **Work in Progress** and that a revision bump has occurred, but you still need to know which engineer last made changes. You click the **>>** (Expand) button and discover that it was your colleague Tim Smith who altered the part. Now you can talk to him about why the part was returned to **Work in Progress**.

### How To: Enable Data Cards

1. In Inventor, log in to the desired Vault and open the desired vault file(s). Click **Data Cards** in the Autodesk Vault ribbon, as shown in Figure 12–4. The data card for the selected file displays in fingertip view.

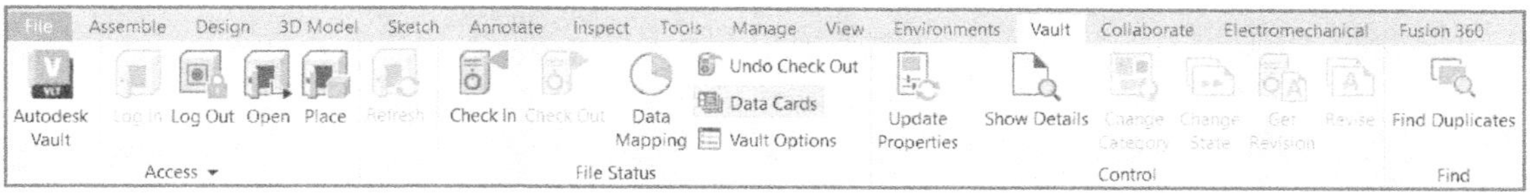


**Figure 12–4**

### How To: View Fingertip Information

1. Enable data cards by clicking **Data Cards** in the Autodesk Vault ribbon. The data card window displays.
2. Select a part in the model. The data card grid updates automatically to show the part's filename, a thumbnail, revision, state, category, and vault status.

### How To: View Full Data Card Information

1. Click **>>** (Expand) in the lower right corner of the data card to switch between the fingertip view and the full data card view. The data card expands to display the properties. Some properties will show a pending icon until the value is retrieved from the server.

   ***Note:*** *Property information displayed on the data card is determined by the administrator in the Configure Data Card dialog box in the Autodesk Vault client.*

2. Click the tabs at the bottom of the grid to see additional properties.

# Understanding Data Card Decks

Multiple data cards can be retrieved to create a card deck. You can specify the scope of the card deck by selecting individual files or an entire open model. A card deck contains one data card for each file specified in the scope and a *Home* card which lists the data cards in the card deck.

## Data Card Deck Controls

At the top of the card deck, a toolbar has been provided for navigating and managing the data cards in the card deck. These commands enable you to retrieve the data cards for a model or a specified group of files and place them into a deck, refresh the data card values, remove a card from the deck, and isolate a card from the deck. There are also navigation buttons (as shown in Figure 12–5) that enable you to move through the deck to the data card you want to review.

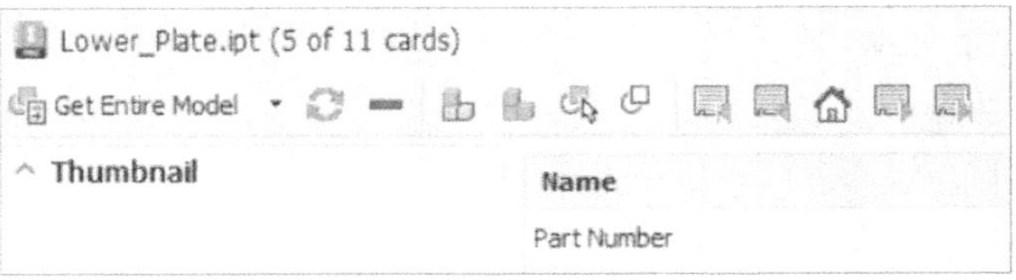


**Figure 12–5**

The following table defines each of the icons located in the data card navigation toolbar.

| Icon | Command | Definition |
|---|---|---|
| 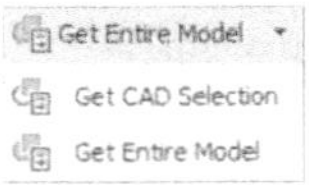  | **Get Data Cards (Get CAD Files or Get Entire Model)** | Retrieves either the selected CAD files or all the files in the open model and creates a card deck. Whichever Get Data Cards command is used last remains displayed. |
|  | **Refresh** | If a single data card displays; the property values for that card are retrieved from the server.<br>If the Summary card is selected, the property values for all data cards defined by the current Get command are retrieved from the server. |
|  | **Remove Card** | Removes the current card or selected cards from the deck. |
|  | **Isolate On** | Toggles on Isolation mode for the selected card or cards. Only the files for the selected data cards remain displayed and all other files in the card deck are rendered transparent on the canvas. |
|  | **Isolate Off** | Toggles off Isolation mode for the selected card or cards. All files that were transparent when Isolate was toggled on, are displayed again. |
|  | **Select in CAD** | Sends the current card selection to the CAD environment as a selection set. |

 

| Icon | Command | Definition |
|---|---|---|
| | **Clear CAD Selection** | Clears the current CAD selection set. |
| | **First** | Goes to the first card in the card deck (also referred to as the *Home* card). |
| | **Back** | Goes back one card in the deck. |
| | **Next** | Goes to the next card in the deck. |
| | **Home** | Goes to the *Home* card. |
| | **Last** | Goes to the last card in the deck. |

# Building a Data Card Deck

You can create a deck of data cards for faster referencing of properties and vault status information. Data cards are gathered from the open model or from a selection set and placed into a card deck. A *Home* card is added as a summary card of the card deck contents.

## How To: Build a Data Card Deck

1. Enable the data cards feature by selecting **Data Cards** in the Autodesk Vault ribbon.
2. Select a model or selection set in Inventor.
3. Click **>>** (Expand) at the bottom of the data card to expand the data card from fingertip view to full view.
4. In the data card deck control toolbar, click the *Get* drop-down arrow and select either **Get CAD Selection** or **Get Entire Model**.
5. The data is retrieved from the vault. Depending on the size of the deck being created, the updates might take some time. You can continue working until all property values have been retrieved.
6. When all the data is retrieved, the *Home* card displays and the navigation controls on the data card deck toolbar are activated.

# Removing Data Cards from a Card Deck

Refine your card deck by removing a data card or group of data cards from the card deck.

## How To: Remove an Individual Data Card from a Card Deck

1. Select the data card you want to remove from the card deck.
2. Right-click and select **Remove Card**. The card is removed from the card deck.

## How To: Remove Multiple Data Cards from a Card Deck

1. Click the **Home** button to go to the *Home* card in the card deck.
2. Select the data cards that you want to remove from the card deck from the data card list.
3. Right-click and select **Remove Card**. The cards are removed from the card deck.

# Home Card

The *Home* card (shown in Figure 12–6) displays the list of the files in the card deck and their property attributes. The property values that display depend on whether a single data card, multiple data cards, or no data cards are selected from the data card list.

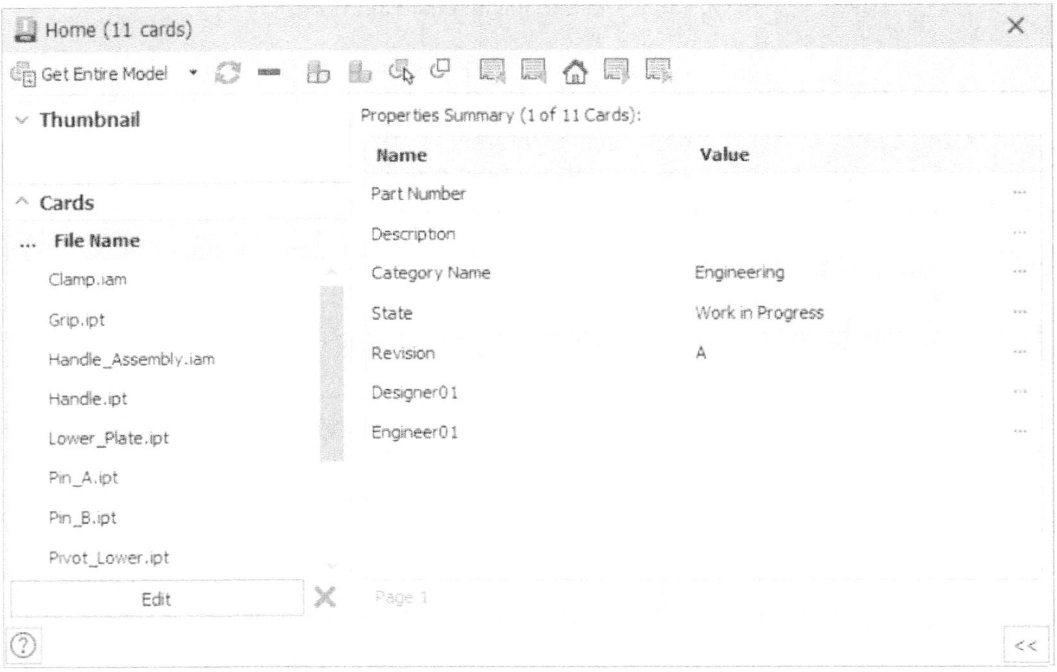


***Home Card with 1 File Selected***

**Figure 12–6**

# Home Card Display Rules

- If a single data card is selected, then the property values for that data card display on the *Home* card.
- If multiple data cards are selected, then the property values shared across the selected data cards display. If the values differ, then the word **VARIES** displays.
- If no data cards are selected in the data card list, then all the property values shared across the entire deck display. If the values differ, then the word **VARIES** displays.

 

You can make edits with individual data cards or use the *Home* card to make bulk edits throughout the entire card deck. When making bulk edits for properties with different values throughout the deck, a value collector is used to list the different values associated with that property.

At the top of the *Home* card, the number of cards in the deck and the number of cards selected for comparison display.

## Isolation Mode

Sometimes, in models with many parts, it is necessary to isolate a part for easier examination. The isolation feature enables you to distinguish specified parts in a model. Select the data card(s) for the part(s) that you want to view and click **Isolate On** from the data card deck controls. The selected parts remain visible on the CAD canvas while all other parts in the card deck become transparent, as shown in Figure 12–7.

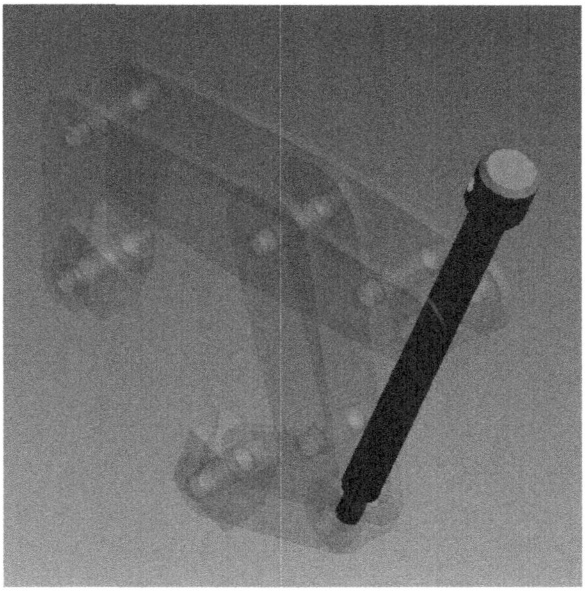

**Figure 12–7**

Click **Isolate Off** from the data card deck controls to make all parts on the CAD canvas visible again.

## Isolating Parts in Autodesk Inventor

You can isolate a part or parts for easier examination by enabling the Isolation feature.

### How To: Toggle Isolation On

1. Click **Home** in the data card deck toolbar to go to the *Home* card.
2. Select the data cards for the parts that you want to isolate on the CAD canvas.

3. Click **Isolate On** in the data card deck toolbar. The parts remain viewable on the CAD canvas and all other parts with unselected data cards in the card deck become transparent.

- Click **Isolate Off** in the data card deck toolbar to make all parts on the CAD canvas visible again.

# Editing Properties with Data Cards

Properties can be edited on both the full data card and in a card deck. Changes with data cards can only be made when the data card is in edit mode. Click **Edit** (as shown in Figure 12–8) to begin changing property values.

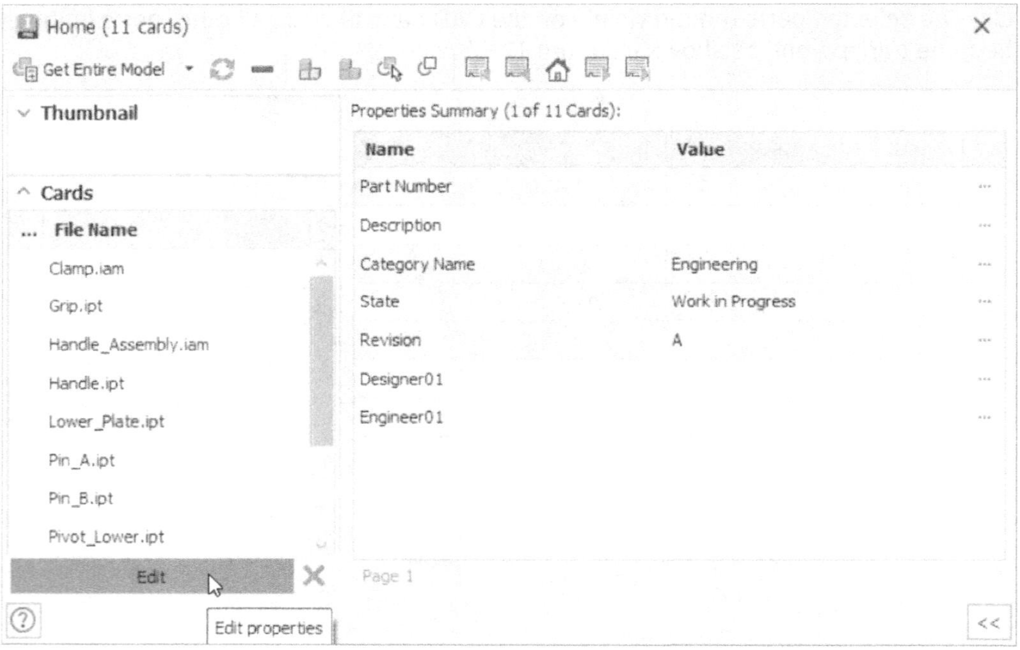


**Figure 12–8**

Files must be checked out before changing anything. If any files in the card deck are not checked out or if a data card is not available for editing, you will receive a message asking you to check out the files or to remove any invalid cards from the card deck. When a property is edited, click **Save** to commit the changes. An asterisk displays beside the filename to indicate that the data card has been modified.

> ***Note:*** *Autodesk Vault operations are disabled when a data card is in edit mode.*

Modified files must be checked back into the vault for the changes to become permanent. If you attempt to close the card deck or to change the data card view while a modified file is checked out, you will be prompted to check the file in or discard your changes before proceeding.

## Tracking Edits

Since edits are not immediately permanent, you can track edits and review them before checking the modified files into the vault. If a property has been modified, an asterisk (*) displays beside the filename on the data card (as shown in Figure 12–9) and beside the filenames in the data list on the home card if you are using a card deck.

Additionally, the font changes for property values that have been modified.

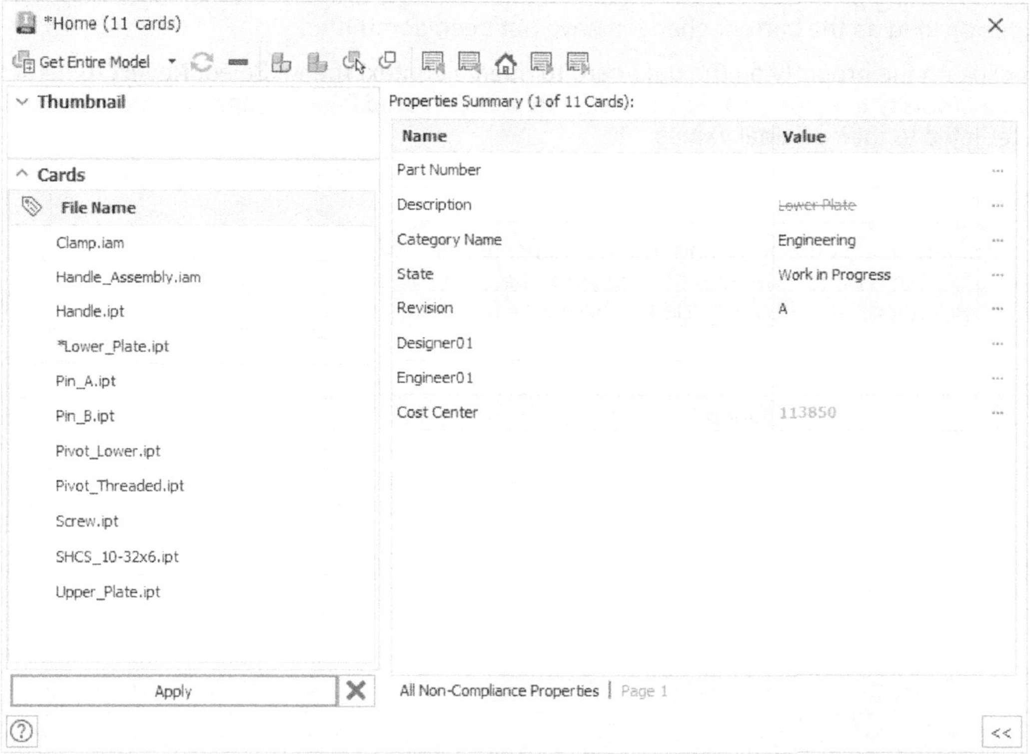


**Figure 12–9**

The following table explains the different text effects and their significance.

| Text | Meaning | Edit |
|---|---|---|
| Normal font | Same as original value (no change) | The value is the same as the original value or has been reset before checking the file back in. |
| Normal font with gray background | Read-only | The property cannot be altered even in edit mode. |
| Strikethrough font | Deleted value | The original value was deleted. When the file is checked back into the vault, this value is blank. |

| Text | Meaning | Edit |
|---|---|---|
| Blue font | Edited value | The original value has changed but the file has not been checked back into the vault to commit the change. |

## Undoing Changes

During the editing process, you can choose to undo a single property change or to undo all changes as long as the current changes have not been committed.

Right-click on the property on the data card to open a context menu. Select **Revert** to reset the selected property to its original value. Select **Revert Selected Files** to reset the properties of the selected files to their original values.

## Compliance Rules

Compliance is a key component in managing properties. When a property is non-compliant, a red exclamation icon is inserted into the value field on the data card. On the *Home* card, a non-compliant icon displays beside the filename to let you know that one of the properties for that file is non-compliant.

Hover the cursor over the exclamation icon to see a tooltip describing the reason why the property is not compliant. Since some data cards contain multiple tabs of properties, the icon will also display on the tab to indicate if there is a non-compliant property not displayed on the data card. There is also a tab that shows all non-compliant properties in one list.

In Figure 12–10, the *Cost Center* value for **Lower_Plate.ipt** is not compliant because it requires a minimum of six characters and only five have been entered.

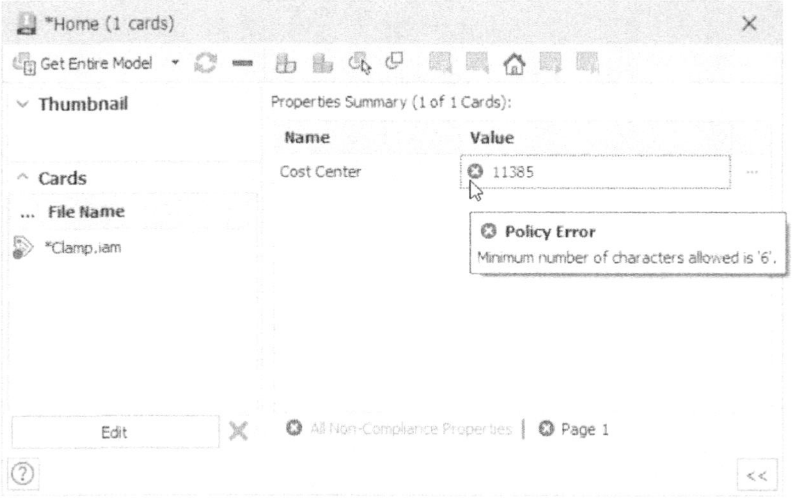


**Figure 12–10**

 

## How To: Edit a Single Data Card

1. Go to the data card for which you want to change a property value.
2. Click **Edit** to enter edit mode. Properties that cannot be edited are disabled.
3. Locate the property you want to change. Use the tabs at the bottom of the values grid to navigate through all available properties.
4. Enter a new value in the property field.
   OR
   Right-click on the field and select **Undo** in the context menu to undo any previous changes.

   ***Note:*** *Changes made to property values are not permanent until the affected files are checked back into the vault. If you attempt to resize the data card or close the data card feature, you will be prompted to check in changed files first.*

5. Click **Apply** to commit the changes. An asterisk (*) displays beside the name of the data card to indicate that it has been modified.

## How To: Edit Properties for Multiple Data Cards

1. Go to the *Home* card.
2. Click **Edit**. Properties that cannot be edited are disabled.
3. Select the data cards in the data card list for which you want to edit property values. Alternatively, clear all selections to change values from the whole deck.
4. Locate the property that you want to change. Use the tabs at the bottom of the values grid to navigate through all available properties.

   ***Note:*** *Changes to the property value affect all cards selected or the entire card deck if no cards are selected.*

5. Enter a new value in the property field. If the field has a value of **VARIES**, select a value from the list or enter a new one.
6. Click **Apply** to commit the changes. An asterisk (*) displays beside the name of the data card to indicate that it has been modified.

# Working with Value Collectors

The value collector is a dialog box that lists the different values associated with a particular property. The values listed are collected from the data cards selected on the *Home* card or the entire deck if no cards are selected. The value collector contains a *Value* column with the list of property values and a *Usage* column that displays how many data cards share that particular value. Value collectors can be accessed from the *Home* card or from a single data card, as shown in Figure 12–11.

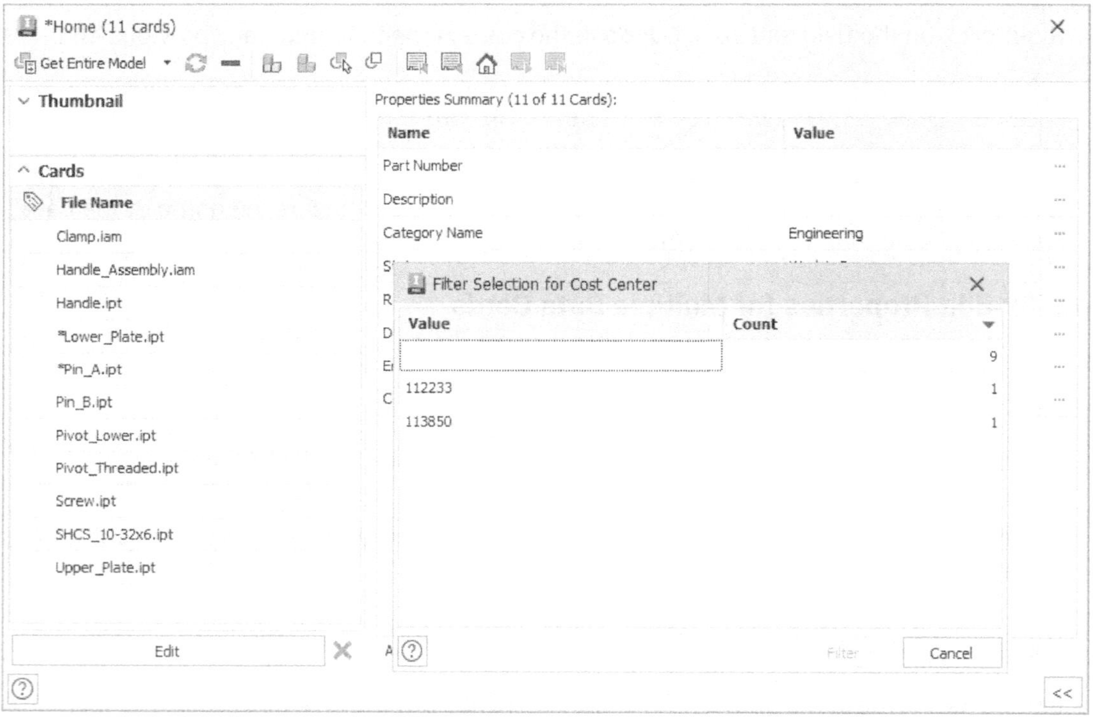


Figure 12–11

## Using a Value Collector with the Home Card

In a card deck, the same properties are repeated for each card, as shown in Figure 12–12. If the selection of data cards shares the same value for that property, then that value displays next to the property name on the *Home* card. However, if the property values differ, then the word **VARIES** displays next to the property. Properties with a value of **VARIES** display with a small ellipsis icon (...). Click the icon to access the value collector.

You can filter property values for review in read-only mode or change them in edit mode.

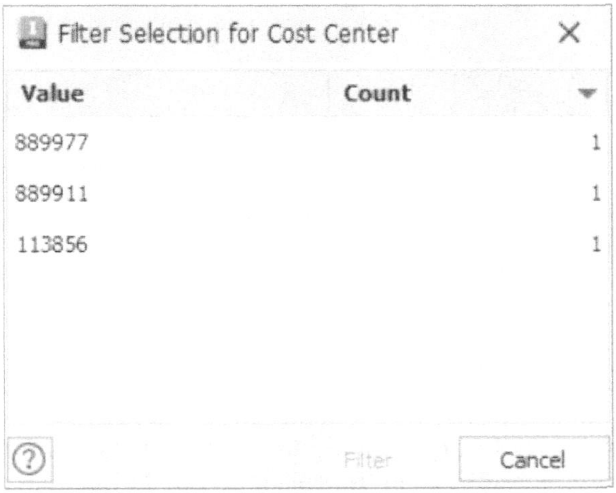


**Figure 12–12**

### Read-Only Mode

In read-only mode, you can filter values collected. Select a value in the value collector and click **Filter** to select the cards in the card list that contain that property value.

> ***Note:*** *The file associated with a data card must be checked out before editing any properties.*

For example, the value collector for the *Cost Center* property lists all of the values for *Cost Center* in the deck. If you select **324657** from the collector and click **OK**, the five cards with **324657** as the value for *Cost Center* are selected in the card list.

This process can be repeated for additional properties, enabling you to refine the data card selection each time.

In edit mode, you can change the values for a file associated with a particular data card or make bulk changes to all cards associated with that value.

The value collector has both a *Values* and a *Count* column, as shown in Figure 12–13. However, unlike read-only mode, an editing field at the top of the value collector enables you to adjust values for the data cards that use that property.

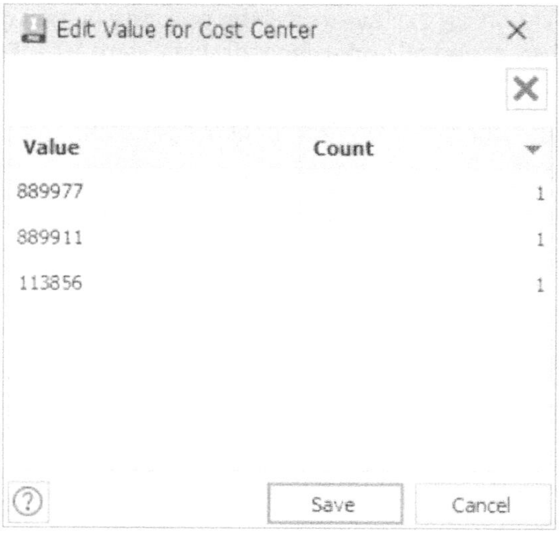


**Figure 12–13**

For example, the value collector for the *Cost Center* property lists all of the values for *Cost Center* in the deck. If you select **889911** in the collector, **889911** displays for editing at the top of the dialog box. The value can then be cleared or modified. Click **Save** to commit any changes.

## Using a Value Collector with a Single Data Card

On a single data card, the properties are the same as those on every other card in the deck. However, only the property values for the selected data card display. A small ellipsis icon (...) displays next to each property. Click the icon to access the value collector.

### Read-Only Mode

In read-only mode, the value collector displays a list of available values in the card deck. These values do not impact the card.

### Edit Mode

In edit mode, the value collector displays a list of available values in the card deck. A value can be selected from the list and applied to the file associated with the current data card.

## Using a Value Collector to Filter Property Values (Read-Only)

### How To: Use a Value Collector to Filter Property Values from the Home Card

1. Go to the *Home* card. Ensure that you are in read-only mode. (**Edit** should be visible.)

2. Select the data cards in the data card list for which you want to collect property values. Alternatively, clear all selections to collect values from the whole deck.
3. Click the ellipsis (...) next to the property value you want to review. The icon is only available for properties displaying a value of **VARIES**.
4. In the *Filter Selection* dialog box, select the value you want to use to filter your data card selection. The data card list is updated to display only those data cards containing that property value.
5. Continue filtering the data card selection using other properties, if required.

### How To: Use a Value Collector to Filter Property Values from a Single Data Card

1. Select a data card in the card deck to review its property values.
2. Ensure that the card deck is in read-only mode. (**Edit** should be visible.)
3. Click the ellipsis (...) next to the property value you want to review. A list of values that already exist in the card deck for that property displays.

## Using a Value Collector to Edit Property Values

> ***Note:*** *The file associated with a data card must be checked out before editing any properties.*

### How To: Use a Value Collector to Edit Property Values from the Home Card

1. Go to the *Home* card.
2. Click **Edit**.
3. Select the data cards in the data card list for which you want to collect property values. Alternatively, clear all selections to collect values from the whole deck.
4. Click the ellipsis (...) next to the property value you want to change. The icon is only available for properties displaying a value of **VARIES**.
5. In the *Edit Value* dialog box, select a new value for the selected property from the *Values* list or enter a value in the editing field.
6. Any changes made to a value affect all data cards using that property value. Refer to the *Usage* column for the number of data cards affected. If required, refine your data card selection using the steps described in the *Read-Only* section above before continuing.

   > ***Note:*** *Changes made to property values are not permanent until the affected files are checked back in to the vault. If you attempt to resize the data card or close the data card feature, you will be prompted to check in changed files first.*

7. Click **Save** to commit the changes and close the *Edit Value* dialog box. An asterisk (*) displays beside the name of the data card to indicate that it has been modified.

### How To: Use a Value Collector to Edit Property Values from a Single Data Card

1. Select a data card in the card deck for which you want to edit property values.
2. Click **Edit**.
3. Click the ellipsis (...) next to the property value you want to change.
4. A list of values that already exist in the card deck for that property displays.
5. Select a new value for the selected property from the *Values* list or enter a value in the editing field. Click **Save** to commit the changes and close the *Edit Value* dialog box. An asterisk (*) displays beside the name of the data card to indicate that it has been modified.

# Managing the Data Card Layout

Administrators can streamline property management with data cards by customizing the data card layout. In the *Configure Data Card* dialog box in the Vault Settings of the client, administrators can determine how many pages a data card uses and which properties display.

Select **Tools>Administration>Vault Settings>*Behaviors* tab** and click **Data Card** to access the *Configure Data Card* dialog box, as shown in Figure 12–14.

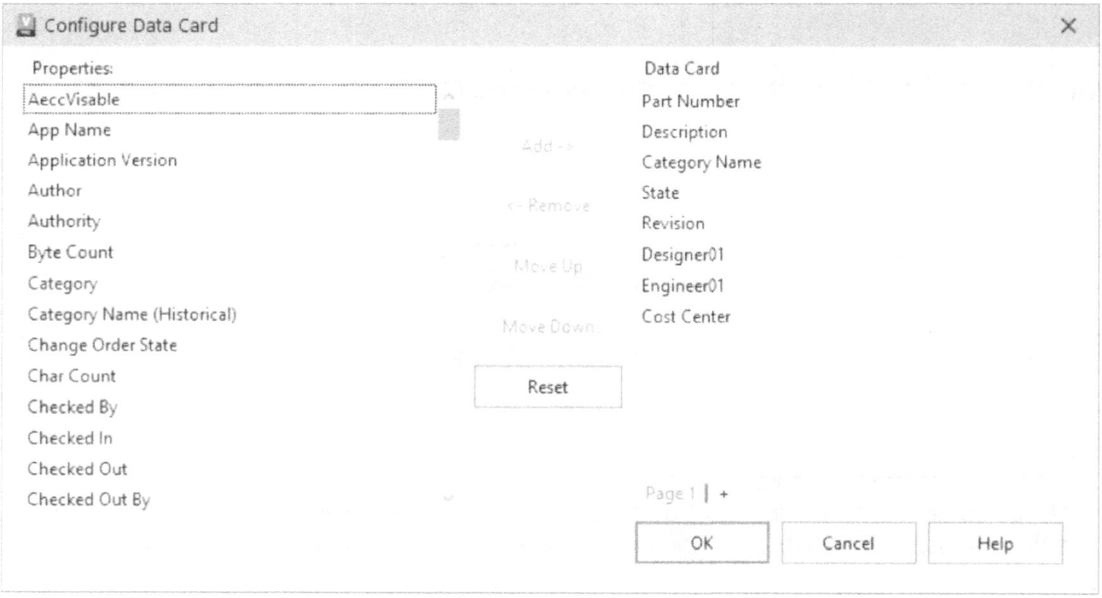


**Figure 12–14**

You can manage tabs and determine which properties are available for the CAD user to modify in the *Configure Data Card* dialog box. A properties list displays all of the properties that can be added to the selected tab. A property can be added to a single tab only once. Several different tabs, however, can list the same property.

| Actions | Description |
|---|---|
| **Add** | Select one or more properties from the properties list and click **Add** to include them in the selected data card tab. |
| **Remove** | Select a property already assigned to a tab and click **Remove** to delete it from that tab. |
| **Move Up** | Moves a property up in the selected tab. |
| **Move Down** | Moves a property down in the selected tab. |
| **Reset** | Returns the current tab to the last layout. |
| **Rename tab** | Double-click on the tab to rename it. |
| **Add new tab** | Click the small tab with a plus sign (+) to add a new tab to the data card. By default, the tabs are numbered sequentially. |
| **Delete a tab** | Click the X in the selected tab to delete the tab itself. |
| **OK** | Saves the changes to the data card layout and closes the dialog box. |

## How To: Configure the Data Card Layout

1. Select **Tools>Administration>Vault Settings>Behaviors tab**. Click **Data Card**.
2. In the *Configure Data Card* dialog box, select one or more properties from the properties list and click **Add** to add them to the selected tab.
    - Select a property and click **Remove** at any time to refine the properties in the selected tabs.
3. If required, click **Move Up** or **Move Down** to reorganize the properties in the tab, as required.
4. Double-click on the selected tab and rename it.
5. Click the + tab to create a new tab.
6. Click the X tab to delete a tab.
7. When finished, click **OK** to save your settings and close the dialog box.
8. Click **Reset** at any time to restore the dialog box to the last saved layout.

# Practice 12a
# Manage a Card Deck

In this practice, you create a custom data card deck for a design.

## Task 1: Create a card deck.

1. Start Autodesk Vault. Log in using the following information:
   - For *User Name*, enter **administrator**.
   - Leave the *Password* field blank.
   - For *Vault*, select **Data Card and Mapping Vault**.
2. In the *Navigation* pane, click **Project Explorer ($)**.
3. Click **Find** in the toolbar.
4. In the *Find* dialog box, search for **Clamp.iam**.
5. Right-click on **Clamp.iam** and select **Open** to launch it in the Autodesk Inventor software, as shown in Figure 12–15. Select **Yes** to checking out the file and select the **Designs.ipj** project file, if prompted.

Figure 12–15

6. Log in to Vault as **administrator**, if required.
7. In the Autodesk Vault ribbon, click **Data Cards**, as shown in Figure 12–16.

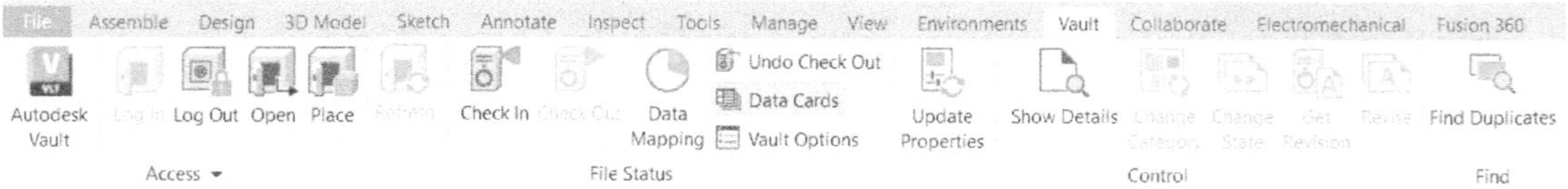


Figure 12–16

8. The fingertip view of the data card for the clamp displays, as shown in Figure 12–17.

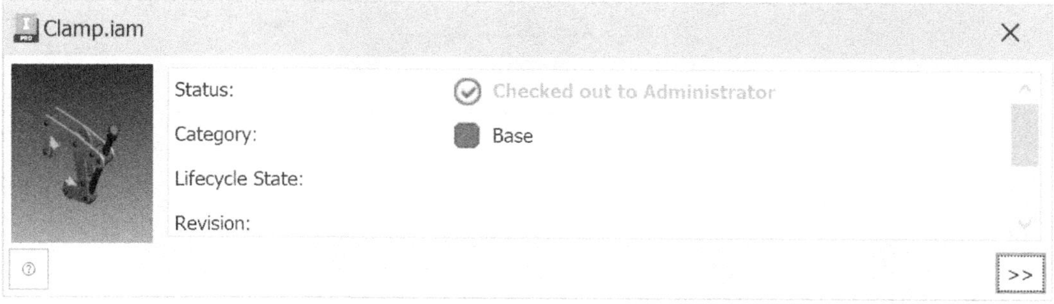


**Figure 12–17**

9. Click the **>>** (Expand) button on the fingertip view to switch to full data card view.
10. Note that the title says **Home** and that there is only 1 card in the deck, as shown in Figure 12–18. Now you will add data cards for referenced parts.

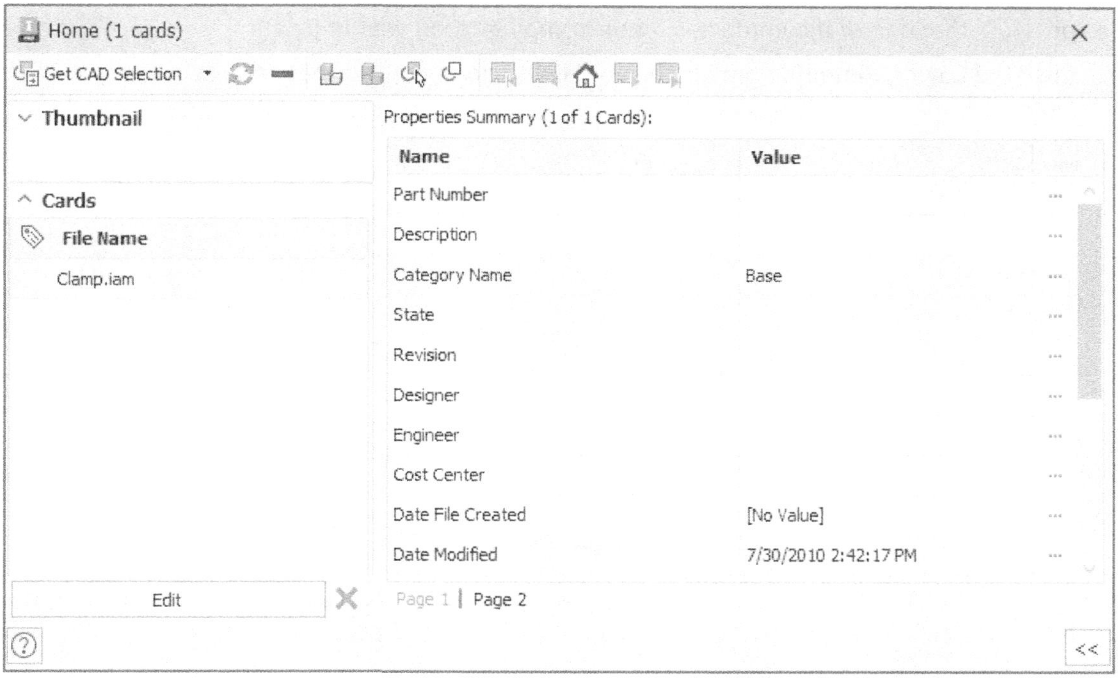


**Figure 12–18**

11. At the top of the full data card view, click **Get Entire Model** from the drop-down list in the toolbar, as shown in Figure 12–19.

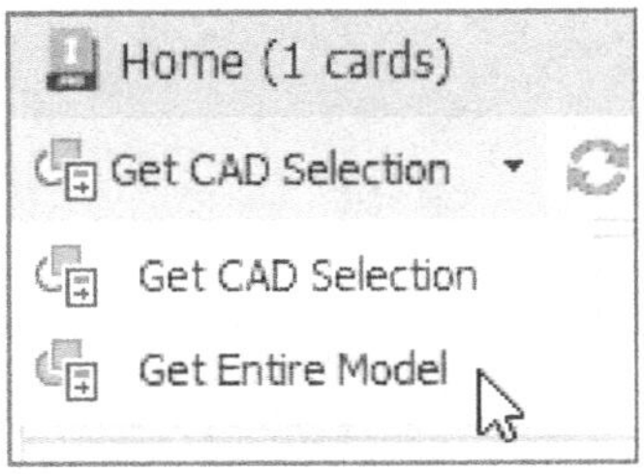


**Figure 12–19**

- Data cards for all of the design components are retrieved.

## Task 2: Edit properties for a single data card.

You now have a card deck consisting of data cards for all of the components in the Clamp.iam design. Note that one of the cards has a non-compliant icon next to it.

1. Click the **Lower_Plate.ipt** name in the card list to go directly to that card, as shown in Figure 12–20.

**Figure 12–20**

2. The *Cost Center* property for the **Lower_Plate.ipt** does not comply with property policy. In this case, the minimum character length for *Cost Center* is six characters.
3. Click **Edit** to enter editing mode.
4. Click the ellipsis (...) in the *Value* field for *Cost Center*.
5. The *Edit Value for Cost Center* dialog box opens. Note that only one card is using the **11385** cost center but no other cards in the deck are using a cost center, as shown in Figure 12–21. You will fix this in a few steps.

 

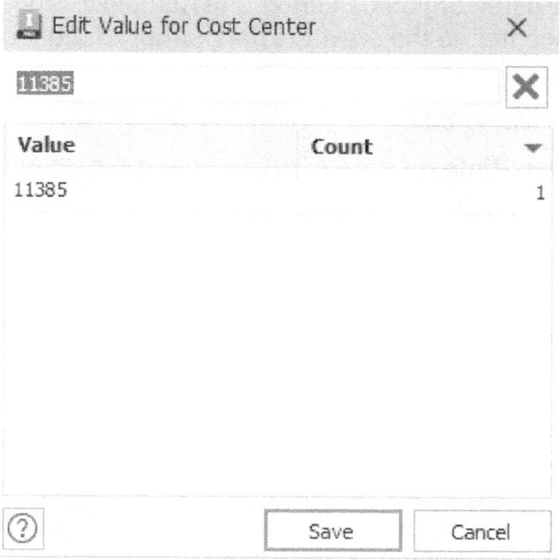


Figure 12–21

6. Enter **113850** in the entry field at the top of the dialog box and click **Save**.
7. The *Cost Center* value has been updated. Note that the new value is in bold blue in the data card field. This means that the value has been changed but it has not been applied yet.
8. Click **Apply** on the data card to commit the change. A *Property Edit Result* dialog box displays whether the change was a success, as shown in Figure 12–22. Click **Close** to exit this dialog box.

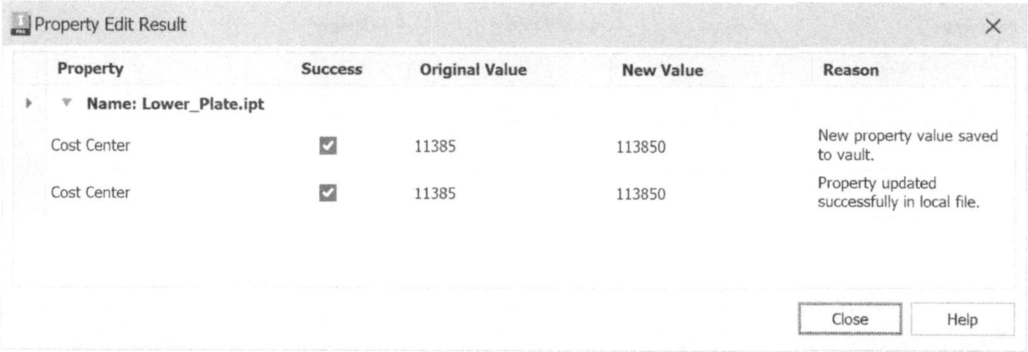


Figure 12–22

9. Click **Home** in the data card toolbar to return to the *Home* card in the card deck. Note that the compliance error has been resolved.
10. Double-click on the **Upper_Plate.ipt** file in the card list to go directly to that card.
11. Since this part is from the same cost center as the **Lower_Plate.ipt**, ensure that this card is updated as well. To do so, click **Edit**.
12. Click the ellipsis (...) beside the *Cost Center* value.

13. All available values are listed or you can enter one manually. Since you know that this part shares the same cost center as the previous part, simply double-click on the **113850** value and it enters that same value in the entry field.
14. Click **Save** to close the dialog box.
15. Click **Apply** on the **Upper_Plate.ipt** data card to commit the changes.
16. Click **Close** in the *Property Edit Result* dialog box.
17. Click **Home** to return to the *Home* card.

## Task 3: Edit properties for multiple data cards.

**Pin_A.ipt**, **Pin_B.ipt**, and **Grip.ipt** share the same cost center but it's different from the one you just did. Rather than edit them one at a time, you can make a mass edit from the *Home* card.

1. Select **Grip.ipt, Pin_A.ipt**, and **Pin_B.ipt** in the data cards list by holding <Ctrl> as you click on the filenames.
2. Click **Edit** in the *Home* card.
3. Click the ellipsis (...) next to the value for *Cost Center*.
4. In the *Edit Value for Cost Center* dialog box, enter **116677** and click **Save**.
5. Click **Apply** to commit the changes.
6. The *Property Edit Result* dialog box shows the multiple changes and whether they were saved to the server successfully, as shown in Figure 12–23.

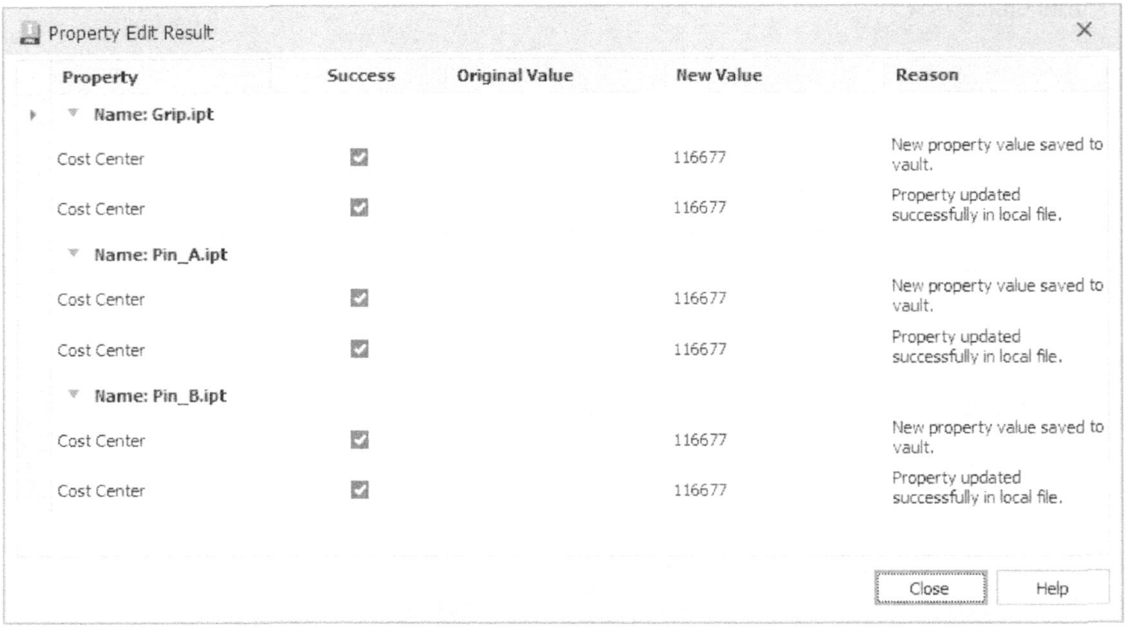


**Figure 12–23**

7. Click **Close** to exit the dialog box.
8. In the *Home* card, select all of the cards in the card list. Note that the *Cost Center* says **VARIES**. This means that more than one value exists for *Cost Center* in the selected group of cards.
9. Click the ellipsis (...) to review the different values for *Cost Center* in the deck. Note that the *Count* column indicates how many cards share each value.
10. Double-click the value that is blank and click **Filter**.
11. The data cards with the empty (blank) value are automatically highlighted in the *Home* card list.
12. Click **Edit**.
13. Click the ellipsis (...) beside the *Cost Center* value.
14. Enter **889921** in the *Edit Value for Cost Center* dialog box and click **Save**.
15. Click **Apply** to commit the changes.
16. Click **Close** in the *Property Edit Result* dialog box. All *Cost Center* values are now updated.

**End of practice**

# 12.2 Data Mapping and Report Generation

The **Data Mapping** feature enables you to easily assess important business data for your model. Report data is mapped on to the model (as shown in Figure 12–24) to provide visual output of the correlation between report results and the open model. Mapping the report to the model colors the model to match the corresponding chart elements. The entire chart can be mapped onto the model, or you can choose which chart elements to map.

Use data mapping to visually evaluate your design.

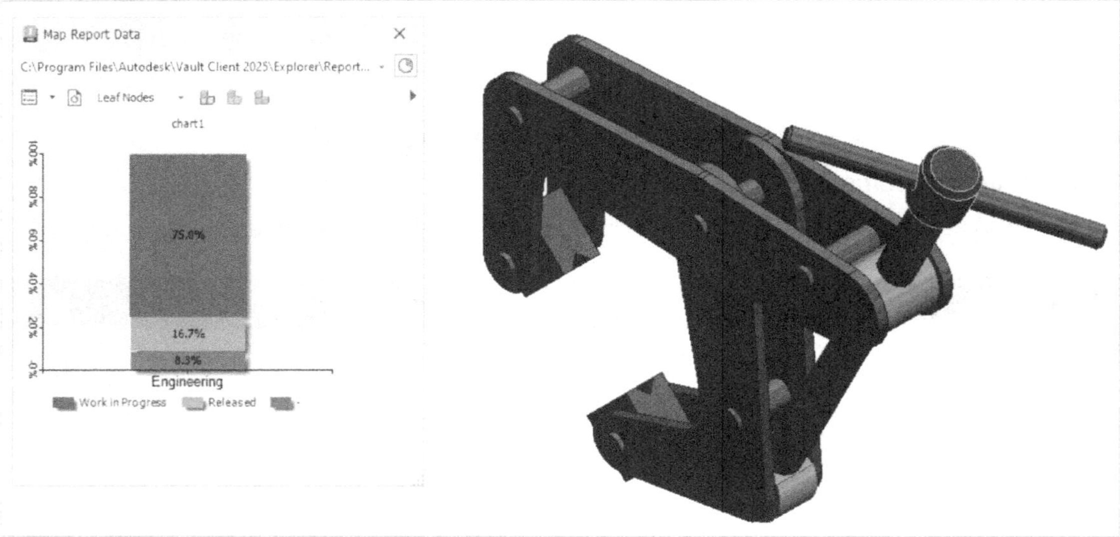


Figure 12–24

## Introduction to the Data Mapping

Data mapping is a useful tool for viewing different levels of data in a model. However, because the model hierarchy can be mapped at different levels, it is important to know from where the data is being collected to accurately interpret the results. Additionally, you should also know how file attachments affect the report results.

> ***Note:*** *Data Mapping is not available in sketch mode.*

## Enabling Data Mapping

Data mapping must be enabled before you can generate reports or map any model data for review. In the Autodesk Vault ribbon, click **Data Mapping** (as shown in Figure 12–25) to launch the *Map Report Data* dialog box.

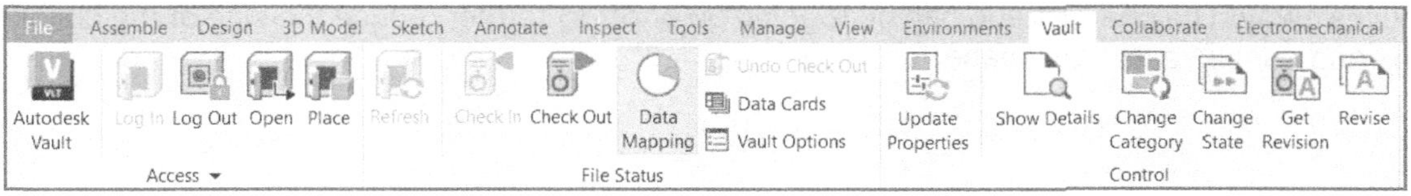


**Figure 12–25**

## File Attachments

A report is generated using all of the files in the current model, including attachments. As a result, the chart might not have a 1:1 correlation with the files displayed in the canvas.

For example, a pie chart slice can indicate that a large percentage of files are currently in the **Work in Progress (WIP)** state. However, when mapping the data onto the model, only a small number of files are color coded to the WIP slice. This difference in display is because the slice is taking into account the attached files and the part files, but only the part files display on canvas. You can view the full report to see a complete list of files that make up a pie slice.

## Mapping Report Data to the Model Hierarchy

When a report is generated, the reporting system evaluates the files without knowledge of their relationships. The resulting chart represents actual flat data. Since a model has several levels to it, you have the option of mapping your data as three different levels to better understand the report data. This versatility enables you to examine model data at the parts level, the assemblies' level, and the first children level. By examining all three levels, you will have the most complete picture of the report results.

## Leaf Node Mapping

Leaf node mapping is the most granular view of the model. Only parts in assemblies are mapped. This level is used most often early in a project to see where components are in the development process.

## All Assemblies Mapping

All assemblies mapping provides a perspective of the report results as they relate to the assembly level and first level parts. The color of an assembly determines the color of its parts but subassemblies are assigned their own colors.

## First Level Children Mapping

First level children mapping is the least granular view. All parts and assemblies within each first level child are given the same color as the first level child.

# Mapping Your Data

The *Map Report Data* dialog box (shown in Figure 12–26) contains several features that enable you to generate reports, map report results, and manage chart elements. The *Map Report Data* dialog box turns opaque when the mouse moves over it and transparent when the mouse moves away. The chart legend can be toggled on or off to further reduce the size of the dialog box and conserve canvas space.

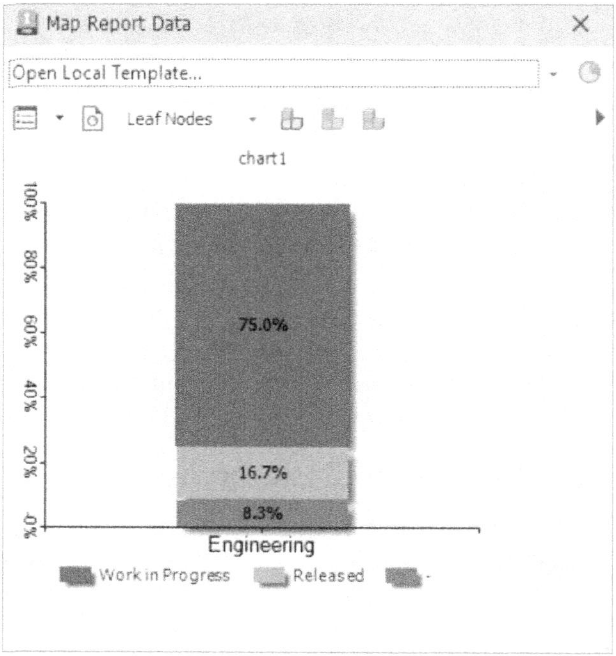


**Figure 12–26**

When the *Map Report Data* dialog box first opens, only the **Report Template** menu and the **Generate Report** button are enabled. All other controls are disabled until a report is generated.

Since the *Map Report Data* dialog box is document-based, each document can have its own dialog box.

## Understanding the Map Report Dialog Box

The following table describes each of the features available in the *Map Report Data* dialog box.

| | Feature | Description |
|---|---|---|
| no icon | **Report Template menu** | The *Report Template* drop-down list contains a list of the most recently used templates and the options for opening an existing template from either a local folder or the vault.<br>**Note:** Opening a template from the vault checks that file out of the vault. The file is checked in after it is saved. |
|  | **Generate Report** | Creates a report based on the selected template. Click the button again to refresh report results after making changes. |
|  | **Display Options** | Enables or disables chart labels and the chart legend. |
|  | **View Full Report** | Displays the full report in a report viewer. |
|   | **Mapping Method menu** | Enables you to select which of the three mapping methods to use when mapping chart data or isolating files. The three options are: leaf nodes, all assemblies, and first level children. |
|  | **Apply Color Mapping** | Assigns the chart element colors to the corresponding model components based on the selected mapping method.<br>This button is a toggle and can be clicked again to toggle off color assignments. |
|  | **Apply Isolation** | Dims the files that are not represented by the chart elements and leaves the selected chart data mapped on the screen at full visibility. The data is isolated based on the current mapping method.<br>This button is a toggle and can be clicked again to toggle off isolation and restore all files to full visibility. |
|  | **Clear Color Mapping or Isolation** | Updates the current mapping and isolation display if any changes are made to the chart element selection.<br>**Note:** If new data is added to the vault, the report must be regenerated. This button does not re-run the report. |
|  | **Chart Selector** | Enables you to select which chart to use for data mapping if more than one chart exists for the template.<br>If data is currently mapped when a new chart is selected, the data is cleared. Click Data Mapping to map the data from the new chart. |

| | Feature | Description |
|---|---|---|
|   | **Chart element context menu** | Enables you to select and manage chart elements for custom data mapping. Access the menu by right-clicking on any of the elements in the.<br>By default, all chart elements are mapped to the model. |
|   | **Chart Legend** | Displays the chart elements and associated color map data graph assignments in a colorful graph. |

## How To: Map Report Data

After generating a report, you can map the results onto the open model in Inventor.

1. Generate a report. See the previous section for more information on generating a report.
2. Once the report is generated, select one of the three mapping methods.
3. Click **Map Report**. The model is colored relative to the report displayed in the data map control.

   ***Note:*** *The report is generated using all of the files in the current model, including attachments. The resulting chart might not have a 1:1 correlation with the files displayed in the canvas. View the full report to see a complete list of files that make up the pie slice.*

# Creating Reports for Your Model

The reporting feature, when used in conjunction with data mapping, lets you map report data to the canvas for visual overview of a model's status and development. This information makes it easier to track designs and projects throughout their lifecycles. You can generate reports of model data based on any of the templates supplied with the client, as shown in Figure 12–27. The report feature is accessed from the *Data Mapping* dialog box.

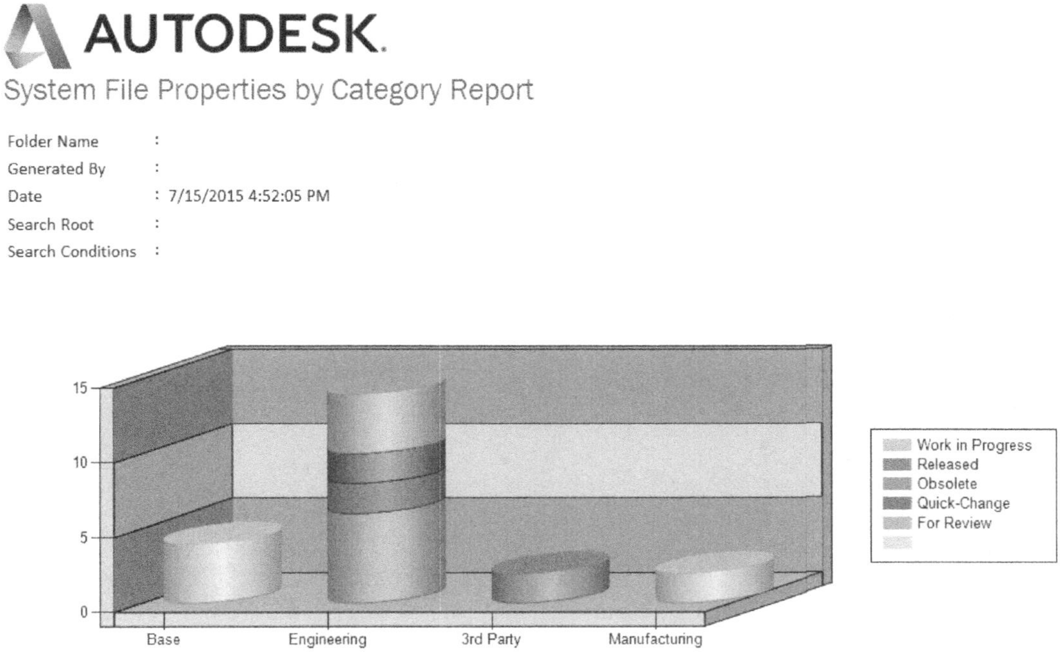


**Figure 12–27**

## Report Templates

Several report templates are provided with the Autodesk Vault client. These report templates contain a color palette for a chart, but the templates do not specify which color is assigned to which chart element. You can specify how chart elements are color coded when you use the data mapping feature. Color coding chart elements enables quick, repeatable viewing of model data.

You can assign standard color mapping in the *Assign Color* dialog box in the Autodesk Vault client. Access the dialog by selecting **Tools>Administration>Vault Settings**. Select the *Behaviors* tab and then select **Define** under *Report Management*.

> ***Note:*** *Refer to the chapter on Reporting for more information on working with report templates.*

## Report Charts

The in-CAD report feature can display data in four different charts:

- Pie chart
- Doughnut chart
- Column chart
- Stacked column chart

> ***Note:*** *If a report contains a chart type not supported by the in-CAD report control, the chart is not displayed on the CAD canvas. The report can be viewed outside the application with a report viewer.*

### How To: View the Full Report

In addition to mapping the data from the report onto the Inventor model, you can view the complete report including any tables and additional layout and formatting, as shown in Figure 12–28.

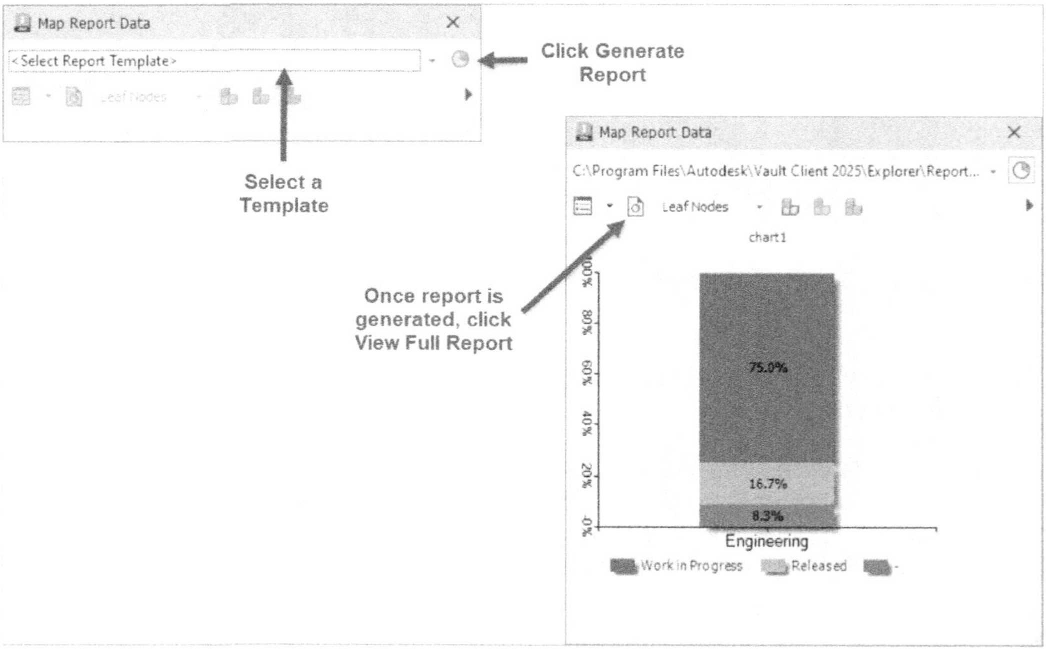


**Figure 12–28**

1. Enable report control by clicking **Data Mapping** in the Autodesk Vault ribbon. The *Map Report Data* dialog box displays.
2. In the *Map Report Data* dialog box, select a report template from the drop-down list, or open a new template from a local folder or the vault.
3. Click the **Generate Report** icon. A progress bar displays with the status of the report. Depending on the size of your model, this process can take a few minutes. You can continue to work while the report is being generated.
   - Once the report has been generated, the report chart displays in the data mapping control.
4. Click the **View Full Report** icon to display the full report.

# Managing Chart Elements

The ability to manipulate chart elements makes it easier to customize how you view your report data when it is mapped, as shown in Figure 12–29. The chart control enables you to override chart colors, create a selection set of files in Inventor based on chart elements and the mapped components, and retrieve a data card deck for the mapped components through a convenient context menu.

**Figure 12–29**

## Selecting Chart Elements

When you map report data, all chart elements are mapped to the model by default. However, you can select individual chart elements in the report and map only those elements. Additionally, you can manipulate the way the data displays on the open model.

There are three ways to select chart elements. Once the chart elements are selected, use the context menu to customize how the data is mapped or viewed.

- Click a single element in the chart to select it. The element is outlined in red, as shown in Figure 12–30.

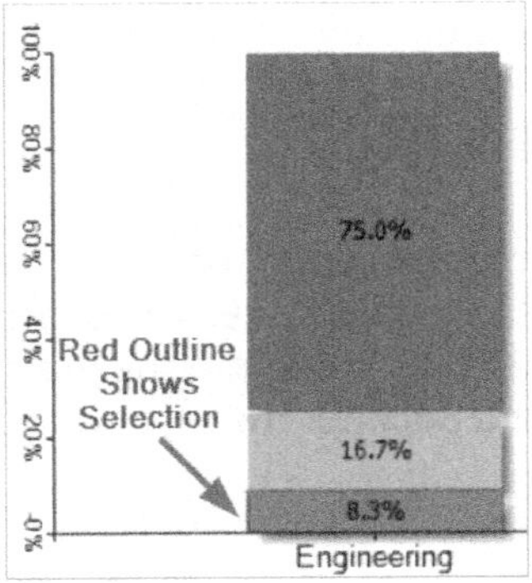


**Figure 12–30**

- Hold <Ctrl> and click multiple chart elements to select multiple chart elements and act on those elements using the context menu, as shown in Figure 12–31.

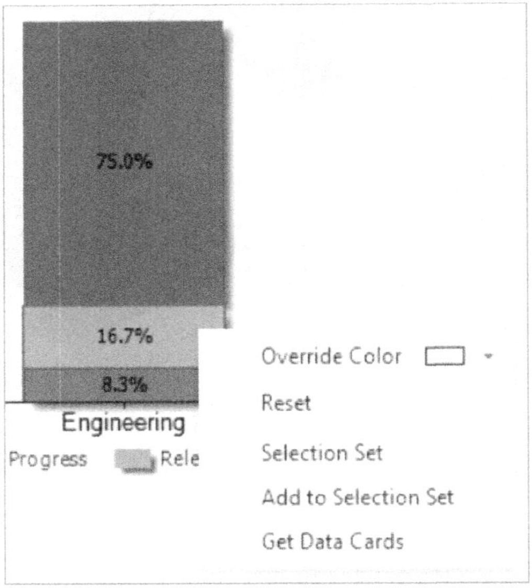


**Figure 12–31**

- Double-click on different chart elements to separate them from the chart. When **Map Data** is toggled on or the data mapping is refreshed, the selected pieces are mapped on the model, as shown in Figure 12–32.

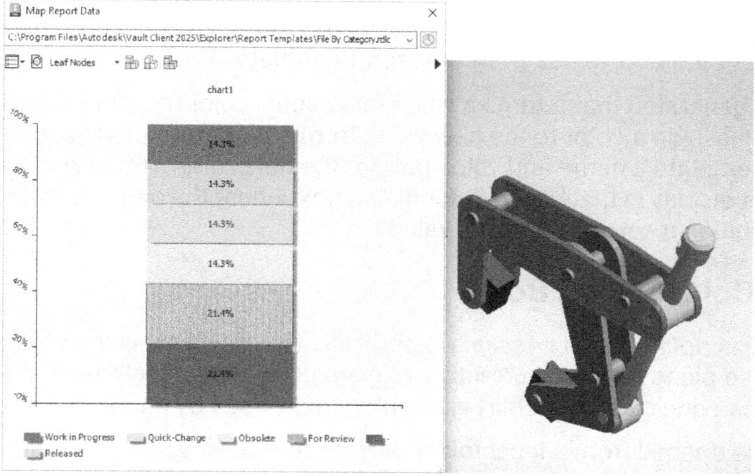


**Figure 12–32**

- Once a selection is made, click **Clear Color Mapping** or **Isolation** to update the data mapping or to update the isolation.

*Note: Changes to element selection and color overrides are not mapped onto the model until you update the mapping.*

## Chart Context Menu

A context menu provides additional options for manipulating mapped data and customizing the view.

| Command | Definition |
|---|---|
| **Override Color** | Enables you to specify a different color for a chart element. |
| **Reset** | Removes a color override. |
| **Selection Set** | Creates a selection set from the components corresponding to the selected chart elements. The corresponding components are selected in the browser and the canvas. |
| **Add to Selection Set** | Includes the components corresponding to the chart element to the current selection set. |
| **Get Data Cards** | Retrieves data cards for each of the currently mapped components. |

 

# Managing Data Mapping Reports

The report management feature enables the administrator to assign colors to values in a report template. When the template is used by the report generation feature in the CAD application, the colors are automatically assigned to their associated values. The administrator can also remove unused or outdated values from the report template.

When a report is generated that returns a value for which a color has not yet been assigned, the report control will assign a color to the new value from a predetermined list of colors and write back the report template a name and value pair for the new color. The new value and default color assignment display in the *Assign Color* dialog box, where the administrator can update the template by assigning a color to this new value.

## The Assign Color Dialog Box

When a template is opened in the *Assign Color* dialog box, the chart elements contained in the template are listed along with the currently assigned color for each element. If the template contains more than one chart, the chart elements are grouped by chart.

Templates can be opened from a local folder or from Autodesk Vault. The *Value* column will be populated with the names of chart elements only if a report has already been generated. If no report has been generated, the fields in the *Value* column are blank.

By default, the *Assign Color* dialog box displays a default palette of eight colors. Unless specified in the template, the colors are assigned to chart elements in this order:

- Grey
- Red
- Orange
- Yellow
- Light Green
- Cyan
- Blue
- Violet

You can enter the exact chart element name in the *Value* field and then select a color to assign that color to the chart element. Remember to save the template to commit the changes.

## How To: Manage Report Templates

1. In the *Tools* menu, select **Administration>Vault Settings**.
2. In the *Vault Settings* dialog box, select the *Behaviors* tab.
3. Select **Define** under *Report Management* to open the *Assign Color* dialog box.
4. From the *File* menu, open a report template from either the vault or a local folder.

   ***Note:*** *If the template is stored in the vault and the administrator has write-permission on the current file, the template is checked out of the vault.*

5. If the template does not contain any custom color properties, the default color palette displays. If the custom color properties have already been added to the template, the value names are extracted and displayed with their assigned color in the dialog box. Any new values without an assigned color display with the next available color in the default list.
6. Do one of the following:
   - Specify a new color assignment for an existing property by selecting a new color in the *Color* field.
   - Enter the exact value name for a new property in the *Value* field.
   - Select a color to assign to the property from the *Color* field.
7. Select **File>Save** to commit the changes. If the template was checked out of the vault, it is checked back in after being saved.

# Practice 12b
# Map Your Data

In this practice, you learn to generate a report based on your model's data and map report data to the open model.

## Task 1: Create a full report.

1. If required, start Autodesk Vault. Log in using the following information:
   - For *User Name*, enter **administrator**.
   - Leave the *Password* field blank.
   - For *Vault*, select **Data Card and Mapping Vault**.
2. In the *Navigation* pane, click **Project Explorer ($)**.
3. Click **Find** in the toolbar.
4. In the *Find* dialog box, search for **Clamp.iam**.
5. Right-click on **Clamp.iam** and select **Open** to launch it in Autodesk Inventor, as shown in Figure 12–33.

**Figure 12–33**

6. In the Autodesk Vault ribbon, click **Data Mapping**, as shown in Figure 12–34.

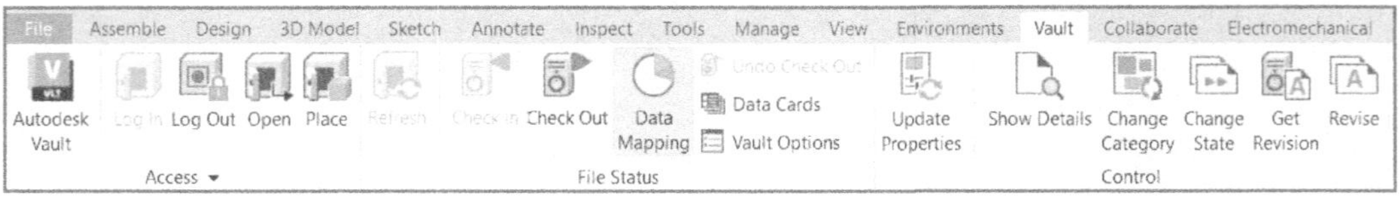


**Figure 12–34**

7. The *Map Report Data* dialog box opens. Select **Open Local Template** from the *Select Report Template* drop-down list, as shown in Figure 12–35.

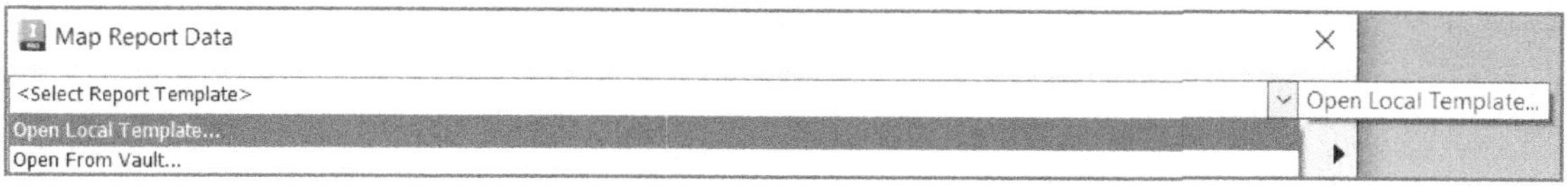


**Figure 12–35**

8. Navigate to *C:\Program Files\Autodesk\Vault Client edition\Explorer\Report Templates* and select the **File By Category.rdlc** report template.

   ***Note:*** *If you receive a warning indicating the template is read-only, a workaround is to check in the File By Category.rdlc template file to the vault and use the Open from Vault command instead of Open Local Template.*

9. Click **Open**.
10. In the *Map Report Data* dialog box, click **Generate Report**.
11. A bar graph report displays in the *Map Report Data* dialog box, as shown in Figure 12–36. The graph shows a percentage breakdown of files in each category based on state. The available states in the example below are **Work in Progress**, **Quick-Change**, **For Review**, **Released, Obsolete**, or **-** (no state).

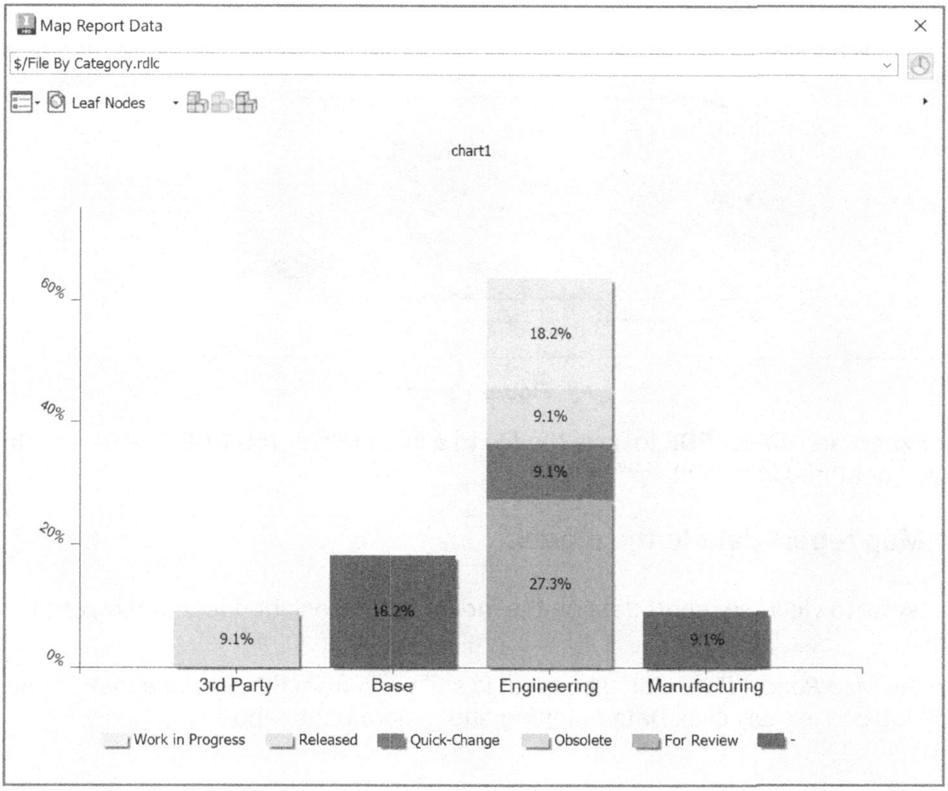


**Figure 12–36**

12. Click **View Full Report** to see the report in printable format, as shown in Figure 12–37.

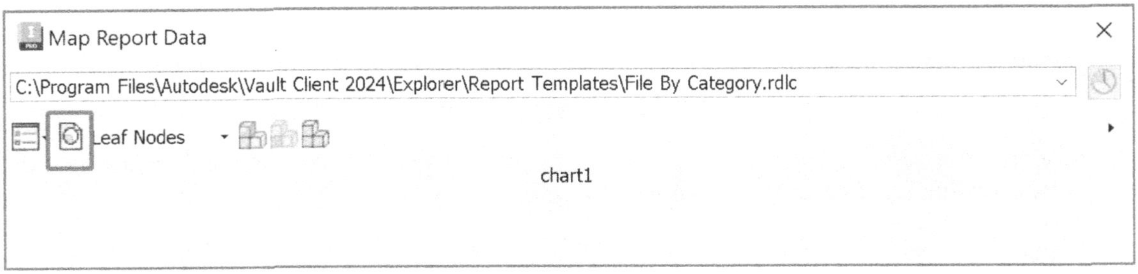


**Figure 12–37**

The report automatically launches in Microsoft Viewer, as shown in Figure 12–38.

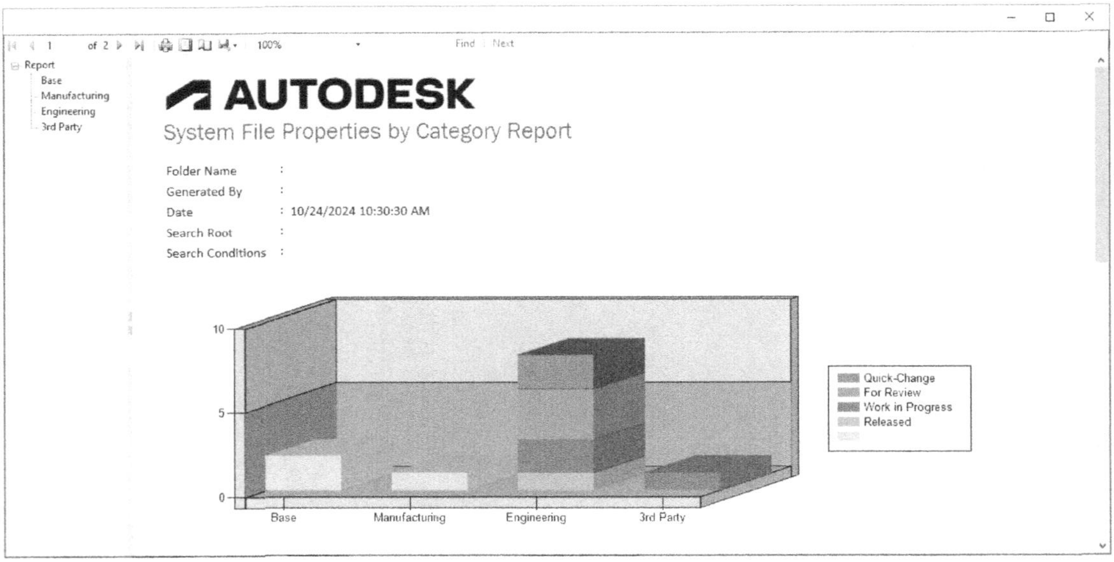


**Figure 12–38**

13. Click **Export** and select **PDF** to save the file to a local folder as a PDF. The file can then be emailed or stored in a vault.

## Task 2: Map report data to the model.

It can be useful to view the report data on the model for an easier understanding of the state of the design.

1. Go to the *Map Report Data* dialog box that is still open from the previous task. If you closed the dialog box, simply click **Data Mapping** and generate the report once more.

2. Click **Apply Color Mapping** to map the report data to the model in its entirety, as shown in Figure 12–39.

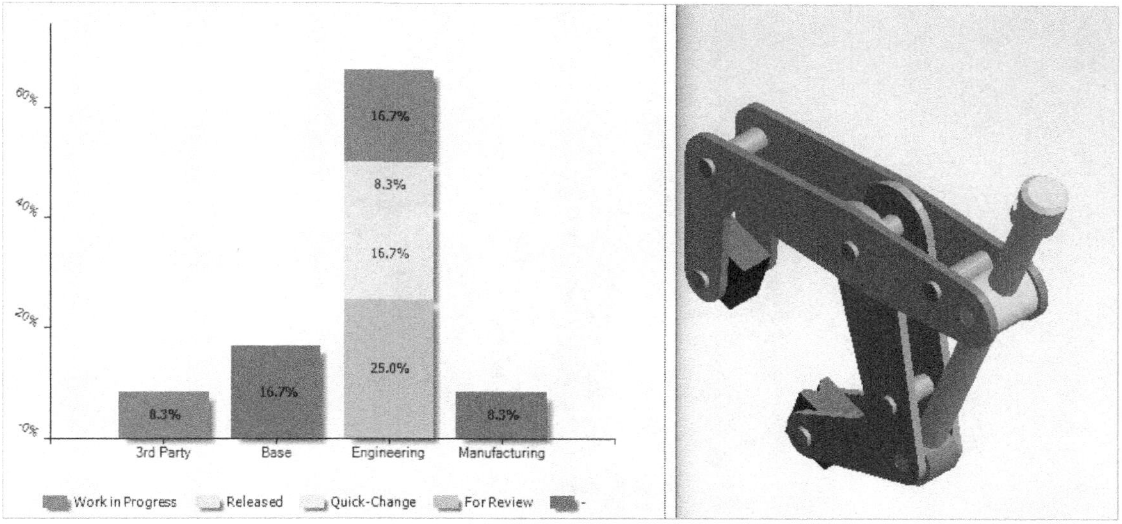


**Figure 12–39**

- By examining the model and referencing the Map Report legend, you can determine the state of each component. For example, the **Lower_Plate.ipt** is in the **For Review** state.

3. In the *Map Report Data* dialog box, double-click on the **For Review** section of the Engineering bar.
4. In the *Map Report Data* toolbar, click **Apply Isolation** to show only the For Review pieces in the model shown in Figure 12–40.

**Figure 12–40**

5. Examine the components in the **Released** and **Quick-Change** states shown in Figure 12–41. In the *Map Report Data* dialog box, double-click on the **Released** and **Quick-Change** pieces as well.

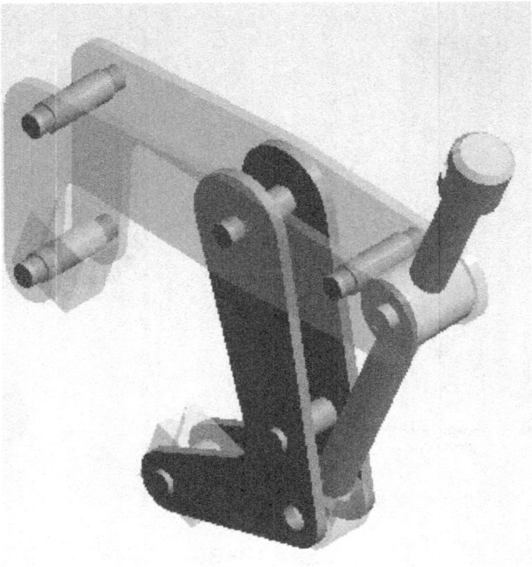

**Figure 12–41**

- The components are mapped on the model and all other components are transparent.

**End of practice**

# 12.3 Sheet Set Manager Integration

Autodesk Vault Professional integrates with the AutoCAD Sheet Set Manager (SSM) for supported AutoCAD products. This integration enables you to add, access, and modify the sheet sets to Vault. You can also access and modify sheet sets in a collaborative environment. In addition, users can rely on up-to-date Vault status on sheet drawings in Sheet Set Manager.

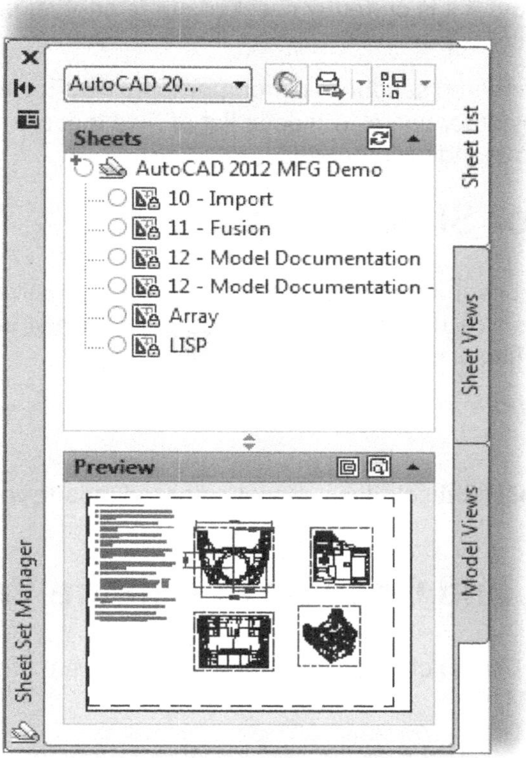


Figure 12–42

Vault also supports all sheet set functionality, including property management, plotting, and publishing tasks. In Vault Explorer, you can use search capabilities to find sheets and sheet sets based on properties inside the sheet set manager. Sheets are represented as files in the Vault which gives you the relationship between sheets and associated drawings.

Once you start working on a sheet set in a Vault environment, there are some changes to how certain Sheet Set commands work.

# Resave All Sheets

When you work on a sheet set with Vault, you are working in a collaborative environment. When you resave all sheets, note the following differences:

- When working in a shared sandbox environment, you can **Resave All** as long as none of the sheets/files involved is currently checked out by other users. The **Resave All** command gets aborted if there are files that cannot be checked out and, therefore, saved. A file might not be available for check out if it is currently checked out to another user or if vault constraints restrict access to the file.
- When working in a non-shared sandbox environment, you can **Resave All** even if some of the files are checked out by other users. You get a list of files that are not available for saving when the sheet set command is completed.

# Remove Sheet or Sheet Subset

When you remove a sheet or subset from a vaulted sheet set, its equivalent vaulted copy is NOT removed automatically. As a result, if you were to reuse the same sheet or sheet subset name, you are informed that the files already exist in the Vault.

> ***Note:*** *Historical references from sheets or sheet set files are lost when they are removed with Vault Explorer.*

If the removed sheet or sheet subset files are expired or redundant, you can remove them via Vault Explorer.

# Move, Rename, and Copy Design in the Vault Client

**Move**, **Rename**, and **Copy Design** changes made in the Vault Client are ignored when you open the edited sheet set in SSM.

Chapter 13

# Administering Autodesk Vault Professional

This chapter describes how to manage the Autodesk® Vault Professional software. You will learn about configuring items, configuring and mapping item properties, and configuring change orders.

## Learning Objectives

- Create units and categories, create new item numbering schemes, and create custom objects.
- Set up change orders, including routing lists, user-defined properties, and change order numbering.

# 13.1 Configuring Items

This section describes how to configure items. You learn how to create units and categories, create new item numbering schemes, and change lifecycle rules.

All of the workflows described in the chapter are accessed from the *Vault Settings* dialog box shown in Figure 13–1. This dialog displays by selecting **Administration>Vault Settings** from the *Tools* menu. You will need to be logged in as an Administrator to complete these workflows.

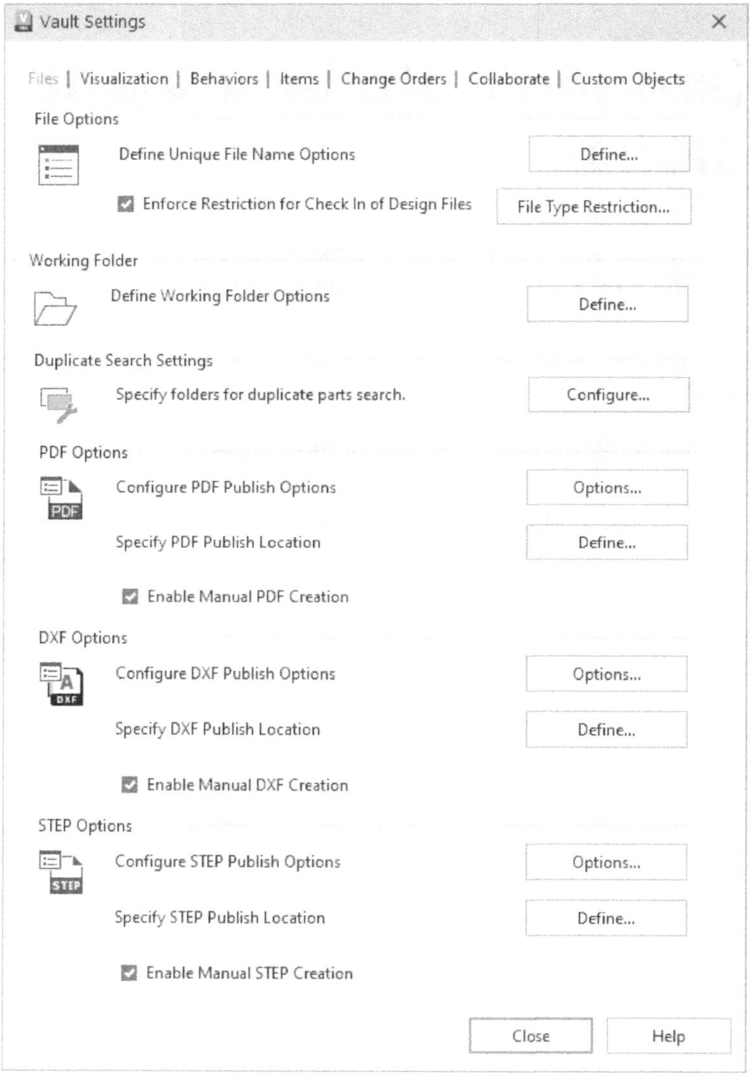


**Figure 13–1**

# Units of Measure

Every item is assigned a unit type. You can create new unit types if the supplied units do not meet your company's requirements. Figure 13–2 shows the complete set of units that ships with Vault Professional.

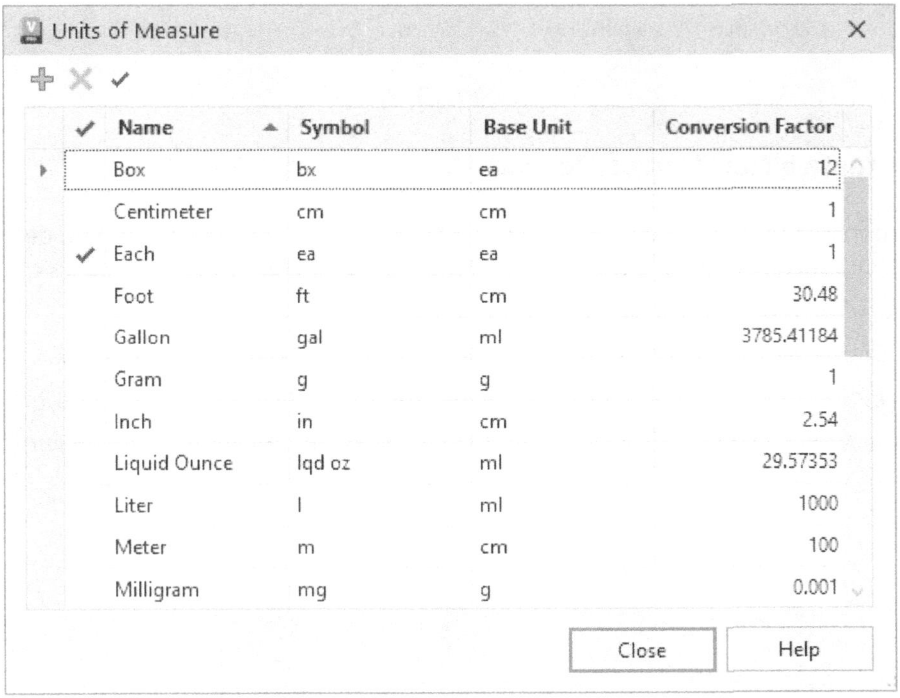


| ✓ | Name | Symbol | Base Unit | Conversion Factor |
|---|---|---|---|---|
| | Box | bx | ea | 12 |
| | Centimeter | cm | cm | 1 |
| ✓ | Each | ea | ea | 1 |
| | Foot | ft | cm | 30.48 |
| | Gallon | gal | ml | 3785.41184 |
| | Gram | g | g | 1 |
| | Inch | in | cm | 2.54 |
| | Liquid Ounce | lqd oz | ml | 29.57353 |
| | Liter | l | ml | 1000 |
| | Meter | m | cm | 100 |
| | Milligram | mg | g | 0.001 |

**Figure 13–2**

## About Units of Measure

Unit types define the units of measure for items. You use unit types to specify the quantity of an item in a bill of materials. Many items use a special unit type, such as each, when the number of required items is countable. Other items are assigned specific unit types, such as meters or grams, when a measurable quantity is required, rather than an item count. Several predefined unit types are supplied, but if those types do not meet your requirements, you can define new ones.

Each unit type is derived from a base unit and a conversion factor. For example, centimeters are the base unit for length and all length units are defined with respect to centimeters. You can create new base units if you cannot define the new unit from the existing base units.

 

Figure 13–3 shows the length units that are defined using the centimeter base unit. The conversion factor relates the unit to the base unit. For example, one inch is 2.54 centimeters and one foot is 30.48 centimeters.

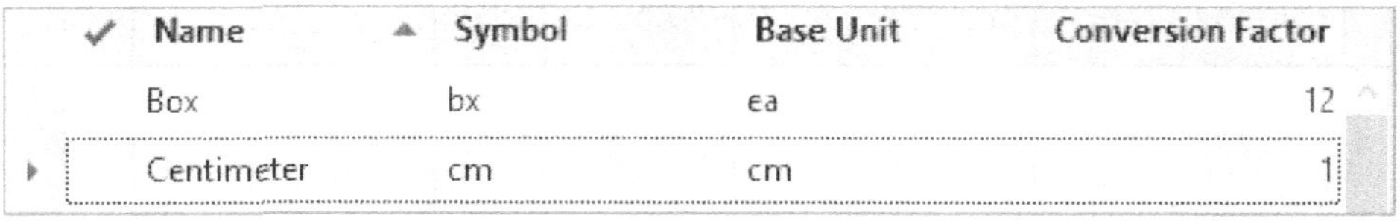


**Figure 13–3**

## How To: Create a New Unit of Measure

One of the items in your product's bill of materials is measured in kilograms. You define a new unit type to support this unit of measure. The new unit uses grams as the base unit.

1. In the *Vault Settings* dialog box, select the *Items* tab.
2. Select **Configure** in the *Units* group to display the *Units of Measure* dialog box.
3. In the *Units of Measure* dialog box, click **Plus sign** to display the *Add Unit* dialog box.
4. Enter the *Name*, *Symbol*, *Base Unit*, and *Conversion factor* information, as shown in Figure 13–4.

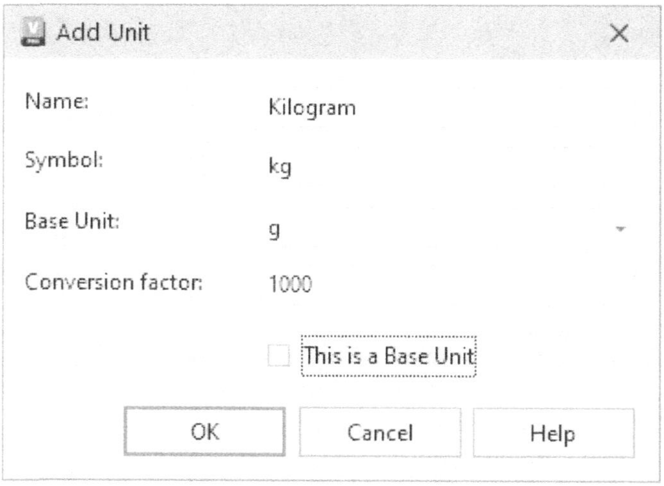


**Figure 13–4**

5. Click **OK** to close the *Add Unit* dialog box.
6. The *Units of Measure* dialog box displays the new unit, as shown in Figure 13–5.

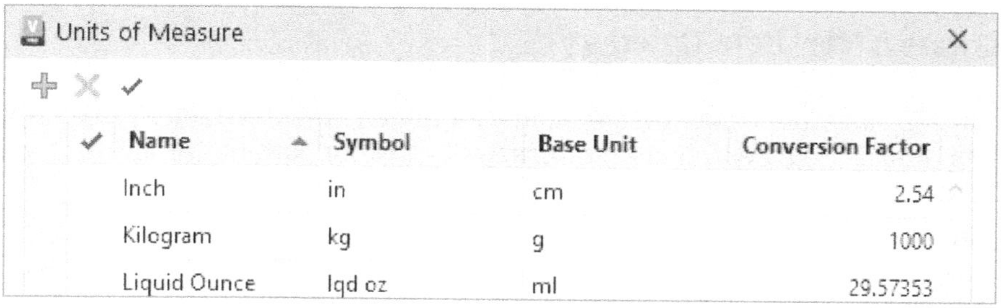


**Figure 13–5**

7. Click **OK** to close the *Units of Measure* dialog box.

# Item Categories

Every item has a category, such as Part, Assembly, or Product, which helps to identify the item. Some categories, such as Part, Assembly, and Purchased, are assigned automatically based on either the type of file or the CAD file's bill of materials (BOM). You assign other categories manually when you create items.

There are several predefined categories, as shown in Figure 13–6. If these do not match the categories you use, you can create new types to meet your requirements.

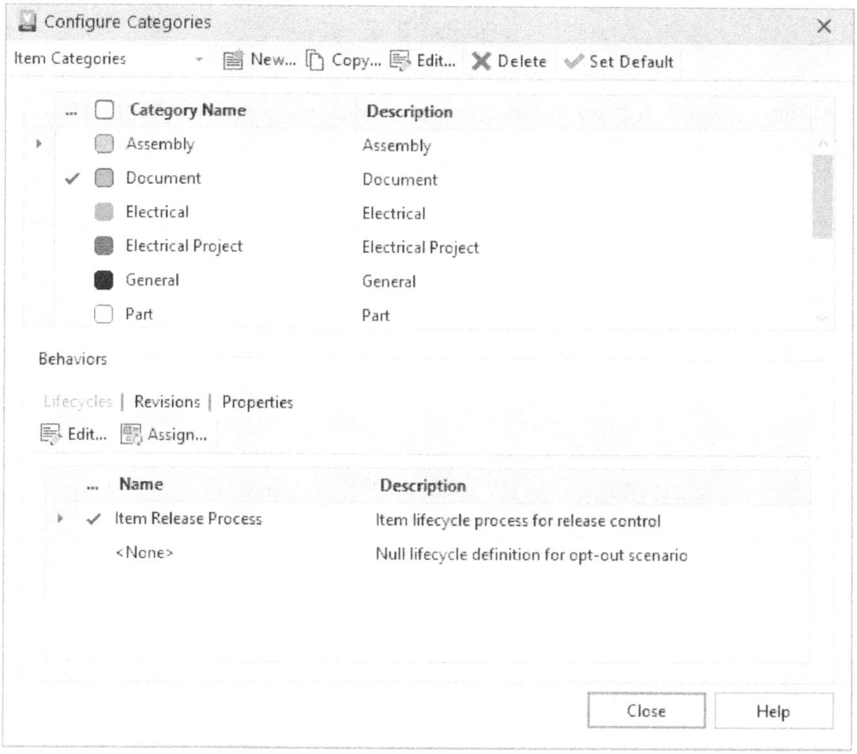


**Figure 13–6**

## How To: Create a New Item Category

Your company manufactures industrial machinery. Frames are often built by one division of the company then brought to a central area for assembly. In your current ERP system, you identify the frame as a weldment.

1. In the *Vault Settings* dialog box, select the *Behaviors* tab and select **Categories** in the *Categories* group to display the *Configure Categories* dialog box.
2. Select **Item Categories** from the drop-down list. The *Item Categories* display as shown in Figure 13–7.

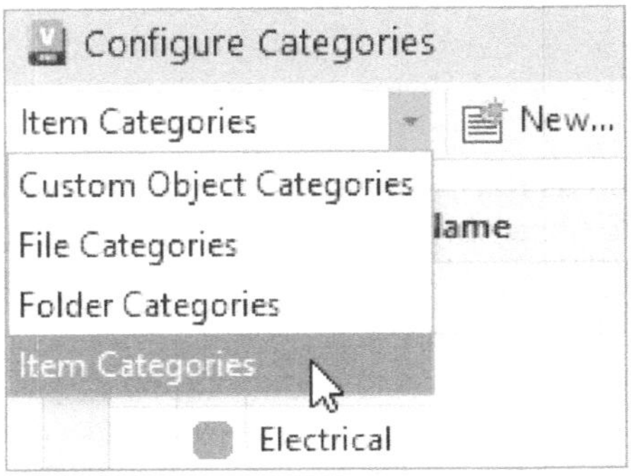


**Figure 13–7**

3. Select **New** from the toolbar to display the *Category Edit* dialog box. Enter the new item category name, pick a category glyph color, and optionally enter a description. Ensure that **Available** is selected, as shown in Figure 13–8.

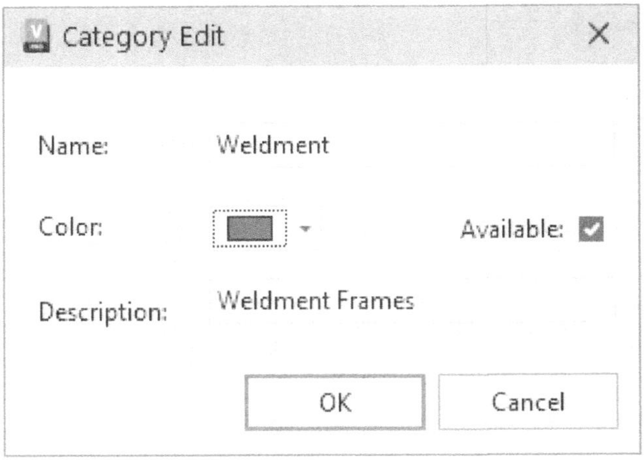


**Figure 13–8**

4. Click **OK** to close the *Category Edit* dialog box. The new item category is added to the list, as shown in Figure 13–9.

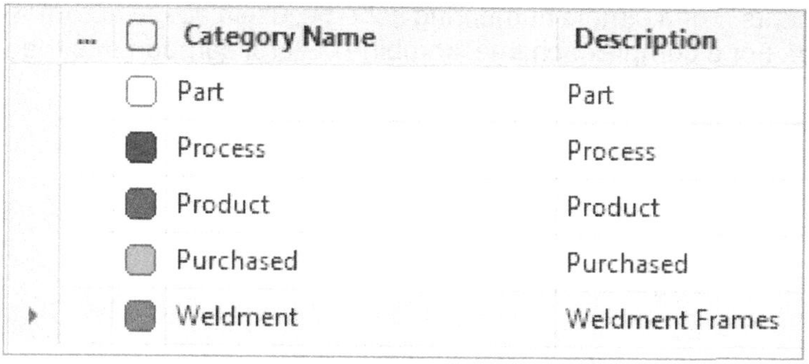


**Figure 13–9**

5. Optionally, assign a different lifecycle definition, a different revision scheme, and set of default properties to add to the item when it is created.
6. Click **Close** to dismiss the *Configure Categories* dialog box.

# Item Numbering Schemes

Item numbers (as shown in Figure 13–10) uniquely identify items. When you set up Vault Professional, create item-numbering schemes to match your company standards.

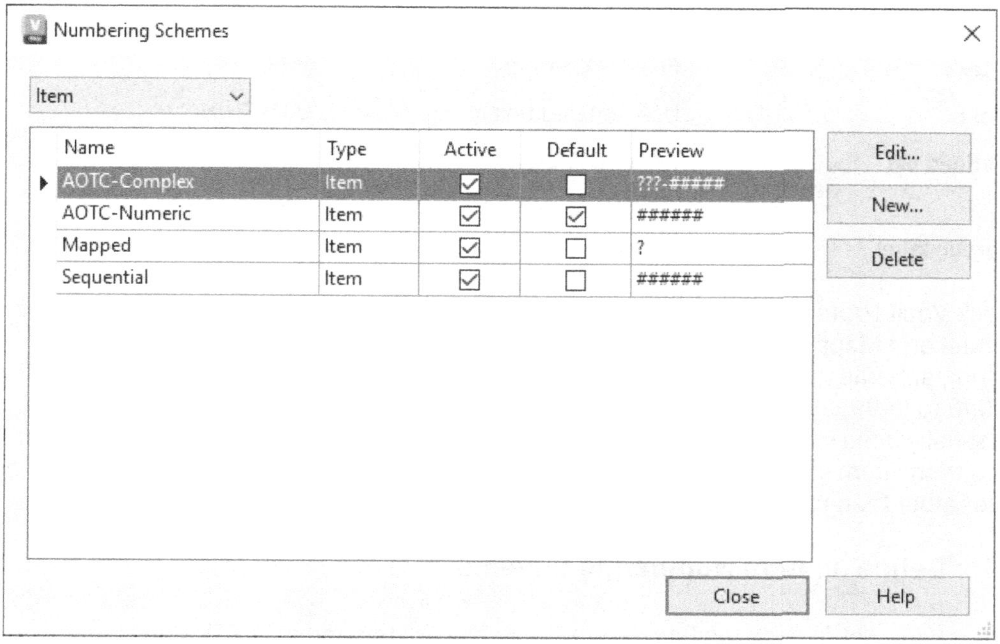


**Figure 13–10**

## Item Number Components

Item numbering schemes (as shown in Figure 13–11) can consist of one or more of the following components. For a simple numbering scheme, use a single automatically generated sequential number. For a complex scheme, combine several components together.

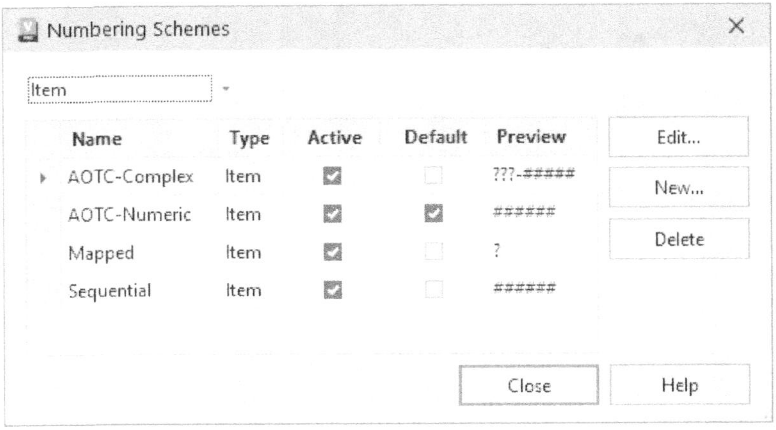


**Figure 13–11**

| Field type | Description | Examples |
|---|---|---|
| **Auto-generated sequence** | Sequential number | 100058 |
| **Delimiter** | Single character | - |
| **Fixed text** | Fixed text string | ABC |
| **Free text** | User-entered text string | ANYTHING |
| **Pre-defined list** | List of choices | FAST, STRU, ELEC, OTHR<br>100, 200, 300, 400, 500 |
| **Workgroup label** | Workgroup ID | WG1 |

Autodesk Vault Professional is shipped with predefined item numbering schemes named **Sequential** and **Mapped**. Neither scheme can be modified. The default **Sequential** item numbering scheme uses a single, automatically generated number that numbers items from 00000000 to 99999999. The **Mapped** item numbering scheme accepts a text string. It is automatically used when you assign an item to a file and the file contains a property that is mapped to the item's *Number* property. It is recommended that you define your own numbering scheme rather than using one of the supplied schemes.

### How To: Define an Item Numbering Scheme

1. In the *Vault Settings* dialog box, select the *Behaviors* tab and select **Define** from the *Numbering* group.

2. The *Numbering Schemes* dialog box opens. Select **Item** from the drop-down list to display the item numbering schemes, as shown in Figure 13–12.

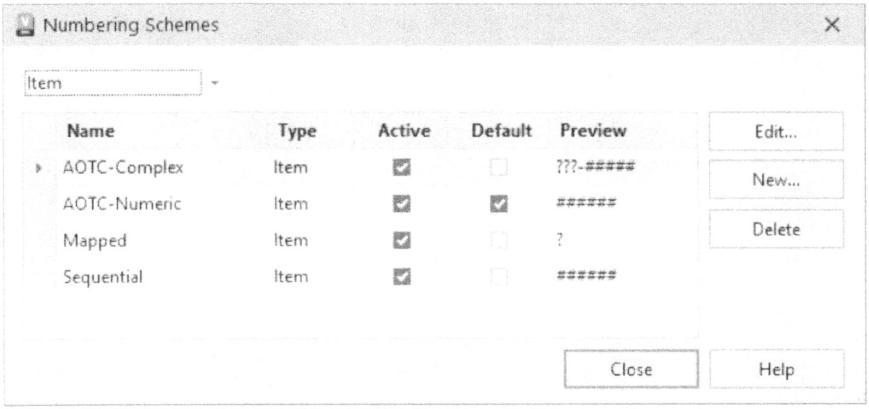


**Figure 13–12**

3. Click **New** to display the *New Numbering Scheme* dialog box. Enter a *Name* for the new numbering scheme and then select **New** in the *Fields* section, as shown in Figure 13–13.

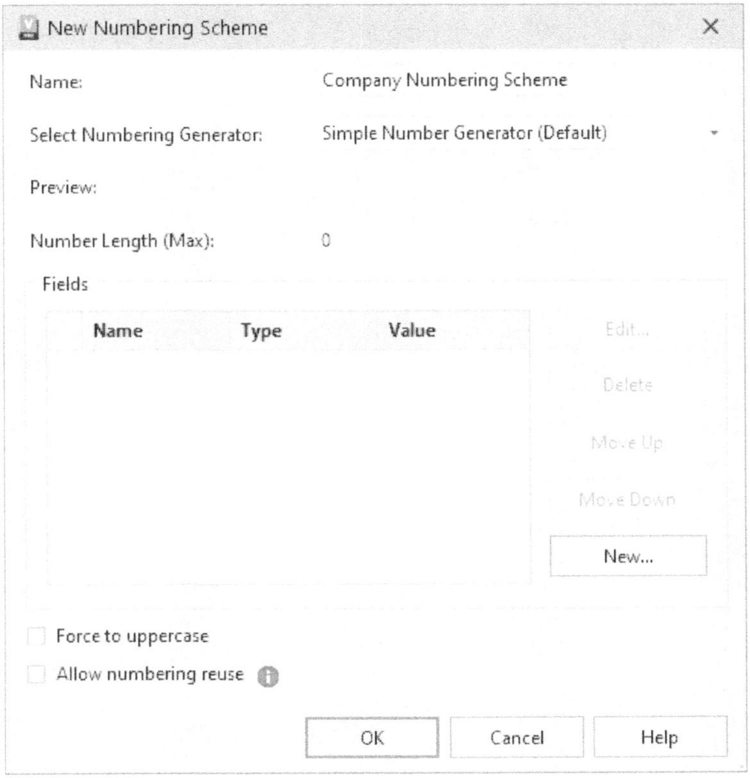


**Figure 13–13**

4. The *Add Field* dialog box opens. Create the first part of the numbering scheme. The example shown below (in Figure 13–14) contains a predefined list with list values 100, 200, and 300 representing Parts, Assemblies, and Purchased items.

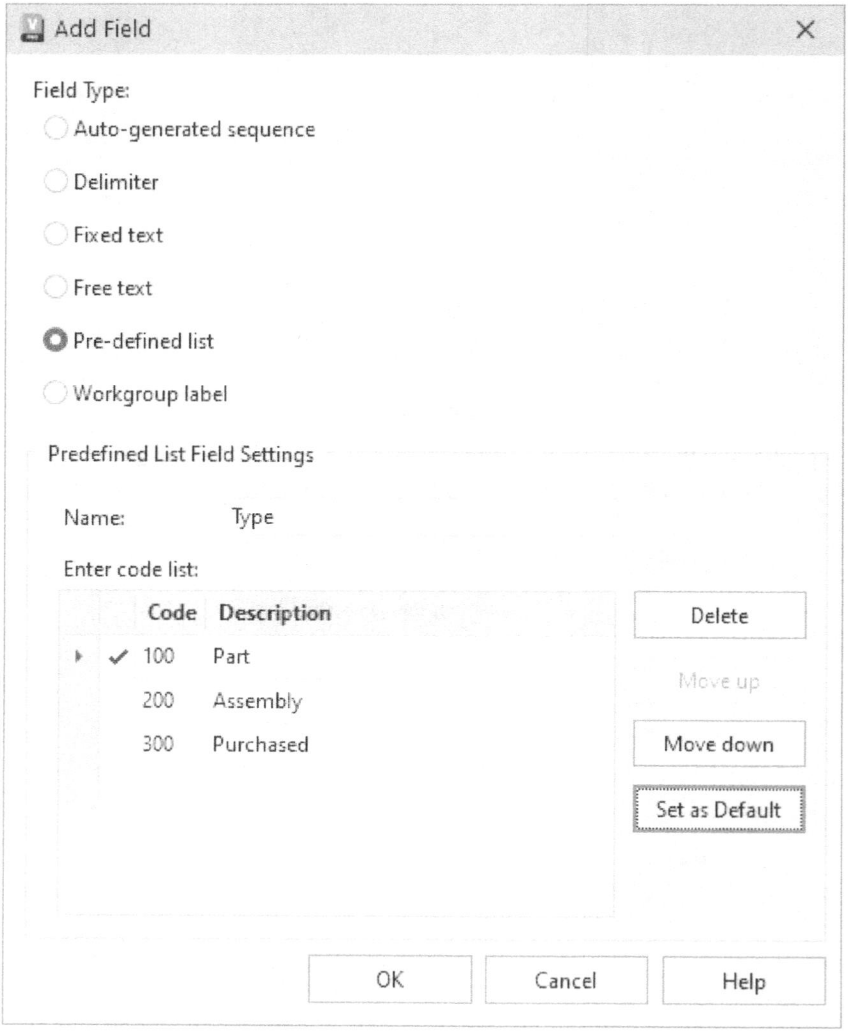


**Figure 13–14**

5. Click **OK** to close the *Add Field* dialog box, as shown in Figure 13–15. The first part of the sequence is shown in the *New Numbering Scheme* dialog box. Note the preview of how the number will look. Add two more parts to the sequence by repeating Step 4.

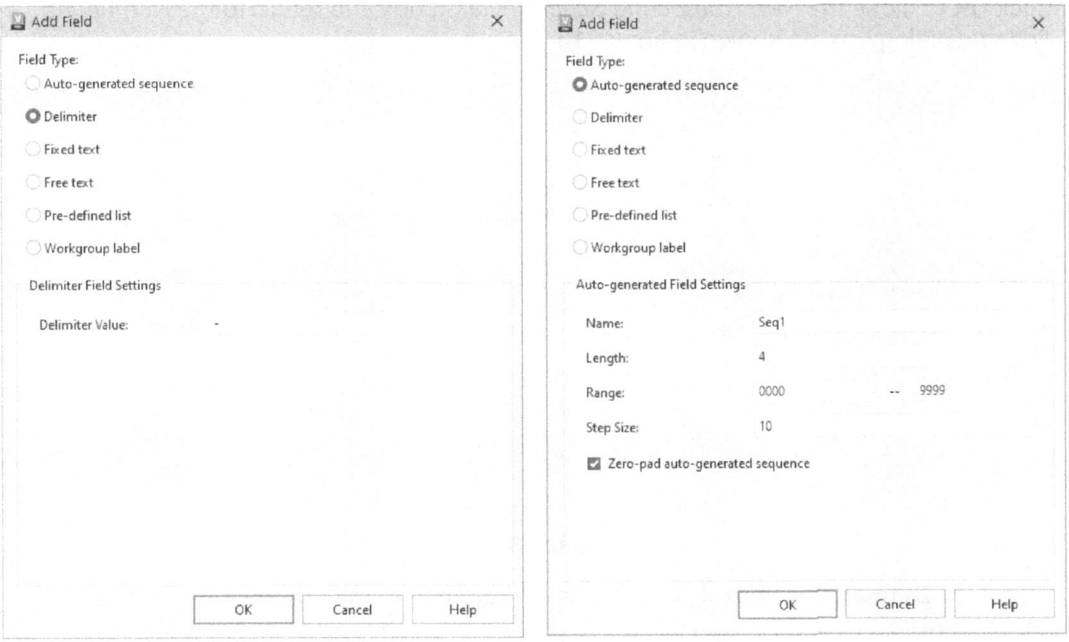


**Figure 13–15**

6. Return to the *New Numbering Scheme* dialog box (shown in Figure 13–16) to view the final sequence.

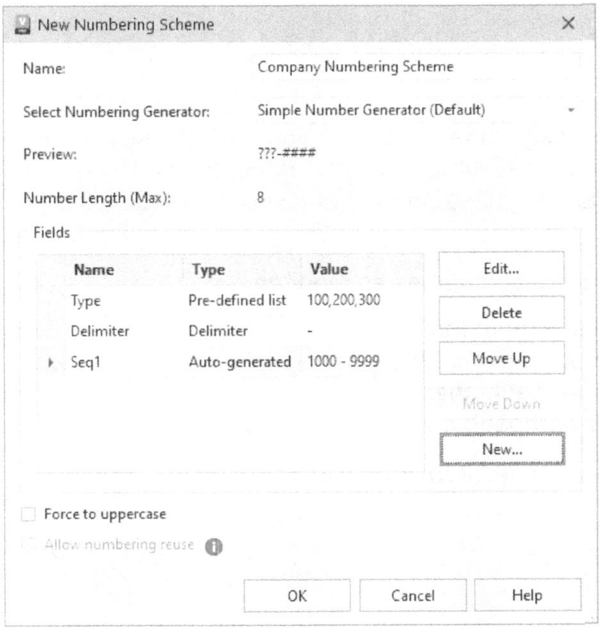


**Figure 13–16**

7. Click **OK** to close the *New Numbering Scheme* dialog box and return to the *Numbering Scheme* dialog box, as shown in Figure 13–17.

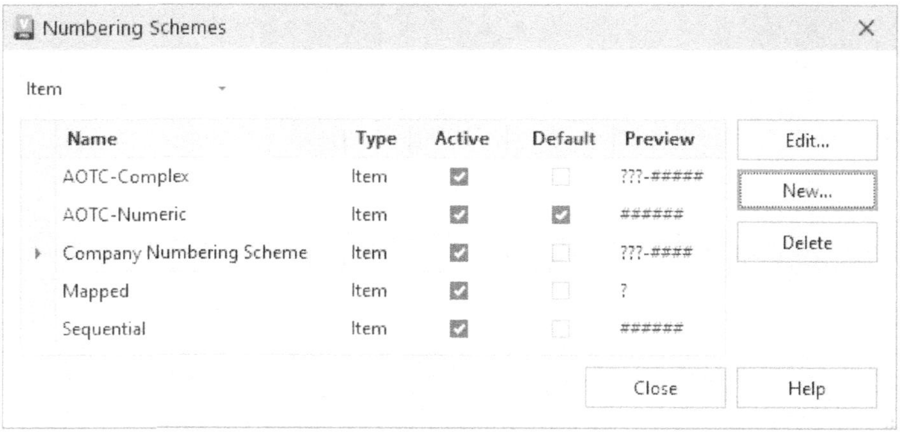


**Figure 13–17**

8. Select the **Default** checkbox if you want this to be the default numbering scheme.

Note that numbering schemes that require user input are not good choices for the default since in automated processes like Assign Item, there is no chance to prompt for the input. In this case, the number generated will always use the default value. You will be required to go back and edit the item if you want to use a different value.

## Guidelines

- Do not use one of the default numbering schemes.

  You should define your own numbering scheme rather than using the default, even if you want to use a simple sequential number. If you want to use a single sequential numbering scheme, start the first item number with a 1 rather than 0 (for example, use 1000001 rather than 0000001) because leading zeros might be suppressed when you share data with other applications.

- Create as many numbering schemes as required.

  You can create and use more than one item numbering scheme if required. For example, you might use a simple sequential numbering scheme for users who assign items. After the items are created, the ERP Manager can renumber items using a more complex scheme to make item numbers compatible with other company systems.

- Consider adding user-defined item properties to enhance searching.

Although complex numbering schemes can be used to identify categories using fields in the item number, you can also use item properties to group and sort items. Properties are more flexible and are more easily searched than complex item numbers. For example, if you use a complex item numbering scheme such as 100-ELEC-10345-545, consider using a simple scheme. Add user-defined properties to items to include the information that is inherent in the numbering scheme. You can search on the properties to find items and new or casual users will be able to better identify and locate items.

# Editing Lifecycle State Security for Files Associated with Items

By default, no security is enabled on files associated with items. You can apply an item's security to its associated files, customize the security for files associated with items, or clear security overrides on associated files.

### How To: Edit Lifecycle State Security for Files Associated with Items

1. In the *Vault Settings* dialog box, select the *Behaviors* tab. Select **Lifecycles** to display the *Lifecycle Definitions* dialog box.
2. Select the state from the *Lifecycle States* list and click **Edit**.
3. Select the *Security* tab.
4. Select the **Security for associated files of items** checkbox to enable security on associated files.
5. Select **Configure**.
6. In the *Security for Associated Files of Items* dialog box, select one of the following actions from the drop-down list:
    - **Apply item security to associated files:** When selected, the Access Control List settings for the item for this state are also applied to the associated file.
    - **Apply custom security to associated files:** When selected, administrators can set an Access Control List that is different from the one applied to the item for that state.
    - **Clear security override from associated files:** When selected, if there is a current override Access Control List on the associated file, the security override is removed when the item enters this state.
7. If you selected **Apply custom security to associated files**, add or remove members and roles, and then configure permissions.
8. Click **OK** to save your changes and return to editing state security.

# Item Revision Schemes

Autodesk Vault Professional includes several predefined revision numbering sequences, as shown in Figure 13–18. You can use one of the predefined sequences or create your own.

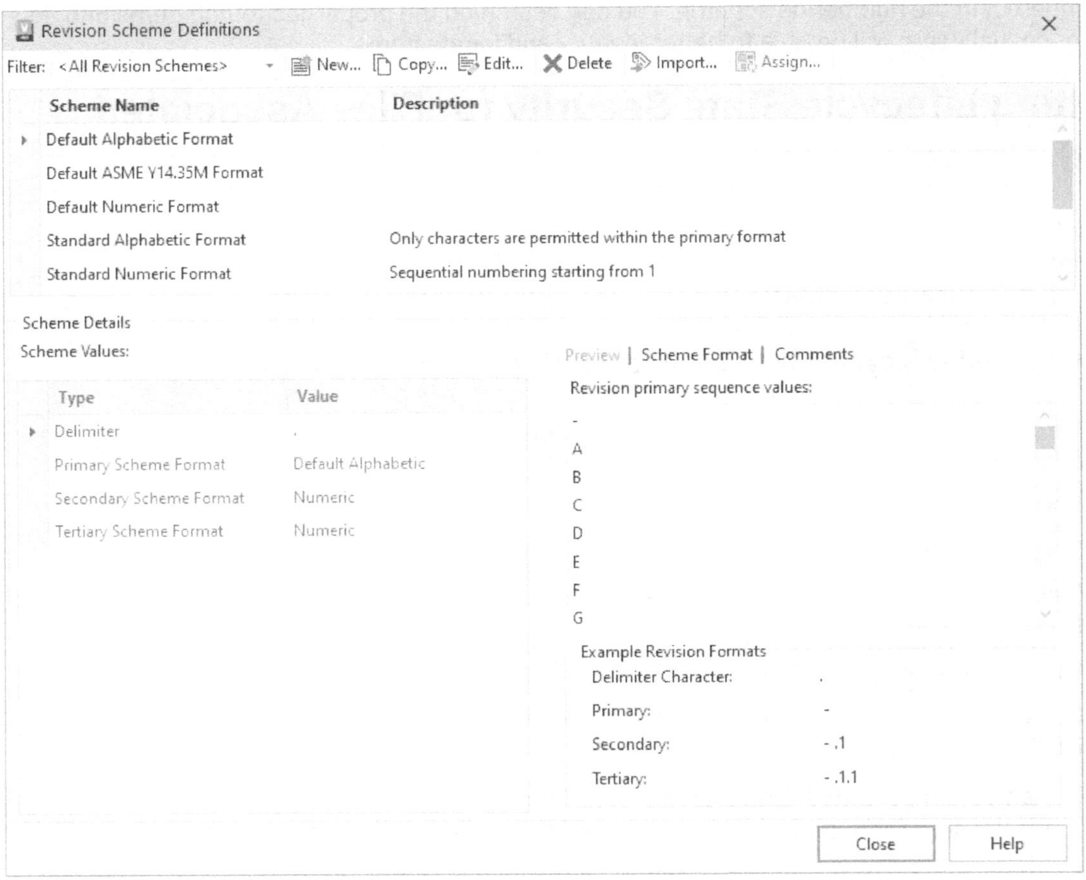


**Figure 13–18**

## How To: Configure Revision Numbering Sequences

The following steps show how to create a revision number sequence for items:

1. Before creating a new revision sequence, you must first create a text file that contains all of the revision numbers. When you specify a new revision, you must either enable the system to choose the next character in the sequence or manually specify a character that is the imported sequence. An example is shown in Figure 13–19.

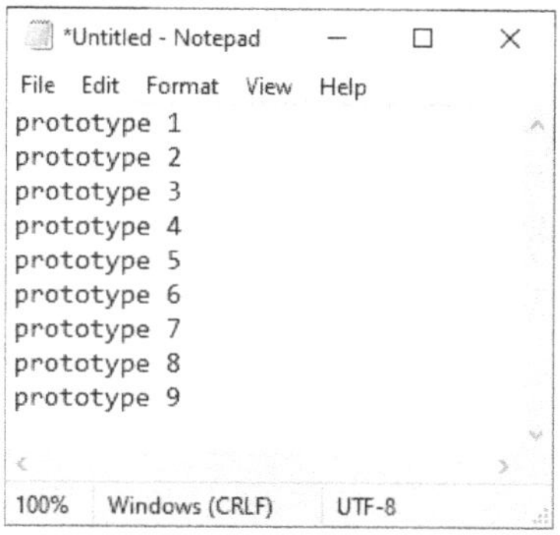


**Figure 13–19**

2. In the *Vault Settings* dialog box, select the *Behaviors* tab and click **Revisions** in the Lifecycle and Revisions section. Click **Import** to create a new revision scheme definition.
3. In the *Import* dialog box, specify the *Name* by browsing to the file. Enter a *Description* and select which of the item *Categories* to associate the revision scheme with, as shown in Figure 13–20.

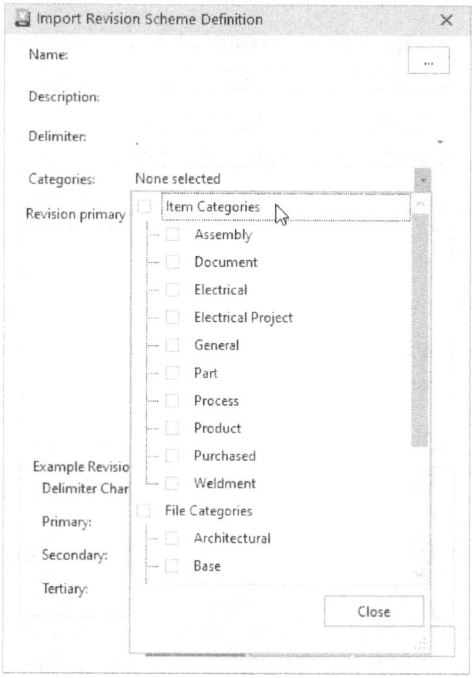


**Figure 13–20**

4. Click **OK** to close the *Import Revision Scheme Definition* dialog box and return to the *Revision Schemes Definitions* dialog box.
5. Click **Close** to close the *Revision Scheme* dialog box.

6. Close the *Vault Settings* dialog box.

# Item Watermarking Configuration

Item watermarks can automatically be generated based on:

- an item's lifecycle state,
- a specified item property, or
- customized text.

The default watermarks are based on the system lifecycle names. Administrators can configure the watermark style and position.

> ***Note:*** *If you customize the display name for a lifecycle state, then you should also change the default watermark.*

## How To: Configure an Item Lifecycle State Watermark

1. Select **Tools>Administration>Vault Settings**.
2. In the *Vault Settings* dialog box, select the *Items* tab.
3. In the *Watermarking* section, select **Lifecycle-based** from the drop-down list and select **Configure**.
4. In the *Lifecycle Watermarks* dialog box, select the lifecycle that you want to use for the state-based watermarks.

   > ***Note:*** *A lifecycle called Item Release Process is provided by the Autodesk Vault software.*

5. Select the lifecycle state for which you want to edit the watermark.
6. Click the ellipsis (...) in the *Watermark Text* column to open the *Watermark Text Entry* dialog box and edit the text of the watermark.
7. Perform one of the following steps:
   - Select the **Input text for display in the watermark** option to enter text of your choice for the watermark.
   - Select a property to display as the watermark from the Insert a property from below drop-down list.
   - Create a multi-line watermark by performing one of the two steps above and clicking **Plus (+)** to add it to the *Watermark Text Display* field. Use **Plus (+)** to add additional watermarks and **Minus (-)** to remove existing watermarks. You can also use the up or down arrows to arrange the order in which the watermarks display.
8. Click **OK** to close the *Watermark Text Entry* dialog box.

9. In the *Customize Watermarks* dialog box, select a location for the watermark from the *Location* drop-down list, as shown in Figure 13–21. The watermark can be placed:
   - Diagonally
   - Horizontally
   - In the Border

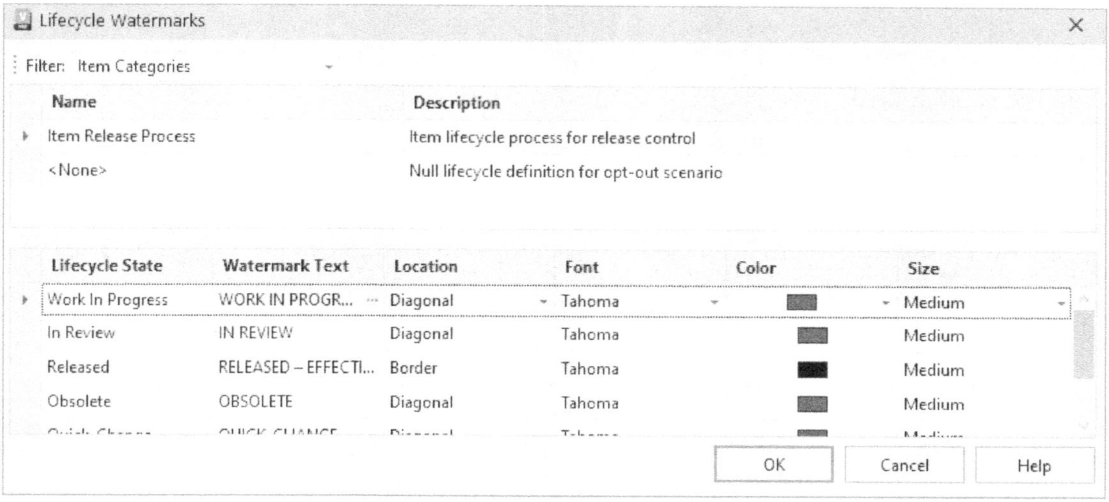


**Figure 13–21**

10. Select a font for the watermark from the *Font* drop-down list.
11. Select a color for the watermark from the *Color* drop-down list.
12. Select a size for the watermark from the *Size* drop-down list.
13. Click **OK**, and the watermark displays as shown in Figure 13–22.

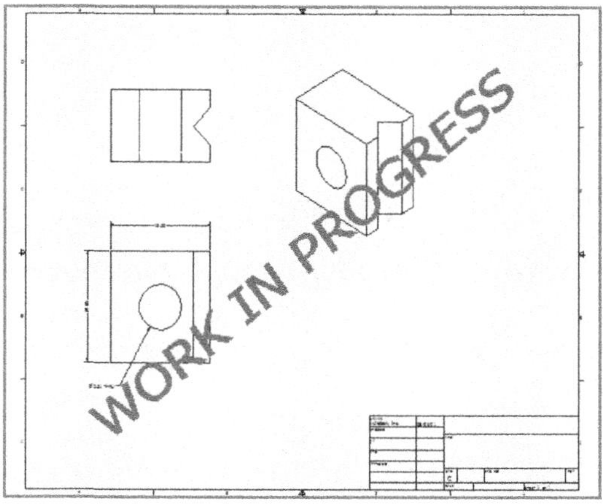


**Figure 13–22**

## How To: Configure a Property-Based Watermark

The watermark value is based on a specific item property that you set using the *Property-based Watermark Settings* dialog box.

> **Note:** *You are automatically prompted to identify an item property the first time you select this option.*

1. Select **Tools>Administration>Vault Settings**.
2. In the *Vault Settings* dialog box, select the *Items* tab.
3. In the *Watermarking* section, select **Property-based** from the drop-down list and select **Configure**.
4. In the *Property-based Watermark Settings* dialog box, select a property from which to draw the text for the watermark from the *Property* drop-down list (as shown in Figure 13–23).

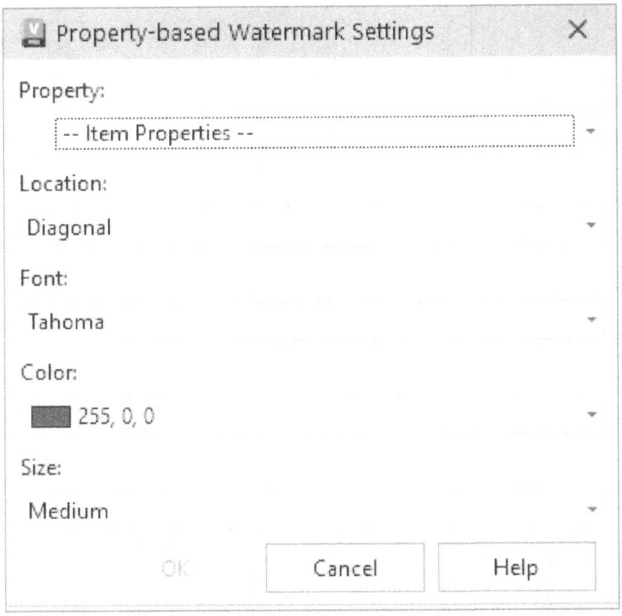


**Figure 13–23**

5. Select a location for the watermark from the *Location* drop-down list. The watermark can be placed:
   - Diagonally
   - Horizontally
   - In the border
6. Select a font for the watermark from the *Font* drop-down list.
7. Select a color for the watermark from the *Color* drop-down list.

8. Select a size for the watermark from the *Size* drop-down list.
9. Click **OK**.

## How To: Configure a Custom Watermark

The watermark value comes from a value you enter in the *Custom Watermark Settings* dialog box.

> **Note:** *You are automatically prompted to identify a text value for the watermark the first time you select this option.*

1. Select **Tools>Administration>Vault Settings**.
2. In the *Vault Settings* dialog box, select the *Items* tab.
3. In the *Watermarking* section, select **Custom** from the drop-down list and select **Configure**.
4. In the *Custom Watermark Settings* dialog box (shown in Figure 13–24), enter the text for the watermark in the *Text* field.

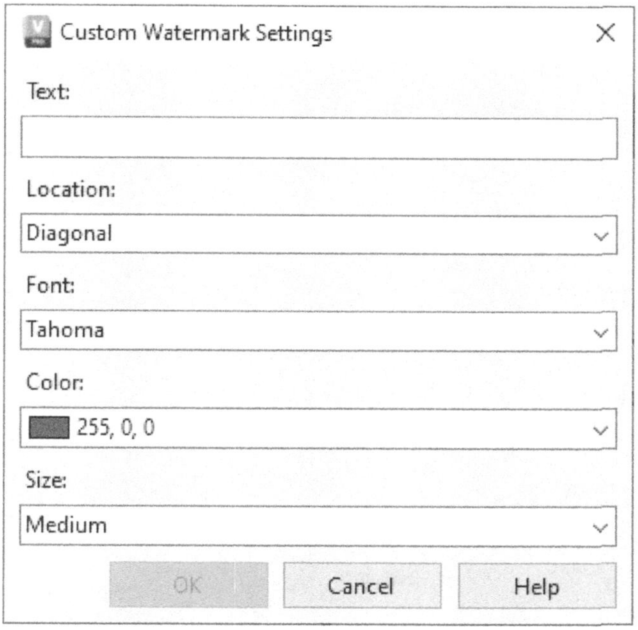


**Figure 13–24**

5. Select a location for the watermark from the *Location* drop-down list. The watermark can be placed:
   - Diagonally
   - Horizontally
   - In the border
6. Select a font for the watermark from the *Font* drop-down list.

7. Select a color for the watermark from the *Color* drop-down list.
8. Select a size for the watermark from the *Size* drop-down list.
9. Click **OK**.

# Assign Item Configuration

You can configure whether BOM rows are automatically displayed or hidden during item assignment.

## How To: Assign Item Configuration

1. Select **Tools>Administration>Vault Settings**.
2. In the *Vault Settings* dialog box, select the *Items* tab, as shown in Figure 13–25.

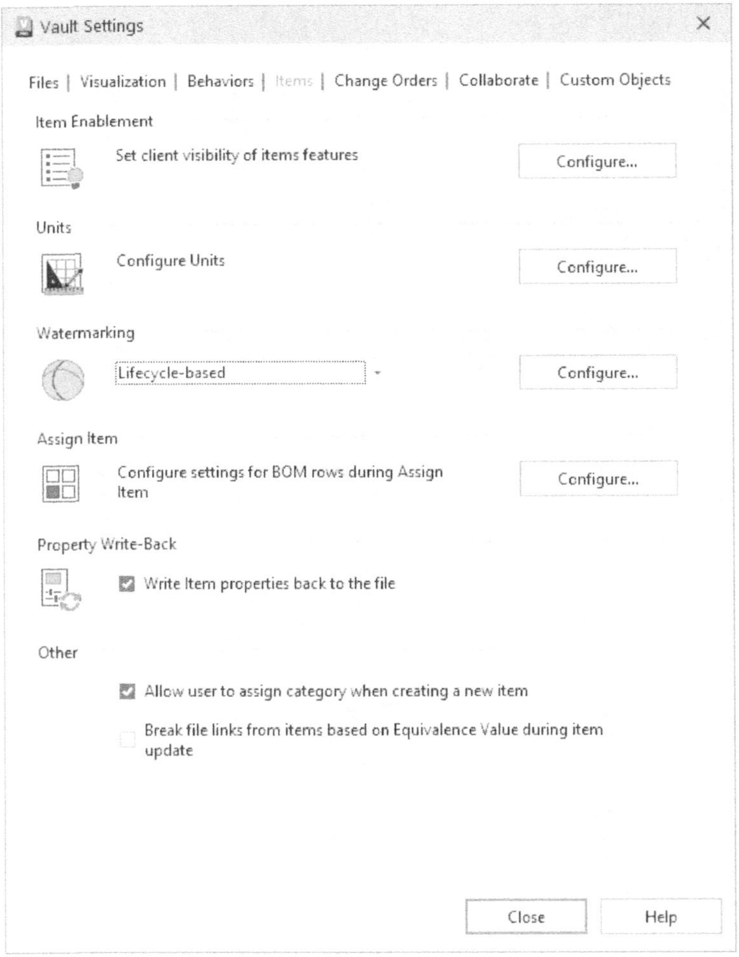


**Figure 13–25**

3. In the *Assign Item* section, select **Configure** to access the *Configure Assign Item* dialog box, as shown in Figure 13–26.

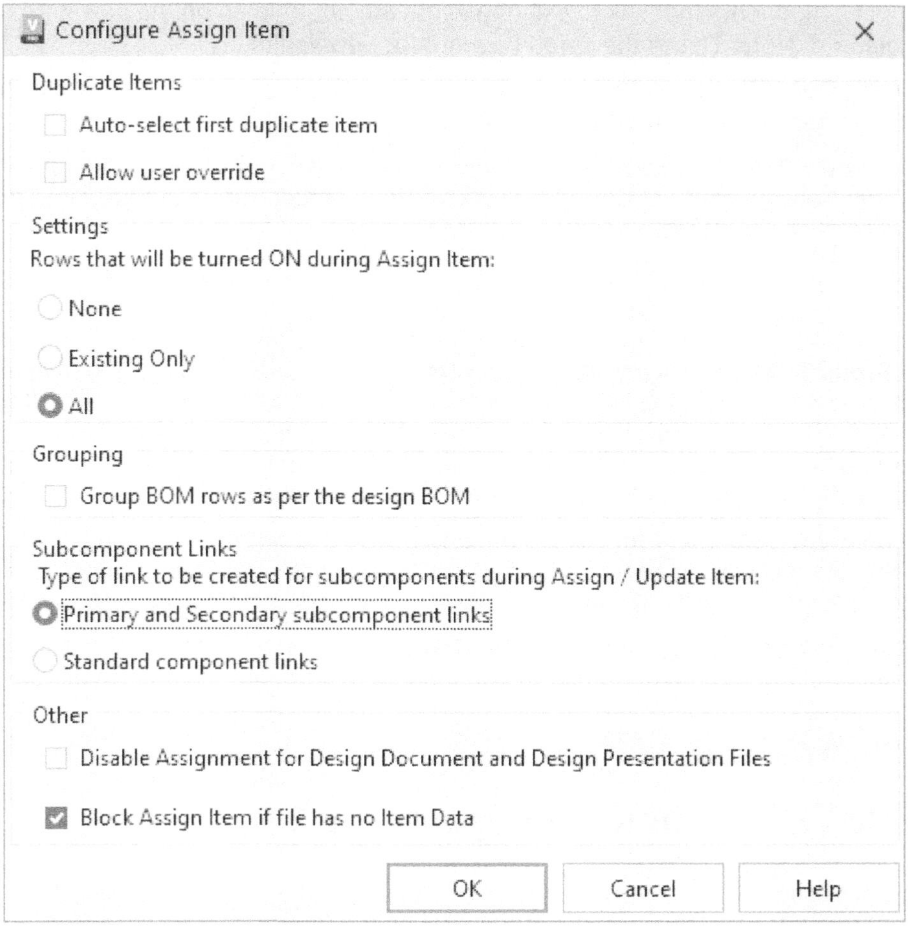


**Figure 13–26**

4. Select whether you want Vault to automatically select the first duplicate item in a list and assign it to the selected file. If you do not select this option, a new item is created instead. If this option is selected, child BOM components will attempt to link to an existing item using the *Equivalence Value* property.

   ***Note:*** *Standard components will always attempt to link to an existing item.*

5. Select the **Allow user override** checkbox if you want the user to be able to choose a duplicate item other than the one automatically selected by Vault.

6. If you want to configure how BOM rows are toggled on during item assignment, select one of the following options:
    - **None:** Components that link to existing items are not toggled on. All new item rows are toggled off. Note: This is the default setting for new vaults.
    - **Existing Only:** Components that link to existing items are toggled on. Components not linked to items remain as BOM components
    - **All:** Components that do not link to existing items have new items created for them. All new rows are toggled on. Note: This is the default setting for Vaults migrated from Vault 2014 or earlier releases.

    **Note:** *These rules apply until a row is linked to an item. Once a row has an item identified, rows are not toggled on or off during subsequent updates.*

7. Select **Group BOM rows as per the design BOM** if you want BOM rows merged or unmerged based on how the CAD application has them. If the checkbox is not selected, BOM rows are automatically merged, regardless of how the CAD application has them. For example, if Inventor has BOM rows unmerged and the checkbox is not selected, the rows are automatically merged in Vault regardless of how Inventor has them.
8. Select **Disable Assignment for Design Document and Design Presentation Files** if you want to disable the ability to assign item to design files such as .IDW files. If this option is checked, design files will only be linked to the items for which they represent.
9. Select **Block Assign Item if file has no Item Data** to prevent items from being assigned to CAD files that can have item data but do not yet have any. This option is selected by default.
10. Click **OK** to save your changes.

# Property Write-Back Configuration

By default, item properties are written back to the associated file from Vault add-ins, Vault Explorer, and the Job Processor. Item properties take precedence over file properties and mappings. If the file's properties are edited and properties are synchronized, the item properties will overwrite the file properties.

**Note:** *Editing and saving a property can result in an item property being written back to a file.*

You can manually synchronize properties on files associated with items.

**Important:** The **Write Item properties back to the file** checkbox on the *Items* tab must be selected (as shown in Figure 13–27) for item properties to be written back to a file.

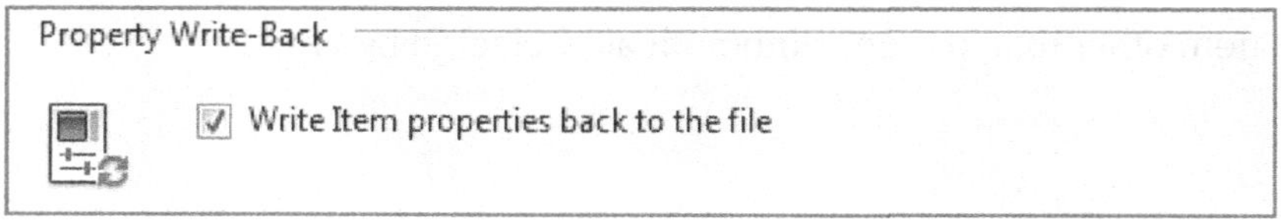


**Figure 13–27**

### How To: Synchronize Associated File Properties

1. In the *Item Master*, select the item for which you want to synchronize file properties.
2. Select the *General* tab in the preview if it is not already selected.
3. Right-click on the *Associated Files* section and select **Synchronize Properties**.
4. Item properties are written back to the associated file.

# Other Configuration

- Determine whether or not a user is able to assign a category to an item when the item is created. By default, this option is selected. Clear the **Allow user to assign category when creating a new item** option checkbox to disable this option.
- When the **Break file links from items based on Equivalence Value during item update** option is selected, Vault automatically breaks the link between an item and a file if the equivalence values do not match during an update of the item. This setting is off by default, as shown in Figure 13–28.

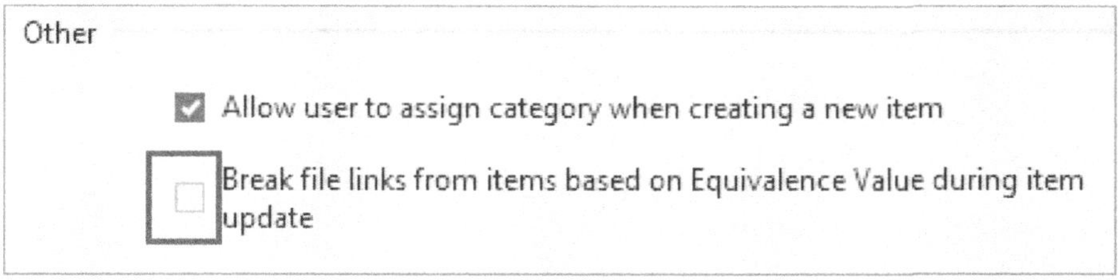


**Figure 13–28**

# Practice 13a
# Configure Items

In this practice, you create a new unit and new category, and configure an item lifecycle state name.

## Task 1: Configure units.

1. Start Autodesk Vault Professional and log in with the following information.
   - For *User Name*, enter **administrator**.
   - Leave the *Password* field blank.
   - For *Vault*, select **AOTCAdminVault**.
2. In the *Tools* menu, select **Administration>Vault Settings** (as shown in Figure 13–29) to display the *Vault Settings* dialog box.

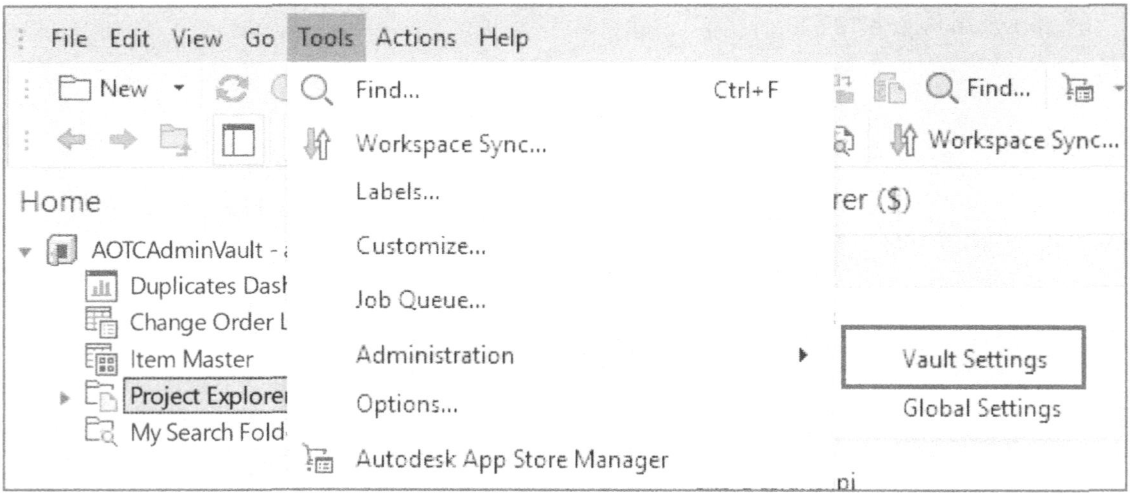


**Figure 13–29**

3. Select the *Items* tab.
4. Select **Configure** in the *Units* section to display the *Units of Measure* dialog box.
5. Click the **Plus sign** to display the *Add Unit* dialog box. This is where you will define the new unit for microns.

6. In the *Add Unit* dialog box, do the following, as shown in Figure 13–30:
   - For *Name*, enter **Micron**.
   - For *Symbol*, enter **um**.
   - For *Base Unit*, select **centimeters (cm)**.
   - For the *Conversion factor*, enter **.0001**.
   - Ensure that **This is a Base Unit** is unchecked.
   - Click **OK** to create the new unit.

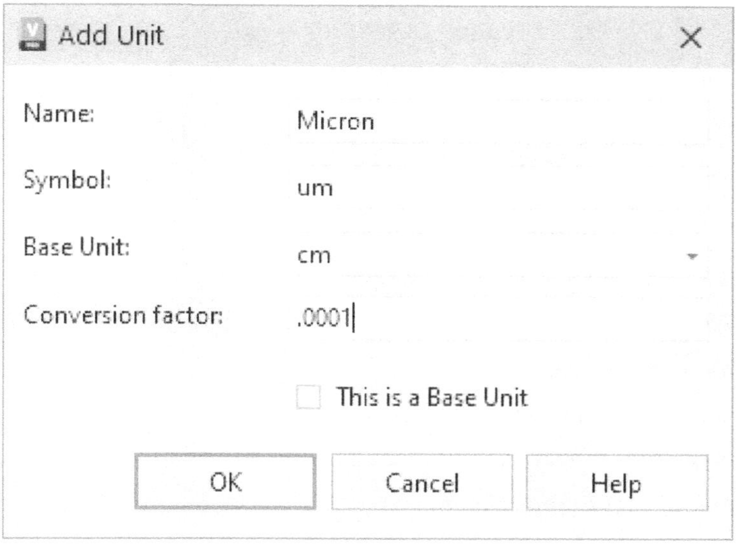


**Figure 13–30**

7. Confirm the new unit is added, as shown in Figure 13–31.

| Name | Symbol | Base Unit | Conversion Factor |
|---|---|---|---|
| Meter | m | cm | 100 |
| Micron | um | cm | 0.0001 |
| Milligram | mg | g | 0.001 |

**Figure 13–31**

8. Click **Close** to dismiss the *Units of Measure* dialog box and return to the *Vault Settings* dialog box.

## Task 2: Configure item category.

1. In the *Vault Settings* dialog box, select the *Behaviors* tab.
2. Select **Categories** in the *Categories* section to display the *Configure Categories* dialog box.
3. Select **Item Categories** from the drop-down list, as shown in Figure 13–32.

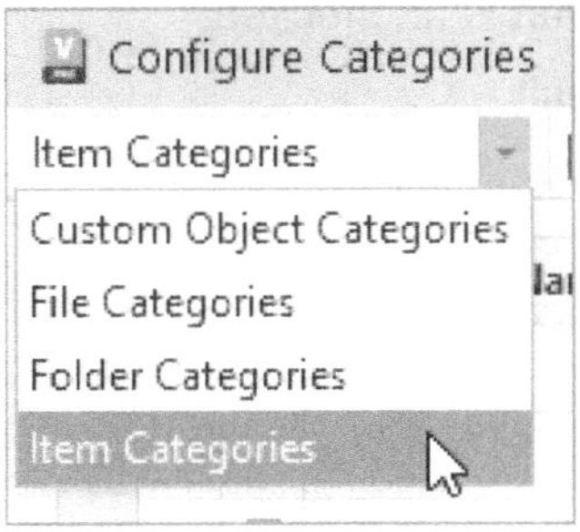


**Figure 13–32**

4. In the *Configure Categories* toolbar, select **New** to display the *Category Edit* dialog box.
5. In the *Category Edit* dialog box, enter the following information, as shown in Figure 13–33:
   - For *Name*, enter **Weldment**.
   - For *Color*, select a color of your choice.
   - Select the **Available** checkbox if not already enabled.
   - For *Description*, enter **Frame Weldments**.

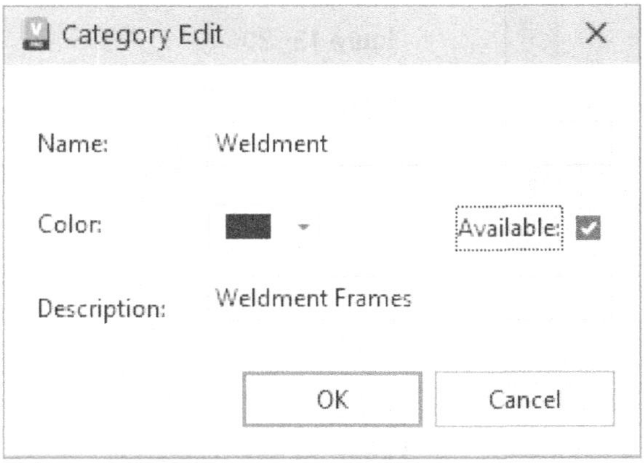


**Figure 13–33**

6. Click **OK** to close the *Category Edit* dialog box and return to the *Configure Categories* dialog box.
7. Click **Close** to close the *Configure Categories* dialog box and return to the *Vault Settings* dialog box.

## Task 3: Check lifecycle state transition action.

1. Select the *Behaviors* tab and select **Lifecycles** to display the *Lifecycle Definitions* dialog box.
2. Select **Item Release Process** and click **Edit**.
3. For the lifecycle state of **Work In Progress**, select the *Transitions* tab, as shown in Figure 13–34.

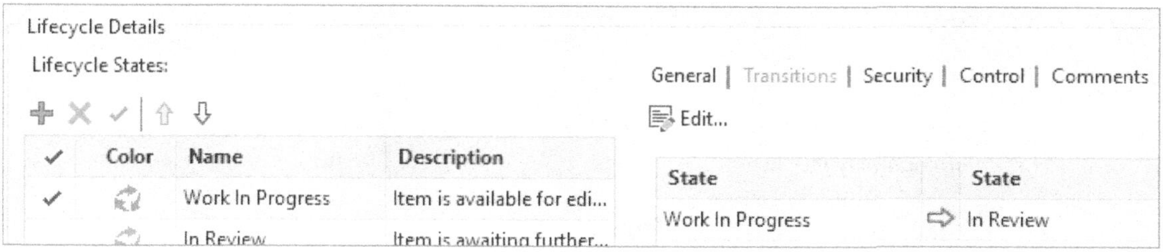


Figure 13–34

4. Select the row that has a *From State* of **Released** and a *To State* of **Work In Progress**, as shown in Figure 13–35.

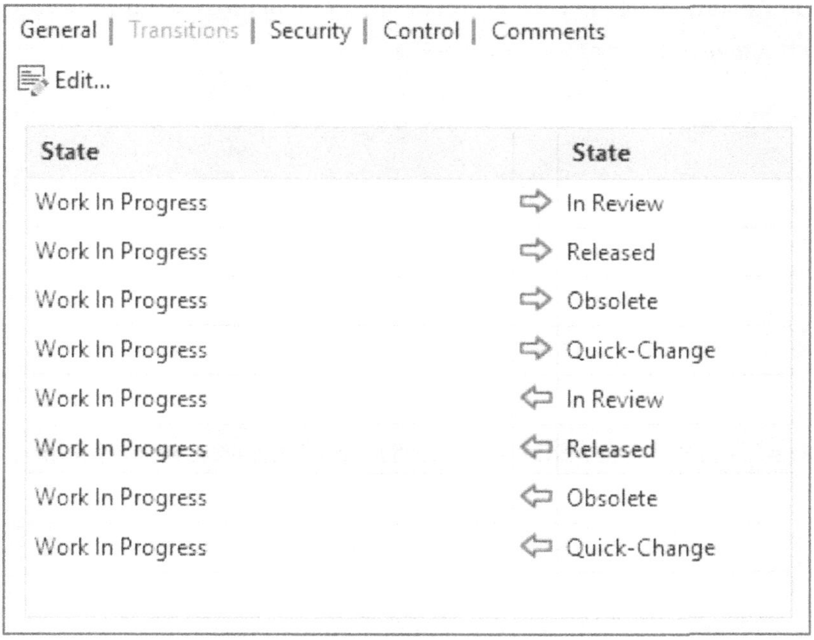


Figure 13–35

5. Click **Edit** and then the *Actions* tab to see the **Bump primary revision** action for this lifecycle state change, as shown in Figure 13–36.

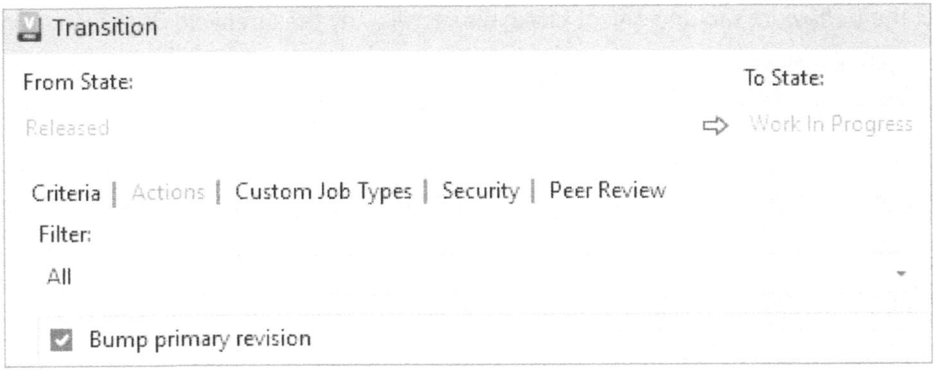


**Figure 13–36**

6. Click **OK**.

## Task 4: Configure item lifecycle state name.

1. Select the **In Review** lifecycle state and click the *General* tab, as shown in Figure 13–37.
2. Replace **In Review** with the string **For Review**.

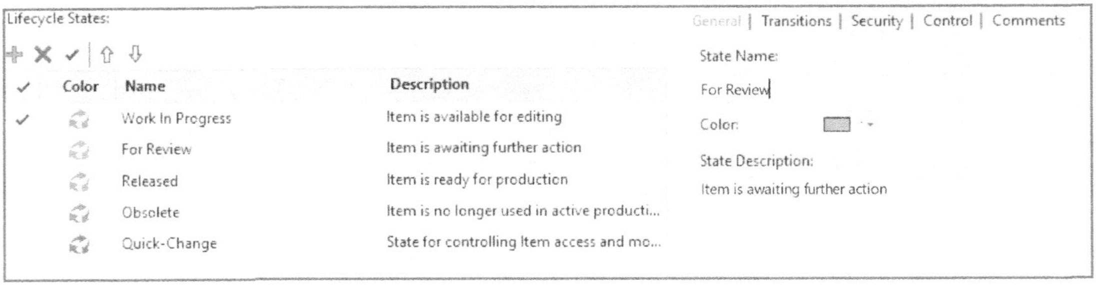


**Figure 13–37**

3. Click **OK**. The lifecycle state name is updated in the list, as shown in Figure 13–38.

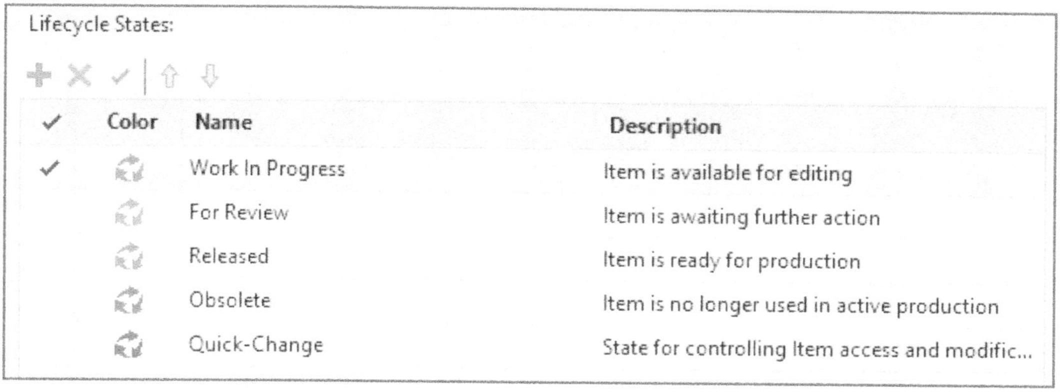


Figure 13–38

4. Click **Close**.

## Task 5: Configure watermarks.

1. Select the *Items* tab, and then in the *Watermarking* section, select **Configure** to display the *Lifecycle Watermarks* dialog box.
2. Select the row for the **For Review** lifecycle state.
3. Change the text to be consistent with the change. Click the button next to the *Watermark Text* **IN REVIEW** to display the *Watermark Text Entry – For Review* dialog box, as shown in Figure 13–39.

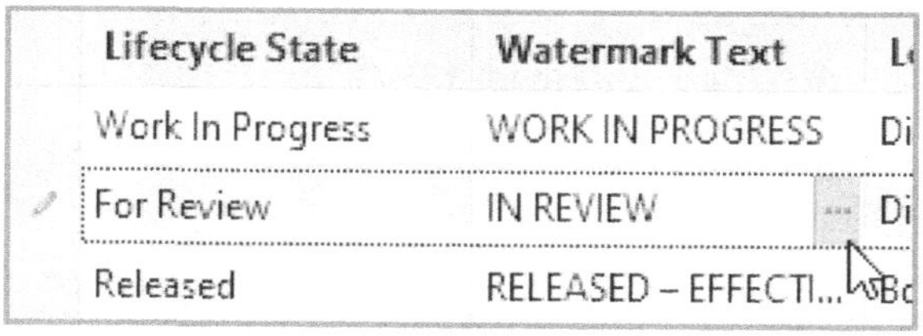


Figure 13–39

4. In the *Watermark Text Display* list, select the current text and then click the - (Remove) button (as shown in Figure 13–40) to remove it.

Figure 13–40

5. Select the **Input text for display in the watermark** radio button and enter the text **For Review**, as shown in Figure 13–41.
6. Click the **+** (Add) button to add this text to the list.

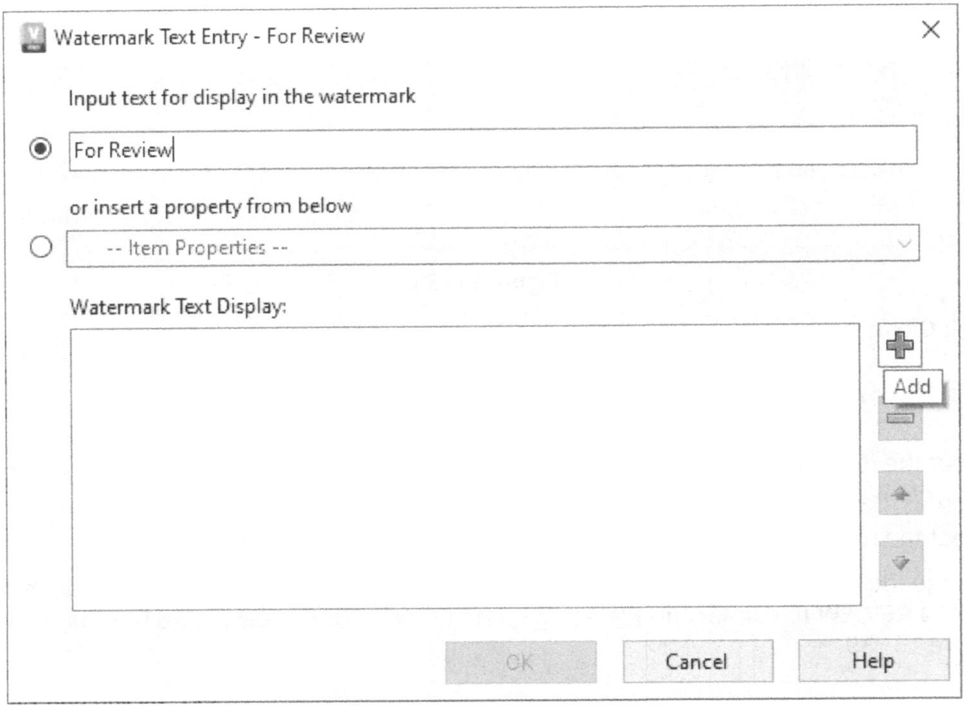


**Figure 13–41**

7. Click **OK** to dismiss the *Watermark text Entry – For Review* dialog box and return to the *Lifecycle Watermarks* dialog box.
8. Note the change in the *Watermark Text* for the **For Review** state shown in Figure 13–42.

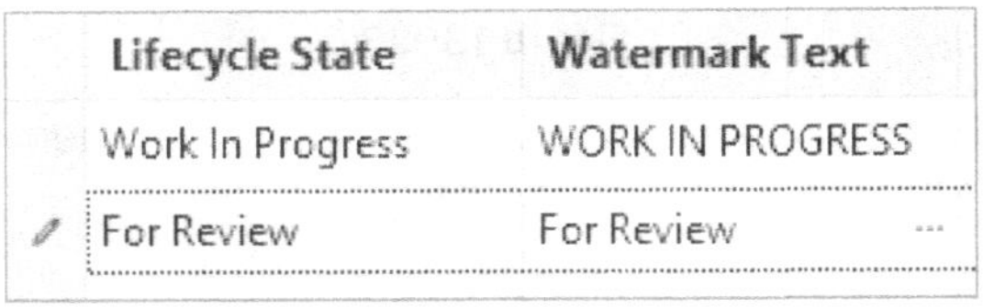


**Figure 13–42**

9. Click **OK** to close the *Lifecycle Watermarks* dialog box and return to the *Vault Settings* dialog box.
10. Click **Close** to close the *Vault Settings* dialog box.

**End of practice**

 

# Practice 13b
# Create Item Numbering Schemes

In this practice, you create two item numbering schemes. One scheme consists of a simple sequential number. The other is a more complex numbering scheme, with a list, delimiter, and sequential number. The completed practice is shown in Figure 13–43.

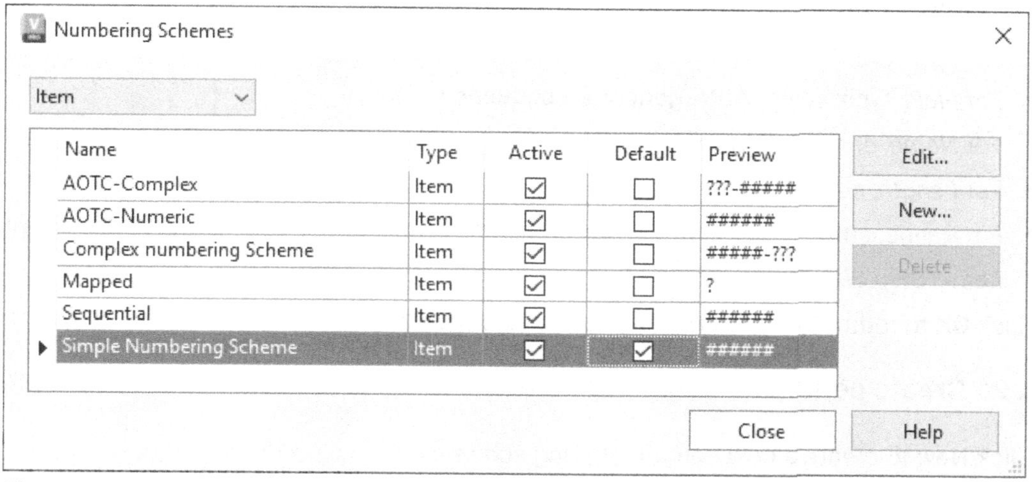


***The completed practice***

**Figure 13–43**

## Task 1: Create simple item numbering scheme.

1. Select the *Behaviors* tab in the *Vault Settings* dialog box.
2. In the *Numbering* section, select **Define** to display the *Numbering Schemes* dialog box.
3. In the *Numbering Schemes* dialog box, in the drop-down list, select **Item** (as shown in Figure 13–44) to display the item numbering schemes.

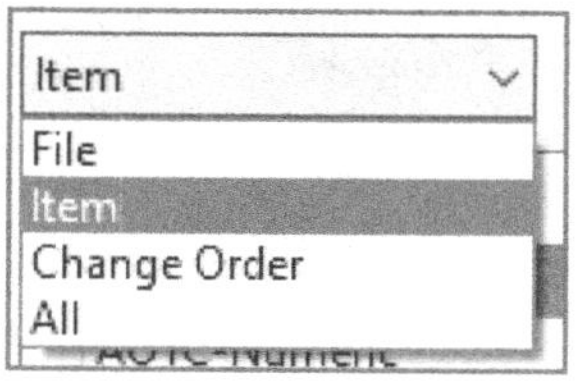


**Figure 13–44**

4. Click **New** to create a new item numbering scheme. The *New Numbering Scheme* dialog box displays.

5. In the *Name* field, enter **Simple Numbering Scheme**, as shown in Figure 13–45.

**Figure 13–45**

6. Click **New** to display the *Add Field* dialog box.
7. In the *Add Field* dialog box, do the following:
   - For *Field Type*, select **Auto-generated sequence**.
   - For *Name*, enter **Number**.
   - For *Length*, enter **6**.
   - For *Range*, enter **100001** for the starting number and do not change the ending number.
   - Leave *Step Size* at the default (**1**).
8. Click **OK** to return to the *Numbering Schemes* dialog box.

## Task 2: Create complex numbering scheme.

1. Click **New** to create a new item numbering scheme.
2. The *New Numbering Scheme* dialog box displays. In the *Name* field, enter **Complex Numbering Scheme**.
3. In this step, you will add an auto-generated sequence field to the new number scheme.
   a. In the *New Numbering Scheme* dialog box, click **New**. The *Add Field* dialog box displays.
   b. Click **Auto-generated sequence**.
   c. In the *Auto-generated Field Settings* area, fill out the information , as shown in Figure 13–46.

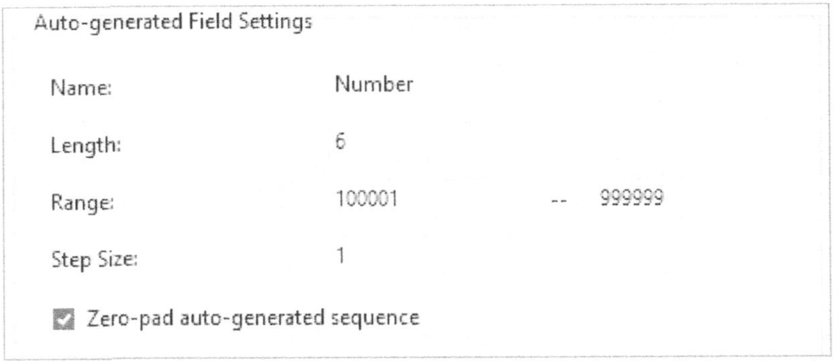


**Figure 13–46**

   d. Click **OK** to close the *Add Field* dialog box.

4. In this step, you will add a *Delimiter* field to the new number scheme.
    a. In the *New Numbering Scheme* dialog box, click **New**. The *Add Field* dialog box displays.
    b. Click **Delimiter**.
    c. In the *Delimiter Field Settings* area, in the *Delimiter value* field, enter **–** (hyphen), as shown in Figure 13–47.

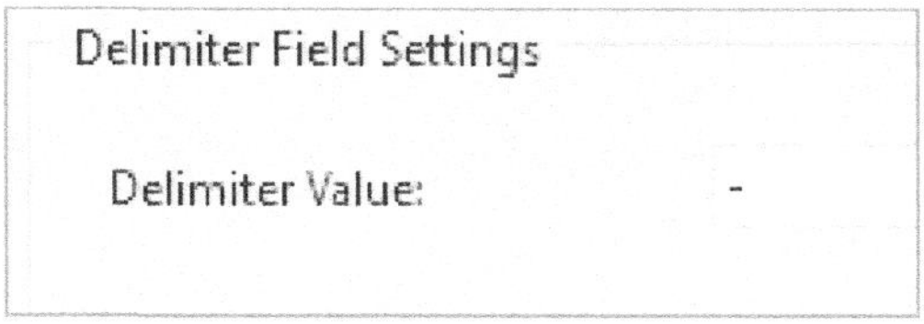


**Figure 13–47**

    a. Click **OK** to close the *Add Field* dialog box.
5. In this step, you will add a *Predefined* list field to the new number scheme.
    a. In the *New Numbering Scheme* dialog box, click **New**. The *Add Field* dialog box displays.
    b. Click **Pre-defined list**.
    c. In the *Predefined List Field Settings* area, click in the *Code* field and *Description* field to fill out the information as shown in Figure 13–48.

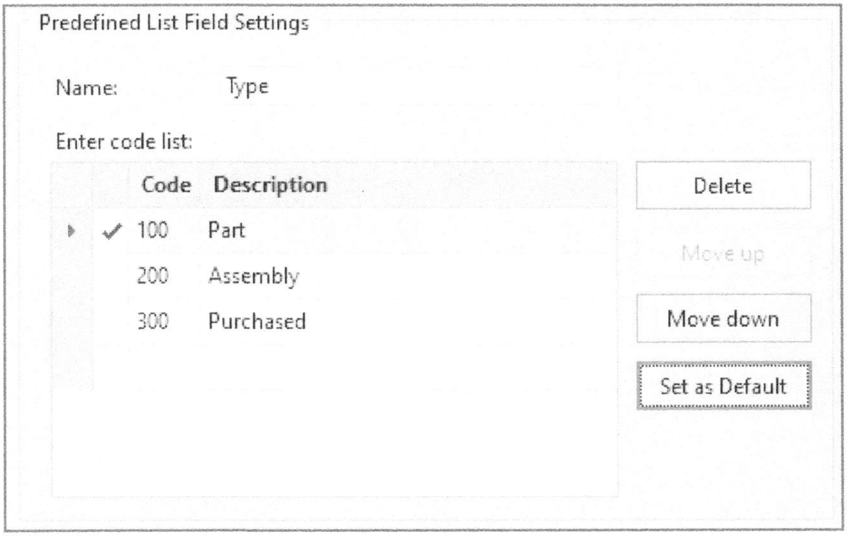


**Figure 13–48**

    d. Click on the 100 row and click **Set as Default**.
    e. Click **OK** to close the *Add Field* dialog box and return to the *New Numbering Scheme* dialog box.

6. Select the **Type** row and click **Move Up** twice to move it to the top of the list.
7. Select the **Delimiter** row and click **Move Up** once to move it between *Type* and *Number*. Your *Fields* list should display like in Figure 13–49.

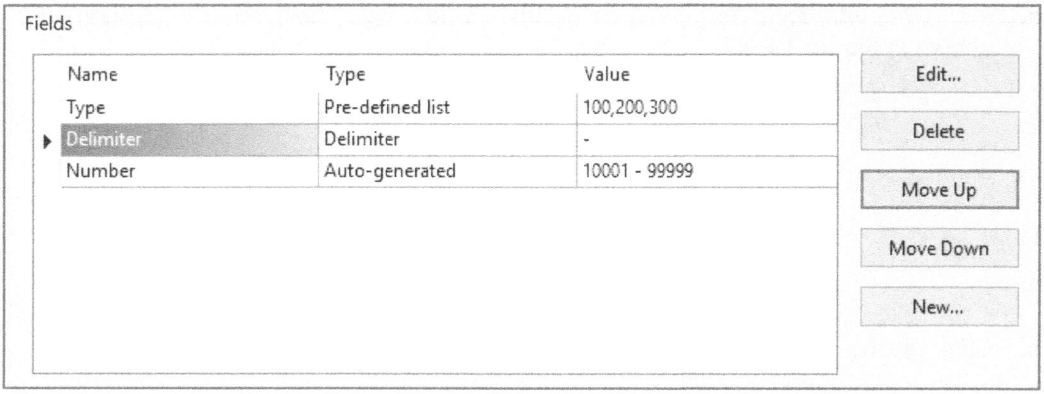


**Figure 13–49**

8. Click **OK** to dismiss the *New Numbering Scheme* dialog box and return to the *Numbering Schemes* dialog box.
9. In the *Numbering Schemes* dialog box, select the **Default** checkbox in the **Simple Numbering Scheme** row as shown in Figure 13–50. This numbering scheme will now be applied to new items. Click **Close** to close the *Numbering Schemes* dialog box.

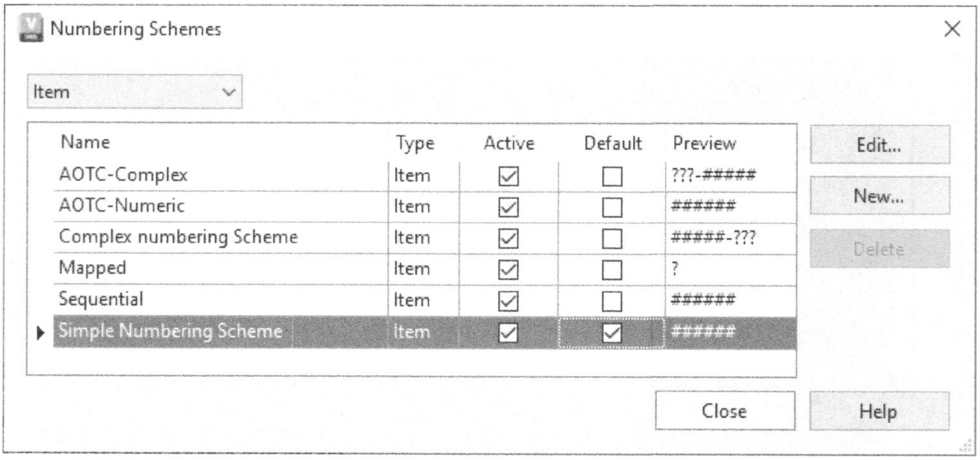


**Figure 13–50**

**End of practice**

# 13.2 Configuring Change Orders

This section describes how to set up and configure change orders (shown in Figure 13–51) to better match your company's requirements.

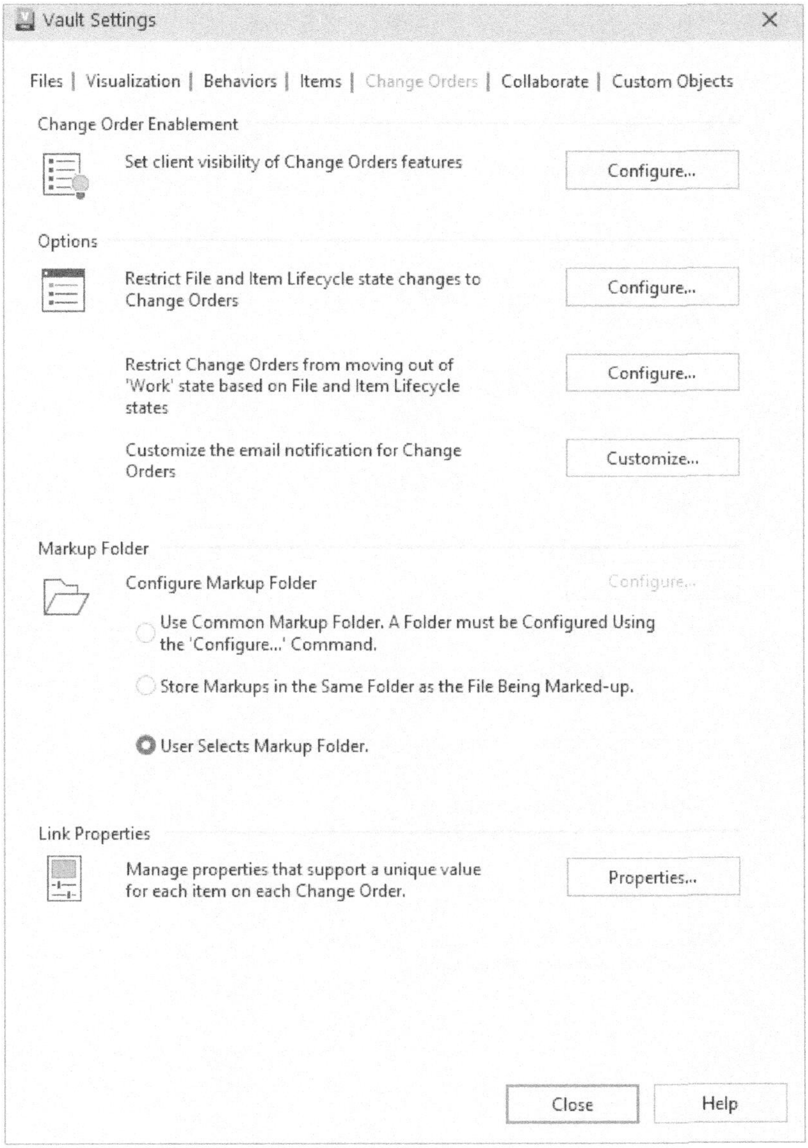


**Figure 13–51**

# Change Order Options

As an administrator, you can set several options for change orders that determine change order workflows. The *Change Orders* tab option settings are shown in Figure 13–52.

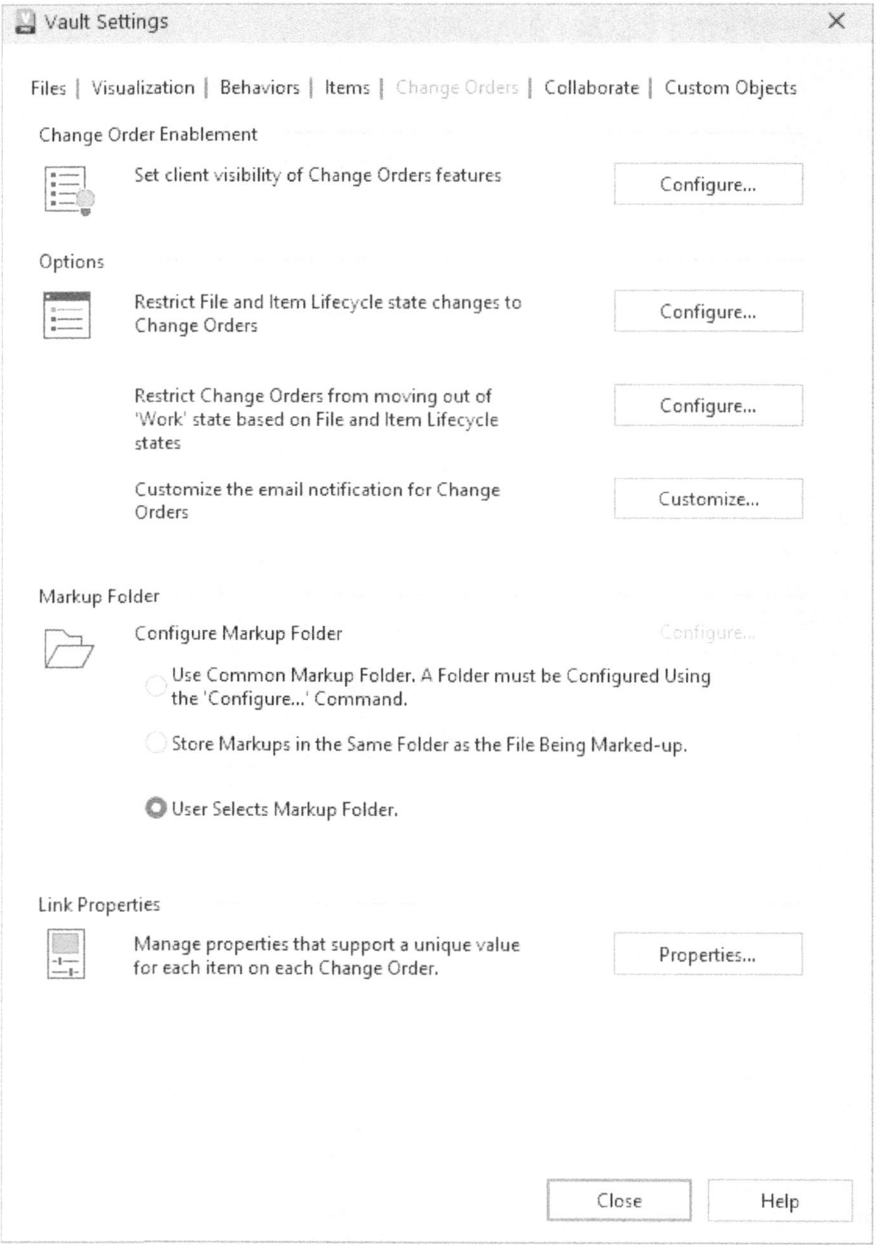


**Figure 13–52**

## Configure Restrictions for Lifecycle State Changes Using Change Orders

Specify whether item or file lifecycle state changes are controlled only by change orders.

When the **Restrict File and Item Lifecycle state changes to Change Orders** setting is enabled, a file or item lifecycle state cannot be changed outside of a change order unless the user is an Administrator. Users must change file and items record states using the **Change State** command inside the change order.

You can select whether users with administrative permissions can override these restrictions.

### How To: Configure Restrictions

1. In the Vault Client, select **Tools>Administration>Vault Settings**.
2. In the *Vault Settings* dialog box, select the *Change Orders* tab.
3. Select **Configure** next to **Restrict File and Item Lifecycle state changes to Change Orders**.
4. Select whether you want to restrict file and item lifecycle changes to change orders.
5. To enable users with administrative permissions to override the restriction for that entity, select **Allow Administrator Override**.
6. Click **Close** to save your changes.

### How To: Prevent a Change Order from Moving Out of a Work State Based on Item and File States

Prevent a change order from leaving its work state unless its item and file records are in selected lifecycle states.

These files and items must be listed in the *Records* tab of the change order, and not the *Files* tab.

1. In the Vault Client, select **Tools>Administration >Vault Settings**.
2. In the *Vault Settings* dialog box, select the *Change Orders* tab.
3. Select **Configure** next to **Restrict Change Orders from moving out of 'Work' state based on File and Item Lifecycle states**.
4. Select the lifecycle states that an item or file cannot be in for the change order to move out of a **Work** state.
5. Click **Close**.
6. Select whether you want these settings to apply to items, files, or both.
7. Click **OK** to save your changes.

# Configuring a Markup Folder

During the change order process, markups are often used to discuss changes. By default, the markup files are placed in the same folder as the associated file. As an administrator, you can enable the user (as shown in Figure 13–53) to select a markup folder or you can configure a markup folder in the vault where all of the markup files are stored.

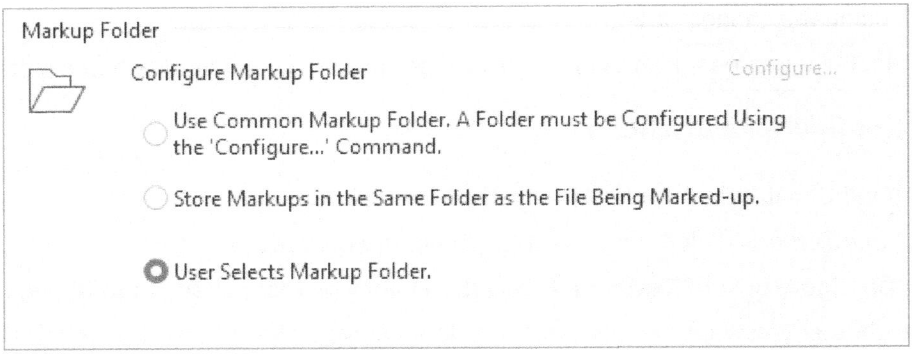


**Figure 13–53**

Figure 13–54 shows a markup folder named *Markups* that was added under the root of the vault.

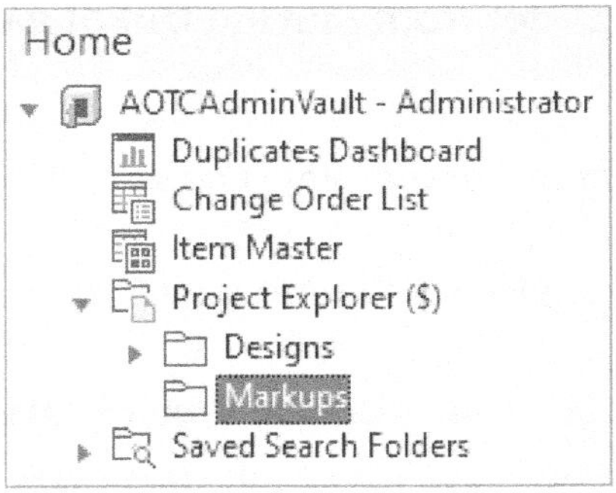


**Figure 13–54**

## How To: Configure a Markup Folder

The following steps describe how to configure a markup folder:

1. In the *Vault Settings* dialog box, select the *Change Orders* tab.
2. In the *Markup Folder* section, click **Use Common Markup Folder**. The **Configure** button, in the same group, is now enabled.
3. Select **Configure** to display the *Select Vault Location* dialog box.

 

4. If the folder already exists, select it (as shown in Figure 13–55); otherwise use the **New Folder** command to create a new folder.

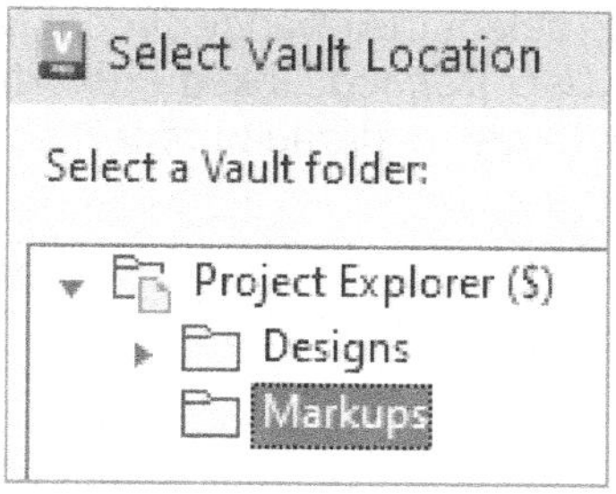


**Figure 13–55**

5. Click **OK** to close the *Select Vault Location* dialog box and return to the *Vault Settings* dialog box.

# Link Properties

## Introduction to Link Properties

Link properties are unique to change orders and enable you to support a unique value for each item on the change order. Link properties are item properties, but only in the context of the change order that they are associated with. If the item is not on a change order, it does not have this property.

Link properties are unique in the sense that they are administered in a dialog box different than file, item, and change order properties. However, they do support Property Compliance. The following change order (shown in Figure 13–56) shows the two ICU Valve Buttons on a change order to remove the paint. The cost of the change for each button is $400 to change the tooling and update the process documentation.

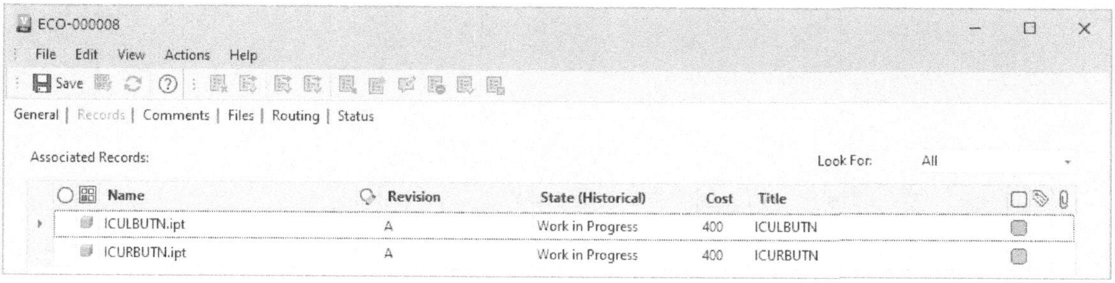


**Figure 13–56**

## How To: Add a Link Property

1. In the *Vault Settings* dialog box, select the *Change Orders* tab. In the *Link Properties* section, click **Properties** to display the *User Defined Linked Properties (Change Orders)* dialog box, as shown in Figure 13–57. There are no default properties shipped with the product.

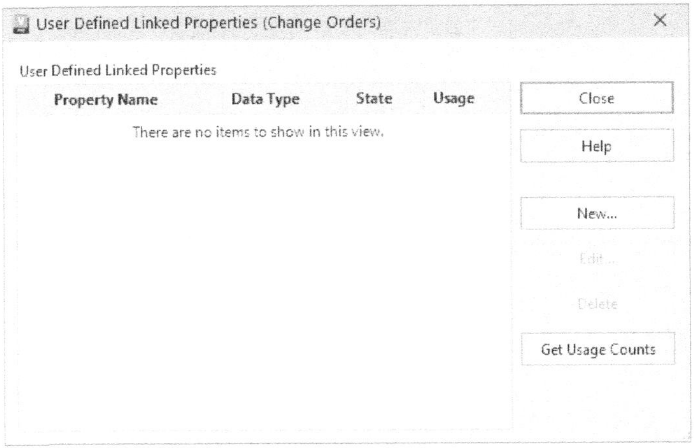


**Figure 13–57**

2. Click **New** to display the *New Change Order Link Property* dialog box. Enter the *Name* and select the *Type* from the drop-down list, then specify the *Settings* for the property (as shown in Figure 13–58). Enter *Initial Value* and *List Values* if required. Click **OK** to dismiss the dialog box and return to the *User Defined Linked Properties (Change Orders)* dialog box.

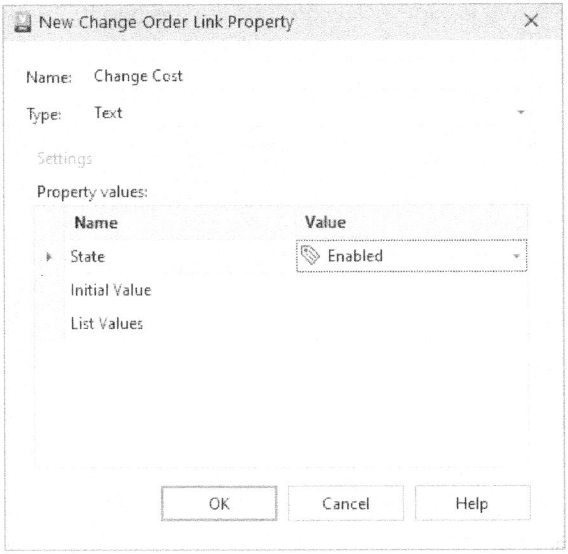


**Figure 13–58**

3. The new link properties display in the list, as shown in Figure 13–59. Click **Close** to return to the *Vault Settings* dialog box.

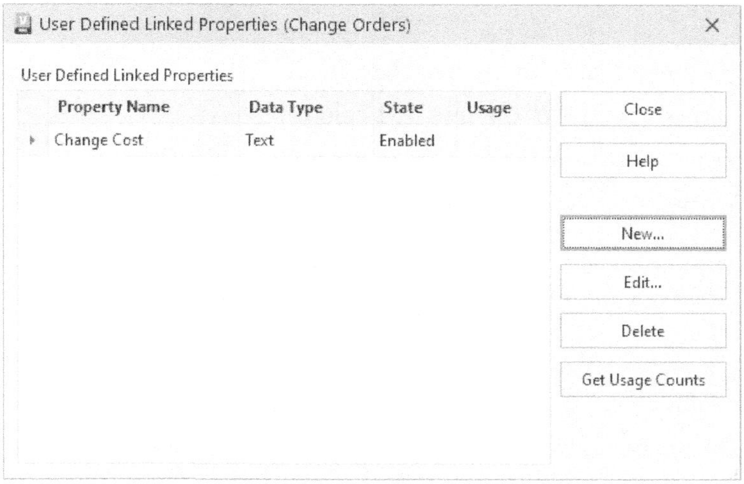


**Figure 13–59**

# Change Order Numbering

The default change order numbering scheme uses a three-letter prefix (ECO) and an auto-generated six-digit number. If the supplied change order numbering scheme does not match your company standards or does not meet your requirements, you can create new change order numbering schemes.

If your company standards require more than one change order numbering scheme, you can create multiple numbering schemes. The person originating the change order can select the appropriate scheme when they create the change order.

## How To: Define a Change Order Numbering Scheme

1. In the *Vault Settings* dialog box, select the *Behaviors* tab.
2. In the *Numbering* section, select **Define**.
3. In the *Numbering Schemes* dialog box, select **Change Order**.
4. Click **New**.
5. Enter the scheme name.
6. Click **New** to add fields for the numbering scheme.

7. In the *Add Field* dialog box, select one of the following field types:
   - Auto-generated
   - Delimiter
   - Fixed text – Enter a name for the fixed text field.
   - Free text – Enter a name for the free text field.
   - Predefined list – Enter a name for the free predefined list field.
   - Workgroup label
8. Click **OK**.
9. The *New Numbering Scheme* dialog box displays a preview of the settings defined in the *Add/Edit* dialog box.
10. To change the settings, click **Edit**. To delete, click **Delete**. To add another numbering scheme, click **Add**.
11. To display text in all capital letters, select the **Force to uppercase** checkbox.
12. Click **OK** to save the scheme.
13. When a new change order is created, the user selects the button next to the *Change Order Number* field (as shown in Figure 13–60) to change the scheme used.

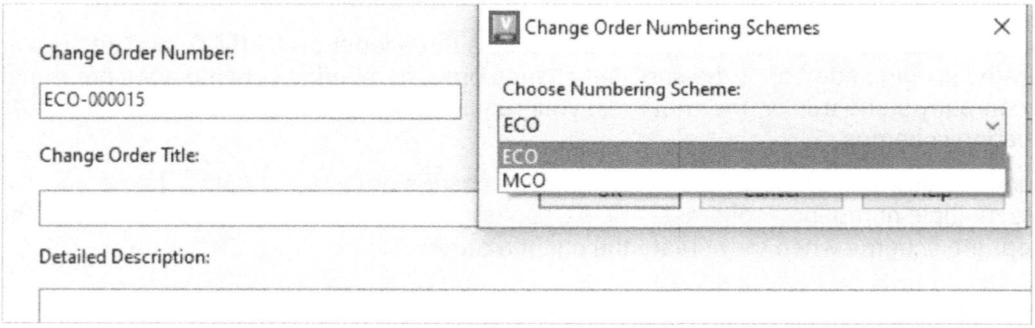


**Figure 13–60**

# Routing Definition – Workflow Selection

There are two possible workflows available with Vault Professional:

1. **Standard:** In the workflow definition, a change order moves from the **Work** state to the **Review** state. The Responsible Engineer or Change Administrator moves the change order out of the **Work** state and the Approvers can either reject the change order to the **Rejected** state or approve it to the **Approved** state. Figure 13–61 shows the default workflow.

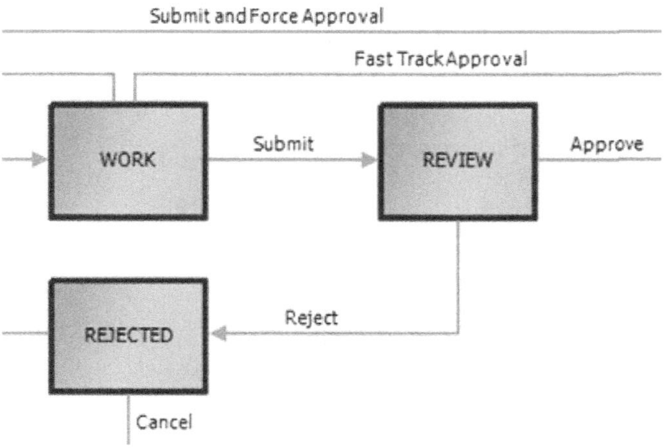


**Figure 13–61**

2. **Check State:** In this workflow definition (shown in Figure 13–62), a new **Check** state and Checker routing participant is added to the standard workflow. This is a common workflow where someone checks the work of the Responsible Engineer to ensure adherence to company standards, etc., before it is submitted to final review. In this workflow, the Responsible Engineer or Change Administrator submits the change order to the **Check** state. There the Checker can either approve it to the **Review** state or reject it back to the **Work** state.

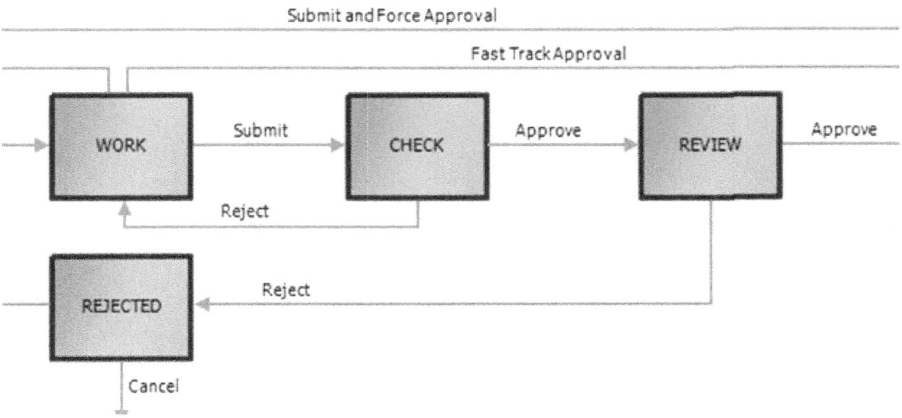


**Figure 13–62**

The workflow can be changed in the *Global Settings* dialog box by selecting **Tools>Administration>Global Settings**, as shown in Figure 13–63.

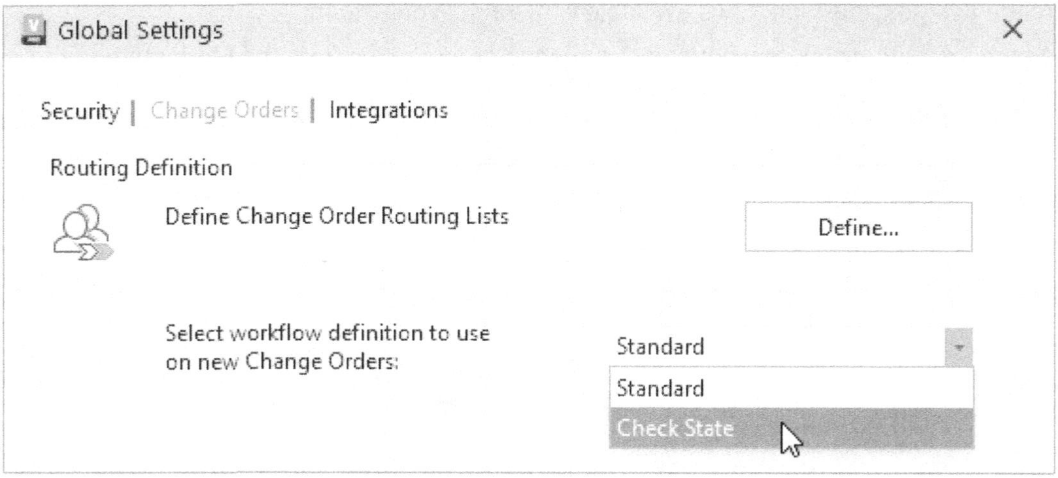


**Figure 13–63**

# Routing Definition – Change Order Routing Lists

As an administrator, you define one or more routing lists to define change order participants and their roles in the change order process. When users create a change order, they select which routing list to use. Small companies might require only one routing list and large companies might require many. Because routing lists are shared across all vaults, only one set of routing lists is required regardless of the number of vaults you use.

Figure 13–64 shows the creation of a change order routing list.

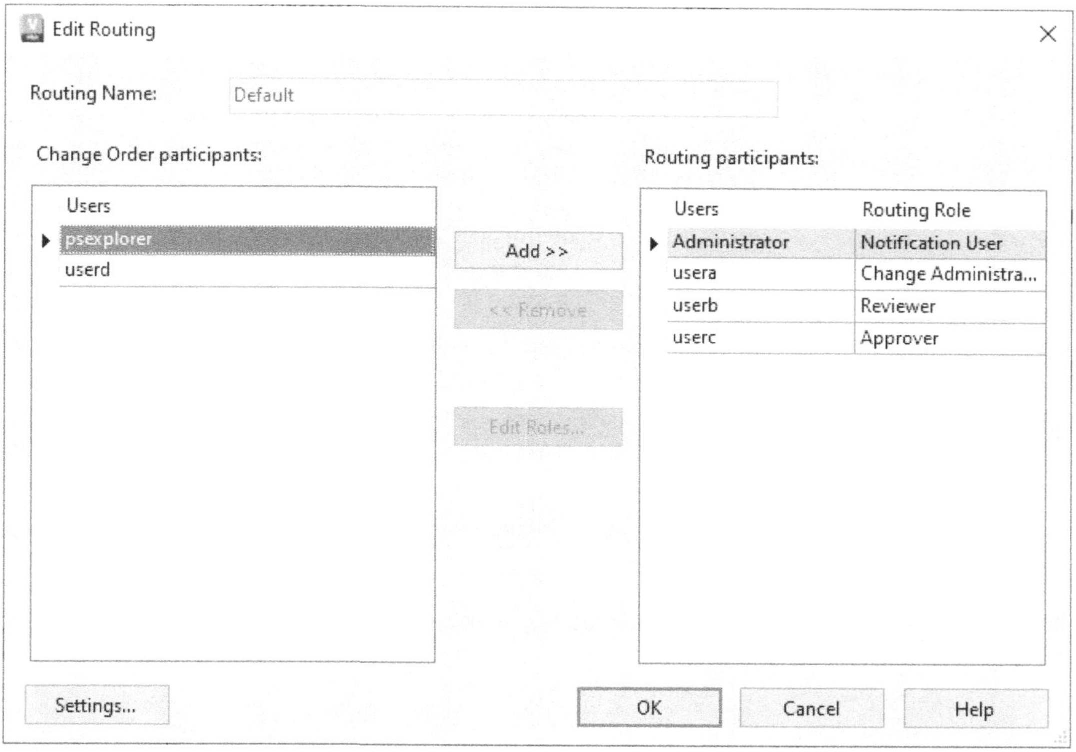


**Figure 13–64**

When a change order is created, you must specify a routing. A routing is a list of participants with predefined roles. Each of the different routing roles has specific permissions and responsibilities.

The Change Administrator, Responsible Engineer, and Approver roles control the progression of the change order. The Reviewer role can add markups, view, add, and reply to comments.

The person creating the change order automatically becomes the Change Requestor.

The task a routing participant can perform depends on the routing participant role.

> **Note:** *Only users with Administrator or Change Order Editor privileges can be assigned routing roles.*

## Change Order Roles

Change order participants are assigned one or more of the following roles.

| Role | Task Availability |
|---|---|
| **Change Requestor** | Initiated the change order. |
| **Change Administrator** | Can add or remove Approvers, Change Administrators, and Responsible Engineers. This participant can edit the title of the change order, add or remove files or items, and modify user-defined properties. Can submit the new change order to the **Open** state.<br>The Change Administrator is also responsible for:<br>• Canceling the change order or reopening a closed change order.<br>• Evaluating change orders in the **Open** state to determine whether they should be processed or canceled, and so is responsible for submitting the Open change order to **Work** or canceling it.<br>• Rejecting change orders to determine whether they should be canceled or can be reworked. When a change order is approved, the Change Administrator is responsible for closing the change order and releasing the associated items and files. |
| **Responsible Engineer** | Can edit the change order when in the **Work** state, make required revisions, and submit the change order for review. |
| **Checker** | Participates only in the **Check** state (when enabled). Can add comments in the **Check** state. Can approve to the **Review** State or reject back to the **Work** state. |
| **Reviewer** | Can only view, add, and reply to comments. |
| **Approver** | Can review, approve, and reject a change order. |
| **Notification User** | Receives notification when the change order is closed. |

 

## Example

A small company wants to track changes. They install Autodesk Vault Professional and need to set up a single change order routing list. Two engineers are responsible for all aspects of the change order process and the production manager wants to be notified of changes.

A change order routing list is created with three participants, as shown in Figure 13–65. Each of the two engineers is assigned as Change Administrator, Responsible Engineer, and Approver. The production manager is assigned as a Notification User.

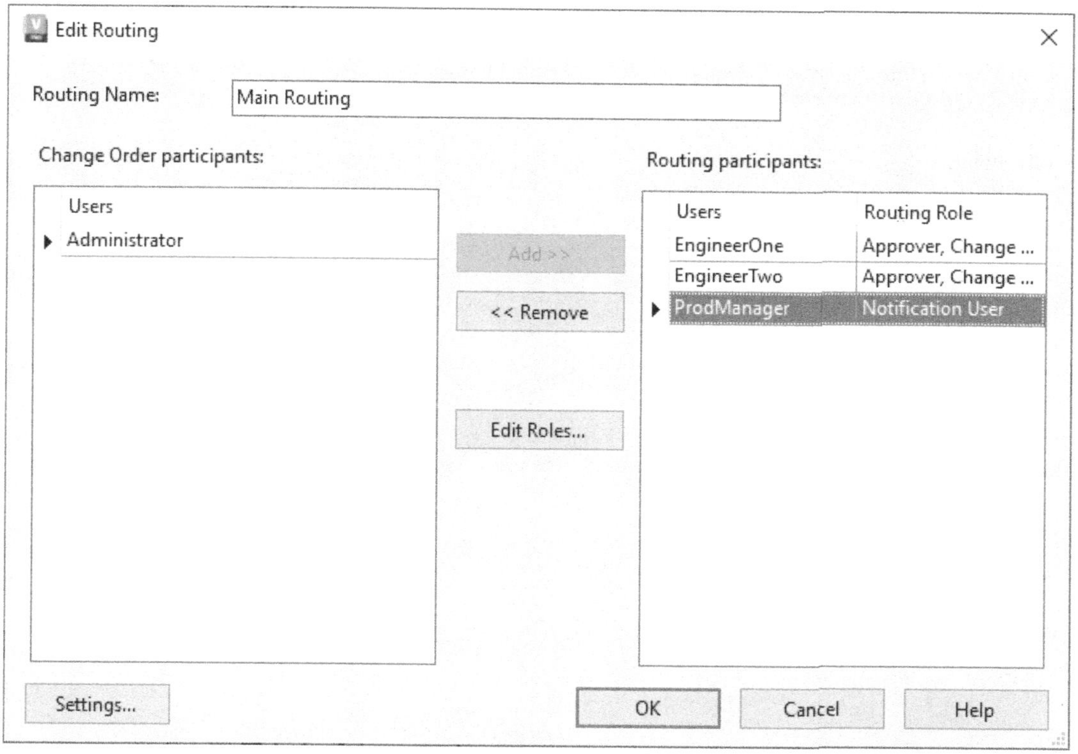


Figure 13–65

## How To: Create a Change Order Routing List

The following steps outline the creation of a routing list:

1. Open the *Global Settings* dialog box (**Tools> Administration>Global Settings**) and select the *Change Orders* tab. In the *Routing definition* section, select **Define** to display the *Routing* dialog box, as shown in Figure 13–66.

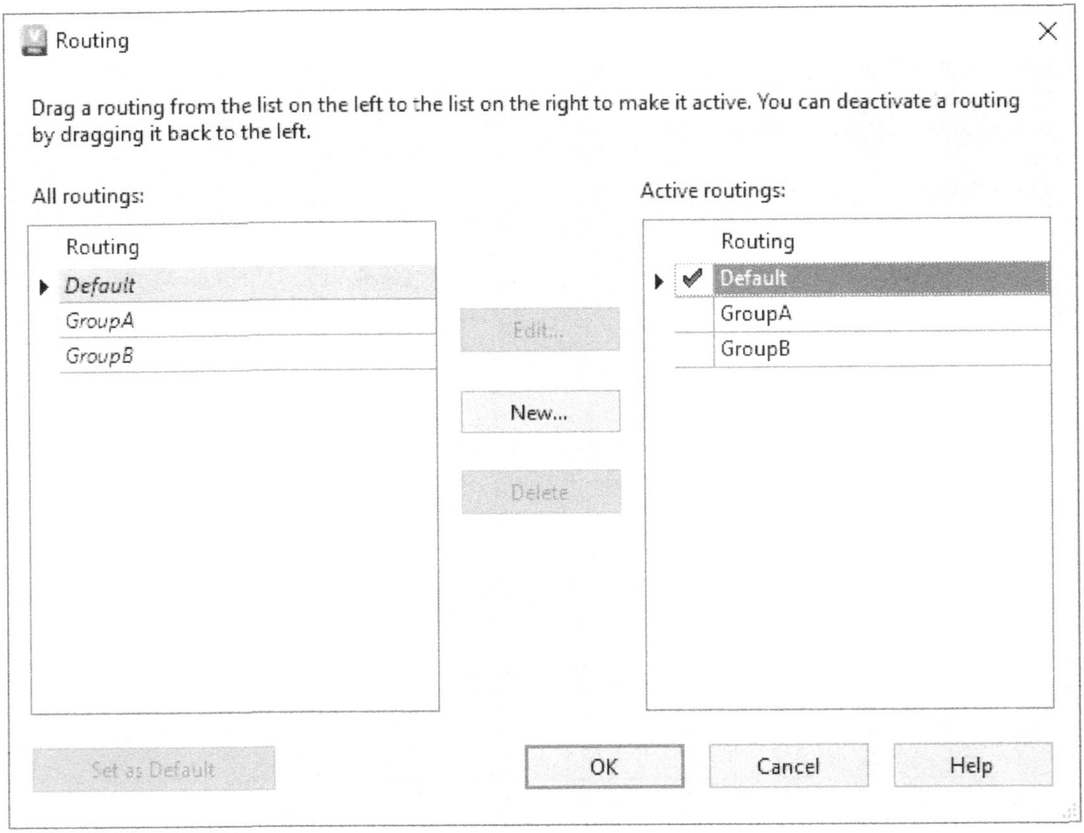


**Figure 13–66**

2. A number of routings have been defined, but only one, **Default**, is currently active and set as the default. Click **New** to display the *Edit Routing* dialog box, as shown in Figure 13–67.

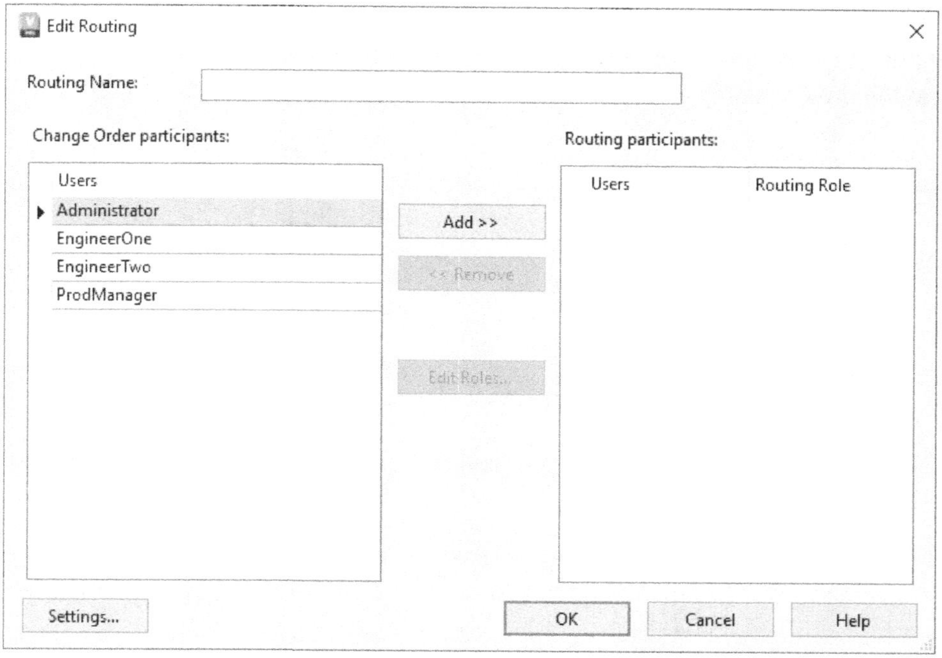


**Figure 13–67**

3. Enter a *Routing Name*, then select one of the users from the *Change Order participants* list and click **Add** to display the *Edit Roles* dialog box, as shown in Figure 13–68.

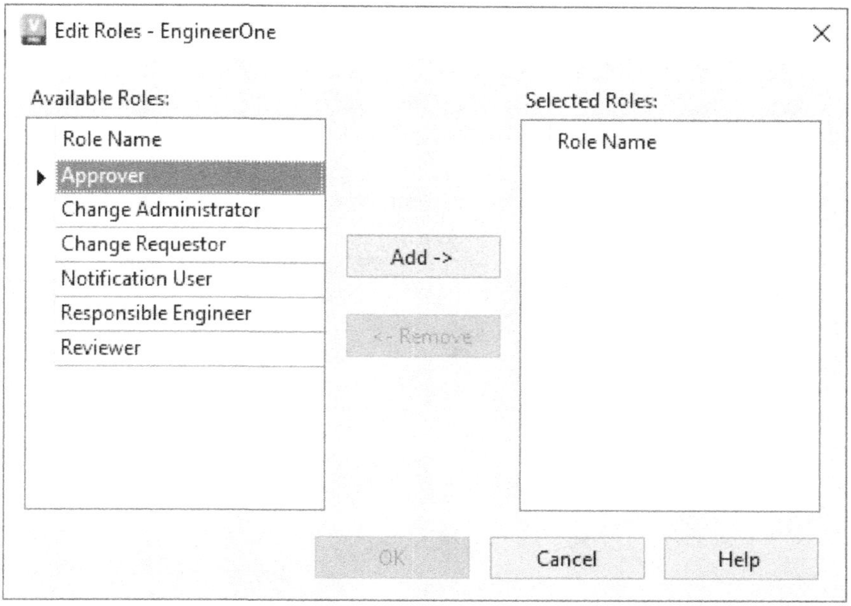


**Figure 13–68**

4. Select a role from the list of *Available Roles* and click **Add** to add it to the list of *Selected Roles*, as shown in Figure 13–69.
5. Repeat the previous step to add any additional roles.

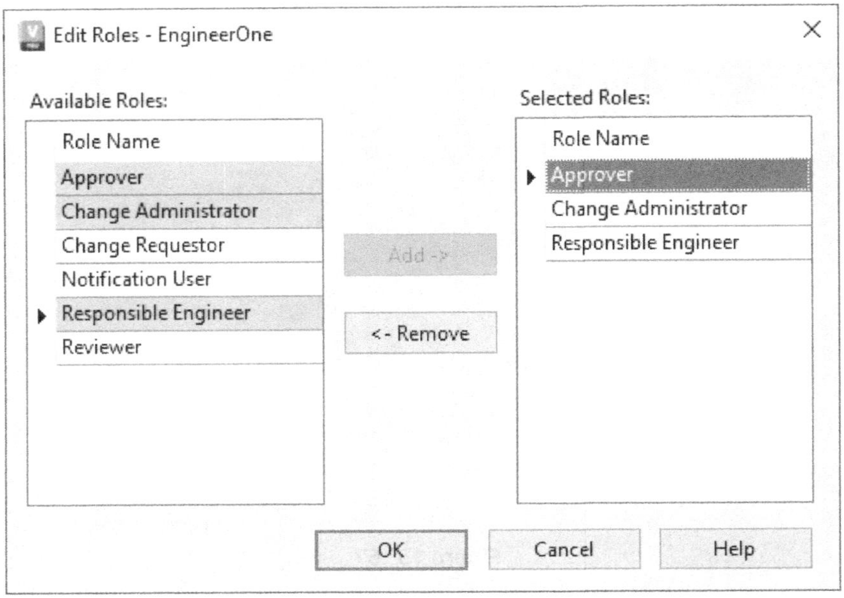


**Figure 13–69**

6. Click **OK** to return to the *Edit Routing* dialog box, as shown in Figure 13–70. Note the *Routing Roles* assigned to the first selected user.

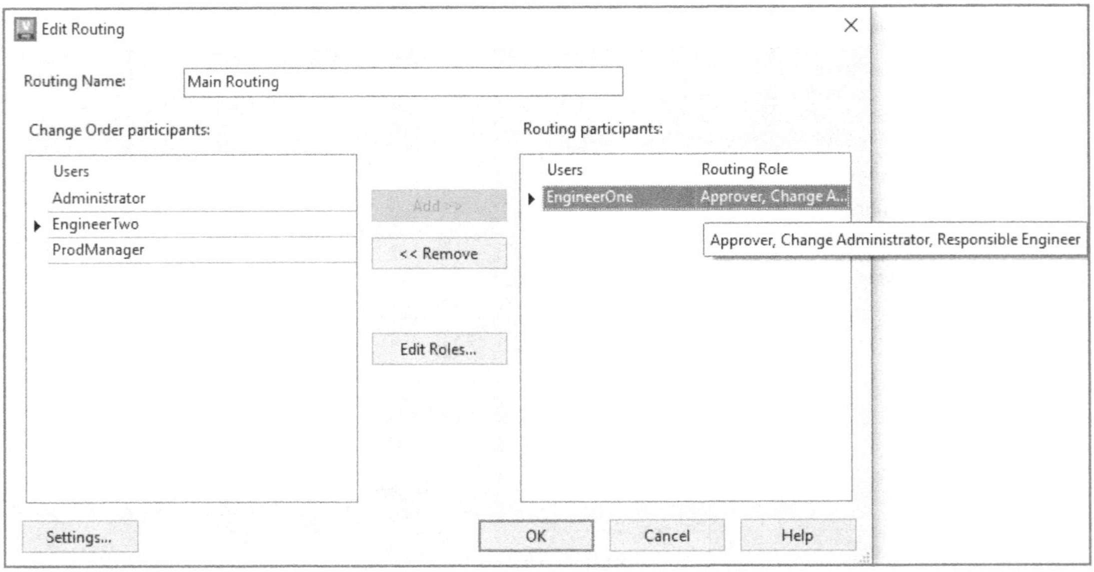


**Figure 13–70**

7. Repeat Steps 3 to 5 to add the rest of the *Change Order participants* and define their *Routing Roles*, as shown in Figure 13–71.

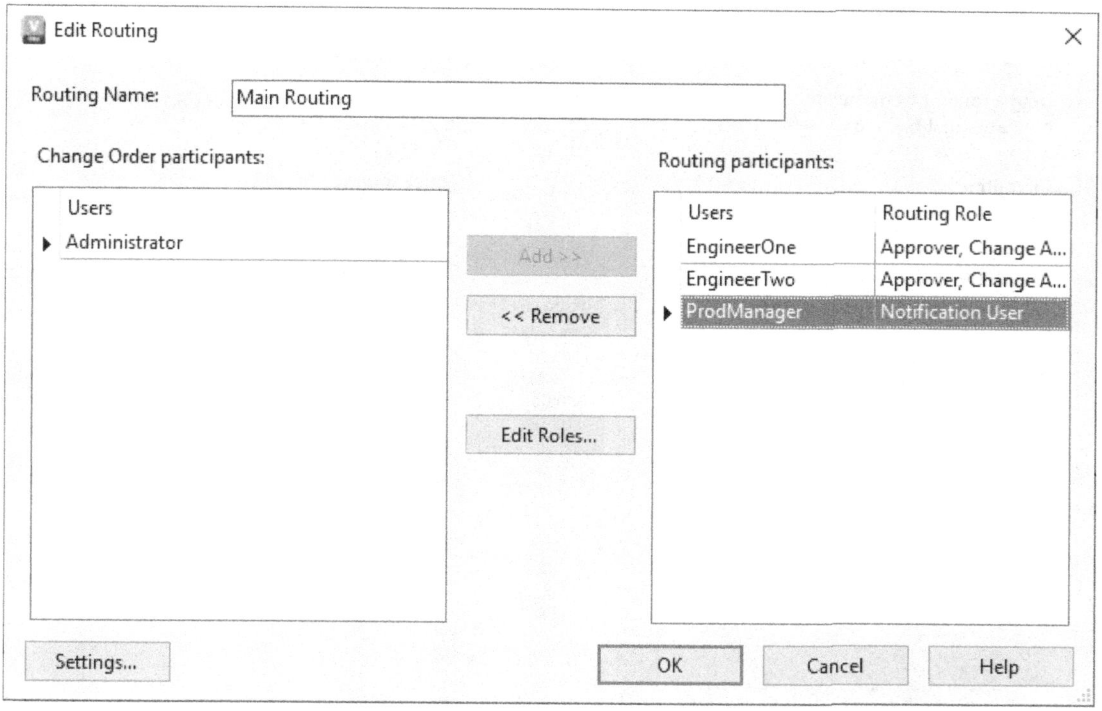


**Figure 13–71**

*Note: You must add users in the Change Administrator, Responsible Engineer, and Approver role. If you are using the optional* ***Check*** *state, a Checker must also be added.*

8. If you have more than one approver, use **Settings** to display and select the approval type required, as shown in Figure 13–72.

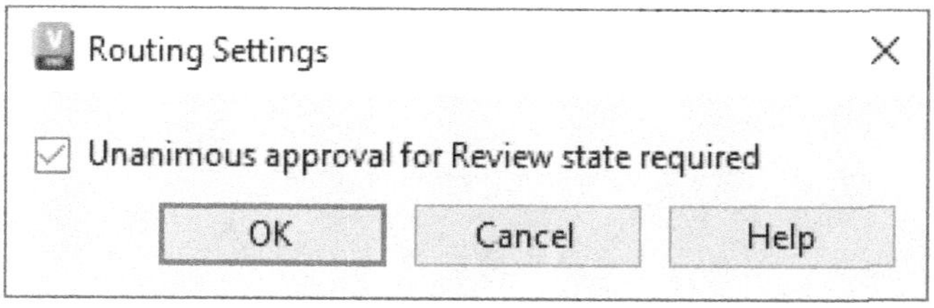


**Figure 13–72**

9. Click **OK** to close the *Edit Routing* dialog box and return to the *Routing* dialog box.

10. In the *Routing* dialog box, select the new routing and drag it from the *All routings* list to the *Active routings* list, as shown in Figure 13–73.

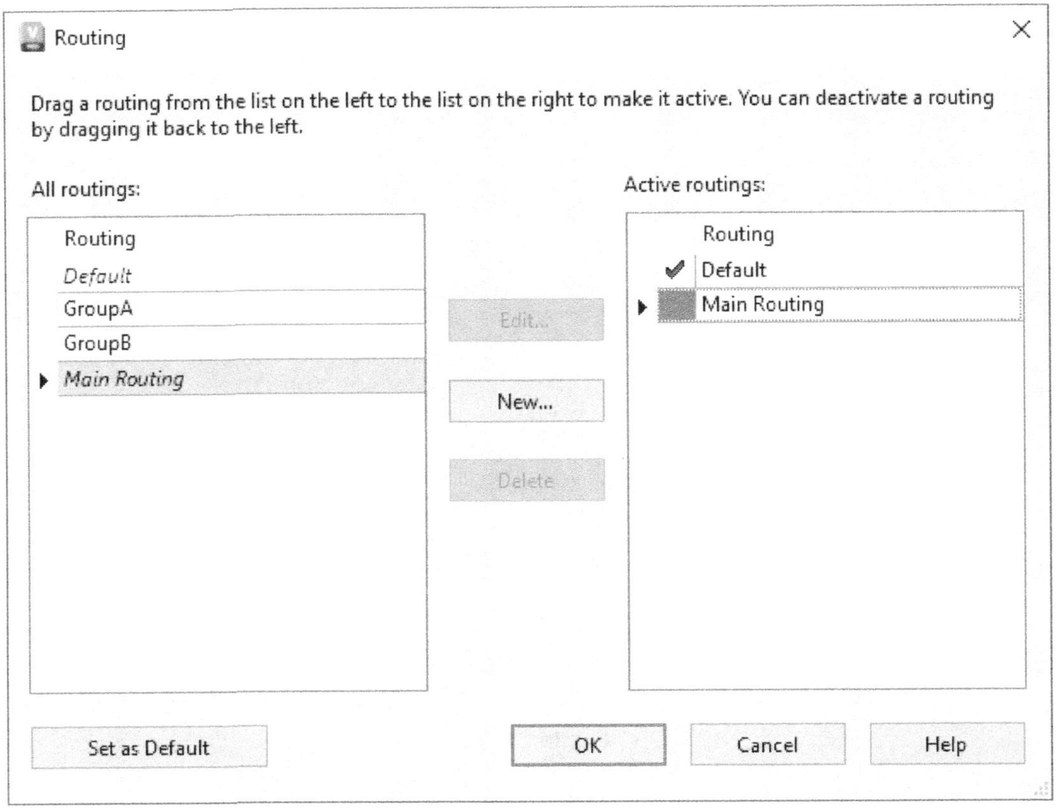


**Figure 13–73**

11. In the *Routing* dialog box, select the new routing. If this is to be the new default routing (as shown in Figure 13–74), click **Set as Default**.

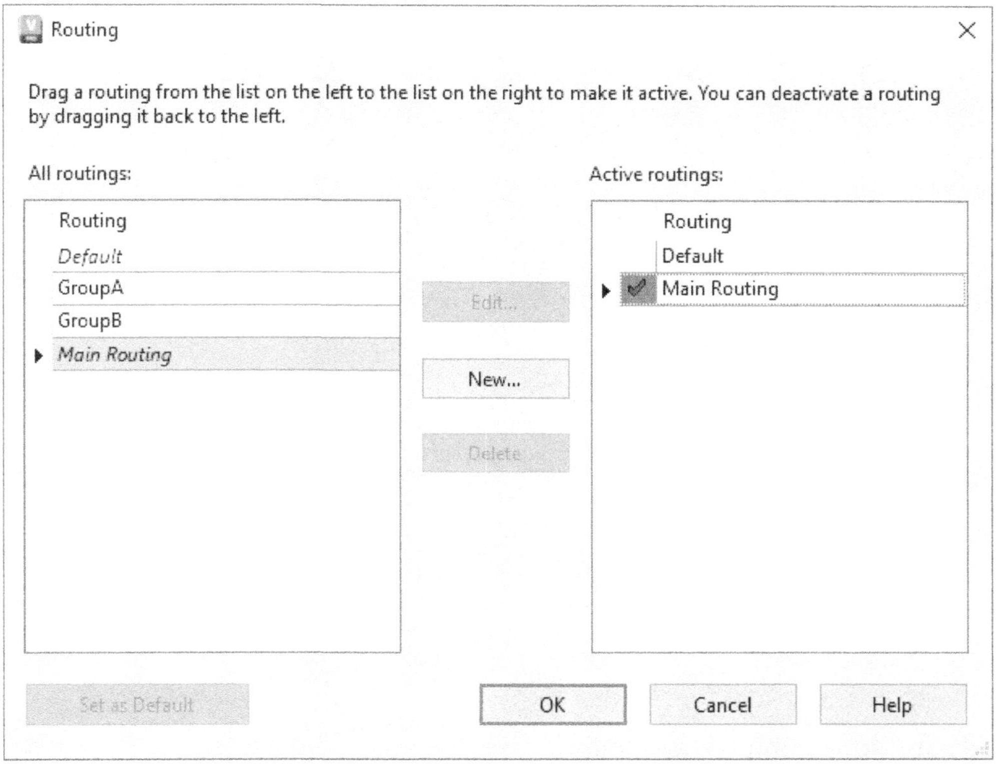


Figure 13–74

12. Click **OK** to close the *Routing* dialog box and return to the *Global Settings* dialog box.

# Configure Email Notification

As an administrator, you must configure email settings if you want notifications emailed to participants on the routing list when a change order enters a state that requires attention. For example, the Responsible Engineer is notified when the change order enters the **Work** state, Approvers are notified when the change order enters the **Review** state, and Notification Users are notified when the change order enters the **Closed** state.

Figure 13–75 displays the *Email Configuration* dialog box in which you enable email notification and enter the email server information.

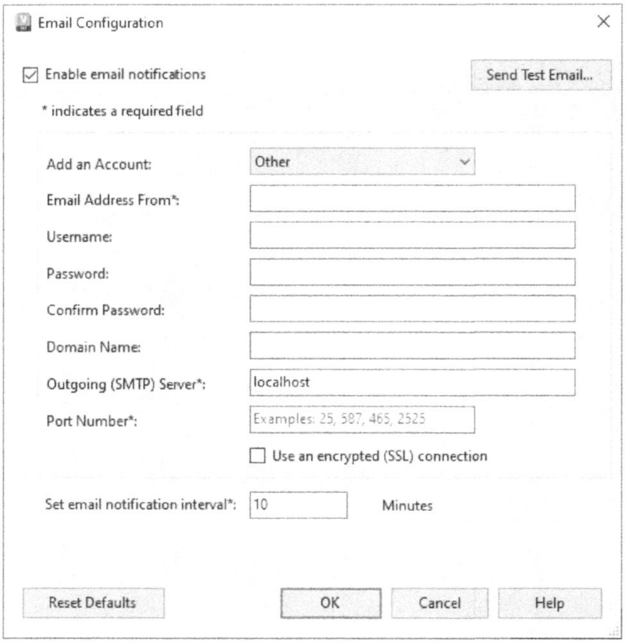


**Figure 13–75**

## How To: Configure Email Notification

The following steps describe how to configure email notification:

1. Ensure that all users that will be participating in change orders have email addresses, as shown in Figure 13–76.

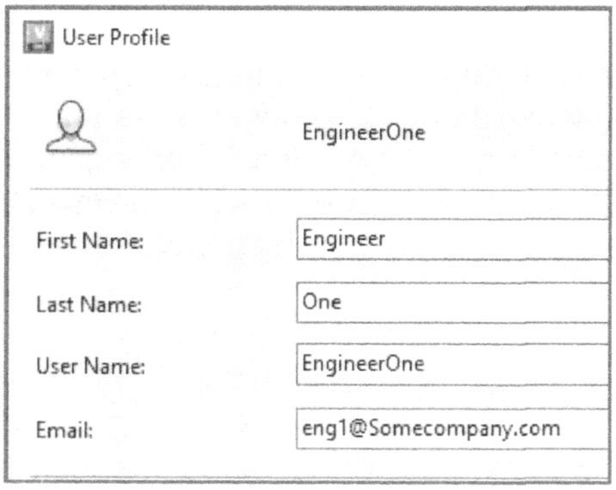


**Figure 13–76**

2. Log in to the Autodesk Data Management Server console as an Administrator.

3. In the *Tools* menu, select **Administration**, as shown in Figure 13–77.

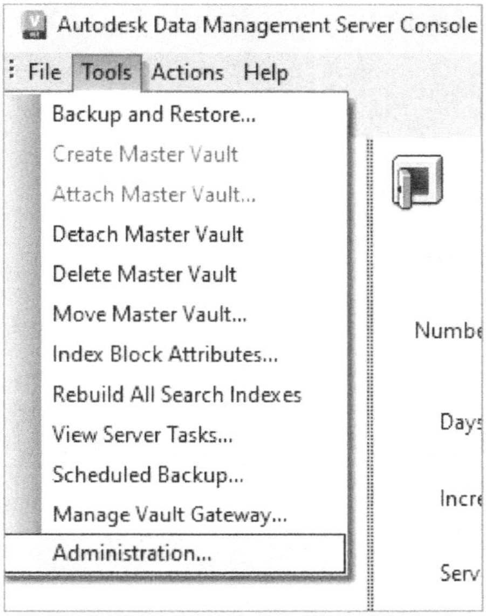


**Figure 13–77**

4. Select the *Advanced Settings* tab. In the *Email* section, click **Email** to display the *Email* dialog box, as shown in Figure 13–78.

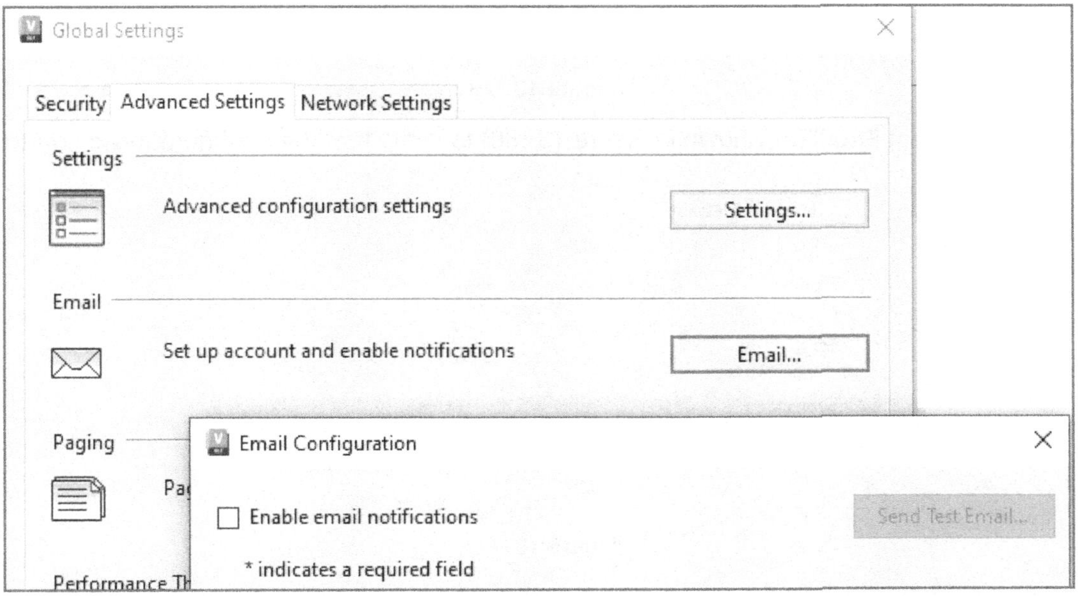


**Figure 13–78**

5. Select **Enable email notifications**, then enter the appropriate Outgoing (*SMTP) Server*, the *Email Address From* (that will show up as the from address in the email), the SMTP Server *Port Number*, and the user credentials, as shown in Figure 13–79.

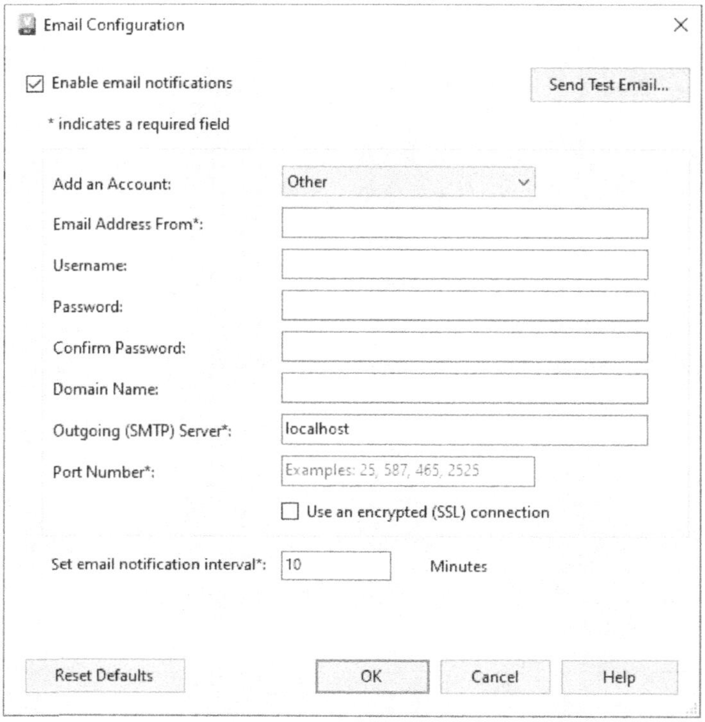


**Figure 13–79**

6. Use **Send Test Email** (as shown in Figure 13–80) to verify that the configuration is correct.

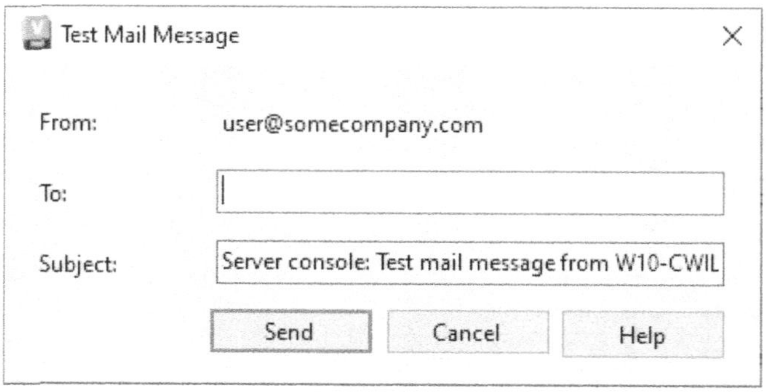


**Figure 13–80**

7. Click **OK** to dismiss the *Email* dialog box and return to the *Global Settings* dialog box.
8. Click **Close** to dismiss the *Global Settings* dialog box and log out of the Autodesk Data Management Server console.

# Practice 13c
# Set Up Change Orders

In this practice, you set up a markup folder, add a user-defined change order property, create a new change order numbering scheme, and add a new change order routing list. The completed practice is shown in Figure 13–81.

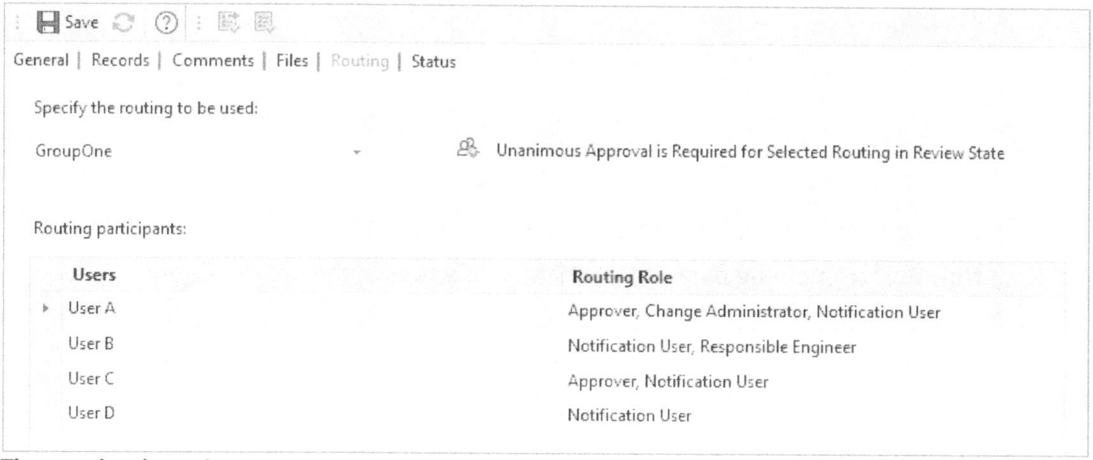


***The completed practice***

**Figure 13–81**

## Task 1: Configure change orders.

1. Start Autodesk Vault Professional and log in with the following information:
    - For *User Name*, enter **administrator**.
    - Leave the *Password* field blank.
    - For *Vault*, select **AOTCAdminVault**.
2. Open the *Vault Settings* dialog box by selecting **Tools>Administration>Vault Settings**.
3. Select the *Change Orders* tab and review the default options.

## Task 2: Set up a markup folder.

1. In the *Markup Folder* section, select **Use Common Markup Folder**s, as shown in Figure 13–82. The **Configure** button, in the same section, is now enabled.

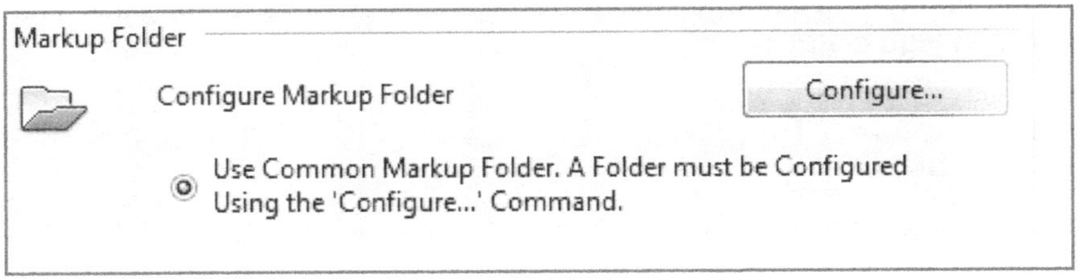


**Figure 13–82**

2. Select **Configure** to display the *Select Vault Location* dialog box.
3. Select **New Folder** to create a new folder named *Markups* in the *Project Explorer ($)* root folder.
4. Enter **Markups** in the *New Folder* dialog box and click **OK**, as shown in Figure 13–83.

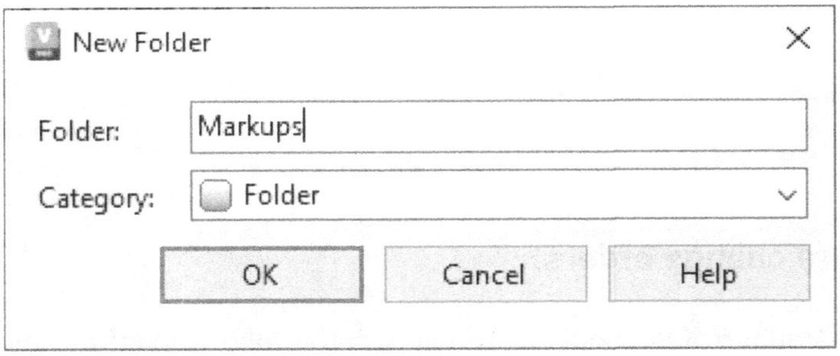


**Figure 13–83**

5. Click **OK** to close the *Select a Vault Folder* dialog box (shown in Figure 13–84) and return to the *Vault Settings* dialog box.

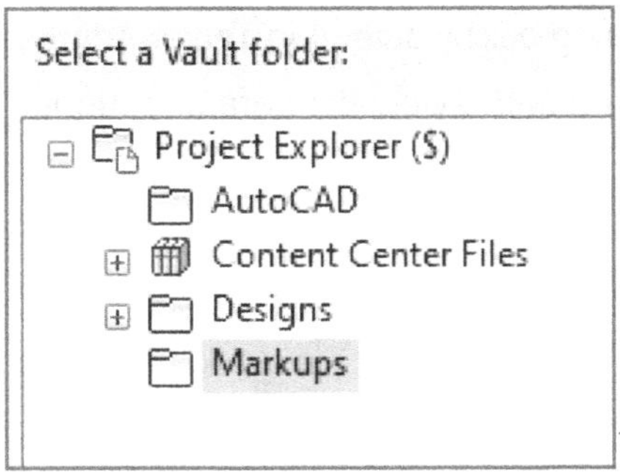


**Figure 13–84**

 

## Task 3: Add link properties.

1. In the *Vault Settings* dialog box, select **Properties** in the *Link Properties* section to display the *User Defined Linked Properties* dialog box, as shown in Figure 13–85.

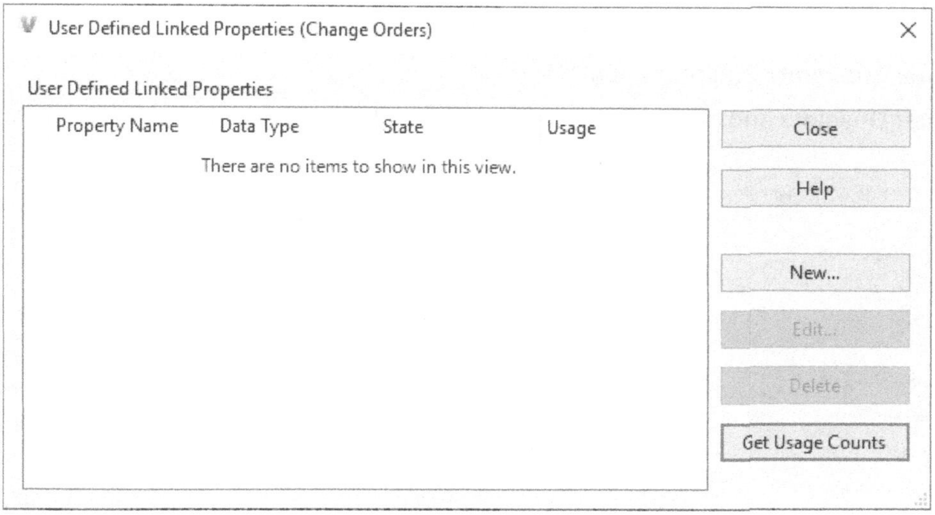


**Figure 13–85**

- Note that unlike other properties, there are no default link properties.

2. Click **New** to display the *New Change Order Link Property* dialog box, as shown in Figure 13–86.

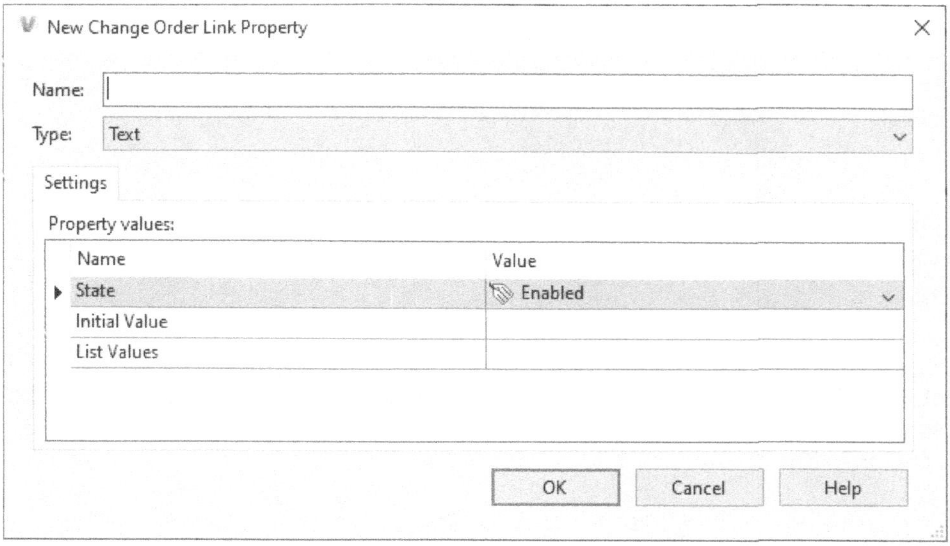


**Figure 13–86**

3. Enter the following information for a new *Disposition* link property:
   - For the *Name*, enter **Disposition**.
   - Keep the default *Type* as **Text**.
4. In the *List Values* field, do the following, as shown in Figure 13–87:
   - In the *Click here to add a new row* section, enter **Revise** and press <Enter>.
   - Enter **Substitute** and press <Enter>.
   - Enter **Obsolete** and press <Enter>.

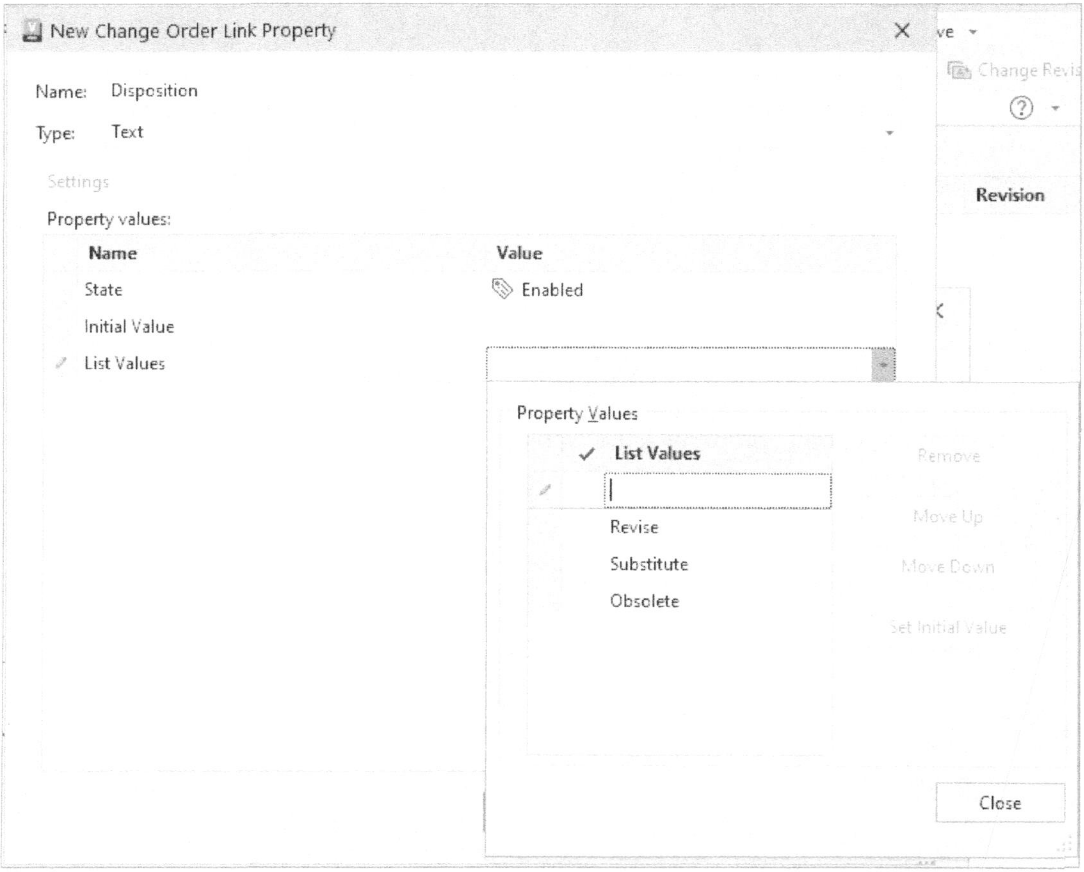


Figure 13–87

5. Select the entry for **Revise** and select **Set Initial Value** to make this the default value, as shown in Figure 13–88.

 

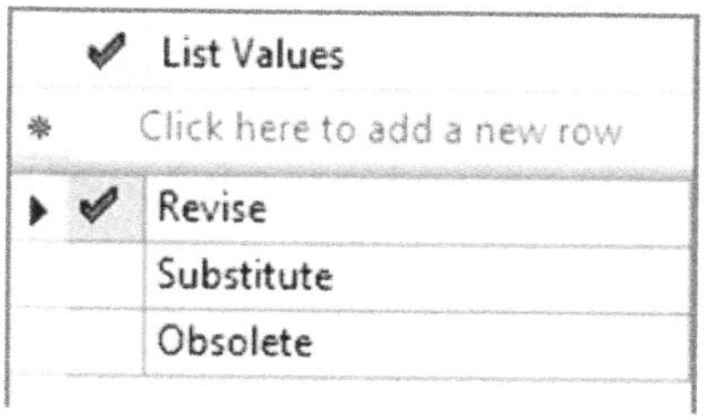


**Figure 13–88**

6. Click **Close** to close this dialog box and return to the *New Change Order Link Property* dialog box.
7. Review the entries. They should look like the following list, as shown in Figure 13–89.

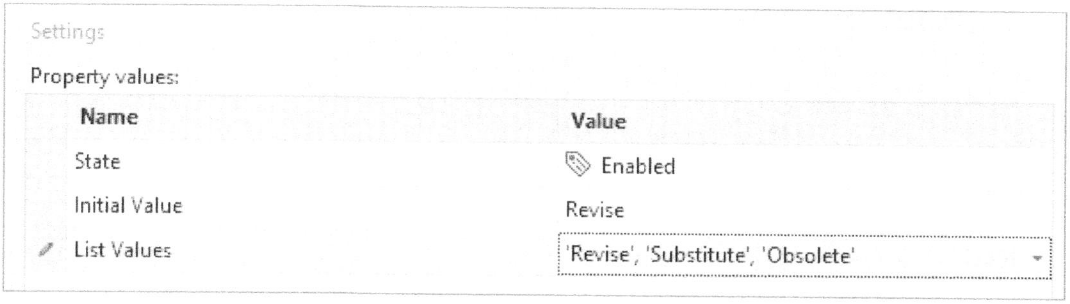


**Figure 13–89**

8. Click **OK** to return to the *User Defined Linked Properties (Change Orders)* dialog box and then click **Close** (shown in Figure 13–90) to return to the *Vault Settings* dialog box.

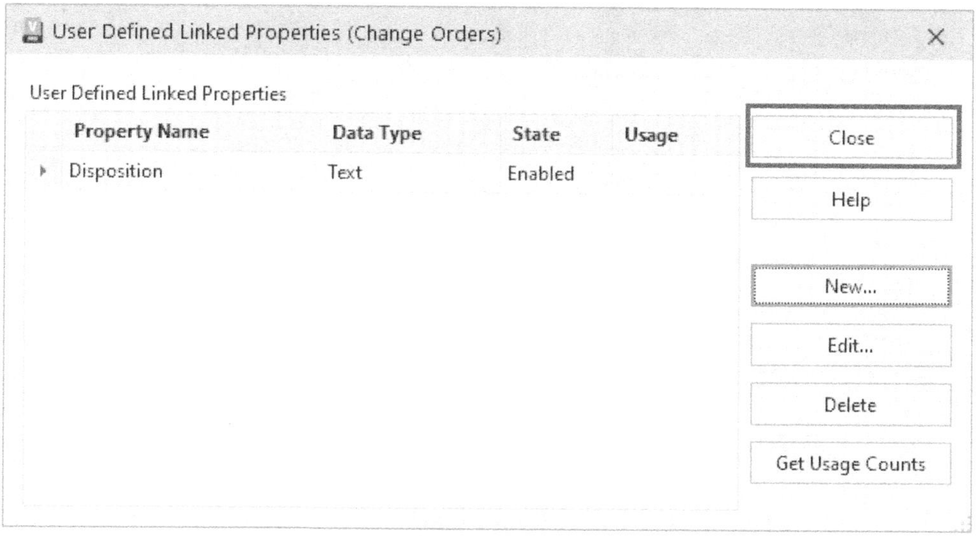


**Figure 13–90**

## Task 4: Change order numbering.

1. In the *Vault Settings* dialog box, in the *Behaviors* tab, in the *Numbering* section, select **Define** to display the *Numbering Schemes* dialog box.
2. Select **Change Order** from the drop-down list.
3. Click **New** to create a new change order numbering scheme with name of **AOTC ECO**.
4. Add the following three fields and the results display as shown in Figure 13–91:
   - Select the **Fixed Text** field type with values of *Name:* **Fixed Text**, *Fixed Text:* **AOTC ECO**.
   - Select the **Delimiter** field type with *Delimiter Value:* **-**.
   - Select the **Auto-generated sequence** field type with values of *Name:* **Auto-generated**, *Length:* **3**, *Range:* **1-999**.

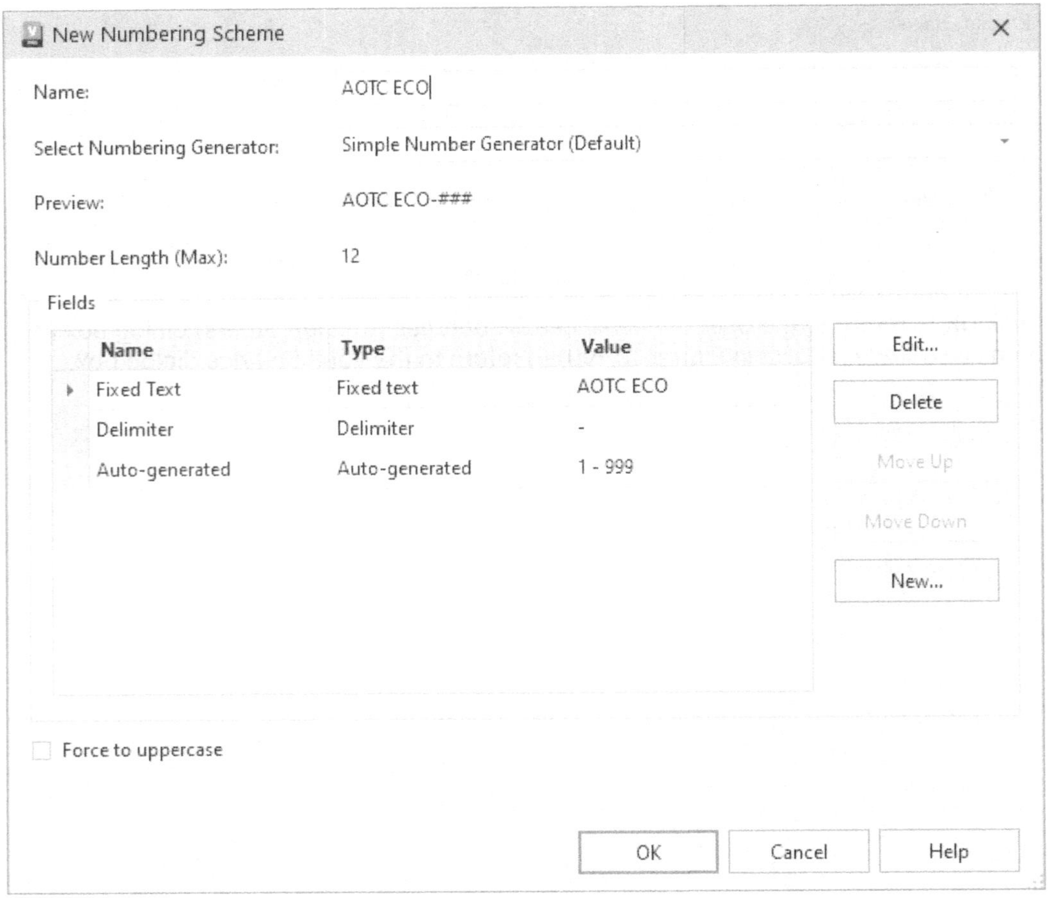


**Figure 13–91**

5. Click **OK** to return to the *Numbering Schemes* dialog box.

6. Select the new numbering scheme and then click the **Default** checkbox (as shown in Figure 13–92) to set it as the default.

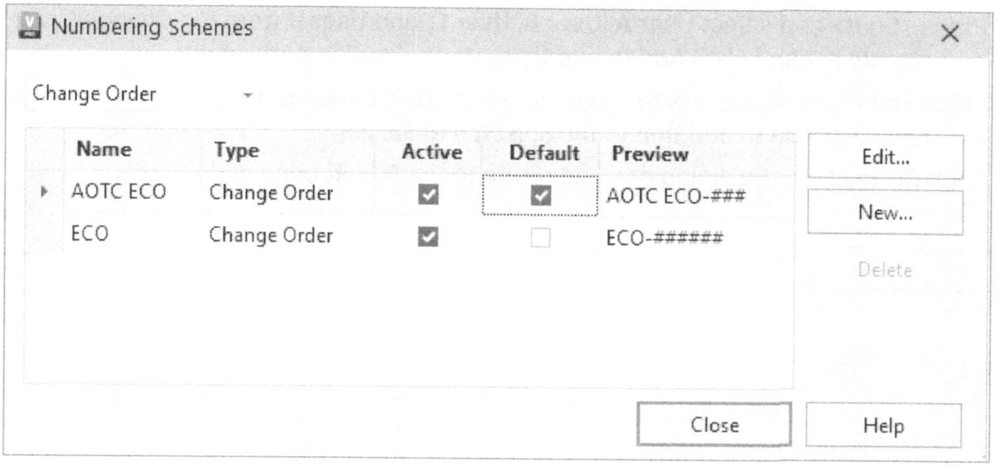


**Figure 13–92**

7. Click **Close** to close this dialog box and return to the *Vault Settings* dialog box.

## Task 5: Create routing list.

1. Click **Close** to close the *Vault Settings* dialog box.
2. In the *Tools* menu, select **Administration>Global Settings** to display the *Global Settings* dialog box.
3. In the *Global Settings* dialog box, select the *Change Orders* tab.
4. Select **Define** to display the *Routing* dialog box.
5. Click **New** to display the *Edit Routing* dialog box.

6. In the *Edit Routing* dialog box, complete the following, as shown in Figure 13–93:
   - For *Routing Name*, enter **GroupOne**.
   - Press <Shift> and select **User A**, **User B**, **User C**, and **User D** from the *Change Order participants* list and click **Add** to add them to the *Routing participants* list.
   - In the *Edit Roles* dialog box that opens, select **Notification User** from the *Available Roles* list, then click **Add** to add that to the *Selected Roles* list.
   - Click **OK** to close the dialog box and return to the *Edit Routing* dialog box.

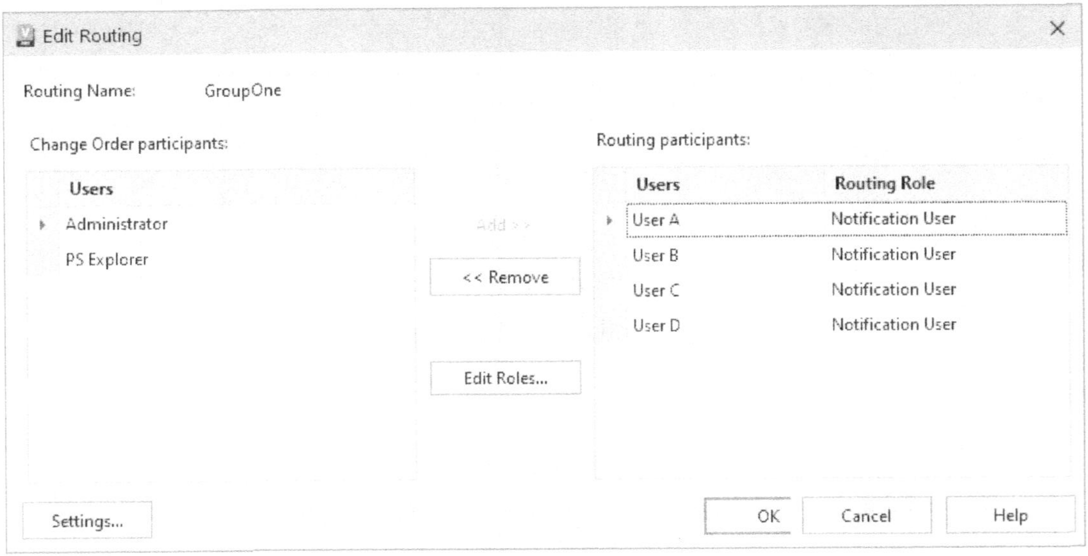


**Figure 13–93**

7. In the *Routing participants* list, select **User A** and click **Edit Roles** to display the *Edit Roles* dialog box.

8. Hold <Ctrl> and select **Change Administrator** and **Approver** from the list, as shown in Figure 13–94.

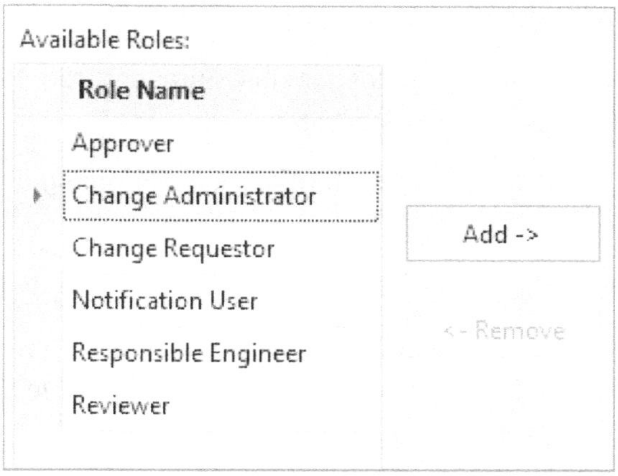


**Figure 13–94**

9. Click **Add** to add these roles to the *Selected Roles* list, as shown in Figure 13–95.

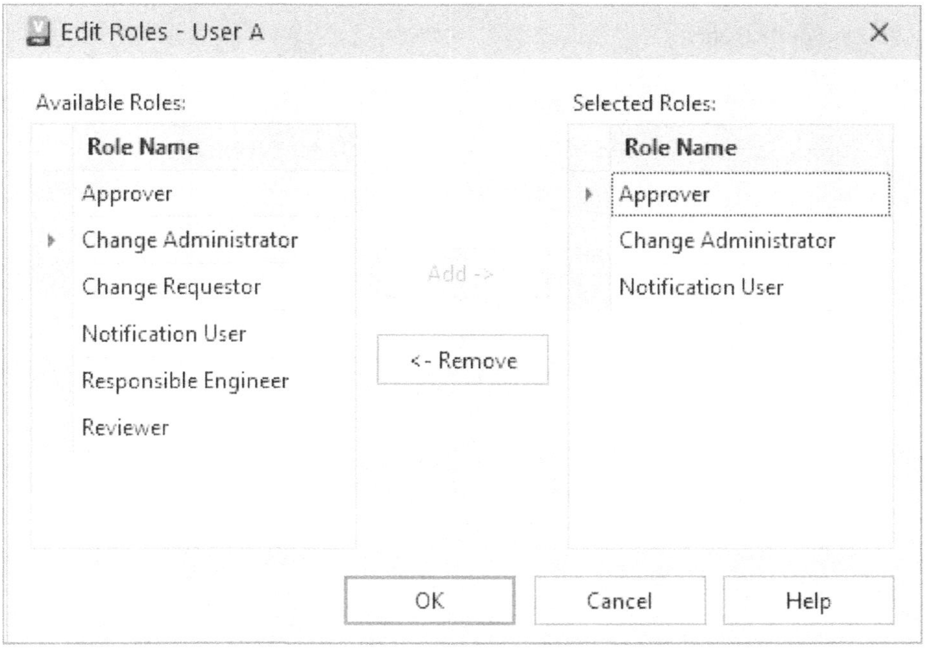


**Figure 13–95**

10. Click **OK** to close this dialog box and return to the *Edit Routing* dialog box.

11. Do the following:
    - Select **User B** in the *Routing participants* list.
    - Click **Edit Roles**.
    - In the *Edit Roles* dialog box, select **Responsible Engineer** from the *Available Roles* list.
    - Click **Add** to add this role in the *Selected Roles* list.
    - Click **OK** to close the dialog box and return to the *Edit Routing* dialog box.
12. Do the following:
    - Select **User C** in the *Routing participants* list.
    - Click **Edit Roles**.
    - In the *Edit Roles* dialog box, select **Approver** from the *Available Roles* list.
    - Click **Add** to add this role in the *Selected Roles* list.
    - Click **OK** to close the dialog box and return to the *Edit Routing* dialog box.
13. Examine the *Edit Routing* dialog box to see the *Routing participants* and their roles that you set up, as shown in Figure 13–96.

**Figure 13–96**

14. Click **Settings** in the lower-left part of the dialog box.
15. Select **Unanimous approval for Review state required**, as shown in Figure 13–97.

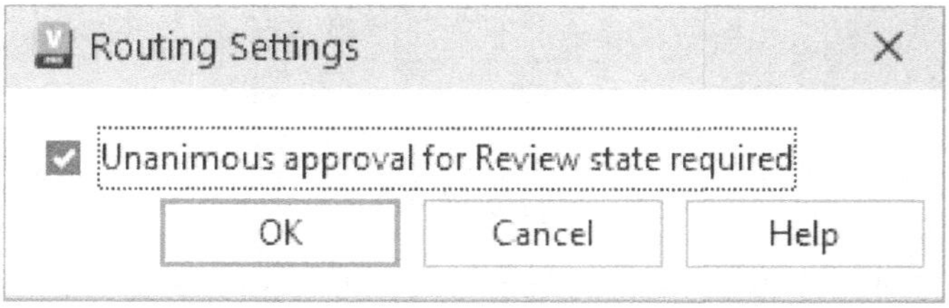


**Figure 13–97**

16. Click **OK** to close this dialog box and return to the *Edit Routing* dialog box.

17. Click **OK** to close the *Edit Routing* dialog box.
18. In the *Routing* dialog box, select the new routing **GroupOne** and drag it to the *Active routings* list, as shown in Figure 13–98.

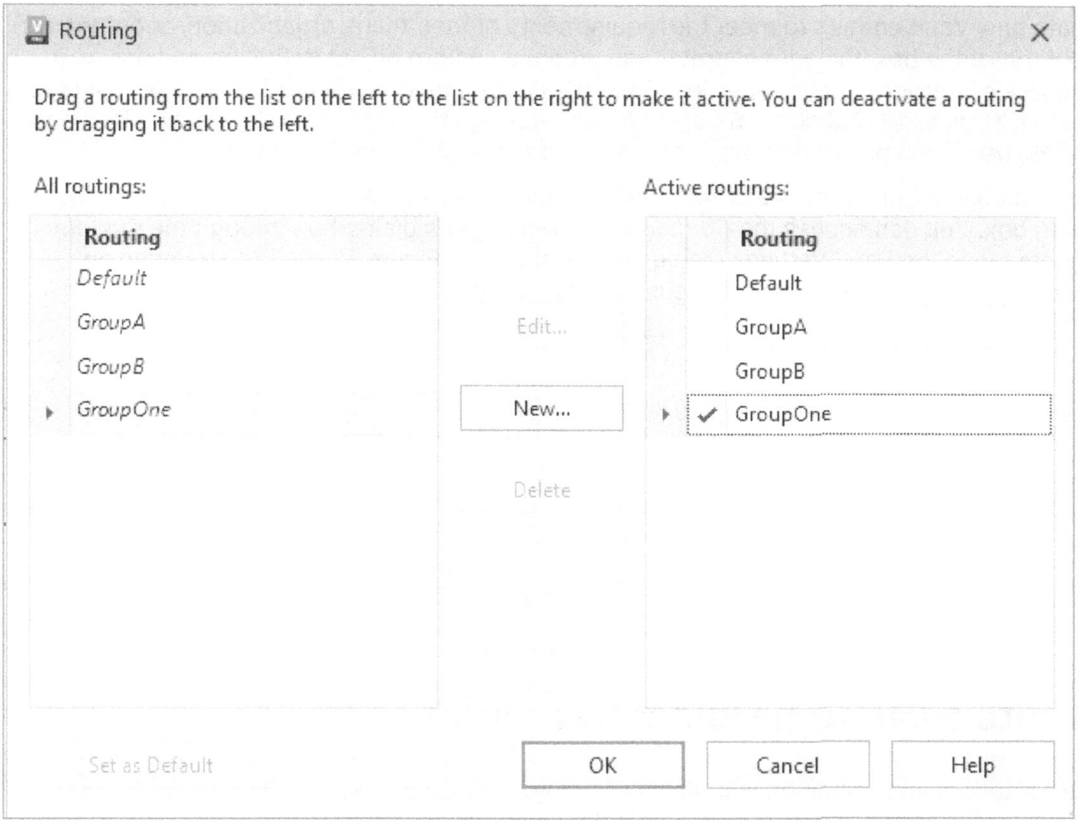


**Figure 13–98**

19. In the lower-left corner of the dialog box, click **Set as Default**.
20. Click **OK** to close this dialog box and return to the *Global Settings* dialog box.
21. Click **Close** to close this dialog box.
22. Exit Vault Professional.

**End of practice**

# 13.3 Custom Objects Definition Administration

This section describes how to create and configure custom objects to suit your company's requirements. Custom objects enable Vault administrators to use an extensible system to create new Vault entities to meet the requirements of their team, organization, or company. Right out of the box, the administrator can create a custom object definition and assign it categories, lifecycles, and properties. Once the custom object definition is created, users can create instances of that custom object directly through the user interface. As with files and folders, users can perform many common Vault tasks with custom objects.

Custom object definitions are created, edited, and deleted in the *Configure Custom Objects* dialog box. You can access the *Configure Custom Objects* dialog box through the *Custom Objects* tab in the *Vault Settings* dialog box, as shown in Figure 13–99. You must be an administrator to create and modify custom object definitions.

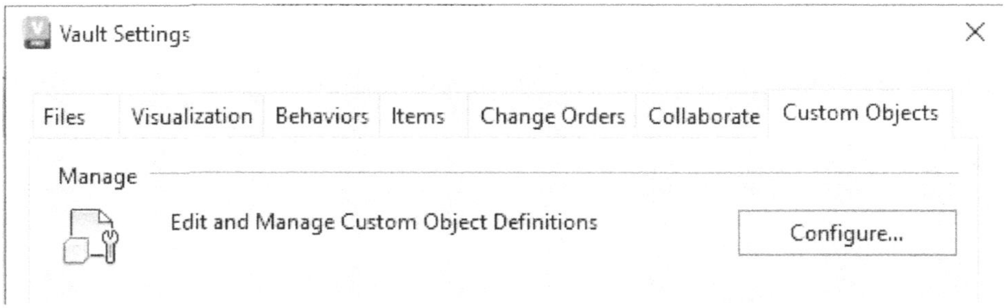


**Figure 13–99**

## Create a Custom Object Definition

The custom object definition is the type of entity that is being created. For example, an administrator can create a custom object definition called Contacts or Tasks.

When the user creates a new custom object based on a definition, it is considered an instance. For example, an administrator creates a custom object definition called Contact. A user could then create an instance of that custom object called Bob Smith.

Users can attach files, folders, and other Vault entities to a custom object with a link. For example, if a custom object definition has been created called Tasks and a user has created a task called Review John's Design, the task (Review John's Design) can be linked to John's design in the vault.

Custom object instances can be checked in or checked out, undergo a change state, and be managed with many common Vault commands. Similarly, linked objects are also affected, depending on the user's settings for the Vault function.

For example, if a user wants to check out a custom object and the custom object has links to files, folders, items, or change orders, the files associated with that linked data are gathered and checked out as well.

## How To: Create a New Custom Object Definition

Follow these steps to create a new custom object definition, as shown in Figure 13–100:

1. In Autodesk Vault Professional, select **Tools>Administration>Vault Settings**.
2. In the *Vault Settings* dialog box, select the *Custom Objects* tab and select **Configure**.
3. In the *Configure Custom Objects* dialog box, click **New**.

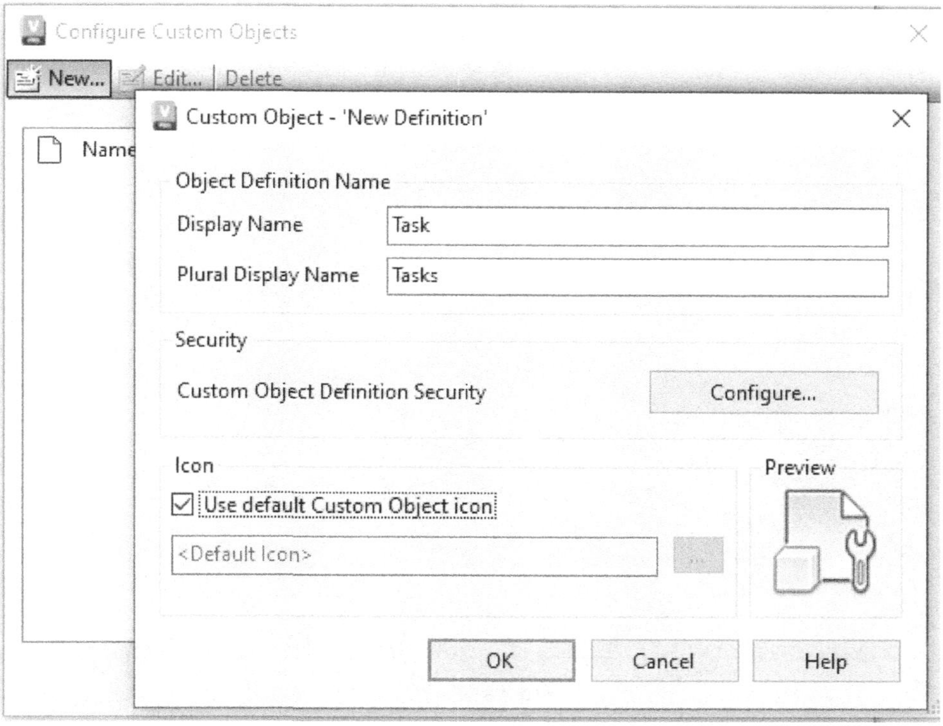


**Figure 13–100**

4. Enter a new *Display Name* for the custom object. This name is used in the Vault user interface when the new custom object displays.

   ***Note:*** *A display name and plural display name are required because Vault uses both contexts throughout the interface. Since there is no universal way to make a name plural, the administrator requirements are to insert the value upon creation.*

5. By default, new custom objects use object-based security. This can be customized by configuring different permissions for individual users and groups.

6. New custom objects can use any icon file (*.ICO). Defining four different sizes of the icon, provides the best-looking icons throughout the Vault interface (16x16, 32x32, 64x64, or 128x128). If only one size is defined, it is stretched or compressed to fit each size. If no icon is available, the **Use default Custom Object icon** option should be selected.The New Task option for creating task custom objects is shown in Figure 13–101.

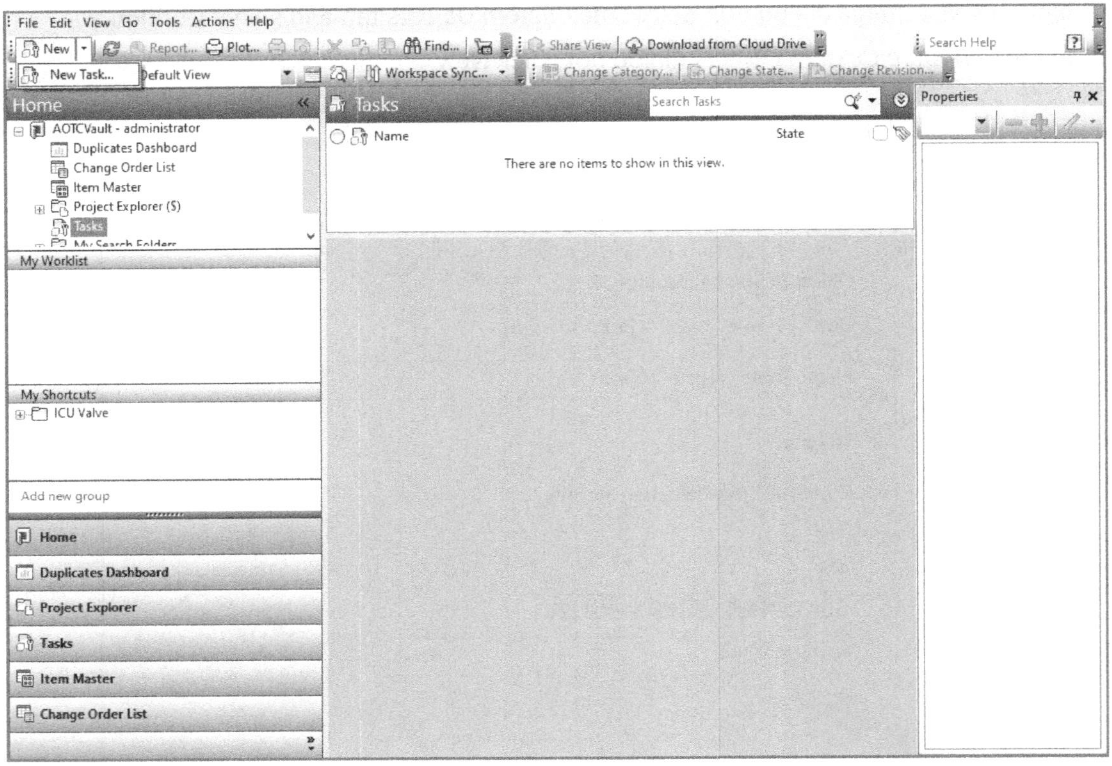


**Figure 13–101**

***Note:*** *New custom objects do not display in the user interface until the user logs out and logs back in after the custom object is created.*

# Edit a Custom Object Definition

Once a custom object definition is created, the administrator can navigate back to the *Configure Custom Objects* dialog box and modify the existing settings.

## How To: Edit Custom Object Definition Name

1. In Autodesk Vault Professional, select **Tools>Administration>Vault Settings**.
2. In the *Vault Settings* dialog box, select the *Custom Objects* tab and select **Configure**.
3. Select a custom object definition and click **Edit**, as shown in Figure 13–102.

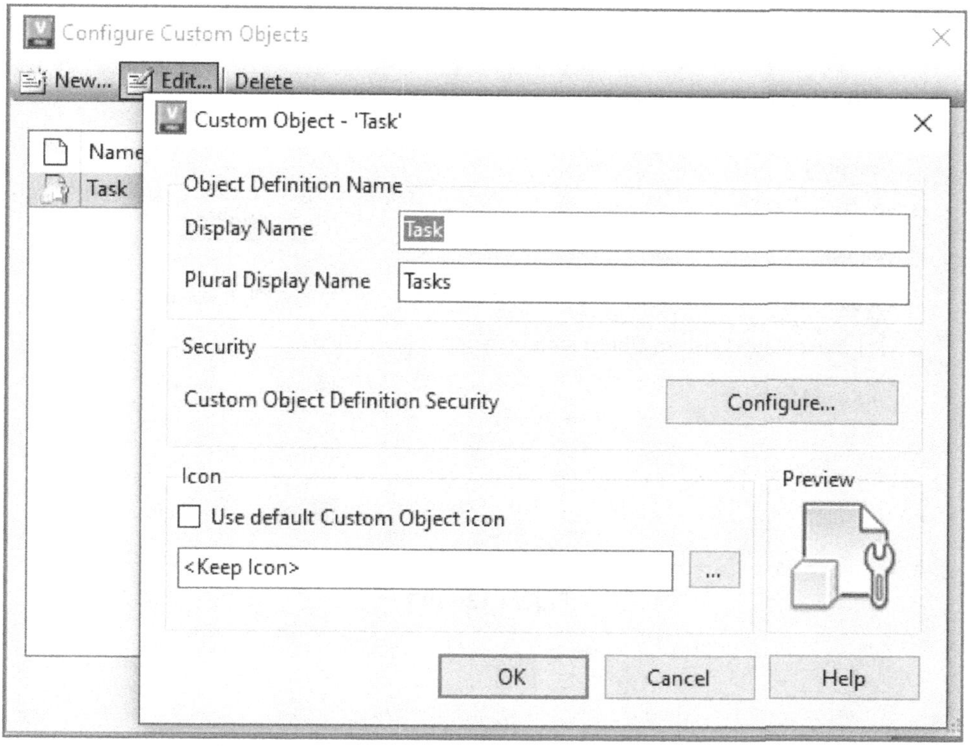


**Figure 13–102**

4. Modify the value in the *Display Name* and *Plural Display Name* fields.
5. Click **OK**.

**Note:** *The changes made to the custom object name are seen after logging out and logging back in to the Vault client.*

## How To: Edit Custom Object Definition Security

1. In Autodesk Vault Professional, select **Tools>Administration>Vault Settings**.
2. In the *Vault Settings* dialog box, select the *Custom Objects* tab and select **Configure**.
3. Select a custom object definition and click **Edit**.
4. Select **Configure** in the *Security* section, as shown in Figure 13–103.

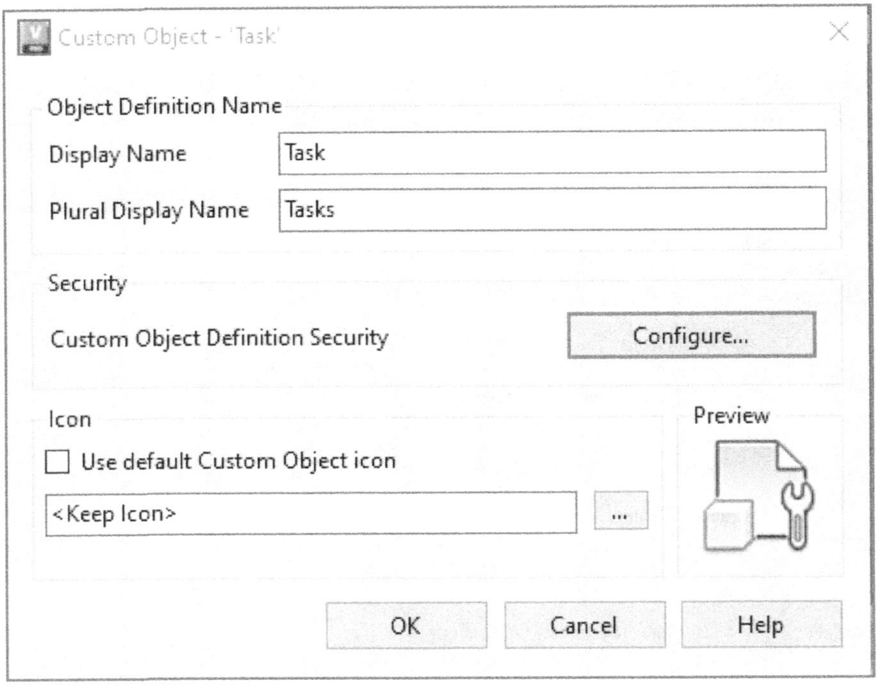


**Figure 13–103**

5. Make edits to the existing access control list, as shown in Figure 13–104.

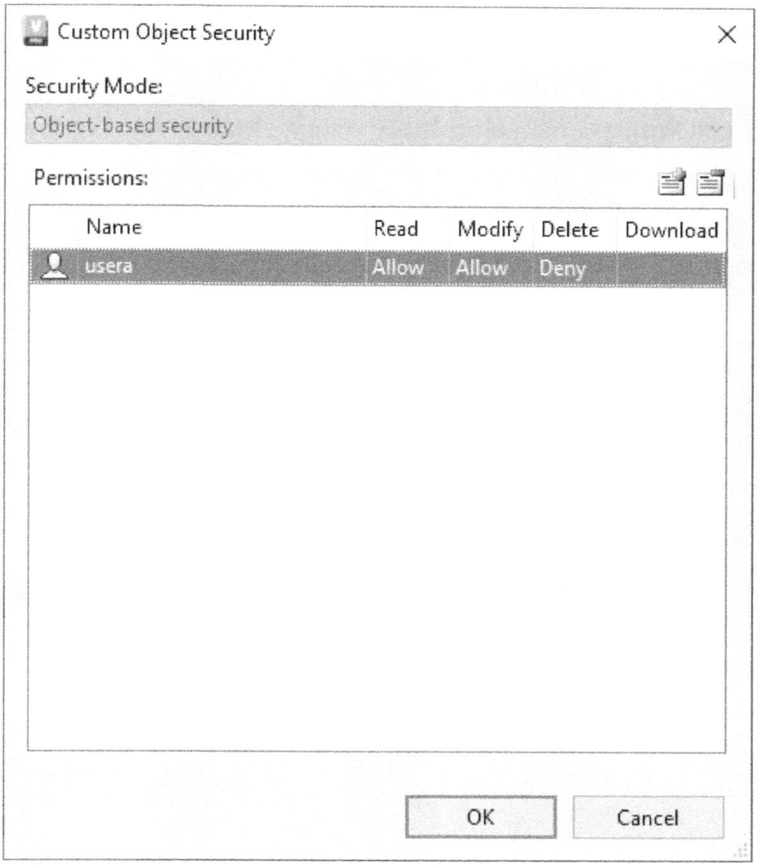


**Figure 13–104**

6. Click **OK**.
   - Edits to the security are made immediately to all instances of the custom object definition.

## How To: Edit Custom Object Definition Icon

The icon associated with a custom object definition can be changed after the definition is created.

1. In Autodesk Vault Professional, select **Tools>Administration>Vault Settings**.
2. In the *Vault Settings* dialog box, select the *Custom Objects* tab and select **Configure**.
3. Select a custom object definition and click **Edit**.
4. Change the icon by either choosing to use the default custom object icon or browsing to a new .ICO file, as shown in Figure 13–105.

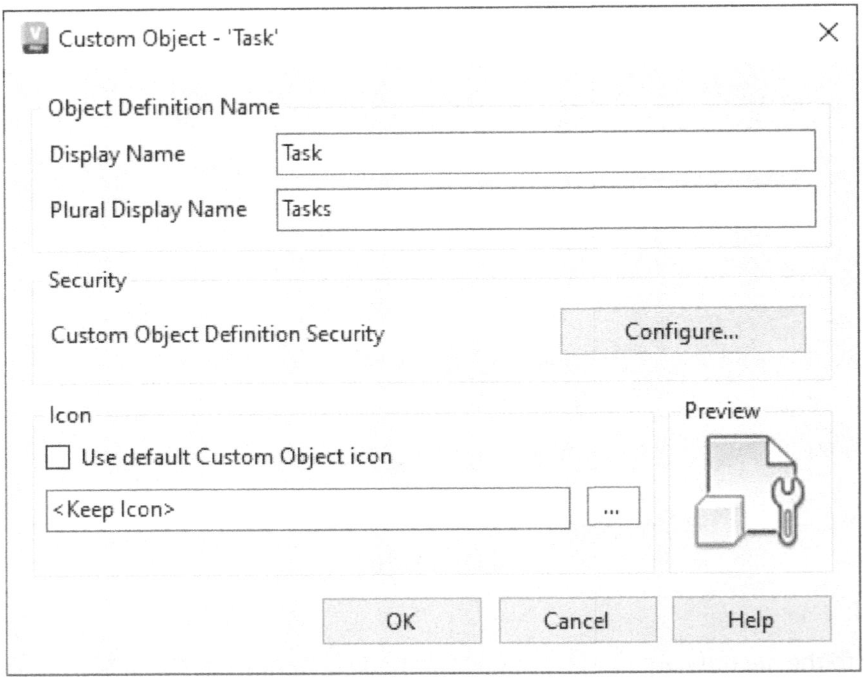


**Figure 13–105**

5. Click **OK**.

*Note: The changes made to the custom object icon are seen after logging out and logging back in to the Vault client.*

# Delete a Custom Object Definition

A user can delete an existing custom object at any time using the *Configure Custom Objects* dialog box. As long as the custom object is not in use, the definition can be deleted from the Vault.

Once an instance of a custom object definition has been created, the definition cannot be deleted.

> **Note:** *All instances of a custom object definition have to be removed from the vault before the definition can be deleted.*

## How To: Delete a Custom Object Definition

1. In Autodesk Vault Professional, select **Tools>Administration>Vault Settings**.
2. In the *Vault Settings* dialog box, select the *Custom Objects* tab and select **Configure**.
3. In the *Configure Custom Objects* dialog box, select the custom object to delete, and click **Delete**, as shown in Figure 13–106.

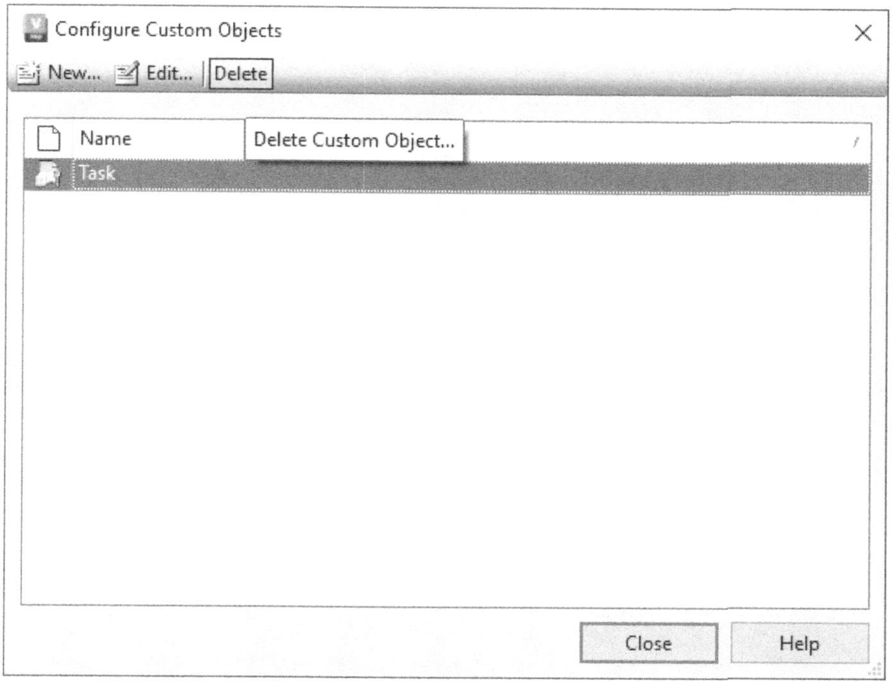


**Figure 13–106**

**4.** Perform one of these tasks:

- If no instances of the custom object were created in the Vault, click **Yes** in the *Confirm Deletion* dialog box.

  OR

- If there are instances of the custom object in the Vault:
  - Click **OK** in the dialog box that confirms the definition is in use.
  - Search the Vault for the custom object instances.
  - Delete the instances.
  - Navigate back to the *Custom Object Configuration* dialog box and select the definition.
  - Click **Delete**.
  - Click **Yes** in the *Confirm Deletion* dialog box.

The custom object definition is deleted. A new definition can be created using the same name, if required.

***Note:*** *If there are properties associated with the custom object definition, the administrator is restricted from deleting it.*

Chapter 14

# Job Server, Vault Revision Tables, and Backups

Topics covered in this chapter include the Job Server, revision tables, and backups. The process of creating and checking in visualization files manually can be time-intensive for some users, especially those responsible for managing large assemblies. The Job Server utility enables users to automatically create and check-in visualization files from their local workstation. The Vault Revision Table feature enables you to automatically update a drawing's revision table with Vault data when properties are synchronized through the Job Server. To prevent data loss, you can use the Backup and Restore functionality.

## Learning Objectives

- Differentiate between the Job Server and Job Processor.
- Enable the Job Server.
- Administrate the Job Server.
- Log in to the Job Processor to view jobs.
- Enable the Vault Revision Table functionality.
- Understand the Vault revision table settings.
- Backup and restore your Autodesk Vault machine.

# 14.1 Enabling the Job Server

With Autodesk® Vault Professional, you can use the Job Server utility to automate specific jobs like DWF or PDF generation when changing the state from **Work in Progress** to **Released**.

## Job Server vs. Job Processor

Administrators can manage the Job Server by tracking jobs, resubmitting stalled jobs, and deleting unnecessary jobs. However, the Job Server must be enabled by an administrator.

Users assign their publishing jobs to a job queue where they are stored until certain parameters are met. The Job Processor then creates the visualization files and checks them into the Vault based on the publishing properties defined in the *Global Settings* dialog box.

### How To: Enable the Job Server

> ***Note:*** *You must be an administrator to enable the Job Server.*

1. Select **Tools>Administration>Global Settings**.
2. In the *Global Settings* dialog box, click the *Integrations* tab.
3. Select the **Enable Job Server** checkbox (as shown in Figure 14–1) to activate the Job Server.

   ***Note:*** *The Job Server permits for publishing jobs to be queued and processed at a later time. You must activate the Job Server prior to sending any jobs to it for publishing.*

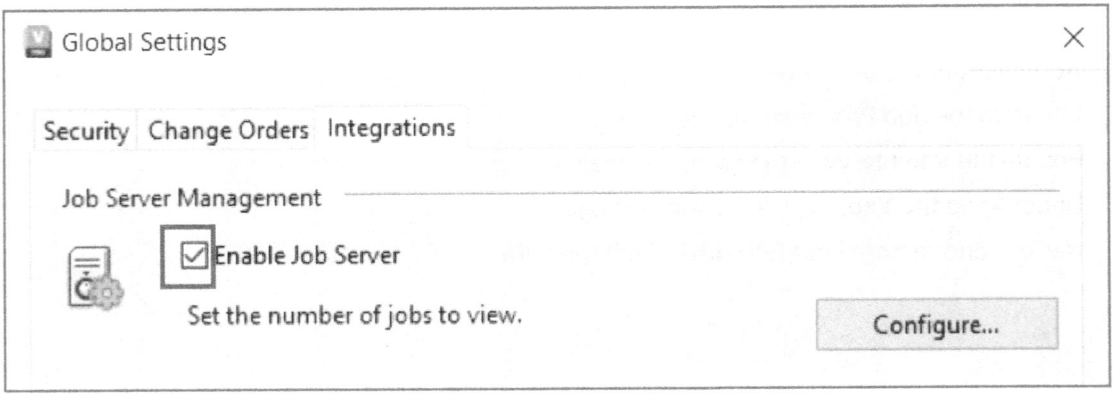


**Figure 14–1**

# Job Processor

The Job Processor is installed at the same time as the Vault Client. As of the 2019 software release, the Job Processor has all of the required CAD applications included with it, so that it can be installed on a computer that does not otherwise have CAD tools installed.

> **Note:** *You must have the Job Server enabled to set up jobs. Having a Job Processor running is not required to submit jobs. The jobs will enter a queue until a Job Processor comes online to request jobs.*

As already explained in the section before, the Job Processor is the engine that controls and completes the jobs.

The first time you access the Job Processor, you must specify the user name, password, and server name. The Job Processor will remember these login credentials each time you log in until changed through the *Administration* menu.

## How To: Install the Job Processor

1. On the workstation where you want jobs to be processed, select **Start menu>All Programs>Autodesk Data Management>Autodesk Job Processor [Edition] for Vault** to launch the Job Processor application, as shown in Figure 14–2.

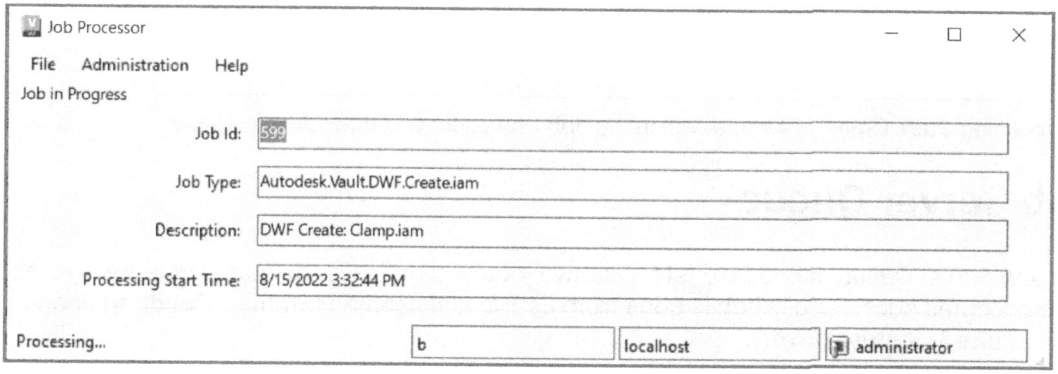


**Figure 14–2**

> **Note:** *Select File>Pause at any time to halt the Job Processor and prevent it from processing any new jobs. If the Job Processor is in the middle of processing a job, it will finish the job first. The Administration>Settings are not accessible unless the Job Processor is paused.*

2. Select **Administration>Settings** to display the *Settings* dialog box.
3. Enter the *User Name* and *Password* of the user for this workstation.
4. Specify the server from which you want the Job Processor to pull jobs for publishing.
5. Click **OK** to save your changes and close the Settings dialog box.

6. Select **File>Resume** to log in to the specified server.

You can find the Job Processor in your taskbar. Click on the arrow-up symbol, shown in Figure 14–3, to see the Job Processor symbol.

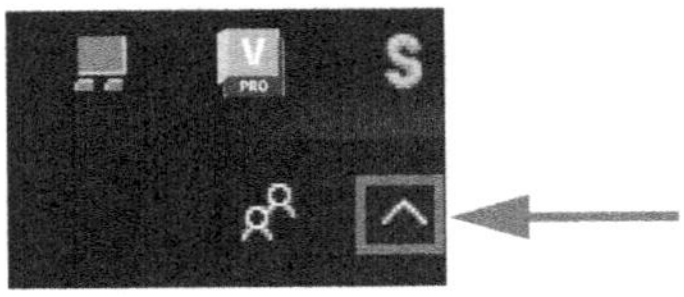

**Figure 14–3**

You do not have to start the Job Processor each time you are starting your machine. There is a mechanism to automate this start procedure by configuration. This is handled in the *Configure Job Server* lesson.

## Job Processor Details

See the following table for an explanation of all fields in Job Processor:

| Detail | Description |
|---|---|
| **Job ID** | Displays the number of the job currently being processed. |
| **Job Type** | Displays a description of the job being processed. |
| **Description** | Displays more information about the job in the queue. |
| **Status** | Displays the current state of the Job Processor. |
| **Processing Start Time** | Time at which the Job Processor began working on a job. |

# Job Server Queue

The *Job Server Queue* dialog box lists all active jobs and displays the status whether the jobs were executed successfully (job is gone from list), is still pending (*Status* = **Pending**) or an error has occurred (*Status* = **Error**).

### How To: Use the Job Server Queue

1. Select **Tools>Job Queue**, as shown in Figure 14–4.

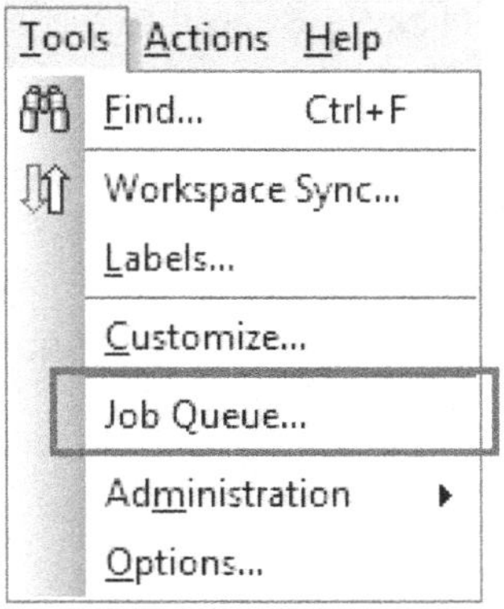


**Figure 14–4**

2. In the *Job Server Queue* dialog box, you can sort the jobs by *ID*, *Priority*, *Status*, *Description*, *Submitted Date*, or by whom they were submitted, as shown in Figure 14–5.

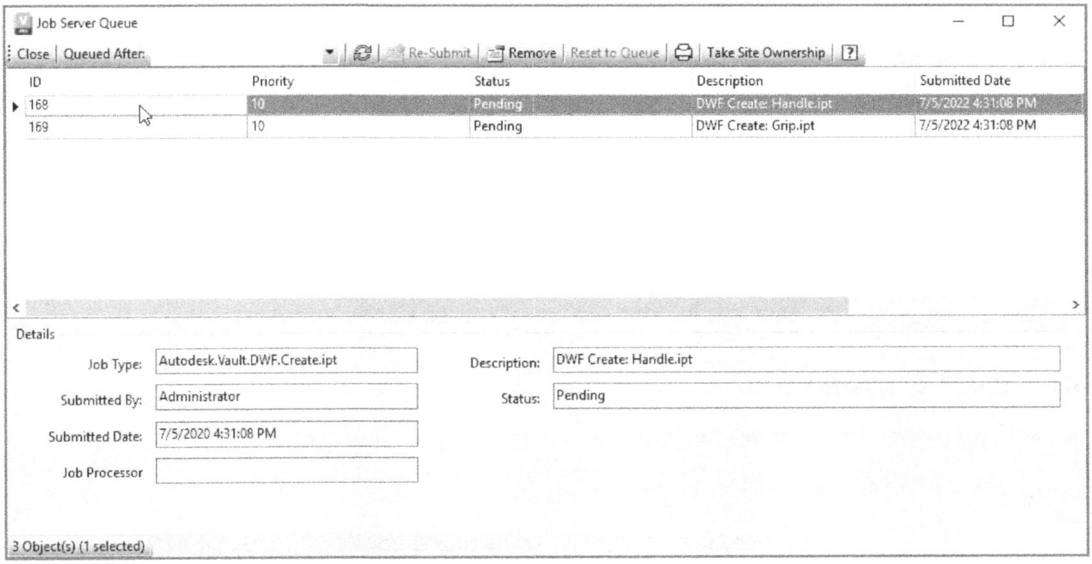


**Figure 14–5**

***Note:*** *The Job Server Queue dialog box displays up to 1,000 jobs. A warning will display to inform the user if there are more than 1,000 jobs in the queue.*

3. Right-click on the column heading to customize the layout and view of the queue.
   - If you want to filter the list so that it only displays the jobs queued after a specific date and time, click the *Queued After* drop-down list and specify when.
4. Select a job that you want to modify and perform one of the following actions:
   - If you want to delete the job from the queue, click **Remove**.

- If the job has an error status, click **Re-Submit** to reprocess the job.
- If you want to remove the Job Processor from the task and leave the job in the queue, click **Reset to Queue**.
- If you want to assign the task to the Job Processor on your workstation, click **Take Ownership**.

5. Click **Print** to send a copy of the grid to the default printer.
6. Click **Refresh** at any time to update the queue.

## Job Server Details

This table describes the details of the *Job Server Queue* dialog box.

| Detail | Description |
|---|---|
| **Job Type** | The type of job that was submitted for processing. Visualization jobs display as Autodesk.Vault.DWF.Create {0} where {0} is the file extension. |
| **Submitted By** | Displays the name of the user who submitted the job to the queue. |
| **Submitted Date** | Displays the date and time the job was submitted to the queue. |
| **Job Processor** | Displays the name of the computer that has taken the job from the queue for processing. |
| **Description** | Displays more information about the job in the queue. This field will also display the DWF Create: filename. |
| **Status** | Displays whether the job's status is Pending, Processing, or Error. |
| **Results** | Displays information only if the job has an error status. |

## Job Server Commands

This table describes the commands in the *Job Server Queue* dialog box.

| Command | Description |
|---|---|
| **Close** | Closes the *Job Server Queue* dialog box. |
| **Queued After** | Filters the list by showing the first 1,000 jobs queued after the specified date and time. |
| **Refresh** | Refreshes the queue. |
| **Re-Submit** | Reprocesses a job that has encountered an error. This button is only enabled when a job has been placed in an error state. |
| **Remove** | Removes any job with the status of Error or Pending. |
| **Reset to Queue** | Removes the reservation of a job by the Job Processor. **Note:** This command is not in the toolbar by default. To add the command, click the toolbar list and select **Add or Remove Buttons**. |

| Command | Description |
|---|---|
| **Take Site Ownership** | Transfers ownership of the job's reservation to the current user's Job Processor. When a site that has reserved jobs is deleted, or a backup is performed but the information is restored to a different site, the pending jobs are deleted from the queue. This feature enables administrators to claim ownership for processing the job before it is deleted. |
| **Print** | Prints the current queue grid to the default printer. |

# Initiating a Job

In your default Autodesk Vault installation, there is already a job integrated, which starts to automatically generate and save DWF files to selected elements.

## How To: Initiate a Job

Use the following steps to view the current queue status:

1. Select one or more CAD files from the list in the main grid.
2. Select **Actions>Update View>Queue Update** (as shown in Figure 14–6) to set up a DWF generation job in the Job Server Queue.

**Figure 14–6**

3. Go to the Job Server Queue by selecting **Tools>Job Queue**.

4. You should see the new DWF job listed as **Pending**, as shown in Figure 14–7.

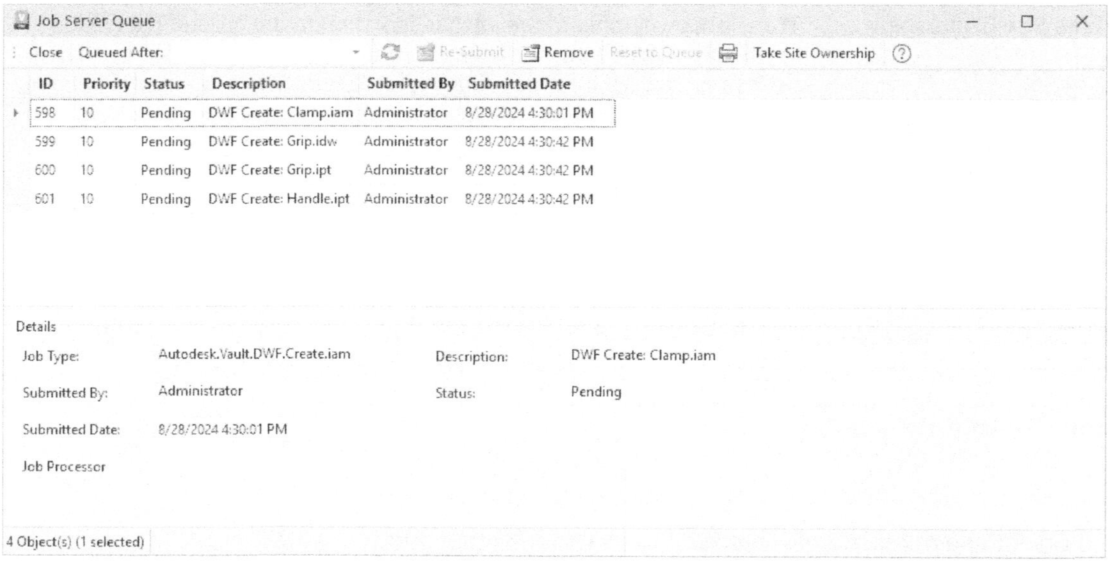


**Figure 14–7**

5. As soon as the DWF is generated successfully, the job will disappear from the queue.
6. Click (Refresh) from time to time to check whether the job is already done.
7. Have a look back to your component list and find the new generated DWF.

In case the job is still hanging in the queue, ensure that your Job Processor is running and completing your job. You can easily check whether your Job Processor is running or not by having a look to the task bar.

# Practice 14a
# Run Some Jobs and Watch Them in the Job Queue

In this practice, you will first enable the Job Server and get the Job Processor running, then you will select multiple CAD files and run the predefined DWF job.

## Task 1: Enable the job server and get the job processor running.

1. Log in to Autodesk Vault as an Administrator. Ensure that **Designs.ipj** is set as the Inventor project file.
2. Go to **Tools>Administration>Global Settings**.
3. Select **Enable Job Server** in the *Integrations* tab (as shown in Figure 14–8), if not already selected.

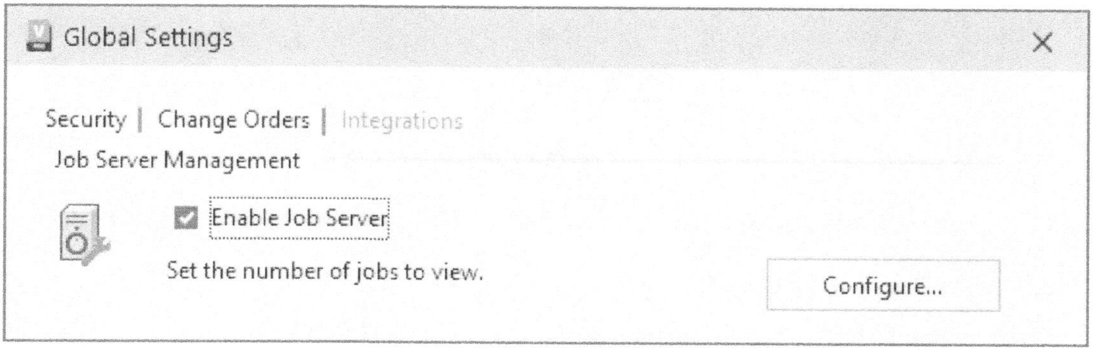


**Figure 14–8**

4. Open your File Explorer.

5. Browse to the *Program Files>Autodesk>Vault Client [Edition]>Explorer* folder and start the **JobProcessor.exe** file, as shown in Figure 14–9.
    - Alternatively, use your Windows *Start* menu and select **All Programs>Autodesk Data Management>Autodesk Job Processor [Edition] for Vault**.
    - If required, enter your name, password, and server to log on.
    - Ensure that the required CAD Applications are installed on the same machine the Job Processor is installed.

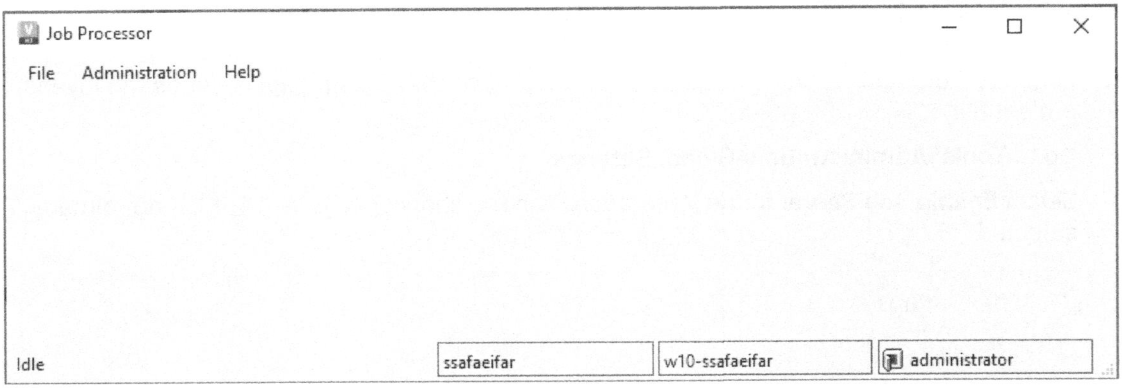


**Figure 14–9**

## Task 2: Multi-select some CAD files and start the automatic DWF generation.

1. Select CAD files from the main Vault grid.
2. Select **Actions>Update View>Queue Update**, as shown in Figure 14–10.

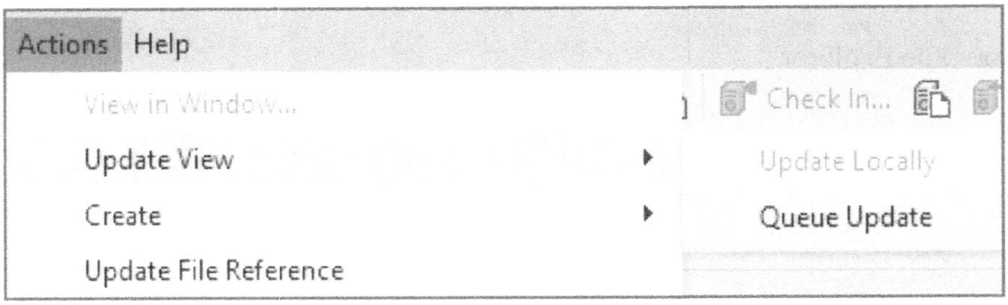


**Figure 14–10**

3. Select **Tools>Job Queue** to open the Job Server Queue to watch the newly created DWF jobs and their status.

4. Select one pending job from the list and remove it by clicking **Remove** in the *Job Server Queue* dialog box, as shown in Figure 14–11.

**Figure 14–11**

5. Wait a few seconds and refresh your list by clicking **Refresh** in *Job Server Queue* dialog box. If no error occurred and the list is empty, exit the Job Server Queue. If the Job Processor is idle, it can take up to 10 minutes to evoke again.
   - **Tip:** To facilitate the job processing, pause the Job Processor and resume it by selecting **File>Pause** and then selecting **File>Resume**.
6. Double-check with your list in Vault whether all DWF's were generated, besides the one you removed from the Job Server Queue.

**End of practice**

# 14.2 Configuring the Job Server

From the administrative point of view, there are several tools that help you to configure and administrate the jobs and events in Vault. The Job Processor can be configured to automatically start each time your machine is started.

## Configuration via Job Processor UI

There are several options and commands in the *Job Processor* dialog box that are explained in the following table:

| Command | Definition |
|---|---|
| **Pause** | On **Pause**, the Job Processor will pause and the jobs remain in the queue. It prevents it from processing any new jobs. If the Job Processor is in the middle of processing a job, it will finish the job first. |
| **Resume** | After you have set the Job Processor to **Pause**, you can click **Resume** to go on completing the jobs in the queue. |
| **Exit** | On **Exit**, the Job Processor will exit and close. |
| **Start on Windows Logon** | Here you can set whether the Job Processor is started automatically on Windows Logon. |
| **Settings** | In the *Settings* dialog box, you can enter your name, password, and server. |
| **Job Types** | Displays the *Job Types* dialog box, which contains all available job types to use. If the workstation does not have the required information to process the particular type of job, that type of file is unchecked. |
| **About Job Processor/Help** | Here you can find useful Help files for handling and administrating the Job Processor. |

An example of a job is shown in Figure 14–12.

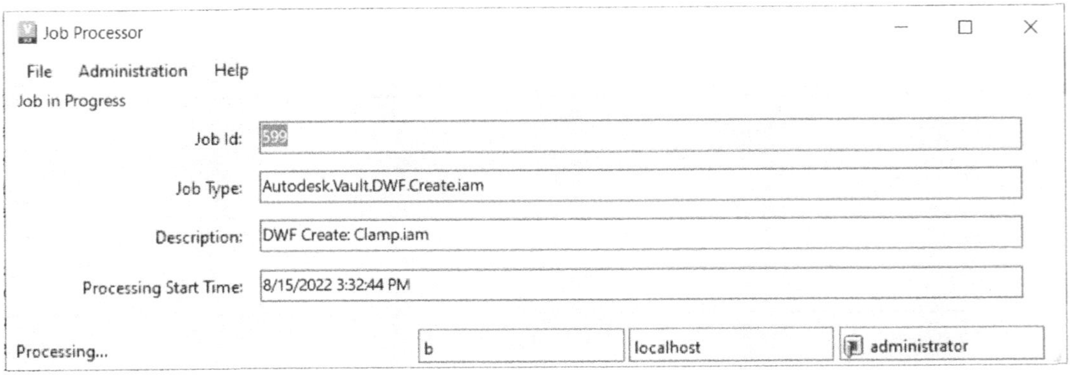


**Figure 14–12**

# The Configuration File

In the Job Processor configuration file, you can add, edit, and delete your custom jobs and set some global settings for the job services.

- Name of configuration file: **JobProcessor.exe.config**.

## Location of the Configuration File

The configuration file can be found in the *Explorer* folder.

- Path to the configuration file: *Program Files>Autodesk>Vault Client [Edition]>Explorer*.

## Settings in the Configuration File

To add a new job to the configuration file, go to the *jobHandler* section in the configuration file.

| | |
|---|---|
| **<jobHandler>** | Add your custom jobs here. As soon as they are implemented correctly in this configuration file, you should check whether the job is available and listed in the Job Processor. Open the Job Processor and select **Administration>Job Types**. The new job should be listed here and is ready to use. |

# Log File

For analyses and control, you can review the Job Processor log file (as shown in Figure 14–13). You can find the log file in the same *Explorer* folder as the configuration file.

- Path to the log file: *Program Files>Autodesk>Vault Client [Edition]>Explorer*.

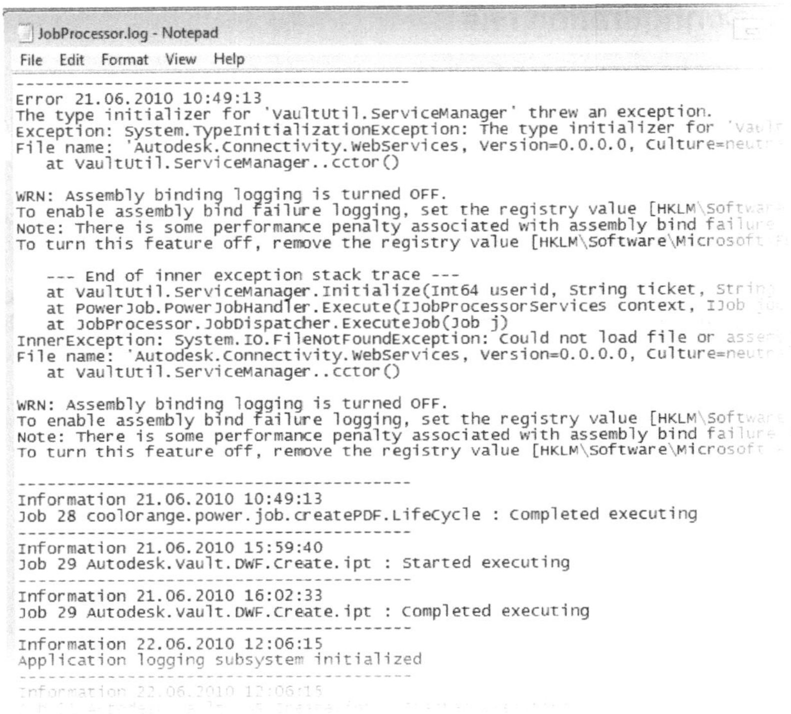


**Figure 14–13**

Here you can find useful information why your job could not be completed successfully or why the Job Processor or Job Server does not work.

# Practice 14b
# Change Settings in the Job Processor

In this practice, you will change the configuration of the Job Processor to start it each time your machine is started. You will then set up some jobs in Vault and pause them in the Job Processor. Finally, you will resume and look at the Job Processor log file to see whether or not all processes were successful.

## Task 1: Configure the Job Processor.

1. Start the Job Processor if it is not started yet.
    - Browse to the *Program Files>Autodesk>Vault Client [Edition]>Explorer* folder and start the **JobProcessor.exe** file or use your Windows *Start* menu and select **All Programs>Autodesk Data Management>Autodesk Job Processor [Edition] for Vault**.
2. From the *Administration* menu, activate the automatic start by selecting **Start on Windows Logon**, as shown in Figure 14–14.

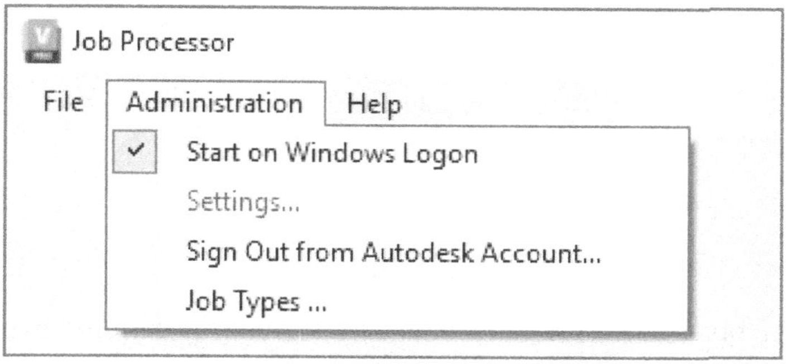


**Figure 14–14**

3. For your information, select **Administration>Job Types** and get an overview of which jobs are available in this Vault installation.

## Task 2: Pause and resume the job process.

1. Select several components and create the DWF job, explained in the first lesson (go to **Actions>Update View>Queue Update**).
2. Go to the Job Server Queue and watch the progress.
3. When only a few jobs are left and still pending, go to the Job Processor and select **File>Pause**, as shown in Figure 14–15.

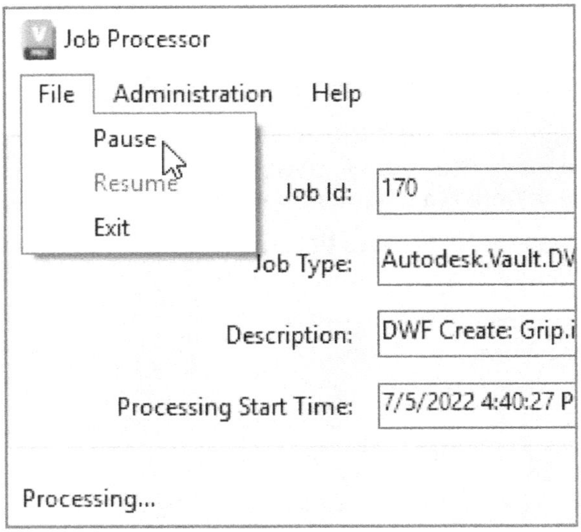


**Figure 14–15**

4. The progress of job execution is paused. The job which was currently in progress will be finished. All jobs queued after this current job are paused and will not be handled as long as the Job Processor is "stopped" (paused).
5. After a while, click **File>Resume** in the *Job Processor* dialog box to go on with job execution.
6. Double-check with your Job Server Queue whether all files were generated successfully. Exit the Job Server Queue and the Job Processor (**File>Exit**).

7. Review the Job Processor log file stored in the *Explorer* directory of your Vault installation (as shown in Figure 14–16), and analyze the content.

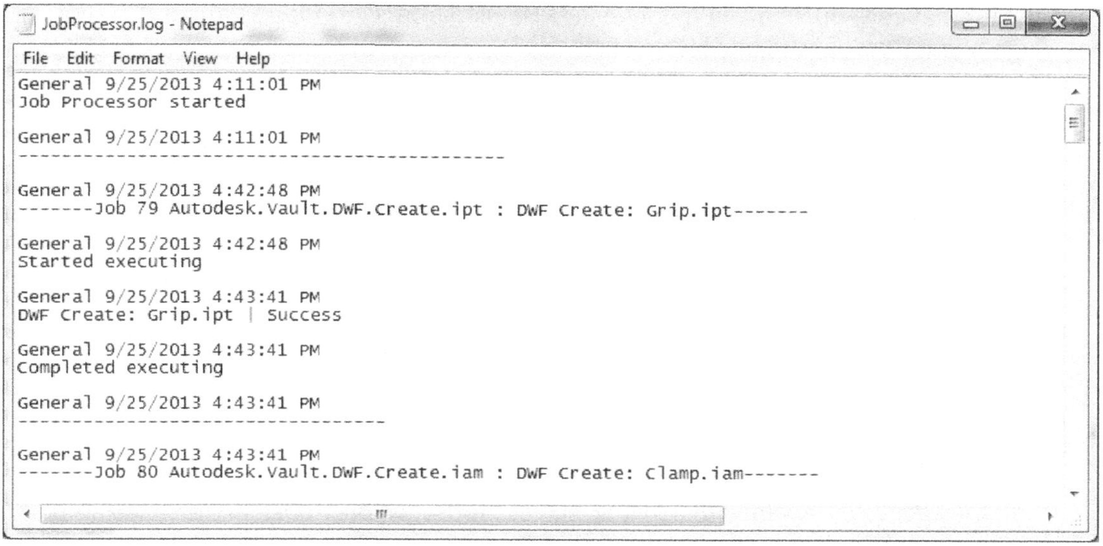


```
General 9/25/2013 4:11:01 PM
Job Processor started

General 9/25/2013 4:11:01 PM
---------------------------------------------

General 9/25/2013 4:42:48 PM
-------Job 79 Autodesk.Vault.DWF.Create.ipt : DWF Create: Grip.ipt-------

General 9/25/2013 4:42:48 PM
Started executing

General 9/25/2013 4:43:41 PM
DWF Create: Grip.ipt | Success

General 9/25/2013 4:43:41 PM
Completed executing

General 9/25/2013 4:43:41 PM
----------------------------------

General 9/25/2013 4:43:41 PM
-------Job 80 Autodesk.Vault.DWF.Create.iam : DWF Create: Clamp.iam-------
```

**Figure 14–16**

**End of practice**

# 14.3 PDF Publishing

You can automatically publish and manage 2D PDF files from CAD files as documentation in the design release process at any lifecycle state.

## How To: Configure PDF Publishing Options

Use the following steps to select the required settings for 2D AutoCAD and 2D Inventor PDF printing (you must have administrative access to peform these tasks):

1. Create a user with access to Released files. See *Assign Roles to Users* for more information.
2. Configure lifecycle definitions.
    a. Select **Tools>Administration>Vault Settings**.
    b. In the *Vault Settings* dialog box, select the *Behaviors* tab and select **Lifecycles**.
    c. Select the definition to be modified and click **Edit**.
    d. In the *Lifecycle Definition* dialog box, select the *Transitions* tab, then (as an example) select **Work in Progress to Released>Edit**.
    e. In the *Transitions* dialog box, select the *Actions* tab.
    f. From the drop-down list, select one of the following options:
        - **Synchronize properties, update view and PDF using Job Server**
        - **Synchronize properties and update PDF using Job Server**

    **Note:** *Selecting one of these options from the list does not automatically select the checkbox as well. Make sure to select the checkbox beside the option, too.*

    g. Select the *Security* tab, add the user created in Step 1, and allow **Modify** access under the **Released** state.
    h. In the *Lifecycle Definition* dialog box, select **Design Representation Process>Edit**.
    i. In the *Lifecycle Definition* dialog box, select the **Released** state.
    j. Select the *Security* tab, add the user created in Step 1, and assign it **Modify** access. See *Edit Lifecycle State Security* for more information.

    **Note:** *You can create PDFs at any lifecycle state.*

3. The sync state job fails if you do not have adequate permission for a particular state to be set on a PDF file, for example, you do not have the *Modify* access on the **Released** state.
4. To enable the Job Server, select **Tools>Administration>Global Settings** and on the *Integrations* tab, select **Enable Job Server**.

    **Note:** *For Job Processor to generate DWF and 2D PDF files, launch AutoCAD DWG Trueview at least once on the Job Processor.*

| 2D AutoCAD PDF Publishing Options | Details |
|---|---|
| **Add As An Attachment** | Shows the published PDF file as an attachment to the file. |
| **Upload to Source File Location** | Automatically stores the published PDF file to the selected file location. |
| **Upload To Selected Vault Path** | Defines a specific location (using Browse) to store the published PDF file. |
| **Sync Lifecycle State and Revision As Source** | Allows both the published PDF and its source file to have the same lifecycle state and a revision value. |
| **Use Page Settings From User DWG** | Eliminates the need to reconfigure page settings in Vault if previously done in the native application. Checked and cannot be unchecked. |
| **Include Model Space** | Enables the published PDF file to contain model space view. |
| **Include Layouts** | Enables the published PDF file to contain model space view only. |
| **Include Layer Info** | Enables the published PDF to contain layer information. |
| **Initialize Layouts** | Enables support for legacy files. |
| **Include Font Handling** | Enables publishing a PDF file with font styles. |

| 2D Inventor PDF Publishing Options | Details |
|---|---|
| **Add As An Attachment** | Shows the published PDF file as an attachment to the file. |
| **Upload to Source File Location** | Automatically stores the published PDF file to the selected file location. |
| **Sync Lifecycle State and Revision As Source** | Allows both the published PDF and its source file to have the same lifecycle state and a revision value. |
| **Upload To Selected Vault Path** | Defines a specific location (using Browse) to store the published PDF file. |
| **Vector Resolution** | Set as 400 DPI for managing large PDF file size and appropriate details. |
| **Plot Object Lineweights** | Enables the published PDF file to display a consistent lineweight for object and consistent lineweight for linetypes. |
| **All Sheets** | Prints all the sheets in the drawing. To print sheets for which the Exclude from Printing option is checked in the *Edit Sheet* dialog box, select Print Excluded Sheets. |
| **All Colors As Black** | Prints the drawing in black and white. Embedded images and shaded views are still printed in color. |

## How To: Publish PDFs from 2D CAD Files

Use the following steps to configure lifecycle definitions and PDF options to publish PDFs from 2D CAD files (you must have administrative access to peform these tasks):

1. Create a user with access to Released files. For more information, see *Assign Roles to Users*.
2. Configure lifecycle definitions.
   a. Select **Tools>Administration>Vault Settings**.
   b. In the *Vault Settings* dialog box, select the *Behaviors* tab and select **Lifecycles**.
   c. Select the definition to be modified and click **Edit**.
   d. In the *Lifecycle Definition* dialog box, select the *Transitions* tab, then (as an example) select **Work in Progress to Released>Edit**.
   e. In the *Transitions* dialog box, select the *Actions* tab.
   f. From the drop-down list, select one of the following options.
      - **Synchronize properties, update view and PDF using Job Server**
      - **Synchronize properties and update PDF using Job Server**

   ***Note:*** *Selecting one of these options from the list does not automatically select the checkbox as well. Ensure that the checkbox beside the option is also selected.*

   g. In the *Security* tab, add the user created in Step 1 and enable the **Modify** access under the **Released** state.
   h. In the *Lifecycle Definition* dialog box, select **Design Representation Process>Edit**.
   i. In the *Lifecycle Definition* dialog box, select the **Released** state.
   j. Select the *Security* tab, add the user created in Step 1, and assign it **Modify** access.

   ***Note:*** *You can create PDFs at any lifecycle state.*

3. The sync state job fails if you do not have adequate permission for a particular state to be set on a PDF file, for example, you do not have the *Modify* access on the ***Released*** state.
4. To enable the Job Server, select **Tools>Administration>Global Settings** and on the *Integrations* tab, select **Enable Job Server**.

   ***Note:*** *For the Job Processor to generate DWF and 2D PDF files, launch AutoCAD DWG Trueview at least once on the Job Processor.*

5. Select **Tools>Administration>Vault Settings** and in the *PDF Options* section, select **Options** to launch the *PDF Publish Options* dialog box and configure the PDF publishing options.

6. Publish a PDF from a CAD file.
   a. Select any AutoCAD DWG file or Inventor 2D CAD file.
   b. Select **Change Category**. In the *Change Category* dialog box, select the **Engineering** category. Click **OK**.
   c. Select **Change State**. In the *Change State* dialog box, select **Released** from the lifecycle state drop-down list. Click **OK**.

   This generates a PDF as an attachment to the selected file. Additionally, a thumbnail for the PDF displays in the *Preview* tab.

   ***Note:*** *To synchronize the revisions of the drawing file and 2D PDF file, set each file's lifecycle revision to be the same.*

   ***Note:*** *To verify the Design Representation classification, click Tools>Administration>Vault Settings>Behaviors>Rules. In the Assignment Rules dialog box, view the Rule Criteria for Design Representation.*

## How To: Create a PDF from 2D CAD Files

When using this command, a PDF can be created without going through a lifecycle state change for a 2D file. As an Administrator, you must enable the **Enable Manual PDF Creation** checkbox in the *PDF Options* section of the Settings dialog in order to use the **Create PDF** capability.

***Note:*** *You must have appropriate access given by your administrator to access the Create PDF command in the different access points.*

Use the following steps to create a copy of a PDF file using a 2D CAD file:

1. Select the 2D CAD file for which you want to manually create a PDF.
2. Right-click and select **Create PDF**, or select the command from the *Actions* menu.
   - **IMPORTANT:** The **Create PDF** command is available only for the latest version of the file and not for any historical version/revision of the 2D CAD files.

## How To: Specify the PDF Publish Location

Use the following steps to specify a desired location outside of Vault Client for PDFs (you must have administrative access to perform these tasks):

1. Select **Tools>Administration>Vault Settings**.
2. In the *Vault Settings* dialog box, select the *Files* tab.
3. Select **Define** next to *Specify PDF Publish Location*.

4. In the *PDF Publish Location* dialog box, select the desired option:
   - **Save in Vault** (local copies will not be created)
   - **Save on a local drive in one folder**
   - **Save on a local drive using the Vault folder structure**
5. Click **OK**.

   ***Note:*** *By default, automatically generated PDF files are hidden in the file list. Select* ***Tools>Options*** *to enable to* ***Show hidden files****.*

# 14.4 Vault Revision Table Administration

The process of manually updating the revision tables on drawings can be time-consuming, especially for changes that require simple property updates throughout a design's lifecycle. The Vault Revision Table feature enables you to automatically update a drawing's revision table with Vault data when properties are synchronized through the Job Server. This functionality eliminates the need to open each drawing in its native CAD application for updates.

**Important**: You must be an administrator with appropriate ownership privileges to enable the Vault Revision Table.

## Vault Revision Table Supported Drawings and Prerequisites

### Supported Drawings

- AutoCAD® drawings (.DWG)
- AutoCAD Mechanical drawings (.DWG)
- Autodesk® Inventor® drawings (.IDW)
- Autodesk Inventor drawings (.DWG)

### Prerequisites

- Autodesk Inventor is installed so that Inventor IDW and DWG drawings can be updated.
- Revision Table functionality is enabled.
- The Job Server is enabled with the **synchronize properties** option selected for the required state transition(s).
- Suitable column headers are created and their property mappings established between the drawings' revision table columns and the Vault properties.

  ***Note:*** *The system property 'Revision' is a key mapping and must be mapped to at least one of the column headers.*

Once all the prerequisites are met, the revision tables for the supported drawings are automatically updated with specified Vault data whenever properties are synchronized with the Job Server. This way, you can be sure that the revision table in your drawing is always up to date with the appropriate information from the vault.

## Vault Revision Table Administration

Administrators can configure the information to be displayed in the revision table of the drawings for standardization across vault through the Revision Table Settings.

The Vault Revision Table feature must be enabled before you can configure revision table settings or use the Revision Table feature in the Autodesk Inventor and AutoCAD Vault add-ins.

### How To: Enable the Vault Revision Table

1. Select **Tools>Administration>Vault Settings**.
2. In the *Vault Settings* dialog box, select the *Behaviors* tab and select **Revision Table**.

   ***Note:*** *You can also open this dialog box from within the add-in by selecting* ***Vault Options*** *in the Vault ribbon and clicking* ***Settings*** *next to Configure Revision Table.*

3. In the *Revision Table Settings* dialog box, select the **Enable Revision Table control** checkbox (shown in Figure 14–17) to enable the Vault Revision Table functionality across Vault.

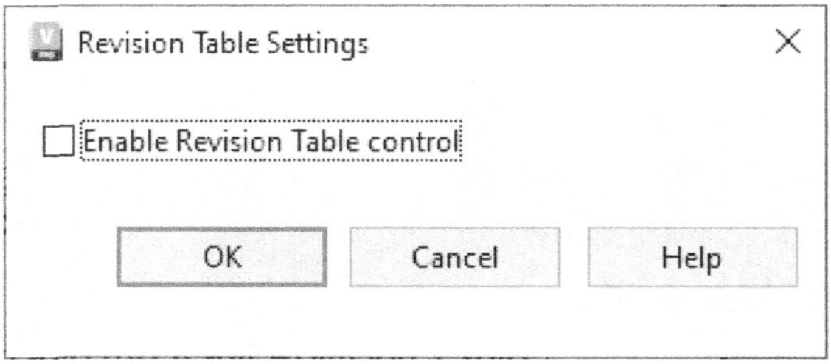


**Figure 14–17**

- When this checkbox is selected, the full view for the Revision Table Settings displays.

## Revision Table Settings Dialog Box

In the *Revision Table Settings* dialog box, you can configure how data displays, which Vault properties are mapped to the revision table, and the type of content displayed. You can also incorporate filters so that only the information you need displays in the revision tables.

| Feature | Details |
|---|---|
|  | Loads suggested settings. |
|  | Loads the default settings for the dialog box. |
|  | Restores all changes in the *Revision Table Settings* dialog box to the settings used the last time the dialog box was opened. |

| Feature | Details |
|---|---|
| **Mappings Tab** | On the *Mappings* tab, you can map Vault properties to the revision table columns.<br>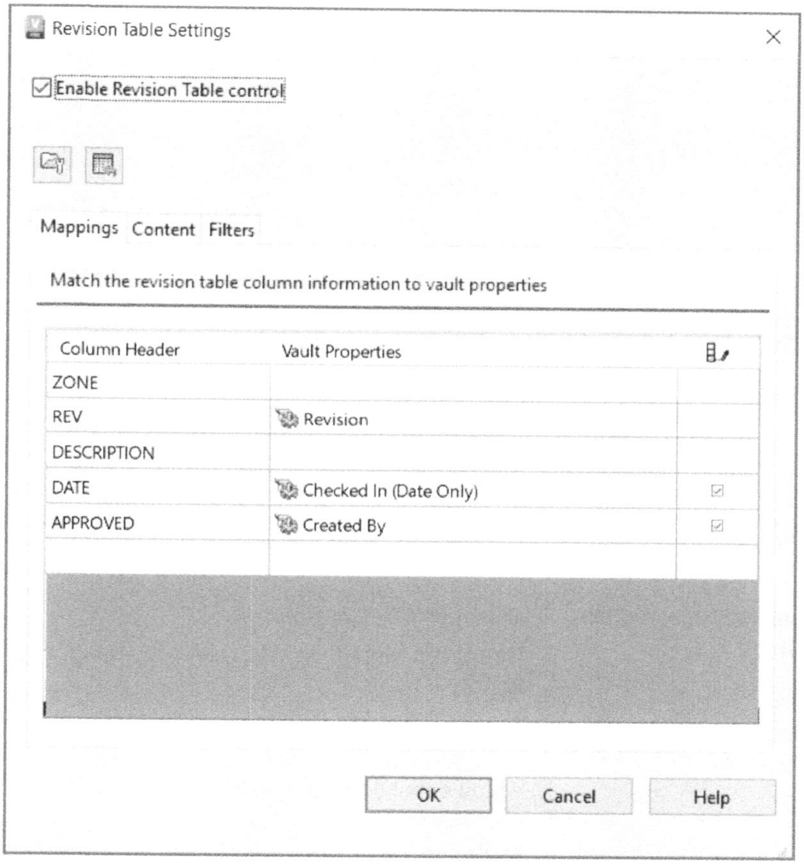<br> |
| **Column Header** | Column name that displays in the revision table. |
| **Vault Properties** | The name of the Vault property that you have mapped to the associated revision table column.<br>The value for this property will automatically display in the column field of the revision table for the drawing. |
|  | Released vs. non-released bias control.<br>Select the checkbox for any row where you want the system to update the revision table only with released information. If the checkbox for a row is not selected, then the latest information from the vault is used. |

<table>
<tr><th>Feature</th><th>Details</th></tr>
<tr><td>Content Tab</td><td>In the Content tab, you can enforce the type of information that displays in the revision table.
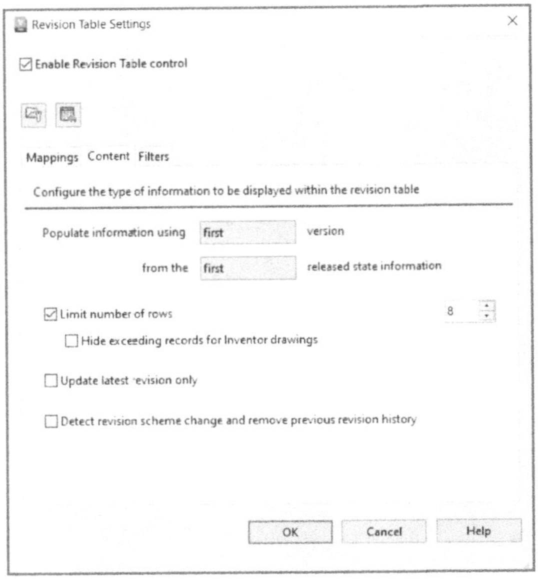
</td></tr>
<tr><td>Populate information using</td><td>Select version control.<br>Select the version and the released state that you want to apply to revision history records.</td></tr>
<tr><td>Limit number of rows checkbox</td><td>If you want to limit the number of rows displayed in the revision table, select the Limit number of rows checkbox. Specify the limit for the number of rows that you want displayed by selecting a value from the value spinner.<br>Note: When the Limit number of rows option is toggled ON, the exceeding records are deleted by default. In Autodesk Inventor drawings, you can also select to hide these exceeding records instead of deleting them.</td></tr>
<tr><td>Hide exceeding records for Inventor drawings checkbox</td><td>Select this checkbox to hide, instead of delete, the additional Autodesk Inventor drawing records.</td></tr>
<tr><td>Update latest revision only</td><td>Select this checkbox to update the mapped values only for the latest revision row in the revision table. All other mapped values in previous historical revision rows do not get updated even if the data is non-equivalent in the vault.<br>Note: Even with the Update latest revision only option enabled, the Vault Revision Table feature continues to remove revision rows that are not found in the Vault.</td></tr>
</table>

| Feature | Details |
|---|---|
| **Detect revision scheme change and remove previous revision history** | If you are using multiple revision schemes, select this checkbox to ensure that the current revision scheme is used. Historical revision rows of an older revision scheme are replaced with the current revision scheme. |
| **Filters Tab** | In the *Filters* tab, you can further refine the data displayed in the revision table by applying revision level filters. 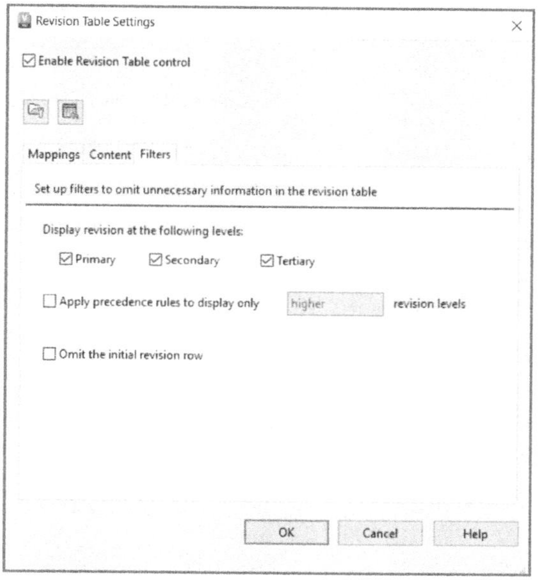  |
| **Display revision at the following levels** | Select the checkbox for each revision level that you want displayed in the revision table. For example, if you have a drawing marked as revision B.2.1, and you only select the **Primary** and **Secondary** checkboxes, then only B.2 displays in the revision table.<br>Refer to *Revision Schemes* for more information about the Primary, Secondary, and Tertiary revision levels. |
| **Apply precedence rules to display only X revision levels** | When multiple revision levels exist in a revision group, it is important to identify the level of revision that you want to be displayed. Enable this checkbox and select whether you want the highest or lowest revision levels displayed in the revision table.<br>This selection takes precedence over the *Display revision at the following levels* option. |
| **Omit the initial revision row** | Select this checkbox to omit the initial revision row from the revision table.<br>Some users find that if the initial revision value (e.g., A) is already in the title block for the revision table, having it repeated as the first revision row is unnecessary. By selecting this checkbox, the first revision row in the revision table becomes the next revision value (e.g., A.1). |

# Practice 14c
# Use Vault Revision Tables

In this practice, you will create a Vault revision table in **Grip.idw**. **Grip.idw** is a drawing of **Grip.ipt**. These files are managed by the *Flexible Release Process* lifecycle definition. To permit the Job Server to run in the **Released** state, the default settings for *Security* for the **Released** state in the *Flexible Release Process* needs to be modified. For the **Released** state, change *Modify* and *Delete* for *Everyone* to **Allow**, as shown in Figure 14–18.

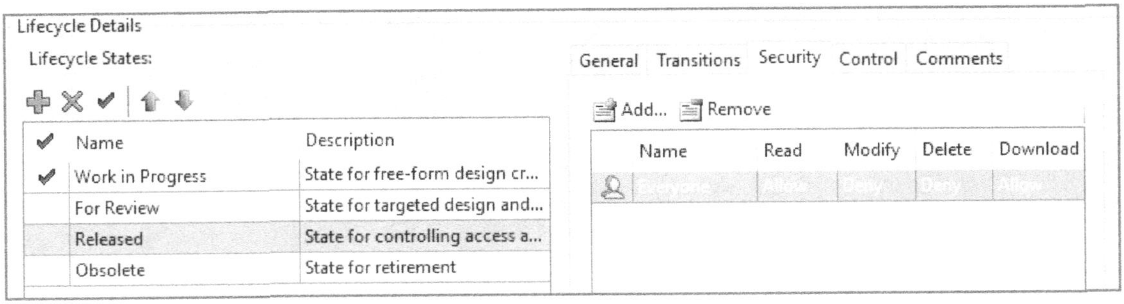


**Figure 14–18**

Also, ensure that the properties get synchronized using the Job Server for the transition of Work in Progress to Released, as shown in Figure 14–19.

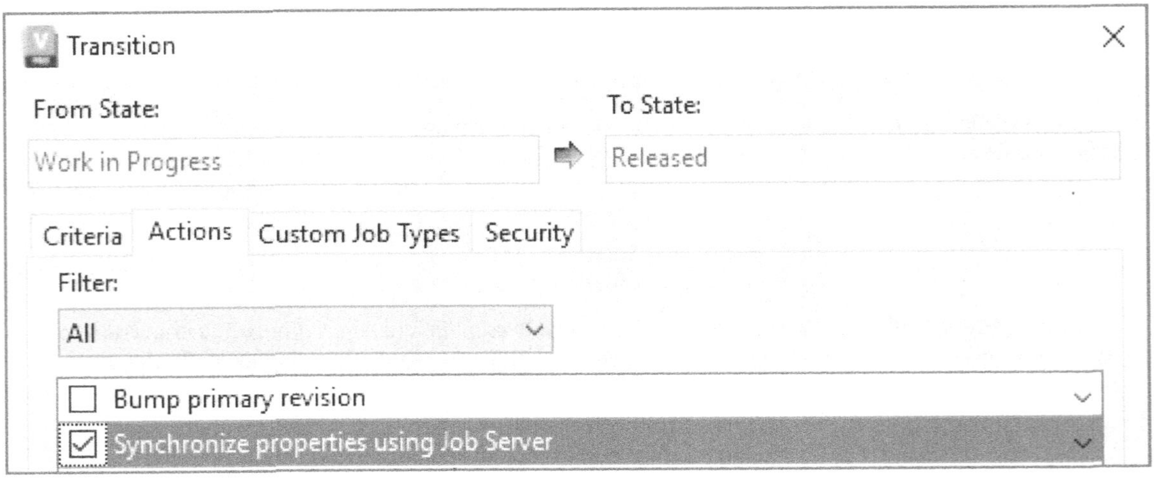


**Figure 14–19**

## Task 1: Enable the Vault Revision Table functionality and map the Description property.

1. Start the Autodesk Vault. Log in using the information below and ensure that **Designs.ipj** is set as the Inventor project file.
   - For *User Name*, enter **administrator**.
   - Leave the *Password* field blank.
   - For *Vault*, select **AOTCVault**.
2. Select **Tools>Administration>Vault Settings**.
3. In the *Vault Settings* dialog box, select the *Behaviors* tab and select **Revision Table**.
4. In the *Revision Table Settings* dialog box, select the **Enable Revision Table control** checkbox to enable the Vault Revision Table functionality.
5. Click **Yes** to load recommended settings. The *Revision Table Settings* dialog box updates as shown in Figure 14–20.

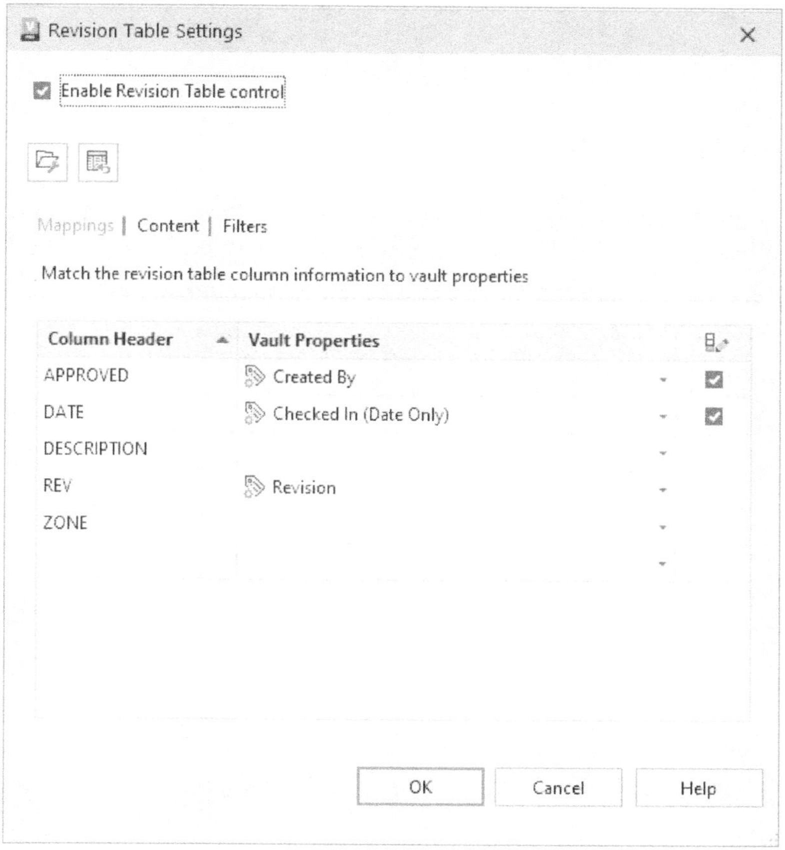


**Figure 14–20**

6. For the Inventor property *DESCRIPTION*, select the Vault system property **Comment**. Note that by default, the *APPROVED* property maps to the **Created By** Vault property, as shown in Figure 14–21. Click **OK**, then click **Close** to close the *Vault Settings* dialog box.

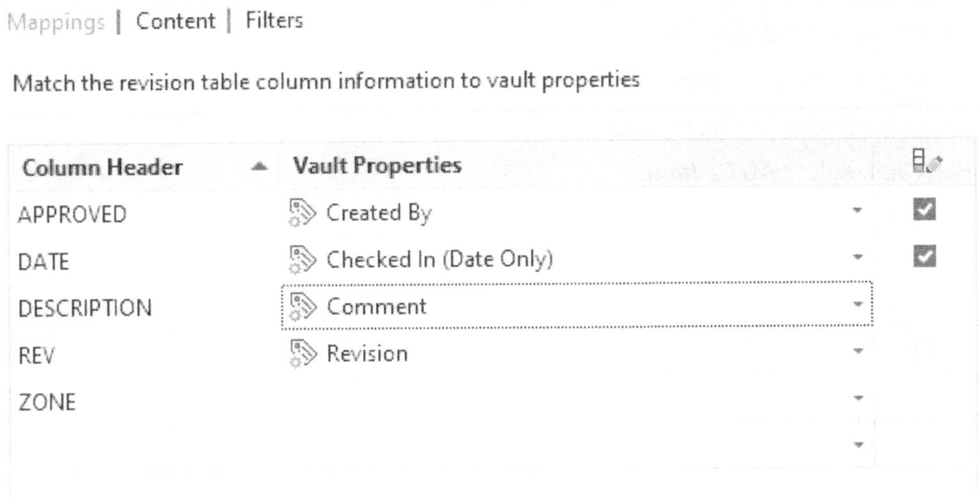


Figure 14–21

## Task 2: Add a Vault revision table to the drawing.

1. In Inventor, log in to Vault and from the *Vault* tab, select **Open**. In the *Designs/Clamp* folder, select **Grip.idw**.
2. In the *Annotate* tab, select **Vault Revision**, as shown in Figure 14–22.

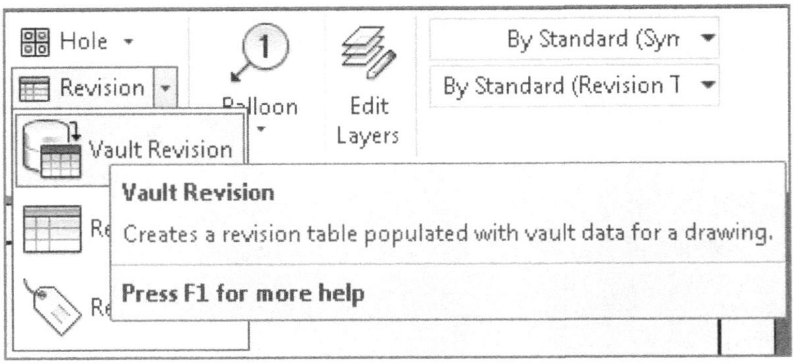


Figure 14–22

3. Insert the table in the top-right corner of the drawing, as shown in Figure 14–23.

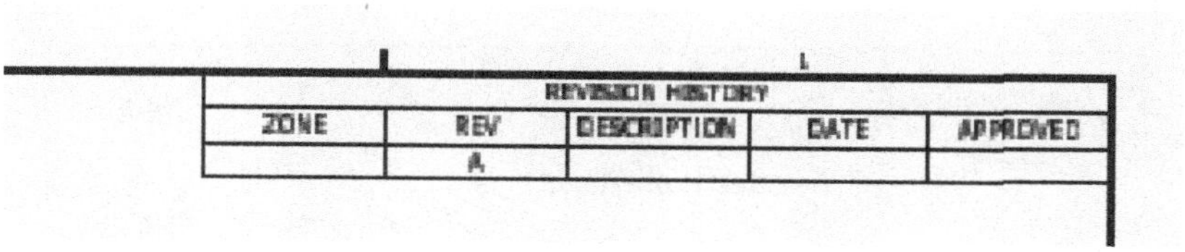


**Figure 14–23**

## Task 3: Edit the Vault revision table.

1. To edit the table, right-click on the revision table and select **Edit**, as shown in Figure 14–24.

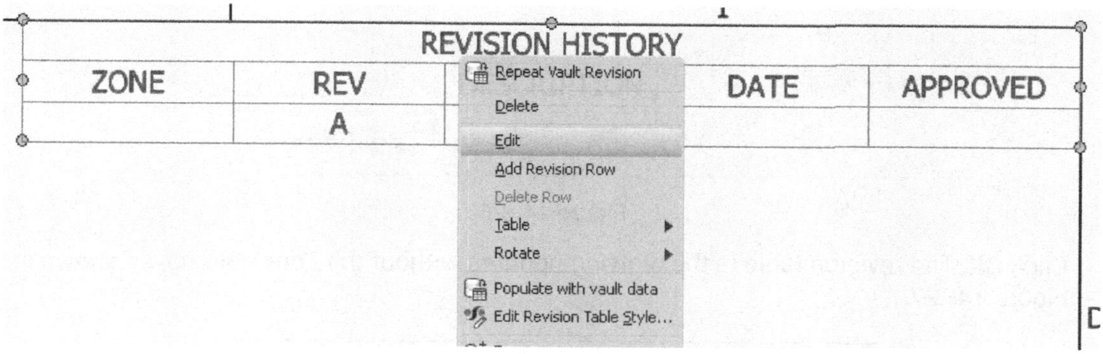


**Figure 14–24**

2. To remove the *Zone* column, right-click on a column header and select **Column Chooser**, as shown in Figure 14–25.

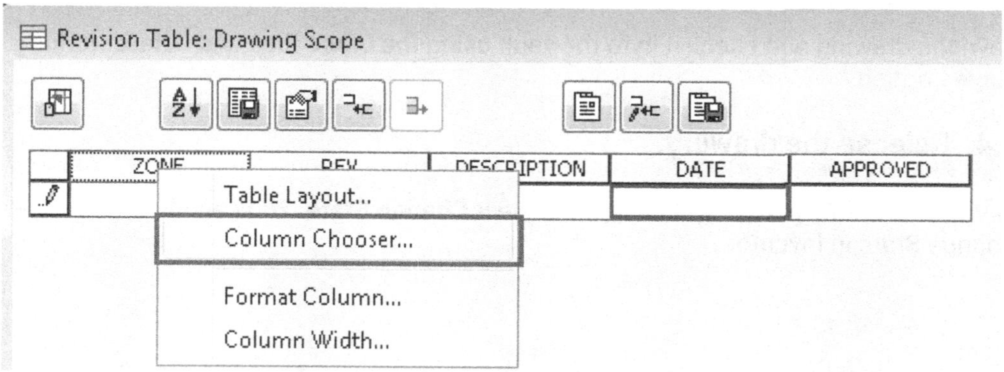


**Figure 14–25**

3. Select **Zone** in the *Selected Properties* list (as shown in Figure 14–26) and click **Remove**, then click **OK**.

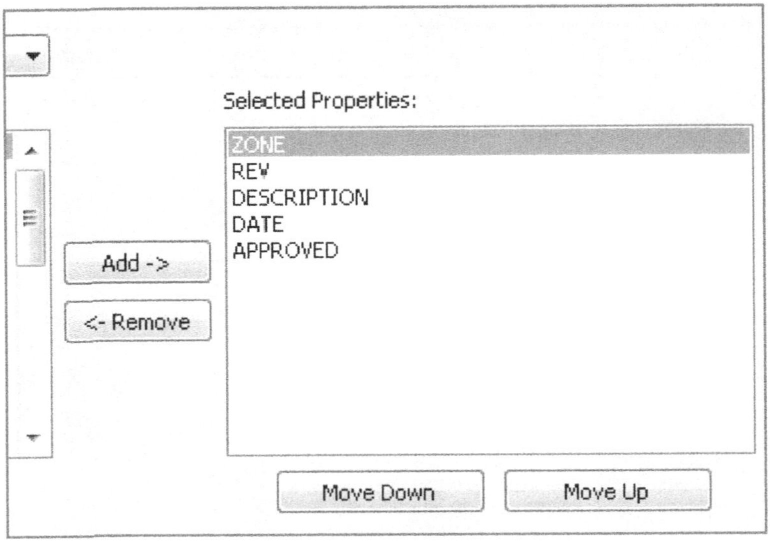


**Figure 14–26**

4. Click **OK**. The revision table in the drawing updates without the *Zone* column, as shown in Figure 14–27.

| REVISION HISTORY | | | |
|---|---|---|---|
| REV | DESCRIPTION | DATE | APPROVED |
| A | | | |

**Figure 14–27**

5. Save the drawing and check it in to the vault using the **Close files and delete working copies** option.

## Task 4: Release the drawing.

1. In Vault, select **Grip.idw**, right-click, and select **Change State**. You can also perform a Change State in Inventor.

2. Select **Released** from the drop-down list, as shown in Figure 14–28.

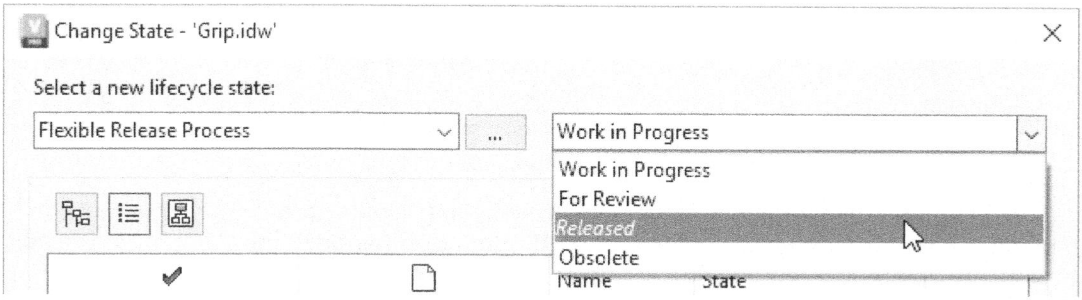


**Figure 14–28**

3. Update the comment to say **Initial Release** (as shown in Figure 14–29) and click **OK**. The state updates to **Released** in the main table.

**Figure 14–29**

4. Now the Job Server will create the visualization files. To force the jobs, open Job Processor and select **File>Pause** then **File>Resume**.

## Task 5: Create a new revision.

1. Now you will create a new revision to make a change to the **Grip.ipt**. In Vault, select **Grip.idw**, right-click, and select **Change State**.
2. Select **Work in Progress**, as shown in Figure 14–30.

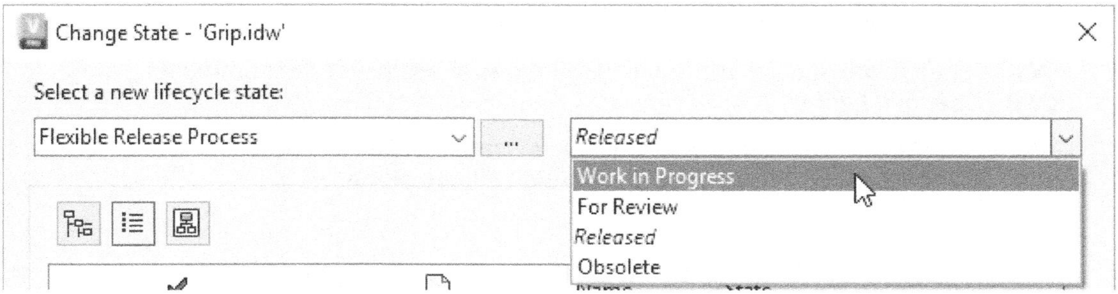


**Figure 14–30**

3. Click **OK**. In the main table, the state updates to **Work in Progress** and the revision changes to **B**, as shown in Figure 14–31.

| | | |
|---|---|---|
| Grip.idw | Work in Progress | B |
| Grip.ipt | Work in Progress | B |

**Figure 14–31**

4. In Inventor, open **Grip.idw** from the vault using **Open (Check Out All)**. Click **Yes to All** to update properties, as shown in Figure 14–32. Note the change to the Vault revision table.

| REVISION HISTORY | | | |
|---|---|---|---|
| REV | DESCRIPTION | DATE | APPROVED |
| A | Initial Release | 5/10/2016 | Administrator |
| B | | | |

**Figure 14–32**

5. In the Vault browser, open **Grip.ipt** (as shown in Figure 14–33) and make a change to the length. Save and close **Grip.ipt**.

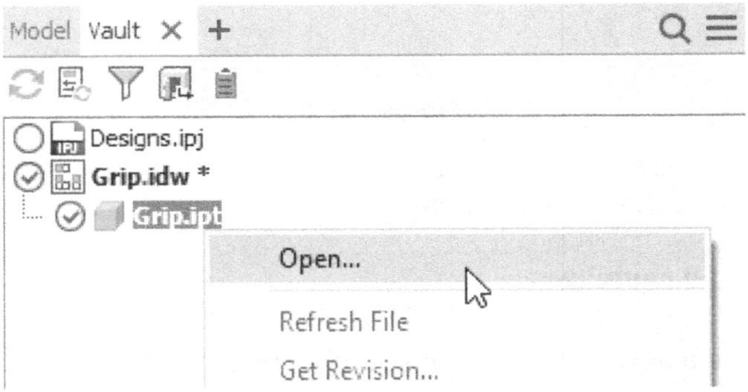


**Figure 14–33**

6. In the Vault browser of **Grip.idw**, save and check in both the drawing and the part. Select the **Close files and delete the working copies** option.
7. In Vault, change the state of the drawing to **Released** again. For the comments, enter **Rev B - Changed Length**.
8. Once again, the Job Server will create the visualization files upon release. To force the jobs, open Job Processor and select **File>Pause** then **File>Resume**.

## Task 6: View the Vault revision table.

1. In Vault, right-click on **Grip.idw** and select **Open** to open the drawing in Inventor.
2. The Vault revision table is updated, as shown in Figure 14–34.

| REVISION HISTORY | | | |
|---|---|---|---|
| REV | DESCRIPTION | DATE | APPROVED |
| A | Initial Release | 5/10/2016 | Administrator |
| B | Rev B - Changed Length | 5/10/2016 | Administrator |

**Figure 14–34**

3. The **Update Properties** feature is integrated with the Vault revision table feature so that the revision block data is synchronized with the vault released information. The manual ways of updating properties if mapped properties are edited include using **Update Properties** in the Vault browser or *Vault* tab, or right-clicking on the Vault revision table and selecting **Populate with vault data**, as shown in Figure 14–35.

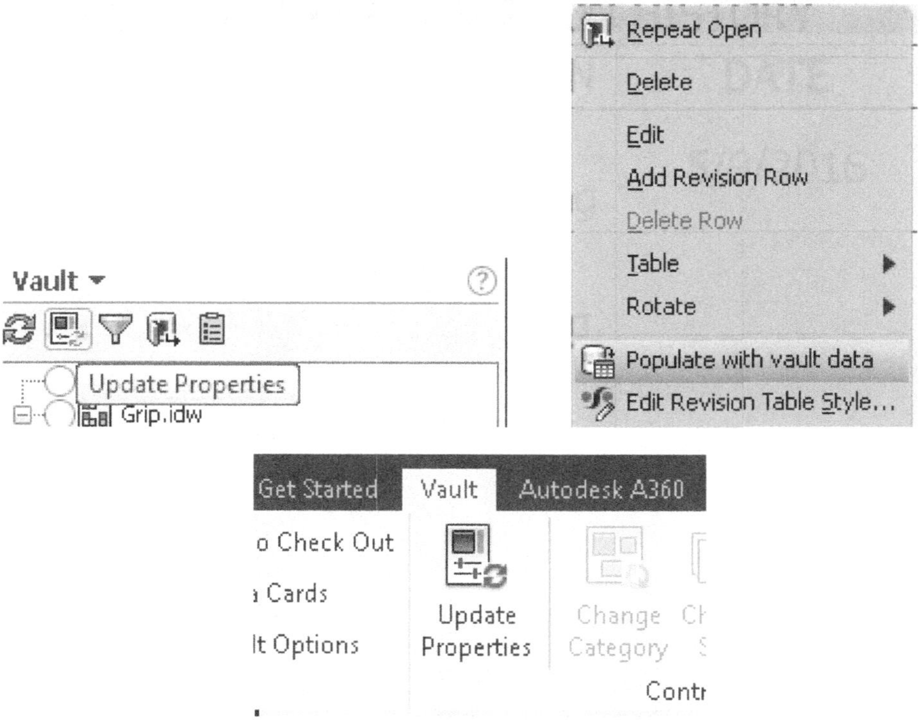


**Figure 14–35**

4. (Optional) If you would like to change the files back to a previous lifecycle state, in Vault, select the files, select **Actions>Roll Back Lifecycle State Change** (as shown in Figure 14–36), and follow the prompts.

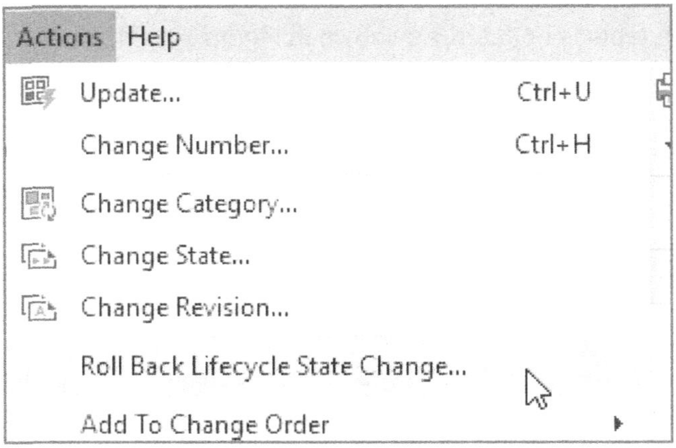


**Figure 14–36**

**End of practice**

# 14.5 Backup and Restore

To prevent data loss, you can select **Backup and Restore** for your Vault.

## How To: Back Up the Vault

1. Log in to Autodesk Data Management Server Console.
2. In the *Tools* menu, select **Backup and Restore**, as shown in Figure 14–37.

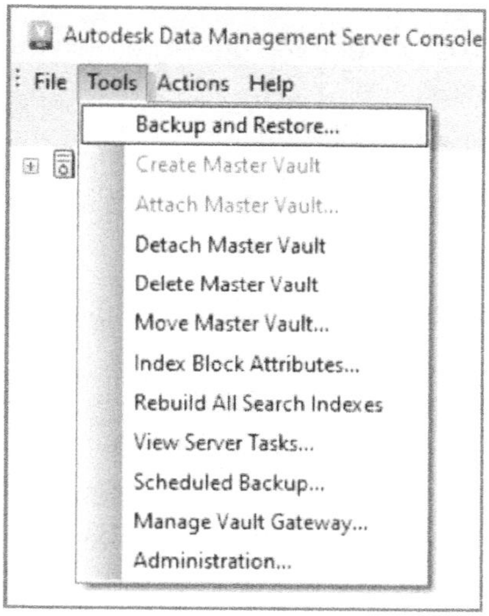


**Figure 14–37**

3. Select **Backup** in the wizard. Before backing up the data, the server console validates the data to ensure that the file store and databases are synchronized. If the database is out of sync, a dialog box displays listing the files that are mismatched. You can cancel the backup to correct the files.
4. Select **Full Backup** or **Incremental Backup**. The Incremental Backup option will not be available if no changes have occurred since the last full or incremental backup.
5. Specify the location to store the backed up data. To browse for a location, click the ellipsis (...) and then locate a directory using the file browser.
6. Toggle on the **Validate** checkbox to verify the archive is good once it is created.
7. By default, standard Content Center libraries are included in the backup process. To exclude standard Content Center libraries from the backup, toggle off the **Backup Standard Content Center Libraries** checkbox.
8. By default, a backup will wait until all files that need to be replicated are replicated before starting. Check the **Ignore non-replicated files** checkbox to start the backup without waiting for these files to replicate.
9. Click **OK**.

# Restoring a Vault

## How To: Restore the Entire Vault

> **Note:** *Access to the vault database is blocked during this task. Data management clients cannot access the database until the task is complete.*

1. In the *Tools* menu, select **Backup and Restore**.
2. Select **Restore** in the wizard.
3. Restoring a vault deletes the data sets and file store. You are prompted for confirmation before proceeding. Click **Yes**.
4. Select **Full Restore** or **Incremental Restore**.

   **Note:** *Access to the Incremental Restore option is available when no changes have occurred since the restore of the previous increment*

5. Specify the location of the backed-up data. To browse for a location, click the ellipsis (...) and then locate a directory using the file browser.
6. Select whether the database is to be restored to the default location or a different location. If you choose **Select Restore Location**, specify a target directory for database
7. Select whether the file store is to be restored to the default location or a different location. If you choose **Select Restore Location**, specify a target directory for the file store.
8. Click **OK**.

The vault data is automatically migrated when it is restored using the server console. If you are restoring the data using the command line, you must migrate the data after it is restored.

**Caution:** If you have another vault on your machine where you want to restore a vault, you need to detach these existing vaults prior to restoring the required vault to avoid any overwriting! When you have finished the restore of the vault, you can attach the other vaults.

## How To: Manually Restore Only the File Store

The file store can be manually restored by itself from a backup package to a remote location in a multi-site environment. This process should only be done by experienced vault administrators.

1. In the selected backup package, open the *FileStores* folder. The *FileStores* folder contains one folder for each vault in the backup. Each folder is named according to the vault to which it belongs.
2. Locate the appropriate file store folder and copy it to the remote location.

# Backing Up Vault Data

Backing up vault data is essential. The following are recommendations for backing up Autodesk® Vault.

## Use the Supplied Backup and Restore Utility

Use the server console to back up all data required to restore a server if a failure occurs. Vault Professional provides a 'hot backup' process (as shown in Figure 14–38), enabling users to continue to access the vault during the procedure. In addition, server console backs up or restores all vaults on the server. There is no way to select individual vaults to back up or restore.

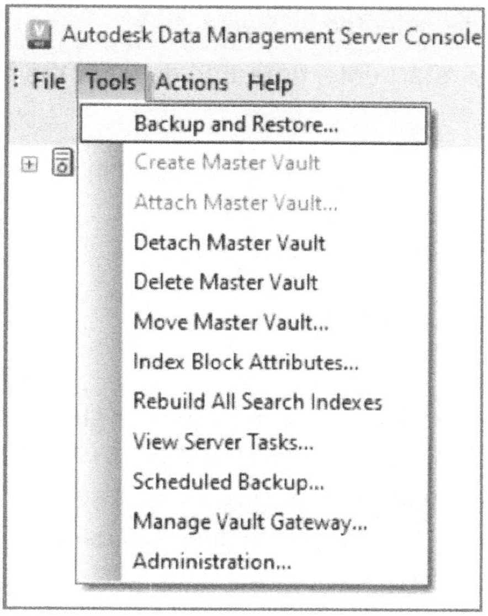


**Figure 14–38**

## Develop a Backup Schedule

The next step is to automate the process. Two common methods are:

- Use **Tools>Scheduled Backup**. This process uses the backup tools included with the server console to create the backup script and task automatically.
- Include the backup as part of a tape backup set. This process uses a tape backup system to back up the vault directly.

The preferred and most reliable method for backing up a vault is to integrate the server console backup tools into your tape backup plan.

## How To: Schedule Backups

1. Inthe *Tools* menu, select **Scheduled Backup**.
2. In the *Backup Configuration* dialog box, specify the location of the backed up data. To browse for a location, click the ellipsis (...) and then locate the directory using the file browser.
3. In the *Vault Credentials* tab, if using a Vault user account, for the Vault account name, specify **administrator**.
4. Select the *Full Backup* tab or *Incremental Backup* tab depending on what type of backup is being scheduled.
5. Select the checkbox for **Schedule a full backup** or **Schedule an incremental backup** depending on which tab was selected in Step 4.
6. Specify the schedule name, start date, time, and days for the backup.
7. Click **OK**.

The batch file is created and a task automatically created in the Windows Task Scheduler.

## How To: Restore Vaults from Backups

1. In the *Tools* menu, select **Backup and Restore**.
2. Select **Restore**.
3. Restoring a vault deletes the current data sets and file store. This action cannot be undone. You are prompted for confirmation before proceeding. Click **Yes**.
4. In the *Restore from directory* field, specify the location of the backed-up data. To browse for a location, click the ellipsis (...) and locate a directory using the file browser.
5. Select whether to restore the database to the original location or to a different location. If you choose **Select Restore Location**, specify a target directory for the database. This selection is sometimes required when restoring data to a different machine that does not have the same drive letters or locations available.
6. Select whether to restore the file to the original location or to a different location. If you choose **Select Restore Location**, specify a target directory for the file store.
7. Click **OK**.

The vault data is automatically migrated when it is restored using Autodesk Vault server console. If you are restoring the data using the command line, migrate the data after it is restored.

 

Chapter 15

# Active Directory, Vault Gateway, and Replication

There are several options to configure and manage your Autodesk® Vault for your needs. User and group and security options make Autodesk Vault highly flexible. The Autodesk Vault Professional software has replication solutions available, such as the ADMS full replication (Connected Workgroups) and Autodesk File Server (AVFS), a file store replication solution. This chapter introduces these replication solutions and their associated components and configuration procedures.

## Learning Objectives

- Manage user accounts regarding the Active Directory.
- Manage groups in Autodesk Vault.
- View and manage Vault gateways.
- Enable and disable workgroup replication.
- Add and delete workgroups.
- Enable and disable a vault for a multi-site environment.
- Replicate a vault, files, and folders.
- Export, import, and configure replication priorities.
- Schedule replication for a multi-site environment.
- Describe the benefits of Autodesk Vault File Server (AVFS).

# 15.1 Active Directory

An administrator can create a vault server account with credentials unique to the vault server or import a Windows Active Directory account. By using an Active Directory account, users can log in to Autodesk data management clients using their Windows account credentials. Users and groups can then be managed using Windows permissions.

## Managing Groups

Individual users have roles and permissions assigned to them that define what actions they can take and to which vaults they have access. You can create groups of users and assign roles and permissions to the group. As a member of a group, a user has all the permissions and roles assigned to the group. By default, every new user is added to a group called **Everyone**. The Everyone group is only available on Access Control Lists. It does not display in the *Groups* dialog box. If the Everyone group is granted membership to a folder, all new users have access to that folder

Groups can be comprised of users or other groups. Groups can be disabled, toggling off all permissions assigned to the group. The permissions and roles assigned to a group are independent of individual user roles and permissions. Groups can also be restricted to specific folders in a vault, so you can keep projects and other data secure between groups.

By assigning users to groups and then granting folder membership to those groups, you can easily manage users and their access to vault folders. This is the best practice for creating a vault security model.

> ***Note:*** *Folder membership is only available with the vault server that is installed with Autodesk Vault.*

### How To: Manage Groups

You must be assigned the role of Administrator to perform this operation.

1. Select **Tools>Administration>Global Settings**.
2. In the *Global Settings* dialog box, select the *Security* tab
3. Select **Manage Access**, then select the *Groups* tab.
4. In the *User and Group Management* dialog box, you can list groups three different ways:
    - Select **View>List** to view the groups in a flat list.
    - Select **View>By Effective Vault** to view the groups as a list grouped by the vaults to which they are assigned.
    - Select **View>By Effective Role** to view the groups as a list grouped by roles.

### How To: Create a Group

1. Click **New** in the *Groups* tab.
2. In the *New Group Profile* dialog box, specify the group settings and click **OK**.

### How To: Edit an Existing Group

1. Select a group from the list.
2. Click **Actions>Edit**.
3. In the *Group Profile* dialog box, specify the group settings and click **OK**.

# Import an Active Directory Domain User Account

Domain user accounts and domain user groups can be imported to the Autodesk vault server. This enables accounts to be created using Active Directory information and enables users to log in to a data management client without requiring a new account. If a user account or group already exists on the server, it can be promoted to an Active Directory account or group. Likewise, an account or group created by importing an Active Directory account can be disconnected or demoted from the Active Directory domain, making the account or group unique to the server.

> ***Note:*** *The Active Directory feature is only available with Autodesk Vault Professional and you must be assigned the role of Administrator to perform this operation.*

You cannot manage Active Directory accounts through the server console. You can only import Active Directory accounts, promote server accounts to the Active Directory accounts, or demote Active Directory accounts to standard server user accounts. To manage Active Directory user accounts and Active Directory group membership, you must use the **User Accounts** controls in the Windows Control Panel.

## How To: Import Users

1. Select **Tools>Administration>Global Settings**.
2. In the *Global Settings* dialog box, select the *Security* tab.
3. Select **Manage Access**, as shown in Figure 15–1.

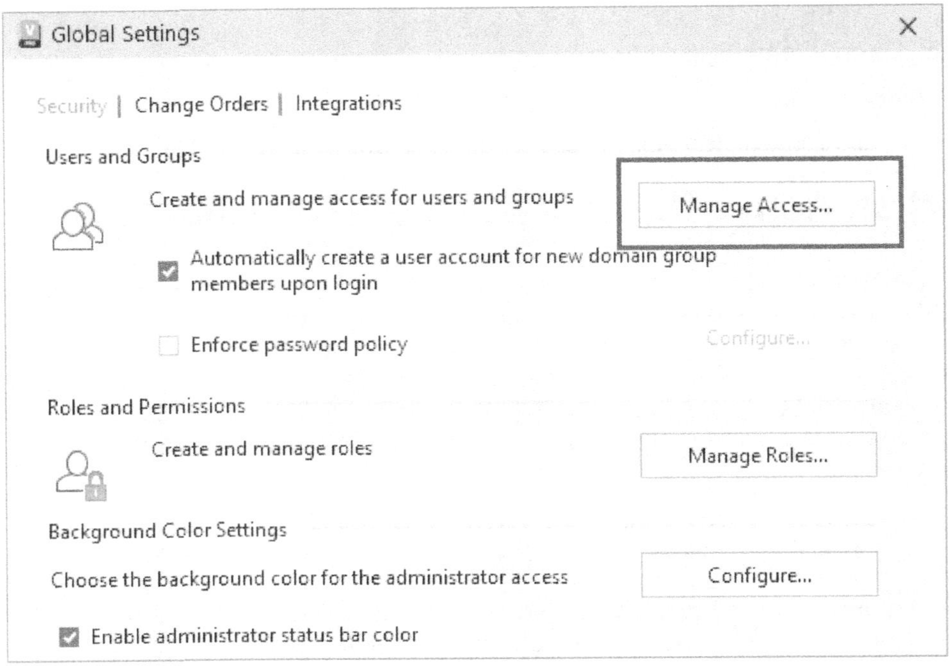


**Figure 15–1**

4. In the *User and Group Management* dialog box, select the *Users* tab, as shown in Figure 15–2.

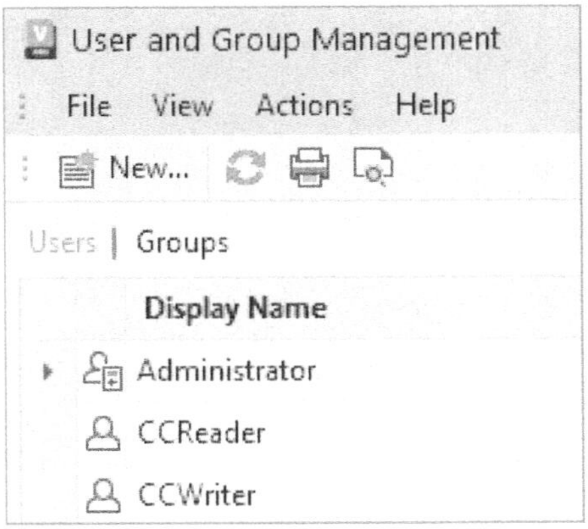


**Figure 15–2**

 

5. In the *User and Group Management* dialog box, you can list user accounts three different ways:
    - Select **View>List** to view the user profiles in a flat list.
    - Select **View>By Effective Vault** to view the user profiles as a list grouped by the vaults to which they are assigned.
    - Select **View>By Effective Role** to view the user profiles as a list grouped by roles.
6. In the *User and Group Management* dialog box, select **Actions>Import Domain User**, as shown in Figure 15–3.

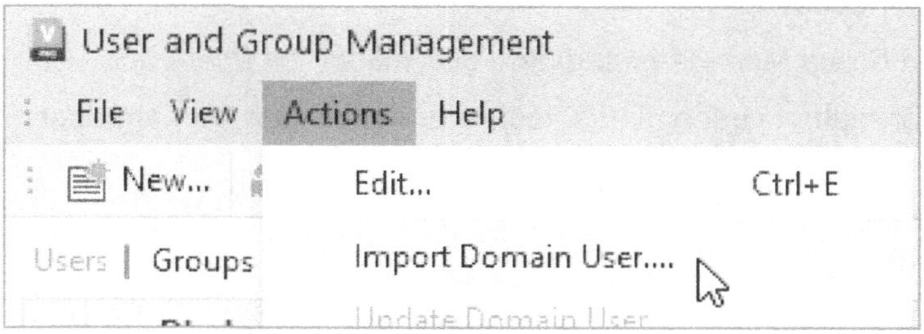


**Figure 15–3**

7. In the *Select User* dialog box, click **Locations** to specify the domain containing the Active Directory accounts to import. In the *Locations* dialog box, select the domain to use and click **OK**.
8. In the *Select User* dialog box, enter the names of the users to add from the Active Directory domain or click **Advanced** to search for the users.
9. Once the uses accounts have been specified, click **OK** in the *Select Users* dialog box. The selected Active Directory domain user accounts are added to the User Management list.

    ***Note:*** *Imported users are not automatically assigned to a group, role, or vault unless they are members of a linked Active Directory group.*

Vault server user accounts imported from an Active Directory domain use the first name, last name, user name, email address, and password associated with the Active Directory account and cannot be edited. The domain name displays in front of the user name. Changes made to the Active Directory user account are updated in the vault server user account automatically.

### How To: Update Domain Users

If users have been added or removed from the Active Directory domain, the Vault server can be updated to reflect the changes to the user account.

**Note:** *You must be assigned the role of Administrator to perform this operation.*

1. Select **Tools>Administration>Global Settings**.
2. In the *Global Settings* dialog box, select the *Security* tab.
3. Select **Manage Access**.
4. In the *User and Group Management* dialog box, select the *Users* tab.
5. Select a user or multiple users and select **Actions>Update Domain User**.

# Import an Active Directory Domain Group

An administrator can create a group of users on the Autodesk vault server or Active Directory groups can be imported. Importing an Active Directory group imports all members of the group, as well as sub-groups.

This enables accounts to be created using Active Directory information and enables users to log into a data management client without requiring a new account. If a user account or group already exists on the vault server, it can be promoted to an Active Directory account or group. Likewise, an account or group created by importing an Active Directory account can be disconnected or demoted from the Active Directory domain, making the account or group unique to the vault server.

### How To: Import Groups

1. In the *User and Group Management* dialog box, select the *Groups* tab and select **Actions>Import Domain Group**.

   **Note:** *Only Security groups can be imported. Distribution groups cannot be imported.*

2. In the *Select Groups* dialog box, click **Locations** to specify the domain containing the Active Directory groups to import. In the *Locations* dialog box, select the domain to use and click **OK**.
3. In the *Select Groups* dialog box, enter the names of the groups to add from the Active Directory domain or click **Advanced** to search for the groups.
4. Once the groups have been specified, click **OK** in the *Select Groups* dialog box. The selected Active Directory domain groups are added to the Group Management list.

All members of the group as well as sub-groups are imported. Groups imported from an Active Directory domain retain the group name and email address from Active Directory. The domain name displays in front of the group name.

## How To: Update Domain Groups

If members have been added or removed from the Active Directory domain group, the Vault server group can be updated to reflect the changes to the group.

> **Note:** *You must be assigned the role of Administrator to perform this operation.*

1. Select **Tools>Administration>Global Settings**.
2. In the *Global Settings* dialog box, select the *Security* tab.
3. Select **Manage Access**.
4. In the *User and Group Management* dialog box, select the *Groups* tab.
5. Select a group and select **Actions>Update Domain Group**.

> **Note:** *One advantage to using groups is when you are adding users to a vault or vaults. First, create a group and add members to the group. Once members have been added to the group, assign a vault to the group.*

# Practice 15a
# Create and Edit Groups

In this practice, you will manage your groups by creating and editing them. You will add roles, databases, and members to the groups.

## Task 1: Create a new group in Vault.

1. Select **Tools>Administration>Global Settings**.
2. Select the *Security* tab and select **Manage Access**.
3. The *User and Group Management* dialog box opens. Select the *Groups* tab, then click **New** to open the *New Group Profile* dialog box.
4. In the *Group Name* field, enter a name for your new group.
5. Enter an email address in the *Email Alias* field to add contact data to this group.
6. Select **Linked to...** to link to an *Active Directory* group.
7. Click **Roles...** to add roles to the group, as shown in Figure 15–4. Repeat with **Vaults...** and **Groups....**

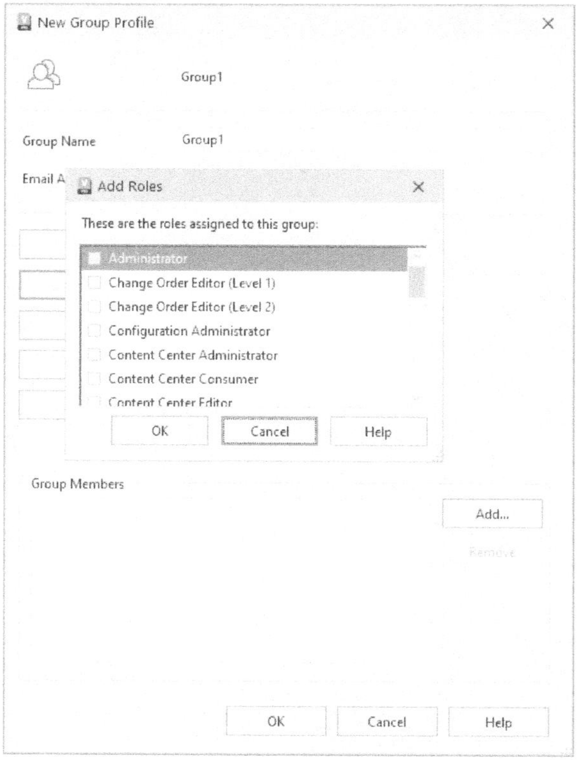


**Figure 15–4**

8. Add or remove *Group Members* to the group by clicking **Add** or **Remove**.
9. Confirm your settings and click **OK** to save the new group in Vault.

## Task 2: Edit the new group.

1. To editing an existing group, select the group you want to edit, right-click, and select **Edit**, as shown in Figure 15–5.

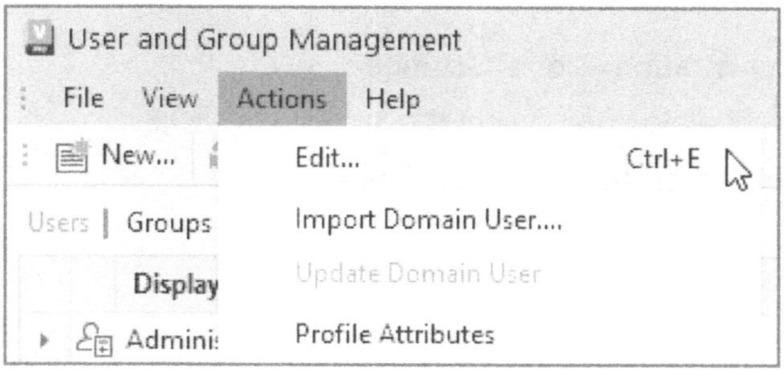


**Figure 15–5**

2. Make the required changes, then click **OK** to save the edited group in Vault.

**End of practice**

# Practice 15b
# Import User/Group via Active Directory

In this practice, you will import users and groups to use the Active Directory functionality in Vault.

## Task 1: Import a user.

1. Select **Tools>Administration>Global Settings**.
2. In the *Global Settings* dialog box, select the *Security* tab.
3. Select **Manage Access**, as shown in Figure 15–6.

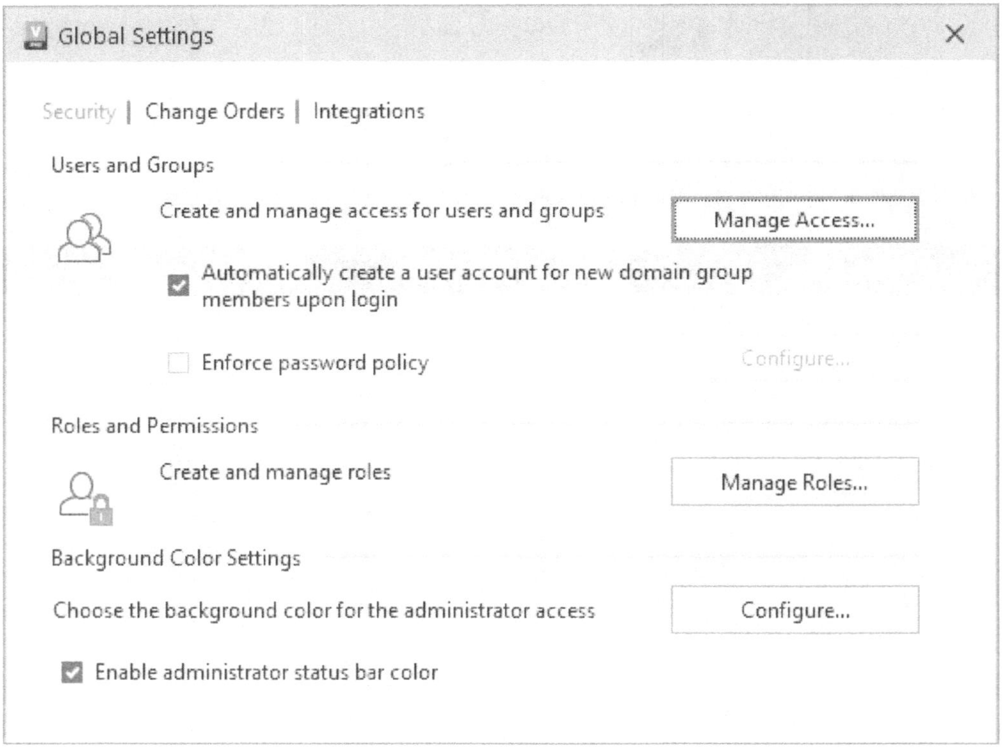


**Figure 15–6**

4. In the *User and Group Management* dialog box, select the *Users* tab and select **Actions>Import Domain User**, as shown in Figure 15–7.

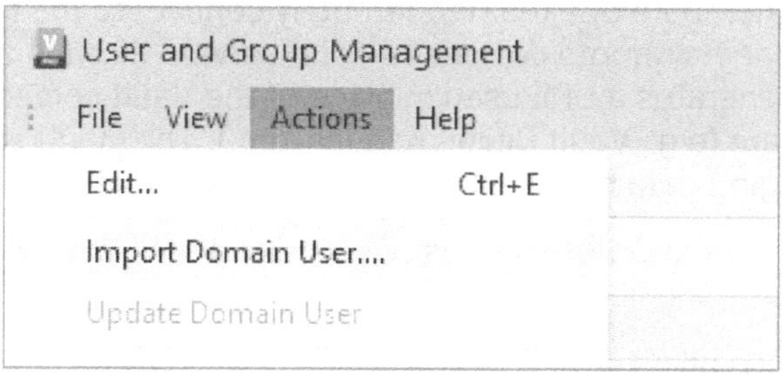


**Figure 15–7**

5. In the *Select Users* dialog box, click **Locations** to specify the domain containing the Active Directory accounts to import. In the *Locations* dialog box, select the domain to use and click **OK**.
6. In the *Select Users* dialog box, enter the names of the users to add from the Active Directory domain or click **Advanced** to search for the users.
7. Once the users accounts have been specified, click **OK** in the *Select Users* dialog box. The selected Active Directory domain user accounts are added to the User Management list.

## Task 2: Import a group.

1. In the *User and Group Management* dialog box, select **Actions>Import Domain Group**.

   ***Note:*** *Only Security groups can be imported. Distribution groups cannot be imported.*

2. In the *Select Groups* dialog box, click **Locations** to specify the domain containing the Active Directory groups to import. In the *Locations* dialog box, select the domain to use and click **OK**.
3. In the *Select Groups* dialog box, enter the names of the groups to add from the Active Directory domain or click **Advanced** to search for the groups.
4. Once the groups have been specified, click **OK** in the *Select Groups* dialog box. The selected *Active Directory* domain groups are added to the *Group Management* list.

**End of practice**

# 15.2 Vault Gateway

Vault Gateway enables members of a team to remotely connect to the vault. Vault Gateway technology securely connects remote devices to Vault servers through a cloud service. The Vault Gateway service generates a URL used in place of the Vault server name when logging in to the Vault client software (e.g., Vault Client, Add-ins, etc.). The cloud service interfaces with the Vault server, exchanging data between the client and server in real time.

- Configuring and using Vault Gateway does not require any of the following network resources:
  - Connection to an on-premise network
  - Connection to a VPN
  - Opened inbound network ports

## Managing Vault Gateways

Administrators configure gateways for individual Autodesk Account teams. A Vault administrator must manage at least one Autodesk Account team to configure a gateway.

### How To: Manage a Vault Gateway

To manage your team's gateway:

1. In the ADMS Console, select the **Tools** option in the menu bar.
2. Select **Manage Vault Gateway**. If you are not signed in, you will be prompted to sign in to an administrator account.
3. The Autodesk Account Teams window displays if you manage more than one team. Select a team and click **OK**.

   ***Note:*** *When a gateway is already configured, the Autodesk Account Teams window does not display.*

4. The Vault Gateways window displays. The Vault Gateways window is the primary dashboard for your team's gateways. It shows information for the local gateway that you manage and other gateways for your team.

### How To: Add a Vault Gateway

Administrators create gateways and share gateway URLs with their team.

To add a new gateway:

1. In the ADMS Console, select the **Tools** option in the menu bar.
2. Select **Manage Vault Gateway**. If you are not signed in, you will be prompted to sign in to an administrator account.
3. If you manage more than one Autodesk Account team, the Autodesk Account Teams window displays. Select a team and click **OK**. The Vault Gateways window displays.
4. The *Local Gateway* section is blank when a team does not have a gateway configured. Select **Configure** in the Vault Gateways window.
5. Complete the following fields in the Configure Local Gateway window:
    - *Region:* Select the region closest to the physical location of your Vault server. Note: A gateway's region cannot be edited after the gateway is configured.
    - *Service Account:* This is the Autodesk ID associated with the gateway. Click **Service Account** to sign in to an account.

    ***Note:*** *The service account must have a Vault Professional license and be part of the team selected in Step 3 above. Additionally, a service account can only be associated with a single gateway.*

6. Click **OK**. The Vault Gateways window displays. Information on the new gateway is updated in the *Local Gateway* section.

## Connecting to a Vault Gateway

After Vault Gateway is configured by your administrator, team members can use the gateway URL to connect to their vault remotely.

Logging in to a gateway follows the same procedure as logging in to a vault through a direct server connection. The Server field takes an HTTPS URL to the gateway (a gateway's host name, displayed when an administrator manages a gateway) instead of a server name. Vault clients cannot connect to the gateway if https:// is omitted from the URL.

> ***Note:*** *Vault Gateway does not support logging in with Windows authentication.*

## Deleting a Vault Gateway

Administrators can permanently delete a gateway and its gateway URL. After deleting a gateway, your team can no longer use the gateway URL. Deleting a gateway is irreversible.

- Team members cannot use the URL to connect to the vault.
- Administrators cannot reuse the URL when configuring a new gateway.

### How To: Delete a Vault Gateway

To delete a gateway:

1. In the ADMS Console, select the **Tools** option in the menu bar.
2. Select **Manage Vault Gateway**. If you are not signed in, you will be prompted to sign in to an administrator account.
3. Select a team and click **OK**.
4. Click **Delete** to delete the local gateway. To delete a gateway in the *Other Gateways* section, select the X icon in the *Action* column to delete the corresponding gateway.

# 15.3 Replication

Replication is the process of copying data from one server to another server usually located in two different physical locations. This process enables the setup of a Vault environment which has two different locations and users will not have to spend time downloading large CAD files across their Wide Area Network (WAN) connection. The replication solutions for Vault Professional include ADMS full replication (Connected Workgroups) for both file store and SQL database replication, and Autodesk Vault File Server (AVFS), which is an alternative file store replication solution.

## Replication Solutions Overview

Data replication is only available in a multi-site environment. A multi-site environment consists of multiple remote sites that can be configured to access the same vault data. A site is comprised of a dedicated Autodesk data management server and a file store. Each site accesses a shared AUTODESKVAULT SQL instance. The SQL database tracks which files and versions are at each site in a multi-site environment. Each site can be synchronized so that newer files and newer versions are shared across sites. Individual vaults can be replicated, or all of the enabled vaults on a site can be replicated. Replication can also be scheduled. By default, replication is set for 12:00 AM (midnight) each weekday when a vault is enabled. During the day, if a user finds that a file is not located on their site, they can replicate the file on demand. Companies that have multiple design organizations that work on the same projects need the ability to collaborate and share files.

Full replication, or Connected Workgroups, is an architecture suited for multiple sites that are distributed over great distances or poor networks. With this architecture, SQL databases are replicated across the multiple locations, as well as the file store.

The Autodesk Vault File Server (AVFS) is an alternative file store replication solution.

## Full Replication (Connected Workgroups)

To enable sites to have their own database server to increase SQL performance, the Autodesk Vault software uses Connected Workgroups. Figure 15–8 shows a workgroup with two different sites connected to a second workgroup with a single site. Note that site B in Workgroup 1 is an AVFS server.

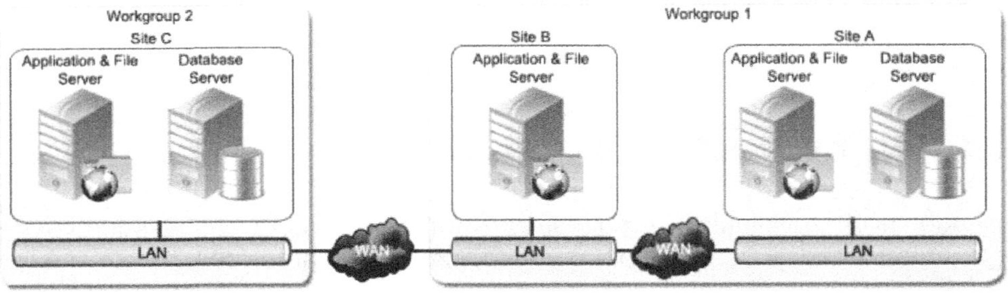


**Figure 15–8**

The Connected Workgroup feature, or full replication, supports the use of multiple database servers using Microsoft SQL Publisher/Subscriber technology. This technology enables the replication of the SQL database at multiple locations.

The terminology used for a Connected Workgroup (i.e., full replication) environment includes:

- **Site:** A location where the Vault server software is installed to which users connect using the client application.
- **Workgroup:** A group of sites connecting to the same SQL database.
- **Publisher:** The first SQL server configured in a full replicated environment.
- **Subscriber:** SQL servers replicating to the publisher in a full replicated environment.

## Autodesk Vault File Server (AVFS)

The Autodesk Vault File Server is a simple file store management system that enables you to move and configure a file store.

Sometimes in multi-site environments, a latency can occur when the Autodesk Data Management Server (ADMS) communicates with SQL. To reduce this latency, the File Server talks directly to the ADMS instead. Similarly, the Vault client(s) communicate directly with the ADMS for metadata and the File Server for file upload/download events, reducing the time it takes to update the file store.

**Important:** The File Server machine must be able to access the machine where the ADMS Console is installed.

> ***Note:** Although the File Server supports a multi-site environment, all file replication must be scheduled from the ADMS Console.*

 

# Managing Workgroup Replication

To create a Connected Workgroup environment, workgroup replication must be enabled. Workgroup replication must be enabled from the publisher site before installing the subscriber sites.

## How To: Enable Workgroup Replication

1. Use File Explorer to create a shared network folder.
2. In the *Navigation* pane, select **Workgroups**.
3. Right-click and select **Enable Workgroup Replication**, as shown in Figure 15–9.

**Figure 15–9**

4. In the *Enable Workgroup Replication* dialog box (shown in Figure 15–10), complete the following:
   a. Enter the path to the shared network folder.
   b. Enter the user account setup to run replication. This account should have access to the shared network folder.
   c. Enter and confirm the password for the replication account.
   d. Click **OK**.

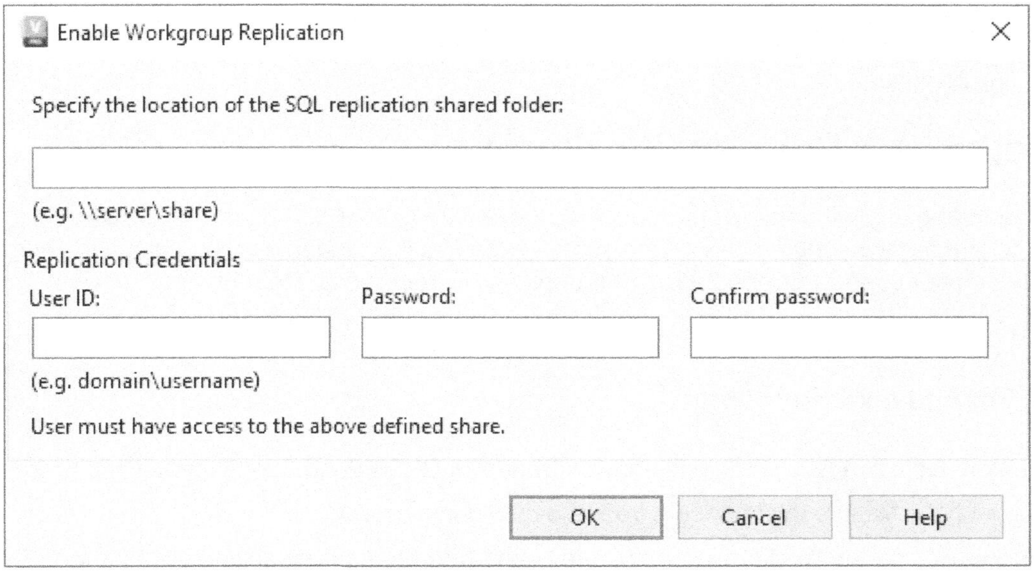


**Figure 15–10**

### How To: Disable Workgroup Replication

To discontinue the use of a Connected Workgroup environment, workgroup replication must be disabled. Before disabling workgroup replication, all workgroups must be deleted.

1. In the *Navigation* pane, select **Workgroups**.
2. Right-click and select **Disable Workgroup Replication**, as shown in Figure 15–11.

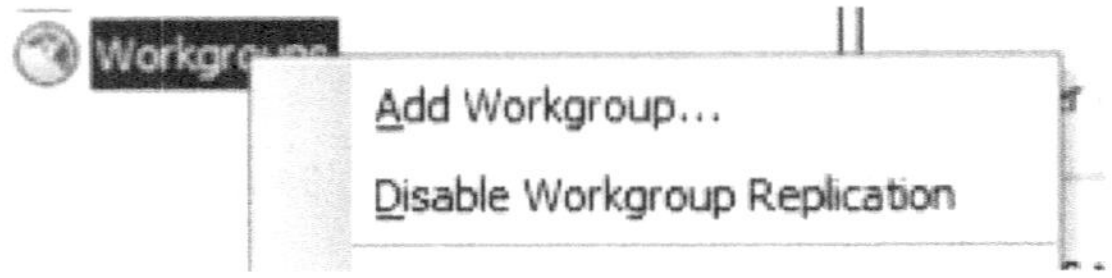


**Figure 15–11**

3. If the subscribing sites have not been deleted, check the box to delete the subscribing sites.
4. Click **OK**.

### How To: Configure Workgroup Replication

Once a workgroup has been added to the Connected Workgroup environment, each vault in the new workgroup has to be configured to replicate. Only vaults selected to replicate from one workgroup will be accessible from a different workgroup.

1. In the *Navigation* pane, select the workgroup of the vault to be replicated.
2. In the right pane, right-click on the vault to replicate and select **Manage Replication**.
3. Use **Add (>>)** and **Remove (<<)** to select which workgroups to replicate the vault.
4. Click **OK**.

# Adding and Deleting Workgroups

Before adding a subscribing workgroup, a supported version of Microsoft SQL Server must be installed on the subscribing server (the same version as is installed on the publishing server). Vault does not support Connected Workgroups on Microsoft SQL Express.

> ***Note:*** *Do not install the Vault server on the subscribing server.*

### How To: Add a Workgroup

1. Install Microsoft SQL with an instance named **AUTODESKVAULT** on the subscribing server.
2. Launch the Vault server console from the publishing server.
3. Right-click on the **Workgroups** node and select **Add Workgroup**, as shown in Figure 15–12.

 

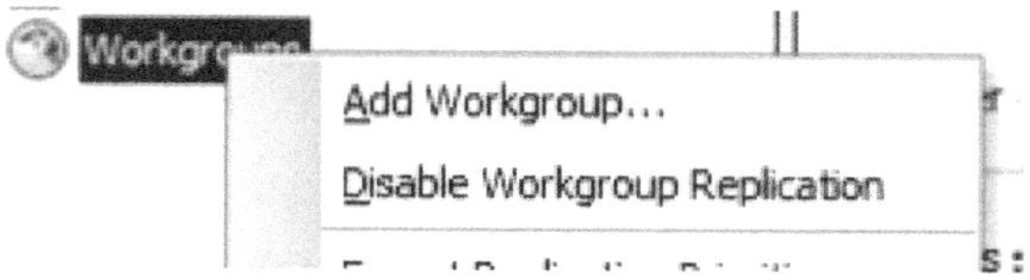


**Figure 15–12**

4. In the *Add Workgroup* dialog box, enter the required information.
   - **Workgroup Name:** The name of the new workgroup.
   - **Workgroup Label:** The unique name for the new workgroup. This name will be tied to all schemes created for this workgroup.
   - **Subscriber Server Name:** The name of the server with SQL installed for the new workgroup.
   - **Remote SQL Credentials:** The login credentials for the new SQL server being used for the new workgroup.
   - **Remote Replication Credentials:** The credentials set up for replication when defined when configuring the publishing server.
5. Click **OK**.

### How To: Delete a Workgroup

A workgroup that is no longer required can be deleted. A workgroup can be deleted using the server console from the publisher workgroup.

1. In the *Navigation* pane, select **Workgroups**.
2. Right-click a workgroup in the list and select **Delete Workgroup**.
3. When prompted for confirmation to delete the workgroup, click yes.
4. If an error occurs where the subscriber database cannot be cleaned up, repeat the process but select Unconditional delete.

## Replicating Vaults, Files, and Folders

### How To: Replicate a Vault

Use the following steps to replicate a vault from the Autodesk Data Management Server console:

1. In the *Navigation* pane, expand the **Workgroups** node.
2. Expand the correct workgroup node.
3. Expand the correct site node.
4. Select a vault located on the current site from the list.

5. Right-click on the site and select one of the replication options shown in Figure 15–13:
   - **Replicate Now:** Synchronize all of the vaults on the current site immediately.
   - **Replicated Folders:** Select which folders and files to replicate.
   - **Replication Schedule:** Establish a synchronization schedule, or toggle off scheduled synchronization.

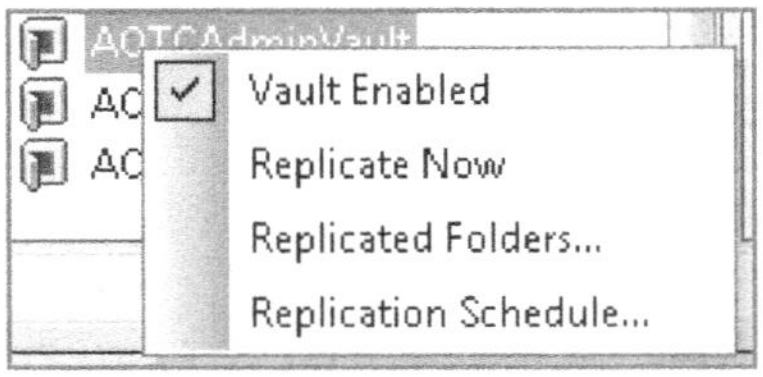


**Figure 15–13**

## Replicating Files and Folders

Folder and file replication can be accessed from the Autodesk Data Management Server console's *Navigation* pane.

> **Note:** *You can also replicate files and folders from the Replication Schedule dialog box by clicking Replicated Folders.*

### How To: Replicate Files and Folders

Use the following steps to access the Folder and *File Replication* dialog box from the Autodesk Data Management Server console:

1. In the *Navigation* pane, select the workgroup of the vault to be replicated.
2. In the right pane, right-click on the vault to replicate and select **Replicated Folders**, as shown in Figure 15–14.

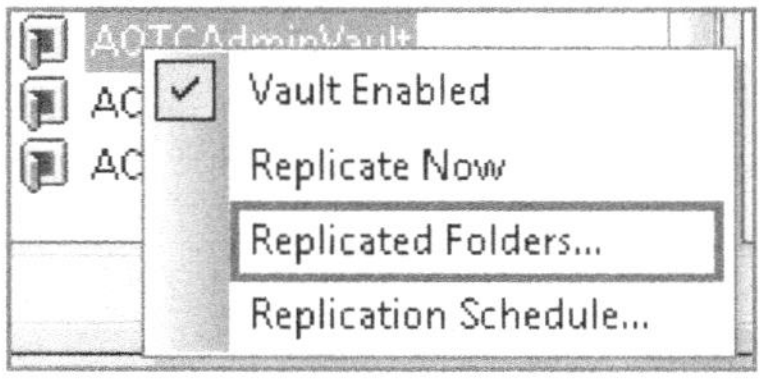


**Figure 15–14**

3. By default all folders will be checked. Uncheck any folders which do not need to be replicated. Check folders which need to be replicated.

> **Note:** *This feature only controls which files will be replicated from the file store and not the metadata about the files. Regardless of what is selected, all metadata is replicated to the subscriber sites. If you want to limit visibility of metadata, you need to apply the correct security on the folders and files.*

 

# Enabling or Disabling a Vault for a Multi-Site Environment

To make a vault accessible to other sites, it must be enabled. When a vault is enabled, it is available to all sites in a multi-site environment. A replicated vault must be enabled on the replicated site. This applies to the subscriber and to the AVFS server. This is not done from the publisher, but rather from the remote site.

## How To: Enable a Vault

To enable a vault:

1. In the *Navigation* pane, expand the **Workgroups** node.
2. Select the site to work with.
3. Select a vault located on the current site from the list.
4. Right-click on the vault name and select **Vault Enabled**.
5. If the file store path for the selected vault is not set or is invalid, you are prompted to specify the file store path for the selected vault. Specify the location of the file store and click **OK**.
6. You are prompted to select whether the vault data is synchronized now or at the next scheduled replication. By default, replication is set for 12:00 AM (midnight) each weekday.

## How To: Disable a Vault

To restrict any other site from accessing a vault, it must be disabled. When a vault is disabled, it is no longer available to any other site in a multi-site environment. A disabled vault is available only to the site where the vault is located. Only vaults at the site from which the server console is running can be disabled.

To disable a vault:

1. In the *Navigation* pane, select **Sites**.
2. Select the line containing the current site and the vault to enable at this site.
3. Right-click on the vault name and select **Vault Enabled** to toggle it off.

### How To: View Site Details

To view site details:

1. In the ADMS console's *Navigation* pane, select **Workgroups**.
2. Select the site that you want to manage.

Each site is listed along with a summary of site statistics, including:

- Server Name
- Description
- Location of File Store
- Vault Name
- Vault Status
- Replication Type
- Last Replication
- Next Replication
- Site Status

## Replication Priorities

Replication Priority (Site Affinity) enables administrators to gain control of how multi-site and database replication files are handled from site to site. Replication priority enables you to set up a preferred list of sites or a selected site for file replication. With replication priority, you can prioritize sites in the *Preferred Sites* list. Once replication priority has been set up for a site, any subsequent file replication (both on-demand and scheduled) uses the preferred list of sites. Replication priorities for all sites can be exported to an XML file, which can then be edited in a text editor and imported back into Vault.

### How To: Configure Replication Priority

1. On the Server Console, select a site by expanding the **Workgroups** node and then expanding the site's workgroup.
2. Right-click on the site and select **Manage Replication Priority**.
3. In the *Manage Replication Priority* dialog box, add sites to the *Prioritized* section by using **Add**.
4. Prioritize sites in the *Prioritized* section by using **Move Up** and **Move Down**.
5. Click **OK** to save your changes.

## How To: Export Replication Priorities

1. In the Server Console, right-click on the **Workgroups** node and select **Export Replication Priorities**, as shown in Figure 15–15.

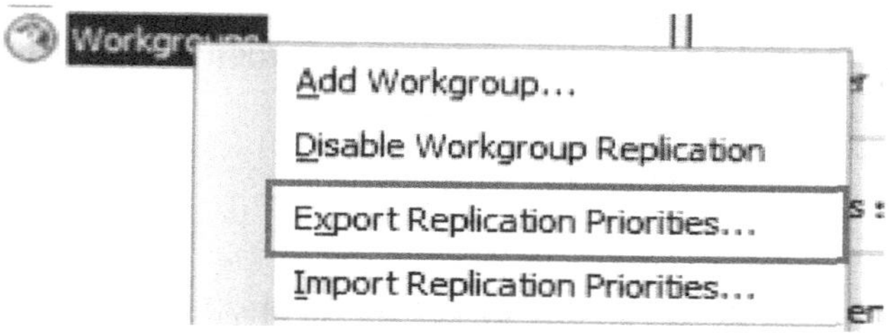


**Figure 15–15**

2. Select a location, enter a name in the *Save* dialog box, and click **Save**.
3. Click **OK** in the confirmation dialog box.
4. Open the XML file in a text editor.
5. Set up replication priority by editing the XML file and saving your changes.

## How To: Import Replication Priorities

1. In the Server Console, right-click on the **Workgroups** node and select **Import Replication Priorities**, as shown in Figure 15–16.

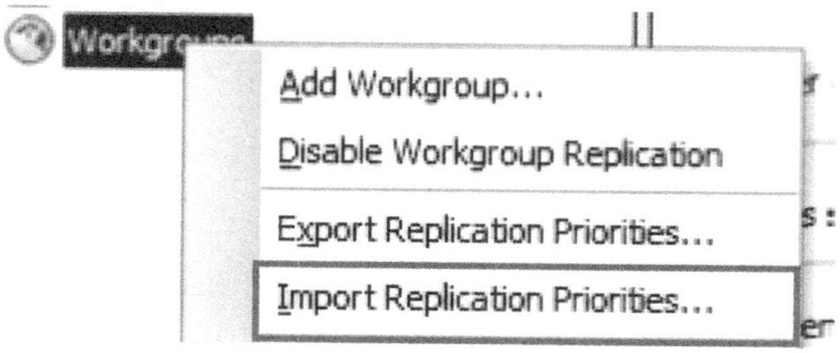


**Figure 15–16**

2. Browse to where the XML file with the replication priority is located.
3. Select the file and click **Open**.
4. Click **OK** in the confirmation dialog box.
5. Validate the import by selecting each site under the **Workgroups** node and viewing the site's Replication Priority table.

# Scheduling Replication for a Multi-Site Environment

## How To: Schedule Replication

Data replication can be scheduled to occur daily, or at a specified intervals. By default, replication is set for 12:00 AM (midnight) each weekday when a vault is enabled.

1. In the *Navigation* pane, expand the **Workgroups** node.
2. Select the workgroup you want to work with.
3. Select the appropriate site.
4. Right-click on the vault and select **Replication Schedule**, as shown in Figure 15–17.

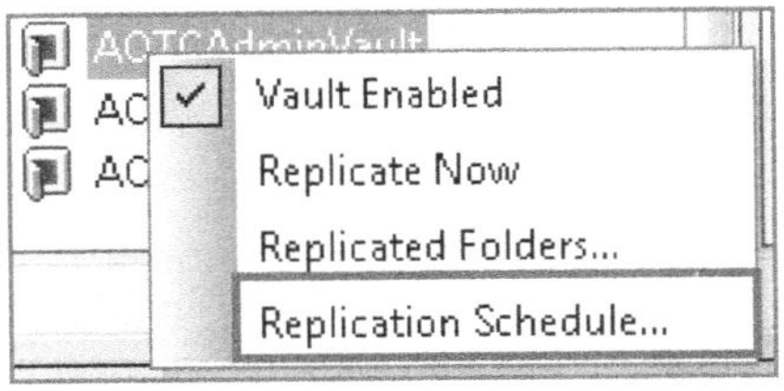


**Figure 15–17**

5. In the *Scheduled Replication* dialog box, select the **Enable scheduled replication** checkbox, as shown in Figure 15–18.

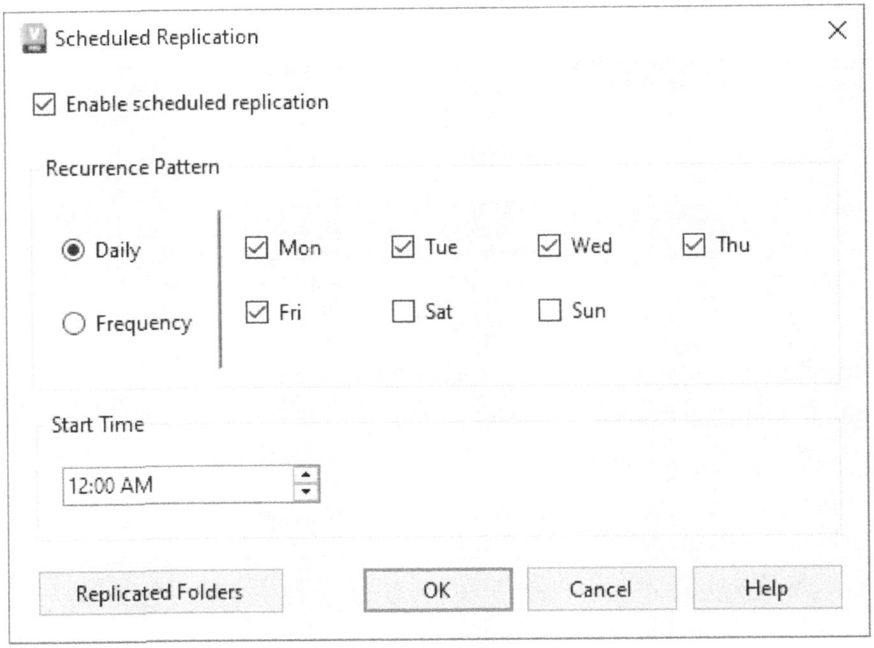


**Figure 15–18**

6. Choose either a daily schedule or a replication frequency.
   - **Daily:** The default daily replication schedule is weekdays at midnight. Specify a start time and select which days to perform the replication.
   - **Frequency:** Specify a start time and then select how often the replication is performed.
7. Click **OK**.

# Autodesk Vault File Server (AVFS) Configuration

Once the Autodesk Vault File Server is installed, ideally you would copy the file store to the AVFS server so that it is not replicating all files from scratch. After configuring the connection between the AVFS server and the primary ADMS server, you need to enable the vault on the AVFS server. This prompts you to specify where the file store folder resides.

Made in United States
North Haven, CT
04 November 2026

21727476R00359